International Handbook of Urban Systems

International Handbook of Urban Systems

Studies of Urbanization and Migration in Advanced and Developing Countries

Edited by

H. S. Geyer

Professor of Regional Planning, Department of Urban and Regional Planning at the University of Potchefstroom

Edward Elgar
Cheltenham, UK • Northampton, MA, USA

Published by
Edward Elgar Publishing Limited
Glensanda House
Montpellier Parade
Cheltenham
Glos GL50 1UA
UK

Edward Elgar Publishing, Inc.
136 West Street
Suite 202
Northampton
Massachusetts 01060
USA

A catalogue record for this book
is available from the British Library

Library of Congress Cataloguing in Publication Data

International handbook of urban systems : studies of urbanization and migration in advanced and developing countries / edited by H.S. Geyer.
  p. cm.
Includes index.
  1. Urbanization—Cross-cultural studies. 2. Rural-urban migration—Case studies. Cities and towns—Growth—Cross-cultural studies. I. Geyer, H.S., 1951-

HT151 .I5855 2002
307.76—dc21

2002072190

ISBN 1 84064 900 3

Printed and bound in Great Britain by MPG Books Ltd, Bodmin, Cornwall

Contents

Tables

Figures

Contributors

 Aguilar, G.A. Adrian is a Senior Researcher at the Institute of Geography, UNAM. He was head of the Social Geography Department, 1989-97 and Tinker Visiting Professor, University of Texas, Austin. With financial assistance from IDRC-Canada and CONACYT-Mexico, he conducted research on middle-sized cities, metropolitan development and urban systems. He has co-authored three books and has written more than 60 articles and chapters for national and international journals and books. He received a PhD from the University of London, U.K.

 Bae, C.C. Chang-Hee (Christine) is an Assistant Professor in the Department of Urban Design and Planning at the University of Washington, Seattle. She holds a Master's in Regional Planning from the State University of New York, Albany, and a Ph.D. in Urban and Regional Planning from the University of Southern California. She has published in leading planning and other journals. Her current research interests include: growth management in the U.S. and abroad, transportation and the environment, environmental justice, and the use of IT in planning education.

 Baeninger, R.R. Rosana has obtained her PhD in Social Science from the Campinas State University (UNICAMP). She is professor of Urban Sociology at the Department of Sociology at UNICAMP and has been associated with the Population Studies Center (NEPO) at UNICAMP since 1986. Her research interest revolves around migration and urban development trends. She has published widely on internal migration and its effects on the urban development process, especially in the State of São Paulo.

 Baycan-Levent, T. Tuzin received her Ph.D. in the field of Regional Planning from Istanbul Technical University in 1999. She is currently an Assistant Professor of Regional Planning at ITU. Her publications are mainly on Urban and Regional Planning, Sustainable Development, Environmental Issues and Water Basin Development and Management. She a member of the RSAI, the Turkish National Committee of Regional Science and the Turkish National Committee of Coastal Zone Management.

Bourne, L.S. Larry is Professor of Geography and Planning, and Director of the Graduate Program in Planning, University of Toronto. He holds a PhD, University of Chicago. He has served two terms as Director of the University's Centre for Urban and Community Studies. His research interests span the fields of urban systems analysis, demography and migration, urban form and development, inner city revitalization, housing markets and urban policy, social polarization and inequalities in cities. He has authored or edited several books and published numerous journal articles and reports, and is actively involved in both professional planning and public policy communities.

 Champion A.G. Tony is a Professor of Population Geography at the University of Newcastle upon Tyne. His research interests include urban and regional changes in population distribution and their policy implications in developed countries. He is chair of the IUSSP's Working Group on Urbanization and is author or co-author of several books and reports and numerous articles in scientific journals. Over the last three years he has carried out research for the Economic and Social Research Council and other national bodies and government departments.

 Fielding, A.J. Tony is a professor of Human Geography, School of Social Sciences, University of Sussex. He obtained his PhD from LSE, was appointed to the University of Sussex in 1964 and has remained there ever since except for Visiting Professorships in the US and Japan (1994/5 and 1998 in Ritsumeikan University, Kyoto: 2001/2 Kyoto University). His main research interests: migration in Western Europe and East Asia; the links between social and geographical mobility; internal migration and regional economic development; the geopolitics of international migration; and Japanese culture and society. He is author / co-author of numerous publications.

 Frey, W. Bill is a demographer and sociologist in the Population Studies Center, University of Michigan and is a also Senior Fellow at the Milken Institute, Santa Monica, CA. He has published widely in the areas of migration, immigration and the demography of metropolitan areas. Research Scholarships include the IIASA, Austria (1980-81), the Andrew W. Mellon Research Scholarship at the Population Reference Bureau in 1988, and the Hewlett Visiting Scholarship at Child Trends (Washington, D.C.) in 1995. He served as a consultant for U.S. government departments and the U.S. Census Bureau.

Gans, P. Paul has been Dean of the Economics Faculty in 1999/2000 and is Professor of Geography at the University of Mannheim. Before moving to Mannheim he taught at the Universities of Kiel (where he obtained his PhD), Hamburg and Erfurt. His main research interests lie in population and urban geography, quantitative methods of geography, and the regions Germany, the European Union, Latin America and India. He has an extensive list of local and international publications.

 Geyer, H.S. Manie is Professor of Regional Planning at the Potchefstroom University. He obtained a D.Phil. in regional planning, at PU. After nine years in practice, which he ended as head of Planning of the Soweto metropolitan government, he joined PU. His research interests lie in urban development theory, migration in the First and Third Worlds, urban systems analysis, and globalization. He has been visiting scholar at the University of Utah, is a regional development consultant and has co-ordinated governmental and academic research projects on a provincial, national and international level. He has published widely, nationally and internationally.

 Goede, E. Esther is a junior researcher at the Department of Spatial Economics at the Free University, Amsterdam. She specializes in urban and transportation issues and is presently a project advisor for a suburban administration in the Greater Amsterdam area in the Netherlands.

 Graizbord, B. Boris obtained his PhD from LSE and is National Program Director for LEAD, Mexico. Since 1979, he has been a research professor at the Center of Demographic Studies and Urban Development in El Colegio de Mexico. His research interests revolve around population studies, industrial pollution, medium-sized cities, metropolitan transport and regional development in Mexico. He has written more than 50 chapters and articles for books and national and international periodicals, magazines and newspapers, and has co-authored four books.

 Heikkilä, E. Elli is the Research Director of the Institute of Migration in Finland. Her licentiate thesis (1986) and dissertation (1989) have dealt with migration and regional development. Population aging was the theme of her post-doctorate research. She has taken part in two international research projects, one on differential urbanization and one on migration and the labour market. She lectures at two universities and has completed 150 scientific and popular publications.

 Ioanos, I. Ion is Director General of Education in Romania and Professor of Human Geography at the University of Bucharest. He obtained his PhD from the University of Bucharest. From 1973 until 1997 he worked at the Institute of Geography, Romanian Academy in Bucharest. He has co-ordinated research projects locally and internationally, has been visiting Professor at the University of Angers, and is author / co-author of 24 books, atlases and maps and 123 chapters in volumes and scientific articles in different national and international journals.

 Järvinen, T. Taru is a Researcher at the Institute of Migration in Finland. She has a M.Sc. and is currently doing her PhD at the Departement of Geography in University of Turku. The subject of her dissertation is the migration dynamics of dual career families in Finland.

 Jaźdźewska, I. Iwona was born in 1958 in Cracow, Poland. She graduated at the University of Łódź, 1984 (M.Sc. in mathematics), and gained a D.Sc. degree at the University of Łódź, 1998 (geographical sciences). She works in the Department of Urban Geography and Tourism, University of Łódź. Her scientific interest lies in geographical information systems, urban networks, urban morphology, and sacral space. She is scientific co-ordinator of Konwersatorium Wiedzy o Mieście (Knowledge about the City).

 Jun, M. Myung-Jin received his Ph.D. in Urban and Regional Planning, University of Southern California. He is Associate Professor of Urban and Regional Planning at Chung-Ang University, Korea. He has been on the faculty at Chung-Ang University in Korea since 1994. His primary field of interest is land use and transportation. He has recently published papers on the transportation costs of Seoul's Greenbelt and on Seoul's New Towns in journals such as the International Regional Science Review and Cities.

 Kemper, F. J. Franz-Josef Kemper is Professor of Population and Social Geography at the Department of Geography, Humboldt University in Berlin. Previously he taught at the Universities of Trier and Bonn. Among his research interests are population geography, in particular migration research, the metropolis, and research on quantitative analysis in geography. He is author / co-author of many publications.

 Mukherji, S. Shekhar obtained two Ph.D.s, one in Demography from the University of Hawaii and one in Urban Geography and Regional Planning from the University of Calcutta. From 1975 to 1976 he conducted post-doctorate research at the Australian National University. He taught for 42 years and recently retired as Chair of the Department of Migration and Urban Studies, International Institute for Population Sciences, Bombay. Over the years he has published 32 books and over 200 research papers.

 Nijkamp, P. Peter, Chair of the Research Council of the Netherlands, is a Professor of Regional and Urban Economics and Economic Geography at the Free University, Amsterdam. His main research interests cover multi-criteria analysis, regional and urban planning, transport systems analysis, mathematical modelling, technological innovation, and resource management. He has expertise in public policy, infrastructure planning / management and environmental protection. He has published many books and numerous articles and has been visiting professor in many universities all over the world. He is past president of the European Regional Science Association and the Regional Science Association International. At present, he is vice-president of the Royal Netherlands Academy of Sciences.

 Petsimeris, P. Petros is Professor of Urban Social Geography at the University of Caen and a member of the Centre de Recherche sur les Espaces et les Sociétés, UMR 6590 CNRS. He obtained his Ph.D. from the University of Caen in 1987 and his Habilitation à Diriger des Recherches in 1992. He lectured as a Visiting Professor at the Institut d'Etudes Politiques de Paris and the Universities of Pise, Trento, Naples, Udine and Turin. He has published widely.

 Pumain, D. Denise is Professor of Geography at the University of Paris I Panthéon-Sorbonne and Director of *Cybergeo,* European Journal of Geography. She is a former chair of the International Geographical Union's Commission on Urban Development and Urban Life (1992-2000) and founder (1984) and Director (1992-2000) of the research laboratory P.A.R.I.S. (UMR Géographie-cités, CNRS). She specialises in urban modelling and theoretical geography and has written several books on urban systems in France and Europe. She is director of the series 'Villes' published by Anthropos.

Richardson, H.W. Harry is the James Irvine Chair of Urban and Regional Planning in the School of Policy, Planning and Development at the University of Southern California, Los Angeles. He has written more than 20 books and 170 research papers. He has consulted for international agencies such as the World Bank and the United Nations, and also for national and local agencies. His current research interests include urban sprawl, the economic and transportation impacts of natural disasters, metropolitan travel behavior, and international urban development.

 Rykiel, Z. Zbigniew received his Ph.D. from the Institute of Geography and Spatial Organisation, Polish Academy of Sciences, Warsaw. He is Head of the Department of Human Geography and Space Economy, Casimir the Great Academy at Bydgoszcz and Professor, College of Finance and Management at Biaystok. His main research interests are urbanization, settlement systems, migration, spatial barriers, regionalization, (regional). social geography, methodology, theory and philosophy of geography, history of Polish geography, political geography, and space economy.

 Simmons, J.W. Jim Simmons is Professor Emeritus in the Department of Geography of the University of Toronto, and Senior Research Fellow at the Centre for the Study of Commercial Activity at Ryerson Polytechnic University in Toronto. He was born in Canada, received his PhD from the University of Chicago, and currently lives in Victoria B.C. For more than thirty years he has mapped and analyzed the Canadian urban system. He is the author / co-author of numerous books, chapters and articles.

 van der Merwe, I.J. Izak received his D.Phil. in Urban Geography, University of Stellenbosch. After 30 years as Lecturer, Professor and Chair in Geography at Stellenbosch, he became Dean of the Faculty of Arts and Social Sciences in 1997. He received the Stals Price for Geography from the South African Academy of Science and Arts and was awarded a fellowship from the South African Geographical Society, of which he was the President in 1995/1996. He has published 45 scientific articles in local and international accredited journals, and is author/co-author of seven books/atlases and nine research reports.

Acknowledgements

The outcome of a publication of this nature is not the product of one person's labour. First, I want to thank the chapter authors and co-authors for their dedication and hard work, often under difficult circumstances. A special word of thanks is owed to the staff of the Edward Elgar Publishing Company, especially Edward Elgar for believing in the viability of the project and Julie Leppard, Alexandra Minton, Nep Athwal, Caroline McLin and Melanie Waller for their professional management of the publication process.

I am also endebted to Brendan Cahill who was responsible for the computer graphics and lay out of the manuscript, Antonia Hebbert, Riana and Wim Voordewind, and Eleanor Geyer who grammar edited the manuscript, and Philip and Kobie Geyer, Elsje Gelderbloem, Laetitia Oosthuizen and Laurette Coetzee, who assisted with the computer editing of the text.

I want to pay tribute to my friend Cees Gorter and my son Christo Geyer, who passed away while this project was in progress. Cees was a gifted researcher who originally formed part of the Netherlands' team. Christo, whose promising teenage-years barely started when his life was ended, remains a large part of my inspiration.

Acknowledgement is hereby given to the South African National Research Foundation for its financial support of an international colloquium that was held in South Africa and for subsequent editorial control while the case studies were in progress. Views that are expressed in this book are those of the authors and do not necessarily correspond with those of the Foundation.

H. S. Geyer
August, 2002.

Preface

The original idea of an edited volume reflecting urban changes that have occurred in selected countries over the past half century, was inspired by the writings of H.G. Wells. Judging from improvements in communication technology a century ago, and mixing fact with a good measure of common sense and creative thinking, H.G. Wells (1902) anticipated great changes in urban development during the twentieth century. The following collage of quotations from his book, in italics, highlights what he foresaw.

Firstly, he predicted that advances in the technology of the combustion engine, which led to developments such as the private motor car, short and long haul trucking and bus services – all of which were designed to improve the transportation of goods, material and people in and between cities – would ultimately result in the development of *giant cities*. Although George Gissing, the nineteenth century novelist and good friend of Wells, stated that giant cities such as London were little more than attractive, tumultuous whirlpools[1] that ultimately would be 'spinning down to death', Wells was much more optimistic. Based on his assessment of the effect new advances in transport technology on land, sea and in the sky would have on urban development, Wells predicted that *these new forces, at present still so potently centripetal in their influence, bring with them, the distinct promise of a centrifugal application that may be finally equal to the complete reduction of all our present congestions.*

The passion for nature, a *house in its own garden*, the *healthful-ness of the country*, and the *wholesome isolation that is possible from much that irritates* in cities, he listed as important *centrifugal attractions* that would cause cities to expand into giant cities. On the other hand, the *greater convenience* of locations close to schools and shopping facilities, department stores which collectively *establish a sort of monopoly of suburban trade* by providing a variety of products *from some one vast indiscriminate shop or store full of respectable mediocre goods*, and *the love of the crowd, the dress*, and *the crush*, as well as *the hot passion for the promenade* are listed as centripetal attractions.

---

[1] See George Gissing's classic book *The Whirlpool*.

Where great cities of the nineteenth century *presented rounded contours* that *grew like puff-ball swells*, the modern city of his time became *star shaped, thrusting out arms along every available railway line*. They looked like *something that has burst an intolerable envelope and splashed*. Referring to these two forms of urban deconcentration, first pushing out towards the fringes of the city and, later on, also along connecting roads between cities, he said: *To the subsidiary centres will be drawn doctor and school-master, and various dealers in fresh provisions, baker, grocer and butcher*. Along the *new roads will be way-side restaurants and tea-houses, and motor and cycle stores and repair places. These coming cities will not be, in the old sense, cities at all; they will present a new and entirely different phase of human distribution*.

Each great city, according to Wells, *is sustained by the trade and production of a certain proportion of the world's surface – by the area it commands commercially*. However, he anticipated an end to urban growth. *Even if we allowed for considerable increase in the production of food stuffs in the future, it still remains inevitable that the increase of each city in the world must come at last upon arrest*.

Communication, he suggested, shall remain pivotal in urban development. *The general distribution of population in a country must always be directly dependent on transport facilities.* · In fact, the position and the population limit of towns are, according to him, determined by *strategic considerations – in a word, communications*.

Considering the effect people's increasing mobility will have on long-term migration trends in England, he summarized the broad features of the redistribution of people during the nineteenth century, as *an unusual growth of great cities* coupled with a *tendency to depopulation in the country*. In his vision of the development of vast megalopolitan areas, he did not regard it as far-fetched that *the London citizen of the year 2000 A.D. may have a choice of nearly all England and Wales south of Nottingham and east of Exeter as his suburb, and that the vast stretch of country from Washington to Albany will be all of it 'available' to the active citizen of New York and Philadelphia before that date*.

These were the visions of Wells at the beginning of the twentieth century, and these same issues are fascinating scholars of urban change today, and will continue to do so in the years ahead. Although the urbanization trends described by Wells continued for many decades, and by the 1960s were expected to continue for much longer, very significant changes in the urban environment had occurred by the end of that decade. A turnaround from urbanization to polarization reversal and later to counter-urbanization was observed in the migration trends of a number of Developed Countries by the end of the 1960s and beginning of the 1970s. During the same period signs of concentration forces beginning to yield to deconcentration forces, were also found in certain Advanced Developing Countries. Later on, during the

1980s, the counter-urbanization trends in certain Developed Countries suddenly and unexpectedly started to subside. In certain cases the second turnaround seems to continue, in others it seems to be short-lived and one may, once again, see the return of fully fledged counter-urbanization.

Sufficient time has now passed since the last concerted efforts were made to reflect back on the duration of each of these phases of urban development in the Developed and Developing World. Questions that need to be investigated are: what long-term migration trends are visible in Developed and Developing Countries in different parts of the world; which factors have been playing an important role in these migration trends in the maturation of urban systems over the years; and what are the consequences of these trends for the future? Addressing these issues is the aim of this book.

Specific questions that are being addressed in the book include: first, what are the similarities and differences in the duration of the phases of urban development that have occurred in Developed Countries and second, how do these phases differ from those occurring in Advanced Developing Countries? Of particular interest are the forces that cause these cycles of population concentration and deconcentration in Developed and Advanced Developing Countries and, especially, the role main and under-current migration streams play in these long-term fluctuations.

The book is divided into two parts. The purpose of the first part is threefold. An introductory chapter defines and explains relevant concepts by moving systematically through the basic ideas and general principles in urban systems analysis. The following two chapters give the current status of views on migration theory and urban systems. Although the first of these two chapters focuses more on the Developing World and the latter on issues in the Developed World, the sets of issues are not mutually exclusive. Some of the issues prevalent in the Developed World also apply to the Developing World, and vice versa, especially those regarding migration theory. Finally, insight gained from views expressed by contributors on current and future trends in migration and in urban maturation are brought together in the final chapter of the first part of the book. Where the first three chapters of Part One deal with the past, the last chapter is concerned with what lies ahead.

Because a wide spectrum of topics is relevant in a study of this nature, not all concepts and principles could be explained in detail in Part One of the book nor is the book intended to serve as an introduction to this field. Students at the under-graduate level who are reading the first three chapters are therefore advised to do some additional reading. For this reason the second and third chapters contain an extensive list of references on each topic that is discussed. Those students who follow this advice will be richly rewarded because as they work their way through the references an intricate but fascinating world will unfold.

In Part Two, a number of prominent researchers are given the opportunity to express their views on the evolution of urban development in a selection of

Developed and Advanced Developing Countries. It is hoped that the inclusion of Developed and Developing Countries in the same study will help overcome the problem of compartmentalization that has plagued research in this field for so many years.

In the chapters in Part Two, an evaluation is first given of the history of urban development trends of each country. Chapters in this part of the book refer to functional urban sub-systems. These include the identification of primary cities and the lower order (intermediate- and small-sized) centres that are functionally related to these primary cities. Sequences in the development of different groups of cities over time are depicted by a geographical analysis of migration gains and losses in these urban sub-systems. Collectively, the study results contained in the case studies in the second part of the book give an insight into the possible longer-term consequences main and sub-stream migration hold for future urban development, and this information may open up new areas for further research.

Based on the selection of themes and the way in which the material was handled by the contributors, the audience should include scholars in the fields of geography, planning, regional studies, economics, social science, history, architecture and public administration. The book will be of interest to under- and post-graduate students as well as advanced researchers in these fields.

Manie Geyer
August, 2002.

PART ONE

Theoretical fundamentals

Chapter 1

The Fundamentals of Urban Space

H. S. Geyer

SPATIAL CHARACTERISTICS OF CITIES

When the maturation of urban systems is studied, as has been done in the case studies in this book, a number of fundamental issues in the relationship between individual towns and cities and their hinterlands needs to be understood. Because this book will also be read by undergraduate students at the entry level, some of the basic concepts will be explained to serve as an introduction to the chapters that follow.

According to Gradmann (1916: 427) an urban centre fulfils two **important functions**: it serves as 'a centre of its rural surroundings and as the mediator of interaction with the world outside'. The size and importance of the city, according to Wells (1902: 47), are determined by its '**sphere of influence**'. The first relationship in the quotation from Gradmann refers to the urban **hinterland** or service area, while the other refers to its sphere of influence. Although the two concepts are sometimes treated in the literature as synonyms they are not exactly the same thing. The hinterland or service area of a town or city is something less than its sphere of influence. The service area is the area dominated by a centre while its sphere of influence can penetrate the service areas of other competing centres. The closest analogy one can find between a centre's hinterland and its sphere of influence lies in Christaller's (1966: 60) distinction between what he terms the 'real' or 'relative' limit of the range of a good or service and its 'ideal' or 'absolute' range.[1] The service area of a town or city refers to its market area, i.e. the area it dominates directly around it, while its sphere of influence refers to the

---

[1] The real limit refers to the catchment area of a business as determined by the competition of competitors in a uniform plain, while the ideal limit is determined by the largest distance a person is willing to travel to visit the business.

outer limits of its interaction field. The size of its hinterland is determined by competition from businesses and organizations of surrounding towns and cities, while the centre's sphere of influence can reach into or even beyond the hinterlands of nearby centres.[2]

The **principle of least effort** (Zipf, 1949; Lösch, 1954) plays a pivotal role in the size of an urban settlement's hinterland because, *ceteris paribus*, people more often than not obtain goods and services from a centre that is the closest to them. This tendency is based on the concept of **friction of distance**. Under varying circumstances the term **distance** can have different meanings. There is '**objective**' and '**subjective**' distance, the former referring to a measure of distance which could be interpreted similarly by all people, and the latter to a measure that could be interpreted differently by different people. Concepts such as '**real**' or '**physical**' distance (e.g. miles or kilometres), or '**economic**' distance (measured in terms of time and cost) are examples of objective distance. Subjective distance is measured in terms of comfort, gratification, laziness, personal choice, etc., none of which would be interpreted exactly the same by two individuals. Generally speaking, there is a direct relationship between the distances people have to travel and their resistance to travel those distances. The longer the distance, the greater the resistance. It is this resistance that normally results in what is known as **distance decay**.

These concepts play an important role in communication. Historically, communication has played a determinant role in the location and development of towns and cities and therefore also in the evolution of urban systems.[3] According to Wells (1902), for instance, 'definite points of convenience' in rural England (i.e. locations which people found desirable for local trade and interaction) were largely determined by general transport modes at the time.

> This distance in England, where traffic has been mainly horse traffic for many centuries, seems to have worked out, according to the gradients and so forth, at from eight to fifteen miles, and at such distances do we find the country towns…If by chance these gathering-places have arisen at points much closer than this maximum, they have come into competition, and one has finally got the better of the other, so that in England the distribution is often singularly uniform. Agricultural districts have their towns at about eight miles, and where grazing takes the place of the plough, the town distances increase to fifteen.

---

[2] It should be noted that reference is made to the competition of businesses and organizations in urban centres, and not competition of urban centres as such. Towns and cities do not compete, their businesses do (Krugmann, 1996; Begg, 1999).

[3] Advances in the computer industry and in information technology had a significant impact on urban change over the past four decades (Castells, 1996; Graham, 1998).

In South Africa, where the largest part of the country was settled by farmers during the Great Trek[4] from 1836 to 1838, rural towns are between 35 and 40 miles apart due to the larger sizes of farms. As communication technology improved, certain central places grew bigger. In a train of cause and effect such larger centres gained centrality because people could travel longer distances as a result of improved transportation which allowed for larger collections of goods and services in regionally convenient points, hence the development of regional centres.

URBAN SYSTEMS

According to **central place theory** a hierarchy of **central places** develops as a result of a wide distribution of people that need goods and services. Christaller (1966) looked at the establishment of such central places from the supply side, Lösch from the demand side[5]. But there are also **non-central places**. These are mining, religious, military, and other kinds of centres that locate as a result of **locational constants,**[6] irrespective of the current distribution of people. Together, central and non-central places represent the full spectrum of towns and cities that can be observed by a person when looking at an atlas.

At this point in the treatment of the fundamentals of urban systems theory, the concept of **hierarchy of urban centres** (Christaller, 1966; Lösch, 1954), which relates to the concept of **urban systems** (Bourne and Simmons, 1978), intersects with a huge body of literature, collectively referred to as **location theory**.[7] This body of theory deals with the factors that determine the location of social and economic activities in space, and **agglomeration economies** (Fujita and Thisse, 1996; Parr, 2002a, 2002b; Malmberg and Maskell, 2002; Richardson, 1973) are one of the important factors in the manifestation of urban hierarchy. Single urban nodes and their hinterlands are examples of **nodal regions**, which are the simplest representation of functional, social and economic space. Clusters of nodal regions are called

---

[4] See the South African Chapter, Part Two for more detail.

[5] The original central place models could be regarded as static representations of a dynamic phenomenon. Various attempts have subsequently been made to highlight the dynamic elements of urban systems (Allen, 1997; Pumain, 2000).

[6] Locational constants according to Richardson (1973: 173) include: "(I) an immobile natural resource (e.g. an area of mineral deposits, a deep water harbour); (ii) a long-established city (its foundation may have been based on a now obsolete locational advantage, pure chance or explained by historical factors); (iii) particular sites that have special advantages due to (a) the heterogeneity of land or (b) being potentially nodal locations from the point of view of future transportation development, and that are developed earlier than other sites".

[7] A few of the many classical works in this field include Weber (1929), Hoover (1963), Isard (1956), Alonso (1964), Smith (1970), and Haggett et al. (1977).

polarized regions (Boudeville, 1967), and depending on the level of aggregation, these clusters of nodal regions could refer to anything between shopping centres in a metropolitan area, to towns and cities that interact more with one another inside the polarized region than with other towns and cities outside the region. The latter could be clusters of towns and cities at the local, regional, national, international, or even global level, each one representing a different level of **territorially organized space** (Friedmann, 1972), and each one individually representing an urban system at a different level of spatial aggregation.

Looking at urban systems from the bottom upwards, and expanding on Perroux's (1950, 1950a) view on the **domination principle** of the firm, all economic interaction patterns can be seen at three levels of aggregation, micro, meso and macro. At the micro level, a socio-economic unit (which could be any firm or organization[8]) normally displays some degree of unity in terms of its organization, but this unity in organization does not necessarily display the same degree of geographical unity,[9] and in such cases cannot be easily shown on a map. As one zooms out of the micro level to the meso level of spatial aggregation, however, the socio-economic unit often begins to show more geographical coherence, and its **area of influence** starts becoming visible. Perroux (1950) calls this the socio-economic unit's 'field of force' which is synonymous with Christaller's (1966) concept of **range of a good** or service.[10] When one continues to zoom out to the macro level, more of the same kind of socio-economic units, each one battling to maintain its own field of force against those of competitors in the same area, can be discerned. Together, the socio-economic units and their areas of influence are constantly in a state of tension, one always trying to gain on another's area of influence within socio-economic space. When one becomes more competitive, its area of influence increases as a result. Together, these units with their areas of influence could be regarded as one layer of activities that are needed to fulfil the needs of people living in an area. But there are many other needs as well resulting in other similar layers of units, each layer with its own spatial characteristics. Based on their social or economic characteristics, these layers can be grouped together in the nine **layers of**

---

[8] Wherever an economic unit locates in geographical space, Christaller's (1966: 17, 24n) 'central place' (which he defines as a firm point in space, a position or place of public interaction) comes into being.

[9] The economic unit's constituent parts may, for instance, not be located in one building which could make it difficult to demarcate at this level of spatial aggregation.

[10] Parr and Denike (1970) demonstrate how factors such as changing technology, government policy and the quality of infrastructure could change the ranges of goods or services.

human activities shown in Figure 1.1.[11] Collections of such socio-economic units at specific locations in space and their generalized areas of influence – the hinterland – result in towns and cities which together form an urban system. Small collections of activities form low-order centres, and large collections large centres.

Figure 1.1 A human activities model

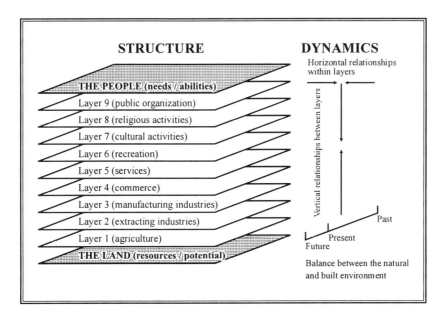

STRUCTURE

DYNAMICS

Horizontal relationships within layers

THE PEOPLE (needs / abilities)

Layer 9 (public organization)

Layer 8 (religious activities)

Layer 7 (cultural activities)

Layer 6 (recreation)

Layer 5 (services)

Layer 4 (commerce)

Layer 3 (manufacturing industries)

Layer 2 (extracting industries)

Layer 1 (agriculture)

THE LAND (resources / potential)

Vertical relationships between layers

Past

Present

Future

Balance between the natural and built environment

Source: Geyer, 2001

In his classic study of the principles that guide the **functional organization of urban areas** in geographical space, Philbrick (1957) identified seven layers of interaction patterns. Looking at urban systems from the bottom upwards, he regards the individual firm or residential unit as a first order unit which makes it possible for firms and organizations to establish. A collection of such firms and organizations could form the business centre of a small village, or a focal point in a larger centre, such as a shopping centre or industrial area. Collectively the areas of influence of the firms and organizations form the area of influence of the village or the

---

[11] In this model (Geyer, 2001), socio-cultural layers that potentially impact on human settlement patterns have been added to the economic layers in Weber's (1929) original industrial development model.

shopping centre, – the second order unit. Philbrick calls this the 'focal point'. A 'cluster of local places' forms a third order central place, and 'clusters of clusters of local places', fourth order or regional centres. Fifth order centres are nodal points at the national level, sixth order centres are nodal points at the international level, and centres at the seventh level have a global influence.

Looking at the **city-size distributions** of a number of countries, ranging from the most to less developed categories, Berry (1961) distinguished between primate, intermediate and log-normal city size distributions. In former distributions one or a few cities dominate the urban system as a whole. During the intermediate phase, centres of the middle order have gained some ground on the primate cities, and during the latter phase they have achieved log-normality. In the study it was found that large countries with long histories of urbanization normally display a large degree of log-normality, while smaller countries with shorter histories of urbanization can be expected to show a larger degree of primacy. The level of development of the country cannot necessarily be determined from the rank-size distribution.

URBAN SYSTEMS EVOLUTION

Building on Friedmann's (1966) **core-periphery model** and adding factors such as 'locational constants' and **social, household and business agglomeration economies** to the picture above, the space economy in which a country's urban system is embedded typically goes through three phases of development according to Richardson (1973). First it goes through a phase of **convergence** when the urban system gains in **primacy**.

> The urban-industrial process of national development begins in one or two regions only, primarily because of the scarcity of investment resources…This initial start becomes a *cumulative causation* process explained by increasing returns to scale and the consequent *polarization* of labor and any surplus capital from other regions. The core-periphery relationship is thus established…where the *core region* consisting of the primate city and its hinterland dominates the rest of the space economy, called the periphery. This periphery is dominated by the core and dependent on it, and its rate of development is controlled and distorted so as to further the core's economic interests.
>
> At a more advanced stage of development, a spatial transformation begins to occur within the core region. The population and agglomeration of economic activities in the primate city become so large that a *monocentric spatial structure* becomes inefficient and costly. Congestion costs and rising land values induce some economic activities to decentralized to *satellite centers* within the core region. These centers may intercept new migrants who are attracted by job opportunities expanding at a more rapid rate than in the primate city (Richardson, 1980, p.67).

This phase of **urbanization** correlates with the 'Early' and 'Intermediate Primate City Stages' shown in Figure 1.2a and 1.2b. Subsequently, polarization forces start giving way to deconcentration forces and economic **divergence** sets in. This phase corresponds with the 'Advanced Primate' and 'Early Intermediate City Stages' shown in Figure 1.2c and 1.2d. According to Richardson (1980, p.68):

> These conditions are probably associated with the generation of agglomeration economies and other scale economies at selected locations in the periphery, and these reflect the diffusion of technical knowledge from the core, rising population and incomes, expanding markets...the exploitation of local resources, lower input costs, improvements in communications, the build-up of infrastructure and other factors making economic expansion at these locations profitable. The dispersion process may be accelerated by obstacles to continued rapid expansion in the core region, such as soaring land and labor costs, increasing congestion...pressure on housing and infrastructure, and above-average rate of increase in living costs. However, the dispersion takes place very unevenly, with most of the growth outside the core region occurring at a limited set of relatively large urban centers. In a sense, the national concentration within the core region is replicated by regional concentration in major regional centers.

At this stage, spatially, the economy has become highly integrated with certain secondary and tertiary centres growing faster than primate cities. Interaction between the closest secondary and tertiary centres and the primate city may lead to the emerging of **development axes**.[12] This phase corresponds with the 'advanced intermediate city' and 'small city phases' in Figure 1.2. The second phase is associated with the concept of **polarization reversal** (Richardson, 1977, 1980)[13] and the final phase with **counter-urbanization** (Beal, 1977).[14] Together these phases, which include main and substream migration, have been termed **differential urbanization** (Geyer and Kontuly, 1993; Geyer, 1996).[15]

Figure 1.2 is a diagrammatic representation of phases of urban evolution from urbanization to counter-urbanization. Although they normally represent

---

[12] For an explanation of the development properties of development axes concept see Pottier, 1963 and Geyer, 1989.

[13] Subsequent studies on polarization reversal are found in Linn (1978), Townroe and Keen (1984), Lo and Salih (1979), Geyer (1990) and Bähr and Wehrhahn (1997).

[14] Many subsequent studies on counter-urbanization have appeared since the mid-1970s, the most notable of which are Berry (1976), Vining and Kontuly (1978), Frey (1987), Fielding (1989) and Champion (1989, 1989).

[15] Studies on differential urbanization include Geyer (1990, 1996, 1998), Geyer and Kontuly (1993), Elliott (1997), Tammaru (2000), and unintentionally also Gilbert (1993).

Figure 1.2 Phases of differential urbanization

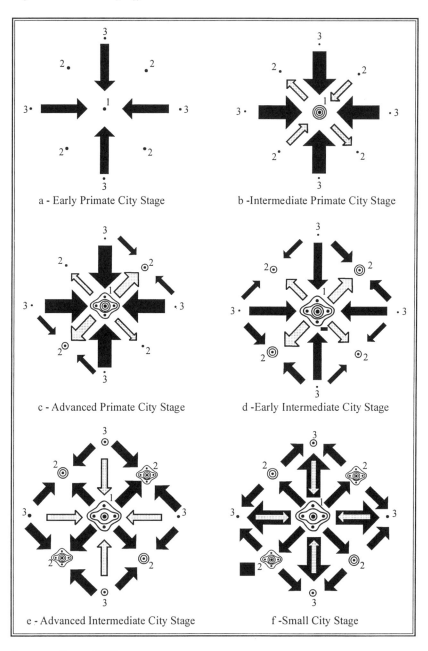

a - Early Primate City Stage

b -Intermediate Primate City Stage

c - Advanced Primate City Stage

d -Early Intermediate City Stage

e - Advanced Intermediate City Stage

f -Small City Stage

Source: Geyer, 1996

a sequence (Geyer and Kontuly, 1993), phases may not necessarily follow chronologically. External circumstances such as the dramatic political changes that occurred in South Africa at the end of the previous century may cause an urban system to re-enter a phase it has gone through already. An idealized picture of the evolution of urban systems as they pass through one complete cycle of urbanization, polarization reversal, and counter-urbanization is shown on Figure 1.3. Migration trends at the peak of the urbanization, polarization reversal and counter-urbanization phases, as well as at the mid-positions in between, are shown in Figure 1.4. During the urbanization phase there is a positive relationship between the net migration rate and settlement size (Figure 1.4B), while, as is shown in Figure 1.4F, the relationship is negative during counter-urbanization (Fielding, 1989). During the polarization reversal phase the relationship is either parabolic or leptokurtic (Figure 1.4D). The other possible intermediate phases are shown in the other parts of the figure.[16]

In general terms urban evolution seems to follow the same pattern all over the world. First there is a phase of **urban settlement establishment** at which time rural settlements are formed. In the European context this phase occurred from approximately the Neolithic era until the Modern era. In the process agricultural oriented communities were gradually transformed into urban oriented communities. The second phase could be called the **urban differentiation phase** when, as a result of improved mobility (Zelinsky, 1971) and the expansion and specialization of urban activities, larger urban settlements are formed, often at the expense of smaller ones. Early stages of this phase are often associated with the problem of **premature urbanization** (Geyer, 1989) resulting in **over-urbanization** (Gugler, 1990). Finally, an urban system enters the urban stabilization phase when concentration forces start giving way to deconcentration. This phase is associated with the concepts of polarization reversal and eventually also counter-urbanization. Whereas urbanization is largely associated with developing countries, polarization reversal is largely linked to more advanced developing countries, and counter-urbanization to highly developed nations. During the urbanization phase, indications are that **productionism** oriented migration (i.e. migration aimed at improving people's ability to find employment) seems to be dominant, while **environmentalism** – i.e. pleasant living conditions – becomes more important during counter-urbanization (Hart, 1983; Geyer and Kontuly, 1993; Geyer, 1996, 1998).

---

[16] These trends are obviously also idealized representations. In reality, as was demonstrated in the case of France (Geyer, 1996), the curves could appear much less smooth.

Figure 1.3 An idealized characterization of one complete cycle of differential urbanization

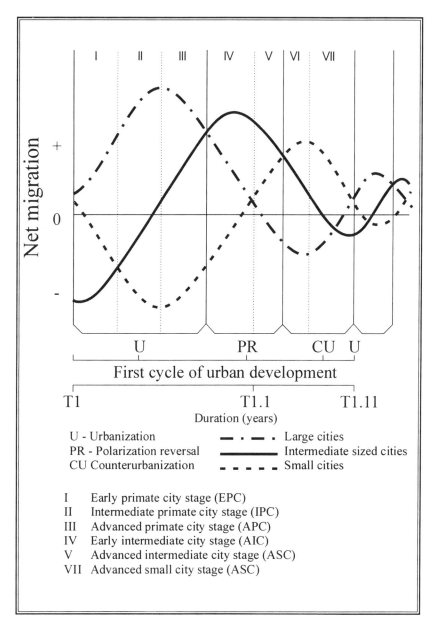

U - Urbanization
PR - Polarization reversal
CU Counterurbanization

— · — · Large cities
———— Intermediate sized cities
■ ■ ■ ■ ■ Small cities

I   Early primate city stage (EPC)
II   Intermediate primate city stage (IPC)
III   Advanced primate city stage (APC)
IV   Early intermediate city stage (AIC)
V   Advanced intermediate city stage (ASC)
VII   Advanced small city stage (ASC)

Source: Geyer and Kontuly, 1993

Figure 1.4 Changing relationships between net migration rate and settlement size during a complete cycle of urban development

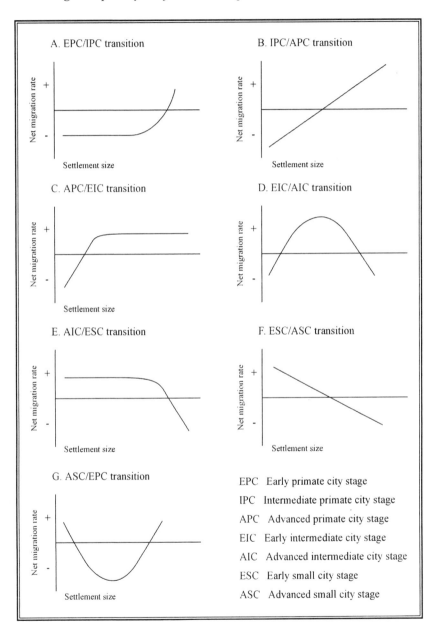

At the international level, governments of the advanced economies of the world[17] have endeavoured to maximise their geo-political dominance throughout the ages. However, **globalization** has attained a new meaning during the second half, but especially the last two decades of the twentieth century. Advancements in computer and communication technology have led to the transformation of modern economies into super-modern **information-driven economies**. Primate cities of these advanced economies – first described as world cities (Hall, 1966; Friedmann and Wolff; Friedmann, 1986) and later as global cities (Sassen, 1991, 2001) – have now become the key financial and transnational corporate command and control centres of the world (Amin and Graham, 1997). While the normal day-to-day social and business transactions of most people in towns and cities still occur within the confines of **local, regional and national urban space** due to the persisting limiting influence of friction of distance (Storper and Scott, 1995), new technologically sophisticated financial and service sectors are evolving which are rendering the traditional concepts of local urban hinterlands increasingly meaningless. As a result, urban systems that were previously largely defined in national terms are now more and more being integrated into a **global urban network**. In the process, Developed Countries have progressed from a Fordist to a post-Fordist industrial era resulting in gradual changes in the **international division of labour** globally. During the Fordist period manufacturing occurred mainly in the First World while the less developed world provided it with production materials. This led to the first international division of labour. Eventually the high cost of labour in advanced countries forced Fordist-oriented production plants towards the low labour cost countries of the world while the former concentrated on economic sectors requiring higher order thinking skills (Marshall, 1995), i.e. the second international division of labour (Forbel et al., 1980). While the three global core regions of the world, North America, Western Europe and the Pacific Core (Japan), tended to vigorously compete in all facets of the global economy during the second period, early indications of closer economic ties between each of the core regions and peripheral areas adjacent to them are emerging, perhaps an indication of the beginning of a new third international division of labour (Lipietz, 1997).

REFERENCES

Allen, P. M. (1997) *Cities and regions as self-organizing systems: models of complexity*, Amsterdam: Gordon and Breach Science Publishers.

---

[17] The term 'Advance Economies' should be interpreted in relative terms here because at every point in the history urban development there were countries that were more developed than others.

Alonso, W. (1974), *Location and land use:Toward a general theory of land rent,* Cambridge Mass.: Harvard University Press.

Amin, A. and S. Graham (1997) 'The ordinary city', *Transactions of the Institute of British Geographers,* **22**, 411-429.

Bähr, J. and R. Wehrhahn (1997), 'Polarization reversal in Sâo Paulo', in T. von Naerssen, M. Rutten, and A. Zoomers (eds), *The diversity of development: Essays in honor of Jan Kleinpenning,* Assen, Netherlands: Van Gorcum, pp. 166-179.

Beale, C. L. (1977), 'The Recent Shift of United States Population to Nonmetropolitan Areas, 1970-75', *International Regional Science Review,* **2**, 113-122.

Begg, B. (1999) Cities and competitiveness, *Urban Studies,* **36**, pp.795-809.

Berry, B. J. L. (1961), 'City size distributions and economic development', *Economic Development and Cultural Change,* **9**, 573-588.

Berry, B. J. L. (1976), 'The counterurbanization process: Urban America since 1970', *Urban Affairs Annual Review,* **11**, 17-30.

Boudeville, J-R. (1967), *Problems of regional economic planning,* Edinburgh: Edinburgh University Press.

Bourne, L. S. and J. W. Simmons (eds) (1978), *Systems of cities: Readings on structure, growth, and policy,* New York: Oxford University Press.

Castells, M. (1996), *The rise of the network society,* Oxford: Blackwell.

Champion, A. G. (ed.) (1989), *Counterurbanization: The changing pace and nature of population deconcentration,* London: Edward Arnold.

Champion, A. G. (1992), 'Urban and regional demographic trends in the Developed World', *Urban Studies,* **29**, 461-482.

Christaller, W. (1933), *Central places of Southern Germany,* Baskin C.W. (trl) Englewood Cliffs, N.J.: Prentice-Hall.

Elliott, J. R. (1997), 'Cycles within the system: Metropolitanisation and internal migration in the US, 1965-90', *Urban Studies* **34**, 21-41.

Fielding, A. J. (1989), 'Migration and Urbanization in Western Europe', *The Geographical Journal,* **155**, 60-69.

Forbel, F., J. Henrichs, and O. Kreya (1980), *The new international division of labour,* Cambridge: Cambridge University Press.

Frey, W. H. (1987), 'Migration and depopulation of the metropolis: regional restructuring or rural renaissance?', *American Sociological Review,* **52**, 240-257.

Friedmann, J. (1966), *Regional development policy: A case study of Venezuela,* Cambridge, Mass.: MIT.

Friedmann, J. (1972), 'A general theory of polarized development', in N.M. Hansen (ed.), *Growth centres in regional economic development*, New York: The Free Press, pp.82-107.

Friedmann, J. (1986), 'The world city hypothesis', *Development and change*, **17**, 69-84.

Friedmann, J. and Wolff, G. (1982), 'World city formation: An agenda for research action'. *International Journal of Urban and Regional Research*, **5**, 309-343.

Geyer, H. S. (1989), 'Apartheid in South Africa and industrial deconcentartion in the PWV area', *Planning Perspectives*, **4**, 251-269.

Geyer, H. S. (1989), 'The terminology, definition and classification of development axes', *South African Geographer*, **16**, 113-129.

Geyer, H. S. (1990), 'Implications of differential urbanization on deconcentration in the Pretoria-Witwatersrand-Vaal Triangle metropolitan area, South Africa', *Geoforum,* **21**, 385-396.

Geyer, H. S. (1996), 'Expanding the theoretical foundation of differential urbanization', *Tijdschrift voor Economische en Sociale Geografie*, **87**, 44-59.

Geyer, H. S. (1998), 'Differential urbanization and international migration: An urban systems approach', in C. Gorter, P. Nijkamp, and J. Poot (eds), *Crossing borders: regional and urban perspectives on international migration*. Aldershot: Ashgate, pp.161-184.

Geyer, H. S. (2001), 'Development planning transition in South Africa', in H. C. Marais, Y. Methien, N. S. Jansen van Rensburg, M. P. Maaga, G. F. de Wet, C. J. Coetzee (eds), *Sustainable social development: Critical dimensions*. Pretoria, Network Publishers, pp 143-152.

Geyer, H. S. and T. M. Kontuly (1993) A theoretical foundation for the concept of differential urbanization. *International Regional Science Review*, **15**, 157-177.

Gilbert, A. (1993), 'Third World Cities: The changing national settlements system', *Urban Studies*, **30**, (3/5), 721-740.

Gradmann, R. (1916), *Schwäbische Städte,* Gesellschaft für Erdkunde zu Berlin, April 8, pp.425-457.

Graham, S. (1998), 'The end of geography or the explosion of place? Conceptualizing space, place and information technology', *Progress in Human Geography*, **22**, 165-185.

Gugler, J. (1990), 'Overurbanization reconsidered', in J. Gugler (ed.), *The urbanisation of the Third World*, Oxford: Oxford University Press, pp.74-92.

Haggett, P., A. D. Cliff, and A. Frey (1977), *Locational analysis in human geography*. London: Edward Arnold.

Hall, P. (1966), *The world cities*, London: Weidenfeld and Nicolson.

Hart, T. (1983), 'Transport and economic development: the historical dimension', in K. J. Button and D. Gillingwater (eds), *Transport location and spatial policy*. Aldershot, Hants. U.K.: Gower. pp. 12-22.

Hoover, E. M. (1963), *The location of economic activity*, New York: McGraw-Hill.

Isard, W. (1956), *Location and space-economy: A general theory relating to industrial location, market areas, land-use, trade, and urban structure*, Cambridge, Mass.: MIT.

Krugman, P. (1996), 'Making senses of the competitiveness debate'. *Oxford Review of Economic Policy*, **12**, 17-25.

Lipietz, A. (1997), 'The post-Frodist world', *Review of International Political Economy*, **4**, 1-41.

Linn, J. F. (1978), *Urbanization trends, polarization reversal, and spatial policy in Colombia*, Münster: Wilhelms-Universität, Institut für Siedlungs- und Wohnungswsen der Westfalischen, Paper No. 12.

Lo, F. and K. Salih (1979), 'Growth poles, agropolitan development and polarization reversal: The debate and search for alternatives', in W. Stöhr and D. R. F. Taylor (eds), *Development from above and below? A radical reappraisal of spatial planning in Developing Countries*. New York: John Wiley, pp. xx.

Lösch, A. (1954), *The economics of location*, New Haven: Yale University Press.

Malmberg, A. and P. Maskell (2002), 'The elusive concept of localization economies: Towards a knowledge-based theory of spatial clustering', *Environment and Planning A*, **34**, 429-449.

Marshall, R. (1995), 'The global jobs crisis', *Foreign Policy*, No.100, 50-68.

Parr, J. B. (2002a), 'Agglomeration economies: Ambiguities and confusions', *Enivironment and Planning A*, **34**, 717-731.

Parr, J. B. (2002b), 'Missing elements in the analysis of agglomeration economies', *International Regional Science Review*, **25**, 151-168.

Parr, J. B. and Denike, K. G. (1970), 'Theoretical problems in central place analysis', *Economic Geography*, **40**, 568-586.

Perroux, F. (1950), 'Economic space: Theory and applications', *Quarterly Journal of Economics*, **LXIV**, 89-104.

Perroux, F. (1950a), 'The domination effect and modern economic theory'. *Social Research*, **17**, 188-206.

Philbrick, A. K. (1957), 'Principles of areas functional organization in regional human geography', *Economic Geography*, **33**, 299-336.

Pottier, P. (1963), 'Axes de communication et developpement Economique', *Revue Economique*, **14**, 50-132

Pumain, D. (2000), 'An evolutionary model of urban systems', in I. Iaonos, D. Pumain, and J. B. Racine, (eds) *Integrated urban systems and sustainability of urban life*, Bucarest: Editura Tehnica.

Richardson, H. W. (1973), *Economic growth theory*, London: MacMillan.

Richardson, H. W. (1977), *City size and national strategies in Developing Countries*, World Bank Staff Working Report, Washington.

Richardson, H. W. (1980), 'Polarization reversal in Developing Countries', *Papers of the Regional Science Association*, **45**, 67-85.

Sassen, S. (1991) *The global city*, Princeton University Press, Princeton.

Sassen, S. (2001) *The global city*, Princeton University Press, Woodstock, Second Edition.

Smith, D. M. (1970) *Industrial location: an economic geographical analysis*, New York: John Wiley and Sons.

Storper, M. and Scott, A. J. (1995), 'The wealth of regions: Market forces and plicy imperatives in local and global context', *Future*, **27**, 505-526.

Tammaru, T. (2000). 'Differential urbanisation and primate city growth in Soviet and post-Soviet Estonia'. *Tijdschrift voor Economische en Sociale Geografie*, **91**, 20-30.

Townroe, P. M. and D. Keen (1984). 'Polarization reversal in the state of Sao Paulo, Brazil'. *Regional Studies*, **18**, 45-54.

Vining, D. R. Jr and T. M. Kontuly (1978), 'Population dispersal from major metropolitan regions: An international comparison', *International Regional Science Review*, **3**, 49-73.

Weber, A. (1929), *Theory of the location of industries*, Friedrich, C.J. (trl) Chicago: University of Chicago Press.

Wells, H. G. (1902), *Anticipations of the reaction of mechanical and scientific progress upon human life and thought*. New York: Harper and Brothers.

Zelinsky, W. (1971), 'The hypothesis of the mobility transition', *Geographical Review*, **16**, 219-249.

Zipf, G. K. (1941), *National unity and disunity: The nation as a bio-social organism*, Bloomington, Ind.: Principia.

Zipf, G. K. (1949), *Human behaviour and the principle of least effort: An introduction to human ecology*, Cambridge Mass.: Addison-Wesley.

Chapter 2

An Exploration in Migration Theory

H. S. Geyer

CONCEPTS THAT SHAPED MIGRATION THEORY

The effect that labour migration had on countries of origin was one of the important issues **classical economists** dealt with in the advanced economies of Europe from the sixteenth to the eighteenth century. At the time, the economic strength of a country was measured by the size of its labour force, and Mercantilists generally argued that the labour force of sending countries would be weakened by emigration.

The **Mercantilist period** was characterized by government control of the economy. Adam Smith's (1776) views on economic liberation and the reduction of government control, however, heralded the blossoming of the free market system (Waters, 1928). This change brought about large scale rural-urban migration, first in Britain and later also in the rest of Europe. The new urban migrants served both as a labour force in the growing industrial sector and as consumers of manufactured goods.

Mechanical inventions such as water-powered and steam-driven machines characterized the **Industrial Revolution** in Britain (Cunningham, 1882; Waters; 1928; Mantoux, 1931), a revolution that later spilled over to other parts of Europe and North America. As in a chain of cause and effect, this mechanization, combined with a continued stream of rural-urban migrants who over-estimated employment opportunities in the industrial sector, resulted in over-urbanization, further urban unemployment[1] and eventually, the **colonization** of the Third World (Shrestha, 1988).

Fuelled by ideas of free trade and the possible economic gains the manipulation of factor shifts could bring, political economists for the first

---

[1] By the nineteenth century Malthusian population economics started to change political thinking (Samuelson, 1970).

time saw the logic of labour shifts to colonies as a means to reduce high levels of unemployment in over-urbanized industrial areas. At the same time markets in colonized areas would have been expanded as potential destinations for the export of manufactured goods. Labour export, they argued, should have a favourable effect on land-person ratios in both the industrialized areas and lagging regions, the ratios in former countries being reduced and in the latter being increased. At the same time the opening up of new markets would expand production options – changes that would ultimately also benefit the local economies of the colonies.

Later the focus in migration shifted from colonization to one responding to the economic needs of the colonizing nations, a process that gained momentum during the twentieth century. This shift '...marked the obsolescence of classical political economy as an approach to immigration and, though seldom noted in contemporary writings, signaled the emergence of new conceptual frameworks...' (Portes and Walton, 1981: 25).

While the focus in classical thinking was mainly on the economic needs of the colonial powers,[2] the emphasis in **neoclassical thinking** shifted to ways in which capital-labour ratios could be improved within developed and developing countries. Industrialization was considered to be an indispensable ingredient in the process of economic development in both developed and developing countries (North, 1955; Ohlin, 1967; Okin and Richardson, 1964; Rostow, 1960; Leven, 1966; House, 1977, 1978; Gottmann, 1973; Tiebout, 1963; Parr, 1999b, 2001).

The focus was placed on concepts such as comparative advantages and agglomeration economies and interregional and international trade, all of which were intended to boost economic growth and eliminate employment imbalances between economic sectors. As if in a delayed replay of history, the views of Lewis (1954) and Ranis and Fei (1961) on the role industrial development could play in economic development, and the application of those ideas internationally, brought about remarkably similar forms of over-urbanization of the Industrial Revolution period to the Developing World.

The neoclassical theory brought new rigid conceptualizations of two-sector economies in which it was argued that un- and semi-skilled labour would migrate mainly in one direction, namely, from over-populated rural regions to industrialized urban areas, restoring the general economic disequilibrium that existed between core and peripheral regions (Lewis, 1954; Ranis and Fei, 1961). At this time migration was simply regarded as a process of factor movement, one in which labour would move between economic sectors (1) to eliminate factor imbalances and (2) to contribute to growth of national output.

---

[2] See Cecil John Rhodes' plea, according to Lenin, that the United Kingdom should acquire additional colonial land for their surplus labour (Shrestha, 1987).

Over the years, however, it became clear that migration alone is not a strong enough force to eliminate imbalances (Yap, 1976).

Instead of eliminating imbalances, the situation of disequilibrium was exacerbated. Induced external investments in the industrial sector in centres where agglomeration economies existed (Hirschman, 1958; Boudeville, 1974; Richardson, 1973) and stagnating agricultural sectors in peripheral regions resulted in high levels of 'premature' rural-urban migration in the Third World. **Spatial imbalances** spiraled wherever the approach was vigorously followed, especially in the developing world (Myrdal, 1957).[3] As happened in Europe during the Industrial Revolution, primary centres in the developing world soon became over-populated, resulting in high levels of urban unemployment and hardship.

The high levels of urban unemployment and the deepening of rural-urban spatial economic disparities that were brought about by this laissez-faire approach necessitated a shift in emphasis away from a balance in employment between economic sectors to a more equitable spatial distribution of economic activities. The **'growth pole' concept**, originally presented in economic sectoral terms (Perroux, 1955), but later translated in industrial development terms (Boudeville, 1974), was regarded as the most appropriate instrument to create economic development in peripheral areas (Lasuén, 1972). Decentralisation policies, aimed at the establishment of industrial 'growth centres' in peripheral regions, were widely implemented in the developed and developing worlds (Hansen, 1972; House, 1977, 1978).

In this approach the emphasis was placed on regional development. Intermediate-sized cities, and in certain instances also specific frontier locations were identified as 'designated' industrial growth points. Based on Friedmann's (1960) core-periphery model, the aim of this policy of spatial intervention was to divert migrants away from large cities to intermediate and smaller sized centres in inner and outer peripheral areas (Geyer, 1989).[4] The ultimate goal was the establishment of flourishing industrial cities in peripheral regions which in time would have caused economic spread effects in adjacent rural hinterlands (Boudeville, 1974; Rodwin, 1972).

The general over-estimation of the 'trickling down' effect of growth centres and the continuing widening of core-peripheral economic differentials

---

[3] The developing world in general (Birg, 1995), but Africa especially is besieged by low productivity, high rates of population growth, and overwhelming instability. A study of 32 African countries has shown that migrants out of agriculture do respond overwhelmingly to market signals based on urban income relative to labour, and that political freedom fuels the process (Barkley and McMillan, 1994).

[4] In the developed world New Towns were often planned to accommodate primate city over-flow, while New Towns in the developing world were mostly planned as industrial centres to divert rural-urban migrants.

in spite of these measures (Myrdal, 1957), led to the discrediting of the growth centre concept as a development instrument (Conroy, 1973; Todd, 1974; Moseley, 1973; Nichols, 1969).[5] Industrial development that was generally too sophisticated for unskilled labour forces in peripheral areas to enable them to capitalize on potential upstream or downstream industrial entrepreneurial opportunities simply compounded the problem.   Also, improved transport infrastructure between core and peripheral areas in many cases further drained, instead of assisting the periphery (Geyer, 1987; Shrestha, 1988).

Subsequently, this led to a shift in policy away from industrial development in a **top-down approach** to **grass roots development** from the **bottom upwards** (Geyer, 1988). 'People's prosperity', an approach where more than just a 'privileged' few labourers were to benefit from economic development, became the buzzword, rather than the 'place prosperity' that was brought about by industrial development policies of the past (Gore, 1984).   Ironically, despite these changes rural-urban migration continued unabated.

ISSUES IN MIGRATION THEORY
NEOCLASSICAL THEORY EXPANDED

In many respects the **Lewis-Ranis-Fei core-periphery model** forms the foundation on which the neoclassical migration theory was built.   It suggests an income-driven migration process in a two-sector economy in which rural-urban migration serves as a mechanism to wipe out economic imbalances. First, redundant labour in the low-wage agricultural sector leaves for the cities to find employment in the high-wage industrial sector and in the process wages in the former sector increase while those in the latter sector decrease. Later on, when all the redundant labour has left, the migration stream tapers off, but according to the model people will continue to leave the agricultural sector as long as there are still differences in income levels between the two sectors.   This migration will continue until imbalances in the productivity and income levels between agriculture and industry have been eliminated.   One of the criticisms that can be leveled against the Lewis-Ranis-Fei core-periphery model is its rigidity.   In his critique on neoclassical migration theory Prothero (1988) contends that the theory tends to be mechanistic, macro in scale, economically oriented, concentrate on sectoral differences, under-emphasize regional differences, exaggerate permanency in migration, and neglect other

---

[5] At the time the view was held that the lack of success of the growth centre approach could largely be ascribed to inaccurate interpretations and, consequently, erroneous applications of the concept (Richardson, 1978), a view that is still held today (Parr, 1999a).

movements. It also does not sufficiently take socio-anthropological explanations into account.

The **theory of relative deprivation** breaks the rigidity of the Lewis-Ranis-Fei core-periphery model. It explains which people in the agricultural labour force are most likely to leave first, and who will keep on leaving although they are gainfully employed in the agricultural sector, i.e. the second stage migrants in the Lewis-Ranis-Fei-model. In the theory of relative deprivation, deprivation is measured by a household's economic position in its own community. The lower a household's position within a community's distribution of income, the greater its relative deprivation and the greater its likelihood to migrate. Communities with relatively equal income distributions will generate less migration. But migration does not only deal with income. Other factors such as access to improved social overhead capital and social and psychological considerations also play a role (Stark, 1984, 1991). Although the relative deprivation will impact on a household's propensity to migrate, its deprivation may not necessarily result in actual migration. Based on the concept of mobility transition (Zelinsky, 1971) the higher the level of development of people, the greater their mobility and the greater their ability to migrate. This weakness in the deprivation theory is partially addressed by the modernization theory.

All over the developing world industrialization has resulted in the deepening of core-peripheral differentials. In terms of the **modernization theory**, two-tier populations tend to develop in such countries. Progressive élites who accept modern western style values and norms become increasingly distanced from the 'traditional' oriented remainder of the population, economically, culturally and intellectually. As a consequence, aspirations of westernizing élites start rising, which increases their propensity to migrate to improve their living and economic environment, first internally, but eventually also internationally (Portes and Walton, 1981).

In terms of their migration outcome, modernization theory, **world systems theory** (Wallerstein, 1974a, 1974b), and **segmented labour market theory** overlap largely. According to world systems theory, capitalism tends to expand outward from core nations to the rest of the world. As market penetration occurs, labour in non-capitalist countries gets displaced, population gets mobilized and international migration becomes fuelled by an ever increasing spatial, economic and social polarization of the globalizing market economy. According to the segmented market theory, migrants from the developing world are often accommodated in the less attractive, low paying, and insecure employment sector in an increasingly segmented labour market of developing countries (Massey et al., 1995). In this way market needs of host countries determine the acceptance and rejection of prospective migrants.

The same mechanisms of core-peripheral migration that are at work in **neoclassical migration theory**, nationally, are also at work internationally. Labour is often regarded by lagging countries as an export commodity to improve their own capital-labour ratios and to gain foreign capital through international remittances.[6]   In certain instances specific international migration systems are created between peripheral and core nations that are linked in super state agreements such as those between European and North American countries.

In these arrangements, pressure is being put on core nations to be more lenient in their international migration policies towards countries included in such agreements (Straubhaar and Zimmermann, 1993).   In these supra regional arrangements, core areas with low fertility rates and peace on the one side act as magnets on peripheral areas with high fertility rates, ecological difficulties and poverty on the other side. Established migration systems that are currently globally visible include those between peripheral European states and Western Europe,[7] the former colonies and their associated former European colonial states, South and Central American states, the USA and Canada, and between the lagging and industrializing areas of Asia and Africa (Zolberg, 1989; Straubhaar and Zimmermann, 1993; Geyer, 1998).

THE INDIVIDUAL VERSUS THE SOCIETY

One of the long-standing problems migration theory faces is the impasse between the individualist and the structural approach to population redistribution processes. **Conventional micro-economic migration theory** tends to look at migration from the individual's perspective – how the individual interprets circumstances when a migration move is contemplated. Even the family unit is sometimes considered as consisting of a number of individuals, not a decision-making unit (Stark, 1984).

Functional or conventional theory assumes that on aggregate, the decisions of individuals are self-regulatory and will eventually lead to a reduction in spatial inequalities and consequently a decline in migration (Goss and Lindquist, 1995; Portes and Walton, 1981). From the perspective of the individual, therefore, improving one's own living conditions is the main purpose of migration.

In the **neo-Marxist dependency theory**, on the other hand, political-economic structures and social class predetermine migration moves. Migration of the individual, according to this view, is guided by a larger

---

[6] The President of Mexico recently explicitly took such a position relative to the United States, for instance.

[7] Particular patterns that are visible are those between Turkey and Germany and countries of the former Yugoslavia and the UK.

system of dominating political-economic forces. Social economic inequalities in the system make it difficult for people to improve themselves. There are three interrelated schools of thought fitting into this theoretical framework: neo-Marxist dependency theory, world systems theory, and **modes of production theory** (Goss and Lindquist, 1995). Dependency theorists blame capitalism, colonialism and the selected exploitation of underdeveloped peripheral labour forces for the spatial imbalance between core and peripheral areas (Shrestha, 1988). Neo-Marxist theorists tend to concentrate on 'historical sequences of events' to justify their views. The continuing of international migration towards core areas after colonialism has come to an end, is either regarded as a legacy of colonialism or is blamed on neo-colonialism, a subtle but equally effective indirect form of (financial) control.

World systems theory to a large extent eliminates this weakness. Global market penetration, it argues, displaces unskilled labour in non-capitalist countries and induces migration (Portes and Walton, 1981; Massey et al., 1995). Prothero (1988) calls the micro-scale circumstances involving individual and personal choices the 'situation', while the latter, the 'setting', involves macro-scale issues of an economic, political, or administrative nature. When macro political, economic or socio-cultural considerations play a dominant role in migration decision making, the focus is on the setting. When the age of a person or his / her competency is the deciding factor, individual considerations, or the situation determine the move.

The two opposing migration approaches attach different values to **individualist and societal** considerations in the migration process. The individualist approach leans towards self-fulfilment. From a community perspective, migration is aimed at the maintenance of the totality. However, the decision to migrate is seldom based on a single consideration. A variety of situation- and setting-considerations normally comes into play when a move is contemplated. Functional, Marxist, and structural theories stress the role society plays in migration decision of individuals. Differences of opinion on the freedom of individuals to make rational decisions, or whether political-economic structures predetermine migration moves, have not been reconciled yet.

Structuration theory (Giddens, 1982, 1984) seems to offer a way out of the current impasse. The theory stresses the importance of the person as 'knowledgeable' in the reproduction of social practices. Human activities have 'intended' and 'unintended' outcomes. 'Institutions' are practices that are deeply sedimented.

Individuals constantly monitor their actions reflectively. 'Reflective monitoring' occurs at three levels. 'Unconscious action' occurs without the agent knowing it, 'practical consciousness' is knowledge that is used but cannot be verbalized, and 'discursive consciousness' is when intentions can be explained.

Every action of a person 'implies structural modification of the social system as a whole' (Moos and Dear, 1996). If a decision is taken to migrate, the move has an impact on both the society that is left and the host society. In terms of structuration theory, action impacts on three time levels, *durée* (immediate social reproduction), *dasein* (medium or biological life) and *longue durée* (institutional reproduction over generations). The longer the time span of the institutional reproduction the more sedimented and durable it becomes (Goss and Lindquist, 1995).

When migrants leave one location and settle in another they leave and enter different environments with particular social and economic features. Some features are more, others less sedimented. Together these features comprise the totality that migrants have to face when migration is contemplated and these are the factors that determine the composition of the 'migration institution'[8] across time and space. When people migrate, changes take place in the social economic composition of both the origin and the destination and in the process both setting and situation are effected.

MIGRATION SYSTEMS AND STREAMS

The **migration system** concept adds another dimension to the current **network approach** to migration and can be defined as specific locations that are linked by streams and counterstreams of migrants (Nogle, 1994). The migration system approach attempts to shed light on the types of migration linkages that exist between countries such as Turkey and Germany, Mexico, Cuba and the USA, or Mozambique, Zimbabwe, Nigeria and South Africa, and it helps to explain differences between permanent and temporary migration considerations (Kritz and Slotnik, 1992). It brings together social, political, demographic and economic factors such as the role receiving countries, geographical proximity, similarities in language, trade flows, colonial heritage, and political alliances and hostilities play in the migration process.

The migration system concept is closely linked to the concept of migration streams. Each, or a combination of the factors mentioned above, can cause or contribute to migration streams. Different terms are being used for **mainstream** and **substream migration**. **Mainstream migration** can be defined as dominant migration flows between locations along specific routes (Lee, 1966). **Counterstreams** are movements in opposite directions. A

---

[8] 'The migrant institution is a complex articulation of individuals, associations, and organizations which extends the social action of and interaction between these agents and agencies across time and space' (Goss and Linquist, 1995: 319).

differentiation should be made between counterstream and **return migrants** (Campbell and Johnson, 1976). Return migrants form part of counterstreams, but not all counterstreams would necessarily contain return migrants. In **differential urbanization** patterns, mainstream migration refers to dominant migration trends, while sub- or counterstream migration refers to Li's (1970) **'reverse stream'**, i.e. minor migration streams that flow in the opposite direction simultaneously (Geyer and Kontuly, 1993).

Substream migration could theoretically occur in the same direction as **mainstream** migration, but the rationale behind substream migration differs fundamentally from that of people who participate in mainstream migration. For instance, lower and higher income groups may be migrating to the same destination for completely different reasons, the larger group forming the mainstream and the smaller group the substream migration. Lower income migrants may be moving to core areas for economic reasons, while higher income groups may be migrating to the same large urban agglomerations because gentrification has improved parts of the urban environment to such an extent that they find the area environmentally acceptable again. An example of this has been found in Toronto (Bourne, 1992). Also, in the USA, higher income groups and African Americans, who, by and large, form part of the lower income group, are currently both migrating to the south.

Finally the concepts of **'productionism'** and **'environmentalism'** (Hart, 1983) are highlighted in the explanation of the differential urbanization concept (Geyer, 1996, 1998; Geyer and Kontuly, 1993; Kontuly and Geyer, 2003), which in turn links the processes of urbanization (Clark, 1967), polarization reversal[9] (Richardson, 1977, 1980), counter-urbanization (Beale, 1977; Fielding, 1989; Vining and Kontuly, 1978), and questions about re-urbanization (Cochrane and Vining, 1988; Frey, 1988; Champion, 1988, 1989). Productionism refers to the phase in people's lives when improved job opportunities, education, income, and upward social mobility are a priority. In the case of unskilled migrants people are often willing to bear poor living conditions in order to find employment in the formal urban sector. Many clandestine migrants fall into this category.

After having had the opportunity to reap the benefits of productionism, people normally enter the environmentalism phase. This phase is entered into when the need to improve one's actual living environment becomes a priority. During the environmentalism phase a person would even trade income for pleasant living conditions and in such cases factors associated with

---

[9] Polarization reversal originally referred to a technical turning point from economic concentration to the reversal of the process. In a migration context it refers to the stage when secondary centres grow faster than small or large metropolitan areas overall. This stage can occur in both developing (Geyer, 1990) and developed countries (Geyer, 1996).

productionism become less important. Many of the older, skilled persons who have spent some time in the formal urban sector fall into this category

Productionism and environmentalism are not entirely mutually exclusive. They go hand in hand, the former enabling a person to achieve the latter. It could, therefore, be argued that productionism and environmentalism are both driven by the same force, that is, the need to improve one's living conditions in all possible respects. But in productionism, improved living conditions can normally not be achieved in the short run, while in environmentalism, improved living and environmental conditions are often an immediate need (Geyer, 1996).

What was a trickle of migrants to the south of the USA in the 1960s became a flood in the 1970s, more of them people in the high income groups. Black migration soon followed. The reason for the wave of counter-urbanization of African Americans from the large metropolitan areas of the United States to the south around 1980 (Beale, 1982) could be fundamentally similar to the rationale behind their migration from the rural south to the large urban agglomerations in the north, decades earlier. Both are based on the same migration principles that led to the neoclassical and neo-Marxist migration theories, i.e. poor people tend to be attracted to areas where there are employment opportunities and where chances for self-improvement are better.

In general people that form a particular migration stream can be classified into different categories. When the young, the less educated, poor, older, and more educated, more enterprising components of the population all migrate in the same direction, the rationale behind each group's movement could differ fundamentally. The younger, more educated, and more enterprising section of the stream would more than likely move to an area to seize economic enterprising opportunities. Once economic development occurs employment opportunities are created, which in turn could trigger lower income migration to the same areas. The latter becomes a delayed reaction to the first stream, both going in the same direction.

RISK FACTORS IN MIGRATION

In his search for answers why rural-urban migration in developing countries continues in spite of well-known high levels of urban unemployment, Todaro (1969, 1982) came to the conclusion that to understand migration trends one must look at expected rather than real prospects of finding employment. He saw migration decision-making as a rational decision of lowly skilled migrants based on the possibility of finding employment only in the informal sector initially but with hopes of finding formal employment over the longer term (Stark, 1984). Gugler (1968) calls this the 'lottery syndrome', i.e.

people taking a chance rather than being sure that they will be able to land a job when they arrive at their urban destination.

Meanwhile migrants will be living off their kin or any other support structure they can find, whether it is legitimate or illegitimate. They may even resort to 'misemployment' such as prostitution, stealing, and drug trafficking in order to make a living (Gugler, 1990). Overall evidence has been found that rural-urban migration does result in personal income gains in the developing world, but positive financial gains do not necessarily mean positive social gains as well (Yap, 1976).

Stark and Levhari (1982) add another dimension to the Todaro hypothesis. According to them risk factors may also play a role in planned rural-urban migration in the developing world. Direct and indirect costs are incurred in the migration process, financially and psychologically (Sjaastad, 1962). Migrants may have to invest in formal education, in-service training and experience before risks factors diminish. That is why older people are often more reluctant to migrate than young people; they have less time to make good the financial and social losses that may result from the migration move (Sjaastad, 1962).

Rural families confronted with survival risks may diversify their income portfolios by 'placing' some of their family members in the urban sector. At this point the two views overlap because Todaro also regards labour as a production factor that can be exported by choice (Harris and Todaro, 1970). Initially, migrants tend to retain their ties with the rural sector for two reasons: remittances to migrants in urban areas when they do not find employment, or remittances back to the rural areas when they do (Gugler, 1968).

The same trends are observable in the developed world. During the phase of urbanization rural-to-urban migration occurred amongst all income groups. When the migration turnaround in the United States started in the late 1960s to early 1970s, lower income groups kept on migrating to metropolitan areas (Berry, 1976; Geyer and Kontuly, 1993).[10] However, the question can be asked whether the large scale migration of higher income groups to states such as California and Florida during the main turnaround phase of the 1970s is not the cause for the subsequent turnaround of lower income groups from the major metropolitan areas in the north to these regions (Beale, 1982). Whether the same rationale applied to the migration of African Americans

---

[10] According to Geyer and Kontuly (1996) the continuing urbanization of the African American minority (see Berry, 1976) represented a sub-stream trend, while the majority of higher income migrants were leaving the major metropolitan areas. Together the sub-stream (migration) and major stream (counter-urbanization) represented differential urbanization. Exactly the opposite trends in differential urbanization were detected in South Africa (Geyer, 1990).

first to the North and later back to the South is a matter that still needs to be determined.

Similar labour movements have been observed within cities. Large concentrations of semi- and unskilled labourers in the CBDs of large and medium sized cities in South Africa, followed by associated crime and violence during the late 1990s forced many businesses that were still viable in the 1970s and 1980s, to relocate in suburban business centres. Soon after the viable businesses were relocated, new concentrations of loiterers started to appear in the suburban business areas. The logic of the concept of productionism lies in the propensity of lower strata migrants, i.e. the semi- and the unskilled, as well as the unemployed and under-employed to migrate to areas where they hope to be able to make a better living.

SHORT TERM MIGRATION

Movements from rural areas to core areas can be complex. In cases where urban systems are well-developed, **stepwise migration** may occur from rural areas through small and intermediate sized towns to large urban agglomerations, each step allowing migrants to become accustomed to a larger urban environment and affording them opportunities to acquire new skills that are necessary for survival. In countries with primate urban distributions (Berry, 1961), i.e. countries that only have a few secondary centres, migrants often directly move from rural areas to primate cities, augmenting core-peripheral disparities (Prothero, 1988).

In stepwise migraton there are indications that many first time unskilled migrants tend to migrate to the nearest cities initially, while maintaining strong ties with their relatives in the rural area (Geyer, 2000, 2000a). Initially, remittances may flow from the rural kinsmen to the pioneering urban migrants. Once migrants have settled in the urban areas, the flow of remittances may be reversed. Pioneering migrants may even be forced to circulate for some time before the migration move becomes permanent. Family ties, chain migration and remittances are also important in international labour migration between developing and developed Countries (Funkhouser, 1995; Borjas and Bronars, 1991). During the 1980s, 70% of all persons who emigrated to the United States were assisted by relatives that were living in the country already and the percentage of migrants who resided with such relatives was also on the increase.

CORE-PERIPHERY RELATIONSHIPS

Although there are areas of agreement among migration theorists, there are also several examples in literature where explanations of migration are criticized and presented as different scenarios, while they actually have much in common. Also, not enough effort is always made to identify the similarities between population dynamics in the developed and the developing world. Several aspects in both bodies of literature that complement each other well have been outlined in the differential urbanization theory (Geyer, 1996; 1998; Geyer and Kontuly, 1993, Kontuly and Geyer, 2003). Interregional migration within developing countries and international migration from developing to developed countries for example are in many respects complementary because both explain migration in terms of spatial differentials in income and wealth (Prothero, 1988).

In this regard the concept of relative deprivation that has been contextualized in a Third World environment, may be expanded to also include migration in the First World. People tend to migrate to areas where their prospects of making a better living are greater, whatever the definition of 'better living' might be. For the poor, better living may more often than not imply finding better employment; for the more affluent, better living may mean moving to a safer, cleaner area with a more moderate climate.

The scale of core-peripheral relationships and the balance between the cores and their peripheries has proven to be crucial in this conceptual framework. Based on Lee's (1966) view of **push** (-) and **pull** (+) **factors**, the greater the difference in the level of 'development' between the core and the periphery, such as is often found in developing countries, or between the More Developed and the less developed world internationally, the greater the difference in the kinetic charge between the two. In such cases a unidirectional migration stream is more likely to flow from predominantly negatively loaded areas (the periphery) to the predominantly positively loaded areas (the core) (Zolberg, 1989; Straubaar and Zimmermann, 1993).[11] Conversely, when the difference between the two becomes less, such as is found in many areas in the developed world, the migratory patterns become more varied and complex, and at the same time, less predictable over time (Champion, 1992).

It is within this core-peripheral framework – which can be differentiated vertically (in terms of their relative level of development) and horizontally (in terms of their scale and absolute and relative location towards each other in space) – that the development of local, regional, national, sub-continental, continental and global urban networks evolve (Geyer, 1998).

---

[11] This does not exclude the possibility of minor counter-streams of migration from core areas to peripheral areas according to the concept of differential urbanization, however.

REFERENCES

Barkley, A. P. and J. Mcmillan (1994), 'Political freedom and the response to economic incentives – labor migration in Africa, 1972-1987', Journal of Development Economics, **45**, 393-406.

Beale, C. L. (1977), 'The recent shift of United States population to nonmetropolitan areas, 1970-1975', *International Regional Science Review*, **2**, 113-122.

Beale, C. L. (1982), 'U.S. population: Where we are; Where we're going', *Population Bulletin*, **37**, 1-59.

Berry, B. J. L. (1961), 'City size distributions and economic development', *Economic Development and Cultural Change*, **9**, 573-588.

Berry, B. J. L. (1976), 'The counterurbanization process: Urban America since 1970', *Urban Affairs Annual Review*, **11**, 17-30.

Birg, H. (1995), *World population projections for the 21st century: Theoretical interpretation and quantitative simulations*, Frankfurt: Campus Verlag.

Borjas, G. J., and S. G. Bronars (1991), 'Immigration and the family', *Journal of Labor Economics*, **9**, 123-148.

Boudeville, J. R. (1974), *Problems of regional economic planning*, Edinburgh: Edinburgh University Press.

Bourne, L. S. (1992), 'Population Turnaround in the Canadian Inner City: Contextual Factors and Social Consequences', *Canadian Journal of Urban Research,* **1**, 66-89.

Campbell, R. R. and D. M. Johnson (1976), 'Propositions on counterstream migration', *Rural Sociology*, **41**, 127-145.

Champion, A. G. (1988), 'The reversal of the migration turnaround: Resumption of traditional trends'? *International Regional Science Review*, **11**, 253-260.

Champion, A. G. (1989), 'Conclusion: Temporary anomaly, long-term trend or transitional phase'? in A. G. Champion (ed.), *Counterurbanization: The changing pace and nature of population deconcentration*, London: Edward Arnold, pp.230-244.

Champion, A. G. (1992), 'Urban and regional demographic trends in the Developed World', *Urban Studies*, **29**, 461-482.

Clark, C. (1967), *Population Growth and Land Use*, New York : St. Martin's Press.

Cochrane, S. G. and D. R. Vining, Jr. (1988), 'Recent trends in migration between core and peripheral regions in Developed and Advanced Developing Countries', *International Regional Science Review*, **11**, 215-243.

Conroy, M. E. (1973), 'Rejection of the growth centre strategy in Latin American regional development planning', *Land Economics*, XLIX, 371-380.

Cunningham, W. (1882), *The growth of English industry in modern times*, Cambridge: Cambridge University Press.

Fielding, A. J. (1989), 'Migration and urbanization in Western Europe', *The Geographical Journal*, **155**, 60-69.

Frey, W. H. (1988), 'The Re-emergence of core region growth: A return to the metropolis?', *International Regional Science Review*, **11**, 261-267.

Friedmann, J. (1960), *Regional development policy: A case study of Venezuela*, Cambridge, Mass.: MIT.

Funkhouser, E. (1995), 'Remittances from international migration: A comparison of El Salvador and Nicaragua', *The Review of Economics and Statistics*, **77**, 137-146.

Geyer, H. S. (1987), 'The development axis as a development instrument in the Southern African development area', *Development Southern Africa*, **4**, 271-300.

Geyer, H. S. (1988), 'On urbanization in South Africa'. *The South African Journal of Economics*, **56**, 154-172.

Geyer, H. S. (1989), 'Industrial development policy in South Africa: The past, present, and future', *World Development*, **17**, 379-396.

Geyer, H. S. (1996), 'Expanding the theoretical foundation of differential urbanization', *Tijdschrift voor Economische en Sociale Geografie*, **87**, 44-59.

Geyer, H.S. (1998), 'Differential urbanization and international migration: an urban systems approach', in C. Gorter, P. Nijkamp, and J. Poot (eds), *Crossing borders: Regional and urban perspectives on international migration*. Aldershot: Ashgate, pp.161-184.

Geyer, H. S. (2000), *A settlement strategy for the North West province*, Department of Local Government and Housing, North West province, Mmabatho, South Africa. Unpublished.

Geyer, H. S. (2000a), *A socio-economic survey of the Western Gauteng province*, Western Gauteng Services Council, Gauteng province, South Africa. Unpublished.

Geyer, H.S. and Kontuly, T.M. (1993), 'A theoretical foundation for the concept of differential urbanization', in N. Hansen, K.J. Button and P. Nijkamp, *Modern Classics in Regional Science: Regional Policy and Regional Integration, Vol. 6* Cheltenham: Edward Elgar.

Giddens, A. (1982), *'Profiles and critiques in social theory'*, Berkeley: The University of California Press.

Giddens, A. (1984), 'Space, time and politics in social theory: An interview with Anthony Giddens', *Environment and Planning D*, **2**, 123-132.

Gore, C. (1984), *Regions in question*, London: Methuen.

Goss, J. and B. Lindquist, (1995), 'Conceptualizing international labor migration: A structuration perspective', *International Migration Review*, **29**, 317-351.

Gottmann, J. (1973), *Megalopolis: The urbanized northeastern seaboard of the United States*, Cambridge, Mass.: MIT.

Gugler, J. (1968), 'The impact of labour migration on society and economy in Sub-Sharan Africa: Empirical findings and theoretical considerations', *African Social Research*, **6**, 463-486.

Gugler, J. (1990), 'Overurbanization reconsidered', in J. Gugler (ed.), *The urbanisation of the Third World*, Oxford: Oxford University Press, pp.74-92.

Hansen, (1972), 'Growth center policy in the United States', in N. M.Hansen (ed.), *Growth centers in regional economic development*. New York: The Free Press, pp. 266-281.

Harris, J. R. and M. P. Todaro (1970), 'Migration, unemployment and development: a two-sector analysis', *American Economic Review*, **60**, 126-142.

Hart, T. (1983), 'Transport and economic development, the historical dimension', in K.J. Button and D. Gillingwater (eds), *Transport, location and spatial policy*, Aldershot, Hants: Gower, pp.12-22.

Hirschman, A. O. (1958), *The strategy of economic development*, New Haven: Yale University Press.

House, J. W. (1977), 'Regions and the system', in J.W. House (ed.), *The U.K. Space: resources, environment and the future*, London: Weidenfeld and Nicolson, pp.1-96.

House, J.W. (1978), *France: an applied geography*, London: Methuen.

Kontuly, T. M. and H. S. Geyer (2003) 'Introduction' / 'Conclusion', *Tijdschrift voor Economische en Sociale Geografie*, **94**. Forthcoming.

Kritz, M. M. and H. Slotnik (1992), 'Global interactions: Migration systems, processes, and policies', in M.M. Kritz, L.L. Lin, and H. Zlotnik (eds), *International migration systems*. Oxford: Clarendon Press, pp.1-18.

Lasuén, J.R. (1972), 'On growth poles', in N. M. Hansen (ed.), *Growth centers in regional economic development*. New York: the Free Press, pp.20-49.

Lee, E.S. (1966), 'A theory of migration', *Demography*, **3**, 47-57.

Leven, C. L. (1966), 'The economic base and regional growth', in Center for Agricultural and Economic Development, *Research and education for regional and area development*, Ames, Iowa: Iowa State University Press, pp. 79-94.

Lewis, A. (1954), 'Development with unlimited supplies of labour', *The Manchester School*, **22**, 139-192.

Li, W. L. (1970), 'A differential approach to the study of migration streams', *Rural Sociology*, **35**, 534-538.

Mantoux, P. (1931), *The industrial revolution in the eighteenth century*, London: Jonathan Cape.

Massey, D. S., J. Arango, G. Hugo, A. Kouaouci, A. Pellegrino, and J. E. Taylor (1995), 'An evolution of international migration theory: The North American case', *Population and Development Review*, **20**, 699-751.

Moos, A. J. and Dear, M. J. (1996), 'Structuration theory in urban analysis: 1. Theoretical exegesis', *Environment and Planning*, *A*, **18**, 231-252.

Moseley, M. J. (1973), 'The impact of growth centres in rural regions: An analysis of spatial 'patterns' in Brittany', *Regional Studies*, **7**, 57-75.

Myrdal, G. (1957), *Economic Theory and Underdeveloped Regions*, London: Duckworth.

Nichols, V. (1969), 'Growth poles: An evaluation of their propulsive effect', *Environment and Planning A*, **1**, 193-208.

Nogle, J. M. (1994), 'The systems approach to international migration: An application of network analysis methods', *International migration*, **32**, 329-342.

North, D. C. (1955), 'Location theory and regional economic growth', *Journal of Political Economy*, **63**, 243-258.

Ohlin, B. (1967), *Interregional and international trade*, Cambridge, Mass.: Harvard University Press.

Okin, B, and H. W. Richardson (1964), 'Regional income inequality and internal population migration', in J. Friedmann and W. Alonso (eds), *Regional development and planning: A reader*. Cambridge, Mass.: MIT, pp.303-318.

Parr, J. B. (1999a), 'Growth-pole strategies in regional economic planning: A retrospective view. Part 1. Origings and advocacy', *Urban Studies*, **36**, 1195-1215.

Parr, J. B. (1999b), 'Regional economic development: An export stages framework', *Land Economics*, **75**, 94-114.

Parr, J. B. (2001), 'On the regional dimensions of Rostow's theory of growth', *Review of Urban and Regional Development Studies*, **13**, 2-19.

Perroux, (1955), 'Note sur la notion de la "pole de croissance"', *Économie appliquée*, **7**, 307-320.

Portes, A., and J. Walton (1981), *Labor, Class, and the international system*, New York: Academic Press.

Prothero, R. M. (1988), 'Populations on the move', *Third World Quarterly*, **9**, 1282-1310.

Ranis, G. and J. C. H. Fei (1961), 'A theory of economic development', *The American Economic Review*, **51**, 533-565.

Richardson, H. W. (1973), *Economic Growth Theory*, London: MacMillan.

Richardson, H. W. (1977), *City size and national strategies in Developing Countries*, World Bank Staff Working Report, Washington.

Richardson, H. W. (1978), 'Growth center, rural development and national urban policy: A defense', *International Regional Science Review*, **3**, 133-152.

Richardson, H.W. (1980), 'Polarization Reversal in Developing Countries', *Papers of the Regional Science Association,* **45**, pp.67-85.

Rodwin, L. (1972), 'Urban growth strategies reconsidered', in N. M.Hansen (ed.), *Growth centers in regional economic development.* New York: the Free Press, 1-19.

Rogers, A. (1981), 'Sources of Urban population growth and urbanization, 1950-2000: A demographic accounting', *Economic Development and Cultural Change*, **30**, 483-506.

Rostow, W. W. (1960), *The stages of economic growth: A non-communist manifesto*, London: Cambridge University Press.

Samuelson, P. A. (1970), *Economics,* New York: MacGraw-Hill.

Shrestha, N.R. (1988), 'A structural perspective on labour migration in underdeveloped countries', *Third World Quarterly*, **12**, 179-207.

Sjaastad, L.A. (1962), 'The costs and returns of human migration', *Journal of Political Economy*, **70**, 80-93.

Smith, A. (1776), *An inquiry into the nature and causes of the wealth of nations*, reprinted in W. B. Todd (ed.) (1976), Glasgow edition of the works and correspondence of Adam Smith, vol. I, Oxford: Oxford University Press.

Stark, O. (1984), 'Rural-to-urban migration in LDCs: A relative deprivation approach', *Economic Development and Cultural Change*, **32**, 475-486.

Stark, O. (1991), *The migration of labor: A review essay*, Cambridge, Mass.: Blackwell.

Stark, O. and Levhari, D. (1982), 'On migration and risk in LDCs', *Economic Development and Cultural Change*, **31**, 191-196.

Straubaar, T., and Zimmermann, K. F. (1993), 'Towards a European migration policy', *Population Research and Policy Review*, **12**, 225-241.

Tiebout, C. M. (1963), 'The urban economic base', in H. M. Mayer and C. F. Kohn (eds), *Readings in urban geography.* Chicago: University of Chicago Press, pp. 105-109.

Todaro, M. P. (1969), 'A model of labor migration and urban unemployment in Less Developed Countries', *American Economic Review*, **59**, 138-148.

Todaro, M. P. (1982), *Economics for a Developing World: An introduction to principles, problems, and policies*, Harlow, Essex, U.K.: Longman.

Todd, D. (1974), 'An appraisal of the development pole concept in regional analysis', *Environment and Planning A*, **6**, 291-306.

Vining, D. R., Jr. and T. M. Kontuly (1978), 'Population dispersal from major metropolitan regions: An international comparison', *International Regional Science Review*, **3**, 49-73.

Wallerstein, I (1974a), 'The rise and future demise of the world capitalist system: Concepts for comparative analysis', *Comparative Studies in Society and History,* **16**, 387-415.

Wallerstein, I. (1974b), *The modern world-system,* New York: Academic Press.

Waters, C.M. (1928), *An economic history of England: 1066-1874,* London: Oxford University Press.

Yap, L. (1976), 'Internal migration and economic development in Brazil', *Quarterly Journal of Economics,* **90**, 119-137.

Zelinsky, W. (1971), 'The hypothesis of the mobility transition', *Geographical Review,* **16**, 219-249.

Zolberg, A. R. (1989), 'The next waves: Migration for a changing wolrd', *International Migration Review,* **23**, 403-429.

Chapter 3

On Urban Systems Evolution

H. S. Geyer

THE HISTORICAL PICTURE

The world has witnessed very remarkable and suprising changes in the **history of urban development** over the past two centuries, but none more surprising than some of the transformations that have occurred since the Second World War. Throughout history, urbanization occurred in waves as and when different peoples pioneered or conquered new territories (Easton, 1954). In Western Europe most of the urban settlements developed between 1250 and 1350 (Mumford, 1961). By 1800 the majority of the people still lived in rural areas and rural villages. Between 1800 and 1950, the world population increased by over 250 per cent, but during the same period urban areas, especially the smaller ones, grew up to ten times faster, mostly in the developed world (Hauser, 1965). In 1950, 17 per cent of the 1.67 billion people lived in urban areas, a percentage that grew to 27 (2.98 billion) in 1975 (Fox, 1984).

Large urban agglomerations were the last to appear. By 1950 only approximately 4 per cent of the world's population lived in places of a million inhabitants or more (Hauser, 1965). Cities grew into metropolitan areas, then into megalopolitan areas (Gottmann, 1978), and based on population growth rates[1] by the end of the 1960s, indications were that certain urban agglomerations will continue to grow until they eventually cover large parts of continents. Doxiadis (1970) termed these continental cities the 'ecumenopolis'. So convinced was Clark (1967: 280) of continued urbanization, that he formulated his **'law of population concentration'**:

---

[1] It took all of the millennia up to the first half of the nineteenth century for the world population to reach the first billion mark. The second billion took around a century, the third, thirty-five years (Hauser, 1965) and, increasing faster and faster all the time, the six billionth baby was born at the end of the second millennium.

The macro-location of industry and population tends towards an ever-increasing concentration in a limited number of areas; their micro-location, on the other hand, towards increasing diffusion, or 'sprawl'.

Ironically, it later turned out that, at that time, urban concentration was already grinding to a halt in certain developed countries, and a new wave of urban deconcentration was about to begin (Beale, 1977; Vining and Kontuly, 1978; Champion, 1989; Fielding, 1989; Frey, 1988).

While urban growth rates in the developed world started to lose momentum towards the end of the twentieth century, urbanization in the developing world gained momentum. In 1950, only seven cities in the world held more than five million people, two of them were in the developing world. By 1984, of the 34 cities that had more than 5 million residents, 22 were located in developing countries (Fox, 1984). By 1975 there were already more people living in urban areas in the developing world than in the developed world (Rogers and Williams, 1982). While 11 of the world's 15 largest cities were located in the developed world in 1950, this number had declined to eight in 1980 (Rogers, 1981).

Much of the urbanization in the developing world can be regarded as **premature urbanization**, i.e people that migrate to urban areas without sufficient skills to effectively compete for employment in the formal urban sector (Geyer, 1989). To aggravate the situation, many parts of the developing world are being left behind by the momentum of economic development in the developed world, especially in Africa (Castells, 1993). Together these two factors are causing the global core-peripheral differentials to widen.

In spite of these alarming statistics, indications are that the net growth rate of the global population has peaked around 1990 and is currently leveling out (Birg, 1995). Although this slowdown is partially due to certain developed countries entering, and others nearing the 'second' **demographic transition** towards the end of the previous century (Champion, 1992; Birg, 1995), the developing world also plays its part. Natural growth rates in the developing world are steadily leveling off, not necessarily as a result of declining fertility rates, but as a consequence of continuing economic, political and health crises[2] causing death rates to soar. While fertility rates of developing countries are still hovering at two to three times the level of the developed world, the latter's rate had dropped below the replacement level by the mid-1970s (Birg, 1995). Although it is expected that the populations of many developed countries will be declining in absolute terms unless they are supplemented by immigration, the 2000 US census results point to a surprisingly high birth rate, the highest since the 'baby boom'.

---

[2] AIDS is reaching catastrophic proportions in many African countries.

LAYERS OF HUMAN ACTIVITIES

Comprehending the complexity of spatial relationships within urban systems is never easy because human life, in Mumford's (1961) words, 'swings between two poles: movement and settlement' and there are so many social, economic and environmental factors that could potentially affect the system. The complexity of core-peripheral relationships within the urban environment and between urban and rural areas in a wider regional context can only be appreciated fully when the geography of human interaction patterns in (and between) each of the **layers of human activities** shown in Figure 1.1,[3] is examined holistically.

The figure depicts the multi-dimensional character and complexity of human activities as they unfold over time. It gives an indication of the range of social, economic, and organizational factors that make up the constituting elements of human activities in an urban system. Looking at the construct from the top downwards, it gives one an overview of the geographical location and density of human settlement patterns in an area. This is what one sees when one looks at an atlas superficially, and unless one reads certain locational factors into the map, the map itself does not reveal many of the intricacies of the activities of the people living in that area, or the reasons why the people settled in that particular fashion in the first place. To be able to understand the logic behind an urban system and the social and economic dynamics that drive the settlement process, one needs to study the layers of interrelated human activities shown in the figure. Only then can one comprehend the complexity of the settlement patterns on the map. The time-scale that is suggested at the bottom of the figure brings dynamism into the model. As the construct, representing human activities in a particular area, moves through time from the past to the present, layers in the model contract and expand all the time as in an imaginary slow symphony of spatial-demographic transformation (Geyer, 2001:145,150).

Throughout history, most urban settlements emanated from agricultural activities, i.e. first layer activities in the human activities model (Figure 1.1), and for long periods of time in almost all parts of the world, **rural villages** dominated the urban scene. In England, for instance, providing goods and services to surrounding agricultural communities was the most important function of most rural villages for centuries. During this time industry and commerce were subordinate (Lipson, 1929). And when the evolution of systems of cities is compared in countries across the development spectrum (Berry, 1961; Haggett et al., 1977) most rural settlements are likely to continue to do so in future. In terms of the central place model (Christaller,

---

[3] In this model (Geyer, 2001), socio-cultural layers that potentially impact on human settlement patterns have been added to the economic layers in Weber's (1929) original industrial development model.

1933; Lösch, 1954) these rural settlements would be regarded as relatively small, widely dispersed, and locally oriented **'central places'** serving as market areas (Gradmann, 1916) and places of social gathering to local rural communities, similar to the market place that was described by von Thünen (1966) more than a century and a half ago.

Although there are significant differences in the types and level of sophistication of agricultural activities between the developed and developing world, there are also significant similarities in the rural centres that serve such communities. Depending on the level of technology used, the type of products produced, and the scale of production, the size of kinetic fields in the agricultural sector on the output side could vary from local to global. On the input side, however, kinetic fields in agriculture usually remain local, whatever its level of sophistication, hence the continued relevance of rural central places in developed and developing countries. Generally it can be said that there is a positive relationship between agriculture and the scale of production, commercial orientation, technological sophistication and the size of its market, nominally and spatially. Small scale, technologically less sophisticated agricultural output is more often aimed at the local market and typical of the developing world, although substantial informal agricultural market activities are also often found in rural towns in the developed world.

Because of technological advances in the developed world, there is a tendency towards higher output levels in the agricultural sector overall. In many respects this trend goes hand in hand with the global distribution of agricultural products (Knox, 1997), which more often than not has a significant curtailing impact on the population and economic profiles of agricultural centres at the lower ends of the urban scale in developed countries. Industrialized agriculture in advanced economies and the commercialization of agricultural products cause certain rural centres to lose their traditional economic function. In developing countries, on the other hand, where informal, subsistence oriented agricultural activities dominate, rural centres are often economically weak because such economic activities are often non-basic (Leven, 1966) in character. Very little income, if any, flows into these villages from elsewhere.

On the other side of the spectrum, however, many of the **larger urban agglomerations** of the developed world started out as **non-central places** associated with activities in the upper layers of the human activities model (Figure 1.1). Their original establishment can be ascribed to the availability of 'locational constants' (Richardson, 1973) such as large exploitable mineral deposits, sea ports, beautiful natural surroundings, strategic commercial or military locations, or locations of historical, cultural or religious significance. Although these centres originated as non-central places from a local (central place) perspective, most of them gained centrality, regionally, nationally, and even internationally through the addition of other attributes over time. In exceptional cases they even acquired global significance through the globalization of manufacturing products, finance, and social monitoring (Knox, 1997).

It seems as if the upper layers of the human activity model (Figure 1.1) have become increasingly important forces in the shaping of urban geography in large parts of the world over the last two decades. It is not surprising, therefore, that anachronistic religious, cultural, or social behaviour is often regarded as the only defense of the lagging nations against the fast pace of what Zelinsky (1971) has termed the 'super advanced' nations.

If the importance of information technology in the networking of business organizations and people in the world is taken as a bench mark, and bearing in mind the visible role culture and religion are beginning to play in local and international spatial politics in large parts of the world, it is clear that a new **fifth economic sector**, the intellectual sector, is emerging in the world today. Essentially, information technology merely serves as a vehicle to distribute information, but a large part of the information that is disseminated across the globe today takes on a new meaning in social-economic space. In many respects the assimilation of social, cultural, political, and economic information for personal fulfillment has become an end in itself. It has become more than just a personal service or luxury. It has become a tangible social-economic entity that helps mould urban space at all levels of spatial aggregation.

URBAN ISSUES IN THE DEVELOPED WORLD
GLOBAL NETWORKS

In his general theory Friedmann (1972) refers to urban systems as **spatially organized space**. At the local and regional levels, a distinction can be made between 'daily', 'weekly', and 'monthly' urban systems (Berry, 1973; Friedmann, 1978). At higher levels of spatial aggregation urban systems can be either regarded as national, sub-continental, continental, world, or global in scale (Geyer, 1998).[4] Whereas the first three scales in the latter group are self-explanatory, Castells (1993) distinguishes between global networks and world systems, the former covering the entire globe while subsets of the global network are covered by the latter.

According to de Vries (1984) the identification of urban systems becomes arbitrary if it is not based on well-defined spatial frameworks. **State boundaries**, he believes, have always served as the most enduring framework of reference for urban systems description. Based on this assumption he refers to 'national' and 'regional' boundaries as the most

---

[4] Looking at functional economic space from the bottom upwards, Philbrick (1957) gave a classical description of economic interaction from the local level to global urban interaction.

appropriate spatial criteria for the delimitation of urban regions. However, ample proof has been given of the universal inability of political-administrative boundaries to contain functional economic interaction (Perroux, 1950, 1950a; Philbrick, 1957). Networks of functional economic interaction rather than political-administrative boundaries seem to be the most appropriate spatial framework for urban systems analysis. **Functional urban space** also goes hand-in-hand with the **core-periphery** concept. Criteria that have been widely used over the years to distinguish core areas from their peripheries, include:

- population densities (Vining and Strauss, 1977; Gordon, 1979),
- population potential (Clark, 1966),
- advanced economic sectors (Perroux, 1955; Ullmann, 1958),
- economic spatial dominance (Sassen, 1996; Knox 1997; Graham 1999, Tellier, 1997; Wallerstein, 1974),
- urban density (Hohenberg and Lees, 1985),
- urban networking (Castells, 1994; Batten, 1995),
- urban scale (Petsimeris, 1998; Chuta, 1998; Geyer, 1998),
- strategic geographical considerations (Marksoo, 1992), and
- urban system maturity (Friedmann, 1966, 1972).

If one considers the factors that are used to differentiate between cores and their peripheries, several types of core as well as core-peripheral relationships could be discerned. Looking at core-peripheral relationships in a global context, Wallerstein's (1974)

> '[w]orld-systems theory argues that the density of economic links among the world's states has created a hierarchy of more and less powerful countries. This perspective divides the world into two main extremes of dependent relations: core and peripheral states. Core states can be defined as having (1) centrality in trade and military interventions, (2) maintained dominance through the use (or threat) of a superior armed force, and (3) centrality in a network of diplomatic information and exchange...Periphery states are those that score lowest on these same dimensions of centrality in military, economic, trade and diplomatic domination.' (Olzak, 1998)[5]

GLOBAL CITIES

Global cities serve as gravity points within Wallerstein's system of global dominance. They are agglomerations located in prominent urban regions dominating the economic, social, political, and cultural networks of the world

---

[5] Nothing illustrates this, and the effect it has on the urban society better than the relationship between the United States and its allies after Osama Bin Laden's attack on the World Trade Centre in New York on September 11, 2001.

Castells, 1994).[6] The concept has remained fuzzy for a long time (Ferguson, 1992) until recently when attempts were made to classify global cities based on particular criteria (Beaverstock et al., 1999; Taylor and Walker, 1999). Generally speaking there are two qualifying criteria used in the designation of global cities, population size and urban function. There are differences in opinion about when cities are of global significance because although they may be 'mega' in terms of size they may not necessarily be regarded as global cities and *vice versa* (Beaverstock et al., 1999). But classifying global cities hierarchically without reference to the inter-city relations in a global context is problematic (Taylor, 1997).

Using Wallerstein's (1974) classification of global regions, primary centres that are located in the **global 'core regions'** of the world[7] are probably the only true global cities at present. Certain primary centres in the **global 'semi-periphery'**[8] could be regarded as emerging global centres. Beyond that, large cities of the world could, in terms of their functional reach, at best be classified as cities of continental, sub-continental, regional, or national importance,[9] many of them dominating their surrounding hinterlands in the same manner as global cities do globally (Geyer, 1998).

INDUSTRIAL RESTRUCTURING

Fordist mass production was instrumental in the creation of a global system of core and peripheral areas (Wallerstein, 1974). Mushrooming industrialization in the large urban agglomerations of Developed Countries that attracted large numbers of labourers from inside and outside their national borders resulted in a mosaic of uneven development around the world. Efficiency, first achieved through **locational advantages**, **agglomeration economies** (Hirschman, 1958; Scott, 1982) and narrowly trained work forces (Piore, 1986), leading to vertical, horizontal and lateral **industrial integration** (Scott, 1983), eventually resulted in the over-accumulation of capital and functional inefficiency (Harvey, 1982; 1989; Smith, 1984; Walker, 1978).

Industrial restructuring followed. Emphasis was placed on 'downsizing', capital mobility, economies of scope, networking and the

---

[6] Primate cities, industrial cities, world cities, and mega-cities are some of the other terms that are often used to describe global cities (Beaverstock, et al., 1999), perhaps an indication of the disagreement amongst authors on what the concept really implies.

[7] These are the well-established, economically dominating postindustrial regions of Western Europe, North America, and Japan in which a concentration of advanced services are found (Friedmann and Wolff, 1982).

[8] These include the newly industrialised regions of the world such as Hong Kong and Singapore whose economies are still heavily dependent on the core regions.

[9] Generally these are stand-alone, self-contained cities with large hinterlands such as Madrid, Toulouse and Johannesburg.

Japanese *kanban* strategy of flexible production systems (Knox, 1997). Three new geographical arrangements of industries emerged: (1) branch-plant 'colonization' by large companies, many of them multinationals that locate in rural areas with quality infrastructure, (2) the mushrooming of localised small-firm growth, some of them linked to major manufacturing plants,[10] others focussing on indigenous production lines, both of which can be spatially concentrated or widely distributed, and (3) the location of high-tech firms and professional services in areas of high environmental quality, some in close proximity to major urban areas, others in small scenic villages in the periphery (Scott, 1988). These changes obviously hold implications for urban development policy.

COMPUTER AND INFORMATION TECHNOLOGY

Innovations in the **computer communication and information technology** (CCIT) sector has probably been the single most important factor that facilitated efficient decentralized management and production. Since the beginning of the 1980s, the technological innovative impetus of the CCIT sector has been growing exponentially, each new wave of innovations expanding the horizon for further innovations. By the end of the 1980s certain authors saw CCIT as becoming such an important factor in developed economies that they would soon be regarded as 'information economies'[11] – economies in which the networks that support linkages between firms, their markets and their suppliers would become vital in competition, causing tension between economies of scale and 'economies of scope' (Gillespie and Williams, 1988).

These innovations are bringing fundamental changes to cities in Western European countries (Dieleman et al., 1993). World cities are gaining in centrality and status because the CCIT brings together new combinations of concentrations of central, financial, institutional, social, informational, and infrastructural industries (Cheshire and Carbonaro, 1996; Graham, 1999). Empirical evidence shows that CCIT is improving the competitiveness of the primary centres of the world and as a consequence allows their economies to attract even more related economic investments (Nijkamp and Jonkhoff, 2000).

---

[10] The spatial conglomeration of 'Just-in-time' industries, linking strongly with key manufacturing industries (Mair, 1993; Hill, 1989; Magid, 1997) such as the automobile manufacturers in Japan, for instance, is an excellent example of the operation of the original growth centre concept and an indication that, given the right kind of industries, local communities can benefit greatly from growth centre activities.
[11] So significant were these advances that the computer and telecommunications revolution has been referred to as the second industrial revolution and the information revolution, the third (Kellerman, 1993).

There is growing penetration of CCIT in all countries, territories and cultures, especially in the Western World, but this penetration is selective and leads to a new global division of labour and a widening **global urban dualism** (Castells, 1993). It impacts on every person's daily life, economically and socially, but only the sizes of the kinetic fields of the urban élite who are travelling on the **'information highway'** are expanded dramatically. The workforce of high-tech economies is polarized and is becoming increasingly stratified (Berry, 1990). Those who find themselves on the CCIT-highway are speeding ahead, those in the urban **information 'ghetto'** are increasingly lagging behind, even within the city (Graham, 1999).

Governments are also re-scaling their activities. Assets are being privatized and space economies are being 'splintered' (Graham and Marvin, 1996). New global-local and even intra-metropolitan core-peripheral communication networks are developing, resulting in an interwoven constellation of communication 'hub-and-spoke' relationships (Graham, 1999). According to Staple (Graham, 1999), CCIT not only breaks down spatial barriers, it helps compress space and time and, as a consequence, societies are increasingly being localized and fragmented. CCIT forms the 'backbone' of all current major structural transformations in the economies of the West because it serves as a vehicle for the creation of a new functionally interrelated global economic system (Castells, 1993).

As a versatile element in the economic process it allows new options of product innovation. It transforms many elements of information into a commodity that is almost totally freed from friction of distance.[12] Innovations in the composition of products and their distribution that were considered to be impossible before, are now possible in manufacturing, retailing, banking, insurance, printing, and the academic world. Business organizations that were previously separated from one another are now electronically linked. It integrates sales and purchasing and reduces transaction costs, and overall, it creates new and exciting production and distributional options (Gillespie and Williams, 1988).

THE NEW ECONOMY AND CONVENTIONAL URBAN SPACE

Despite the growing concentration of corporate headquarters, high level service industries, global financial services, and supra governmental institutions in many large cities in the world, there is a growing need for **face-to-face contact** in this technologically advanced sector (Beaverstock et al., 1999). There is an isolated perception that the CCIT revolution will result in the collapsing of conventional hierarchies at all levels of spatial

---

[12] Despite this advantage the CCIT is increasingly becoming burdened by new forms of friction – that of financial and technological access.

aggregation, and that geographical space will be completely dominated by technological space (Graham, 1998). Because of the tendency of electronic interaction in the 'network society' to transcend conventional geographical arrangements and the fact that international electronic interaction in many respects supersedes local communication as the dominant process, it was thought that conventional hierarchical concepts such as city, region, state and continent will soon become redundant (Graham, 1999). The question can be asked whether humans will not be freed from the burdens imposed by the friction of distance, to such an extent that urban areas will ultimately lose their spatial cohesion. Batty (1993) believes such extreme views of technological determinism are unfounded, because cyberspace is 'layered on top of, within and between the fabric of traditional geographic space'. There are indications that CCIT may even increase the necessity for face-to-face interaction in a post-Fordist industrial era.

Similar fears of the collapsing of geographical space were expressed when the telephone, telex and later the facsimile came into use (Graham, 1998), but this technology did not eliminate the necessity for face-to-face contact. In fact, they consolidated existing economic and social relationships (Thrift, 1996). New communication technology tends to add to existing methods of communication and in the process impacts on the friction of distance and on time-space convergence. It also seems to affect the arrangement of significant elements of economic, administrative and social interaction patterns, and therefore, also core-peripheral relationships. In certain instances some forms of communication are complemented, others are substituted, and still others are made more flexible, but conventional forms of personal and face-to-face communication remain a dominant limiting force in human interaction patterns.

Although the reach of certain individuals in certain fields are expanding globally, and only certain economic sectors become spatially integrated (Gillespie and Williams, 1988), **conventional** forms of **communication** such as physical delivery services are still subject to physical and economic friction of distance (Michelson and Wheeler, 1994). This friction causes the constellation of interaction fields in and between urban areas to be as relevant today as it was when explained by Philbrick (1957) more than four decades ago.

Due to traffic congestion and social overhead costs in the areas where people physically live, the direct relationship between urban size and the friction of distance will continue to be a limiting factor in the size of cities for some time to come. In an extensive survey of important factors that determine the location of industries in Mexico and Canada, Polèse and Champagne (1999) for instance warned us not to discard textbooks on 'traditional' industrial **location theory**, based on agglomeration economies and the friction of distance as yet, because it still very much applies.

Concentration is still the most outstanding feature of economic activity and a clear indication of the pervasiveness of increasing returns to scale. In fact, the presence of the city is evidence of the impact of increasing returns to scale, despite post-modernistic changes that are evident in its structure (Knox, 1994). The persistence of concentration of manufacturing is an indication of the continuing importance of economies of scale, agglomeration economies, and of social-institutional externalities (Krugman, 1991; Boddy, 1999).

In the treatment of CCIT on the development of urban systems, scholars are facing two significant problems. First, there is a tendency among scholars to treat CCIT as one collective unit, which it is not. Certain technology is being used regularly, others are used less frequently. Some technology is being substituted by more efficient and advanced technology, while redundant technology is still being used elsewhere. This is a major obstacle in the realistic assessment of the impact CCIT has on human life, and therefore on urban systems. Hägerstrandt's (1952) view that the assimilation of innovation depends on its availability, threshold limitations and time of exposure probably still applies to CCIT just as it did to the diffusion of television sets in the USA from 1953 to 1965 (Berry, 1972).

Finally, the mere treatment of CCIT as an extension of existing economic sectors is problematic. Although it penetrates all current economic sectors, from the primary to the quaternary, the explosion of environmental, medical, political, educational, social, and entertainment information and the propagation of cultural and religious consciousness through the telecommunication media is an indication of the beginning of the new **fifth economic sector**, the intellectual or pentanary sector. It no longer merely forms part of the service sector. It serves as a vehicle to inform, educate, entertain and satisfy people's intellectual curiosity in all corners of the world.

DEMOGRAPHIC CHANGE AND MIGRATION

In many respects CCIT could be regarded as an external influence on urban systems. But there are several other equally important internal factors that influence urban communities directly. Demographic variables, and in particular, fertility rates, are among them.

Extending the **demographic transition** in the developed world into what has been described as the 'second transition', fertility rates fell below the replacement level of 2.13 live births per woman in Europe for the first time in the mid-1960s (Champion, 1992), followed by the rest of the developed world ten years later (Birg, 1995). Falling fertility rates combined with rising life expectancy levels had a significant impact on the aging and social stratification of the population and on the sizes and composition of households (Beale, 1982; Champion, 1992). **Family sizes** are decreasing, family members are aging overall, and single parent families are becoming a common phenomenon. Changing needs and mobilities result in diverging redistribution trends.

Over the past two decades, for instance, **elderly migration** had a significant impact on overall migration trends in England and Wales.[13] Between 1970 and 1980, England's southern coastal area and East Anglia gained many older people, while the South East, particularly London was the chief loser of this population group. More than a third of the elderly migrants of counties that gained more than 10 per cent of this population group, originated from London (Grundy, 1987). Less of this group have been migrating to the coastal regions lately. Many now choose not to move at all or to move to small inland villages and towns (Fielding, 1992). According to Speare and Meyer (1988) shifts to the Sunbelt and to non-metropolitan areas in general are features of migration of elderly people in the United States, many of them older people with children leaving high immigration metropolitan areas (Frey and Liaw, 1998). Moreover, Zelinsky's (1971) claim that higher skilled persons are more prone to migrate than lower income people, has been proven to be correct in the United States (Beale, 1982). Anglo-American experience showed that there are three phases in elderly migration, each phase very much linked to changes in people's life-course. Those in their early retirement move to desired locations. When minor disabilities develop, they move to areas where support is readily available. When major disabilities set in, they tend to move to locations where assistance is obtainable (Speare and Meyer, 1988; Champion, 1992).

While older people tend to leave large cities to find more scenic environments, cities seem to serve as **social escalators** for younger people (Fielding, 1992a). These trends have been linked to the concept of **productionism** and **environmentalism** (Hart, 1983), the former referring to younger, less affluent people migrating to cities to find employment opportunities and the latter to older more affluent people migrating to more pleasing environments (Geyer and Kontuly, 1993; Geyer, 1996, 1998). Over-all these demographic changes in the developed world played a significant part in the turnaround from **urbanization** to **counter-urbanization**.[14]

In contrast to the developing world where migration trends seem to be more predictable, higher levels of mobility of people in the developed world make them more susceptible to short term migration. Long distance

---

[13] The propensity to migrate is significantly higher amongst older people in more developed societies than less developed societies during their life-course (Warnes, 1992).

[14] Although it has been found that factors such as locational preferences of consumers and employers played a more significant role than regional restructuring in the deconcentration tendencies in the United States during the 1970s and 80s (Frey, 1987), the two groups of factors are inter-linked, the one affecting the other.

shuttling, **circulation** and seasonal migration are becoming particularly evident in countries such as the United States.

International migration has also been on the increase since the 1980s (Champion, 1992).[15] A dualistic migration pattern is being observed, highly skilled workers entering the upper end of the labour market and unskilled workers filling in at the lower end (Champion, 1994). Categories of international migrants include: 'invisibles', i.e. people that mesh in with the local people, 'gap-fillers', i.e. people filling vacancies that cannot be filled by locals, political refugees, and privileged foreigners, i.e. people that are treated as locals by virtue of blood lineage (Böhning, 1991). The rise in **international labour migration** in Europe, especially that of low-skilled labour has provoked some stern reaction from affected quarters. This is becoming an increasingly important factor in urban dynamics in the developed world today.

POLARIZATION IN THE URBAN ENVIRONMENT

The postmodern world is increasingly becoming a normative driven society in which the urban élite, whose norms are determined by the quality of life they can afford, are pitted against the urban poor, whose norms are determined by what they need to do to survive in, for them, a harsh economic environment. At the other end of the scale, social polarization is the result of economic progress in most large cities of the world. In the postindustrial economies of these modern cities, where shifts occur from manufacturing to advanced business services, increasing polarization of occupation and incomes becomes visible at the extreme upper end of the economic spectrum. Growth in technologically advanced activities in the upper strata is accompanied by an increase in the economically unsophisticated **informal sector** that 'services' the upper strata. In the process informal activities are booming (Lambooy and Moulaert, 1996). A new economic structure evolves. Informal activities tend to flourish in economically depressed commercial and manufacturing zones, a situation that is not conducive to the expansion of the middle strata. This growing **economic polarization** in the large cities of the world is increasingly spilling over into the social arena (Sassen, 1996). But this process in not limited to the large modern cities of the Developed World only. It is a world wide phenomenon of the postmodernistic urban society.

The rate at which the gap has been deepening between high technology, low technology and informal industrial activities and between the income levels of the people that are economically active in these three sectors in cities in the First World and developing world has been increasing. Also the

---

[15] This is one of the reasons given for the slowdown in the turnaround in Europe since the 1980s.

numerical balance between the three sectors is becoming increasingly skewed. This can severely raise the levels of competition for the same urban space between opposing factions (Sandercock, 1998) – one group overcoming Malthusian economics, the other increasingly being overcome by it.

Lagging communities often regard **economic enclaves** as the only way to create and protect employment opportunities for themselves. Social, cultural and economic 'safe havens' are enclaves that are caused by urban polarization. They allow people to migrate to urban areas that would have been inaccessible to them otherwise. Socially integrated urban societies present a much tighter and more competitive environment to infiltrate than societies where enclaves are known to exist.

In many parts of modern urban society economic enclaves co-exist peacefully. Examples of such enclaves are the well-known China Towns in certain cities in the United States. In other cases tension boils over into what can be termed strained 'social enclosurism' such as in cities in the Balkan states. The enclave economy concept is closely related to the 'dual-labour-market' hypothesis which, in turn, is sustained by current international labour migration practices. In the dual-labour-markets of industrialized economies, vacancies in the manual labour categories tend to be more regularly filled by migrants and unskilled nationals, while skilled nationals tend to work in the more stable categories (Piore, 1986).

Polarization differs as the city structure changes in terms of the size of the labour market, income distributions, divisions of labour, unemployment, household compositions and age structure (Hamnett, 1996). The **Todaro** (1969, 1982) **migration hypothesis** and the related issue of social mobility (Fielding, 1989, 1992) are both of particular relevance in this field of research.

URBAN CHANGE
URBAN COMPETITION

Collectively, the citizens of cities and their economic and social organizations compete with other cities[16] to attract (i) the most skilled labour, (ii) have the most effective infrastructure and governance, and (iii) offer the highest environmental standards and the best quality of life (Lever and Turok, 1999; Krugman, 1991). Technical improvements are constantly raising the level of increasing returns to scale in manufacturing and services

---

[16] Urban competition is not a one dimensional phenomenon. Citizens in urban areas compete with citizens in other urban areas individually and collectively through their social, economic and administrative activities. The complexity of the matter only becomes apparent when the areas of competition between cities are broken down into the layers of activities indicated on Figure 1.1.

in the most advanced cities of the developed world. Only in exceptional cases like Singapore, Hong Kong and Taiwan has the developing world succeeded in matching the innovative pace set by the leading developed economies of the world. Large parts of the developing world are falling out of touch. This difference in pace is bound to change the global urban system from a pyramidal-shaped hierarchy into a pagoda-shaped one.

Advances in the CCIT-field have an important role to play in this change. The rate at which the CCIT-sector is advancing is likely to widen the spectrum of increased kinetic energy of people in the future. The most important current obstacle that prevents modern cities from functioning effectively, lies in the differences between the sizes and expansion rates of the **kinetic fields** of the urban élite and those of the urban poor. Indications are that this situation is likely to continue in the future. In fact, new advances may even exacerbate it. While the kinetic energy of those who have access to CCIT and who can capitalize on the latest advances in the field, will continue to expand exponentially, the kinetic energy of those who operate outside or on the fringes of the field will remain static or expand only linearly. If this situation continues, and it likely will, growing proportions of the urban population will be forced to make a living outside the formal urban environment, in both the developed and less developed urban environment.

Advances in technology in general, and in CCIT in particular will allow more **freedom of choice** to those individuals who have access to it. People who have the financial and technical ability to utilize available technology will have greater personal freedom and lead more individualistic urban life styles, and in a chain of cause and effect, cohesion of the urban élite will more than likely wither. Similarities in technology should result in the narrowing of cultural, economic and social differences of the economically advanced in different parts of the world. However, contact between individuals and between them and nature is a basic need that will ensure the continued existence of communities.

Those that live outside this privileged circle are bound to become more altruistic. As a spontaneous defence, the technically disenfranchised are becoming increasingly culturally conscious and enclosure oriented, inside cities, within regions and state boundaries, as well as internationally. The more people are excluded from technology and the more they are dependent on one another for their existence, the stronger will their communal cohesion become, socially, politically and culturally.

Although information technology is becoming increasingly important in all economic activity in advanced economies, it is unlikely that manufacturing and services are, or will become subordinate to CCIT in the near future as Castells (1993) would have us believe. Manufacturing output has been the mainstay of urban economic development and is likely to remain so in future (Scott, 1988).

As the **pentanary sector** grows in importance, however, new functional economic relationships (which will benefit a small **privileged minority** more than the masses) may cause a deepening of urban dualism in cities. This may cause a divide between the urban élite and the disadvantaged in a postmodern urban environment, a phenomenon that has already been surfacing in many developed cities (Sandercock, 1998). The reason for this is that the urban élite in advanced urban economies tends to prosper in a cosmopolitan environment while the vulnerable **under-skilled majority** of the urban population increasingly have to resort to underground and informal ways of existence to survive, a situation that will augment economic and social urban polarization, and ultimately, enclosurism. Increasing gap filling from developing countries (Böhning, 1991), which will be necessitated by the aging of the developed world populations, will increase the likelihood of enclavism in cities in developed countries (Castells, 1993). Enclosurism may even deepen if immigration policies in developed countries remain as lenient as they are at present on the issue of cultural assimilation of immigrants (Straubaar and Zimmermann, 1993).

URBAN MATURATION

Based on analyses of long term migration trends, Vining and Strauss (1977) suggest a more or less fixed spatial **development sequence** for developed countries. First urbanization takes place, followed by intra-urban diffusion, then interregional deconcentration from urban to rural regions takes place, and finally the process ends with deconcentration within these rural regions.[17] Borrowing from Kondratieff's long-wave theory, Berry (1988), through his extension of the **long-wave theory**, expanded significantly on Vining's one-cycle hypothesis by showing significant repeated correlations between urban and other economically related growth cycles in the United States over a 250 year period. Focussing on growth sequences of individual urban agglomerations the Klaassen-group identified various phases of urban evolution:

❑ Initially, cities go through an **'urbanization'** phase at which time they grow at the cost of their surrounding countryside,

❑ later on, **'suburbanization'** sets in when the urban ring starts growing at the cost of the core,

---

[17] At first, deconcentration was regarded as a regional phenomenon, i.e. people leaving large metropolitan regions for peripheral regions in a clean break from past trends (Vining and Strauss, 1977). Later it was discovered that the redistribution process occurred in waves (Gordon, 1979), the centres the closest to metropolitan areas being the first recipients of population that are leaving the large cities, followed by deconcenration downward along urban hierarchies in a process of counter-urbanization (Frey, 1988).

❑ then the **'dis-urbanization'** phase starts, when the population loss of the core exceeds the population gain of the ring, resulting in the agglomeration losing population overall.

❑ Finally, the city returns to a phase of **'re-urbanization'** when either the rate of population loss of the core tapers off, or when the core starts regaining population, although the ring might still be losing population (Klaassen et al., 1981, 1981a; van den Berg et al., 1981, 1982).

Richardson's (1977, 1980) view of the spatial relationship between industrial and urban development is almost identical to the Vining group's description of the evolution of urban systems in the developed world. Highlighting only the migration implications of Richardson's description of the urban development process, population accumulates firstly in the primate city. This is followed, first, by decentralization within the core[18] resulting in a multi-nodal urban structure, then by interregional deconcentration towards a limited number of nodes within the inner periphery, and later on, by deconcentration towards the outer peripheral regions. He refers to the early stages of the turnaround as the **'polarization reversal'** phase, i.e. when the deconcentration process takes hold. This phase is followed by counter-urbanization when the core loses population in absolute terms. Although Richardson (1977, 1980) only linked the polarization reversal concept to developing countries, indications are that developed countries do indeed also go through the polarization reversal phase (Geyer, 1996). In fact, because Richardson mainly focussed on economic (industrial) deconcentration in developing countries, the signs of demographic polarization reversal may only set in long after economic deconcentration has started, hence the apparent anomaly of polarization reversal also occurring in developed countries.

Based on these observations the following general statements can be made regarding sequences in the economic development of urban systems (Geyer and Kontuly, 1996):

❑ National urban systems initially go through a primate city phase. During this phase a large proportion of economic development and large numbers of migrants are attracted to one or a few primary centres (Richardson 1973) and a core-peripheral system develops.

❑ As the national urban system expands and matures, new urban centres are added to the lower ranks while many of those that already exist, develop and move up through the ranks. In this process, economic development gets dispersed, while the urban system becomes spatially more integrated (Friedmann 1966; Richardson 1973).

---

[18] For an elaboration on current views on the spatial dynamics inside the metropolitan area, see Bourne (1992).

❏ Such expanding national urban systems develop into various strata of territorially organized core-peripheral subsystems, from the macro-level through the regional and sub-regional levels to the local or micro-levels (Friedmann, 1972; Bourne and Simmons, 1978). The polarized region as a functional entity is an example of such a core-peripheral subsystem (Boudeville, 1967). On aggregate, there is more economic interaction between urban centres within the region than with centres outside.

❏ The sequence of tendencies observed in the development of urban systems, first toward concentration and then toward dispersion or deconcentration, is not limited to systems at the national level, but can manifest at each of the lower levels of core-peripheral systems, because the same spatial forces that operate at the national level, also operate at the subnational and local levels.

❏ In a growing urban environment, the odds normally favour the development of secondary centres closer to primary centres (Richardson 1977, 1980; van den Berg et al., 1982; Gordon 1979; Richter 1985), unless an outlying centre is located in an area with exceptional locational attributes (Friedmann, 1966).

The world systems theory suggests an evolving **core-periphery** dispensation which is created by the globalization of the market economy and which greatly influences international migration patterns. Capitalism extends outward from Europe, North America, and the Far East as the core nations of the world. New York, London, and Tokyo serve as apexes within these cores at the international level. According to the theory the world-wide penetration of the developed world's market forces displaces unskilled labour in the peripheral regions of the world. This creates mobilized populations prone to migrate. Globalization creates employment opportunities in global cities for highly skilled labour in management, finance, and services and as a spin-off, employment opportunities are also created in these centres for ancillary workers in entertainment, accommodation, construction, maintenance and services.

If the principles outlined in the propositions regarding the development of national urban systems were to be applied to the global urban system, the world systems theory could be extended as follows:

❏ The **global urban system** has gone through several primate city (economic growth) phases in history. Initially, when economic power was concentrated in the Middle and Far East, large economically vibrant cities developed there. Later on, when capitalism dawned, the balance of power and city growth shifted to Europe and North America, and although the major cities of the latter regions are still in a strong position, the focus seems to be slowly shifting back to Asia in recent years.

❑ As the primate urban centres on the different continents of the world expand and mature, new urban centres of international importance are added to the lower ranks, while many of those that already exist, develop and move up through the ranks. In this process, new **global economic focal points** emerge on the world map and economic development gets dispersed, while the world urban system becomes spatially more integrated.

❑ Various **strata of core-peripheral subsystems** develop in this expanding international urban system, from the global through the continental and the sub-continental, to the national and the local levels.

❑ The sequence of tendencies observed in the development of urban systems, first towards concentration and then towards dispersion or deconcentration, is not limited to systems at the state level only. It also manifests at higher levels of aggregation because the same spatial forces that operate at the national and subnational levels also operate at higher levels of aggregation.

❑ Due to locational advantages, the intensity of **spatial economic networking and integration** are higher between large world centres and satellite cities and intermediate-sized cities closer to them than between world centres and other similar sized centres further away.

As a result of the impact of these propositions on the development of the global urban system, further generalizations could be made:

❑ The **world cities** and large urbanized regions around them have become spatially highly integrated **core regions**. Therefore, what holds true for individual global cities in terms of capital accumulation and access to markets and resources globally, also holds true for larger areas surrounding these apexes.

❑ Based on the location of these global economic apexes and their economically integrated surrounding areas, the global urban system can also be divided into **inner and outer core areas** as well as freestanding intermediate-sized city regions and peripheral regions. Together these global apexes and their surrounding urban areas constitute core-peripheral subsystems at the highest level of aggregation.

❑ Core-peripheral subsystems displaying the same spatial economic characteristics can also be identified at the continental, sub-continental, and national levels.

❑ In terms of human resource potential the focus of urban settlements at the global scale is likely to shift increasingly towards the East in the future. As the gateways to large territories of the developing world, certain strategically located developing cities are becoming important continental and sub-continental cores.

❑ On aggregate, continental and sub-continental cores dominate large peripheral areas economically around them in much the same way as world cities do at the global level. Global, continental, sub-continental, national, sub-national, and local cores and their respective hinterlands should therefore be regarded as similar urban subsystems that form different strata of the same urban system.

Figure 3.1A shows how the positions of cities in the graph generally shift from the lower-left quadrant to the upper-right as their populations and economies expand over time. Figure 3.1B shows how the rate of economic development of cities (shown along the y-axis) generally increases, while their population growth rate tapers off over time. In this way the relative positions of cities of all sizes in developed and developing countries can be indicated on the same graphs. An empirical analysis of this kind should greatly complement the work that has been done on global city analysis by scholars such as Friedmann and Wolff (1982), Beaverstock et al. (1999), Sassen (1991, 1996), and Taylor and Walker (1999).

Figure 3.1 The growth of urban centres over time

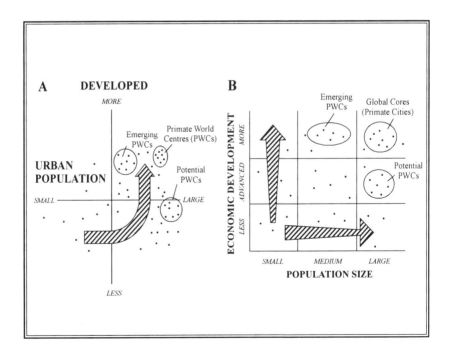

Source: Geyer, 1998

REFERENCES

Batten, D. F. (1995), 'Network cities: Creative urban agglomerations for the 21st century', *Urban Studies*, **32**, 313-327.

Batty, M. (1993), 'The geography of cyberspace', *Environment and Planning, B*, **20**, 615-661.

Beale, C. L. (1977), 'The Recent Shift of United States Population to Nonmetropolitan Areas, 1970-75', *International Regional Science Review*, **2**, 113-122.

Beale, C. L. (1982), 'U.S. population: Where we are; Where we're going', *Population Bulletin*, **37**, 1-59.

Beaverstock, J. V., R. G. Smith and P. J. Taylor (1999), 'A roster of world cities', *Cities*, **16**, 445-458.

Berry, B. J. L. (1961), 'City size distributions and economic development', *Economic Development and Cultural Change*, **9**, 573-588.

Berry, B. J. L. (1972), 'Hierarchical diffusion: The basis of developmental filtering and spread in a system of growth centers', in N. M. Hansen (ed.), *Growth centers in regional economic development*, New York: The Free Press, pp.108-138.

Berry, B. J. L. (1973), 'Growth centers in the American urban system', in *Geographical perspectives on urban problems,* Washington: National Academy of Sciences, pp.94-107.

Berry, B. J. L. (1976), 'The counterurbanization process: Urban America since 1970', *Urban Affairs Annual Review*, **11**, 17-30.

Berry, B. J. L. (1988), 'Migration reversals in perspective: The long-wave evidence', *International Regional Science Review*, **11**: 245-251.

Berry, B. J. L. (1990), 'Urban systems by the Third Millennium: A second look', *Journal of Geography*, **89**: 98-100.

Birg, H. (1995), *World population projections for the 21st century: Theoretical interpretation and quantitative simulations*, Frankfurt: Campus Verlag.

Boddy, M. (1999), 'Geographical economics and urban competitiveness: A critique', *Urban Studies*, **36**, 811-843.

Böhning, W.R. (1991), 'Integration and immigration pressures in Western Europe', *International Labour Review*, **130**, 445-458.

Boudeville, J-R. (1967), *Problems of regional economic planning*, Edinburgh: Edinburgh University Press.

Bourne, L. S. and J. W. Simmons (eds) (1978), *Systems of cities: Readings on structure, growth, and policy*, New York: Oxford University Press.

Castells, M. (1993), 'European cities, the informational society, and the global economy', *Tijdschrift voor Economische en Sociale Geografie*, **84**, 247-257.

Castells, M. (1994), *The rise of the network society,* Oxford: Blackwell.

Champion, A. G. (ed.) (1989), *Counterurbanization: The changing pace and nature of population deconcentration,* London: Edward Arnold.

Champion, A. G. (1992), 'Urban and regional demographic trends in the Developed World', *Urban Studies,* **29**, 461-482.

Champion, A. G. (1994), 'International migration and demographic change in the Developed World', *Urban Studies,* **31**, 653-677.

Cheshire, P. and G. Carbonaro (1996), 'Urban economic growth in Europe: testing theory and policy prescriptions', *Urban Studies,* **33**, 1111-1128.

Christaller, W. (1933), *Central places of Southern Germany,* Baskin C.W. (trl) Englewood Cliffs, N.J.: Prentice-Hall.

Chuta, B. (1998), 'World cities, globalization and the spread of consumerism: A view from Singapore', *Urban Studies,* **35**, 981-1000.

Clark, C. (1967), *Population growth and land use,* New York: St.Martin's Press.

Clark, C. (1966), 'Industrial location and economic potential', *Lloyds Bank Review,* **82**, 1-17.

De Vries, J. (1984), *European urbanization 1500-1800,* London: Methuen.

Dieleman, F., H. Priemus, and W. Blauw (1993), 'European cities: Changing urban structures in a changing world', *Tijdschrift voor Economiesche en Sociale Geografie,* **84**, 242-246.

Doxiadis, C. A. (1970), 'Man's movement and his settlements', *Ekistics,* **29**: 296-321.

Easton, S. C. (1954) *The heritage of the past: from the earliest times to the close of the Middle Ages,* New York: Rinehart and Co.

Ferguson, M. (1992), 'The mythology about globalization', *European Journal of Communication,* 7, 679-693.

Fielding, A. J. (1989), 'Inter-regional migration and social change: A study of South East England based upon data from the Longitudinal Study', *Transactions of the Institute of British Geographers,* **14**, 24-36.

Fielding, A. J. (1989a), 'Migration and Urbanization in Western Europe', *The Geographical Journal,* **155**, 60-69.

Fielding, A. J. (1992), 'Migration and social change', in J. Stillwell, P. Rees, and P. Boden (eds), *Migration processes and patterns: population redistributiion in the United Kingdom, Vol 2,* London: Belhaven, pp.xx.

Fielding, A. J. (1992a), 'Migration and social mobility: South East England as an escalator region', *Regional Studies,* **26**, 1-15.

Fox, R. W. (1984), 'The world's urban explosion', *National Geographic,* **166**, 179-182.

Frey, W. H. (1987), 'Migration and depopulation of the metropolis: Regional restructuring or rural renaissance?', *American Sociological Review*, **52**, 240-257.

Frey, W. H. (1988), 'Migration and metropolitan decline in Developed Countries: A comparative study', *Population and Development Review,* **14**, 595-628.

Frey, W. H. and K. Liaw (1998), 'Immigrant concentration and domestic migrant dispersal: Is movement to nonmetropolitan areas "White Flight"?', *Professional Geographer,* **50**, 215-232.

Friedmann, J. (1966), *Regional development policy: A case study of Venezuela*, Cambridge, Mass.: MIT.

Friedmann, J. (1972), 'A general theory of polarized development', in N. M. Hansen (ed.), *Growth centers in regional economic development*, New York: The Free Press, pp.82-107.

Friedmann, J. (1978), 'The urban field a human habitat', in L.S. Bourne and J.W. Simmons, J.W. (eds), *Systems of cities: Readings on structure, growth, and policy*. New York: Oxford University Press, pp.42-52.

Friedmann, J. (1979), *The good society*, Cambridge, Mass: MIT.

Friedmann, J. and G. Wolff (1982), 'World city formation: An agenda for research action'. *International Journal of Urban and Regional Research*, **5**, 309-343.

Geyer, H. S. (1989), 'Apartheid in South Africa and industrial deconcentartion in the PWV area', *Planning Perspectives*, **4**, 251-269.

Geyer, H. S. (1996), 'Expanding the theoretical foundation of differential urbanization', *Tijdschrift voor Economische en Sociale Geografie*, **87**, 44-59.

Geyer, H. S. (1998), 'Differential urbanization and international migration: An urban systems approach', in C. Gorter, P. Nijkamp, and J. Poot (eds), *Crossing borders: Regional and urban perspectives on international migration*. Aldershot: Ashgate, pp.161-184.

Geyer, H. S. (2001), 'Development planning transition in South Africa', in H. C. Marais, Y. Methien, N.S. Jansen van Rensburg, M.P. Maaga, G.F. de Wet, C.J. Coetzee (eds), *Sustainable social development: Critical dimensions*. Pretoria: Network Publishers, pp.143-152.

Geyer, H. S. and T. M. Kontuly (1993), 'A theoretical foundation for the concept of differential urbanization', in N. Hansen, K.J. Button, and P. Nijkamp (eds), *Modern Classics in Regional Science: Regional Policy and Regional Integration*, Vol. 6, Cheltenham: Edward Elgar. pp.135-160.

Gillespie, A. and H. Williams (1988), 'Telecommunications and the reconstruction of regional comparative advantage', *Environment and Planning A*, **20**, 1311-1321.

Gordon, P. (1979), 'Deconcentration Without a "Clean Break"'. *Environment and Planning A*, **11**, 281-290.

Gottmann, J. (1978), 'Megalopolitan systems around the world', in L. S. Bourne and J. W. Simmons (eds), *Systems of cities: Readings on structure, growth, and policy*. New York: Oxford University Press, pp.53-60.

Gradmann, R. (1916), *Schwäbische Städte*, Gesellschaft für Erdkunde zu Berlin. April, 8, pp.425-457.

Graham, S. (1998), 'The end of geography or the explosion of place? Conceptualizing space, place and information technology', *Progress in Human Geography*, **22**, 165-185.

Graham, S. (1999), 'Global grids of glass: On cities, telecommunications and planetary urban networks', *Urban Studies*, **36**, 929-949.

Graham, S. and S. Marvin (1996), *Telecommunications and the city: Electronic spaces, urban places*, London: Routledge.

Grundy, E. (1987), 'Retirement migration and its consequences in England and Wales', *Aging and Society*, **7**, 57-82.

Hägerstrandt, T. (1952), *The propagation of innovation waves*, Lund Studies in Geography, Series B, Human Geography, No.4. The Royal University of Lund, Sweden.

Haggett, P., A.D. Cliff, and A. Frey (1977), *Locational analysis in human geography*. London: Edward Arnold.

Hamnett, C. (1996), 'Social polarization, economic restructuring and welfare state regimes', *Urban Studies*, **33**, 1407-1430.

Hart, T. (1983), 'Transport and economic development: The historical dimension', in K. J. Button and D. Gillingwater (eds), *Transport location and spatial policy*. Aldershot, Hants. U.K.: Gower. pp. 12-22.

Harvey, D. (1982), *The limits to capital*. Oxford: Basil Blackwell.

Harvey, D. (1989), *The condition of post-modernity*. Oxford: Basil Blackwell.

Hauser, P. M. (1965), 'Urbanization: An overview', in P. M.Hauser and L. F. Schnore (eds), *The study of urbanization*. New York: Wiley, pp.1-48.

Hill, R. (1989), 'Comparing transnational production systems: The automobile industry in the USA and Japan', *International Journal of Urban and Rgional Research*, 13, 462-480.

Hirschman, A. O. (1958), *The strategy of economic development*, New Hven: Yale University Press.

Hohenberg, P. M. and L. H. Lees (1985), *The making of urban Europe, 1000-1950*. Cambridge, Mass.: Harvard University Press.

Klaassen, L. H., J. A. Bourdrez, and J. Volmuller (1981), *Transport and Reurbanization*. Aldershot, Hants, U.K: Gower.

Klaassen, L. H., and G. Scimemi (1981a), 'Theoretical Issues in Urban Dynamics', in L. H.Klaassen, W. T. M. Molle and J. H. P. Paelinck (eds), *Dynamics of Urban Development,* New York: St.Martin's Press, pp. 8-28.

Knox, P. L. (1994), *Urbanization: An introduction to urban geography.* London: Prentice-Hall.

Knox, P. L. (1997), 'World cities in a world-system', in P. L. Knox and P. J. Taylor (eds), *World cities in a world-system,* Cambridge: Cambridge University Press, pp.3-20.

Krugmann, P. (1991), 'Increasing returns and economic geography', *Journal of Political Economy*, **99**, 483-499.

Lambooy, J. G. and Moulaert, F. (1996), 'The economic organization of cities: and institutional perspective', *International Journal of Urban and Regional Research*, **20**, 217-237.

Leven, C. L. (1966), 'The economic base and regional growth', in Center for Agricultural and Economic Development, *Research and education for regional and area development*, Ames, Iowa: Iowa State University Press, pp. 79-94.

Lever, W. F. and Turok, I (1999), 'Competitive cities: Introduction to the review', *Urban Studies*, **36**, 791-793.

Lipson, E. (1929), *The Economic history of England.* London: A. and C. Black.

Lösch, A. (1954), *The economics of location,* New Haven: Yale University Press.

Mair, A. (1993), 'New growth poles? Just-in-time manufacturing and local economic development strategy', *Regional Studies*, **27**, 207-221.

Magid, L. (1997), 'Moving people and goods in a global, information-based economy', *Transportation Quarterly*, **51**, 25-27.

Marksoo, A. (1992), 'On the role of urban centres of fringe areas in Estonia', in M. Tykkylainen (ed.), *Development issues and strategies in the new Europe: local, regional and interregional perspectives.* Aldershot: Avebury, pp.163-170.

Michelson, R. L. and J. O. Wheeler (1994), 'The flow of information in a global economy: The role of the American urban system in 1990', *Annals of the Association of American Geographers*, **84**, 87-107.

Mumford, L. (1961), *The city in history: Its origins, its transformations, and its prospects.* San Diego: Hatcort Brace Jovanovich Publishers.

Nijkamp, P. and W. Jonkhoff (2000), 'The city in the information and communication technoloty age: a comparative study on path dependency', Proceedings of the International Regional Science Association conference, Port Elizabeth, January, 24-26.

Olzak, S (1998), 'Ethnic protest in core and periphery', *Ethnic and Racial Studies,* **21**, 187-217.

Perroux, F. (1950), 'Economic space: Theory and applications', *Quarterly Journal of Economics*, **LXIV**, 89-104.

Perroux, F. (1950a), 'The domination effect and modern economic theory'. *Social Research*, **17**, 188-206.

Perroux, F. (1955), 'Note sur la notion de 'pole de croissance', *Économie appliquée*, **7**, 307-320.

Petsimeris, P (1998), 'Urban decone and the new social and ethnic divisions in the core cities of the Italien Industrial Triangle', *Urban Studies*, **35**, 449-465.

Philbrick, A. K. (1957), 'Principles of areas functional organization in regional human geography', *Economic Geography*, **33**, 299-336.

Piore, M. J. (1986), 'The shifting grounds for immigration', *Annals of the American Academy of Political and Social Science*, **485**, 23-33.

Polèse, M. and É. Champagne (1999), 'Location matters: Comparing the distribution of economic activity in the Canadian and Mexican urban systems', *International Regional Science Review*, **22**, 102-132.

Richardson, H. W. (1973), *Economic growth theory*. London: MacMillan.

Richardson, H. W. (1977), *City size and national strategies in Developing Countries*. World Bank Staff Working Report, Washington.

Richardson, H. W. (1980), 'Polarization reversal in Developing Countries', *Papers of the Regional Science Association,* **45**, .67-85.

Richter, K. (1985), 'Nonmetropolitan growth in the late 1970s: The end of the turnaround?', *Demography*, **22**, 245-263.

Rogers, A. (1981), 'Sources of Urban population growth and urbanization, 1950-2000: A demographic accounting', *Economic Development and Cultural Change*, **30**, 483-506.

Rogers, A. and J. G. Williams (1982), 'Migration, and Third World development: and overview', *Economic Development and Cultural Change*, **30**, 463-482.

Sandercock, L. (1998), *Towards cosmopolis*. Chichester: Wiley.

Sassen, S. (1991), *The global city: New York, London, Tokyo*, Princeton, NJ: Princeton Universit y Press.

Sassen, S. (1996), *Cities in a world economy*, Thousand Oaks, Cal.: Sage Publication.

Scott, A. J. (1982), 'Locational patterns and dynamics of industrial activity in the modern metropolis', *Urban Studies*, **19**, 111-142.

Scott, A. J. (1983), 'Industrial organization and the logic of intra-metropolitan location: 1 theoretical considerations', *Economic Geography*, **59**, 233-250..

Scott, A. J. (1988), *Metropolis: From the division of labor to urban form.* Berkeley: University of California Press.

Smith, N. (1984), *Uneven development*, London: Allen and Unwin.

Speare, A. and Meyer, J. W. (1988), 'Types of elderly residential mobility and their determinants', *Journal of Gerontology*, **42**, S74-S81

Straubaar, T., and K. F. Zimmermann (1993), 'Towards a European migration policy', *Population Research and Policy Review*, **12**, 225-241.

Taylor, P. J. (1997), 'Hierarchical tendencies amongst world cities: A global research proposal', *Cities*, **14**, 323-332.

Taylor, P.J. and Walker (1999), *World cities: A first multivariate analysis of their service complexes*, GaWC Research Bulletin No.13, www.lboro.ac.uk/gawc

Tellier, L. (1997), 'A challenge for regional science: Revealing and explaining the global spatial logic of economic development', *Papers in Regional Science*, **76**, 371-384.

Thrift, N. (1996), 'New urban eras and old technological fears: Reconfiguring the goodwill of electronic things', *Urban Studies*, **33**, 1463-1493.

Todaro, M. P. (1969), 'A model of labor migration and urban unemployment in Less Developed Countries', *American Economic Review*, **59**, 138-148.

Todaro, M. P. (1982), *Economics for a developing World: An introduction to principles, problems, and policies.* Harlow: Longman.

Ullman, E. L. (1958), 'Regional development and the geography of concentration', *Papers and Proceedings of the Regional Science Association,* **4**, 179-162.

van den Berg, L., L. H. Klaassen, W. T. M. Molle, and J. H. P. Paelinck, (1981), 'Synthesis and conclusions', in L .H. Klaassen, W. T. M. Molle, and J. H. P. Paelinck (eds), *Dynamics of Urban Development*, New York: St.Martin's Press, pp.251-267.

van den Berg, L., R. Drewett, L. H. Klaassen, A. Rossi, and C.H.T. Vijverberg, (1982), *A Study of Growth and Decline*, Oxford: Pergamon Press.

Vining, D. R. Jr. and A. Strauss (1977), 'A Demonstration that the Current Deconcentration of Population in the United States is a Clean Break with the Past', *Environment and Planning A,* **9**, .751-758.

Vining, D. R. Jr and T. M. Kontuly (1978), 'Population despersal from major metropolitan regions: An international comparison',   *International Regional Science Review*, **3**, 49-73.

Von Thünen, J. H. (1966), *Von Thünen's isolated state.* Wartenberg, C.M. (trl) Oxford: Pergamon Press.

Wallerstein, I. (1974), 'The rise and future demise of the world capitalist system: Concepts for comparative analyses', *Comparative Studies in Society and History*, **16**, 387-415.

Walker, R, (1978), 'Two sources of uneven development under capitalism', *Review of radical Political Economy*, **10**, 28-37.

Warnes, T. (1992), 'Migration and the life course', in T. Champion and T. Fielding (eds), *Migration processes and pattern: Research progress and prospects, Vol.1*, London: Belhaven, pp.175-187.

Weber, A. (1929), *Theory of the location of industries*, Friedrich, C. J. (trl.) Chicago: University of Chicago Press.

Zelinsky, W. (1971), 'The hypothesis of the mobility transition', *Geographical Review,* **16**, 219-249.

Chapter 4

The Urban Future

H. S. Geyer

WHAT LIES AHEAD?

THE RATE OF CHANGE

When H.G. Wells published his book in 1902 on what shape urban life was expected to take in the twentieth century, based on mechanical and scientific progress at the time, it is safe to say that many of his readers would have been astonished by what he predicted for the future. But as it turned out, inventions were to follow that not even his creative mind could have imagined. Now, one hundred years later, we yet again stand at the beginning of a century where equally interesting and, safe to say, **unforeseeable changes lie ahead**. In fact, prospects for change are increasing by the day. If the view is correct that the world's current pool of knowledge doubles every two years, then today's knowledge will only form one per cent of the pool of knowledge by 2030!

According to the human activities model[1] there are several layers of human activities that have significantly impacted upon human settlement patterns over the centuries (see Figure 1.1). As the focus of civilizations shifted through the layers over time, specific **discoveries and innovations** revolutionized human life at specific time periods. Each subsequent revolution tended to open up new prospects for discoveries and innovations in uncharted territories, and at the same time they created space for new developments in areas that have already been revolutionized. In the process the rate of **revolutionary change** tended to increase exponentially as time went by.

---

[1] The human activities model is partially based on Weber's (1929) layers of economic activities and expanded by taking Dooyeweerd's (1926) fifteen human modalities into consideration.

The agricultural revolution occurred 10000 years ago. It took another 5000 years for the metallurgical revolution to occur. The telescopic revolution started in the beginning of the seventeenth century. The Industrial Revolution, which should actually be regarded as a series of individual revolutions intermingled by waves of innovations, started in the late eighteenth century. The first flight of the Wright brothers a century ago set the aviation revolution in motion. Fifty years ago the first operational computer initiated the digital revolution. This revolution was instrumental in triggering the communication revolution twenty years ago, which in turn led to the information revolution a decade ago. If one looks at how the tempo of change increased as humans advanced from one revolution to the next it seems inevitable that exciting times are lying ahead.

If, according to Muller's (2001) initial idea, all the historical events of the past 3000 years could be indicated on the 60 minutes of the face of a mantle clock, most of the revolutionary inventions that have changed the form of human settlements in one way or another, would have occurred during the last eleven minutes of the hour. Gutenburg's printing press, a product of the Renaissance, was invented at eleven minutes before the hour. Seven minutes later, the telegraph and the steam locomotive were developed. Two minutes to the hour, the telephone, the wireless, the combustion engine and the airplane came into regular use and one minute later, the laser beam, the television, the mainframe computer, the jet plane and the manned space rocket. These inventions paved the way for broadcast satellites, quartz watches, personal computers, and in the last seconds of the hour, the Internet.

THE AGE OF THE PENTANARY SECTOR

The impact of the **electronic and computer innovations** on corporate business over the last twenty years has been quite remarkable. Due to a plethora of changing cost factors such as increasing labour costs, altered production structures that were made possible by computer-aided communication and information technology, and the decreasing impact of agglomeration economies, many **Fordist mass-production processes** were no longer economically viable in areas where they had been previously. Today these plants are often found in advanced developing countries with good infrastructure and large pools of relatively productive, cheap labour where capital-labour ratios are more favourable for such production. developed countries, in contrast, tend to concentrate more on services and knowledge-based forms of output.

The impact of electronic and computer innovations has been equally remarkable on the social behaviour of individuals. While they traditionally had to move to the experience, the experience is now increasingly being moved to them (Berry, 1997). Through the Internet, the television set and the sound system, they have almost limitless sources of pleasure within the confines of their homes. As a result new social networks are being formed, many of them in the virtual environment, while traditional ones are either being transformed or discarded or are fast becoming redundant. Today, individuals are, for the most part, able to amuse themselves without the need of others. Socially, people interact more with make-believe characters on computer or with one another through telephonic and electronic devices than through personal physical contact, and when they do meet, their social association is often nothing more than an agglomeration of strangers based on an external attraction such as a sports match, a political gathering, a visit to a shopping centre or an entertainment attraction. As a result the glue that holds families, social groups, political parties and religious denominations together in the developed world is becoming weaker by the day.

It therefore seems evident that the new **knowledge-driven economy** has an effect on the entire range of actors in the economies of countries, from the corporate business sector at the upper end of the economy to the unskilled individual at the lower end – the former manipulating the market, the latter being manipulated by it. In old industrialized countries the focus tends to shift away from the traditional economic activities in the lower layers of the human activities model to the upper layers, while the focus in Newly Industrialized Countries shifts from agriculture to manufacturing industries. Overall, the New Economy has been instrumental in the establishment of the **pentanary sector** over the last decade or so. It serves the intellect of people in an entertaining manner and in the process info-tainment, edu-tainment, and religi-tainment reign supreme.

As the pentanary sector evolves, a greater premium will in the future be placed on the qualifications of individuals, measured not only in terms of their academic knowledge, but in their ability to gainfully participate in the new economy. Young people will be facing the prospect of having to improve their qualifications all the time in order to remain competitive and most of them will have to constantly expand their horizons because they will find it difficult to find employment in areas in which they have been educated initially. Households will increasingly become multi-wage and multi-generation oriented and the single-wage-earner nuclear family will soon vanish (Berry, 1990). Only those able to participate in the new economy will prosper. The others will increasingly become isolated from the new economic mainstream, and the gap between those that prosper in the new economy and those that remain behind is destined to become greater as time goes by.

According to Halal (Muller, 2001) manual labour in the United States will decline from 20 per cent of the total labour force to 10 per cent by 2010. Office workers will decline from 40 per cent to between 20 and 30 per cent. The remainder of the labour force will consist of knowledge workers – computer experts, managers with specialized knowledge, professional consultants, educators, scientists, etc. Pearson (Muller, 2001) predicts that fully automated factories will be operative by the second half of the first decade of the 21st century. Intelligent robots will become commonplace and virtual companies will become central in the new economy by 2010. According to Joseph Pelton (Muller, 2001) there will be 100 million global communication workers by 2015. The likely outcome of the new knowledge economy is the fragmentation of large companies and an increase in the number of knowledge workers operating from airplanes, motorcars, and homes. Most of these 'global nomads' will also be working for more than one company at a time. Based on these observations it seems clear that the new communication economy will have an opposite effect on the economic environment than it seems to have on the social environment. Increasing communication abilities on the economic terrain are likely to stimulate more activities, many of them necessitating eye-to-eye contact. While communication technology therefore tends to isolate people from one another physically within society, it tends to increase contact between them within the workplace. The workplace becomes the work-cum-socializing arena, while the home becomes a place of seclusion, a hideout for the exhausted body and spirit to recuperate (Geyer, 2001).

Countries that have gained an advantage in the new economic race will increasingly monopolize their advantage through electronic-, info- and bio-technology. A typical example of this is the encoding of genes to prevent grain from germinating from seed. And unless there is a dramatic change in the attitude of governments and clerics in a large percentage of Third and Fourth World Countries, such countries will keep on producing basic products, will keep on having high fertility rates matched by high death rates, will keep on having high unemployment rates, and continue to be unable to feed their populations properly. And unless a cure is found for HIV/AIDS, the high death rate among people in the highly sexually active age groups will keep on eliminating the positive effects education could have had on younger generations.

PROSPECTS OF SUPER-ADVANCEMENT

URBAN DEMOGRAPHIC DIVISIONS

Most of the First World countries have reached the end of the 'first' **demographic transition** towards the latter part of the twentieth century and have entered or are entering what could be regarded as the 'second' transition. A majority of the citizens of these countries are well educated, have employment, live in relative comfort, and have sufficient shelter. Because of the reluctance of many of those living in large metropolitan areas to enter into manual, low paid jobs, and simply because the supply of labour in those categories as well as in certain specialized fields falls below the level of demand in these cities, **international immigration** becomes an important mechanism to provide labour to employment categories in which there is a shortfall. Low skilled international migrants aiming to enter the lower end of the employment market tend to head for the large cities where prospects of finding work are considered to be better. Well-trained immigrants on the other hand normally have the ability to find jobs more easily in locations of their choice and often also blend in with host communities sooner.

Because of the large influx of immigrants to large metropolitan areas of advanced countries, a large percentage of them illegal and unskilled, they tend to undercut the remuneration levels of locals that are competing in the same labour market. This forces many of the latter to deconcentrate to areas where older and more affluent people used to move to during an earlier phase of counter-urbanizaion, the latter moving for environmental reasons, the former for employment reasons.[2] As a result of these opposing migration trends the character of larger cities in developed countries seems to become more cosmopolitan as time goes by (Berry, 1997), hence the term **'cosmopolis'** (Sandercock, 1998). The cosmopolitan character of large urban societies in large First World cities brings its own brand of challenges. In the current post-modernistic era, foreign cultures in the metropolitan areas of developed countries are demanding more recognition for their own style of commercial, social and cultural activities and because there are enough of them, their impact on the broader society becomes quite visible.

The current high concentrations of immigrants in large metropolitan areas in the First World are likely to cause new divisions amongst them. Faction-forming is likely to increase, and so will the tension between them. This is likely to set in motion the **next phase of counter-urbanization**, i.e. immigrants undercutting one another, forcing those that cannot make a living to join the local lower income groups that are currently moving to the same non-metropolitan areas to which the higher income groups have moved during an earlier phase of counter-urbanization. While the deconcentration trends (of mostly higher income groups) that have periodically been observed in developed countries over the past three decades may confirm the income divergence that was predicted by Kutznets (1955) and Williamson (1965) earlier on, the current deconcentration of lower income groups is destined to change the core-peripheral concept from a regional to a local phenomenon, internalising it in larger metropolitan and non-metropolitan cities throughout the First World. In this process, the clear dichotomies which we have become accustomed to in the Third World are bound to also become visible in the larger cities of the First World.

---

[2] It should be noted that there is a nuance difference between this phase of counter-urbanization and the counter-urbanization that was first detected in the United States in the early 1970s. The deconcentration of high income groups was environmentalism driven, the lower income groups productionism driven. This is a typical example of 'differentiated deconcentration', the main and substream migration moving essentially in the same direction (see Chapter 2).

In the process the tendency of developed countries to form super blocks, each block applying its own brand of strict immigration selection to reduce the influx of large numbers of unwanted migrants, is likely to increase. The outcome of this immigration policy is likely to reinforce the new third wave of **international division of labour**[3] that is currently gaining momentum.

URBAN SPATIAL DIVISIONS

Many of the large **old industrial cities** of the developed world, which still tend to form the gravity centres of core regions, are struggling to maintain their erstwhile attractiveness to new manufacturing industries. New companies tend to use new technology and they often prefer to locate their businesses in cleaner, **less congested urban environments**, often in satellite centres in large metropolitan fringe areas or further afield. However, as financial, corporate, and tourist centres of global or sub-continental significance, core cities tend to maintain strong economic and cultural ties with their surrounding urban and peri-urban hinterlands. Together they make up the cores and core fringe areas of developed countries.

It seems as if the mutual relationship between the old cores and their less densely urbanized fringes is instrumental in the survival of both, the former providing financial and corporate services and the latter more attractive living and business conditions. As a result very few parts of the more densely settled areas of developed countries can today still be regarded as truly rural. Due to improved communication infrastructure the cores and their fringes cover large parts of the developed world. In England the 'South East', in Europe the 'Blue Banana' and in the United States the 'North Eastern Seaboard' are examples of such expansive polarized (multi-nodal) core regions. Individually some them straddle state boundaries and together they form polynucleated urban networks (Geyer, 1998) globally linking people by intercontinental flights and through tele-optic and satellite connections on a daily basis.

The availability of good communication infrastructure within core and core fringe areas and the increasing mobility of their inhabitants are destined to significantly change the settlement and migration patterns in developed countries in years to come. During the early phase of urbanization most migration of countries that are today considered to be 'developed', was directed towards primate cities, making population redistribution patterns in them relatively predictable. Productionism[4] was a prime migration force during this period. By the time the urban system reached maturity, however,

---

[3] Colonialism caused the first international division of labour, Post-Fordism ('global industrial sprawl') the second, and the forming of global superblocks ('global federalism') the third.

[4] That is, when people migrate primarily for financial reasons.

differences between what could be regarded as main and substream migration became much more subtle, and although productionism is today still an important factor, environmentalism[5] becomes a more prominent and visible migration force (Hart, 1983; Geyer and Kontuly, 1993).[6] And because of the greater mobility of the population, their locations are more readily influenced by changing economic and social conditions. Visible shifts in the **population redistribution patterns** of developed countries between core areas and non-metropolitan areas are often influenced by cyclic changes in their economies. The latter impact on factors such as trade-offs between income elasticities for housing space and commuting (Gordon et al., 1991). Generally speaking, however, people's ability to commute over relatively long distances is beginning to impact more visibly on the development of the urban system at the advanced stages of maturity.

Signs of the developed world reaching **urban system maturity**, therefore, seem to be similar in many respects. The local populations of large, old metropolitan areas tend to stagnate or decline in absolute terms and are largely supplemented by international migrants. Although certain sections of the metropolitan populations have traditionally preferred to live in residential areas close to the metropolitan centres (Weaton, 1977), and are still doing so today,[7] factors such as urban decay, capital redundancy,[8] high land prices, and traffic congestion cause a majority of people that still work in these cities to move to less congested, esthetically more pleasing areas towards the outskirts of the core areas.

Massive **commuting** becomes a regular feature of these cities, which tends to further compound the problem of residential flight from large parts of the inner core areas to outer core and satellite cities towards the fringes of cities. First cities that are closer to the core regions (which leads to the expansion of the core fringe) tend to respond (Gordon, 1979), but later small towns deeper into the periphery also start attracting migrants. As transport and other

---

[5] That is, when people migrate primarily to improve their living conditions.

[6] Back in 1970, Brian Berry called this a new inversion – the environments historically least valued are now becoming the most desired.

[7] Factors such as economic restructuring, labour market segmentation, and demographic aging make inner city residential locations more preferable to 'certain kinds of high income and often childless households' than suburban areas (Bourne, 1992). Old prestigious residential areas close to city centres remain popular amongst this section of population. In recent years old redundant industrial buildings converted into prestigious office blocks and high-income residential buildings (such as the waterfront developments that have sprung up in many cities in the world), have become equally popular amongst this group of people.

[8] Capital redundancy, which is associated with the concept of agglomeration diseconomies, sets in when buildings and infrastructure that were designed for use during an earlier era, become ineffective and as a result, start falling into disrepair and disuse. Old industrial areas are typical examples of this phenomenon.

communication technology further improves, the **daily urban systems** of core regions should keep on expanding. In the process even more environmentally diversified urban structures than the current post-modern metropolitan areas of the Developed World should emerge.

Despite the **short-term swings in migration trends** between urbanization and counter-urbanization (Fielding, 1989; Champion, 1989; Geyer, 1996), the overall trend in societies that find themselves in the mature stage of development is likely to be towards continued counter-urbanization. All indications are that societies that are in an advanced stage of economic development, whose focus is shifting from industry to advanced services in the quaternary and pentenary sectors, will become less tied to central locations. If the prediction of the emergence of super-advanced societies is correct (Zelinsky, 1971), it can be expected that less congested urban areas and more serene rural environments further and further away from the large urban agglomerations will become increasingly popular amongst the most mobile sections of the population and their economic concerns. In view of this, a **new division of cities** seems to be evolving in the First World. Not all mega-cities are 'centres of excellence'. There are those that have the baggage of significant amounts of 'old' industries, large percentages of lower income groups and a visible presence of urban decay. These cities will find it increasingly difficult to attract and to keep new large-scale economic investments, unless urban authorities decide to 'clean up' their cities.[9] Then there are 'good addresses'. These are the cities that have maintained good environmental control. They are often smaller stand-alone metropolitan areas that attract and keep New Economic investments.[10]

KINETIC FIELDS

Cities do not interact, their citizens do, and their **interaction** can either occur in person or through economic, administrative or social organizations that were devised by them. As Philbrick (1957: 303) suggests occupancy can be regarded as 'the sum of the activities of persons focussed in establishments, localized in places, within structures or facilities made by people, interconnected by communication, transportation, and organization built or devised by them'. The latter determines the size and form of people's social and economic kinetic fields from the local to the global scale (Geyer, 2001).

Over the centuries, the **kinetic fields** of people have expanded and contracted as development circumstances changed (Doxiadis, 1970), and as

---

[9] Portland is a case in point. Although it contains a fair amount of old styled industries, the local authority is actively creating an economic environment that will attract new styled industries by engaging in urban renewal schemes and by keeping the city small and clean (Muller, 2001).

[10] Vancouver, Denver, and Atlanta are examples of such cities in North America.

time went by, they also became more complex. Today the cellular phone, the facsimile machine, and the Internet are liberating people socially and economically more than ever, and this is just the beginning. New inventions such as multi-purpose portable devices that simultaneously can serve as a cellular phone, a television unit, a sound system, a computer, a virtual entertainment centre and a host of other related household functions all in one, are already being contemplated. They hold the potential to expand people's networking options almost indefinitely. **Networks of cities**, based upon dominant patterns of economic and technical interaction between citizens of those cities are more likely to determine future geographical relationships than the boundaries of nation-states. Just as Fox and Kumar (1965) showed that, due to improved transport technology local functional economic space in Ohio in the United States exceeded the average size of counties nine fold over a period of one hundred years, new urban networks are currently also emerging across nation-state boundaries with much the same effect at a larger scale. Lille (formally Rijssel) and its medieval sister-city, Kortrijk, are currently developing into one large industrial axis, while Maastricht, Aachen and Luik, once prospering cities that have stagnated during the rise of the nation-states, are once again expanding as a regional urban network (Muller, 2001).

If one considers the range of scales and the complexity of the layers of networks possible in and between each of the layers of human activities shown in the Human Activities Model (see Figure 1.1) it is no wonder that larger **associations of nation-states** such as the European Union are becoming an imperative to better accommodate the new emerging forms of human networking. In many respects, the traditional nation-state has simply outgrown its usefulness and is fast becoming too limiting as a geo-political unit for the effective management of newly evolving human networks.[11] At the same time local economic networks that are created by the farmer who gets his equipment fixed in the local industrial area, or a member of a household doing shopping in the nearest shopping centre, are destined to remain important for many years to come.

CONDITIONS SHAPING THE BUILT ENVIRONMENT
THE DEVELOPED WORLD
What is written above refers largely to the economic activities of the **advanced sector** of the global society. But there is also the **lagging sector** within the developed world to consider. These are people that were born in

---

[11] Traditionally, the difference between regions and countries lay in the mobility of production factors (Krugman, 1998). Today, there is a need for as much freedom of movement of production factors between nation-states as there was between regions in a country in the past.

the developed world but who could not keep up with it, as well as increasing numbers people that originate from less developed countries and are currently living in First World cities. Both groups find it increasingly difficult to keep up with the advanced sector and to be able to survive they have to find alternative forms of survival in what many perceive as a hostile urban environment. Layers of informal activities[12] that are evolving underneath the current layers of formal economic activities are destined to become a more visible phenomenon in First World cities in the future. Covert economic practices such as 'misemployment' (Gugler, 1990) are also likely to increase in the future. Those that cannot keep up with the advanced sector will either have to revert back to their traditional ways of making a living, or they have to try and find a way to live off, or be linked to the advanced sector. Whatever the case, economic activities that are linked to the lagging urban communities of the First World are destined to remain in the 'ancillary' category, and unless ways can be found to 'take them along', vertical (economic) and horizontal (geographical) polarization, and the tension it brings,[13] is likely to increase in these cities.

DEVELOPING COUNTRIES

Generally there are two **categories of developing nations**. One is the 'emerging' or 'newly' industrialized group *enroute* to the economic super-highway, regarded as **'developing' countries**. The others are either stagnant or losing ground relative to the advanced nations of the world and can be regarded as the **'lagging' countries**.[14] If one compares the features of the urban systems of these Third World countries it soon becomes evident that it is often the development approach of the people in a particular country and its government, as well as certain key cities in it, that play a dominant role in the way the world perceives them.

The image of the labour force of prospering developing countries is often one of diligent, hard working people with a proven record of high productivity, and their governments are usually seen as accommodating and

---

[12] There are generally three layers of informal activities in First and Third World countries, the traditional sector (technologically unsophisticated, often agriculture-oriented), the intermediary sector (technologically more advanced, often providing intermediary products and basic services), and the quasi-formal sector (technologically sophisticated products, often informal branch activities of formal businesses) (Geyer, 1989).

[13] See Friedmann (1972) for ways in which the tension between the more and less enterprising elites in the urban environment tend to play out over time.

[14] This distinction between the terms 'lagging' and 'developing' Countries should not be confused with the terms: 'Third' and 'Fourth World'. In the latter the focus is on chronology and level of development (Wolf-Philips, 1987), in the former it is on development thinking.

supportive of industrial development. But more often than not it is the standing of single cities such as Hong Kong, Singapore, Bangkok, and Seoul in the global financial-industrial urban network that gives the countries such a prosperous image. In many respects the remainder of the urban systems of these countries is still very much lagging behind. The former often appear as prosperous, modern First World urban economic islands in a sea of under-development, an environment where the jet airplane and the donkey cart literally operate side-by-side. In most advancing developing countries it is the reaction of their governments to high Gini-quotient levels that poses the greatest potential threat to their continued long-term economic growth.

THE SITUATION IN LAGGING COUNTRIES

Lagging countries on the other hand are often those with people and governments that base their views and policies on outdated political ideas or on cultural-religious **fundamentalism**. Typical examples are governments that base their social and economic policies on constricting **religious** fundamentalism, preventing their citizens, especially women, from fulfilling their own intellectual, social and economic potential. Others tend to cling to outdated egalitarian **socio-political** doctrines that seem to favour shared poverty approaches merely for the sake of economic equality rather than rewarding enterprising innovation. Another brand of the same kind of fundamentalism is reflected in the well-known **cultural** slogan, 'mayebuye iAfrica' ("come back, Africa"), that lives in the hearts and minds of certain people in parts of Africa.[15] The degree to which those people are slowly sliding back into **archaic ignorance** is clearly visible in the increasing measure of their **dependence** on the developed world to feed and heal their exploding populations and in their vocal accusing demands for support to stay afloat. In many of these cases the First World components of their cities have either collapsed or are on the brink of total collapse and most of their inhabitants are slowly sliding back to traditional pre-modern forms of urban existence. Large parts of former prospering cities in these countries are now little more than heaps of rubble and refuse, with infrastructure that is in a partial or complete state of disrepair. Contrary to developed countries the capital redundancy factor in these cities is spinning out of control, not as a result of progress (as is often the case in developed countries) but as a result of technological and economic regression. And more often than not the urban systems of these countries are deteriorating because of the general unhealthy state of their **stagnating economies** and the inability of such communities to

---

[15] Although the term 'African Renaissance' resonates well with the developed world, it is still regarded as a surrogate for 'mayebuye iAfrica' in certain African circles. The developed society of the world associates it with the concept of 'enlightenment', while the traditionalists interpret it literally, i.e. back to the African tradition. In the process both groups are happy.

maintain even the most basic current infrastructure, a condition that undermines the building of a strong investment culture. Large numbers people in these cities live in squalid conditions[16] while the more enterprising people barricade themselves against the poor.[17]

Most urban systems of lagging countries are still in the **'premature' urbanization** phase, i.e. unskilled urban migrants that are unable to effectively compete for jobs in the urban sector. These people tend to add to the burden of those that already live in the cities, forcing the enterprising sector to either isolate themselves financially and otherwise from the rest, or move to countries that offer a more promising future. Although countries such as Brazil, Mexico, Venezuela, and South Africa[18] seem to be approaching the polarization reversal phase of development, most Lagging Countries are likely to remain in the premature urbanization phase for some time to come.

CONCLUSION

Due to technological changes over the past two decades, the global urban society has evolved into two main categories: the advanced sector that travels on the technological super highway and those that are lagging behind.[19] People in these two categories are found across the development spectrum, in advanced, developing and lagging countries, and it is the necessity for these people to find a way to coexist in the same urban environment that makes the study of this environment so exciting.

Challenges the urban society faces include:

❑ Having to cope with exploding, stagnating, or declining populations,
❑ growing gaps between prosperous and lagging communities in and between cities,
❑ a clash of new and existing cultures,
❑ making complex social structures work,
❑ continuing renewal of constantly aging urban structures, and
❑ finding ways of continuously attracting new investments.

---

[16] See the chapter on India, for instance.
[17] Heavily guarded high-income residential areas, some even with guard towers to protect people's property are not an uncommon sight in Third World cities today.
[18] Since the political transition, South Africa has slipped back into the premature urbanization phase.
[19] Mimicking the inverted 'U'-income model (Kutznets, 1955; Williamson, 1965) at the global scale, Krugman and Venables (1995) believe declining friction of distance leads first to the differentiation of the world into high-wage industrialized cores and low-wage agricultural peripheries and later to income divergence as the periphery industrializes.

In a potentially polarized society there are several ways in which adversaries can deal with one another: suppression, neutralization, cooperation, and replacement (Friedmann, 1972). All over the world indications are that the most open and progressive urban societies are the ones that succeed best in overcoming these challenges through cooperation. The reasons for this are because such societies have the ability to attract creative personalities, their openness creates space for human and material resource innovation, and they tend to reward people socially, economically and politically for their ingenuity. These are minimum requirements for people living in the rapidly changing urban environment we face in the twenty first century.

REFERENCES

Berry, B. J. L. (1970), 'The geography of the United States in the Year 2000', *Transactions of the Institute of British Geographers*, **51**, 21-53.

Berry, B. J. L. (1990), 'Urban systems by the Third Millennium: A second look', *Journal of Geography*, **89**: 98-100.

Berry, B. J. L. (1997), 'Long waves and geography in the 21st Century', *Futures*, **29**, 301-310.

Bourne, L. S. (1992), 'Population turnaround in the Canadian inner city: Contextual factors and social consequences', *Canadian Journal of Urban Research*, **1**, 66-89.

Champion, A. G. (ed.) (1989), *Counterurbanization: The changing pace and nature of population deconcentration*, London: Edward Arnold.

Dooyeweerd, H. (1926) *De beteekenis der wetsidee voor rechtswetenschap en rechtsphilisophie*, Kampen: Kok.

Doxiadis, C. A. (1970), 'Man's movement and his settlements', *Ekistics*, **29**: 296-321.

Fielding, A. J. (1989), 'Migration and Urbanization in Western Europe', *The Geographical Journal*, **155**, 60-69.

Fox, K. A. and T. K. Kumar (1965), 'The financial economic area: Delineation and implication for economic analysis and policy', *Regional Science Association Papers*, **15**, 57-85.

Friedmann, J. (1972), 'A general theory of polarized development. In N.M. Hansen (ed.), *Growth centers in regional economic development*, New York: The Free Press, pp.82-107.

Geyer, H. S. (1989), 'The integration of the formal and informal urban sectors in South Africa', *Development Southern Africa*, **6**, 29-42.

Geyer, H. S. (1996), 'Expanding the theoretical foundation of differential urbanization', *Tijdschrift voor Economische en Sociale Geografie*, **87**, 44-59.

Geyer, H. S. (1998), 'Differential urbanization and international migration: An urban systems approach', in C. Gorter, P. Nijkamp, and J. Poot (eds), *Crossing borders: Regional and urban perspectives on international migration*. Aldershot: Ashgate, pp.161-184.

Geyer, H. S. (2001), 'Development planning transition in South Africa', in H. C. Marais, Y. Methien, N. S. Jansen van Rensburg, M. P. Maaga, G. F. de Wet, C. J. Coetzee (eds), *Sustainable social development: Critical dimensions*. Pretoria: Network Publishers, pp.143-152.

Geyer, H. S. and T. M. Kontuly (1993), 'A theoretical foundation for the concept of differential urbanization', in N. Hansen, K. J. Button, and P. Nijkamp (eds), *Modern classics in regional science: Regional policy and regional integration*, Vol. 6, Cheltenham: Edward Elgar. pp.135-160.

Gordon, P. (1979), 'Deconcentration without a "clean break"', *Environment and Planning A*, **11**, 281-290.

Gordon, P., H. W. Richardson, and M. Jun (1991), 'The cmmuting paradox', *Journal of the American Planning Association*, **57**, 416-421.

Gugler, J. (1990), 'Overurbanization reconsidered', in J. Gugler (ed.), *The urbanization of the Third World*, Oxford: Oxford University Press.

Hart, T. (1983), 'Transport and economic development: The historical dimension', in K. J. Button and D. Gillingwater (eds), *Transport location and spatial policy*. Aldershot, Hants. U.K.: Gower. pp. 12-22.

Krugman, P. (1998), 'Space: the final frontier', *Journal of Economic Perspecitives*, **12**, 161-174.

Krugman, P. and A. Venables (1995), 'Globalization and the inequality of nations', *Quarterly Journal of Economics*, **110**, 857-880.

Kutznets, S. (1955), 'Economic growth and income inequality', *The American Economic Review*, **45**, 1-28.

Muller, P. (2001), *Môre is 'n nuwe spel: 'n Toekomsblik*. Pretoria: Lapa Publishers.

Philbrick, A. K. (1957), 'Principles of areas functional organization in regional human geography', *Economic Geography*, **33**, 299-336.

Sandercock, L. (1998), *Towards cosmopolis*. Chichester: Wiley.

Weaton, W. C. (1977), 'Income and urban residence: An analysis of consumer demand' *American Economic Review*, **67**, 620-631.

Weber, A. (1929), *Theory of the location of industries*, Friedrich, C.J. (trl.) Chicago: University of Chicago Press.

Wells, H. G. (1902) *Anticipations of the reaction of mechanical and scientific progress upon human life and thought*. New York: Harper and Brothers.

Williamson, J. G. (1965), 'Regional inequality and the process of national development : A description of the patterns', *Economic Development and Cultural Change*, **13**, 3-84.

Wolf-Philips, L. (1987), 'Why "Third World"?: origin, definition and usage', *Third World Quarterly*, **9**, 1311-1327.

Zelinsky, W. (1971), 'The hypothesis of the mobility transition', *Geographical Review,* **16**, 219-249.

PART TWO

Empirical findings

A. WESTERN EUROPEAN COUNTRIES

Chapter 5

Population Change and Migration in the British Urban System

A. G. Champion

INTRODUCTION

Britain's experience of urbanization is quite distinctive in several ways, though it exhibits some parallels with other countries. It was the first country in the world to undergo mass urbanization, with the urban share of its population passing the 50 per cent mark by the middle of the nineteenth century. Following more than a century of very rapid population growth through to the First World War, its high overall population density was already at that time leading to the fusion of adjacent urban places, making it more difficult to identify the separate components of its urban system. The introduction of a powerful land-use planning framework after the Second World War, allied with an overarching policy of urban containment and the 'green belt' philosophy, has subsequently kept cities and towns much more separate in physical terms than would otherwise have been the case. Nevertheless, as for most other countries, improvements in personal mobility and increases in other forms of spatial interaction have led to steadily greater functional interdependence between settlements. Moreover, though a major trading nation on the world stage well before the term 'globalization' was coined, in recent decades Britain has seen its urban system being impacted ever more strongly by international events.

This account of urbanization and migration in Britain begins by providing more detail on the historical context, focusing mainly on the developments of the past half-century but also reviewing the legacy of the nation's long history of settlement. The following section examines the implications of this evolution for the task of developing frameworks for representing the national urban system, with especial attention to the problems of defining urban centres and identifying the territorial extent of their hinterlands. Thirdly, a selection of these frameworks is used to document the main features of urban system change as revealed by data on total population and migration since the 1951 Census. This section also examines the roles of population subgroups in contributing to the observed patterns and trends. The final section assesses what currently evolving trends seem to presage for the future and highlights the main challenges for policy and research.

BACKGROUND TO THE BRITISH CONTEXT

While the focus of this book is on urban change during the last fifty years, plus a look into the future, an understanding of Britain's changing urban system must take into account its earlier history. The national population was already highly urbanized at the beginning of the twentieth century, let alone by mid-century. More than this, the vast majority of the basic nuclei around which the country's urban system has evolved have been in existence as settlements for over a thousand years. Thirdly, the land-use planning regulations that have been in operation since the 1940s have to a considerable extent worked to preserve the inherited pattern of urban centres. These fundamental aspects of the historical legacy provide the starting point for outlining the principal forces affecting the British urban system since 1950 and for describing the most important spatial outcomes.

THE HISTORICAL LEGACY

Urbanization, as conventionally measured in terms of the share of population living in urban places, was very largely a phenomenon of the nineteenth century as far as Britain is concerned. According to what is still the most thorough study on this subject (Law, 1967), 34 per cent of the population of England and Wales was already living in 'urban areas' at the time of the first Census in 1801. The proportion had risen to 54 per cent by 1851 and reached 78 per cent by 1901.

Subsequent censuses providing data on numbers living in administrative urban units (i.e. urban municipalities) show that these areas' share of the total population of England and Wales, which stood at 77.0 per cent at the 1901 Census, grew only marginally thereafter. By 1911 the figure was 78.1 per cent, by 1921 79.3 per cent, and by 1931 80.0 per cent, and it reached its highest census-year point in 1951, at 80.8 per cent. By 1971, the level had fallen back to 78.0 per cent, as population spilled over the boundaries of these areas into the officially defined 'Rural Districts' (see Champion, 1975).

Obviously, data based on administrative areas is of limited validity in the context of the burgeoning suburbanization of the twentieth century. It is therefore appropriate that, following each of the most recent two censuses (though unfortunately not before 1981), counts were made of the population of physically defined 'urban areas', using a basis similar to that of Law

(1967). The 1991 Census put the urban share at 89.7 per cent for England and Wales and 89.6 per cent for Great Britain as a whole, i.e. including Scotland (but not Northern Ireland for which no equivalent data is available). The latter is exactly the same as the equivalent figure calculated from the 1981 Census, suggesting that even on a properly defined basis the conventional urbanization process had been completed by then.

Clearly, Britain was already highly urbanized at the beginning of the last century and, in particular, probably saw little further increase in the urban share of its population after mid-century. Between 1901 and 1981 its level of urbanization would seem to have risen by no more than 12 percentage points in round figures. Most of this increase is likely to have taken place in the first half of the century. Since 1951, it is very unlikely that any significant level of net rural-to-urban migration has occurred, with the continuing shake-out of traditional rural employment being offset by urbanites moving into the countryside. This means that, in studying urban systems development in Britain over the last 50 years, the emphasis must be almost exclusively on the changing distribution of the already urban population.

A second fundamental point about the British context is the stability of the settlement system. In one sense, here we look even further back – to the 11th century, if not earlier. The vast majority of all settlements in Britain today have existed for over a thousand years. This is indicated by their place-names (drawn principally from British/Celtic, Jutish, Anglo-Saxon and Danish origins) and is confirmed by their mention in the Norman Domesday Book of 1086.

Rather more topical for the present review, however, is that most of Britain's 'urban areas', as reported in the 1991 Census, already existed as urban centres in 1901. Since then, most of them will have spread laterally and in some cases fused with other urban centres to form agglomerations. Nevertheless, only in relatively few cases will settlements that were non-urban in 1901 (on the basis of Law's approach) have become urban subsequently, except where they have been enveloped by the expansion of nearby urban centres. Even the majority of the places designated under the New Towns Act 1946 were based on pre-existing settlements (Osborn and Whittick, 1969; Champion et al., 1977).

Moreover, the land-use planning arrangements that were introduced immediately after the Second World War, most notably by the Town and Country Planning Act 1947, have served very largely to fossilize the physical pattern of settlement inherited from the first half of the twentieth century. By regulating the location and density of virtually all new property development, this very largely marked the end of 'urban sprawl' in Britain (Best, 1981). In particular, it imposed strict limits on the lateral growth of the physical urban areas of the large conurbations and many other cities, with the explicit aim of preventing their coalescence with neighbouring settlements. This policy was reinforced where necessary by the declaration of a formal 'green belt' and by plans to decant surplus development pressures to cities and towns beyond this *cordon sanitaire*. It also placed a virtual prohibition on the physical extension of the smallest settlements in the countryside, where new building had either to be in the form of infilling of sites within the settlement boundary or to be diverted to larger 'key settlements' with an already urban character (see Cullingworth and Nadin, 1997; Hall, 1992).

In sum, over the past half-century the physical pattern of urban areas has changed relatively little in extent. Rural-urban land conversion has never returned to the peak levels recorded in the 1930s, even in the heyday of New Town development between the late 1940s and mid 1970s. Moreover, in recent years, around half of all new house building has been taking place on recycled urban land. Similarly, the number of physically discrete urban areas in the year 2000 will be almost exactly the same as in 1950. Planning controls have worked to keep the existing urban areas separate and have largely prevented the emergence of new ones.

FORCES AFFECTING THE BRITISH URBAN SYSTEM SINCE 1950

Despite this relatively stable physical framework, a number of powerful forces have wrought massive changes in Britain's urban system during the past half-century. In terms of broad headings, the main developments can be summarised as follows:

1. Counter-urbanization, specifically population redistribution down the urban hierarchy, already underway in the 1960s, peaking in the 1970s but still a very clear dimension in the 1980s and 1990s in terms of overall population change and especially internal migration (Champion, 1994; 2001a; Champion et al., 1998).

2. De-industrialization, involving a massive shake-out in manufacturing and mining employment, with the biggest relative effects impacting on the places that had the greatest specialization in these sectors, most notably the larger towns and cities in northern Britain but also smaller mining settlements and other one-industry towns (Champion and Townsend, 1990; Martin and Rowthorn, 1986; Sadler, 2000).

3. Urban employment deconcentration, comprising an even stronger 'urban-rural shift' than for population dispersal since the early 1970s (Fothergill and Gudgin, 1982; Turok and Edge, 1999). This partly reflects the effects of large-city de-industrialization, but is also a reaction to the shifts in residential population and an attempt by employers to seek out better operating conditions (land, labour, enterprise, transport links).

4. Decline of employment in traditional rural industries (Hodge and Whitby, 1981; Bowler, 2000). This is partly due to long-term decline in the farm-related population as a result of greater mechanization and

scientific developments. It has been compounded by a switch from relative prosperity for most farmers in the 1950s and 1960s (helped by buoyant world markets and large subsidies) to deep depression in the late 1990s (with reduced support, poorer markets, higher costs and problems caused by animal diseases).

5. Net immigration from outside the UK, which has in recent years emerged as a major element of national population growth (over 50 per cent) in marked contrast to the net emigration of the 1950s (Champion, 2000). Given that this influx has been disproportionately concentrated on London, it is now a major cause of increasing regional imbalance and has helped to offset the urban exodus of the domestic population.

6. A socio-demographic transformation (Scase, 2000). In particular, this involves rising female participation in the workforce (with implications for household incomes, residential preferences, etc) and changes in household composition (with growing numbers of households with elderly-only, one-person only, lone-parent families and unrelated sharers).

7. A continuing revolution in transport and (tele)communications (Turton, 2000). This permits greater flexibility in commuting and other journeys and offers the potential for more economic activity to be carried out away from a fixed workplace, either at home or on the move.

8. The rise of the conservation movement (Park, 2000). This brought to an end the era of mass clearance and redevelopment in British cities during the 1970s and has steadily been increasing its influence on the planning of more rural areas, alongside the NIMBY (Not In My Back Yard) syndrome.

Most of these changes have been taking place concurrently, though some are more relevant to recent years and others are longer-term. Some refer to processes that tend to operate nationally, even if they have uneven spatial incidence, while others are much more localized in their effects.

GEOGRAPHICAL IMPACTS ON BRITAIN'S SETTLEMENT SYSTEM

These broad forces have produced major changes to the national settlement system, not only in terms of the economic, social and environmental characteristics of places but also in the functional relationships existing between and within the separate physical units that make up urban Britain. These changes have been widely documented, including by Champion et al. (1996), Mohan (1999) and Turok and Edge (1999). Among the most notable are:

1. The reinforcement of the 'North-South divide' within Britain, with people and jobs becoming more concentrated in the southern half of the country. The qualitative differences in economic structure, occupational composition and personal wealth are even greater, such that the London region is often considered to be 'another country'.

2. Even more marked variations between urban regions within macro economic regions, with fastest relative population growth for certain types of towns, especially resort and retirement settlements and places with universities, high-tech industry and business services.

3. Gentrification of certain neighbourhoods in central/inner parts of the largest and/or most dynamic cities (e.g. London, Bristol, Edinburgh), plus smaller-scale central-city redevelopments elsewhere (e.g. Manchester, Leeds, Glasgow, Newcastle).

4. Long-term transformation of (many) inner city areas from white 'working class' areas of the 1950s to predominantly ethnic-minority areas, which are now expanding out into inner/older suburbs.

5. More general economic decline of, and net domestic out-migration from, inner city areas. This is in spite of substantial housing renewal in the 1960s and 1970s, and is largely prompted by the changing geography of work, though also reflecting problems in neighbourhood quality.

6. Strong increase in numbers of jobs in the suburban and outer areas of larger conurbations, though with a rather fragmented spatial distribution: some in large 'sub-centres', especially where these are based on pre-existing town centres that have been incorporated into the conurbation, but also much in a wide variety of employment and retail sites designated by the land-use planning process.

7. Massive growth of population, jobs and associated urban development in physically separate cities and towns lying 'beyond the green belts' of the major metropolitan areas, up to 150km away in the case of London, places that to an increasing extent are developing their own growth dynamics aided by proximity to airports and intercity motorways (which in some cases also form city beltways).

8. Rapid growth of the more rural districts that comprise 'the countryside', especially the most accessible areas around cities and towns but also smaller urban centres and rural settlements in regions relatively remote from the major metropolitan centres. This has been accompanied by a 'rural gentrification' owing to the better-off nature of the commuters and retirees that predominate in this influx, combined with the decline of traditional rural activities.

In sum, for over 50 years the UK has possessed a powerful (though not necessarily very coherent) planning system that largely prevents the emergence of new urban centres and aims at compact, non-haphazard patterns of new urban development. Nevertheless, major changes have been occurring in the distribution of population, jobs and services and in travel behaviour, substantially altering the size and complexion of settlements and the functional relationships between them. Establishing exactly what all this means for the changing structure of the British urban system poses a considerable research challenge.

CONCEPTUALIZING THE BRITISH URBAN SYSTEM

The delimitation of the zones to be used in the study of urbanization trends itself constitutes a major task, not least because of this being very much a 'Catch 22' problem. It is necessary to analyse the urban system in order to identify its underlying structure, yet some preconceived framework is required for doing this and may well influence the picture observed. In practice, it is most common for trends to be observed on the basis of a geographical framework developed on the basis of past experience, while looking out for new developments that would suggest the need for revising the framework and reworking the analyses. At the same time, choice of the 'filter' through which to observe the changing urban system will also be influenced by the particular aim of the study and the theoretical perspective in which it is set. The aim of this section is to introduce alternative approaches used to represent urban Britain, whereas the next section examines the results of using these to observe trends. A broad distinction is drawn between approaches based on administrative areas and those that have been specially devised for the study of urban-system change.

APPROACHES BASED ON ADMINISTRATIVE AREAS

A substantial amount of the work carried out to help understand urban change in Britain has been based on administrative areas, the most common being the 'local authority' (LA, or local government district, equivalent to 'municipality' in some other countries). This approach comprises at least three variants.

Using the Administrative Status of LAs

Until the local government reorganization of 1974, there were around 1400 LA units in England and Wales outside London. Emerging out of the earlier sanitary and health districts and formalised in the Local Government Acts of 1888 and 1894, these fell into four main types with different levels of powers: Rural Districts, Urban Districts, Municipal Boroughs and County Boroughs (in rising order of administrative status). Studies of urbanization levels could be based on the proportion of people not living in Rural Districts (see above). However, though in some cases they were modified over the near-century of their existence to incorporate lateral expansion of the built-up areas, in most cases their boundaries failed to keep up with the pace of expansion, with the result that urbanization levels calculated on this basis fell increasingly short of reality.

Using LAs Classified on Criteria Other Than Administrative Status

This approach became the norm for some types of statistical reporting and academic study after the reorganization of local government in the mid 1970s. This was because of the introduction of a two-tier framework of counties and districts in England and Wales (and a similar pattern for Scotland) that made no official distinctions, apart from six counties (with 36 districts) being designated as 'metropolitan'. One example is the Office of Population Census and Survey's 11-fold classification of the 403 districts of England and Wales, based on a mixture of administrative and socio-economic data, with types ranging from Inner London Boroughs to Remoter, Mainly Rural Districts. OPCS (now ONS, Office for National Statistics) has also produced purely socio-economic classifications of districts after each Census from 1971 and another following a further round of local government reorganization in the mid 1990s (Wallace et al., 1995; Bailey et al., 2000). Academics have also produced district-level classifications customised to their own research needs, the most quoted being a five-fold typology based on degree of rurality (Cloke, 1977).

Aggregating Contiguous LAs to Form Larger Territorial Units That Better Represent the Settlement Pattern

The recognition of six 'metropolitan counties' (see previous paragraph) represents one example of this, broadly differentiating England into metropolitan and non-metropolitan parts. This follows previous official practice of defining 'conurbations', used for reporting Census and other population data up to the mid 1970s, and is considerably different from the US Metropolitan Area concept, given that the English 'non-metropolitan counties' contain many large cities. Nevertheless, this basic distinction is seen as so important in the country's settlement structure that, following Mrs Thatcher's abolition of these counties in 1986, official statistical agencies have continued to report data for these units. Other examples of aggregations of LA units include academics using them to produce best-fit approximations to the reality of the functional urban system (see below).

APPROACHES SPECIFICALLY DEVISED TO REPRESENT THE URBAN SYSTEM

Though there were early studies of the urban hierarchy along Christaller lines (for example, Smailes, 1944) and there has also been a recognition of the value of city regions for analysing inter-regional migration (Fielding, 1971), customised representations of the British urban system have been based mainly on the US approach to defining Metropolitan Areas (US Bureau of the Budget, 1964) and Daily Urban Systems (Berry, 1967). This started with the US-based work of International Urban Research, which during the 1950s produced a set of 'comparable metropolitan units' for the whole world (IUR, 1959). This was followed by a series of somewhat different representations of the British urban system, with most of them based on the concept of an urban core plus surrounding commuting field but with some based mainly on identifying the degree of self-containment of places. The main examples are as follows.

Metropolitan Areas

Apart from the 'conurbations' recognised by the Census, the first attempt at defining 'metropolitan areas' was made by IUR (1959) and applied in a pioneering study of urban growth and decentralization by Schnore (1962). In all, this identified 58 MAs: Belfast in Northern Ireland, 5 in Scotland and 52 in England and Wales. Each MA should have a total population of not less than 100,000, comprising a continuous urban area ('City') of not less than 50,000 people and (where appropriate) a 'Ring' of contiguous LA units with at least 65 per cent of its economically active population engaged in non-agricultural industries and close enough to the principal city to make commuting feasible.

Standard Metropolitan Labour Areas (SMLAs) and Derivatives

SMLAs were devised by Peter Hall for a study of urban development in England and Wales in the 1960s. The approach was similar to IUR in identifying a core and ring, but the criteria were rather different, as far as possible replicating the SMSAs of the US Census Bureau (as this work was carried out in association with a parallel study in the USA). The criteria in this case were: a core comprising an LA or a number of contiguous LAs with a density of at least 12.5 workers per hectare or a single LA with at least 20,000 workers; and a ring of contiguous LAs each of which sent at least 15 per cent of its resident workers to the core and a total SMLA population of at least 70,000. This yielded 100 SMLAs for England and Wales. In addition, influenced by Berry's (1967) alternative approach to the US case, a Metropolitan Economic Labour Area (MELA) was delineated for each SMLA core that included an Outer Ring, comprising contiguous LAs that supplied any commuters to the core or more commuters to that core than any other (see Hall, 1971; Hall et al., 1973). The 100 MELAs were much more extensive than the SMLAs, but even so did not completely exhaust the national territory, with the remainder being treated 'non-metropolitan'. This framework was expanded by Spence et al. (1982) to include Scotland, adding an extra 26 MELAs. Variants on this theme, either selecting only those of over a certain size or status or using somewhat different definitions, were used in European comparative studies by Hall and Hay (1980), Berg et al. (1982), and Cheshire and Hay (1989; see also Cheshire, 1995).

The CURDS Functional Regions Framework

This urban-centred-regions approach, produced by the Centre for Urban & Regional Development Studies (CURDS) at Newcastle University, was specifically devised for use in analysing 1981 Census data and changes in the British urban system since the previous Census (see Coombes et al., 1982; Champion et al., 1987; Champion and Dorling, 1994). It grouped pre-1974/5 LAs into a set of urban centres based on a minimum level of employment and retailing and delineated their contiguous commuting fields in a way that exhausts national territory. A total of 281 spatial units were identified, of which 53 were termed Rural Areas because they fell below a population threshold, while the remaining 228 were termed Urban Regions. Each of the 281 Urban Regions and Rural Areas (URRAs) can be classified according to size, urban status, economic structure, etc., for the purposes of urban-system monitoring and analysis.

In one of several elaborations of this approach, the Rural Areas are assigned to the Urban Region with which they have the strongest commuting ties to form 228 Functional Regions (FRs). Secondly, Urban Regions are subdivided into Core (delineated on the basis of the main settlement's continuously built-up area), Ring (those LAs sending at least 15 per cent of employed residents to jobs in the Core and more to that particular Core than any other), and Outer Area (sending more to that Core than any other). As a result, the FRs can be analysed on the basis of the four-fold division of Core, Ring, Outer Area and Rural Area. Finally, adapting an approach explored by Champion (1976) and the principle of Consolidated SMAs developed by the US Census Bureau, FRs with strong commuting links between each other were distinguished by being put into a higher-level grouping called Metropolitan Regions. In each of these, the FR that formed the main commuting destination was termed Dominant and the remainder Subdominant.

Regionalizations Based on Self-Containment and Separation Measures

This approach is based very largely on interaction data, primarily journey to work. The main application has been in the identification of Travel To Work Areas (TTWAs), traditionally used by central government for monitoring unemployment and for other purposes such as designation of areas for business assistance and training programmes. TTWAs are designed as areas with a certain minimum level of commuting self-containment, though also subject to modification in the light of consultation by interested parties. They are revised after each Census, with 322 being defined with 1981 Census data and 297 with 1991 Census data (ONS and Coombes, 1998). A similar approach, using a wider range of information including data on journey to bank and a large set of service-area boundaries, has been used by Coombes (2000) to regionalise the whole of Great Britain into 307 'localities', which nest into 43 'city regions'.

In conclusion, there is clearly a variety of ways in which the British urban system has been conceptualised during the past half-century. This variety is partly due to the fact that different approaches have been required for different types of application, with a notable gulf existing between government and academic researchers. In particular, though specific government departments have recognised the value of functionally defined areas (especially TTWAs), most branches of government operate through the LA framework, with no explicit recognition of settlement-system geography. Meanwhile, academics have expressed reservations about the value of so-called 'general purpose' regionalizations, instead developing spatial frameworks more suitable for their own particular purposes. Even the academic sector, however, would seem to be having difficulty in keeping up with the pace of change on the ground, as we shall see.

OBSERVED PATTERNS AND TRENDS

This section presents the results of applying a selection of the approaches to delimiting urban areas described above. First, a long-term perspective is taken, examining intercensal change from 1951 to 1991 (the latest census for which data is available at the time of writing). Then a more detailed look is taken at population change between 1981 and 1991 and internal migration in the year leading up to the 1991 census. Both these analyses use versions of the CURDS Functional Regions framework. Finally, a classification of local authority districts is used to test for the existence of a counter-urbanization tendency across Britain's settlement system. The predominant picture revealed by these analyses is one of long-established and continuing urban deconcentration or 'counter-urbanization', tempered only somewhat by a revival of larger cities in recent years.

LONG-TERM TRENDS, 1951-1991, FOR URBAN REGIONS AND RURAL AREAS

This part of the analysis examines population trends for two classifications of the Urban Regions and Rural Areas (URRAs) element of the Functional Regions framework (see previous section). One of these is based on overall population size, with 11 groups, while the other uses a six-fold typology of urban status. The former can be used to examine the prevalence of urbanization versus counter-urbanization tendencies in the manner pioneered by Fielding (1982), while the urban-status typology can be collapsed to produce the three levels of cities needed to test for the urban system's position according to Geyer and Kontuly's (1993) 'differential urbanization' model.

The results of the analysis based on size groups are shown in Figure 5.1, where for each of four intercensal periods the weighted average rate of population change is plotted for URRAs classified according to size at the start of each decade. The overall impression is of a downward slope from left to right, signifying a negative relationship between size and growth. This de-

Figure 5.1 Population change by URRA size group, 1951-91

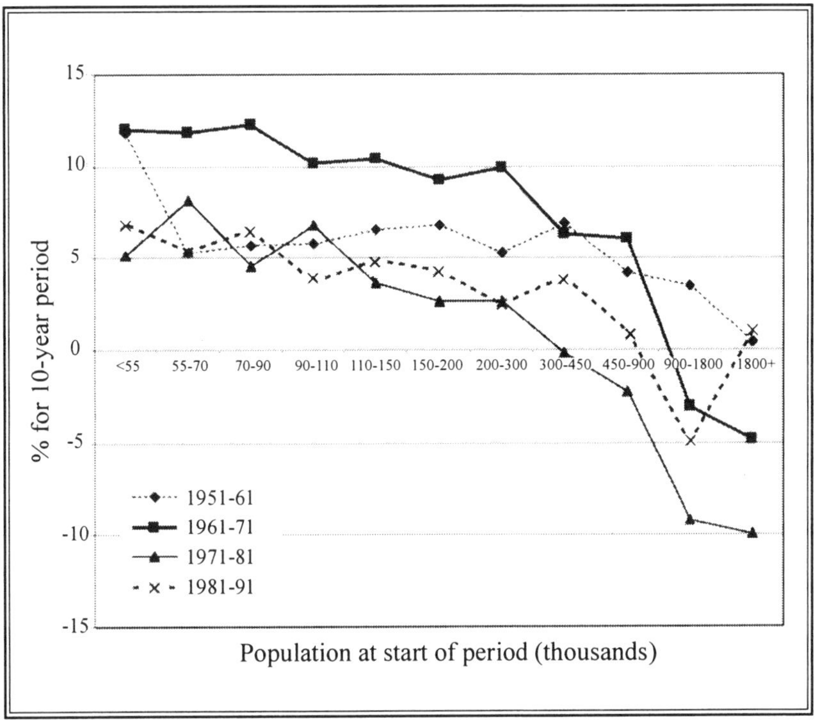

Notes: 'Counter-urbanization' in Fielding's (1982) formulation and means that population is shifting down the settlement-size hierarchy. This interpretation is largely powered by the significantly below-average performance of the largest size groups, with the gradient across the others being less steep. On this basis, it would therefore seem that population deconcentration has been the prevailing tendency of the British urban system for at least the past half-century.

Source: Calculated from Population Census data.

At the same time, some differences between decades are evident. Disregarding variation in the overall level of the lines (which mainly reflects the much faster national population growth of the first two decades) and concentrating on the gradients, the pace of deconcentration appears to have been strongest in the middle two decades. In the 1950s the majority of the size groups recorded growth rates very close to the national level of 5 per cent, with only the largest category (comprising London alone) lying substantially below this and only the smallest category (containing many New Towns designated in 1946-50) lying much above this rate. The slope is much steeper in the 1960s and 1970s, when a marked gap can be seen between the well below average rates of the largest groups and the well above average rates of the others. The gradient becomes shallower again in the 1980s, when in particular London put in a much stronger performance than would be 'expected' from its size (Figure 5.1).

The analysis by urban-status types (Table 5.1) provides a more summary view emphasising position in the urban hierarchy rather than population size *per se*. The pattern matches quite closely those just shown in spite of using a fixed classification based on URRAs' circumstances at the middle of the reference period rather than the floating one of the size-group analysis. All four decades exhibit a general negative relationship between growth and urban status. The relationship is most fully developed in 1971-81, with the population change rate rising with each successive step down the urban hierarchy, but it is almost complete in the other three decades, too. In the 1980s, it is only London that is out of line, paralleling the results of the size-group analysis. In both the 1950s and 1960s it is the Rural Areas category that breaks the sequence, a result that differs from the previous analysis due

Table 5.1 Population change 1951-91, for a six-level urban hierarchy for Great Britain, % for period

Hierarchical level	1951-61	1961-71	1971-81	1981-91
Great Britain	5.0	5.3	0.6	2.5
London Dominant	0.4	-4.9	-8.6	1.0
Conurbation Dominants	3.4	-3.1	-8.3	-5.1
Provincial Dominants	4.3	4.8	-1.5	-0.2
Cities	6.9	8.8	2.0	2.6
Towns	7.9	11.6	6.4	5.1
Rural Areas	-0.6	5.4	8.8	7.8

Source: Calculated from Population Census data.

to the fact that here this category omits the majority of original New Towns, these having qualified as 'Towns' by the 1970s.

Table 5.2 shows the results of converting this six-fold typology into the large, middle-sized and small city categories needed to classify the British urban system on the basis of Geyer and Kontuly's (1993) 'differential urbanization' model and establish whether Urbanization, Polarisation Reversal (PR) or counter-urbanization predominates. Classifying the top three urban-status types as the large-city category and considering the Rural Areas to lie outside the system, it is found that Britain has been consistently in the grip of counter-urbanization since 1951. At the same time, the range of rates across the three city categories reinforces the observation above about the changing pace of the process, with only some 6 percentage points separat-

Table 5.2 Stages of differential urbanization, 1951-91, for Great Britain

City category and DU model classification	1951-61	1961-71	1971-81	1981-91
Change rate (% for period)				
Large	2.1	-2.6	-7.1	-1.3
Intermediate	6.9	8.8	2.0	2.6
Small	7.9	11.6	6.4	5.1
Range of rate (% point)	5.8	14.2	13.6	6.4
Change rate ranking (1=high)				
Large	3	3	3	3
Intermediate	2	2	2	2
Small	1	1	1	1
DU model classification				
Pattern	CU	CU	CU	CU
Stage	V	V	V	V

Notes: City categories are based on the hierarchical levels in Table 5.1: Large comprises London Dominant, Conurbation Dominant and Provincial Dominant; Intermediate comprises Cities; Small comprises Towns. U Urbanization, PR Polarization Reversal, CU Counterurbanization.

Source: Calculated from Population Census data.

ing large and small city categories in the 1950s and 1980s compared to around 14 in the two middle periods.

The same approach is taken in Table 5.3 to discover whether this consistency applies to regional subsystems within Britain as well as to the country as a whole. Using basically the same regionalization into four divisions as used by Coombes et al. (1989; see also Champion et al. 1987), a somewhat different picture emerges, at least for the earlier years. In the 1950s three of the four regional divisions were characterised by the PR pattern of the 'differential urbanization' model (stage III or IV), with only London Metropolitan Region experiencing counter-urbanization. Subsequently, however, the latter has come to prevail across the whole of Britain, with the Rest of the South and the Industrial Heartland moving into stage V in the 1960s and the Periphery in the 1970s. These findings confirm that urbanization – defined as the increasing concentration of urban population into larger cities – was already a spent force in Britain by the middle of the twentieth century and that urban-system deconcentration has formed the prevailing tendency over the past 50 years, albeit varying in its intensity over time and space.

POPULATION CHANGE AND MIGRATION, 1981 TO 1991, FOR FUNCTIONAL REGIONS

A more detailed look is now taken at population change for the intercensal decade 1981 to 1991 and internal migration in the year leading up to the 1991 Census. We again use the CURDS framework, though in this case the higher level of the Functional Regions (FRs) where Rural Areas are treated as one of four types of constituent zones alongside Cores, Rings and Outer Areas (see above). This permits us to see the main features of the internal population restructuring of urban regions and the way in which this relates to differences in population dynamics of whole urban regions across the size hierarchy. This section is based on work by Rees et al. (1996), which crosstabulates zone types against a size classification of FRs and also looks at net migration rates by gender and age.

Grouping the FR zones into three categories (with Outer and Rural Areas combined), it can be seen from the upper panel of Table 5.4 that strong decentralization of population was taking place within FRs during the 1980s. In aggregate, Cores lost population, while Rings gained people and Outer/Rural Areas recorded an even higher overall rate of growth. Furthermore, this decentralization tendency is found at all five levels of the FR size hierarchy distinguished here.

Looking down the columns of the upper panel of Table 5.4, it is found that the population change rate of Cores displays a very clear negative relation-

Table 5.3   Stages of differential urbanization, 1951-91, for four regional divisions of Great Britain

Regional division, City category, and DU model classification	1951-61	1961-71	1971-81	1981-91
Change rate (% for period)				
London Metropolitan Region				
Large	0.2	-4.9	-8.6	1.0
Intermediate	17.2	20.4	4.8	4.5
Small	30.7	23.6	8.7	5.4
Rest of the South				
Large	7.3	8.7	0.7	2.7
Intermediate	10.1	12.7	5.7	7.2
Small	8.2	15.6	10.1	9.4
Industrial Heartland				
Large	4.1	-0.9	-6.6	-3.8
Intermediate	4.7	6.6	0.4	0.2
Small	3.2	9.6	5.6	3.5
Periphery				
Large	2.1	-1.4	-5.9	-3.7
Intermediate	3.7	3.4	-1.3	-0.1
Small	2.8	2.5	1.1	1.1
Stage in DU model				
London Metropolitan Region	V	V	V	V
Rest of the South	IV	V	V	V
Industrial Heartland	III	V	V	V
Periphery	IV	IV	V	V

Notes: Key to stages: I/II, III/IV and V are the Early/Advanced Stages of Urbanization, Polarization Reversal and Counterurbanization respectively.

Source: Calculated from Population Census data.

Table 5.4   Rates of population change, 1981-91 (%) and net within-Britain migration, 1990-91 (per 1000 people), by population size of functional region and FR zone type

Functional Region size	Functional Region zone			
(000s)	Cores	Rings	Outer & Rural Areas	Total
Population change*				
800+	-6.3	-1.7	3.4	-5.6
400-799	-3.0	4.3	6.9	-0.2
200-399	-0.9	4.7	5.8	1.5
100-199	-0.6	3.1	5.7	1.5
<100	0.5	4.6	5.5	3.4
Total	-2.9	3.3	5.7	-0.2*
Within-Britain migration				
800+	-6.7	1.6	6.2	-5.5
400-799	-3.9	3.3	9.4	-0.9
200-399	-2.5	4.2	6.7	0.6
100-199	-0.1	4.8	7.4	2.7
<100	0.9	5.6	7.0	4.5
Total	-3.4	4.1	7.2	0.0

Notes: * Population change is measured on the 'population present' definition, which at -0.2% nationally understates the estimated real change rate of 2.5% though the between-area relativities are not likely to be much affected.

Source: Rees et al. (1996), Tables 11 and 12.

ship with FR size. This is clearly the main driver of the growth/size gradient for the whole FRs, as there is no similarly strong growth/size relationship for the Rings and Outer/Rural Areas. At the same time, in this respect the largest FRs are distinctive in that, despite the very high rate of loss from their Cores, their other zones do not appear to be benefiting proportionately. Both the Rings and Outer/Rural Areas of this group of FRs were growing significantly more weakly than is the case for the other four size groups, doing little to offset the losses from the Cores and thereby contributing to this group's high overall loss of population.

The second panel of Table 5.4 presents the results of the same form of analysis for net within-Britain migration for the 12 months leading up to the 1991 Census. This demonstrates clearly that migration is the key component behind these differences. Indeed, looking along both dimensions of the table, the range of values is higher than for population change. Moreover, given that the migration data relate to only one year as opposed to the full 1981-91 decade, the pattern they show is remarkably similar to that presented by the population change data. This suggests that the relativities must have been pretty stable over time despite some marked fluctuations in national economic growth and in housing and labour market conditions during the decade.

Rees et al. (1996) have also used the 1991 Census counts of migrants by sex and broad age group to obtain extra insight into the nature of migration across the urban system. Figure 5.2 shows the results of an analysis of six size groups of FRs. This reveals a pretty regular counter-urbanization gradient for four of the five age groups, the exception being the 16-29 year olds group for whom the smallest FRs (with under 50,000 residents and containing sizeable rural areas) record net migration loss rather than strong gain. A more complex analysis based on the crosstabulation of metropolitan-status group and zone type (Rees et al., 1996, Figure 12) revealed a particularly large net shift of families (people aged 30-44 and 1-15) from the Cores to the Rings of all three types of FRs, as well as major spillover from the Dominants to the other two types of FR. The Outer and Rural Areas of all three FR types were found to have recorded net gains of all ten age/sex groups, except in two of the 60 cases.

TESTING FOR A 'COUNTER-URBANIZATION CASCADE', 1990 TO 1991, WITH A TYPOLOGY OF LOCAL AUTHORITY DISTRICTS

This section provides a more detailed examination of urban-rural migration in Britain. Its starting point is the observation above that counter-urbanization is the most important dimension of population redistribution today, and that this has been the case for several decades. Given that population is shifting from larger to smaller urban regions and into more rural areas, one question concerns the way in which different levels of the urban hierarchy are linked by net migration flows. Also important is the extent to which these flows are selective in their socio-demographic characteristics as opposed to involving all types of people, as this will shed light both on the factors involved and on the implications for the places affected most.

Figure 5.2 Net migration for functional region size groups, by age and sex, Great Britain, 1990-91

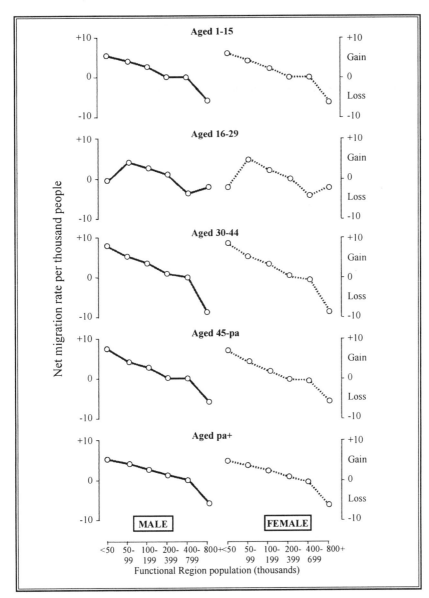

Notes: pa = pensionable age (65+ for males, 60+ for females)

Source: After Rees et al. (1996), Figure 13.

Because the most relevant census data is available in no more spatial detail than local authority districts, this series of tests is conducted for a 13-fold classification of these districts that broadly represents different levels of the settlement hierarchy. Table 5.5 shows the level of net within-Britain migration for these 13 district types for 1990-91. This confirms the broadly regular progression from the highest rate of net migratory loss at the top of the urban hierarchy, as represented here by Inner London, to the highest rate of net gain for the Remoter Rural category, comprising rural districts situated more than 65 km from a 'metropolitan' district.

Table 5.6 allows an examination of the direction of net flow between each possible pairing of all 13 district types. A positive figure indicates that the flow between any pairing is 'down the urban hierarchy' in terms of the ordering of district types in Table 5.5 — in other words, it is in a counter-urbanization direction. In all, out of the total 78 pairings possible, 66 are

Table 5.5 Population change resulting from within-Britain migration, 1990-91, by district type

District type	Code	Population 1991 (000)	Net migration 1990-91	%
1. Inner London Boroughs	IL	2,504	-31,009	-1.24
2. Outer London Boroughs	OL	4,175	-21,159	-0.51
3. Principal Metropolitan Cities	PMC	3,923	-26,311	-0.67
4. Other Metropolitan Districts	OMD	8,428	-6,900	-0.08
5. Large Non-metropolitan Cities	LNC	3,493	-14,040	-0.40
6. Small Non-metropolitan Cities	SNC	1,862	-7,812	-0.42
7. Industrial Districts	ID	7,476	+7,194	+0.10
8. Districts with New Towns	NT	2,838	+2,627	+0.09
9. Resort, Port and Retirement	RPR	3,592	+17,736	+0.49
10. Accessible Urban/Rural	AUR	7,919	+19,537	+0.25
11. Remoter Urban/Rural	RUR	2,303	+13,665	+0.59
12. Accessible Rural	AR	1,645	+10,022	+0.61
13. Remoter Rural	RR	4,731	+36,450	+0.77

Notes: PMC and OMD include the Central Clydeside Conurbation.

Source: Calculated from 1991 Census Special Migration Statistics and Local Base Statistics (ESRC/JISC purchase). Crown copyright. Adapted from Champion and Atkins (1996).

Table 5.6 Net migration between pairings of 13 district types, 1990-91, Great Britain

District type	IL	OL	PMC	OMD	LNC	SNC	ID	NT	RPR	AUR	RUR	AR
OL	17442											
PMC	-240	-661										
OMD	175	517	11652									
LNC	-128	24	-23	-2								
SNC	-657	70	17	109	57							
ID	1866	3213	2710	4056	2267	906						
NT	1281	2863	1640	1538	637	416	-387					
RPR	2461	5741	1116	1889	617	1100	1423	911				
AUR	5162	18329	4486	5068	2725	2318	-337	765	-3980			
RUR	1081	2493	542	679	3717	1177	264	788	613	2765		
AR	557	1395	1215	2116	378	-7	2054	413	-58	3169	-131	
RR	2009	4617	2055	3791	3513	1498	4807	2484	947	9065	585	1079

Notes: See Table 4.5 for key to district types. Positive figures denote net flows from column headings to rows (down-hierarchy); negative figures denote net flows from row headings to column headings (up-hierarchy). Net flows within same district type (diagonals) are zero and therefore are not shown.

Source: Calculated from 1991 Census Special Migration Statistics (ESRC/JISC purchase). Crown copyright. Adapted from Champion and Atkins (1996).

found to be in this direction, and several of the remaining 12 comprise pairings between adjacent levels of the hierarchy (i.e. along the diagonal), where there may not be a great deal of difference in the degree of 'urbanness'. Also important to note is that the largest net flows are by no means confined to the diagonals, indicating that there is no simple spillover from one level to the next, as would be found with water flowing down a simple cascade. Instead, there would appear to be a much more diffuse type of cascade in which, for the most part, each level of the hierarchy is receiving net in-migration from all levels above it and losing net migrants to all levels below it.

Table 5.7 presents the results of the same form of analysis repeated for cross-sections of the migrants classified on the basis of three characteristics in order to see how selective this counter-urbanization tendency is within the population. It can be seen that the tendency is extremely pervasive for the majority of age groups, with down-hierarchy net shifts for at least 73 of the 78 pairings of district types for all but the age groups in the 16 to 29 year old range. Among the latter, it is the 16 to 19 year olds that are especially prone to net migratory movement up the urban hierarchy, as has already been found in Figure 5.2 and is well known internationally in the form of young adults moving towards the 'bright city lights'.

The patterns for economic activity and ethnicity partially reflect the age factor. In relation to the former, the highest proportions of down-hierarchy moves are for the retired and the self-employed, the latter most commonly being people nearing retirement age, while the lowest ones are for full-time students and the unemployed. As regards ethnicity, non-white populations do not fit the 'counter-urbanization cascade' model as well as whites, an outcome that may be partly attributable to their youthful age structure as well as their lack of desire and/or ability to move away from the larger cities. Nevertheless, even for the least well-fitting ethnic group, blacks, it is found that well over two-thirds of their 78 pairings are down-hierarchy. Clearly, while this particular analysis says nothing about the pace of between-hierarchy redistribution, the overwhelming pattern – with the principal exception of young adults – is towards net migration down the hierarchy.

Unfortunately, this data source provides no information on the socio-economic characteristics of people moving up and down the urban hierarchy, but a broad indication of this is available from a separate analysis. According to Champion (1999), net out-migration from Britain's major conurbations in the year leading up to the 1991 Census was disproportionately skewed towards professional and managerial occupations. For seven of the eight places analysed in that study, at least two of the three higher-skill categories (professional, managerial and technical) recorded higher rates of net migratory loss to the rest of the UK than the three lower-skill categories

Table 5.7 Pairings of district types exhibiting down-hierarchy net flows, 1990-91, by selected characteristics, Great Britain

Characteristic	Down-hierarchy net flows	All net flows	%
Age group			
All ages	66	78	84.6
1-15	74	78	94.9
16-19	27	78	34.6
20-24	38	78	48.7
25-29	68	78	87.2
30-44	74	78	94.9
45-pa	73	78	93.6
pa+	75	78	96.2
Economic position (16 years & over)			
All aged 16+	62	78	79.5
Employed	61	78	78.2
Self-employed	72	78	92.3
Unemployed	47	78	60.3
Retired	71	78	91.0
Student (inactive)	44	78	56.4
Other inactive	74	78	94.9
Ethnicity			
All ethnicities	66	78	84.6
White	68	78	87.2
Black	54	78	69.2
South Asian	62	78	79.5
Chinese & Other	51	78	65.4

Notes: pa = pensionable age (65+ for males, 60+ for females)

Source: Calculated from 1991 Census Special Migration Statistics, ESRC/JISC purchase. Crown copyright. Adapted from Champion & Atkins (1996).

(other non-manual, skilled manual, other manual). The exception was Greater London, where a higher rate of net exodus was found for skilled manual workers than for professionals.

ANTICIPATING THE FUTURE

The analyses presented above convey a strong element of consistency in showing that the British urban system has not experienced any further concentration at least since the middle of the twentieth century, when a counter-urbanization tendency was already in place nationally and all four regional divisions had seen the eclipse of their large cities. Nevertheless, as shown by the 'counter-urbanization cascade' test, not all population groups have been participating equally in net migration down the urban hierarchy. Moreover, the pace of overall deconcentration has varied across the decades, accelerating between the 1950s and the 1960s and then falling back substantially in the 1980s. The latter, in particular, raises the question as to what can be expected in the future, which in its turn challenges our understanding of the dynamics of evolving settlement systems as well as affecting policy-making.

LATEST DEMOGRAPHIC DEVELOPMENTS

Thus far, attention has been focused on the four decades 1951-91. This is mainly because it is only at the time of a Census that population and migration data is available for the non-standard areas that are needed to represent the urban system accurately. It is also because post-1991 local government reorganization makes it impossible to study the past half century on a comparable basis with administrative areas. Nevertheless, official population estimates can be used to reveal developments between the 1980s and 1990s at a broad level of geography, while population projections for the new local government framework provide an indication of what current trends hold for the future.

Overall population change for eight conurbations and the rest of the UK for the 1990s is shown in Table 5.8, beside a comparison with the previous decade. Taken together, the eight grew more slowly than the nation as a whole, 0.22 per cent per annum compared to 0.36 per cent, signifying a continuing shift of population to the rest of the country. On the other hand, in the context of their previous experience of substantial population loss, the mere fact of increase in the 1990s is impressive. Their overall upward shift in annual growth rate by 0.34 percentage points from their 1980s level is markedly higher than the national shift and occurred at the expense of the rest of the UK, which saw a reduction in rate against the national trend.

Nevertheless, there are marked variations between the eight conurbations both in their latest growth rates and in the change in their situation since the

1980s. Greater London is in a class of its own, not just in its massive size compared with the other conurbations but also in its pattern of growth. As noted in the previous analyses based on functionally defined areas (cf. Figure 5.1 and Table 5.1), London was already back in surplus in the 1980s and has built very strongly on this in the 1990s. Growing at twice the national rate

Table 5.8 Population change for eight large conurbations and rest of UK, 1991-99 and 1981-91

Conurbation	Population 1999	Change 1991-99		Change 1981-91		Shift in rate*
	000s	000s	% p.a.	000s	% p.a.	% point
Greater London	7285.0	395.1	0.72	84.3	0.12	0.60
West Midlands	2626.5	-2.9	-0.01	-43.7	-0.16	0.15
Greater Manchester	2577.0	6.6	0.03	-48.6	-0.19	0.22
Merseyside	1403.6	-46.1	-0.40	-72.5	-0.48	0.08
South Yorkshire	1302.4	0.5	0.00	-15.2	-0.12	0.12
West Yorkshire	2115.4	30.9	0.19	17.7	0.09	0.10
Tyne and Wear	1108.5	-21.9	-0.24	-24.8	-0.21	-0.03
Clydeside	1719.1	-17.0	-0.12	-134.7	-0.72	0.60
7 conurbations	12852.5	-50.0	-0.05	-321.8	-0.24	0.19
8 conurbations	20137.5	345.2	0.22	-237.5	-0.12	0.34
Rest of UK	39363.3	1342.3	0.44	1693.7	0.47	-0.03
UK total	59500.8	1687.5	0.36	1456.2	0.26	0.10

Notes: * Shift in rate refers to movement of % p.a. rate from 1981-91 to 1991-97. p.a. = per annum. Clydeside comprises the post-1996 district authorities containing parts of the former Central Clydeside Conurbation.

Source: Calculated from mid year estimates from Office for National Statistics and Registrar General for Scotland

since 1991, it has captured almost one-quarter of the UK's total population growth according to the official estimates. Its upward shift of 0.6 percentage points between the two decades is matched only by Clydeside, but the latter was still losing population in the 1990s, as were also Tyne and Wear, Merseyside and West Midlands. While the overall picture for the seven provincial conurbations is one of improvement in position, with an upward shift in growth rate in the 1990s somewhat greater than the national figure, they are still failing to achieve a positive balance in aggregate.

The principal reason for the greater demographic dynamism of the conurbations in the 1990s can be found in increased migration gains from outside the UK, as also can that for the widening gap between London and the others. Since the 1970s the UK has switched from net loser to net gainer of international migrants, with the main beneficiaries being the conurbations in general and London in particular. As shown in Table 5.9, on average in the 1990s overseas migration was adding over 100,000 a year to the UK population, with nearly three-quarters bound for these eight places and over

Table 5.9 Components of population change for eight large conurbations and rest of UK, 1991-99, thousands

Conurbation	Births minus deaths	Net migration			Boundary change	Total change
		Total	Within -UK	Overseas		
Greater London	315.6	79.7	-387.6	467.3	-0.2	395.1
West Midlands	66.6	-79.1	-123.9	44.8	9.6	-2.9
Greater Manchester	38.6	-31.1	-63.6	32.5	-0.9	6.6
Merseyside	0.9	-47.0	-43.2	-3.8	0.0	-46.1
South Yorkshire	10.2	-10.2	-23.0	12.8	0.5	0.5
West Yorkshire	43.3	-12.2	-36.8	24.6	-0.3	30.9
Tyne and Wear	-2.5	-20.5	-26.0	5.5	1.1	-21.9
Clydeside	2.9	-19.9	-36.3	16.4	0.0	-17.0
7 conurbations	160.0	-220.1	-352.8	132.7	10.1	-50.0
8 conurbations	475.6	-140.4	-740.4	600.0	9.9	345.2
Rest of UK	382.0	970.3	740.4	229.9	-9.9	1342.3
UK total	857.6	829.9	0.0	829.9	0.0	1687.5

Notes: Within-UK migration is as measured by the NHS Central Register and excludes movements of prisoners, armed forces personnel, etc. These will be included in 'Overseas migration', as this is calculated as a residual. Clydeside comprises the post-1996 district authorities containing parts of the former Central Clydeside Conurbation; its within-UK migration is estimated from data for Health Board Areas.

Source: Calculated from mid year estimates and within-UK migration data from Office for National Statistics and Registrar General for Scotland.

three-quarters of that destined for London alone. These net gains, primarily of young adults, have served to boost the rate of natural increase of the most affected conurbations, chiefly London but also West Midlands, Greater Manchester and West Yorkshire. By contrast, the total volume of net migration loss from the conurbations to the rest of the UK is, at just over 90,000 a year for 1991-99, almost identical to its average for the 1980s.

Not surprisingly, official population projections indicate the same tendency of continuing population deconcentration, though admittedly they do not take full account of the latest increase in net immigration in the late 1990s. The 1996-based projections for England suggest that London's growth rate will remain above the national average through the projection period to 2021, generating a population increase of 9.4 per cent as opposed to England's 6.9 per cent increase. By contrast, England's six provincial conurbations in aggregate are expected to lose 2.1 per cent of their population over this 25-year period. Combined with London, this means an overall population gain of 2.3 per cent for 'conurbation England', just one-third of the national level of increase. Higher than expected net immigration would perhaps narrow this gap somewhat, but the extent of this would depend on how far the extra gains for the conurbations were offset by a higher net exodus to the rest of the UK.

DYNAMICS OF BRITAIN'S EVOLVING URBAN SYSTEM

What do these latest developments, taken in conjunction with earlier trends, tell us about the key dimensions and principal drivers of change in the British urban system? At the broadest level, two dimensions have dominated: the north-south drift and the urban-rural shift (Champion and Townsend, 1990). The southern half of the UK has been recording the stronger population growth for many decades, while population movement down the urban hicrarchy has been occurring in all Britain's major regions. At the intersection of these two dimensions, the 'urban north' has recently proved the weakest element, while the 'rural south' has grown the fastest. Meanwhile, London has emerged from a situation of heavy net migration loss in the 1960s and 1970s to a positive migration gain, albeit only modest and due to large-scale net immigration from overseas offsetting a continuing net exodus to the rest of the UK.

The divide between north and south shows little sign of abating, as the part of the urban system most strongly dominated by London becomes more distinctive not only quantitatively but also in qualitative and functional terms. What were analysed separately above as the London Metropolitan Region and the Rest of the South (cf. Table 5.3) are becoming increasingly intertwined as longer-distance employment deconcentration from the core of London has followed the earlier residential exodus and as these two processes continue to reinforce each other. Moreover, while much of the job growth in the middle-sized and smaller urban regions of southern England is associated with consumer services, as in the equivalent levels of the urban hierarchy elsewhere in the UK, the south is distinctive in capturing the majority of the UK's increases in high-skill work. Reflecting London's pre-eminent role not only in the British urban system but also as one of three leading 'world cities', its wider region has recorded strong growth in research and development, finance and banking, other producer services, the media and public administration.

This growing cleavage between north and south is confirmed by the migration exchanges affecting the British urban system. On the one hand, the net shift of residents from north to south is now quite slight at an average of only around 30,000 a year, despite the continuing divide in job growth and unemployment rates. On the other, the south's role as an 'escalator region' (Fielding, 1992) persists, notably with London drawing in younger and more enterprising people from the rest of the UK and with the region as a whole losing older workers and retirees. The increasing scarcity and rising price of housing in the London region forms a powerful deterrent to in-migration from the rest of the UK, with those who are less wealthy or aspiring turning to weekly commuting or resorting to lesser jobs and the informal economy nearer home. At the other end of the life course, the same factor is a major stimulus for the outward movement of families in search of cheaper housing and of older self-employed and retired people who do not need daily access to a metropolitan workplace and can realise substantial equity by trading down in the housing market.

Counter-urbanizing moves and international migration contribute to this evolving dislocation and imbalance in the British urban system. Despite the net movement of older people from south to north, the vast majority of the net exodus of some 90,000 a year from the main conurbations is destined for medium-sized and smaller settlements within their own wider regions. At the same time, the grossly disproportionate concentration of net immigration on London has further polarised the national urban system. In demographic terms, it has helped to rejuvenate London's age structure while other major cities have aged. Also, being largely bimodal in its skills composition, immigration to London from outside the UK has both helped to increase the high-level social capital needed to enhance its world-city status and boosted labour supply for the types of jobs that traditionally have been taken up by migrants from the de-industrialising northern cities.

Rather less clear but no less important for the evolving dynamics of the British urban system is whether counter-urbanization and immigration are related to each other causally. Much debate has taken place, notably in the USA (see Frey's chapter in this volume), about whether large-scale immigration to certain areas has prompted a net exodus of residents and is leading towards a 'demographic balkanization' of national space by ethnicity. In the British case, London provides the nearest equivalent of this situation, with its net gains from overseas in the 1990s being almost identical to its net losses to the rest of the UK (Table 5.9) and with non-whites already making up one-third of 0-15 year old Londoners in 1991. Even so, it remains unclear whether the departure of whites is due to 'white flight' or to other factors such as increasing housing market pressures or, alternatively, whether the ability to sell their houses at a high price is merely permitting London residents to realise a long-held desire to move out of London into a less urbanized setting. Elsewhere in Britain, while racial tensions have been recorded in some cities, the exodus to surrounding areas has been running ahead of the immigrant influx, with some neighbourhoods now verging on total depopulation. There, at least, it would seem that quality of life considerations, combined with easier travel and the relocation of jobs, are the main driving force.

ISSUES FOR POLICY AND RESEARCH

Current and evolving trends pose big challenges for both policy makers and researchers. The last 50 years in Britain have seen a major change in urban policy. The framework introduced immediately after the Second World War aimed at the dispersal of residents and jobs from the congested conurbations, albeit within a planning framework designed to minimise the physical spread of built-up areas. Following the decision in 1976 to terminate the New Towns programme, a succession of government programmes has attempted to boost the flagging fortunes of the larger cities and their more deprived neighbourhoods. Judging by the evidence of Figure 5.1 and Table 5.8, some success has been achieved, at least in terms of the progressive upward shift in the population growth rates of the larger cities in the two decades since the 1970s.

Despite the slowdown in the pace of urban population deconcentration, two major planning issues remain. One relates to the situation in the main conurbations, where government is keen to see further physical regeneration and improvement of living conditions, as reflected in its latest policy document *Our Towns and Cities: The Future – Delivering an Urban Renaissance* (DETR, 2000). Success in this arena, however, depends most especially on securing a sustained increase in employment, something that has proved extremely elusive for decades as far as the largest provincial cities are concerned. In the case of London, the principal challenge is that of expanding its residential capacity while also making it a more pleasant place to live and work. London is projected to require an increase in housing stock of around 1 per cent a year if it is to accommodate the population growth expected from natural increase and international migration, let alone achieve a reduction in its net migration losses to the rest of the UK. For a city that is already very heavily built-up and also hemmed in by its 'green belt', this is a tall order.

The other major planning issue relates to the accommodation of growth at the lower levels of the urban hierarchy that have been gaining from the 'counter-urbanization cascade'. In this context, it is important to recognise that planning policy is probably the single most important reason why urban population deconcentration has been more persistent and geographically widespread in Britain than in most other countries. The 'green belts' designed to restrict the lateral growth of the larger cities have forced their 'overspill' populations to relocate further away than would otherwise have been the case, while the tightness of development controls generally has provided an extra centrifugal push into more remote rural areas. Over 50 years of such 'urban containment' policy has left little spare capacity within the 'urban fence' of the settlement system, so a major controversy now rages over 'where will the people go?' (Breheny and Hall, 1996; Secretary of State for the Environment, 1996; Champion, 2001b). The main choices seem to lie between a revival of the idea of entirely new settlements, building on the New Towns experience, and a move towards the 'compact city', which would require the physical extension of existing settlements and a review of 'green belt' policy. Depending on the outcome, the UK urban system would either receive a further boost to its deconcentration or see a reinforcement of its larger urban places.

The current agenda for researchers in this field also revolve mainly around these two broad arenas, with the principal challenge being to see them as part of a single whole. It is probably fair to say that, ever since the waning of interest in a systems approach to modelling and planning urban change in the 1970s, research has followed policy in becoming most concerned with the targeting of policy initiatives on specific localities, with the wider picture being relatively neglected. This has now begun to change, with greater academic interest being shown in the evolving nature of the settlement system. The European Spatial Planning Directive, along with its associated research programme, is focusing attention on the emergence of a polycentric structure in urban regions and on the intensification of interactions across the urban-rural interface. Meanwhile, changes in transport and telecommunications are being seen as underpinning a shift towards a more physically fragmented and 'splintered' urban form, represented in terms like the 'network city' and 'multiplex city' (see Champion, 2001b, for a review).

At the present time, one can only speculate on the implications for how the urban system is evolving on the ground and how it should be conceived in conceptual terms. On the one hand, there would seem to be an urgent need for central government to move away from its current treatment of the nation as basically a single set of local government districts or indeed a much larger set of separate residential areas. On the other, there exists no universally agreed framework of wider areas, even within the academic community. The CURDS Functional Regions approach based on urban-centred regions remains useful in examining the broad trends of the past half century, but may no longer have the same relevance, as evidenced by the search for a new framework by one of its original designers (Coombes, 2000). Hopefully, the forthcoming results of the 2001 Census, coupled with a recent expansion of neighbourhood-level administrative statistics, will provide a sufficient basis for a fundamental review of conventional ideas and practices.

ACKNOWLEDGEMENTS

This paper includes material from two studies funded by the UK's Economic and Social Research Council: a Census Programme project on migration between metropolitan and non-metropolitan areas in Britain (Grant H507255132) and a Cities Programme project on migration, residential preferences and the changing environment of cities (Grant L130251013). The information in all Tables and Figures is calculated from Crown Copyright data and published by permission of the Office for National Statistics and the General Register Office Scotland. Tables 5.4 to 5.7 and Figure 5.2 contain data derived from the 1991 Census Special Migration Statistics as modified by Oliver Duke-Williams and Philip Rees, of the School of Geography at the University of Leeds. These data were accessed from the ESRC/JISC Census purchase held at Manchester Computing, using the software written by Oliver Duke-Williams. The author is also grateful to Ann Rooke for preparing the Figures.

REFERENCES

Bailey, S., J. Charlton, G. Dollamore, and J. Fitzpatrick (2000), 'Families, groups and clusters of local and health authorities: Revised for authorities in 1999', *Population Trends*, **99**, 37-51.

Berry, B. J. L. (1967), *Functional economic areas and consolidated urban regions of the United States*, Chicago (mimeo).

Best, R. (1981), *Land use and living space*, London: Methuen.

Bowler, I. (2000), 'Agriculture', in Vince Gardiner and Hugh Matthews (eds), *The changing geography of the United Kingdom*, Third Edition, London and New York: Routledge, pp. 84-107.

Breheny, M. and P. Hall (eds) (1996), *The people – where will they go?* London: Town and Country Planning Association.

Champion, A. G. (1975), 'The United Kingdom', in R. Jones (ed.), *Essays in World Urbanization*, London: George Philip and Son, pp.47-66.

Champion, A. G. (1976) 'Evolving patterns of population distribution in England and Wales, 1951-71', *Transactions of the Institute of British Geographers New Series*, **1** (4), 401-420.

Champion, A. G. (ed.) (1989), *Counterurbanization: The changing pace and nature of population deconcentration*, Arnold, London.

Champion, A. G. (1994), 'Population change and migration in Britain since 1981: Evidence for continuing deconcentration', *Environment & Planning A* **26**, 1501-1520.

Champion, A. G. (1999), 'Migration and British cities in the 1990s', *National Institute Economic Review*, **170**, 60-77.

Champion, A. G. (2000), 'Demography', in Vince Gardiner and Hugh Matthews (eds), *The Changing Geography of the United Kingdom*, Third Edition, London and New York: Routledge, pp. 169-189.

Champion, A. G. (2001a), 'The continuing urban-rural population movement in Britain: Trends, patterns, significance', *Espace, Populations, Sociétés*, **2001-xx1-2**, 37-51.

Champion, A. G. (2001b), *The Containment of Urban England: Retrospect and Prospect*, Milan: Franco Angeli.

Champion, A. G. and D. Atkins (1996), *The counterurbanization cascade: An analysis of the 1991 census special migration statistics for Great Britain*, Seminar Paper 66, Department of Geography, University of Newcastle upon Tyne.

Champion, A. G., D. Atkins, M. Coombes, and S. Fotheringham (1998), *Urban exodus*, London: Council for the Protection of Rural England.

Champion, A. G., K. Clegg, and R. L. Davies (1977), *Facts about the New Towns: A socio-economic digest*, Corbridge: Retail and Planning Associates.

Champion, A. G. and D. Dorling (1994), 'Population change for Britain's functional regions, 1951-91', *Population Trends*, **83**, 14-23.

Champion, A. G., A. E. Green, D. W. Owen, D. J. Ellin, and M. G. Coombes (1987), *Changing places: Britain's demographic, economic and social complexion*, London: Edward Arnold.

Champion, A. G. and A. R. Townsend (1990), *Contemporary Britain: A geographical perspective*, London: Edward Arnold.

Champion, A. G., C. Wong, A. Rooke, D. Dorling, M. G. Coombes, and C. Brunsdon (1996), *The population of Britain in the 1990s: A social and economic atlas*, Oxford: Clarendon Press.

Cheshire, P. (1995), 'A new phase of urban development in Western Europe? The evidence for the 1990s', *Urban Studies*, **32** (7), 1045-1063.

Cheshire, P. and D. G. Hay (1989), *Urban problems in Western Europe: An economic analysis*, London: Unwin Hyman.

Cloke, P. J. (1977), 'An index of rurality for England and Wales', *Regional Studies*, **11** (1), 31-46.

Coombes, M. (2000), 'Defining locality boundaries with synthetic data', *Environment and Planning A*, **32**, 1499-1518.

Coombes, M. G., L. R. Dalla and S. Raybould (1989), 'Counterurbanization in Britain and Italy: A comparative critique of the concept, causation and evidence', *Progress in Planning*, **32**, 1-70.

Coombes, M. G., J. S. Dixon, J. B. Goddard, S. Openshaw, and P. J. Taylor (1982), 'Functional regions for the population census of Great Britain', in D. T. Herbert and R. J. Johnston (eds), *Geography and the urban environment: Progress in research and applications*, vol. 5, Chichester: John Wiley, pp. 63-112.

Cullingworth, B. and Vincent N. (1997), *Town and country planning in the UK*, Twelfth edition, New York and London: Routledge.

DETR (2000), *Our towns and cities: The future – delivering an urban renaissance*, Cm 4911, London: Department of the Environment, Transport and the Regions, London.

Fielding, A. J. (1971), *Internal migration in England and Wales: A presentation and interpretation of 'city-region' data*, University Working Paper 14, Centre for Environmental Studies, London.

Fielding, A. J. (1982), 'Counterurbanization in Western Europe', *Progress in Planning* 17, 1-52.

Fielding, A. J. (1992), 'Migration and social mobility: South East England as an "escalator" region', *Regional Studies* 26 (1), 1-15.

Fothergill, S. and G. Gudgin (1982), *Unequal growth: Urban and regional change in the UK*, London: Heinemann.

Geyer, H. S. and T. M. Kontuly (1993), 'A theoretical foundation for the concept of differential urbanization', *International Regional Science Review,* 15, 157-177.

Hall, P. (1971), 'Spatial structure of metropolitan England', in M. Chisholm and G. Manners (eds), *Spatial policy problems of the British economy*, Cambridge: Cambridge University Press, pp. 96-125.

Hall, P. (1992), *Urban and regional planning*, Third edition, London: Routledge.

Hall, P. and D. Hay (1980), *Growth centres in the European urban system*, London: Heinemann.

Hall, P., R. Thomas, H. Gracey, and R. Drewett (1973), *The containment of urban England, Volume One, Urban and metropolitan growth processes or megalopolis denied*, London: George Allen & Unwin.

Hodge, I. and M. Whitby (1981), *Rural employment: Trends, options, choices*, London and New York: Methuen.

IUR (1959), *The world's metropolitan areas*, Berkeley and Los Angeles: International Urban Research.

Law, C. M. (1967), 'The growth of the urban population in England and Wales, 1801-1911', *Transactions of the Institute of British Geographers*, 41, 125-143.

Martin, R. and R. Rowthorn (eds) (1986), *The geography of de-industrialization*, Basingstoke: Macmillan.

Mohan, J. (1999), *A United Kingdom? economic, social and political geographies*, London: Arnold.

ONS and M. G. Coombes (1998) *1991-based travel-to-work areas*, London: Office for National Statistics.

Osborn, F. J. and A. Whittick (1969), *New Towns: The answer to megalopolis*, Second Edition, London: Hill.

Park, C. (2000), 'Conservation and preservation', in V. Gardiner and H. Matthews (eds), *The Changing Geography of the United Kingdom*, Third Edition, London and New York: Routledge, pp. 437-458.

Rees, P., H. Durham, and M. Kupiszewski (1996), *Internal Migration and Regional Population Dynamics in Europe: United Kingdom Case Study*, Leeds: School of Geography, University of Leeds.

Sadler, D. (2000), 'Manufacturing industry', in V. Gardiner and H. Matthews (eds), *The changing geography of the United Kingdom*, Third Edition, London and New York: Routledge, pp. 129-149.

Scase, R. (2000), *Britain in 2010: The new business landscape*, Oxford: Capstone.

Schnore, L. F. (1962), 'Metropolitan development in the United Kingdom', *Economic Geography*, **38** (3), 215-233.

Secretary of State for the Environment (1996) *Household growth: Where shall we live?* London: HMSO.

Smailes, A. E. (1944), 'The urban hierarchy in England and Wales', *Geography*, **29**, 41-51.

Spence, N., A. Gillespie, J. Goddard, S. Kennett, S. Pinch, and A. Williams (1982), *British cities: Analysis of urban change*, Oxford: Pergamon.

Turok, I. and N. Edge (1999), *The jobs gap in Britain's cities: Employment loss and labour market consequences*, Bristol: The Policy Press.

Turton, B. (2000), 'Transport', in V. Gardiner and H. Matthews (eds), *The changing geography of the United Kingdom*, Third Edition, London and New York: Routledge, pp. 108-128.

US Bureau of the Budget (1964), *Standard Metropolitan Statistical Areas*, Washington, D.C.: Government Printing Office.

van den Berg, L., R. Drewett, L. H. Klaassen, A. Rossi, and C. H. T. Vijverberg (1982), *Urban Europe: A study of growth and decline*, Oxford: Pergamon.

Wallace, M., J. Charlton, and C. Denham (1995), 'The new OPCS area classifications', *Population Trends*, **79**, 15-30.

Chapter 6

The French Urban System

D. Pumain

INTRODUCTION

France is an example of a Developed Country which exhibits original features in its urbanization process, compared to common trends as they are usually recorded, especially when they are compared with the American or British experience. The urban evolution of the last half-century, especially when urban sprawl is considered, can be partly interpreted through the intermediary position of France between Northern and Southern Europe. But the main features of the French urban system proceed from a much longer history. With about ten million inhabitants, Paris is the largest European city. It appears relatively modest in size when compared to the megapolises of other continents, whereas it remains enormous as the head of the French territory, with a lengthy political and administrative centralism. Towns and cities are scattered all over the territory but, probably because of its relatively low population density, they rarely form large conurbations as in Britain or the Rhine countries (Figure 6.1). While the last fifty years of urban growth has not significantly altered the spatial structure of the national urban system, because of a wide diffusion of urban change, the future of French cities now has to be examined in the European context.

A HALF CENTURY OF URBAN GROWTH

As in other countries of the European and Asian continents, the development history of towns and cities in France goes back a very long way, to Roman times two thousand years ago. But the main stage of accelerated urban growth, as in other Developed Countries, started during the Industrial Revolution in the nineteenth century. However, the French urbanization of

Figure 6.1 The French urban system, 1999

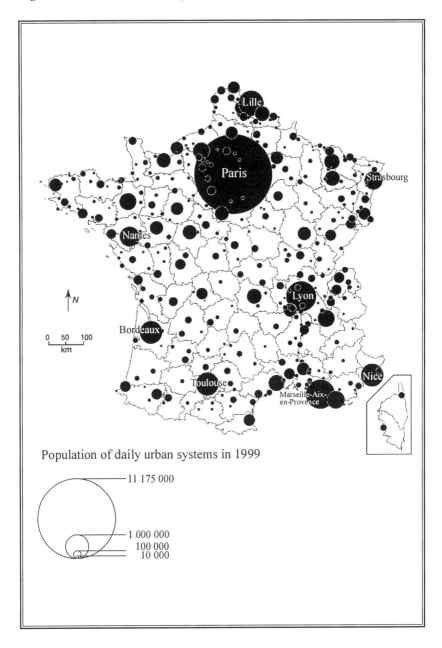

Population of daily urban systems in 1999

Source: INSEE, Recensements de la Population, 1999

that time was not as intense or as rapid as in countries in Northern Europe (Bairoch, 1996). The average annual growth rate of the urban population during the nineteenth century was about 1 per cent in France, whereas it was 2 per cent per year in the UK. This may be attributed to the early impact of the demographic transition in France. The decline in urban growth started before the end of the eighteenth century, which reduced the potential number of migrants from the countryside. This was tentatively linked to the prosperity of the country at the time, especially its agriculture. The relative slowness in the pace of urbanization may also be explained by the diffusion of Industrial Revolution technology to only parts of the country. Capital investments in heavy industries and manufacturing did not reach many of the southern and western parts (this is traditionally represented by an unequal level of industrial development on each side of a line drawn between Le Havre and Marseille). Whatever the reasons, the urban population only exceeded the rural population around 1930, whereas 50 per cent of the population was already urbanized in the UK in 1850 and in Germany in 1880. France was still a rather rural country after the Second World War.

BELATED BUT INTENSE URBANIZATION

After the Second World War, urbanization in France became very intense compared to previous periods and to urbanization trends in neighbouring European countries. The growth rate of the urban population evolved in a cyclical manner, increasing to a maximum of 1.8 per cent per year during the 1960s and decelerating afterwards. Roughly, two periods of two decades each can be distinguished. Between 1954 and 1975 the annual average growth rate was almost 1.5 per cent per year, while it dropped to less than 0.5 per cent between 1975 and 1999. As a result, the overall urbanization rate (i.e the urban population as a share of the total population) continued to increase. It has grown from 54 per cent in 1950 to 73 per cent in 2000. Measured in terms of daily urban systems the country's level of urbanization reached 76 per cent at the end of the previous century.

The cyclical aspect of the wave of urbanization is a combination of the demographic and economic trends of the period, which also displayed a cyclical evolution. The post-war Baby-Boom was intense until the middle of the sixties and was followed, as in other western European countries, by a decrease in fertility. However, the decline in France never equalled the very low fertility rates that were observed in northern Italy, Germany, or even Spain after 1990, but it has more or less stabilised around the value of 1.8 since the eighties. This can be partly explained by social policies such as the financial assistance to families with three children or more and various measures helping women to keep their jobs during their maternity period. During the cycle of economic growth known as 'the thirty glorious years' the net income per person increased by a factor of three. Basic manufacturing activities including steel industry and mechanics were booming first in the 1950s, followed by the automobile industry, aeronautics and electric supplies in the 1960s. In a second wave of development, the electronic industry and the tertiary activities provided most of the new employment, including a very large increase in private and business services, whereas retail activities were losing jobs because of the concentration of firms. Foreign immigration became an important factor during the first decades. This was accompanied by an upsurge in low-skilled job opportunities, but it was reduced to almost none after the middle-1970s, when economic growth entered a deceleration phase and new jobs required higher-skilled labourers. Meanwhile, agriculture was deeply transformed. The transformation of farming from family poly-cultural production towards more specialized and business oriented farming led to an increase in productivity and production output. Foreign migrants as well as agricultural workers leaving their farms also contributed to urban growth.

CHANGING THE DEFINITIONS OF URBAN UNITS

Measuring urban development became a challenge for the French Statistical Institute. The statistical concept of an urban agglomeration (or urban unit) was created in 1954. The definition of an urban agglomeration was based on two criteria : its size (more than 2000 inhabitants) and its spatial continuity (less than 200 metres between two buildings – excluding areas where the construction of building was not allowed). Very often the urban agglomeration expands over several administrative subdivisions (i.e. the communes) and a common distinction is made between the central commune (or central town) and the surrounding communes which constitute the suburbs (*banlieue* in French). The whole urban unit carries the name of the central town which is usually the most populated commune of the agglomeration and corresponds with the historical centre.

The *Zones de Peuplement Industriel et Urbain* (ZPIUs) were created in 1962 to take into account the fact that more and more communes could be included in the daily urban system of a town without belonging to the built-up area contiguous to this urban centre. Functional criteria that were used to select types of communes included (i) the level of daily commuting, (ii) the share of households working in the agricultural sector and (iii) the rate of demographic growth. ZPIUs included industrial activities or dormitory towns, which had to be considered as urban and linked to an agglomeration in the statistical definition.

Since 1996, ZPIUs were replaced by *aires urbaines* retrospectively from the 1990 census. The former had become too extensive. More than 75 per cent of the 36 000 French communes and 96 per cent of the total population became part of ZPIUs in 1990. There was also a need to make the definition less arbitrary, using more standardized criteria and taking other national definitions into consideration. An *aire urbaine* is centred on an 'urban centre' concentrating more than 5000 jobs.[1] The urban centre is surrounded by an urban ring consisting of communes with at least 40 per cent of their inhabitants working in the centre or adjacent communes already forming part of the urban ring. A complementary *"espace à dominante urbaine"* (space with prevailing urban character) is defined and includes communes whose working population is shared between several urban centres without reaching the threshold of 40 per cent in any of them.

Two different images of French urbanization are given when urban agglomerations and *aires urbaines* are considered. Approximately six thousand communes and more than 18 per cent of the surface of the country are included in approximately two thousand urban agglomerations. In the more extensive and functional definition of about 350 *aires urbaines*, more than a third of the surface and one out of three communes forming part of daily urban systems are included (Table 6.1). When measured in the framework of the *aires urbaines*, the urban population growth rate has been

Table 6.1 Expansion of urbanization in France in terms of two different definitions

	1968	1975	1982	1990	1999
Agglomerations					
Number	1520	1642	1781	1890	1995
Number of communes	3958	4450	4879	5300	5956
Population (000s)	34817	38334	39508	418942	44201
Surface (km²)	68 827	76227	83323	89642	100052
Aires urbaines					
Number				361	354
Number of communes				10687	13908
Population (000s)				41278	45053
Surface (km²)				132090	175997

Source : INSEE and F. Paulus (2001)

---

[1] For the sake of comparison it should be mentioned that in the United States, SMSAs were based on cores providing at least 50 000 jobs.

twice the one measured in the limits of the agglomerations during the last three decades.

URBAN SPRAWL AND DECONCENTRATION

People living in urban areas at the local level have been deconcentrating since 1975, a process that started a little earlier in larger cities. The deconcentration of the urban population first started with a decrease of the population in urban centres and an increase in their suburbs and rural peripheries. This resulted in a large expansion of urban spots on maps (see on Figure 6.2 the spatial limits of the *aires urbaines* in 1999 compared to what they had been in 1968 under the same definition at that time). The share of the urban population in the peri-urban ring is still increasing: 21 per cent in 1999 against 17 per cent in 1990. When differentiated according to the urban centres (the main commune), traditional suburbs (communes of the *banlieue*) and the outer urban ring,[2] the demographic evolution remains very consistent since the migration turnaround in 1975: the further away from the centre, the higher is the average growth rate. Of course, one must keep in mind that the growth rates of the rural communes belonging to the outer ring concern smaller numbers of population than other types of places. As an example, the average growth rates per year were, during the last decade, +1.19 per cent for the outer rings, + 0.41 for the suburbs and 0.15 for the central communes. Moreover, a slowing down of the process of urban sprawl has been observed since the beginning of the 1990s and was confirmed by the 1999 census. When urban sprawl occurred the fastest between 1975 and 1982, the relative evolution of urban centres, suburbs and outer urban rings became very contrasted: the mean annual population growth rates of the urban centres were negative, those of the suburbs slightly positive and those of outer rings were the highest. Since 1982, the decrease of population in the urban centres is becoming less important and in the last period the evolution has even become positive again, whereas the growth rates of suburbs and of the communes of the outer rings are decreasing (Figure 6.3). The process of urban sprawl was actually cyclical in time and wave-like in space, and at the end of the period, there was a convergence towards a mean growth rate in all the parts of the *aires urbaines*.

This process of urban sprawl corresponds to the expanding trend of daily urban space as permitted by the increasing speed of local transportation modes. The departure of inhabitants from a city centre towards a rural periphery could be interpreted as (i) encouraged by clever housing estates

---

[2] I.e. communes that do not belong to the urban agglomeration but that are functionally part of the *aires urbaines* through a high commuting rate.

Figure 6.2 Urban sprawl in France, 1968-99

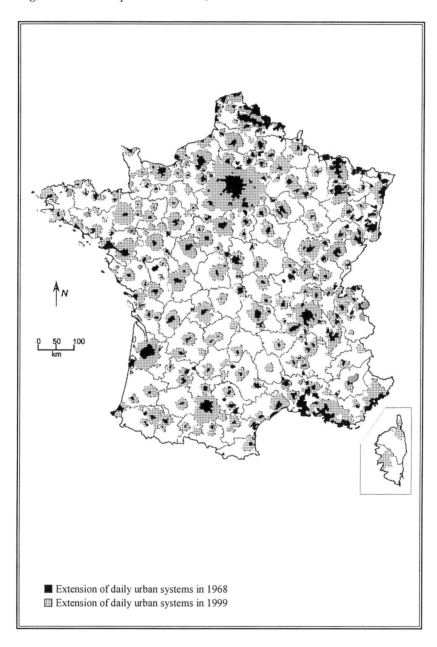

■ Extension of daily urban systems in 1968
▦ Extension of daily urban systems in 1999

Source: INSEE, Recensements de la Population

Figure 6.3 Changing growth rates of different zones of daily urban systems, 1968-99

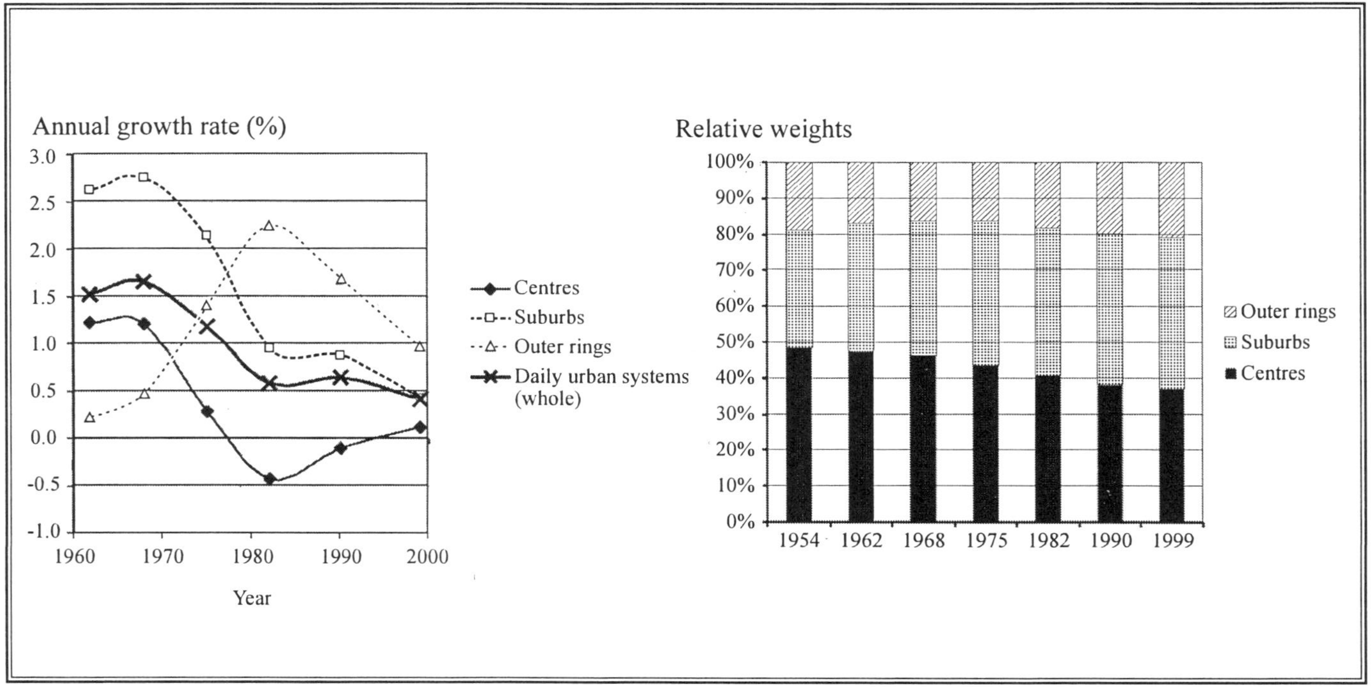

Source: INSEE. Recensements de la Population

traders, (ii) a sign of rejection of the urban way of life and (iii) a marked preference for a country lifestyle. However, the spatial distribution of the houses of these neo-rural people around the main urban centres shows how strongly they are attached to these centres (Figure 6.2). Urban deconcentration is not a sign of urban decline, however. For example, during the last decade, 113 *aires urbaines* lost population but the number of their housing units increased at a rate of 0.5 per year. In the 248 other *aires urbaines* whose population was growing at an average of 0.5 per cent per year, the number of housing units increased more than twice as fast (1.2 per cent per year). In terms of the spatial diffusion process, the French case may be representative of an intermediary position in Europe. The phenomenon of urban sprawl has both similar and unique features which could be regarded as an intermediary position between the countries of Northern and Southern Europe. This situation leads to apparent contradictions in the strength of urban expansion: France is a country where the main stage of peri-urbanization occurred rather late during the 1970s and 1980s, but the process of urban sprawl has had a more profound impact than in the case of Spain and even Italy, for instance.

The French urban evolution also may be a reflection of the European urban development process collectively, which demonstrates the combined advantages of compact cities and more dispersed settlements. Despite its extensiveness, there is no conclusive proof that urban sprawl in France represents a strong feeling against an urban way of life. On the contrary, there is a real predilection for urban centres and urban values among French society, perhaps an expression of the strength of the Mediterranean cultural reference in the French way of life. However, the closeness of the older generation to a rural lifestyle[3] and their memories may explain the deep desire for countryside. But the urban heritage still has an enormous symbolic and economic value in France, and although it is not as rich as in Italy, there is a large diversity among European cities on this issue. According to the evolution of urban land prices and the location of jobs and main urban amenities it seems unlikely that French cities evolve in the same way as American cities. The American model of urban sprawl can therefore not be directly applied to the French situation. The French case is also interesting for the peculiarity of its political framework for urban development. Although the French local government system is not as interventionist in monitoring urban planning as that of countries such as the Netherlands and Sweden for example, the French State maintains a strong indirect effect on urban sprawl through its general housing and transportation policies. The extreme spatial fragmentation of decision-making is partly counterbalanced

---

[3] Fifty percent of the French population was still rural in 1950.

by general planning tools and a growing awareness of the necessity for municipalities to co-operate.

In conclusion, it should be emphasized that although urban sprawl has occurred in France rather extensively at the local scale of each daily urban system, whatever its size, this phenomenon should not be interpreted as counter-urbanization.

PERSISTENCE OF CONCENTRATION TRENDS AT THE SCALE OF THE URBAN SYSTEM

A high level of primacy is a distinctive feature of the French urban system. A ratio exceeding 7 between the population size of the first and the second city has remained unchanged for at least two centuries. This is the only example of an urban system with such a strong primacy among the large Developed Countries (Pumain and Moriconi-Ebrard, 1997) and can perhaps be explained by the very centralised political and administrative model of organization that stemmed from the French monarchy in the fifteenth century (and perhaps earlier). The emphasis on Paris as the national gravity point has subsequently been re-inforced by the spatial economic-political organization of the country. For instance, the infrastructure of the rapid transportation networks, i.e. paved roads in the eighteenth century, and railways in the nineteenth century as well as the highways of the mid-twentieth century and TGV trains in the last decades have all followed a star-like pattern with Paris as a centre.

In every region, this hierarchical organization – which regularly alternates a large number of small towns close to one another with more distant big cities – brings in more or less significant size differences between metropolises, large regional capitals and small urban centres. It is highly informative to know what is the actual extent of inequalities in city sizes inside a region, since it reflects the cumulative processes of accumulation and concentration which have occurred in the past and were very often linked to the administrative and political organization of society in territories (Pumain, 2000)). The unequal concentration of urban population also has important consequences when choosing appropriate policies for regional planning and sustainable development, because among other things economic location factors and indicators of urban pressure on local environment are tightly linked to agglomeration sizes. However, the relative importance of each category of city size in one region cannot be measured easily in a comparative way, for instance by a simple proportion of the urban population living in each class of towns and cities. Such an indicator would be biased primarily by the size of the largest city in the region. Models of city size distribution, which reflect the systematic dependency between the sizes of towns and cities of the same regions have to be used for providing comparable measures of urban concentration.

When the question of the continuity in urban concentration is considered, based upon urban agglomerations and *aires urbaines*, each urban category provides a different answer. When the restrictive definition of the urban agglomeration is used, the historical data series show a trend of increasing concentration since at least 1850, with a clear reversal from 1975 onwards. A conclusion could be that, thanks to changes in French society including a broader interest in the environment, quality of life, and heliotropism, and appropriate planning policies, the traditional trend of increasing spatial inequalities in a very centralised country have been victoriously turned around. As a result more attention and development opportunities were given to remote parts of the territory. But if the notion of *aires urbaines* is used, as a better measure of their real size, for the 350 largest urban centres, the result is quite different (Table 6.2 and Figure 6.4). Instead of a reversal, the graph shows a clear trend of increasing concentration of urban population. This is confirmed by a comparison of the mean growth rates of urban units and *aires urbaines* during the last third of the twentieth century (Table 6.3). Although large urban agglomerations seemed to grow less rapidly than the smallest, when observed in the more relevant spatial limits given by the *aires urbaines* definition, the trend is more in favour of the large urban centres.

Table 6.2   Change in the concentration index of city size distribution, 1968-99

Year	Minimal population	Number of daily urban systems and urban units	Slope of the fitted Pareto distribution*
1968	2000	1450	1.099
1975	2000	1489	1.103
1982	2000	1486	1.167
1990	2000	1453	1.202
1999	2000	1357	1.247

Notes: * The R-square of the fitted Pareto distribution exceeds 0.99.

Source: RGP-INSEE. Bretagnolle, Paulus, Pumain, 2001.

We therefore conclude that the proliferation and diffusion of communication technology and of the society of information have not yet interrupted the powerful trend towards a more concentrated urban system in France. This evolution corresponds with Pred's (1977) observations of urban systems dynamics in the past showing a process of hierarchical diffusion of innovations which accumulates the effects of initial advantages in the largest urban centres and a process of short circuit which tends to eliminate the smallest centres from the competition, because the increase in speed and facilities of communication is extending the spatial range and the attractiveness of the largest centre (Bretagnolle, Pumain and Rozenblat, 1998).

Table 6.3 Growth rates by city size (% per year)

Size class (thousands)	Urban agglomerations				Aires urbaines	
	1954-75	number	1975-99	number	1975-99	number
2-5	1.64	510	0.76	739		
5-10	1.88	257	0.54	351		
10-20	2.48	111	0.45	164	1.11	80
20-50	2.41	84	0.46	112	1.19	109
50-100	2.85	31	0.30	51	1.26	53
100-200	2.82	18	0.67	25	1.16	26
200-2000	2.34	11	0.85	23	1.43	30
Paris	1.48	1	0.53	1	0.89	1

Source: RGP- INSEE.

Figure 6.4 Concentration index of city size distribution, 1954-99

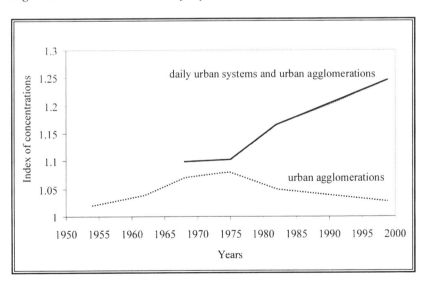

Source: RGP-INSEE UMR Géographie-cités, 2001

COMPETING CITIES IN A SELF-ORGANIZING SYSTEM

First of all it has to be remembered that in a very old and tightly connected national urban system, as in the case of France, qualitative changes in the economic and social profiles of cities follow the pattern of competitive distribution of urban growth. Empirical evidence of this kind of distributed change has been put forward by several comparative studies (Pumain and Saint-Julien, 1984). Data on the availability of jobs in approximately thirty categories of economic activities and in twenty categories of social status (and occupation) are available for each of the seven population censuses that were held between 1954 and 1999[4]. Evidence of the distributed changes described above is given for each census year in terms of the expanding spatial framework of the urban agglomerations (and also according to the *aires urbaines* for the last two census years). The best way of comparing such economic and social profiles was to use multivariate analysis. In order to avoid the effect differences in city sizes could have on the outcome of the study, a principal component analysis was done for each census year, based upon the proportions of each category to the total labour force for each city. The study showed a rather similar outcome over time. The main differentiating factors are first the multidimensional and mutually exclusive specializations in manufacturing activities, versus services, which are mostly an inheritance of the Industrial Revolution. A second differentiating factor that has progressively emerged during this period is the disparities between cities that have succeeded in modernizing their economies and societies over time, and those that have not.

Because the pattern has remained rather stable over time, it was possible to use the principal component analysis method in a quasi-longitudinal manner to compare the profiles of employment of each city according to the same spectrum of activities at the different census years simultaneously. Figure 6.5 is a diagrammatic scheme of the results of this analysis, presented here for about twenty cities described by a dozen aggregated economic activities for five census years. The five points representing the position of each city in the structure at each census year have been connected to form trajectories. These trajectories show changes in the specialization of a city relative to the others in the system over time. The main feature of the study result is the remarkable parallelism between the trajectories, which shows how similar the qualitative transformation processes of all cities during the whole period have been. This qualitative change mainly implies a substitution of jobs in manufacturing by jobs in the tertiary sector. The share of services in total urban employment was less than 50 per cent in 1954 and is around 70 per

---

[4] Only minor differences occur in the data due to modifications in the nomenclature.

Figure 6.5 Trajectories of main cities in the space of economic activities, 1968-90

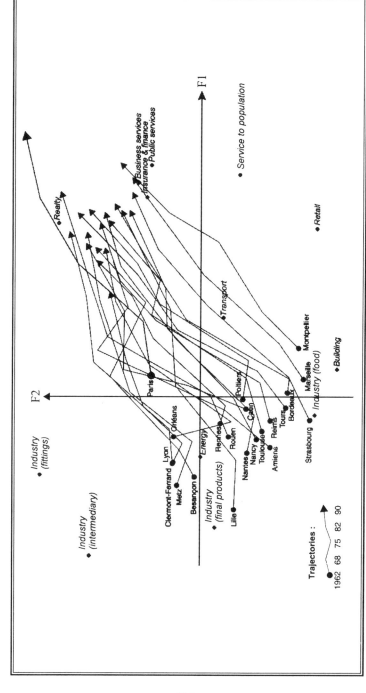

Source: INSEE. Recensements de la Population

cent currently. Jobs in the manufacturing of final consumption goods have decreased less than jobs in basic industries, whereas the retail trade sector has lost its importance compared to public, business, and financial services.

Figure 6.5 shows that Paris, whose employment structure was already ahead of all other cities in the urban system in this direction, has maintained its advantage in the transformation process by the end of the study period. Comparatively, the situation between the other cities has not changed much, despite the degree of the renewal of their activities over the last approximately twenty years. What does not appear on the figure but can be observed from the computed results, however, is the subtle but very fluctuating character of common changes that occur in the urban system. At each time interval, certain cities may gain a little on the general direction of the evolution or lag behind it, but these ups or downs do not continue for long periods of time. Overall, change in an urban system seems to follow the general transformation trends. This is typical of a very tightly connected system, where information is circulated very rapidly and processes of imitation of innovation, wherever it happens, are very powerful. Actually the trajectories of cities in Figure 6.5 display a rather uniform spatial diffusion process.

The result of all this is a remarkable degree of stability in the economic and social structure of cities in the urban system. Once a specific innovation does not follow the 'normal' spatial process of diffusion, it becomes unevenly distributed and leaves a trace in the structure of the urban system which cannot be erased before a very long period of time. This has been the case in heavy industries during the Industrial Revolution, a century and a half ago, as it has been the case more recently in highly skilled activities such as high-tech industries, international finance and other business services. The latter tend to concentrate in the largest metropolitan areas although they have a relatively small impact on the number of jobs in the cities overall.

It is only by sophisticated methods of analysis and after a systematic filtering out of common trends of change that specific evolutions can be revealed. They consist in small deviations from the general trends, which tend to affect not one but a set of indicators, and which are amplified over time. These relative changes often have the same multidimensional composition as the general trends. Such an evolution is analogous to observations made about the dynamics of self-organized systems in other scientific fields (Allen, 1997). Extraordinary specialization and growth of subsets of cities may lead to transformations in the structure of an urban system which could be described as bifurcation in the dynamics of a self-organizing system. Occurrences of this sort in France seem to be accompanied by public spatial planning policies launched by DATAR

(*Délégation à l'Aménagement du Territoire et à l'Action régionale*). Four main trends in the re-shaping of the urban system should be mentioned:

(1) *Diffusion of growth and modernization within a centre-periphery framework*. This process is the result of a combination of public policies and "spontaneous" economic trends. A range of spatial planning policies was designed to counterbalance the historical spatial imbalance that stemmed from the longstanding central oriented government system in the country. At the same time, private investments tried to profit from the existing differentials between regions in terms of salaries and equipment. A first growth impulse that occurred in regions along the west and south of Paris (mainly Brittany), during the sixties, is linked to laws supporting industrial decentralization from Paris as well as the creation of the electronics and automobile industries employing a residual rural labour force in those regions. During the seventies and eighties, the concentric circles of development enlarged and reached regions of Poitou and Aquitaine, the regions belonging to the 'Atlantic Arc' having also benefited from their general attractiveness as coastal regions during the last two decades of the century. This brought in new developments in an area that did not benefit from development that occurred in France during the Industrial Revolution. Investment in higher education and in housing significantly increased the mean income level of these regions which were well under the national average at the beginning of the 1950s.

The second diffusion of development impulses from the 'centre' towards the 'periphery' occurred hierarchically; it did not occur in a wave-like fashion as described in the former process. This hierarchical diffusion was set in motion by public policy specifically designed to modernize and develop a list of eight designated 'métropoles d'équilibre' in 1964. It preceded the law on political decentralization and was instrumental in improving the business centres' high level services of the main regional capitals.[5]

Although both diffusion movements succeeded in preventing the strong primacy of the French urban system from increasing any further, it did not succeed in reversing the trend. Contrasts between the Paris urban region and the other cities remain as sharp as they were before, quantitatively and qualitatively.

(2) *An erosion of excessive specialization*. Since the middle of the 1960s a relative and sometimes absolute decrease in population and an absolute loss in the degree of their specialization have been a characteristic of almost all

---

[5] These are Lyon, Marseille, Lille, Toulouse, Nantes, Bordeaux, Nancy-Metz and Strasbourg.

cities of the northern and north eastern regions of France. Many of the cities in these regions specialized in mining, steel production, or textile industries. These cities have lost jobs over the entire period due to competition or relocation of firms in other parts of the world. Despite the implementation of policies aimed at supporting the local labour force,[6] continuing streams of out-migration are indicative of how difficult it is to diversify activities in an area where the education level and the rate of female participation in the labour force are among the lowest in the country.

A slow and difficult recovery process started as early as the sixties and is still under way in these regions. Part of the recovery process entails investment in public infrastructure, such as two new universities that were opened, one in the 1980s and one in the 1990s in Valenciennes and Dunkerque, and in the provision of urban services in the mining basin where they had long been neglected. Regional capitals such as Lille, Nancy and Metz now act as focal points for new developments. These developments can rely on research and technical capacities, as well as on stronger capitalist structures in the case of the North region.

(3) *The booming South.* Cities in the southern regions, especially those along the Mediterranean coast, have become more and more attractive, not only to elderly people, but to all population categories, from almost every region. The attraction of these 'sun belts' is representative of trends in many other Developed Countries such as the US, England or Germany. This has been reinforced by factors such as the in-migration of hundreds of thousands of people from the former French colony of Algeria during the early 1960s. Many of them have re-invested their capital in the developing region of Bas-Languedoc in the vicinity of Montpellier where they helped boost the economy. Even though this in-migration has had well diffused effects, the urban development has been selective. Cities which already had an academic tradition and a more 'bourgeois' society, like Montpellier or Toulouse, were favoured, while smaller and more industrial towns with a working class society like Nîmes or Béziers were relatively neglected. This trend however has been continuing for more than forty years and it explains the diversification of the economy in the cities of these regions, including high tech activities in centres such as Nice, Marseille, Toulouse and later Bordeaux.

(4) *Technopolitan development* There is a strong spatial link between high tech industries and public and private research institutions. Although such

---

[6] This was done through assistance in industrial conversion or helping workers who previously rented from the manufacturing firms to obtain housing at affordable prices.

complexes are present in various degrees in every regional capital, this association is the main explanation for the rapid and continuous dynamism of cities located in valleys of the northern Alps and middle-Rhône valley. The growth of Grenoble is emblematic of this success story, and this city's development has also boosted the development of other Alpine towns, both the previously manufacturing oriented towns like Annecy or those specialising in the tertiary sector such as in Chambéry, as well as in Lyon, the large metropolis of the region. Chemistry, bio-technologies and computer industries and services are the main activities driving this specific urban development.

In conclusion it could be remarked that interurban competition is a major process in the evolution of urban systems. It explains the very quick adoption of technological, economic and social innovations in a whole range of cities as well as the delays and inequalities stemming from the fluctuations in the spread of diffusion. While it is often hierarchical, this diffusion or filtering down of innovations is not a process forced upon passive communities from above. On the contrary, a most active competition is observed among cities. This is a conscious process which becomes an important factor when conflicts arise, for instance when two cities compete for the same infrastructural equipment. It is also apparent in advertising campaigns and has been especially visible in urban marketing policies of local authorities since the middle of eighties.

POPULATION REDISTRIBUTION THROUGH MIGRATION

Residential mobility continuously increased in France between 1954 and 1975, then decreased a little again. This slow-down was first observed in the long distance migration between departments (about 100 subdivisions in France) or regions (22), and then affected the short distance moves (changes in housing or between communes inside the same department or region). Long distance migration mainly means change in profession whereas short distance migration are more frequently related with familial events like marriage or births. As in other countries, the highest mobility rates are observed for population in the 20 to 29 year age group. The mobility level of the population in France remains however of about the same magnitude as in other European countries or Japan (10% changes in housing per year). It is roughly half of that observed in North America.

Two major regional shifts have occurred in the spatial distribution of net migration since the 1950s. First, the Paris region attracted as much as 25 per cent of the population increase through migration during the sixties, while the metropolitan area as such accommodated 18 per cent of the total French population. The metropolitan region lost some of its attractiveness, however, and by the 1970s had started losing population to other regions, mainly to the south and west. This may be interpreted as a centre-periphery reversal in spatial concentration trends. It should be noted however that Paris has kept a positive migratory balance with the other regions for the more mobile age group, of 20 to 29 years, and is still attracting young people for studies and their first job. The largest losses were primarily people in retirement age, from 60 to 69, and secondary families, people aged 35 to 39 years, with children.

The second shift is a reversal in attraction from the industrial regions of Northern and North-eastern France, which were very attractive until the beginning of the 1960s. These regions started encountering severe losses in population mainly due to residential migration after the mining and steel industries started waning. At the same time regions of the south and west have become increasingly attractive.

Migration flows are important. Between 1990 and 1999, 5.5 million people changed their places of residence, but most of these movements were simple replacements of one individual by another. Only 15 per cent of inter-regional migration contributed to an effective modification of the spatial distribution of population (Baccaïni, 2001). In the case of towns and cities, the efficiency index of migration, i.e. the ratio between net migration and total migration, measured in number of in-migrants plus out-migrants, is approximately 10 per cent (Baccaïni and Pumain, 1996). This finding is important for the theoretical interpretation of the role of migration flows in the evolution of an urban system. As much as 90 or 95 per cent of migration from one city to another is simply movements of substitution, in-migrants come and occupy the positions left by the out-migrants. The high number of individual replacements has to be compared to the small aggregate gain by the cities. The relative persistence of the structure of the urban system is compatible with (and probably determined by) the intense activities at the micro-level.

MINOR SELECTIVE EFFECTS OF MIGRATION
Migration flows entering and leaving cities between two population censuses have been analyzed systematically according to their age structure and by occupational groups (Baccaïni and Pumain, 1996). There is a great resemblance between the proportions of each social group among the in- and out-migrants as well as in the resident population. This means, for instance, that larger proportions of workers enter and leave the manufacturing cities, whereas more senior executives also come to or leave the leading capitals. The spatial pattern of social groups in migration flows almost entirely follows the spatial pattern of social categories in urban agglomerations. However, if

migrations reproduce the spatial division of labour, they reinforce the segregation by age groups between cities. Migration tend to reinforce the aging of cities whose populations are already older on average, especially along the Mediterranean coast. While the aging process due to migration differentials is a regional process, dispersed nodes in the urban network are rejuvenated by the process. The latter are typically cities with secondary and tertiary educational functions that attract students and keep them until they find their first job.

The classification of cities according to their coefficients of migration differentials by age or social group confirms the popularity of Mediterranean cities as retirement centres for the elderly. Except for two or three old mining centres there are no longer any high migration differentials for workers. Cities in the West, the Paris Basin, Northern Alps and Rhône valley tend to attract executives and their employees. Almost all large cities lose executives, which corresponds to their function of the production of a highly skilled population, mainly through their educational institutions.

On the whole, it may be said that migration is determined by the existing socio-economic structure of the urban system, more than it contributes to the change in the city's structure. However, a distinction has to be made between migrations according to age, which are more selective, and migrations according to occupation, which are more adaptive. On the quantitative side, migration still causes differences between cities, even if their share in urban demographic growth, which was dominant until the end of the 1960s, has progressively become less important than natural growth of urban population.

FUTURE TRENDS

The future shape of the urban system can be discussed at different scales of analysis. At the local level, a slow down in demographic growth will not necessarily stop urban sprawl in the long run because the expansion of built-up areas is supported by other processes. The diminution of the mean size of households, the increase in the number of second homes and in new building stock in the urban outskirts, are contributing to development in the urban fringe. The general participation of women in the labour force, longer life expectancy, the growing instability of couples, structural unemployment or the proliferation of less stable modes of employment may also cause a growing demand for new housing. It has been shown that the expansion of built-up areas depends more on the speed of journeys and on the accessibility of cities than upon their demographic growth (Bretagnolle and Paulus, 2001).

THE POSSIBLE IMPACT OF NEW TECHNOLOGIES

The question of the impact of new technologies on urban form is often debated in connection with the location of residence and jobs. Can teleworking have a strong effect on the de-concentration of settlements? In the assessment of the possible impact of teleworking on urban form in France the small share of this type of organization has to be weighed against the size of the rest of the economy. Whatever the way of counting, this share does not go beyond one per cent of the labour force. Is it possible that the new technologies may have a more significant impact on the location of economic activity? This question is raised in France because the former public company (DGT) had a policy of providing infrastructure across the entire country. The French universal network appeared to be very advanced at an early stage. The information and communication technologies (ICT) take part in the process of reorganization of production activities. At the urban and metropolitan scales, they contribute to various processes of restructuring and relocation. Concerning the latter, surveys have shown however that among location decision factors, a good connection to ICT was much less important than the rent price of offices and accessibility to a central position. Connection to ICT plays an important role for the organization of work but not as much for location (Massot, 1995).

The question of the possible effect of teleworking on a diminution of urban traffic by reducing the need for daily journeys is still very controversial. There is no evidence of a substitution between physical transport of people and telecommunications: on the contrary, the more people own telecommunication tools, the more they move! The impact of teleworking may be contradictory; it appears to increase the need to travel as well as reduce it. Perhaps, instead of diminishing or increasing urban traffic, the main effect of teleworking may be to increase the flexibility in the individual movement patterns (Guérois and Pumain, 2001).

In any case, it should be remembered that we are only at the very beginning of the Information Revolution. The automobile was invented a century ago and its effects on the form of cities only became apparent thirty years later. On the other hand the telephone had very little impact on locations and urban forms, whereas it may have contributed to the explosion of mobility. So, many of the suggestions which are now made about the possible impact of new communication technologies are highly speculative.

POLITICAL REGULATION FOR LOCAL URBAN DEVELOPMENT

Political decision making is highly fragmented in France since all of the 36000 communes have the power to approve their own building plans and determine their own construction programmes. Recently, a set of new laws raised the decision making power to a supra-communal management level.

Various tools, competence and tax resources have been provided for setting up a more integrated development strategy for urban areas. Two new types of institutions are created by the law of 12 July 1999. The *communautés d'agglomération* includes a set of contiguous communes which group 50 000 and more people around a central town of at least 15 000 inhabitants. The *communautés urbaines* are defined for larger metropolises only and must include at least half a million inhabitants. The law on urban solidarity and renewal of December 2000 improves the co-ordination between the communes. The political agglomeration is the spatial framework for the management of social housing and public transport, while the *aire urbaine* becomes the framework for spatial planning and road transportation. More generally, one major objective of the law is to promote the spatial and social cohesion of urban areas by limiting their outward expansion and by ensuring housing rights. The question of urban sprawl is taken into account by a modification of the town planning documents which includes a better articulation between urbanization, housing and transportation policies, and by new local policies for collective transport. It is clear that a complete overhaul of the transportation system is needed before a significant containment of urban sprawl can be achieved. At the moment the responses are only technical. Public transport policies are being discussed as regulators of the transportation system, while they would only be really efficient if the social values in our urban world were to be re-examined. New hopes are coming from other ways of playing with time inside the urban realm, but currently there are only a few local associations that negotiate for different time schedules in firms in France compared to Italy for instance.

THE IMPACT OF THE EUROPEAN UNION

The most obvious consequence of the opening up of frontiers and the globalization of the economy is the powerful trend to metropolization and to concentration in the higher levels of the urban hierarchy. Despite transformations in the political and economic sphere, the higher levels of the urban hierarchy remain surprisingly stable (Cattan et al.,1994) and significant changes can only be expected over very long periods. It would be unrealistic, for example, to expect to see a change in the dominant positions of London and Paris in the European urban system. Except for Paris, French cities are small compared to second level cities of neighbouring large European countries. In the beginning, the opening up of inter-urban competition at the European level might therefore be detrimental to most of the French regional capitals. At a lower level, an indication of the degree to which cities participate in the spatial re-organization of economic activities at the European level is derived from the location of multinational firms (Rozenblat and Pumain, 1993). Only approximately twenty French cities have benefited from this process, since only agglomerations above 200 000 inhabitants have until now attracted such firms. Metropolization trends are likely to continue over the next decades, even though a wider diffusion of international urban functions is expected over the long run.

Other urban changes will be affected by the geographical location of cities within Europe, rather than size. Spatial proximity is still important despite our world of networks! *Ceteris paribus*, cities located in the vicinity of international borders have until now been more active in the integration of their activities at the European level. This may prove to be favourable for spatial re-equilibrium on French territory, but at a larger scale France may lose some of the advantages of its relatively central position as new countries are being added to the old core of the European community.

CONCLUSION

The recent evolution of the French urban system is an example of how their general trends of the global economic and social evolution and banal dynamic are interfering with the specific inherited features of a particular urban system. This 'path dependency' is by no means a sign of inertia within the system but it rather demonstrates its ability to adapt to changes that occur as a result of reactive adjustments to different parts in the system. This, of course, should be linked in more detail to the behaviour of urban actors that are mutually informed of what the others are doing through the network system in the urban system.

Although strong demographic and economic growth have dominated the urban development scene during the second half of twentieth century, it was their spectacular spatial expansion that stirred up attention among urban analysts. During the last decade of the twentieth century, the focus in the minds of Europeans has shifted towards more compact cities and effective measures to protect the environment. A new attraction of urban centres is visible in changes in the population growth rates. It is by no means a 'revival' since there was no real 'urban decline' before, but it may express a will to re-equilibrate the presence of activities and residence in central locations. A series of policy measures have been devised to remove two major obstacles that have impeded the effective and consistent management of urban sprawl in France until now, (i) reducing political fragmentation in decision-making by moving the decision-making power on town and transport planning matters to inter-communal structures, and (ii) reducing the dominant role of the private car in urban transportation by developing policies that favour public transport systems. The articulation between policies coming from different agencies at various levels of decision making still seems to be a major challenge for French urban planning authorities.

Despite the certitudes which are claimed in some political declarations,[7] one has to be cautious in the interpretation of urban sprawl and moreover in its evaluation. There is for instance an obvious lack of knowledge about the effects of the form and structure of cities on their economic development. On the one hand, comparative studies have to be promoted to improve the scientific quality of social and political debates. Such studies may reveal, as our analysis of the French case suggests, that because European cities, like other cities of the world, are adapting to a global process, it does not mean they necessarily have to become similar to the North American cities which initiated the process. Urban sprawl is just one innovation that is transforming cities, and as for the use of motor cars, it has a major impact on their space-time dimensions for social interactions. There are many other innovations to come, and some will probably be related to communication technologies. Whatever form they take, they will have to correspond with what societies want as part of an urban way of life, and they may come from elsewhere than America. With regard to this, the European urban model could make a new contribution to world geographical diversity, which should perhaps remain an objective, and there should also be a consensus around the need for biodiversity.

Acknowledgment: I wish to thank Fabien Paulus for his invaluable help in preparing data and figures.

REFERENCES

Allen, P. (1997), *Cities and regions as self-organising systems: Models of complexity*, Amsterdam: Gordon and Breach.

Baccaïni, B. (2001), 'Les migrations internes en France de 1990 à 1999', *l'Appel de l'Ouest: Economie et Statistique*, **344**, 39-79.

Baccaïni, B. and D. Pumain (1996), 'Migration in France between 1975 and 1990: A limited degree of decentralisation', in P. Rees, J. Stillwell, M. Kupiszewski and A. Convey (eds), *Population Migration in the European Union*, London: Wiley, pp. 192-206.

Bairoch, P. (1996), 'Cinq millénaires de croissance urbaine', in Sachs I. (ed.), *Quelles villes pour quel développement*, Paris: PUF.

Bretagnolle, A., D. Pumain and C. Rozenblat (1998), 'Space-time contraction and the dynamics of urban systems', *Cybergeo*, **61**, 12.

Bretagnolle, A., F. Paulus and D. Pumain (2001), 'Time and space scales in the measurement of urban growth', *Cybergeo*.

---

[7] For instance, in its meeting in April 2000 the G8 regarded urban sprawl as the main obstacle to sustainable development.

Cattan, N., D. Pumain, C. Rozenblat and T. Saint-Julien (1994), *Le système des villes européennes*. Paris: Anthropos, coll.Villes, pp. 201.

Pred, A (1977), *City systems in advanced societies*, London: Hutchison.

Pumain, D. (2000), 'Settlement systems in the evolution', *Geografiska Annaler*, **82b** (2), 73-87.

Pumain, D. and F. Moriconi-Ebrard (1997), 'City size distributions and metropolisation', *GeoJournal*, **43** (4), 307-314.

Pumain, D. and T. Saint-Julien (1984), 'Evolving structure of the French urban system', *Urban Geography*, **5** (4), 308-325.

Pumain, D. and T. Saint-Julien (eds) (1996), *Urban networks in Europe*. Paris: John Libbey-INED, Congresses and Colloquia, 15, 252 p.

Rozenblat, C. and D. Pumain (1993), 'The location of multinational firms in the European urban system', *Urban Studies*, **10**, 1691-1709.

Chapter 7

Urbanization in Germany Before and After Unification

P. Gans and F. J. Kemper

INTRODUCTION

At the end of 1998 Germany registered a population of 82 million, 71.8 per cent of them living in settlements of more than 10,000 people and 30.7 per cent in cities with more than 100,000 inhabitants. Figure 7.1 verifies the relatively high proportion of the population in medium sized settlements. The relation between rank and size of the larger cities in Figure 7.2 indicates an almost ideal distribution according to Zipf's model. Berlin with 3.44 million inhabitants, the biggest city in Germany, cannot be regarded as a primate city. Hamburg (1.70 million), Munich (1.21 million), Cologne (0.96 million) and Frankfurt/Main (0.64 million) fill positions 2 to 5 in the rank-size order. There are several reasons why a functional distinction can be drawn between these centres, all of which are centres of international importance (Blotevogel, 1998).

Firstly, in comparison to many other European countries, Germany is a relatively young national state. Before 1871 Germany was largely regarded as a linguistic-culturally defined community with strong regional identities. The capitals of former historically independent territories such as Heidelberg, Weimar or Gotha and their associated local urban systems, which together form part of the current German urban system, resulted in an extraordinarily wide variety of regional city types in terms of historical heritage, function and size.

Secondly, traces of this historically based territorial organization are still recognizable in the present federal structure of Germany, with relatively positive prospects for the state capitals, for example Erfurt, Kiel, Mainz or Schwerin.

Figure 7.1 Proportion of population by settlement size, 1998

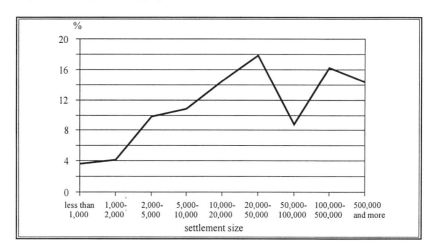

Source: Statistisches Bundesamt (ed.) (2000), *Statistisches Jahrbuch 2000 der Bundesrepublik Deutschland,* Wiesbaden: Metzler-Poeschel

Figure 7.2 Rank-size distribution of cities with at least 100,000 inhabitants, 1939 and 1998

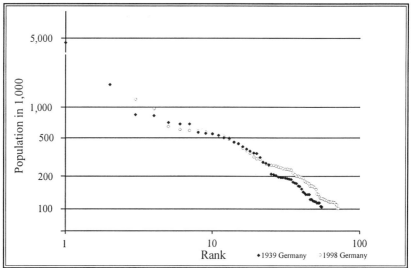

Source: Laufende Raumbeobachtung; Statistisches Bundesamt (ed.) (2000), *Statistisches Jahrbuch 2000 der Bundesrepublik Deutschland,* Wiesbaden: Metzler-Poeschel; calculations by the authors

Thirdly, the Second World War, provoked by Nazi Germany, resulted in the division of the German Empire and Berlin in two states with different social, economic and political systems, the Federal Republic of Germany (FRG) and the German Democratic Republic (GDR) with Bonn and East Berlin as respective capitals. This had a significant impact on the urban system of unified Germany. After 1945 the divided Berlin lost its functional importance in favour of West German urban centres, especially Hamburg, Munich, Cologne/Düsseldorf/Bonn, and Frankfurt/Main. Leipzig, in East Germany, fell from the 5th position in rank in 1939 overall to the 15th position in 1998 by population. Before 1945, the city was the seat of the Constitutional Court of the German Empire and as a city of fairs was well known world-wide. Subsequent to the division of the country after The Second World War these functions were moved to the West German cities of Frankfurt/Main (book fair), Hanover (industry fair) and Karlsruhe (Constitutional Court). Today, the citizens of Leipzig are struggling to regain the city's former status as a centre of national or even international importance. Other cities in the former GDR that have been experiencing functional problems and difficulties sustaining their erstwhile levels of development after unification are:

❑ those that lost their administrative functions as district capitals before unification,

❑ those that lost a large part of their economic base, and

❑ those that lagged behind during the time of the GDR.

Although the rank-size distribution of German cities may appear well-balanced overall, the urban systems of the Eastern and Western parts of the country are neither functionally nor spatially balanced, as a consequence of the social and political upheavals caused by the period between The Second World War and the unification of 1990.

The cities in West Germany show a relatively even spatial distribution between Hamburg in the north and Munich in the south (Figure 7.3). There are two areas with an exceptional concentration of cities, one along the river Rhine from the Swiss border via Karlsruhe, Mannheim, Mainz, Bonn and Cologne to Duisburg in the Ruhr conurbation, and the other from west to east along the zone between the low mountain range and the North German lowlands stretching from Aachen via Cologne/Düsseldorf, the Ruhr conurbation, Hanover to Halle/Leipzig and Dresden. In the remaining areas large centres such as Berlin, Bremen, Nuremberg and Stuttgart are evenly dispersed.

In East Germany the urban agglomerations are more concentrated in the south. The regions around Halle/Leipzig, Dresden, and Chemnitz are in stark

Figure 7.3 Cities by size and types of regions according to settlement structure

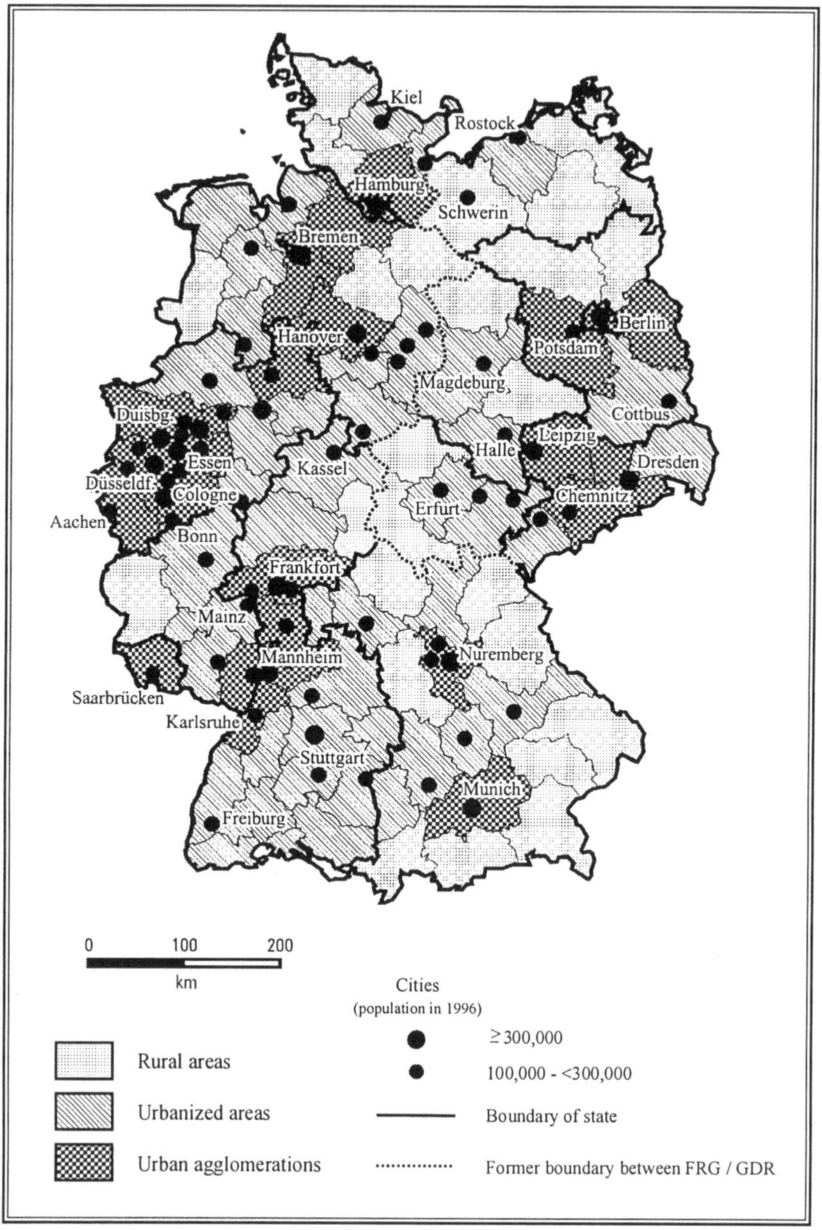

Source: According to Heineberg, 2000

contrast to the sparsely populated rural areas in the north. The settlement structure displays more pronounced regional disparities between rural areas and urban agglomerations than in West Germany. Urbanized regions possess an intermediary position regarding the population density and the size of the core city which could be regarded as secondary in a national context (Figure 7.3).

The structure of large urban agglomerations in Germany is typically either monocentric or polycentric. Examples of the first type are Berlin, Hamburg and Munich, where the biggest city dominates all other towns in its immediate hinterland in terms of size and functions. Examples of the second kind are centres such as the Rhine-Main and Rhine-Neckar agglomeration and the Rhine-Ruhr conurbation. These agglomerations consist of several large cities with specialized and complementary functions which have their origin in different historical periods. The biggest agglomeration, the Rhine-Ruhr conurbation, has more than 11 million inhabitants and consists 'of several fused but differently structured city regions' (Blotevogel and Hommel, 1980: 157) like that of Bonn, Cologne, Düsseldorf, Duisburg, Essen and Dortmund.

Despite all the transformations that have occurred in Germany since the Second World War, the urban system of Germany today is based on two epochs: the period of town establishment from the 11th to the 13th century and the period of industrialization since the mid-19th century. During the latter phase locational advantages in terms of natural resources and communication played a vital role in the evolution of the urban system. Cities without such advantages stagnated and even shrank in size.

INDUSTRIALIZATION AND THE DEVELOPMENT OF THE URBAN SYSTEM UNTIL THE SECOND WORLD WAR

As in other European countries, industrialization in Germany was closely linked with urban population and economic growth. Industrial development caused profound demographic, social and economic changes in society. During the most intensive phase of industrialization, between the foundation of the German Empire in 1871 and the outbreak of World War I in 1914, the population increased from 41 million to 64.6 million with an average growth rate of 12 per 1,000 annually (Figure 7.4). The beginning of the demographic transition caused a maximum growth rate of 15 per 1,000 during the first decade of the 20th century, due to declining mortality and only a small downward tendency of fertility. Figure 7.4 shows how emigration, as a result of population pressure, was more than offset by a high birth rate before 1910. Subsequently, emigration started to decline because of employment opportunities that were caused by industrial development.

Figure 7.4 Population development in the German Empire, 1871-1940

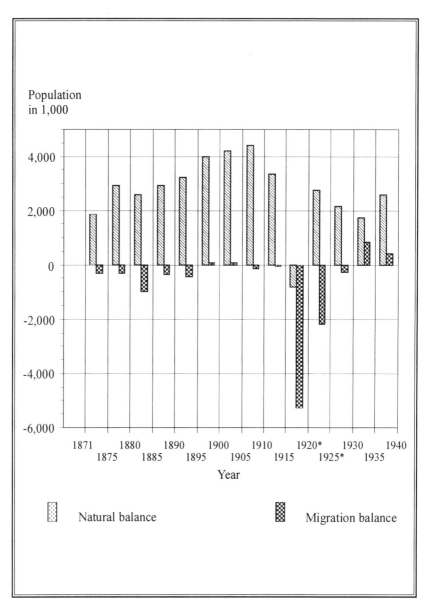

Notes: * 1920 and 1925 losses by territorial assignments included

Source: Marschalck, 1984, p. 146

Soon after World War I fertility rates started to decline markedly. Despite a rising life expectancy the annual growth rate declined to approximately 6 per 1,000 during the 1920s and 30s. This decline in fertility rates was caused by factors such as the modernization of society, shifting the emphasis from agriculture to industry, compulsory education, the prohibition of child labour, the introduction of health and retirement insurance, the general rise in living standards, and the beginning of the emancipation of women. In the process, social advancement depended increasingly on the individual's personal abilities and level of education. In order to improve the education of their children, parents reduced family sizes. Fertility decline can, therefore, be interpreted as behavioural adjustment of couples to social and economic change. Signs of this attitude were first observed in the large cities but soon also took hold in smaller cities down the urban hierarchy. As a result of increasing competition for jobs in the private and public sector in the larger cities, people in the upper income brackets started limiting the number of their children in order to improve their chances of advancement, while lower income groups reduced their family sizes in order to survive in the urban environment. Traditional values and norms about the size of the family lost their influence. In this regard, the decrease in the fertility rate can be interpreted as an innovation process in the society's generative behavior. Declining birth rates and a rising life expectancy changed the population structure. The proportion of children below the age of 15 years declined from 34.3 per cent of the total population in 1871 to 24.2 per cent in 1933. At the same time the ratio of people above 65 years of age increased from 4.6 per cent to 7.1 per cent, and the average household size declined from 4.64 in 1871 to 3.27 in 1939.

The importance of industrialization corresponded with the increase in urbanization. The proportion of the population living in cities with at least 100,000 inhabitants amounted to only 4.8 per cent in 1871. In 1910 this percentage increased to 21.3 per cent and by the beginning of the Second World War, in 1939 it was 31.6 per cent. At the other end of the scale the (rural) population declined in municipalities of less than 2,000 inhabitants. These trends show how spatially concentrated the population became during the intensive phase of industrialization between 1871 and 1910. The number of the large cities increased from 8 in 1871 to 59 in 1939, and the census results of 1907 indicate that natural population growth, urban coalition and, above all, migration gains were the three most significant causal factors in this urban growth pattern. The percentages of long distance migrants that were attracted to cities such as Berlin, Gelsenkirchen and Dortmund (see Table 7.1) confirm the dominant position of these cities in the urban system at the time. Before World War I the capital and the Ruhr region were preferred destinations of migrants coming from the former German regions east of Oder

Table 7.1 Origins of the population in large cities of Germany, 1907

City	inhabitants born in respective city (in %)	short distance migrants (in %)	long distance migrants (in %)
Königsberg	40.8	50.6	7.4
Berlin	40.5	18.0	39.1
Kiel	32.2	30.5	35.6
Hamburg	48.2	22.2	26.4
Gelsenkirchen	38.6	28.5	31.2
Dortmund	41.9	30.7	25.1
Aachen	65.4	24.7	5.7
Stuttgart	41.5	45.3	10.4
All cities	42.4	32.0	22.9

Source: Bähr, 1997, p. 337

and Neisse. In 1939 four of the eleven cities with 500,000 inhabitants or more were situated in the Ruhr region. These four cities had a total population of 2.3 million which exceeded that of Hamburg (1.7 million in 1939). The high proportion of long distance migrants to Hamburg and Kiel can be ascribed to specific reasons. As a seaport, Hamburg was the last intermediate stop on the continent for many emigrants to destinations abroad, while many civil servants and soldiers were transferred to Kiel because of its naval base. The migrants to Stuttgart and Aachen originated predominantly from surrounding areas, which suggests a less dominant position in the urban system before World War I, despite the fact that Stuttgart had only a little less than 500,000 inhabitants in 1939.

The rank-size distribution of the German urban system at the outbreak of the Second World War confirms the dominance of Berlin over the other cities. Its population was approximately 2.6 times larger than that of Hamburg, the second largest city in the country (Figure 7.2). Then there was a group of seven regional centres with at least 500,000 inhabitants, like Munich, Cologne and Düsseldorf, to which the cities in the Ruhr region viz, Leipzig, Dresden, Frankfort/Main and Stuttgart were assigned. According to an analysis of Blotevogel (1998), Berlin topped the German urban hierarchy because of its importance in administration, economy, culture and science.

From a spatial point of view, industrialization began during the nineteenth century in Saxony and Rhineland-Westphalia. The development of raw material-dependent coal and steel industries in the Ruhr-conurbation led to the development of a number of large cities in the area especially after the founding of the German Empire in 1871. The political and economic unification of Prussia, Bavaria and Württemberg and other independent states, required their spatial integration. This was achieved by expanding the railway and waterway network in the national territory. During this period Berlin became the most important city in Germany (Blotevogel and Hommel, 1980).

However, transportation costs and the dependence on raw materials started to decrease as a result of technical advances. The locational and agglomerative advantages of the Ruhr area began to diminish significantly after 1918, while other regions far from the Ruhr such as Rhein-Main (Frankfurt/Main), Rhein-Neckar (Mannheim) and Mittlerer Neckar (Stuttgart) gained importance (Petzina, 1987). A highly exhausted labour market, the intertwinement of the interests of municipal administrations and large enterprises of coal mining and the steel industry, bottleneck problems with regard to green field development and to facilities such as the traffic network, power and water supply, made it difficult for innovative small or medium-sized businesses to settle in the Ruhr conurbation,[1] while southern Germany, particularly Württemberg, started to attract these businesses between the two World Wars.

After the Second World War the trend continued. Many businesses relocated from the divided Berlin because of political reasons, to the American occupied zone, especially to Frankfurt/Main (banks) and Munich (electronics). Other factors that played a part include the specific promotion of enterprises requiring intensive research by the federal state government of Bavaria, a strategic location within the European Community and non-economic factors, such as easy access to leisure amenities and areas of natural beauty (Kunz, 1986). As the traffic network expanded and new technologies developed, constraints on industrial location diminished, and non-economic factors gained importance. The Munich area profited greatly from this.

---

[1] Small and medium-sized businesses are usually better equipped to develop new products than large industries with inflexible production and labour structures designed for standardized mass production (Sinz and Strubelt, 1986; Häussermann and Siebel, 1986).

FEDERAL REPUBLIC OF GERMANY (UNTIL 1990)
DEMOGRAPHIC AND SOCIO-ECONOMIC DEVELOPMENT

The continuation of the urbanization process in Germany during the twentieth century has been strongly marked by singular events and political upheavals. As a consequence of the Second World War, Germany lost large areas east of the Oder and Neisse rivers to Poland and the Soviet Union. More than 10 million refugees and expellees flocked to the newly established German states from these and other East European states between 1945 and 1950. During the 1950 census of the Federal Republic of Germany, 7.9 million expellees and 1.6 million refugees were registered from the Soviet occupied zone (including East Germany), a total of 20 per cent of the entire population. The spatial distribution of this population was characterized by striking regional disparities. The rural areas of Schleswig-Holstein, eastern Lower Saxony and eastern Bavaria attracted most of these people. Since most of the war damages occurred in cities and metropolitan areas, a substantial part of the urban population, particularly women and children, were evacuated to rural regions during the war. As a result of this the population of the FRG, excluding West Berlin, increased from 40.2 million to 48.7 million between 1939 and 1950. This equalled an increase of 21 per cent in the population, yet the population of the large cities decreased by more than 3 per cent.

During the 1950s the 'de-urbanization' of the Second World War period was followed by a new round of urbanization caused by large-scale urban and industrial reconstruction. Many displaced persons and refugees were officially resettled from Schleswig-Holstein, Lower Saxony and Bavaria to areas such as Northrhine-Westphalia, and from the Ruhr-conurbation to Baden-Württemberg and Rhineland-Palatinate. In 1950 a high percentage of expellees was unemployed, but later during the 1950s and early 1960s, due to high occupational mobility (often downwards) and a change to work in manufacturing industries, many of them were assimilated into the labour market. Moreover, from 1950 to 1961 more than 3 million people moved from the GDR to West Germany because of political and economic reasons (Köllmann, 1983).

After August 1961, when the Wall in Berlin was erected and the border between East and West Germany was blocked, the migration flows from East to West suddenly stopped. Yet the FRG, like other West European countries, still experienced shortages in unskilled and semi-skilled labourers, particularly in the Fordist mass production sector and in certain sections of the personal service sector. To alleviate these shortages, 'guest workers' from Mediterranean countries were recruited. From 1968 to 1973 as many as 2.4 million guest workers migrated to the FRG. At first, in the early 1960s, these foreign migrants moved to southern Germany, then to metropolitan areas of West Germany and eventually to northern Germany and West Berlin. The largest concentrations of foreign workers were found in the cities, metropolitan areas and industrial regions (Giese, 1978). During the oil crisis in 1973 all bilateral guest worker agreements with the countries of origin were cancelled. Many foreign workers returned to their home areas. Others stayed in Germany and were followed by their families, a process that unintentionally turned temporary migrants into permanent residents.

Towards the late 1960s the birth rates of both German countries started to decline. In West Germany, after the net reproduction rate reached a peak of 1.14 in 1964 it started to decline steadily from 0.95 in 1970 to 0.65 in the late 1970s. Since then it has showed only slight variations. Despite the inflow of foreign migrants to Germany the population stagnated during the period between the censuses of 1970 and 1987. By the late 1980s the situation changed again. The dramatic political events in Germany and the former communist countries of Eastern Europe led to large scale migration from East to West Germany, as was the case during and directly after the Second World War. In 1989, when the borders between East and West Germany were re-opened, nearly 400,000 persons moved from the GDR to the FRG. In addition, many ethnic Germans from different countries of eastern Europe came to Germany. By 1996 the latter already totalled 2.6 million. Other migration flows to Germany consisted of refugees and asylum applicants (Münz et al., 1997). By means of controlled resettlements within the country a large proportion of refugees as well as ethnic Germans were redistributed evenly throughout the country.

From 1970 to 1990 the FRG was transformed from an industrial society to a post-industrial service-dominated economy. The proportion of the workforce in the secondary sector rose from 43 per cent in 1950 to 48 per cent in 1970. During the 1970s and 1980s de-industrialization began to occur, beginning with the large areas of coal, iron and steel industries of the Ruhr conurbation and the Saar area. By 1991 the proportion of the secondary sector declined to 40 per cent, whilst the tertiary sector had risen from 33 per cent in 1950 to 43 per cent in 1970 and 56 per cent in 1991. Not only large cities and urban agglomerations were affected by the economic restructuring. Rural areas also lost large numbers of agricultural workers resulting in a decline in the percentage of the primary sector in the FRG from 25 per cent in 1950 to 5 per cent in 1980.

POPULATION DEVELOPMENT AND SETTLEMENT SYSTEM

In this section the influence of the demographic and socio-economic developments on the settlement structure of the FRG is investigated, based on the West German counties (Kreise) which are homogeneous in settlement structure (Bundesamt für Bauwesen und Raumordnung, 1999). The counties are aggregated to functional planning regions, discerning three types of regions: urban agglomerations, urbanized regions, and rural regions (Figure 7.3).[2] Changes in the population of each of these regional types between censuses are shown in Figure 7.5.

Figure 7.5 Population change by type of region and time period, West Germany

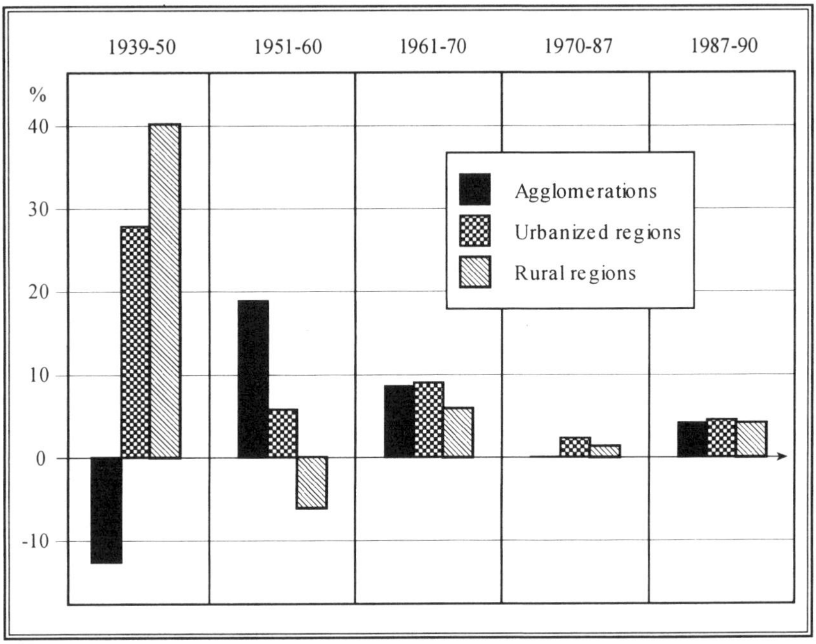

Source: Laufende Raumbeobachtung

The first phase between 1939 and 1950 mirrors the population change of the post-war era with a large degree of relocation from destroyed cities and urban agglomerations to more sparsely populated regions. This process of de-urbanization, triggered by political-military events, was followed by re-urbanization caused by the subsequent economic recovery and the reconstruction of cities. During the latter period the urban agglomerations and urbanized regions gained population through internal and international migration whereas rural areas only gained population through natural growth. The 1970-1987 period is characterized by a shift in industrial activities away

---

[2] In this classification urban agglomerations are regarded as large metropolitan areas while urbanized regions are areas containing cities which could be regarded as secondary in a national context.

from Fordist to post-Fordist production. This shift was also associated with the deconcentration of industrial activities and the expansion of the tertiary sector in large cities. In the process the urbanized regions showed a marginal over-all gain in their population. Also rural regions showed some increase whilst urban agglomerations began to stagnate. Finally, from 1987 to 1990, the population increase in the country was evenly distributed among the different regional categories due to the application of regional quotas for in-migrants from abroad.

Indications are that the disruptions affecting the population, economy and settlement system of West Germany during the Second World War had largely been overcome by the late 1950s. From then on, the country entered a period of relative normalization and stabilization. As can be seen in Figure 7.5 the population of the intermediate sized city regions grew faster after 1961 than the other two categories. In terms of the differential urbanization model (Geyer, 1996) West Germany entered the polarization reversal phase during the 1970s and 1980s after a transition from urbanization to polarization reversal in the 1960s. However, it should be stressed that the regional types were over-bounded which makes the possible obscuring of micro changes within the regional boundaries more than likely.

Figure 7.6 shows the changes in the shares of the population of the three types of region. Except for the period directly after the Second World War

Figure 7.6 Proportion of population by year and type of region

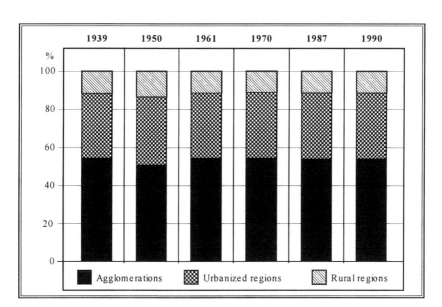

Source: Laufende Raumbeobachtung

the shares have remained remarkably stable, which, according to Blotevogel and Hommel (1980), and Blotevogel and Möller (1992) is a general feature of the West German urban system as a whole. Between 1939 and 1990 the population of West Germany increased from 40 million to over 61 million, but the proportion of agglomerations and of rural regions only slightly declined in favour of the urbanized regions over the period. While the shares of the rural regions increased before the 1960s, the agglomerations lost ground slightly after the 1970s.

Despite the stability, important relocations occurred within the different groups of regions. County types are used to demonstrate these subtle changes in Figure 7.7. The figure shows that the phases of de-urbanization in the 1940s and of urbanization in the 1950s were accompanied by corresponding shifts between cores and suburban rings. In the 1960s the growth of core cities fell behind the growth in suburban areas, while in the 1970s and early 1980s core cities lost population, larger cities faster than smaller ones. West Germany is therefore characterized by suburbanization after the 1960s. Applying the descriptive model by Klaassen et al. (1981) which only differentiates between metropolitan and non-metropolitan areas, the urbanization of the 1950s was followed by a phase of suburbanization in the 1960s and later by inter-regional de-concentrations of de-urbanization.

To trace the transition from suburbanization to de-urbanization in more detail, it is necessary to distinguish between population redistribution trends in the 1970s and the 1980s. Several studies have shown that intra-regional de-concentration with population losses in the core cities and gains in the suburban zones have shifted to losses in the agglomerations overall while rural regions gained population. Both Kontuly and Vogelsang (1988) and Kanaroglou and Braun (1992) demonstrated how internal migration patterns changed from suburbanization to counter-urbanization around 1980, as has been experienced in some other Western industrialized countries since the early 1960s. However, this was not a steady process in West Germany. Trends of counter-urbanization and even re-urbanization strengthened and weakened all the time. To study these changes in more detail, annual data series on internal migration flows are very helpful.

INTERNAL MIGRATION PATTERNS IN THE 1980S.

To enable one to compare the annual changes in internal in- and out-migration in West Germany (old Länder) after 1980, the data are presented in terms of the 'prognostic regions' of the Federal Office for Building and Regional Planning (Kemper, 1999). These areas consist of all counties within a planning region which are homogeneous in settlement structure. After excluding counties with extreme values, due to large agglomerations of ethnic Germans and asylum seekers, the correlation coefficients of successive years

Figure 7.7 *Population change in West Germany by types of county*

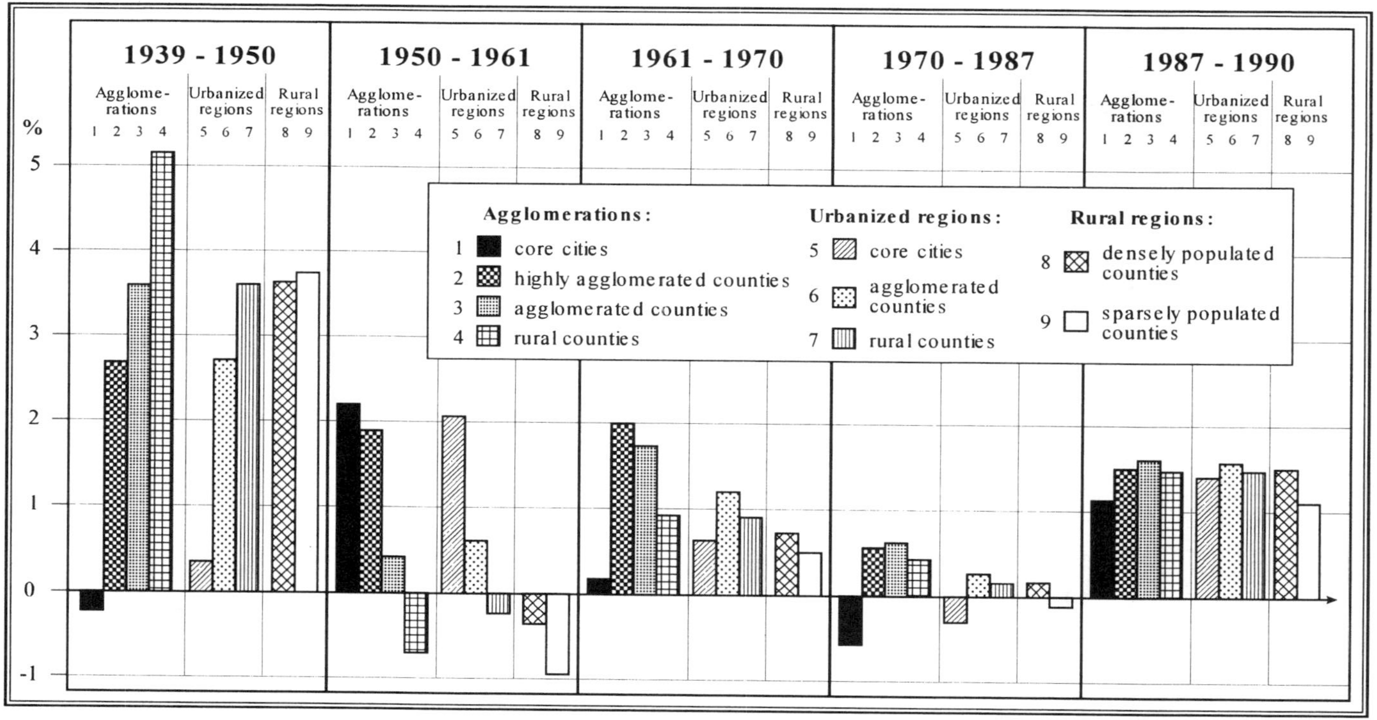

Source: Laufende Raumbeobachtung

161

were calculated to measure the similarity of the internal migration patterns of two successive years. These coefficients were obtained as part of a factor analysis containing four factors, each one interpreted as a different phase of migration in West Germany.

The first phase started in 1980 and ended in 1983 and is characterized by intra-regional as well as inter-regional de-concentration, typical of the counter-urbanization process. The suburban zones and rural regions recorded migration gains while the core cities lost population (Table 7.2). Since the mid-1980s the pattern has changed. The migration balance has now turned negative in urbanized and peripheral (rural) regions, while in-migration has

Table 7.2 Rate of migration balance with reference to type of counties and time period (West Germany or old Länder)

Type of county	1980-83	1985-87	1989-91	1992-96
Agglomerations				
core city	·-3.53	-0.54	0.47	-3.26
highly agglomerated counties	1.45	1.98	3.88	2.13
agglomerated counties	4.10	3.04	7.73	6.87
rural counties	4.00	1.51	6.68	9.24
Urbanized regions				
core city	-0.85	-2.27	1.99	-2.95
agglomerated counties	1.61	0.07	4.00	4.91
rural counties	1.07	-0.67	5.53	6.31
Rural regions				
densely populated counties	1.83	0.46	4.43	4.67
sparsely populated counties	0.75	-0.91	3.61	4.95

Source: Laufende Raumbeobachtung; calculations by the authors

exceeded out-migration in metropolitan areas. Gains in metropolitan areas were not uniform, however. Agglomerations and core cities in southern Germany gained population while core cities in the central and northern parts of West Germany kept on losing population. The re-urbanization in southern Germany is associated with favourable economic development conditions. The third phase between 1989 and 1990 is characterized by migration gains in all the regions of West Germany, even in the old industrialized Ruhr conurbation after decades of migration losses. The overall population growth was caused by the inflow of migrants from East Germany and abroad.

When the migration of the different age groups over the study period is considered the relative stability in the trends is an outstanding feature. Younger age groups tend to move towards the core cities and the highly agglomerated counties whereas older people prefer less densely inhabited areas, the peripheral hinterlands and rural regions. Yet the migration patterns of the 25 to 29 year age group changed markedly over the period. A factor analysis of the net migration patterns of this group showed four phases which are fairly similar to the general periods for the total population (Table 7.3).

Table 7.3   Rate of migration balance of 25 to 29 year olds (10,000) with reference to type of county and time period (West Germany or old Länder)

Type of county	1980-85	1987-88	1990-92	1994-96
Agglomerations				
core city	-6.5	6.8	1.8	2.0
highly agglomerated counties	6.9	4.2	4.6	1.9
agglomerated counties	8.5	4.9	11.5	5.6
rural counties	7.3	-0.8	0.4	10.4
Urbanized regions				
core city	-19.2	-10.2	-3.8	-16.9
agglomerated counties	2.1	-2.4	4.3	1.1
rural counties	4.1	-4.4	5.1	3.7
Rural regions				
densely populated counties	3.0	-3.1	2.3	-0.3
sparsely populated counties	2.8	-7.3	0.2	-0.5

Source: Laufende Raumbeobachtung; calculations by the authors

During the first half of the 1980s the group left the inner areas of the agglomeration areas, large and medium core cities while gains were recorded in the suburban rings. The distribution changed significantly in 1987 and 1988. Most people in this age group moved to the south as part of the above-mentioned period of southerly directed re-urbanization. Only the counties of the agglomerative areas had positive balances with the highest values in the core cities. This re-urbanization continued also in the early 1990s after unification. Therefore, the migration patterns of the age group from 25 to 29 mirrors the changing internal migration balances of the population. On the one hand, this group, which largely consists of people seeking employment, seems to react to changing conditions in the labour market. On the other hand, immigrants are over-represented in this age-group, especially during the early 1990s, and their migrations patterns are heavily influenced by the official redistribution policy for immigrants in the country.

FACTORS EXPLAINING SPATIAL DE-CONCENTRATION IN THE SETTLEMENT SYSTEM

To explain changes in the population and settlement redistribution special attention should be given to recent de-concentration trends because the transition from an industrialized to a post-industrial society seems to be accompanied by spatial de-concentration. De-concentration occurs at two different levels, intra- and interregional, and different factors are responsible for each of the two forms of de-concentration. Whilst suburbanization as one of the forms of intraregional de-concentration has been documented in detail in the literature (Gaebe, 1987), the more recent interregional de-urbanization and polarization reversal trends deserve particular attention.

The first important group of explanatory factors relates to economic restructuring and a new regional division of labour. It is well known that the process of de-industrialization has been associated with declining numbers of workers, employees and population in many old-industrial areas, particularly metropolitan areas and large industrial districts like the Ruhr conurbation. In contrast, less densely inhabited counties in West Germany have experienced a growth of employment opportunities in the manufacturing sector since the 1970s, as a result of savings in production costs, and as a consequence, there are proportionally more employment opportunities in many of the rural areas in the secondary sector than in the metropolitan areas. This corresponds with the thesis of a new spatial division of labour which according to Fielding (1989) is partially responsible for counter-urbanization. Within the secondary sector, headquarters, management functions and research and development are concentrated in big cities and metropolitan areas, whereas routine work has been shifted to rural areas, or to other countries with low wages.

Apart from de-industrialization, there is also a process of re-industrialization. New industries using advanced technologies based on flexible economies of scope are typically not found in old contaminated industrial areas but in regions which offer a combination of good accessibility and high quality human capital and amenities. In the FRG such regions are over-represented in the southern states, with the consequence of a north-south shift in economic growth and job opportunities which attract migrants (Friedrichs et al., 1987). Moreover, in the 1980s growth of employment has been particularly high in the suburban rings of metropolitan areas and in rural regions, especially in the south (Irmen and Blach, 1994).

Residential preferences for low-density housing, more rural residential areas and attractive landscapes are also responsible for de-concentration. In representative surveys usually a large majority of the population vote against big cities as preferred places for living in favour of towns and small settlements. However, in the FRG there are only few detailed studies about the role of residential preferences in migration decisions. Many of such studies focus on the elderly and within this group environmental factors and amenities are important determinants of retirement migration (Friedrich, 1995; Kemper and Kuls, 1986). Obviously, the relationship between productionism and environmentalism changes during the life course. Yet it seems that in recent times more people are trying to combine both factors in their choice of location for work, housing and family life. Whether such combinations are possible depends, among other factors, on the structure and growth of regional labour markets and on changes in the business cycle. In the FRG there is a general positive relationship between the growth rate of the GDP and the degree of internal migration (Kemper, 1997). Furthermore, it is argued that the changing preferences of the 25-29 year old migrants during the second half of the 1980s in favour of metropolitan areas and big cities are related to an economic boom and growth of job opportunities during this time (Kontuly and Schön, 1994).

The interregional de-concentration of population and jobs would not have been possible without strong improvements of transportation and infrastructure in many rural areas, often assisted by public regional policy programmes. Claval (1990) argues that outdated center-periphery models should not be used any more to describe regional developments within industrialized countries which normally have as many centres as there are metropolitan areas. This is particularly relevant to West Germany whose urban system can be regarded as spatially decentralized and regionally balanced. The former dominance of Berlin in the urban system has not been taken over by another city because important functions of West Berlin have been distributed to several West German cities. Because of its isolated location, West Berlin lost its more than a quarter of its population between 1939 and 1987. Moreover, as Laux (1990) has shown, according to employment in higher-order services, West Berlin ranked number 6 in 1987, whilst each of the top three cities, i.e. Hamburg, Munich and Frankfurt/Main, had more than twice the number of employed persons Berlin had at the time. As a consequence of the Second World War, 'the Federal Republic of Germany is an extreme case of decentralization of all leading functions' (Schöller et al., 1984: 194). Obviously, the historical development of the country as well as the federal structure of the FRG with many important state capitals has contributed to this de-centralization.

GERMAN DEMOCRATIC REPUBLIC

DEMOGRAPHIC AND SOCIO-ECONOMIC DEVELOPMENT

As a consequence of the Second World War, two German states were founded in 1949: the FRG was located in the American, British and French occupied zone, the GDR in the Soviet zone. Conditions for development were substantially less favourable in the GDR than in the FRG. The Soviet Union's socio-economic model, which differed fundamentally from that of the West, was one of the important causes for these unfavourable conditions (Strubelt, 1996, p.19). Another factor was the way in which the boundaries were drawn. Firstly, the GDR covered the centrally situated areas of the 1937-version of the former German Empire, extending from the Baltic Sea in the north down to the low mountain ranges in the south. Berlin was divided into East and West Berlin, the former corresponding with the eastern sections of the former capital and the latter forming an independent territorial enclave in the national territory of the GDR.

Secondly, there was a pronounced contrast in the settlement structure between the rural areas in the north dominated by agriculture and the agglomerations in the south, characterized by industry. The South-North division, based on the industrialization process during the 19th century, was further accentuated by the construction of chemical plants near Halle/Leipzig for the utilization of the brown coal deposits before the Second World War.

Thirdly, the economic conditions in the east were characterized by bottlenecks in the industrial production process. Enterprises were cut off from their traditional suppliers and sales markets by the new boundaries. Above all, heavy industries and hard coal, the latter was necessary for effective power provision, were missing. The GDR had sufficient supplies of brown coal and potash, but hard coal, iron ore and non-ferrous metals had to be imported. The GDR also did not have sufficient access to the sea.[3] As early as the 1950s this disadvantage was dealt with by developing suitable overseas

---

[3] The largest Baltic Sea port Stettin became Polish property in 1945 and the traditional trade route via Hamburg was blocked since the city was situated in the FRG.

harbours, especially at Rostock, and this had positive effects on the city's population development. In addition, the main traffic routes to Berlin ran mainly in an east-west direction which made it more difficult to transport goods from industrial areas in the South to cities on the Baltic Sea.

Fourthly, after 1945 the economic system, especially the distribution of property, was fundamentally transformed. In the GDR a planned economy was introduced, which was only possible if the means of production were centrally controlled by a national planning administration. This was brought about by land reform by means of the collectivization of agricultural farms, the expropriation and nationalization of key industries, banks and insurance companies and the introduction of national shares in private enterprises (Eckart, 1989: 55-56).

The social and economic transformation of the GDR had several negative effects on the population development. From 1939 to 1950 the number of inhabitants increased by 1.6 million, i.e. 9.6 per cent. As in the case of the FRG, this was caused by the influx of refugees and expellees into rural areas (Figure 7.8). But from then on until the reunification in 1990 the GDR lost

Figure 7.8 Population development of the GDR by settlement size

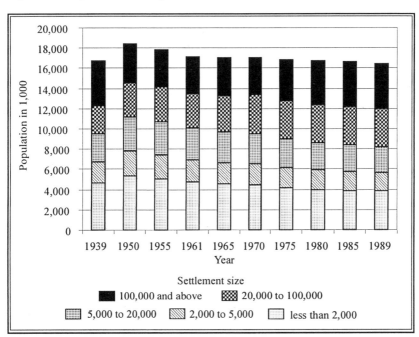

Source: Statistisches Bundesamt (ed) (1993), *Bevölkerungsstatistische Übersichten 1946 bis 1989*, Sonderreihe mit Beiträgen für das Gebiet der ehemaligen DDR, 3, Wiesbaden: Metzler-Poeschel; calculations by the authors

population annually. Before the building of the Wall in 1961 the greatest loss in one year had been 433,000 persons or 2.2 per cent of the total population. These losses were caused by migration to the FRG, partly because people were dissatisfied with the political system in the GDR and partly because they wanted to participate in the economic upswing of the FRG. Figure 7.9 verifies the diminishing migration losses after the building of the Wall in 1961.

While the migration imbalance between GDR and FRG continued, the fertility decline in the GDR from the mid-1960s was similar to that in the FRG (Figure 7.9). Thus, the highest net reproduction rate was 1.17 in 1964

Figure 7.9 Population development of the GDR, 1950-89

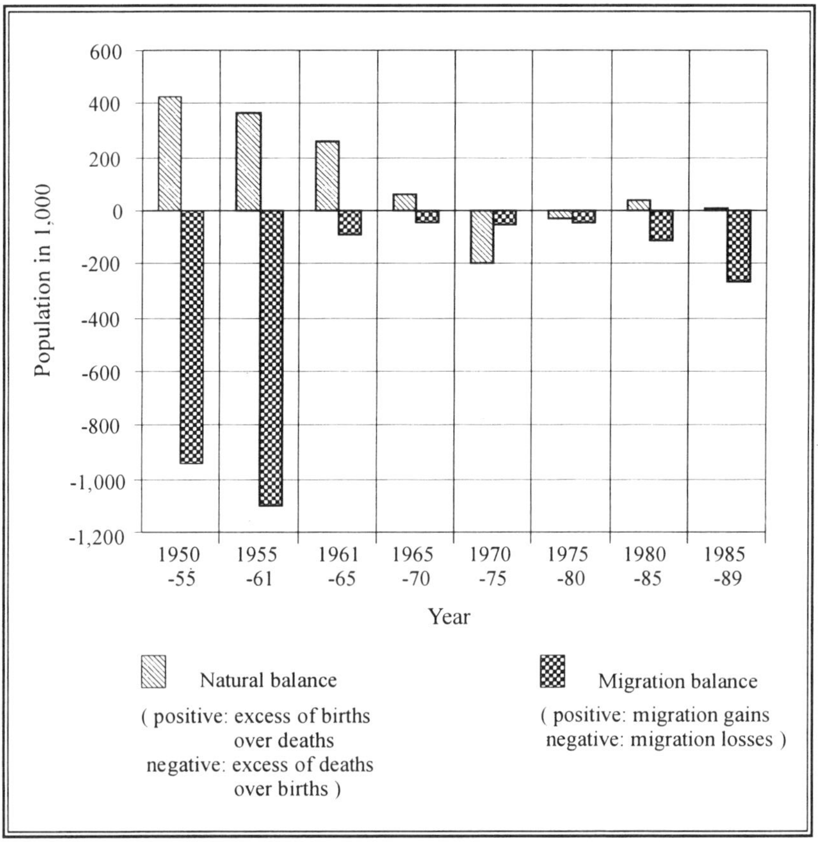

Source: Statistisches Bundesamt (ed.) (1993*), Bevölkerungsstatistische Übersichten 1946 bis 1989*, Sonderreihe mit Beiträgen für das Gebiet der ehemaligen DDR, 3, Wiesbaden: Metzler-Poeschel

and it decreased to a minimum of 0.73 in 1975. In contrast to the FRG, after the government had introduced its pro-natalistic population policy in the mid 1970s, fertility started rising again before 1980 (Gans, 1996). Despite these measures, however, the total fertility rate never reached the replacement level. Changes in the natural population growth in the 1980s were based on the aging of the population rather than on changes in the fertility rate.

POPULATION DEVELOPMENT AND THE SETTLEMENT SYSTEM

The effect of the Second World War is clearly visible on the spatial population distribution from 1939 to 1950. Evacuations from large cities that had been damaged during the war and the influx of refugees, predominantly to smaller settlements that had been less affected, caused a decrease in population in the core cities in agglomerations of approximately 21 per cent.[4] In contrast the less densely populated rural regions registered an increase of 30 per cent (Figure 7.10). Cities with at least 100,000 inhabitants decreased by 15 per cent or 663,000 persons, while all other settlements, independent of their size, recorded an increase of 19 per cent or 2.3 million inhabitants (Figure 7.8).

This phase of de-urbanization was followed by a less intensive concentration process. With the exception of city centres in urbanized regions, all other large cities suffered an average population loss of 6.6 per cent overall from 1950 to 1961 (Figure 7.8 and 7.10). Before the building of the Wall in 1961 almost all counties had been affected by the migration to West Germany. In the second half of the 1950s the population redistribution turned into urbanization (Figure 7.8), because cities with at least 100,000 inhabitants registered the smallest losses of all settlement sizes. After 1961 the urbanization process gained momentum, but this time only settlements with more than 20,000 people attracted population, the larger ones faster than the smaller ones (Figure 7.8). During the 1960s the population redistribution trends per county and region type varied somewhat. Core cities, like rural regions, gained population at this time. After 1970, however, although the total population of the GDR declined, only core cities registered an increase, and until the opening of the border in November 1989, the continuing concentration process kept on favouring the larger cities. This process was stimulated by the building of satellite towns consisting of blocks of flats in the large cities. They were mainly intended to house the workforce for nearby industrial centres, as examples of Halle-Neustadt, Leipzig-Gruenau, Berlin-Marzahn and others show. Compared to the average housing, especially to the tenement housing built during the industrialization these new blocks of flats ('Neubaublocks') were attractive because of facilities like bathrooms or

---

[4] In Berlin the population decrease was 23 per cent over the period.

Figure 7.10 Population development of the GDR by types of region and county, 1939-90

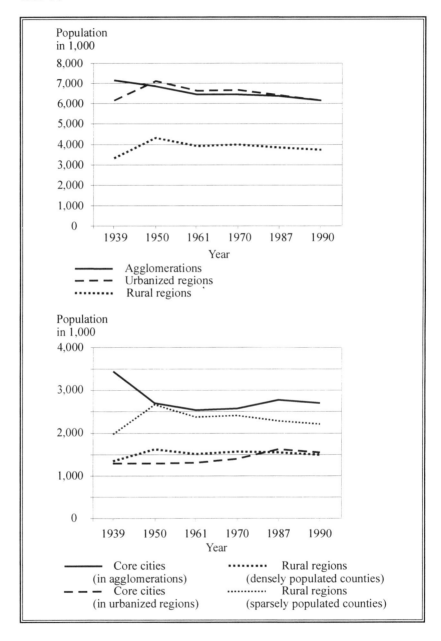

Source: Laufende Raumbeobachtung

central heating and were difficult to obtain until 1989. Due to a permanent demand for labour in the industrial centres, the government used the provision of such flats to attract needed people.

Generally, it seems as if the post-war population redistribution pattern in the GDR – weak de-concentration between 1950 and 1970, and concentration since then – can be ascribed to the initial economic conditions after the war, contrasts in the settlement structure between the south and the north, and on the political-economic system of the GDR.

EXPLANATIONS FOR THE POPULATION REDISTRIBUTION TRENDS IN THE GDR

Since the foundation of the GDR the government had always endeavored to reduce the country's economic dependence, particularly on the FRG. Urgent projects that were lodged included the construction of an international port on the Baltic coast as a base for imports and exports as well as the establishment of primary industries that were necessary for the economic and urban reconstruction of the country. The implementation of the latter was based on the Soviet model of the establishment of large-scale industrial projects (Strubelt, 1996: 25):

❑ Rostock as an international port of the GDR,
❑ Hoyerswerda as a location for brown coal refinement,
❑ Cottbus as a centre of brown coal and power production,
❑ Eisenhüttenstadt with its steel plant based on hard coal imported from Poland and iron ore from the Soviet Union.

The locations were close to sources of raw material and waterways and were far from the western boundary for military reasons. These developments led to the concentration of job opportunities, the provision of housing, the installation of infrastructure, and a substantial increase in the number of inhabitants in these cities, especially in the 1950s and 1960s (Figure 7.11). Not only were the regional disparities between south and north reduced by these projects but also the urban-to-rural migration. The government also supported development in central places such as Neubrandenburg in the north of Berlin in order to even out regional imbalances and to improve the supply of goods and services in sparsely populated rural areas (Figure 7.11).

The increase in the number of people in the designated cities during the 1950s and 1960s was caused by natural growth, the resettlement of refugees, and the influx of redundant labourers from the rural hinterlands to the cities after the collectivization of the agricultural sector. Investment preferences in favour of cities and centres outside the agglomerations in the south induced migration, especially to East Berlin whose reconstruction required a large

Figure 7.11 Population development of selected cities in the GDR, 1939-90

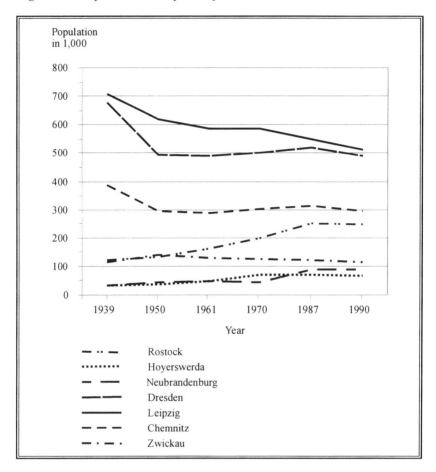

Source: Laufende Raumbeobachtung

labour force. The stagnating and even declining populations of Dresden, Chemnitz, Leipzig and Zwickau are indicative of the levelling out of population imbalances in the country during those years (Figure 7.11). The decrease in regional disparities until the mid-1970s was less associated with development plans than with centrally controlled economic planning (Strubelt, 1996: 21).

District administrations, which formed the territorial foundation of all planning systems according to the Marxism-Leninism model, played a pivotal role in this centrally controlled economic planning. The aim with these districts (Bezirke) as functional areas was the minimization of transport cost, which in turn gave rise to economic specialization and as a consequence the creation of regional mono-structures. The district capitals as administrative and industrial centres were subordinate to the urban system of the GDR; functionally they formed a second level of the urban hierarchy below the capital East Berlin. Adding to the economic purpose of the district capitals, the GDR-government also pursued a political objective through these district capitals since their categorizing could strongly influence the hierarchy of the regional urban system. Existing regional centres (i.e. capitals of former principalities where traditional central place functions were located), did not become district capitals because they represented a non-socialist civil society. Instead neighbouring municipalities were favoured as district capitals, e. g. Suhl and not Meiningen, or Neubrandenburg and not Neustrelitz.

During the 1970s the idea of the spatial balancing-out of regional disparities was abandoned because the re-establishment of industries in rural areas turned out to be economically unviable. Instead, the GDR-government began to promote the creation of population centres and started favouring the concentration of investments in cities, especially in district capitals and above all in East Berlin. Tables 7.4 and 7.5 reflect the continuous inflow of the population from rural areas to cities during the 1980s and thereby confirm the urbanization process. While the cities with at least 100,000 inhabitants attracted the balance of the internal migration, these cities registered losses above average by international migration during the 1980s. The positive relationship between settlement size and the balance of migration within the GDR indicates step-wise migration from small municipalities through county and district capitals to East Berlin as the capital (Schmidt and Tittel, 1990: 245). The rural areas did not only experience a brain drain but also the degradation of living conditions compared to those of the cities (Schmidt and Tittel, 1990: 251). Several reasons are pointed out by Grundmann (1994: 85) for the urbanization trend in the GDR: the centrally controlled economy with its emphasis on investments in large-scale enterprises in large cities, the expansion of administration in favour of East Berlin at first, but later also in district capitals, and the insufficient infrastructure and in accessibility of smaller settlements.

Not all cities profited equally from this concentration process though. The number of houses that were built varied according to functional criteria and in the process the number of inhabitants increased above average in East Berlin (13.3 per 1,000). The capital recorded migration gains from all over the country (Schmidt and Tittel, 1990: 247; Grundmann 1994: 85). Smaller district capitals such as Suhl (20.5 per 1,000), Neubrandenburg (19.4 per 1,000) and Frankfort/Oder (12.0 per 1,000) also experienced exceptionally high growth rates because of in-migration from the district. On the other

Table 7.4 Population change of the GDR according to settlement size, 1980-89

Population development	Settlement size in 000s				
	-2	2-10	10-50	50-100	100+
Population in 1980 (000s)	4007.0	3249.7	3873.2	1308.0	4302.5
Internal migration (per 1,000)	-55.0	-25.9	9.9	4.9	57,0
Internat. migrations (/ 1000)	-3.0	-3.7	-6.1	-11.0	-18.3
Balance, births and deaths (/ 1000)	22.7	-63.9	22.2	31.0	13.1
Population in 1988 (000s)	3867.8	2959.2	3975.6	1341.2	4531.0

Source: Statistisches Bundesamt 1993; computations by the authors

Table 7.5 Balance of internal migration by settlement size, 1970-89

Origin	Destination (settlement size 000s		
	-10	10-100	100+
Less than 10,000	-	561,610	309,782
10,000 to 100,000	-561,610	-	247,291
100,000 and more	-309,782	-247,291	-

Source: Statistisches Bundesamt 1993; computations by the authors

hand, the population of the industrial and district capitals stagnated or even declined (Figure 7.11), e.g. Hoyerswerda (-2.4 per 1,000), Schwedt (-2.6 per 1,000), Chemnitz (-1.6 per 1,000), Leipzig (-3.6 per 1,000) or Zwickau (-1.1 per 1,000). In Halle/Leipzig negative environmental conditions acted as strong push factors (Schmidt and Tittel, 1990).

With regard to emigration during the 1980s (Figure 7.9) larger cities, especially East Berlin and the district capitals lost more migrants than smaller settlements (Table 7.4). It seems as if the emigrants assumed that their needs could not be met within the GDR because the cities represented the highest standard of living (Schmidt and Tittel, 1990: 246; Gans, 1995: 79).

MIGRATION, URBANIZATION AND THE URBAN SYSTEM IN UNITED GERMANY

In 1991 East Germany added five new states to the Federal Republic. The two parts of Berlin merged in a reunited city of 3.44 million inhabitants. As a result the rank-size distribution of German cities (Figure 7.2) appears to be 'normal'. Overall, the four biggest cities are relatively evenly distributed in four parts of the country – Berlin in the East, Hamburg in the North, Cologne in the West and Munich in the South.

If one looks at the high-order functions of the cities, it can be seen that there is no domination of the German urban system by any one metropolis. Although Berlin is the capital and the biggest city it has deficiencies in many economic sectors. Blotevogel (1998) has analyzed the high-order service functions of the 12 most important metropolitan areas in Germany in 1995 and the analysis shows that Berlin has a rather unbalanced composition of business services. It is over-represented in employment in science, education, art and the media while it has shortcomings in finance, insurance, legal services and wholesale trade. The same structural deficiencies characterize the other East German metropolitan areas of Dresden and Halle/Leipzig. In contrast to this, the composition of metropolitan areas in West Germany are more balanced although some specialize in certain areas. The Rhine-Main area with Frankfurt/Main as the core specializes in finance, Hamburg in wholesale trade, Munich in technical services, art and media, and publishing services, and the Rhine-Ruhr conurbation in wholesale trade, insurance and legal services. Germany, therefore, has several regional metropolises each specializing in certain areas, but no one completely dominates the urban system.

The period around 1990 is characterized by the highest inflow of migrants from abroad to Germany in the 20th century. In West Germany, the flows of ethnic Germans from eastern Europe, asylum applicants, refugees from civil wars in former Yugoslavia etc. were supplemented by migrants from East Germany. As a consequence the population of West Germany increased by almost 3 per cent from 1989 to 1991. The influx applies to metropolitan areas as well as to rural regions, big cities as well as small settlements. For the first time in decades even cities in old-industrial districts gained migrants. Gans (2000) has demonstrated that the 'reurbanization' registered in the large cities differed from earlier urbanization processes, because it was a temporary phenomenon that was linked to the political upheavals in eastern Europe during the early 1990s. After some years of population gains the core cities of agglomerations and urbanized areas again started losing population (Table 7.2).

Urban development in East Germany during the 1990s occurred rather differently. From 1991 to 1996 the distribution of annual net internal migration was analyzed by factor analysis on the basis of the prognosis areas. It turned out that two different patterns corresponding to two phases have to be distinguished (Table 7.6). At the beginning of the 1990s all prognosis areas of the new Länder were marked by migration losses which were particularly high in the rural regions. The opening of the border between the

Table 7.6 Rate of migration balance with reference to type of county and time period (East Germany or new Länder)

Type of county	1991/92	1995/96
Agglomerations		
core city	-4.3	-16.7
highly agglomerated counties	-9.6	-14.8
agglomerated counties	-16.5	21.5
rural counties	-11.4	26.5
Urbanized regions		
core city	-22.8	-36.4
agglomerated counties	-17.0	2.0
rural counties	-18.0	9.7
Rural regions		
densely populated counties	-15.7	-8.8
sparsely populated counties	-28.6	-8.6

Source: Laufende Raumbeobachtung; calculations by the authors

two German states resulted in a precipitous rise in the number of East-West migrants. From November 1989 to March 1990 about 370,000 persons or 2.3 per cent of the total population left East Germany. After the first free elections in spring of 1990 the number of moves clearly dropped, but in 1994 it still amounted to 168,000. At the same time growing counter migration from West to East Germany increasingly started to offset the earlier migration flows from the East to West Germany.

During the second phase from 1995 to 1996, densely inhabited suburban counties in the agglomeration areas and the urbanized regions started to show a positive migration balance, while core cities and rural regions were still being marked by migration losses. The period after 1995 is marked by strong intra-regional de-concentration tendencies with suburban areas gaining significantly more migrants than had ever been seen in the old Länder before. Supported by tax reductions, many investors from West Germany built new houses and housing estates, shopping centres, and business parks in the suburban rings of core cities. In contrast to West Germany, rural regions lost population through internal migration. Also the losses in the medium-sized core cities were significantly higher than in the West, but in spite of that the clear division during the early 1990s between East and West Germany became much less marked during the mid-1990s.

After the turbulent years before the 1990s, West Germany had returned to its regular internal migration pattern of intra-regional and inter-regional de-concentration by 1992 (Table 7.2). Core cities in the agglomerations and urbanized areas had lost population to outer suburban rings. Rural regions had also started gaining population again, peripheral counties slightly faster than more densely populated counties.

The migration of the different age groups in the 1990s displayed much more striking transformations in the new Länder than in the old ones. During the first phase at the beginning of the 1990s negative balances were indicated in almost all age groups. Only large-sized core cities registered gains, the 18-24, and 25-29 year old groups, while medium-sized core cities gained some older people above the age of 64 (Figure 7.12). In the second phase changes to the direction of the western pattern could be observed. On the one hand, the preferred migration of the 25-29 year old migrants to agglomeration areas was similar to that of West Germany. On the other hand, significant losses of the 30-49 year old group as well as the group below 18 years in the core cities and the high gains in the hinterlands are indicative of substantial suburbanization. While the rural regions in the former FRG register positive migration balances of the elderly age groups during the mid 1990s, only the sparsely populated, peripheral counties of the new Länder recorded gains. This may be regarded as a first sign of interregional de-concentration – de urbanization which was first observed in the old Länder in this age-group before spreading to other age groups.

In both parts of the Federal Republic an intraregional de-concentration process has been observed after the mid-1990s. But the suburbanization that occurred in the new Länder was not simply a repetition of the same processes in West Germany because conditions in the new Länder were quite different (Sailer-Fliege, 1998; Franz, 2000). Most housing in East Germany was constructed in the suburban rings around core cities during the 1990s because of the tax advantages that were allowed for the depreciation of buildings and because the process of permission for land use and building plans in suburban communities was significantly streamlined and simplified. In East Germany a larger percentage of the new buildings are blocks of flats than in the former West Germany, and many of them were built by West German investors because they could save tax, while detached family houses are less common. The excessive building of these tax-saving complexes resulted in many of them now being empty and not used at all. The demographic selectivity of persons moving into the new suburban housing is relatively low, because different groups by age and household size move into these areas, whereas the

Figure 7.12 Rate of migration balance according to age groups, types of county and time period (East Germany or new Länder)

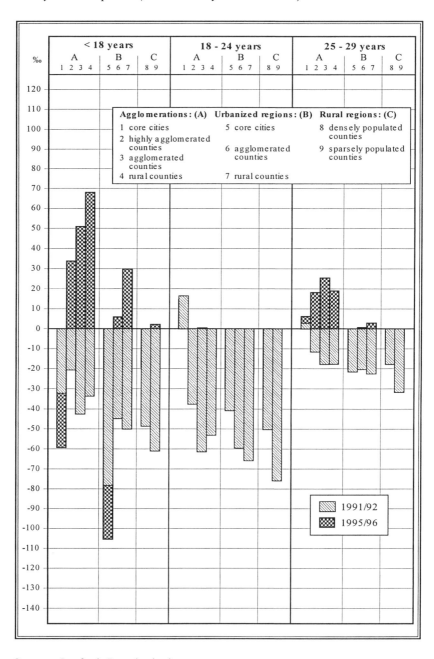

Source: Laufende Raumbeobachtung

socio-economic selectivity is high since only high-income groups in East-Germany up to now could afford to buy or to rent a house or a modern flat.

CONCLUSION

During the nineteenth century Germany saw a rapid process of urbanization which proceeded parallel to industrialization and gave rise to a growing concentration of population, employment and housing. Borries (1969) has shown that an index of concentration computed on the basis of 30 regional units slightly increased from 14.8 in 1816 to 15.4 in 1871. During the subsequent period of high industrialization, it increased to 20.8 by 1910. The continuation of urbanization in the 20th century was interrupted by specific political events, especially the two World Wars. As a consequence of the Second World War, rural regions gained population, resulting in de-concentration. In both German countries the 1950s were characterized by a renewed phase of concentration and urbanization, a process that was strongly linked to the reconstruction of cities and towns. During the next decades, the developments in West and East Germany clearly differed. After the 1960s suburbanization was important in West Germany. This process of intraregional de-concentration culminated in the 1970s. Interregional de-concentration started to occur after the late 1970s. Intermediate and rural regions gained population while many metropolitan areas started losing population. The decline of large cities and agglomerations tapered off and by the late 1980s they had experienced renewed growth, which was part of the nationwide increase effected by a wave of in-migration from other countries. This 're-urbanization' should therefore be interpreted as an externally induced short-term interruption of long-term trends.

East Germany of the 1950s and 1960s was characterized by a policy that was designed to stimulate the development of rural regions through industrialization and new town development. Yet in the 1970s and 1980s urbanization trends dominated. Large cities and administrative centres gained population while smaller towns declined. After unification, and after some years of high population losses due to out-migration and birth-decline, the new Länder experienced a period of strong suburbanization, a process that had been prevented by the State during Soviet control. However, by that time interregional de-concentration had not yet occurred. Some cities in East Germany, particularly the capitals of the new Länder and big cities in Saxony could strengthen their central functions, whereas almost all industrial centres had to suffer from strong decline of employment and population. In West Germany de-urbanization again gained momentum after the upheavals of the time around unification. This process of interregional de-concentration is supported by an administrative policy of regular distribution of large groups of in-migrants (ethnic Germans, asylum-applicants, refugees).

Overall, the development of urbanization and counter-urbanization, concentration and de-concentration in Germany can be seen as a reflection of trends with varying duration. Long-term and deep-seated changes in the economic system and in the society resulted in industrialization and the emergence of a post-industrial society. Whereas industrialization was strongly associated with urbanization and growing concentration, it seems as if the movement towards post-industrialism is linked to moderate forms of de-concentration. Political changes caused medium-term changes during the 1970s and 1980s. Regional economic and housing policy in the centralized GDR during the 1970s and 1980s caused a distinct phase of urbanization.[5]

Despite all of the political upheavals of the 20th century, the German urban system has remained remarkably stable. The most far-reaching change concerns the position of Berlin in the urban system. Until the Second World War, Berlin had a dominating position which it has not yet regained. Instead, the historical regional variety of the German urban system has been confirmed by the emergence of 'regional metropolises' in different parts of the country. This will be particularly important to the large cities in the new Länder which still show deficiencies in many functional sectors and have suffered from strong population decline during the 1990s. Perhaps they will recover and regain some of their traditional positions in the German urban system of the future.

However, if current population trends continue, east-west demographic differences will deepen. According to the regional policy forecast 2015 of the Federal Office for Building and Regional Planning, most regions of the old states will register population gains until 2015, while nearly all regions of the new states will have suffered considerable losses (Bucher, 2001). The latter will be particularly high in urbanized regions with old industries and in sparsely populated peripheral areas. By contrast, according to the projection, West Germany will follow the previous trends of de-concentration and therefore the rural regions will record the highest population gains, even if the parts with low density will only show increases slightly above average.

In East Germany, only suburban rings of metropolitan areas will have rising population figures, whereas the core cities have to expect continuing high losses. If the population trends of the late 1990s according to the size distribution of cities are prolonged into the future, the big cities in East Germany will show the highest decreases, because out-migration is particularly relevant. On the one hand, young people will go to West Germany, especially to southern parts, in search of better employment opportunities, on the other hand families and the elderly wishing for improved

---

[5] It should be mentioned that certain short-term trends which have not been dealt with in this chapter could be linked to the business cycle

housing conditions will move to suburbs. To steer against these tendencies, further support of urban development and housing improvement is needed as well as strengthening of the urban economy. In West Germany, big cities have only slight population losses because of de-concentration, but vacancies on the housing market are not to be expected.

Apart from mere population figures, the structure of the population will change in the future. The most important process is demographic aging. This process will be especially rapid in East German cities, and caused by birth deficits as well as out-migration of younger persons. By contrast, in many West German urban agglomerations the current pattern of higher average age in the core cities and young suburban populations will change to the opposite, because many suburbanites of the 1970s are now reaching the age of retirement. A further distinguishing feature of big cities in West Germany will be a rising proportion of immigrants and their descendants.

In addition to the demographic differences between east and west, economic disparities can only be slowly diminished. Yet other regional disparities, within the old as well as the new states, should not be neglected. In both parts of Germany economic growth is more concentrated in regions, cities, and urban agglomerations of the south. But despite these regional disparities, it is not expected that the regionally balanced German urban system will change rapidly in the near future.

REFERENCES

Bähr, J. (1997), *Bevölkerungsgeographie*. Third Edition. Stuttgart: UTB, Verlag Eugen Ulmer.

Blotevogel, H. H. (1998), *Europäische Metropolregion Rhein-Ruhr, Schriften des Instituts für Landes- und Stadtentwicklungsforschung des Landes Nordrhein-Westfalen*, **135**, Dortmund: ILS.

Blotevogel, H. H. and M. Hommel (1980), 'Struktur und Entwicklung des Städtesystems', *Geographische Rundschau*, **32**, 155-164.

Blotevogel, H. and H. Möller (1992), 'Struktur und Entwicklung des Städtesystems der Bundesrepublik Deutschland', in H. Köck (ed.), *Städte und Städtesysteme*, Köln: Aulis, pp. 244-250.

Borries, H. W. von (1969), *Ökonomische Grundlagen der westdeutschen Siedlungsstruktur*, Hannover: Gebrüder Jänecke Verlag.

Bucher, H. (2001), 'Die Bevölkerung der Zukunft', in Institut für Länderkunde (ed.), *Nationalatlas Bundesrepublik Deutschland, Bevölkerung, Heidelberg and Berlin*: Spektrum Akademischer Verlag, pp. 142-143.

Bundesamt für Bauwesen und Raumordnung (1999), 'Aktuelle Daten zur Entwicklung der Städte, Kreise und Gemeinden'. Ausgabe 1999, *Berichte des BBR*, **3**, Bonn: Selbstverlag.

Claval, P. (1990), 'A critical review of the centre-periphery model as applied in a global context', in A. Shachar and S. Öberg (eds), *The world economy and the spatial organization of power*, Aldershot: Avebury, pp. 13-27.

Eckart, K. (1989), *DDR*, Suttgart: Ernst Klett Verlag, 3rd edition.

Fielding, A. J. (1989), 'Population redistribution in Western Europe: Trends since 1950 and the debate about counter-urbanization', in P. Congdon and P. Batey (eds), *Advances in regional demography*, London: Belhaven , pp. 167-179.

Franz, P. (2000), 'Suburbanization and the clash of urban regimes. Developmental problems of East German cities in a free market environment', *European Urban and Regional Studies*, **7**, 135-146.

Friedrich, K. (1995), *Altern in räumlicher Umwelt. Sozialräumliche Interaktionen älterer Menschen in Deutschland und in den USA*, Darmstadt: Steinkopff.

Friedrichs, J., H. Häussermann and W. Siebel (eds) (1987), *Süd-Nord-Gefälle in der Bundesrepublik?*, Opladen: Westdeutscher Verlag.

Gaebe, W. (1987), *Verdichtungsräume. Strukturen und Prozesse in weltweiten Vergleichen*, Stuttgart: Teubner.

Gans, P. (1995), 'Wanderungsverflechtungen unterschiedlich strukturierter Regionen in den neuen Ländern', in P. Gans and F.-J. Kemper (eds), *Mobilität und Migration in Deutschland*, Erfurter Geographische Studien, **3**, Erfurt: Selbstverlag des Geographischen Instituts, pp.79-88.

Gans, P. (1996), 'Demographische Entwicklung seit 1980', in W. Strubelt et al. (eds), *Städte und Regionen – Räumliche Folgen des Transformationsprozesses*, Berichte der Kommission für die Erforschung des sozialen und politischen Wandels in den neuen Bundesländern, **5**, Opladen: Leske + Budrich, pp. 143-181.

Gans, P. (2000), 'Urban population change in large cities in Germany, 1980-94', *Urban Studies*, **37**, 1497-1512.

Geyer, H. S. (1996), 'Expanding the theoretical foundation of differential urbanization', *Tijdschrift voor Economische en Sociale Geografie*, **87**, 44-59.

Giese, E. (1978), 'Räumliche Diffusion ausländischer Arbeitnehmer in der Bundesrepublik Deutschland 1960-1976', *Die Erde*, **109**, 92-110.

Grundmann, S. (1994), *Wanderungen, Regionale Bevölkerungsentwicklung in den neuen Bundesländern. Analysen, Prognosen und Szenarien*, Graue Reihe der KSPW 94-05, Berlin: GSFP, pp. 81-122.

Häußermann, H. and W. Siebel (1986), 'Die Polarisierung der Großstadtentwicklung im Süd-Nord-Gefälle' in J. Friedrichs, H. Häußermann and W. Siebel (eds), *Süd-Nord-Gefälle in der Bundesrepublik?*, Opladen: Westdeutscher Verlag, pp. 70-96.

Heineberg, H. (2000), 'Germany after unification: Urban settlement system in the 1990s' in A. Mayr and W. Taubmann (eds), *Germany ten years after reunification*, Beiträge zur Regionalen Geographie 52, Leipzig: Selbstverlag Institut für Länderkunde e.V., pp. 24-39.

Irmen, E. and A. Blach (1994), 'Räumlicher Strukturwandel. Konzentration, Dekonzentration und Dispersion', *Informationen zur Raumentwicklung*, **7/8**, 445-480.

Kanaroglou, P. S. and G. O. Braun (1992), 'The pattern of counterurbanization in the Federal Republic of Germany 1977-85', *Environment and Planning A*, **24**, 481-496.

Kemper, F.-J. (1997), 'Internal migration and the business cycle: The example of West Germany', in H. H. Blotevogel and A. J. Fielding (eds), *People, jobs and mobility in the New Europe*, Chichester, Weinheim: Wiley, pp. 227-245.

Kemper, F.-J. (1999), 'Binnenwanderungen und Dekonzentration der Bevölkerung. Jüngere Entwicklungen in Deutschland', in H.-D. Schultz (ed.), *Quodlibet Geographicum. Berliner Geographische Arbeiten* **90**, Berlin: Selbstverlag des Geographischen Instituts, pp. 105-122.

Kemper, F.-J. and W. Kuls (1986), *Wanderungen älterer Menschen im ländlichen Raum am Beispiel der nördlichen Landesteile von Rheinland-Pfalz*. Arbeiten zur Rheinischen Landeskunde, **54**, Bonn: Ferd. Dümmlers Verlag.

Klaassen, L. H., W. T. M. Molle and J. H. P. Paelinck (eds) (1981), *Dynamics of urban development*, New York: St. Martin's Press.

Kontuly, T. and K. P. Schön (1994), 'Changing western German internal migration systems during the second half of the 1980s', *Environment and Planning A*, **26**, 1521-1543.

Kontuly, T. and R. Vogelsang (1988), 'Explanations for the intensification of counterurbanization in the Federal Republic of Germany', *Professional Geography*, **40**, 42-54.

Köllmann, W. (1983), 'Die Bevölkerungsentwicklung der Bundesrepublik', in W. Conze and M. R. Lepsius (eds), *Sozialgeschichte der Bundesrepublik Deutschland*, Stuttgart: Klett-Cotta, pp. 9-50.

Kunz, D. (1986), 'Anfänge und Ursachen der Nord-Süd-Drift', *Informationen zur Raumentwicklung*, **11/12**, 829-838.

Laux, H. D. (1990), *Hauptstadt oder Hauptstädte? Zur Stellung Bonns im Städtesystem der Bundesrepublik Deutschland. Ein Beitrag zur Hauptstadtdiskussion*, Bonn: Stadt Bonn.

Marschalck, P. (1984), *Bevölkerungsgeschichte Deutschlands im 19. und 20. Jahrhundert*, Frankfurt/Main: Suhrkamp.

Münz, R., W. Seifert and R. Ulrich (1997), *Zuwanderungen nach Deutschland*, Frankfurt and New York: Campus.

Petzina, D. (1987), 'Wirtschaftliche Ungleichgewichte in Deutschland. Ein historischer Rückblick auf die regionale Wirtschaftsentwicklung im 19. und 20. Jahrhundert' in Landeszentrale für politische Bildung Baden-Württemberg (ed.), *Nord-Süd-Gefälle in Deutschland?* Vorurteile und Tatsachen, Stuttgart: Verlag W. Kohlhammer, pp. 59-81.

Sailer-Fliege, U. (1998), 'Die Suburbanisierung der Bevölkerung als Element raumstruktureller Dynamik in Mittelthüringen. Das Beispiel Erfurt', *Zeitschrift für Wirtschaftsgeographie*, **42**, 97-116.

Schmidt E. and G. Tittel (1990), 'Haupttendenzen der Migration in der DDR', *Raumforschung und Raumordnung*, **48**, 244-250.

Schöller, P., H. H. Blotevogel, H. J. Buchholz, and M. Hommel (1984), 'The settlement system of the Federal Republic of Germany'. in L. S. Bourne, R. Sinclair and K. Dziewonski (eds), *Urbanization and settlement systems. International perspectives*, Oxford: Oxford University Press.

Sinz, M. and W. Strubelt (1986), Zur Diskussion über das wirtschaftliche Süd-Nord-Gefälle unter Berücksichtigung entwicklungsgeschichtlicher Aspekte, in J. Friedrichs, H. Häußermann and W. Siebel (eds), *Süd-Nord-Gefälle in der Bundesrepublik?*, Opladen: Westdeutscher Verlag, pp. 12-50.

Strubelt W.(1996), 'Regionale Disparitäten zwischen Wandel und Persistenz', in W. Strubelt et al. (eds), *Städte und Regionen – Räumliche Folgen des Transformationsprozesses*, Berichte der Kommission für die Erforschung des sozialen und politischen Wandels in den neuen Bundesländern, **5**, Opladen: Leske and Budrich, pp. 11-110.

Chapter 8

Urban Development in the Netherlands: New Perspectives

P. Nijkamp and E. Goede[1]

EARLY URBAN HISTORY OF THE NETHERLANDS[2]

Cities are the furnaces for economic growth and play a critical role in the economic history of the Developed World. They create unprecedented, and as yet unexploited agglomeration economies to the benefit of the whole country (Glaeser, 1998). This observation is also reflected in the urban history of the Netherlands.

New cities originated along the banks of the large Dutch waterways in the feudal era between circa 1000 and 1433, mainly due to the revival of trade. From the thirteenth century onwards, Dutch fishing, shipping and trading showed rapid growth. The city of Dordrecht, which had a favourable location, was the first city to attract economic activities of major significance. The IJssel-delta (Kampen and Deventer) also became a focal point of business in the thirteenth to sixteenth centuries.

In the year 1500, the Netherlands consisted of seventeen provinces that had emerged from the Roman Empire. In 1587, the country was officially referred to as the Republic of the United Netherlands. Despite its impressive name, no such thing as a single Dutch State ever existed. The Eighty Years War (1568-1648) led to the independence of the Republic and turned the United Netherlands into a formidable sea power. In the course of the

---

[1] The authors wish to thank Cees Gorter for his helpful suggestions during the preparation of this paper. Sadly he passed away in October 2001.
[2] Data has been drawn from the Historische Winkler Prins Encyclopedie (1959), Grote Winkler Prins Encyclopedie (1976), Grote Winkler Prins Encyclopedie (1992) if not elsewhere indicated.

sixteenth century the city of Amsterdam took a leading position as the most important (financial) trading town of Holland.

At the end of the sixteenth century, colonial expansion started. The first journey to India occurred in 1595 and led to the founding of the Dutch East India Company in 1602. In 1621 the Company of the West Indies was founded, which enabled the Dutch to expand to the New World. Between 1580 and 1675 the economy of Holland showed continuous growth. For this reason, the seventeenth century is regarded as the Golden Age of the Republic of the United Netherlands.

In 1622, almost 60 per cent of the Dutch population, which numbered about 400000 people, lived in cities. By then 33 cities already existed, although eighteen had a population of less than 5,000 residents each. Amsterdam was the largest city in 1670 with approximately 200000 inhabitants. This was about half of the total population, but even on an international level, it was quite considerable. The most important cities at that time, besides Amsterdam, were Leiden, Haarlem, Delft, Gouda, Hoorn, Enkhuizen, Rotterdam and Middelburg. In certain areas even the countryside was urbanized and especially the Zaan region near Amsterdam developed into an important industrial area (van der Ham, 1998).

Also foreigners were attracted by Dutch prosperity. Between 1580 and the beginning of the eighteenth century, about half a million immigrants settled in the Republic. In those days one out of every two employees was of foreign origin. At the same time, approximately 500000 people were emigrating to the colonies or started working on one of the many ships (van der Ham, 1998).

As a result of the urban upsurge in the seventeenth and eighteenth centuries, Amsterdam and Rotterdam, and to a lesser extent The Hague and Utrecht, expanded strongly. At the same time, the previously important towns in the South and East of the country began to stagnate. In this way a pattern of several large towns, a number of medium-sized towns, and many small towns emerged. In 1849 more than 40 per cent of the Dutch population lived in these towns. By 1930 this percentage had risen to 65.6 per cent, but it gradually dropped to just below 53 per cent in 1970 (Deurloo et al., 1980). At the beginning of the twentieth century, the Netherlands was still largely rural in nature, but over a period of one century it changed into an urbanized country. The Industrial Revolution prompted the development of new infrastructure (harbours, rail infrastructure, roads) which, in turn, stimulated the growth of the most accessible urban centres from the beginning of the twentieth century.

URBAN CLASSIFICATIONS IN THE NETHERLANDS[3]

Urban development in the Netherlands over the past 50 years cannot be fully understood without an explanation of the different approaches to urban classifications that were implemented over the years. The history of measuring the degree of urbanization in the Dutch Central Bureau of Statistics (CBS) dates back to the 1950s when a multi-dimensional classification of the smallest administrative geographical unit, the municipality, was developed. In this classification a distinction was made between: rural municipalities, urbanized rural municipalities, and urban municipalities. These degrees of urbanization were based on population density, the structure of the economically active population, and the urban character of the built-up area (Hoekveld, 1981).

Each of the above categories of urbanization can be further subdivided. For this paper only the subdivision of category C is relevant. Depending on the population size of the municipalities category C can be subdivided into 5 categories. Small rural cities with between 2 000 and 10 000 inhabitants fall in category C1. Small cities with 10 000-30 000 inhabitants belong to category C2. The third and the fourth categories are the medium-sized cities. C3 numbers 30 000-50 000 inhabitants and C4 consists of 50 000-100 000 inhabitants. The final category C5 covers large cities with more than 100 000 inhabitants.

Although the degree of urbanization (or ABC-classification) was widely used in the past, doubts about its usefulness have been raised in recent years. However, an update of the classification is not possible because of the decision to abandon a national population census (the last one dates back to 1971). Since 1992 a new measure has been introduced: the address-density of an area. It is based on the concept of concentration of human activities according to building addresses. The degree of urbanization of an area has been defined as the average number of addresses in an area with a radius of 1 km around a central address. Five categories have been identified: very strongly urbanized, strongly urbanized, moderately urbanized, under-urbanized and non-urbanized.

For the description of urbanization patterns in the Netherlands from 1950 to 1992, the degree of urbanization (or ABC-classification) has been widely used. For the period from 1992 to 2000 address densities are being used. Another classification that is of interest was used by van den Berg et al. (1987). They classified twenty-four Dutch agglomerations (see also Table 8.1 and Figure 8.1) for the period 1950 to 1982 according to three development stages: cores (urban areas), rings (suburban areas) and agglomerations.

The classifications of the CBS and the van den Berg group overlap to a large extent. If the two classification systems are compared one could say

---

[3] Data in this section have been drawn from Den Dulk et al. (1992).

that 'cores' correspond to 'urban municipalities' (category C) and 'rings' to 'urbanized rural municipalities' (category B). 'Agglomerations' could be regarded as a combination of categories B and C. The remaining A-category or 'rural municipalities' falls outside the scope of the division of van den Berg et al. (1987), but can be regarded as peripheral areas.

It should be noted that a direct comparison of the latter two classifications is hard to achieve because the sizes of cities in category C vary greatly, and this complicates the specification of this category simply as 'cores' or urban areas. We have tried to overcome this by subdividing it into the five subdivisions, which have previously been described, and by analyzing these separately. Consequently, category C1 consists of peripheral or rural areas, category C2 and C3 are suburban areas (rings) and category C4 and C5 are regarded as 'urban areas' (cores). Also urbanized rural municipalities cannot simply be categorized as 'rings'. To give an accurate picture, they do not only consist of urbanized rural municipalities (B1 and B2), but also of commuter municipalities (B3).[4]

Table 8.1 The sample of Dutch agglomerations

Size	Randstad	Emanation zone	Peripheral zones
> 500,000 inhabitants	Amsterdam (12) Rotterdam (16) The Hague (15)	-	-
250,000 to 500,000 inhabitants	Utrecht (9)	Arnhem (6) Eindhoven (22)	Groningen (1) Enschede/Hengelo (5) Heerlen/Kerkrade (23)
100,000 to 250,000 inhabitants	Leiden (14) Hilversum (13) Amersfoort (8) Dordrecht/ Zwijndrecht (17) Haarlem (11)	Nijmegen (7) Breda (19) Alkmaar (10) Tilburg (20) Den Bosch (21)	Leeuwarden (2) Zwolle (4) Emmen (3) Maastricht (24) Vlissingen/ Middelburg (18)

Notes: Numbers in brackets identify the locations of agglomerations on the map of The Netherlands shown in Figure 1.

Source: van den Berg et al. (1981 and 1987).

---

[4] For the sake of this discussion this subdivision has not been made. For the same reasons mentioned in this section, a comparison between the degree of urbanization and address density is not feasible and therefore has not been attempted.

Figure 8.1 Agglomerations of the Netherlands, 1987

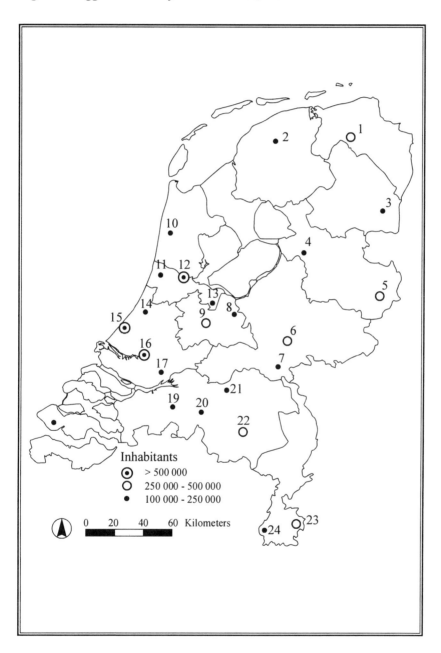

Source : Van den Berg et al., 1987

MIGRATION AND URBANIZATION: GENERAL OVERVIEW FOR THE PERIOD 1950-2000

To describe 50 years of urban developments, we start with a general overview of the entire period. Around 1950 about 10.11 million people lived in the Netherlands. This number has increased by 58 per cent to 15.86 million by the year 2000. This growth has not been equally dispersed over the period. In the twentieth century the population of the Netherlands grew on average by 100 thousand inhabitants per year. Although the surface of the country has expanded somewhat through land reclamation in the former Zuiderzee, this was not sufficient for the strong increase in population. It has also caused an increase of population density. Table 8.2 shows the population numbers and population densities of the periods considered. The continuous increase of population and population density in the Netherlands has resulted in migration flows and strong urbanization. The largest population concentration has always been in the west of the country, where the four largest municipalities are located: Amsterdam, Rotterdam, The Hague and Utrecht (Prins and Verhoef, 2000).

Table 8.2 Population size and density development for the period 1950-2000

Population	1950	1960	1970	1980	1990	2000
Total	10026773	11410843	12953731	14091014	14892574	15863950
density / km^2	309	352	384	415	439	468

Source: compiled from: CBS data

Over the past forty years the percentage of people living in urban municipalities, has remained around 50 per cent of the total Dutch population. This accounted for 6 million people in 1960 and 7.5 million people in 1990. This percentage is more difficult to determine for people living in rural municipalities and urbanized rural municipalities because it has changed over the course of the years. Between 1960 and 1990 the share of the population living in rural municipalities has declined continuously but not constantly from almost 25 per cent in 1960 to below 11 per cent in 1990, a drop of 13.25 per cent over the period. In this period 1 119 276 people left the rural municipalities. During the same period, the share of the urbanized rural municipalities increased. Where in 1960 more than 20 per cent of the Dutch population lived in urbanized rural municipalities, in 1990 this share had increased to almost 38 per cent. In absolute terms, the number of people living in urbanized rural municipalities has more than doubled from 3 201 248 to 5 643 381 inhabitants. The largest leaps occurred in the 1970s. During this period the rural municipalities lost 10 per cent of their population share (1 204 914 residents) and the share of urbanized rural municipalities increased by 11 per cent (1 844 899 residents). For specific numbers and percentages, we refer to Table 8.3. A graphical overview of these periods is provided in Figure 8.2 and 8.3.

Table 8.3 Population sizes and shares of municipalities by degree of urbanization, 1950-90

Population	1960	Share	1970	Share	1980	Share	1990	Share
Rural	2800463	24.54	2843908	21.95	1638994	11.63	1681187	11.29
Urbanized rural	2442133	21.40	3271385	25.25	5116284	36.31	5643381	37.89
Urban	6168247	54.06	6838438	52.80	7334190	52.06	7566370	50.82

Source: Compiled from CBS data

Figure 8.2 Development of population distribution related to degree of urbanization, 1960-90

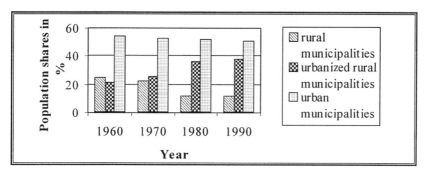

Source: Deduced from Table 8.3

Figure 8.3 Changes in population distribution between 1960 and 1990

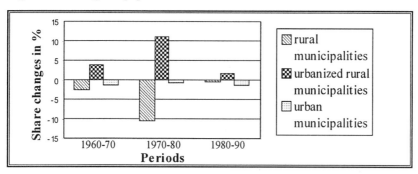

Source: Deduced from Table 8.3

As has been previously mentioned, the Netherlands has experienced a continuous growth in population since 1950. This growth diminished from 13.8 per cent in the 1950s to 5.7 per cent in the 1980s. The 1990s showed a different picture, however, because in this decade the population rose suddenly by 6.5 per cent. At the level of urbanization, population increases occurred, except for the rural municipalities in the 1970s. In that period the rural municipalities were faced with a population decrease of more than 42 per cent, while the population of the urbanized rural municipalities increased by 56.4 per cent. This is in line with the changes that have previously been recorded. The growth percentages of urban municipalities declined gradually, but remained positive. In Table 8.4, the growth percentages of population are shown for the period 1950-2000.

Table 8.4 Percentage population growth related to degree of urbanization, 1950-2000

Population growth (%)	1950-60	1960-70	1970-80	1980-90	1990-2000
Rural municipalities		1.55	-42.37	2.57	
Urbanized rural municip.		33.96	56.4	10.3	
Urban municipalities		10.87	7.25	3.17	
Total population	13.8	13.52	8.78	5.69	6.52

Source: deduced from Tables 2 and 3

Table 8.5 gives an overview of the number of municipalities over the course of the years, and where available, the degree of urbanization. From this Table it can be concluded that the total number of municipalities has decreased by 47 per cent from 1015 in 1950 to 537 in 2000. With regard to the degree of urbanization per decade, data are only available for the years 1980, 1990 and 1992. From this data it can be seen that during those years, rural municipalities on average represented 27 per cent, urbanized rural municipalities approximately 56 per cent, and urban municipalities 17 per cent of the total number of municipalities in the Netherlands. In absolute terms, the number of municipalities has diminished in all three categories of the ABC-classification, although the number of urban municipalities declined only slightly by 2.5 per cent and has been stable at 117 municipalities since 1990. Compared to the total number of municipalities, the urbanized rural municipalities and the urban municipalities have gained in share and only the rural municipalities have diminished, but it should be noted that the changes are relatively low.

Table 8.6 has been compiled because of the lack of data in Table 8.5. In Table 8.6 the number of municipalities is specified in categories of numbers of inhabitants for the period 1950-1999. It shows that some of the smallest municipalities had a large decrease from 624 in 1950, to only 20 in 1999. The second category gained municipalities until 1980 (from 314 in 1950, to 407 in 1980), after which it dropped to 292 municipalities in 1999. Categories 3, 4 and 5 all showed increases, and category 3 increased by almost one third from 53 in 1950, to 167 in 1999.

Table 8.5 Number of municipalities related to degree of urbanization, 1950-2000

Municipalities	1950	1960	1970	1980	Share	1990	Share	1992	Share	2000
Rural				239	29.5	177	26.3	165	25.5	
Urbanized rural				452	55.7	378	56.3	365	56.4	
Urban				120	14.8	117	17.4	117	18.1	
Total	1015	994	913	811		672		647		537

Source: compiled from CBS data

Table 8.6 Number of municipalities related to categories of numbers of inhabitants, 1950-1999

Number of municipalities	1950	1960	1970	1980	1990	1999
1: > 5000 inhabitants	624	556	406	246	105	20
2: 5000-20000 inhabitants	314	344	389	407	384	292
3: 20000-50000 inhabitants	53	61	78	114	130	167
4: 50000-100000 inhabitants	13	19	26	27	36	34
5: > 100000 inhabitants	11	14	14	17	17	25
Total	1015	994	913	811	672	538

Source: compiled from CBS data

The population increases in the different urban zones and in the Netherlands as a whole, are not only the result of natural growth, but also of internal and international migration. According to the Central Bureau of Statistics, the definition of internal migration is the number of changes of residence of the population within the Netherlands, i.e. a move from one municipality to another.[5] When studying interregional moves, it could generally be said that more people want to move to the west of the country. Moreover, the agricultural provinces (the northern and south-western parts of the country) are normally confronted with a surplus of people wishing to

---

[5] Except for changes caused by municipal border changes.

move away to another part of the country. The eastern and southern parts of the country fluctuate in general around the neutral line.[6]

Immigration relates to all individuals whose arrivals result in entries in Dutch population registers. Up to September 1994 the entry criterion was 30 days of residency for Dutch nationals, and an expected residency of at least 180 days for non-Dutch residents. Since October 1994 the criterion has changed to residency for two thirds of a year irrespective of nationality. Emigration relates to all individuals departing from the Netherlands whose departure results in cancellations from the Dutch population registers. The basis for removal from the registers has changed from 8 months abroad to 12 months, irrespective of nationality. Net migration equals the number of arrivals minus the number of departures (CBS, 2001).

The post-war period showed an emigration surplus in the Netherlands. The Dutch emigration reached its peak in 1952 when 81,000 people emigrated from Holland. From then on emigration diminished somewhat with some recovery in the 1970s and 1990s at an absolute level and a continuous decrease with regard to the annual growth figures. Immigration has risen since 1960 with a small decline in the 1980s, both at an absolute and relative level. The rise of immigration occurred because foreign employees were attracted by Dutch welfare and were recruited by companies that could not find enough labourers in the Netherlands. It is assumed that the Dutch welfare was also a reason why emigration decreased in the Netherlands. Between 1960 and 1990 the number of foreigners in the Netherlands increased more than five times. In 1960 less than 120 000 foreigners were living in the Netherlands. By 1990 the country had approximately 640 000 foreigners, which equaled 4.3 per cent of the total population. Especially because of family reunions and the influx of refugees, the Netherlands can currently be regarded as an immigration country, although in comparison to other countries immigration to the country is still at a relatively low level (Grote Winkler Prins, 1992). Table 8.7 illustrates the immigration and emigration figures for the Netherlands between 1950 and 1999. Subsequently, we discuss the decade periods separately and in more detail.

MIGRATION AND URBAN DEVELOPMENT IN THE PERIOD 1950-1960[7]

In the period 1950-1960, the population of the Netherlands increased by 13.8 per cent from 10 million inhabitants to 11.4 million inhabitants. This was the largest increase in the past 50 years. Also in regard to the economy, the years after the war can be described as a boom. The 1950s showed significantly lower unemployment figures than in the years before the war. Because of

---

[6] This picture has been portrayed by Ter Heide (1965) for the period 1880-1960.

[7] Based on Ter Heide (1965), CBS-data and other indicated references.

Table 8.7   Immigration and emigration figures for the period 1950-1999

(* 1000)	1950-1959	1960-1969	1970-1979	1980-1989	1990-1999
Immigration	486	644	934	850	1129
Emigration	621	558	605	587	605
Average annual increase of immigration*	4.5	5.3	6.9	5.9	7.3
Idem of emigration*	5.8	4.6	4.5	4.1	3.9

Notes: * Per 1000 of population
Source: adapted from Prins et al., 2000

advanced industrialization, the southern part of the Netherlands had to deal with a positive balance of migration and the agricultural provinces (north and south-west) were consequently faced with out-migration. The western part of the country still showed positive migration although this balance was relatively low in the early 1950s. In 1954 the migration balance in the west increased and reached a peak in 1956, after which the balance declined sharply but remained positive, albeit at a relatively low level. The drop in migration in the western part of the country can partly be attributed to the decentralization of industry and to the expense cuts in 1956. The eastern part of the country showed a sudden increase in migration at the end of the 1950s and it even reached a higher peak than the western part in 1960.

Although an impression may have been given that the level of internal migration has been high, the volume of internal migration was always rather low. This was especially the case in the short distance markets (within the provinces). The intra-and outer-provincial migration was more or less at the same (low) level (about 42 percent). This was exceptional because before the war intra-provincial migration was always at a much higher level (around 75 per cent), than outer-provincial migration. One reason for the lower intra-provincial volume was the increase in the average sizes of municipalities. A decrease of 60 municipalities between 1940 and 1960 (respectively 1054 and 994) indicates that the municipalities became larger and that the migration volume between adjacent municipalities consequently declined. Moreover, the population density increased from 268 in 1940 to 352 in 1960. The demographic composition did not change dramatically over this period and can therefore not be used as grounds for this phenomenon. One effect of the low short-distance migration was the 6.8 per cent increase in commuting between homes and work between 1947 and 1960.

From the 1950s urbanization mainly resulted from migration flows to the smaller cities. After 1950 the largest cities faced the heaviest migration losses, while the population of many other municipalities increased

(Hoekveld, 1981). This can be deduced from Table 8.8, where the municipalities together show a bigger increase (but at a slower pace) than the individual municipalities. Due to the limited territories of the large cities, other locations were sought to accommodate the increasing city population. The three largest agglomerations suburbanized in the 1950s, but generally speaking, the period 1950-1960 was one marked by urbanization (see Table 8.9).

Table 8.8 Average annual population growth of the individual C-municipalities, of the C-municipalities as a whole and of the Dutch population between 1950 and 1970

Average annual growth in %	1950-1960	1960-1970
Of individual C-municipalities	1.6	1.9
Of all the C-municipalities	1.2	1.2
Of the total Dutch population	1.3	1.3

Source: adapted from Hoekveld, 1981

Table 8.9 Urban developments between 1950 and 1978

Agglomerations	1950-1960	1960-1969/70	1969/70-1978
Large Randstad	Suburbanization	Sub-disurbanization	Disurbanization
Remaining Randstad	Urbanization	Urb.-suburbanization	Suburbanization
Emanation-zone	Urbanization	Urb.-suburbanization	Suburbanization
Peripheral	Urbanization	Urbanization	Suburbanization

Source: deduced from van den Berg et al., 1987

The CBS-classification in the study of Ter Heide (see Table 8.10) shows a more or less similar picture when urbanized rural municipalities are considered as smaller cities.[8] From this study it turns out that in the 1950s especially the rural municipalities (or peripheral areas) were faced with large migration losses, whereas the urbanized rural municipalities saw an increase in inhabitants. These two flows, together, indicate an urbanization process, all the more because the urban municipalities were only confronted with minor migration losses. Also the study of van den Berg et al. comes to the same

---

[8] This also appears from the figures of the subdivision of category C, see Ter Heide (1965) p. 209.

conclusion, that urbanization dominated in the 1950s. They discovered that in the 1950s, an overall increase in cores and rings of the agglomerations occurred, where the cores grew the fastest. This is termed an urbanization phase, because the agglomerations grew at the cost of the surrounding rings. The urban developments between 1950 and 1982 are shown in Table 8.11.

Table 8.10 Number of municipalities, degree of urbanization, and migration balance of the determined categories for the period 1948-1960

Type of municipality	Migration losses (in ‰)					Migration gains (in ‰)				
	0.0-3.9	4.0-7.9	8.0-11.9	> 12.0	Total	0.0-3.9	4.0-7.9	8.0-11.9	> 12.0	Total
Rural municipalities	173	135	181	16	505	132	17	8	3	160
Urbanized rural municipalities	44	29	7	1	81	100	11	20	11	142
Urban municipalities	36	12	7	1	56	26	16	5	4	51

Source: adapted from Ter Heide, 1965

Table 8.11 Annual growth rate of 24 selected Dutch agglomerations in % of the total agglomeration population 1950-1982

Location	1950-1960	1960-1970	1970-1974	1974-1978	1978-1982
Cores	+0.82	+0.19	-0.66	-0.47	-0.10
Rings	+0.51	+0.81	+0.90	+0.64	+0.51
Agglomerations	+1.32	+1.00	+0.24	+0.17	+0.41
Netherlands	+1.38	+1.35	+1.03	+0.75	+0.70

Source: derived from van den Berg et al., 1987

In the period 1951-1956, 17.9 per cent of the migrants were family members and 82.1 per cent, single persons. Single persons not only dominated the migration market; they also migrated over longer distances. Among the outer-provincial migrants, a minority of 16.1 per cent consisted of families and among the intra-provincial migrants, families represent only 19.9 per cent. The dominance of single persons in the migration process can be linked to the age of the migrants. Table 8.12 gives the percentages of migrants related to age for the years 1951 and 1960. It can be concluded that in the 1950s the largest number of migrants were between 20 and 24 years of age and that more than 50 per cent were between 15 and 30 years. The dominance of adolescents and young adults and therefore mostly single people in migration is a normal phenomenon. It can further be noted that seniors above 65 years tend to change residence more often in the analyzed period. This can be explained by the decline in the involvement of older people in economic activities, which gives them more freedom in choosing a new place to live.

Table 8.12 Percentages of internal migrants in relation to age for the years 1951 and 1960

Age category	1951	1960
0-15 (1951) or 0-14 (1960)	8.2	7.0
16-19 (1951) or 15-19 (1960)	11.1	15.0
20-24	24.5	24.6
25-29	20.5	18.1
30-39	17.3	15.7
40-49	7.7	7.3
50-64	5.7	6.0
65+	5.0	6.3

Source: adapted from Ter Heide, 1965

Table 8.13 gives a rough classification of occupations together with the corresponding percentages of migrants and of the total working population.[9] From this table it is clear that the employers and the self-employed are represented by a low migration percentage, but that this category of occupation at the same time represents a relatively large share of the total working population. The low migration percentage can be explained because this category frequently consists of owners of companies, who tend to stay at the same place for years. The migration percentage of employers and self-

---

[9] Because of a lack of data the total working population here only refers to working male heads of families, and therefore, Table 8.12 can only be used as a rough indication.

employed rose somewhat in the 1950s while the share of the working population declined.   Furthermore, the employees were relatively more mobile than the manual workers in 1951, whereas the opposite was the case in 1960. For the total working population both these categories rose in share. As regards the migrants without an occupation, it turns out that the women dominated and that, logically, the youngest and oldest age categories were strongly represented in the migration flows of the 1950s.[10] The migrating women were probably divorced women, widowers and brides.

Table 8.13 Labour migration relative to labour force in The Netherlands (migrants with an occupation and labour force male heads of families)

Occupation	Migrants		Total working population	
	1951	1960	1947	1960
Employers and self-employed	4.0	5.8	33.6	23.6
Employees	42.0	51.0	19.8	27.9
Manual workers	54.0	43.2	46.6	48.4

Source: adapted from Ter Heide, 1965

With regard to income and status in the 1950s, it can be said that in general migration to the suburbs tended to attract high-income and high-status occupational groups, except around the youngest cities such as Arnhem and Eindhoven (Ter Heide, 1965). To study the urban income distribution for the period 1950-1978, the Netherlands has been divided into three areas (van den Berg et al. 1987):

❑   *The Randstad*, the most intensively urbanized section of the Netherlands that contains the three largest agglomerations;

❑   *The periphery*, the economically weaker frontier of the nation on which the central government has focused its socio-economic development policy since the 1950s;

❑   *The emanation zone*, the transitional zone between Randstad and periphery.

In the 1950s the urban incomes of the Randstad area and of the emanation zones rose, although the income of the Randstad rose at a much higher level. The peripheral areas declined in income. From Table 8.14 it appears that during this period the Randstad agglomerations were the only regions that could be classified as prosperous. The remaining Randstad agglomerations

---

[10] For detailed figures we refer to Ter Heide (1965) p. 309.

had above average incomes, but were not growing, and those in the emanation and peripheral zones stood below the national average. In Table 8.15 it is shown that the cores absorbed the largest part of the income of the agglomerations. While the share of the cores declined, the share of the ring zones increased in the 1950s due to sub-urbanization of the three largest agglomerations. The peripheral rings, however, were faced with the lowest income of the entire Netherlands in 1960 (Van den Berg et al. 1987).

Table 8.14 Income development between 1950 and 1978

Agglomerations		1950-1960	1960-1969/70	1969/70-1978
Large Randstad	Aggl.	Prosperity	Recession	Recession
	Core	Prosperity	Recession	Recession-depression
	Ring	Prosperity	Prosperity	Recession*
Remaining Randstad	Aggl.	Prosperity	Prosperity	Recession
	Core	Recovery	Prosperity	Recession-depression
	Ring	Prosperity	Prosperity	Recession*
Emanation-zone	Aggl.	Recovery	Recovery-prosperity**	Recession
	Core	Recovery	Recovery-prosperity**	Recession-depression
	Ring	Recovery	Recovery-prosperity	Prosperity
Peripheral	Aggl.	Depression	Recovery	Recovery
	Core	Depression*	Recovery	Depression
	Ring	Depression	Recovery	Recovery

Note: * on a relatively high level ** on a relatively low level

Source: adapted from van den Berg et al., 1987

Table 8.15 Income shares of cores and ring zones between 1950 and 1978

	Share of cores (%)	Share of ring zones (%)
1950	77.7	22.3
1960	74.8	25.2
1969	70.4	29.6
1978	63.7	36.3

Source: deduced from van den Berg et al., 1987

MIGRATION AND URBAN DEVELOPMENT IN THE PERIOD 1960-1970

Between 1960 and 1970 the Dutch population remained at a fairly high overall growth percentage of 13.5 per cent. In absolute terms this amounts to more than 1.5 million people. The number of municipalities declined from 994 in 1960 to 913 in 1970, whereas the population density obviously increased. It appears that among the urban population, this proportion diminished only marginally from 80.3 per cent in 1960 to 79.7 per cent in 1970 (Van den Berg et al. 1981).

When studying the different urban zones, Hoekveld (1981) shows that the largest cities (such as Amsterdam, The Hague, Haarlem, Groningen and Arnhem) continued to lose people in the early sixties. This is due to the fact that the number of municipalities with reducing or stagnant populations diminished, especially in the eastern part of the country. This suggests, therefore, that the emphasis in urban development in the Netherlands moved more towards sub-urbanization in the 1960s.

Looking at Table 8.11, the agglomerations still show a large increase (1 per cent annually) albeit lower than in the 1950s and lower than the growth of the Dutch population as a whole. The growth of the agglomerations was mainly the result of a strong increase in the rings. The growth in the rings occurred at the expense of the cores where there was only a small increase. Therefore it can be concluded that spatial deconcentration became the dominant urban development trend in the Netherlands during the 1960s (van den Berg et al., 1987). Comparing this with Figure 8.3, it is indeed clear that the share of the rings (the urbanized rural municipalities) grew by 3.9 per cent while the shares of the urban and rural municipalities both dropped. This becomes even more evident in Figures 8.4 and 8.5, where the development of the different C-municipalities is illustrated. Here it can be seen that the large cities were confronted with a substantial share-loss of 5.5 per cent while the small and especially the medium-sized cities (+3.7 per cent) experienced an influx of inhabitants.

This data is in accordance with Table 8.8. Here the same trend as in the 1950s appears, but the individual municipalities show a higher growth percentage, which points to sub-urbanization. The major Randstad agglomerations (Amsterdam, The Hague, and Rotterdam) declined even into dis-urbanization. This means that the population of the agglomerations declined through an excess of population gains in the ring by population losses in the core (see also Table 8.9). These agglomerations were further faced with problems such as rising unemployment, deteriorated facilities and services, and public deficits (van den Berg et al., 1987). This is contrary to the general trend of a large expansion in most of the employment categories between 1930 and 1971 (Hoekveld, 1981).

Figure 8.4 Population distribution of C-municipalities between 1960 and 1990

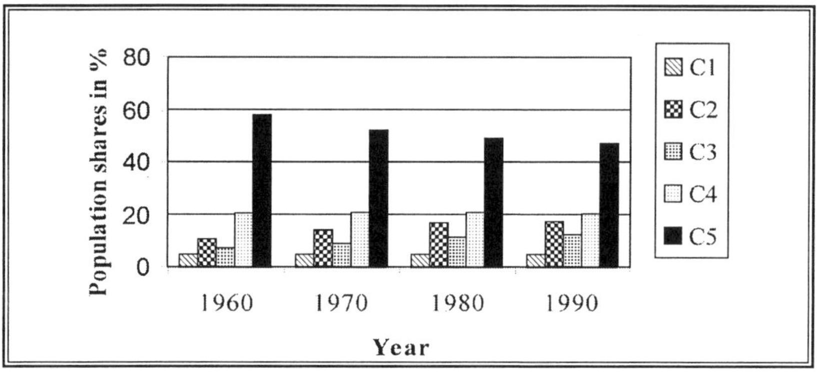

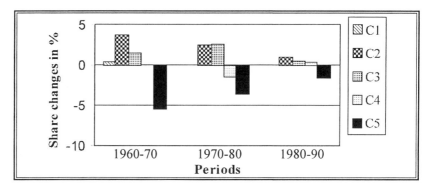

Source :   compiled from CBS data

Figure 8.5 Changes of population shares of C-municipalities between 1960 and 1990

Source :   deduced from Figure 8.4

During these decades, incomes rose and relative transportation costs dropped, which facilitated covering longer distances by car and broadened the urban population's range of residence and workplace choices. Many households made the decision to relocate further from their workplaces, which led to the described process of sub-urbanization, and for the largest cities such as The Hague, to dis-urbanisation (van den Berg et al., 1987).

With the assistance of Table 8.16, we can look closer at the migration flows in the 1960s and 1970s (see next section). From here it turns out that the cores were confronted with a large negative net-effect, which resulted in a negative migration balance for all agglomerations.

Table 8.16 Migration effects in the 24 agglomerations (*1000) between 1960 and 1978.

Area	Migration movement	1960-1970	1970-1978
Cores	Migration losses	324.4	432.9
	Migration gains	19.4	15.6
	Net effect of migration	*-305.0*	*-417.3*
Rings	Migration losses	11.0	
	Migration gains	243.4	267.9
	Net effect of migration	*+232.4*	*+267.9*
Agglomerations	Migration losses	145.9	202.8
	Migration gains	73.6	56.3
	Net effect of migration	*-72.3*	*-146.5*

Source: adapted from van den Berg et al., 1981

In this period income declined in the Randstad agglomerations, while it increased in the emanation and peripheral zones. In terms of income (see Table 8.14), the three largest agglomerations were overtaken by the five small Randstad agglomerations and closely challenged by three medium-sized agglomerations (Utrecht in the Randstad and two others located in the emanation zone). During this period, the downward development of the peripheral agglomerations recovered. With the exception of the three largest agglomerations, the income in all other agglomerations remained positive during the 1960s (van den Berg et al., 1987). As a continuation of the 1950s, the income shares of the cores further declined, whereas the shares of the ring zones increased (Table 8.15) in line with the direction of the urban developments towards sub-urbanization. Especially the ring areas of the emanation zone agglomerations increased in income during this period.

MIGRATION AND URBAN DEVELOPMENT IN THE PERIOD 1970-1980

In this period, the trends of the previous decade continued with regard to total population, population density and number of municipalities. This implies that total population and population density both increased (although total population growth was almost 5 per cent lower than in the 1960s) and the number of municipalities decreased (see general overview for specifics).

The distribution of population over the country as a whole changed significantly during the 1970s (see Table 8.3, Figure 8.2 and 8.3). The share of the population of rural municipalities decreased by 10.3 per cent, while that of urbanized rural municipalities increased by 11 per cent and urbanized municipalities remained stable around 52 per cent. This implies a further continuation of the sub-urbanization process that was started in the 1960s. From these figures it appears that this sub-urbanization occurred at the expense of the rural municipalities. This becomes clearer when one looks at Table 8.4; the population of the rural municipalities decreased by more than 42 per cent and that of urbanized rural municipalities increased by more than 56 per cent. The population figures of urban municipalities increased by only 7.3 per cent.

From the analysis of agglomerations, the conclusion is that the 1970s could be characterized as a period of true sub-urbanization (see also Table 8.9). From Table 8.11 it clearly appears that throughout that period, the growth in the ring population was greater than the decrease in the core population. Although both figures declined gradually during the 1970s, sub-urbanization continued. With regard to the population of the agglomerations, they were first faced with retardation of growth, after which this reverted to an increase in the growth rate. Also the relative share of the agglomerations increased with regard to the national total. Although the central cities still exerted a negative influence on growth of the collective agglomerations in this period, their development was generally positive. The reduced volume of population loss in the three largest cores was particularly remarkable (van den Berg et al., 1987).

In this decade the growth in income ended and went into decline in all groups of agglomerations; only the peripheral agglomerations maintained their relatively low incomes (see Table 8.14). The income of the agglomerations in general converged towards the national average except for the small Randstad agglomerations, which were relatively prosperous. At the end of the 1970s, the ring zones represented an income share of more than 36 per cent (see Table 8.15), due to sub-urbanization in general and dis-urbanization in the three largest cores.

When one looks at the age of the migrants, every age category had negative migration balances in the Randstad in 1975 (see Table 8.17). Also with regard to the composition of migration, it turns out that in that specific year many families migrated from the Randstad to other parts of the Netherlands, while the attraction for single people to migrate to the Randstad was relatively low (see Table 8.18).

MIGRATION AND URBAN DEVELOPMENT IN THE PERIOD 1980-1990

The period of the 1980s was from a spatial perspective an era of rather stable developments, without clear disturbances in migration and urban growth patterns. This period may be characterized as a steady state.

Table 8.17: Migration between Randstad and remaining Netherlands related to age categories in 1975, 1980 and 1985

		0-14	15-29	30-49	50-64	65+	Total
1975	To Randstad	10,985	34,195	10,210	2,230	2,015	59,635
	From Randstad	20,350	36,975	17,785	7,440	5,490	88,040
	Balance	*-9,365*	*-2,780*	*-7,575*	*-5,210*	*-3,475*	*-28,405*
1980	To Randstad	8,440	30,545	9,365	2,125	1,780	52,255
	From Randstad	13,945	30,355	15,585	5,355	3,405	68,645
	Balance	*-5,505*	*+190*	*-6,220*	*-3,230*	*-1,625*	*-16,390*
1985	To Randstad	8,840	32,505	11,885	2,690	2,675	58,595
	From Randstad	9,445	22,320	12,595	5,050	3,380	52,790
	Balance	*-605*	*+10,185*	*-710*	*-2,360*	*-705*	*+5,805*

Source: deduced from Jobse et al., 1989

Table 8.18: Migration balances of families and singles in 1975, 1980 and 1985

Living environment	1975		1980		1985	
	Single	Family	Single	Family	Single	Family
Four largest cities	-1,705	-51,430	715	-32,445	8,550	-16,370
Growth municip.	2,790	10,835	4,770	14,750	6,110	9,470
Medium-sized municipalities	1,375	-5,140	0	-6,405	570	-4,570
Agglomeration municipalities	-505	5,035	-1,420	2,230	-2,340	2,690
Remaining Randstad	-360	10,770	-1,635	3,070	-3,075	4,765
Remaining Netherlands	-1,595	29,930	-2,430	18,800	-9,815	4,015

Source: deduced from Jobse et al., 1989

In the 1980s the increase in population continued, albeit at a slower rate than previously (i.e. 5.7 per cent or 801,560 people). Population density further increased whereas the number of municipalities declined by 139, the largest decline between 1950 and 2000.

The distribution of population over the country shows minor changes between 1980 and 1990 (Table 8.3). The urbanized rural municipalities still grew in share, but by only 1.6 per cent. The rural and urban municipalities both declined in share with respectively 0.3 per cent and 1.3 per cent. This still points to sub-urbanization, albeit at a relatively low rate.

The distribution of municipalities shows a different ratio than the distribution of population over the country (Table 8.5). The direction of change of the shares of rural and urbanized rural municipalities in the 1980s remained the same as in Table 8.3. The urban municipalities are an exception. The share of population of urban municipalities declined, but the share of number of municipalities increased.

When studying the population shares of different C-municipalities, it appears that only the largest municipalities decreased in share by 1.7 per cent in the 1980s. It is remarkable, however, that the share of C4 has risen because, in the 1970s, these municipalities experienced a decline. The smallest municipalities were still stable in population share. In this picture C2 shows the largest increase in share of approximately 1 per cent in the period 1980-90.

The total mobility pattern is strongly determined by migrants between 15 and 29 years of age (almost 50 per cent of the total number of migrants) in the 1980s. This category of migrants showed a large positive migration balance in the Randstad in 1985 (see Table 8.17). All negative migration balances of the age categories have dropped to modest levels, except for the migrants between 50 and 64 years of age.

During the 1980s the migration balance of families approached an equilibrium, while the attraction of the Randstad for single people became quite strong. In particular, the position of the four largest cities was dominant. The number of families that moved away from the large cities declined dramatically, especially in the early 1980s, while an equally significant number of single people migrated to the Randstad (see Jobse and Musterd, 1989 and Table 8.18). Also, the number of migrants between 15 and 29 years, who migrated to the large cities, was remarkable. The number of those who settled in the large cities was twice the number of those who moved away from the large cities (Jobse and Musterd, 1989).

MIGRATION AND URBAN DEVELOPMENT IN THE PERIOD 1990-2000

The last decade of the twentieth century showed signs of new trends. Whereas the growth in population declined after 1950, the 1990s showed a different pattern of increase. The population growth of 6.5 per cent was almost 1 per cent higher than in the 1980s. The country had a population density of 468 persons per square km and numbered only 537 municipalities at the beginning of the new millennium. The distribution of population and municipalities between 1992 and 2000 has been determined by means of the most recent CBS classification, i.e. address density.

Regarding the distribution of municipalities, there were 322 and 192 non-urbanized municipalities in 1992 and 2000 respectively (Table 8.19). This is by far the largest number of municipalities in the country, which can be explained by their small size. From this it can be concluded that the more urbanized and larger the municipality, the fewer the number of municipalities. If one looks at Table 8.6, however, it is remarkable that the previous statement relative to the smallest municipalities has not been valid since 1980. The smallest municipalities are not only small in size but also in number; this was especially noticeable in 1999. In the 1990s this category was confronted with a decline of more than 80 per cent. Since 1980 the largest number of municipalities was found in the second category (with between 5 000 and 20 000 inhabitants), but also the third category (with between 20 000 and 50 000 inhabitants) rose sharply during this period.

Table 8.19: Urban developments in 1992 and 2000 according to address density

	Year	Non-urban	Slightly urba-nized	Moder-ately urba-nized	Strongly urba-nized	Very strongly urba-nized	Total
Number of municipalities	1992	322	182	87	44	12	647
	2000	192	184	94	55	12	537
Population number (mil.)	1992	2.93	3.10	3.13	3.25	2.74	1.51
	2000	2.35	3.40	3.27	4.10	2.77	1.59
Shares of population in %	1992	19.36	20.37	20.7	21.47	18.08	-
	2000	14.8	21.39	20.62	25.71	17.48	-
Population growth in %	1992-2000	19.84	10.09	4.46	25.54	1.37	4.86

Source: compiled from CBS data

From Table 8.19 and Figures 8.6 and 8.7, it further appears that with regard to the distribution of population, the strongly urbanized areas had the largest population share. These areas have even grown by more than 4 per cent in share due to a large population increase of more than 25 per cent between 1992 and 2000. At the same time the non-urbanized areas lost almost 20 per cent of their population and therefore almost 5 per cent in share. This can partly be explained by a large decline in number of municipalities (from 322 to 192). For reasons previously mentioned, it is difficult to compare this classification with the degree of urbanization in 1990 or 1992, which is shown in Table 8.3 (population numbers and shares) and Table 8.5 (number of municipalities and shares).

The number of persons that changed residence is significantly higher (see Table 8.20) than the internal migration figures indicated in Table 8.21. This can be attributed to the fact that internal migration is defined as the volume of change in residence between different municipalities. Nevertheless, Table 8.20 gives a useful overview of the developments in the 1990s. From this table it appears that the number of people switching houses constantly rose during the 1990s, except for 1999 when this number suddenly declined by almost 5 per cent. The rise in the number of persons switching homes in the 1990s can be attributed to the economic growth in this period. Because the growth continued, the prices of houses increased extraordinarily, which is probably the reason for the decline in 1999. It further shows that the ratio of migrations within municipalities, within provinces and between provinces is about the same during this period, viz. 63 per cent, 21 per cent and 16 per cent, respectively.

Figure 8.6 Population distribution according to address density in 1992 and 2000

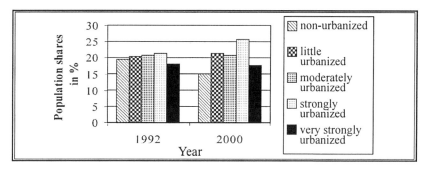

Source: deduced from Table 8:19

Figure 8.7 Change of population distribution between 1992 and 2000

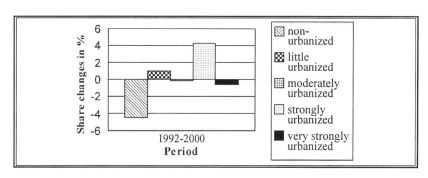

Source: deduced from Table 8:19

Table 8.20: Basic figures of removals within the Netherlands

(*1000)	1990	1995	1996	1997	1998	1999
Persons changing residence	1553	1717	1714	1740	1774	1696
- Within municipalities	986	1111	1084	1107	1108	1058
- Within provinces	321	358	370	367	383	371
- Between provinces	243	248	260	266	283	267

Source: derived from Prins et al., 2000

Table 8.21: Some components of internal migration in the Netherlands, 1988-98

Year	Total (*1000)	Within the same province (%)	With family (%)
1988	589	58.8	43.9
1989	596	57.8	42.0
1990	566	56.6	40.1
1991	562	56.3	39.7
1992	577	57.2	40.0
1993	588	58.2	40.3
1994	594	58.8	39.2
1995	606	59.1	37.5
1996	630	58.7	37.5
1997	643	57.1	37.2
1998	666	57.5	37.4

Source: compiled from CBS data

In Table 8.21 some components of internal migration are shown. Here it also appears that migration has risen in the 1990s, while the share of migrating families has gradually been decreasing and has been stable at around 37.5 per cent since 1995. The average share of migrations within the same province is almost 58 per cent in the 1990s.

URBAN POLICIES IN THE NETHERLANDS BETWEEN 1950 AND 2000[11]

Urban developments in the Netherlands of the past 50 years can partly be explained by the urban policies that have been devised and implemented during this period. Since policies tend to follow development trends this section on urban policies describes urban developments that have actually occurred in the Netherlands. The chapter finishes with an examination of predictions for the urban future of the Netherlands.

After the Second World War, the Netherlands had to recover from the destruction and find a solution for the housing shortage. In this period of recover, a remarkable effort was made in the area of public housing, industrialization and road construction. In 1951 a special Work Commission 'The West of the Country'[12] was established and in 1960 the First Memorandum on Town Planning was published. In this document special attention was paid to the limited capacities of the existing cities to cope with the increasing population. In particular, the large flows of people to the west of the country resulted in additional pressure on the housing market and threatened the existing urban agglomerations there. The government was afraid that the favourable economic, social, cultural and especially geographic position of the western part of the country would cause an unequal balance in relation to other parts of the country. Therefore, a spread policy was formulated to stimulate the areas outside the Randstad and to assimilate larger population shares. This was aimed at reducing the Randstad's population growth and to create a healthy business environment in the peripheral regions.

The Second Memorandum on Town Planning appeared in 1966. At that time it was predicted that by the year 2000 the Dutch population would number about 20 million people. Therefore, policies were focussed on bundled (concentrated) deconcentration over the country. To accommodate the fast growing population it was necessary to form urban districts (urban areas around a large city, the so-called 'growth cores') and to enlarge the infrastructure network. The people who stayed behind in the cities were, however, ignored and at that time the use of cars was not seen as a problem. The proposals of the Second Memorandum have hardly been implemented. The Randstad grew more than expected and instead of bundled deconcentration, an overflow to 'little green cores' took place.

The Third Memorandum on Town Planning was introduced in different stages between 1973 and 1983. The motive for this report was a new population projection. Instead of the terrifying prediction of 20 million

---

[11] Based on: Vijfde Nota Ruimtelijke Ordening , Nijkamp (1982), VROM-website and Sorber (2001).
[12] Original: "Werkcommissie Westen des Lands"

people for the year 2000, a maximum of 17 million was forecast. The Third Memorandum has become a collection of three sub-Memoranda: the Orientation Memorandum of Town Planning, the Urbanization Memorandum and the Rural Areas Memorandum.

In the Orientation Memorandum of 1974 explicit attention was paid to the environment and to urban problems. It was still the aim to spread population and employment, but this was combined with environment care, protection of open spaces and the reduction of inequality and deprivation. Therefore, 11 growth poles were indicated. In the Orientation Memorandum the growth of mobility and the related congestion were noticed for the first time and were seen as a problem that was closely associated with the total spatial and socio-economic development of the country. But action only was taken when mobility got out of hand.

The Urbanization Memorandum of 1976 planned a strengthening of the urban functions to prevent the erosion of large cities and the corrosion of the small cores. Furthermore, attention was paid to the concentration of a limited number of growth cities and cores to control the wave effects of urbanization out of the Randstad.

In 1988 the Fourth Memorandum on Town Planning was published under the motto of 'the Netherlands in the year 2015, work today'. The Fourth Report was part of the policy to achieve an economic recovery of the country. This would be carried out by aiming for appropriate locational conditions and by exploiting the existing advantages of the Netherlands (Schiphol Airport, Rotterdam Port and the favourable hinterland connections). The ultimate goal was the creation of an ideal locational climate for foreign main offices. With regard to the cities, a new spatial concept of the compact city was introduced. This meant the bundling of activities such as living, working and services as a way to reduce the enormous growth in traffic volumes. Therefore, the emphasis was put on compact urbanization and a restrictive policy for open spaces. In 1991 the Fourth Memorandum Extra appeared and here the so-called VINEX locations were developed as a continuation of the Fourth Memorandum. VINEX locations were aimed at combining living and working space within urban districts.

Presently, the Fifth Memorandum on Town Planning is in progress. In December 2000 the Government approved the first part of it. The Fifth Memorandum will consider the period up to the year 2020, but a further study will be provided for the period leading up to 2030. In contrast to previous plans, which dictated building locations and the volume of what was to be built, this plan will only outline the rules of the game to the lower governments of provinces and municipalities. Special attention is again given to investments in spatial quality, and to a lesser extent, to the main ports and the hinterland connections.

From this section it is obvious that the policies of the Netherlands for town planning can until very recently be described as demonstrating a strong belief in a feasible environment.

FUTURE URBAN PERSPECTIVES

It is of course difficult to map out the urban future of the Netherlands. Nevertheless, it may be possible to offer some perspectives based on the driving forces described in the previous section.

First, we observe a strong tendency towards settlement in the western part of the Netherlands. This is the destination of most immigrants, with the emphasis on concentration in the larger cities. Consequently, it is likely that urban areas in the western part will continue to grow in the future. If density becomes too high, sprawl from the Randstad to the next ring may take place, but this is just a case of ongoing urbanization with the Randstad still as the functional socio-economic heart of the Dutch economy.

A second future perspective on the Dutch space-economy concerns land-use planning. A significant part of the western part is protected, including much of the current green space. Strict land-use zoning has favoured concentration in the bigger agglomerations while suppressing unlimited expansion of villages in the western part. This has led to a poly-nuclear structure of the western part of the country characterized by an intense network connectivity between the medium-sized and large cities in a circular form as the green belt around the Green Heart of the Randstad (see also Ipenburg and Lambregts, 2001). With a first trend towards deregulation of land use-planning, in particular a larger responsibility for local authorities, a more selective dispersal of settlement patterns may emerge in the Randstad. Given the infrastructure constellation (and limitation), it is likely that those places located on accessible infrastructure links may become the fast growers in the near future.

REFERENCES

Centraal Bureau voor de Statistiek (diverse dates). *Annual reports of population and municipality statistics.* Centraal Bureau voor de Statistiek (2001). www.cbs.nl

Den Dulk, D., H. van de Stadt en J. M. Vliegen (1992). Een nieuwe maatstaf voor Stedelijkheid: De omgevingsadressendichtheid, in Centraal Bureau van de Statistiek, *Maandstatistiek Bevolking*, nr. 7, p. 14-27.

Deurloo, M. C. and G. A. Hoekveld (1980). *The population growth of the urban municipalities in the Netherlands between 1849 and 1970, with particular reference to the period 1899-1930.* Amsterdam: Free University Institute for Geographical Studies and Urban and Regional Planning.

Glaeser, E. L. (1998). Are cities dying? *Journal of Economic Perspectives*, **12 (2)** , 139-160.

Grote Winkler Prins Encyclopedie (1992). Ninth Edition. Amsterdam: Elsevier.

Grote Winkler Prins Encyclopedie (1976). Seventh Edition. Amsterdam: Elsevier.

Historische Winkler Prins Encyclopedie (1991). Amsterdam: Elsevier.

Hoekveld, G. A. (1981). *On the development of the Dutch urbanisation pattern between 1930 and 1971.* Working paper Voorburg: N.I.D.I

Ipenburg, D. and B. Lambregts (2001), *Polynuclear urban regions in North West Europe*, Delft: Delft University Press.

Jobse, R. B. and S. Musterd (1989). *Dynamiek in de Randstad – een analyse van woningbouw- en migratiestatistieken voor de periode 1970-1986.* Zoetermeer: Ministerie van Onderwijs en Wetenschappen.

Klaassen, L. H., W. T. M. Molle and J. H. P. Paelinck (1981), *Dynamics of urban development.* Aldershot: Gower Publishing Company.

Ministerie van Volkshuisvesting, Ruimtelijke Ordening en Milieu (2000). *Vijfde Nota Ruimtelijke Ordening.* The Hague.

Nijkamp, P. (1982). *De toekomst van de stad.* Groningen: Vuurbaak.

Nijmeijer, H. (2000). *Nederland in delen – groot en klein.* Centraal Bureau voor de Statistiek. Index no. 1, January, The Hague

Prins, K. and R. Verhoef (2000). 'Demografische ontwikkelingen in Nederland', in NIDI. *Bevolkingsvraagstukken in Nederland Anno 2000*, Voorburg: N.I.D.I, pp. 21-37

Sorber, M. (2001). *Volgt wonen werken of volgt werken wonen?* Master's Thesis. Amsterdam: Free University.

Ter Heide, H. (1965). *Binnenlandse migratie in Nederland – Rijksdienst voor het nationale plan.* Publicatie nr. 16. Den Haag: Staatsuitgeverij 's-Gravenhage.

van den Berg, L. and J. van der Meer (1981). Urban change in the Netherlands, in Klaassen L. H., W. T. M. Molle and J. H. P. Paelinck. *Dynamics of urban development.* Aldershot: Gower Publishing Company, pp. 118-138

van den Berg, L., L. S. Burns and L. H. Klaassen (1987). *Spatial cycles.* Brookfield: Gower Publishing Company.

van der Ham, G. (1998). *Geschiedenis van Nederland.* Amsterdam: Nieuwezijds.

Vliegen, M. (1999). *Nederland regionaal – stadsbevolking.* Centraal Bureau voor de Statistiek. Index no. 7, August, The Hague.

Chapter 9

Counter-urbanization in Italy

P. Petsimeris

INTRODUCTION

As has already been documented, in the last three decades counter-urbanization has become a dominant force shaping the settlement patterns in a number of countries on both sides of the Atlantic (Berry, 1976; Illeris, 1979; Fielding, 1982; Vining, 1989, Ceresa et al., 1983; and Champion, 1989). This process is characterised by decreasing urban size, falling population densities, and decreasing heterogeneity of urban forms and activity distribution within urban regions.

This phenomenon has mainly affected the 'mature' urban systems of North America and Western Europe, while over the last twenty years the urban systems of other Less Developed Countries of Southern Europe have experienced changes that, in some respects, seem likely to lead to similar outcomes in the future. The aim of this chapter is to examine the process of urban deconcentration in Italy during the period 1951-2001.

Our main hypothesis is that the Italian urban system is highly heterogeneous, and the processes of urban diffusion are for this reason very different in the various regions. A number of studies oversimplified the case of the Mediterranean countries, including Italy, by attributing to them the early stages of maturity of their urban systems.

We will try to answer a series of simple questions:

❑ Are the processes of counter-urbanization affecting the entire territory of the peninsula, or are there areas where the phenomenon is more intense?

❑ What is the temporality of this process?

❑ What is the relationship between the deconcentration models of Berry (1976), Fielding (1982) and the city life model (van den Berg et al., 1982) and the empirical evidence?

THE ANALYSIS OF POPULATION DECONCENTRATION IN ITALY.

A number of international comparative studies considered the Italian settlement system (van den Berg et al. 1982; Fielding, 1986; and Ceresa et al. 1983;).

The diachronic analysis of urban networks (Ceresa et al. 1983) has established a typology. This extremely simple typology reunites the countries of Europe in four distinctive groups, and is based on the degree of de-concentration of the urban networks in question:

❑ Countries like Great Britain, Holland and France where the tendency of urban de-concentration, already in place during the 1970s, has continued throughout the 1980s.

❑ Countries like Italy, Austria and Germany where counter-urbanization only appeared during the 1980s.

❑ Countries like Greece, Spain, Portugal, Ireland and the Southern Italian macro-region where the tendency towards urban concentration continued during the 1980s, and which, according to the 1981 censuses, present strong sub-urbanization tendencies in the largest agglomerations.

❑ Finally, the socialist countries where the tendency towards urban concentration continued despite the anti-urban policies put in place by their governments.

From these groupings it is clear that the diversity of processes of urban de-concentration do not depend mainly on the size of the country or of the region. At the same time we can observe that counter-urbanization generally manifests itself in the economically mature regions.

The analysis of Fielding (1989) of the European countries situated to the west of a line drawn from the Adriatic to the Baltic showed that:

❑ In the 1950s urbanization was the dominant characteristic of the models of population distribution for all of the countries examined.

❑ In the 1970s urbanization only affected one country (Spain). In six countries (Austria, Ireland, Italy, Norway, Portugal and Swizerland) the processes of population concentration had ceased, and in the remaining seven countries (Belgium, Denmark, Germany, France, Sweden, Holland and the United Kingdom) counter-urbanization was dominant.

❑ In the 1980s Italy and Germany were affected by strong counter-urbanization processes. At the same time the process of counter-urbanization had diminished in Belgium, Denmark, Norway, Holland, Sweden and Switzerland. For the six remaining countries the author did not have the most recent data at his disposition.

❑ France passed from urbanization to counter-urbanization at the end of the 1960s.

A number of important analyses have been made in Italy of the migration phenomena of the city system, the historical evolution of the urban network (Gambi, 1973), the functional structuration of the urban network (Bottai and Costa, 1981; Scaramellini, 1991; and Dematteis and Petsimeris, 1989), and the position of the Italian cities within the European urban network (Conti and Spriano, 1990; Camagni and Pio, 1988). Most studies of Italian cities have focused on urbanization processes and urban networks (Cori, 1984 and 1986; Dematteis 1992; and Martinotti, 1993). A certain number of studies focused on individual regions or cities and studied deconcentration processes among other things (Mainardi, 1969; Muscarà, 1978; Dalmasso, 1971 and 1984; Seronde-Babonaux, 1983; Emanuel (1989), Petsimeris (1989) Coro et al., 1987; Cristaldi, 1994). Finally, a number of scholars insist on the selectivity of urbanization and counter-urbanization processes in terms of functional structures (Celant, 1988; Scaramellini 1991), and the increasing levels of social segregation in cities (Petsimeris 1989 and 1998). In this chapter we will concentrate mainly on the population change in relation to settlement size and regional differentiation, and try to understand which stage of urban deconcentration the different regions and metropolitan areas of Italy have reached at the end of the 20th century.

THE AREA AND THE DATA

In our analysis we used ISTAT decennial census data (1951, 1961, 1971, 1981 and 1991 – the most recent). The data for the 2001 census are not yet available, so we used the Public Records Office data. This data set is published every year, and indicates the natural and migratory movements and the resident population on the 31st December.

Italy is subdivided into 20 regions which are aggregated into four macro-regions : The North West (Piedmont, Liguria, Vale d'Aosta and Lombardy); the North East (Trentino Alto Adige, Venetia, Friuli-Venetia-Julia, Emilia Romagna); the Centre (Tuscany, Umbria, Latium and Marche); and the South, also known as the *Mezzogiorno* (Abruzzi, Molise, Calabria, Basilicata, Apulia, Campania, Sicily and Sardinia).

The intermediate administrative level is the province: 107 units that include a main city (*capoluogo*) and the administrative hinterland. In terms of toponymy the capital city also gives the name of the Province. For instance the city of Milano is the *capoluogo* of the province of Milano and so forth.

Finally the basic administrative unit is the *comune*. Italy is subdivided into 8000 *comuni*. The largest is Rome and the smallest has a population of less than 100 inhabitants. It is important to emphasise the huge differences in terms of distribution of the *comuni* in three of the macro-regions. Two regions of the North, Piedmont and Lombardy, contain 2755 *comuni* and the seven regions of *Mezzogiorno* contain 2199 *comuni*. In terms of population Piedmont and Lombardy have 13.3 million in 1998 and the *Mezzogiorno* 20.8 million (i.e. the *Mezzogiorno* has 556 *comuni* less but 7.5 million inhabitants more than Lombardy and Piedmont).

Another important factor that makes the study of urbanization in Italy more difficult is the differentiation of the *comuni* in terms of area, and the fact that the *comuni* which are large in terms of population are not equally large in terms of area. This difference is very important in terms of economic, social and spatial heterogeneity of the core and of the ring and makes the interpretation of the processes of suburbanisation more difficult. Rome has the largest area: 2000 sq. km, i.e. more than the area of Milan, Turin, Genoa, Florence and Bologna.

During the period 1951-1999 Italy's population grew from 47.5 million to 56.7 million. In 1951 there were 24 cities with more than 100,000 inhabitants, 15 of which were located in the North, 3 in the Centre and 6 in the South. During the same period the settlements with a population of more than 100,000 represented 20 per cent of the total Italian population. In 1991 the number of cities doubled (46) and represent 25.5 per cent of the Italian population. In terms of distribution 50 per cent of the cities were located in the North, 17.4 per cent in the Centre and 32.6 per cent in the south. But the changes concern also the other segments of the urban hierarchy and the suburban and peri-urban areas of the country. These changes were not isolated, continuous or forecastable in an easy and linear historical process. During the second half of the twentieth century Italy experienced significant growth and became one of the most important industrialised nations.

In the same period Italy was also transformed from a country of out-migration into a country of in-migration. Furthermore the massive interregional and interurban migration from the poor southern areas to the North, mainly Milan and Turin, ceased. During the period more than 6 million people left the marginal areas of the south, and the rural and peripheral areas of the north to concentrate in the metropolitan areas of the North and Rome. All these transformations had important consequences in terms of land use, infrastructure, housing production and suburbanization. We obviously will not analyse all of this, but it is important to take into account when analysing the processes of urban deconcentration.

THE REGIONAL DIFFERENTIATION

Milan, Turin and Genoa form the industrial triangle of Italy. In this area the Industrial Revolution started at the end of the nineteenth century and, it was here that Fordist development was manifest until the early 1970s. This area was also the main concentration of economic resources, and it became the central destination of biblical flows of population originating from the countryside, the areas of low economic development of the North East and the most remote areas of the Mezzogiorno. Inter urban, core-hinterland and intra-urban mobility have greatly affected the economic and social geography of the three metropolitan areas. These changes have an immediate consequence, not only on the urban form of the core areas, but also on the regional landscape. The urban form of the Italian cities shows strong uniformity in the periphery (high rise housing), formal, functional and social heterogeneity in the peri-central quarters with a mix of building types, and heterogeneity in the rings with the coexistence of *palazzoni*, single family housing, industrial buildings and the remains of farm buildings (Pizzorno, 1972; Gambi, 1973; Cardia et al., 1978; Crosta, 1978; Carozzi and Rozzi, 1984; and Cori, 1984).

In stark contrast with the wealthy, industrial North is the Mezzogiorno, i.e. the south of Italy, that in terms of resources, and social, political and economic organisation constitutes the less developed part of Italy. In the early seventies, Gambi (1973) used the term 'pre-industrial' to designate a model of urbanization and a type of economic organisation for this area. This macro-region's development was also dominated and controlled by the criminal organisations of the mafia. Geographers and sociologists concerned with the area have used a variety of terms to describe its character. For example, Conti (1983) used the term 'a territory without geography'; Leone (1988) employed the term 'Italia non metropolitana'; and Trigilia (1992) defined its development as 'development without autonomy' in order to underline the huge transfer of public resources that are still insufficient to stimulate autonomous growth. One can also find in the literature a distinction between 'northern' Mezzogiorno (the more developed regions of Campania and Apulia) and southern Mezzogiorno (the less developed areas).

Bagnasco in the late seventies used the suggestive term of 'third Italy' (*terza Italia*) in order to indicate that the dichotomic interpretation of the Italian territory (north-south) was not the most appropriate in order to understand the complexity of the Italian space (Bagnasco, 1977). In fact between the industrial north (mainly north-west) and the under-developed south there were other areas that were characterised by an increase in the development of small and medium firms, and by diffused development. This development was taking place in the central and north-eastern parts of Italy (the third Italy). The main characteristic of this area was that it had never experienced Fordist development based on big industry and on large metropoles. This territory is characterised by the presence of a dense urban network formed by medium sized cities i.e. former medieval *comuni* with strong traditions in terms of autonomy and handcraft skills. In this area there was a new economic, social and territorial organisation based on a flexible work force that associates work in family firms, and a strong specialisation in the sectors of textiles, fashion, furniture, shoes, ceramics, and mechanics.

Our main hypothesis is that this variety of economic and social organisations corresponds to different models of production of urban space and of urbanization processes in terms of concentration and deconcentration, and also in terms of centralisation and decentralisation.

DEFINITIONS AND MEASURES OF COUNTER-URBANIZATION AND DE-URBANIZATION

The process of urban de-concentration is increasingly termed counter-urbanization, a strong but suggestive term which owes its popularity to Berry (1976) who used it in order to open up the way to a new type of regional studies. The process of counter-urbanization has as its fundamental characteristic a decrease in size, density and heterogeneity. A more operational definition of counter-urbanization is given by Fielding (1982). According to this author, counter-urbanization is the inverse negative correlation between the size and the net migration of the settlements of one region or of one nation. In other words the larger the city, the larger the urban decline due to negative net migration. We should underline that the concept of urbanization is to be understood in its widest sense (concentration of population and a positive correlation between size and net migration). But we must not forget that the concept of urbanization is rich in significance, in that it encompasses spatial, historical, demographic, economic, social and behavioural aspects.

Both the abovementioned definitions of counter-urbanization concern the urban system of a nation or a region. At the metropolitan level, van den Berg et al. (1982) proposed the city cycle model in order to analyse the evolution of a single functional urban region in time. The urban area is called the Functional Urban Region (FUR) and is composed of a core (city centre) and a periphery (ring) defined according to a threshold of commuting between the core and the ring). According to this model there are four main stages in the life of a city: urbanization, sub-urbanization, de-urbanization and re-urbanization.

❑ Urbanization is characterised by a rapid expansion of urban zones. This is the phase of industrial urbanization. During this phase the main population concentration processes take place in the core. The origin of this population is the hinterland or the rest of the region or other regions.

❑ Sub-urbanization is characterised by a strong process of de-concentration of both population and economic activities from the centre towards the hinterland that puts into effect a process of urban diffusion; in parallel we can witness an increase in interactions between the urban zones in terms of mobility, migrations and innovations.

❑ De-urbanization is characterised by a decrease in population and employment, which affects the whole agglomeration (FUR). During this phase, the little centres of peri-urban space register an increase in economic activities and population.

❑ Re-urbanization is characterised by the regeneration of the centre. In this phase, we witness a return to growth in the core, due to rehabilitation or renewal of the historic centres.

On the bases of the above definitions we will measure the processes of deconcentration in Italy.

THE ANALYSIS OF URBAN DECONCENTRATION AT THE NATIONAL AND REGIONAL LEVELS

To study processes of counter-urbanization in Italy's urban system according to Berry's definition (population deconcentration) one can make use of Hoover's index, which gives a measure of the degree of population concentration in certain areas in relation to the total population of the country. For this purpose, three kinds of spatial disaggregations of the country can be used. The first one corresponds to the twenty administrative regions; the second consists of the 107 provinces; and the third represents the elementary administrative level: the *comune*.

Hoover's index of population concentration (Hc) at a specific point in time for a given subdivision of a territorial unit is as follows:

$$Hc = \frac{1}{2} \sum_{i=1}^{n} [Pi\text{-}ai]\ 100$$

where:

n = the number of sub-areas into which the territorial unit (nation, region or metropolitan area) is subdivided;

Pi = the ratio of the population of the sub-area I to the total population (nation, region or metropolitan area); and

ai = the ratio of the surface of sub-area I to the total surface of all sub-areas.

Hc ranges from 0 to 100. When Hc=0 the population distribution in the country examined is uniform, which may be considered an 'ideal' state of population diffusion. The opposite end of the range of the value Hc=100 is obtained when there is one single sub-area in which the whole population of the country is concentrated.

From Table 9.1 we can observe that at the regional and provincial levels the concentration process increased throughout the period examined, even if after 1981 the rate of increase slowed considerably. At the *comune* level we can observe that the concentration increased continuously until 1971 (4 points per decade). During the period 1971-1981 the growth was very weak, after which it stabilises. These remarks are relevant because they hide important differ-entces concerning the process of deconcentration for the various regions.

Table 9.1 Concentration indices of Italy at the regional, provincial and commune level, 1951-1999 (Number of areas in brackets).

Area	1951	1961	1971	1981	1991	1999
Region (20)	17.4	18.5	19.6	20.1	20.6	20.9
Province (107)	25.2	27.2	29.9	30.4	30.5	30.7
Commune (8000)	41.2	45.3	50.0	50.9	50.7	50.8

Source: Own calculations

The analysis of the population concentration at the commune level for the twenty Italian regions can be summarised as follows. In 1951 two regions had structural concentration values above to 50 (Liguria and Campania). Seven other regions have intermediate values bettwen 40 and 50 (Valle d'Aosta, Latium, Lombardy, Friuli V. G., Piedmont, Emilia Romagna and Tuscany). All the other regions recorded low values, the weakest of which were Basilicata (17.95) and Molise (18.03). During the period 1951-1999 all regions increased their concentrations from 2.8 (Liguria) to 16.6 (Marche). The higher increases were recorded by Marche, Molise, Abruzzi, Piedmont, Emilia Romagna, Umbria, Tuscany and Basilicata. If we subdivide the last half-century into two sub-periods (1951-1971 and 1971-1999) we can have a clearer picture of the trends.

During the first period seven regions increased their concentration: Marche, Piedmont, Emilia Romagna, Latium, Tuscany, Lombardy and Abruzzi. With one exception all of the regions are in the Northern and Central Italy, and three of them contain the three main Italian metropolises.

After 1971 there was an important change. The regions that were characterised in the previous decades by processes of concentration are now experiencing important deconcentration processes: Latium, Liguria, Lombardy, and to a lesser degree Piedmont and Emilia Romagna.

The majority of the Southern regions increased their population concentrations at a lower but a continuous pace: Molise, Basilicata, Abruzzi, Calabria, Sardinia and Sicily. The same phenomenon can be observed for Marche and Umbria in Central Italy.

Figure 9.1 represents the trends of Hoover values for selected Italian regions, while Table 9.2 represents a typology that takes into account five

Figure 9.1 Trends of Hoover values for selected Italian regions, 1951-99

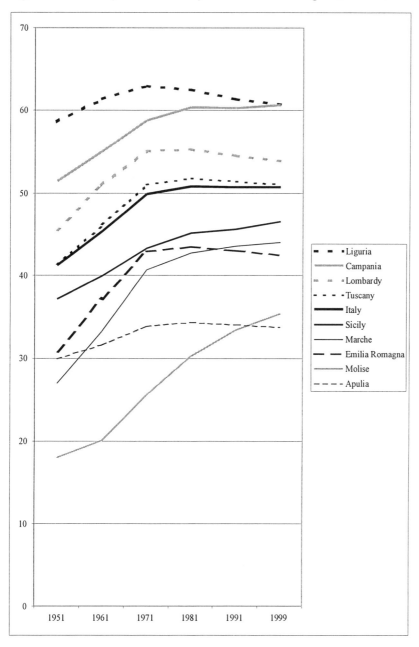

▪ ▪ ▪	Liguria
	Campania
▪ ▪ ▪	Lombardy
▪ ▪ ▪	Tuscany
	Italy
	Sicily
	Marche
▬ ▬	Emilia Romagna
	Molise
─ ─ ─	Apulia

Source: Own calculations

Table 9.2 Typology of Italian regions according to their structural concentration and their deconcentration trends.

	North West	North East	Centre	South and Islands
Type 1: High structural con-centration, with concentration until 1971 followed by de-concentration	Liguria Piedmont Lombardy		Latium	
Type 2: High structural con-centration, with concentration until 1971 followed by stability after 1981	V. d'Aosta			Campania
Type 3: Medium structural concentration, with concentration until 1971 followed by stability		Emilia Romagna Friuli V. J. Trentino A-A.	Tuscany	
Type 4: Low structural con-centration, with de-concentration after 1981		Venetia		Apulia
Type 5: Low structural concentration, with concentration throughout the period weakening after 1991			Umbria Marche	Basilicata Molise Calabria Sardinia Abruzzi Sicily

main types of regions by using the criteria of structural concentration (the degree of concentration at the beginning of the observation), and the evolution of the concentration or deconcentration process in time. From this classification we can observe that the first type concerns mainly four out of five metropolitan regions, three of which are in the industrial triangle and one in the Centre, the region of the capital (Latium). The second type concerns one region of the North and one region of the South. The third type groups mainly the regions of the centre of the North East (known as the 'third Italy'). The forth type concerns the booming region of Venetia in the North East which belongs also to the 'third Italy' and one of the most dynamic regions of the South: Apulia. Finally, the fifth type groups the majority of the Southern regions and two regions of the centre: Umbria and Marche.

This analysis shows the complexity of deconcentration processes in the various Italian regions. These are the result not only of the inherited urban network but also of the huge impact of industrial Fordism and the rural exodus towards the main Italian cities. However, this index is synthetic and does not allow us to understand the contribution of the different size of settlements to the actual structure of the regions.

In order to study the relation between population growth and settlement growth we constructed a series of graphs that represent Italy and three regions of the North, Centre and South of Italy: Piedmont, Tuscany and Calabria. We considered 1991 as the date of reference and we subdivided the settlement of each region into 11 groups or less. These groups are: less than 500 inhabitants; 2: 500-1,000; 3: 1,000-2,000; 4: 2,000-5,000; 5: 5,000-10,000; 6: 10,000-25,000; 7: 25,000-50,000; 8: 50,000-100,000; 9: 100,000-250,000; 10: 250,000-500,000; 11: 500,000 and over. We successively calculated the population for each group for the five other decades (1951, 1961, 1971, 1981, 1991).

Figure 9.2 indicates the relationship between size of settlement and population growth for Italy between 1951 and 1999. During the 1950s the six groups of settlements with a population less than 25,000 inhabitants recorded a decline. The group of cities that recorded the highest population growth were those between 250,000 and 500,000 inhabitants (23.9 per cent). The same group also recorded the highest growth in the 1960s (20.5 per cent). During the first two decades only the settlements less than 5,000 lost population, while all of the other groups of settlements increased their population. The group of 5,000-10,000 grew by 6.5 per cent, and the groups between 10,000 and 250,000 recorded increases that varied between 13 per cent and 16 per cent. In the 1980s the decline of the cities above 500,000 became more dramatic (−10.8 per cent). We also observed the decline of the group 50,000-100,000 (-2.1 per cent) and the decline of the most dynamic group of the previous decades (250,000-500,000) which lost -3.8 per cent, while the cities between 100,000 and 250,000 were in stagnation (+0.3 per cent). During this period the settlements of less than 2,000 continued to lose population. Finally during the 1990s the biggest settlements continued their decline, the medium large cities were declining or stagnating and only the settlements between 1,000 and 50,000 recorded an increase. If this is the general situation in Italy the different regions present a less uniform image.

Figure 9.2 The relationship between settlement size and population growth, Italy, 1951-99

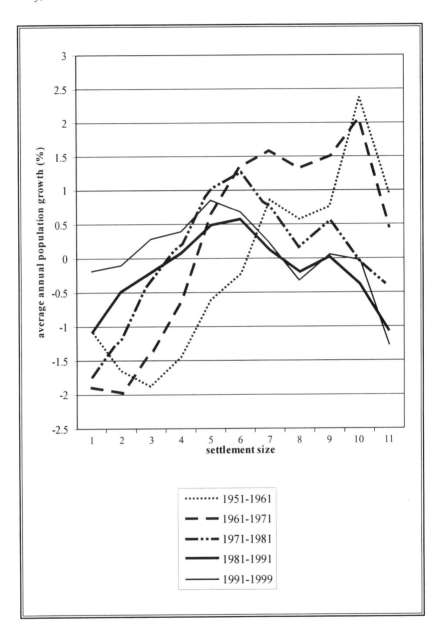

Source: Own calculations

Figure 9.3 indicates the relationship between population growth and settlement size in Piedmont during the 1950s. This shows a positive correlation between population growth and settlement size. The cities were growing proportionally according to their size. The largest degree of growth was recorded by Turin. The settlements with a population of less than 5,000 were in decline. During the 1960s we can observe that it was mainly the medium sized cities that were increasing. Turin continued its growth but the rhythms slowed down. The smaller settlements continued their decline.

In the 1970s the larger cities experienced a decline, while the medium sized cities grew and the smaller settlements continued their decline. In the nineties we can see that we are far from the correlation of the seventies: The large cities continued in their decline but this tendency slowed down. Similar trends were found for the small settlements, and the medium cities recorded a weak increase.

In Tuscany (Figure 9.4) the cities with a population over 10,000 were growing during the period 1951 to 81. The highest rate of growth was recorded by the group of cities with a population of between 100,000 and 250,000. During the period 1961-1971 the cities with a population of between 25,000 and 250,000 recorded growth of between 15 per cent and 20 per cent but during the following decade the growth of these cities decreased and ranged from 2 per cent to 7 per cent. The largest city, Florence, after a growth of 16 per cent during the 1950s, reduced its growth to 5 per cent and 2 per cent during the next two decades. During the 1980s Florence entered a phase of decline (-10 per cent) that persisted in the 1990s (-7 per cent). After the 1980s, in addition to the decline of Florence, we can observe the stagnation or the decline of the group of cities with over 50,000 inhabitants. The settlements of less than 10,000 were losing population during the 1950s and 1960s. During the 1970s the decline affected the settlements less than 5,000 and during the 1990s the settlements of less than 2,000.

In Calabria (Figure 9.5) we can observe that the groups of settlements with a population of more than 10,000 have recorded growth since 1951. The highest rates of growth concerned the cities between 25,000 and 50,000. The largest City (Reggio di Calabria) recorded population increases throughout the period, even if after 1981 their rhythm slowed down. The settlements with a population below 10,000 lost population throughout all the period examined. The only exception was the group 5,000-10,000, which increased weakly after the 1970s and stagnated during the 1990s.

From this analysis it emerges that the correlation between population growth and size of settlement is very different in the three regions that represent the North, the Centre and the South of Italy. In the North the counter-urbanization processes are stronger and they started earlier. In Tuscany we can see that the deconcentration process is not as important as in Piedmont, and in the south we can observe a continuation of the concentrtion

Figure 9.3   Correlation between settlement size and population growth,
Piedmont, 1951-99

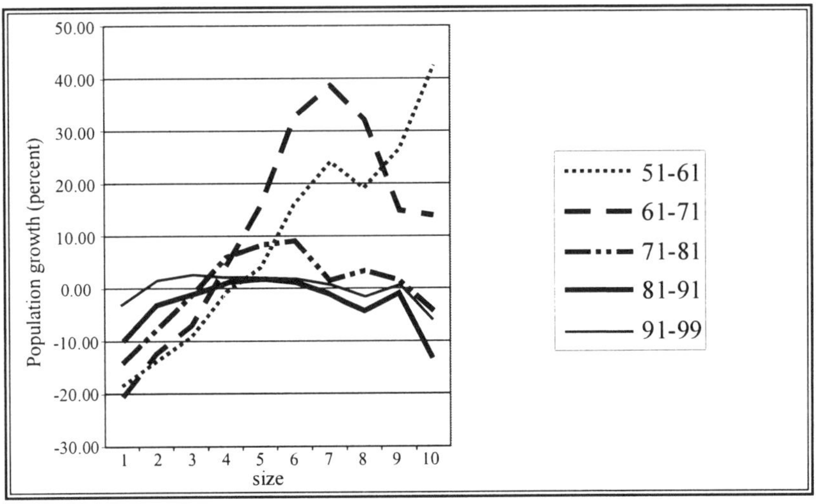

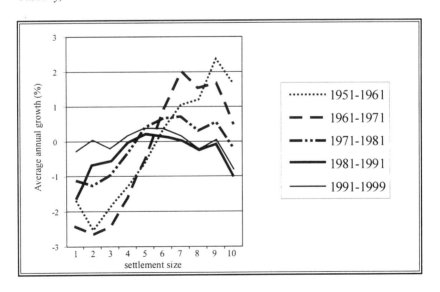

Source: Own calculations

Figure 9.4   Correlation between settlement size and population growth,
Tuscany, 1951-99

Source: Own calculations

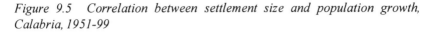

Figure 9.5   Correlation between settlement size and population growth, Calabria, 1951-99

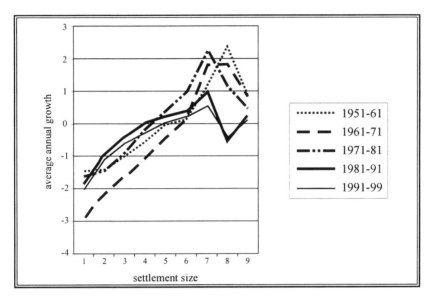

Source: Own calculations

processes even if their rhythms are not as strong as during the seventies and the eighties. A further analysis (Petsimeris, 2002) showed that the main difference is between the type of growth. The decline in the North is mainly due to the natural balance, while in the South the growth is due to the natural balance. In the large cities in the North net migration cannot compensate for the huge losses in terms of natural balance, while in the South a part of the population growth is due to the positive natural balance.

THE MAIN METROPOLITAN AREAS

For the analysis of the metropolitan areas we took into consideration the five main metropolitan areas as delimited by Sforzi for ISTAT (1997). According to this study the national territory (8,000 *comuni*) is subdivided to 784 Labour Market Areas (*Sistemi Locali del Lavoro*). Each area has a core and a ring which are interdependent in terms of residential and job location. According to this delimitation Rome is composed of 65 sub-areas, Milan 99, Turin 43, Naples 42 and Genoa 36. These aggregations change from census to census according to the intensity of the flows, and the interdependence between the core and the suburban areas. In order to be able to make diachronic comparisons we used the 1991 delimitations calculated on the data for 1951, 1961, 1971, 1991 and 1999 as elaborated by Buran and Mela

(2001) (Figure 9.6).

Between 1951 and 1971 the cores showed strong growth, while from 1971 onwards they have all lost population. During the first period, also known as the period of Fordist growth, the cores of Turin and Milan increased by 450,000 inhabitants each, Genoa by 130,000, Rome by 1.1 million and Naples by 215,000. In the second period the populations increased by 212,000 in Turin, 300,000 in Milan, 120,000 in Genoa, 200,000 in Rome and 200,000 in Naples. In other words the five cities increased their population by 2.4 million inhabitants during the period 1951-1971, and lost one million inhabitants over the next twenty years. This is equivalent to a net increase of 1.4 million inhabitants during the half a century. Even if an increase of this order shared between five large cities for a period of half a century could seem normal, it is an important quantitative and qualitative change which has brought about a dramatic transformation of the urban landscape: in its social, economic, cultural and political components; in terms of mass production of housing; in terms of uniformisation of the urban landscape (*periferie*); and in terms of property speculation. By contrast, the rings showed a continuous pattern of growth. During the period 1951-1999 the ring of Turin increased by 400,000 inhabitants, Milan by 970,000, Rome by 320,000, Naples by 700,000 and Genoa by only 10,000. While there was a decline in the core, the rings were still growing. However, after 1981, the rings were not growing sufficiently to compensate for the losses of the cores. Infact, the decline for the five metropolitan cores was of 684,000 inhabitants and the growth of the rings 374,000. This means that the metropolitan areas of Italy are in the phase of de-urbanization: the difference between the total growth of the ring and the total decline of the core is -310,000 inhabitants.

Table 9.3 Population change in the Italian FURs (core+ring), percent.

	1951-1961	1961-1971	1971-1981	1981-1991	1991-1999
Turin	41.2	28.7	1.3	-6.9	-2.4
Genoa	11.6	4.6	-5.1	-9.8	-5.4
Milan	30.1	25.3	1.9	-4.6	-1.0
Rome	31.6	27.4	5.0	0.6	0.4
Naples	18.0	13.3	9.1	0.5	2.5

Source: Own calculations

As we can see from Table 9.3, Genoa entered the phase of deurbanization during the period 1971-81, and Milan and Turin followed in the next decade. Rome and Naples were in the stage of mature suburbanization (decline of the

Figure 9.6 Population change in selected Italian FURs

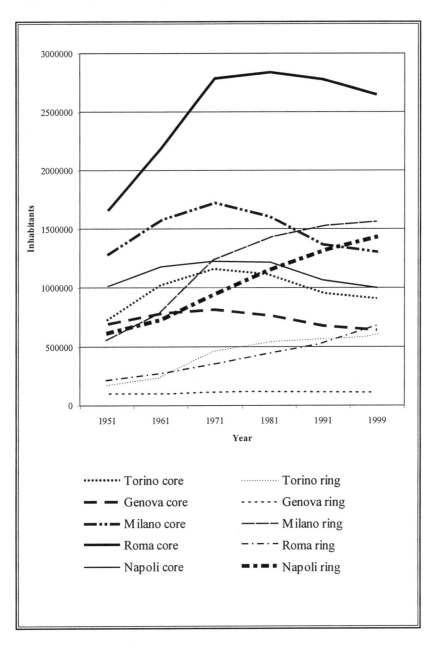

Source: Own calculations

core, and growth of the ring that compensates for the losses of the core) which slowed down considerably after the 1980s. We can also note that the decline of the northern metropolitan areas slowed down in the 1990s. These patterns show an important differentiation between the northern and the central and southern agglomerations but they do not allow us to forecast a process of re-urbanization in quantitative terms according to the prediction of the city lifecycle model.

THE SPATIALITY OF URBAN DIFFUSION

Figure 9.7 represents Italian *comuni* by period of maximum population. This map helps us to see the morphology and the temporality of urbanization processes in Italy during the 20th century. As we can see, the areas that recorded their highest population level before 1936 were mainly the Alpine areas of the north western and northern parts of the country, the Appenine areas, and the internal parts of the peninsula and islands. These areas were characterised by a weak economic base, and highly dependent on agriculture. During the period 1971-81 we can observe the importance of Turin, Milan, Genoa and the other major industrial cities of the north, the cities of the Gulf of Venice, and the hill areas in the centre of the country.   In 1981 Rome recorded its maximum population, in the same period we can also see forms of overspill in the main metropolitan areas (Milan and Turin).

In 1991 the importance of the growth of the metropolitan rings of Milan, Turin, Rome, Naples and Genoa was apparent. Maximum population levels were also recorded in the same period in Via Emilia, Venetia, Bolzano and Tuscany. The importance of urban diffusion along the Adriatic coast (the Marche and Molise littoral strip) was highly marked in this period. We can also see historically high levels of population in the Gargano area in Apulia and the whole area of the Tavoliere della Apulia. A similar pattern was found on the west coast extending from Rome northwards until Grossetto (the south of Tuscany) and southwards to Salerno (south of Naples). On the islands, maximum population was recorded in 1991 in the north and south of Sardinia, and the southern and eastern coasts of Sicily.

CONCLUSIONS

The analysis of the process of concentration has shown us that in Italy the process of counter-urbanization has touched most of the industrial regions of the North, and in turn has affected certain regions of the Centre and the South. In the South the processes of population concentration persist. In the metropolitan areas, we observe an opposition between the urban industrial concentrations of the North, and the other urban areas of the Centre and the South.

In contemporary Italy we can observe a de-urbanization process in the

Figure 9.7 Communes classified by period of maximum population

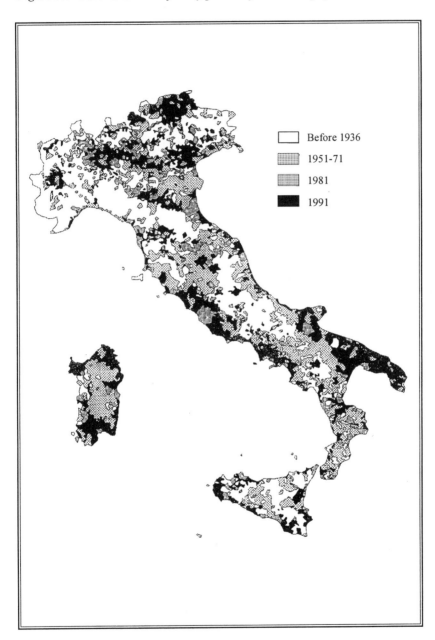

Source: Istat, 1994

largest metropolitan areas. The decline is also affecting the majority of the cities with a population of more than 100,000. This is due to important quantitative and qualitative changes in the functional and social structure of the upper ranks of the Italian urban hierarchy: tertiarisation and social polarization.

At the same time there is an increase of population in the outer suburban areas, the linear conurbation of Via Emilia, along the eastern and western coast and the regions of flexible economy. This pattern applies to all areas with the exception of the core areas of the main cities (Bologna, Parma, Modena, Reggio nell'Emilia).

However it is important to underline that there are neither processes of re-urbanization in terms of growth in the cores of the large metropolitan areas nor has there been a turn-round in terms of an increase in the population of the remote rural areas and the small settlements. A number of case studies have demonstrated that the medium sized cities that experienced most growth during the 1970s and 1980s were mainly those belonging to the metropolitan areas (Petsimeris 1989; Martinotti 1993). The increase of the population in the South must be attributed more to natural growth than migration (Coppola et al., 1992). And the huge losses of the North are attributable to the negative natural balance, which is not compensated for by migration flows (Petsimeris, 2002).

In qualitative terms, we are faced by processes of urban deconcentration which are not processes of decentralisation. What is taking place is a process of selective centralisation of functions (Celant, 1988) in the metropolitan cores accompanied by a process of socially selective in-migration and working class out-migration: an important increase of managers and huge decline of employees and blue collars (de-proletarisation) (Petsimeris 1998). The forthcoming publication of the results of the Italian census 2001 will provide the opportunity to examine the further development of the trends we identified in this paper.

REFERENCES

Bagnasco, A. (ed.) (1977), *Tre Italie. La problematica territoriale dello sviluppo italiano*, Bologna: Il Mulino.

Bagnasco, A. (1986), *Torino un profilo sociologico*, Torino: Einaudi.

Bagnasco, A. (1990), *La città dopo Ford, il caso di Torino*, Torino: Boringhieri.

Berry, B. J. L. (1976), *Urbanization and counterurbanization*, Beverly Hills, California: Sage.

Bottai, M. and M. Costa (1981), 'Modelli territoriali delle variazioni demografiche in Italia', *Rivista Geografica Italiana*, **88**, pp. 267-295.

Camagni, R. and S. Pio (1988), *Funzioni urbane e gestione metropolitana europea : la posizione di Milano nel sistema dell'Europa meridionale*, Milano: Franco Angeli.

Cardia, C., I. Insolera, P. Krammerer, B. Secchi, and B. Trentin (1978), *La città e la crisi del capitalismo*, Bari: Laterza.

Carozzi, C. and R. Rozzi (1984), 'Le processus d'urbanisation de la partie centre-orientale de la plaine du Pô', in Actes du Colloque, *La Géographie Historique des villes d'europe occidentale*, Paris: Cahiers du CREPIF, pp. 141-154.

Celant, A. (ed) (1988), *Nuova città e nuova campagna*, Pàtron: Bologna.

Ceresa, G., A. Mela, M. Pellegrini, and P. Petsimeris (1983), 'L'evoluzione del fenomeno urbano in Europa analizzata attraverso la legge rango-dimensione, in G. Leonardi and G. Rabino (eds), *L'analisi degli insediamenti umani e produttivi*, Milano: Franco Angeli, pp. 149-171.

Champion, A. G. (ed) (1989), *Counterurbanization: the changing pace and nature of population deconcentration*, London: Edward Arnold.

Conti, S. (1983), *Il Mezzogiorno d'Italia; Un territorio senza Geografia*, Milano: Franco Angeli.

Conti, S. and G. Spriano (1990), *Effetto città. Sistemi urbani e innovazione : prospettive per l'Europa degli anni Novanta*, Fondazione G. Torino: Agneli.

Coppola, P. and L. Viganoni (1992) Il Mezzogiorno urbano: la complessità del retardo, in G. Dematteis (ed.) *Il fenomeno urbano in Italia: interpretazioni, prospettive e politiche*, Milano: Franco Angeli, pp. 55-90.

Cori, B. (1984), 'The national settlement system of italy, in L.S. Bourne, R. Sinclair and K. Dziewonski (eds), *Urbanization and Settlement Systems: International Perspectives*, Oxford: Oxford University Press, pp. 283-300,.

Cori, B. (1986), 'The national settlement system of Italy: a general view', in L. S. Bourne, B. Cori and K. Dziewonski (eds), *Progress in settlement systems geography*, Milan: Franco Angeli, pp. 97-137.

Coro, G., M. Gambuzza, F. Occari (1987), 'Dinamiche demografiche e sviluppo insediativo nel Veneto negli anni '80', *Oltre il Ponte*, **18**, pp. 44-80.

Cristaldi, F. (1994), *Per una delimitazione delle aree metropolitane. Il caso di Roma*, Milano: Franco Angeli.

Crosta, P. (1978) : *Settore e Blocco edilizio: produzione e governo del territorio*, Milano: CLUP.

Dalmasso, E. (1971), *Milan, capitale économique de l'Italie*, Paris: Orphys.

Dalmasso, E. (1984), 'Aspects de l'évolution du système urbain italien, in Actes du Colloque (ed), *La Géographie Historique des villes d'europe occidentale*, Paris: Cahiers du CREPIF, pp. 72-76.

Dematteis, G. (1992), Il fenomeno urbano in Italia: interpretazioni, prospettive, politiche, Milano: Franco Angeli.

Dematteis, G. and P. Petsimeris (1989), 'Italy: counterurbanization as a transitional phase in settlement reorganization, in A. J. Champion (ed), *Counterurbanization: the changing pace and nature of population deconcentration*, London: Edward Arnold, pp. 187-206.

Emanuel, C. (1989) : 'Oltre la crisi : centralizzazione e decentramento, polaroïd e retirons nel Piemonte degli anni 80', in P. Petsimeris (ed.), *Le reti urbane tra decentramento e centralità, nuovi aspetti di geografia delle città*, Milano: Franco Angeli, pp.101-130.

EUROSTAT, (1992), *Le concept statistique de la ville en Europe*, Luxembourg: Office des Publications officielles des Communautés européennes.

Fielding, A. J. (1982), 'Counterurbanization in Western Europe, *Progress in Planning*, **17**, 1-52.

Fielding, A. J. (1989), 'La contro-urbanizzazione nell'Europa occidentale', in P. Petsimeris (ed), *Le reti urbane tra decentramento e centralità, nuovi aspetti di geografia delle città*, Milano: Franco Angeli, pp.83-100.

Gambi, L. (1973), 'Da città ad area metropolitana', *Storia d'Italia*, **V**, 367-424.

Gambi, L. (1991), 'Incongruenze e deficienza della legge di riforma delle autonomie locali (142/90), sui concetti di area metropolitana e di comunità territoriale', *Storia Urbana*, **54**, 223-229.

Illeris, S. (1979), 'Recent development of the settlement system of advanced market economy countries', *Geografisk Tidsskrift*, **78/79**, pp. 49-56.

ISTAT (1994), *I grandi comuni, 13° Censimento Generale della Popolazione 1991*, Roma: ISTAT.

ISTAT (1997), *I sistemi locali del lavoro 1991*, Roma: ISTAT.

Leone, U. (1988), 'Le trasformazioni dell'Italia non metropolitana, il Mezzogiorno', in U. Leone (ed.), *Valorizzazione e sviluppo territoriale in Italia*, Milano: Franco Angeli, pp. 71-102.

Mainardi, R. (ed) (1968) : *La rete urbana nell'Italia Settentrionale*, Milano: Centro di Documentazione di Ingegneria Civile, Architettura e Pianificazione Territoriale.

Martinotti, G. (1993), *Metropoli, La nuova morphologie della città*, Bologna: Il Mulino.

Mela, A. and P. Buran (2001), 'Imagini territoriali dello sviluppo piemontese', in P. Buran (ed) *Scenari per il Piemonte del Duemila, verso l'economia della conoscenza*, Torino: IRES, pp. 315-354.

Muscara, C. (ed.) (1978), *Megalopoli Mediterranea*, Milano: Franco Angeli.

Petsimeris P. (1989), *Les processus d'urbanisation au Piémont, analyse géographique des transformations socio-fonctionnelles d'une région mûre*, Thèse de Doctorat de 3ème cycle, Caen: Université de Caen.

Petsimeris P. (1989), 'Deconcentrazione urbana e ripolarizzazione selettiva in Piemonte: verso una nuova dialettica dell'urbanizzazione', in P. Petsimeris (ed.), *Le reti urbane tra decentramento e centralità, nuovi aspetti di geografia delle città*, Milano: Franco Angeli, pp.131-155.

Petsimeris, P. (1998), 'Urban Decline and the New Social and Ethnic Divisions in the Core Cities of the Italian Industrial Triangle', *Urban Studies*, **35**, 449-466.

Petsimeris, P. (2002), 'A Re-examination of the Role of Migration in Urban Diffusion in Italy', *Ekistics* (forthcoming).

Pizzorno, A. (1972), 'Sviluppo economico e urbanizzazione', in A. Cavalli (ed.), *Economia e società*, Bologna: Il Mulino, pp. 277-300.

Scaramellini, G. (1990), *Funzioni centrali, funzioni metropolitane, reti urbane*, Milano: Franco Angeli.

Scaramellini, G. (ed.) (1991), *Città e poli metropolitani in Italia*, Milano: Franco Angeli.

Seronde-Babonaux, A.-M. (1983), *Roma la crescita di una metropoli*, Roma: Editori Riuniti.

Trigilia, C. (1992), *Sviluppo senza autonomia. Effetti perversi delle politiche nel Mezzogiorno*, Bologna: Il Mulino.

van den Berg, L., R. Drewett, L. H. Klaassen, A. Rossi and C. H. T. Vijverberg (1982), *Urban Europe: a study of growth and decline*, vol. 1, Oxford: Pergamon.

Vining, D. R. Jr. (1982), 'Migration between the core and the periphery', *Scientific American*, **247**, pp. 36-45.

B. NORDIC AND CENTRAL EUROPEAN COUNTRIES

Chapter 10

Past, Present and Future of Urbanization in Finland

E. Heikkilä and T. Järvinen

THE HISTORY OF URBANIZATION IN FINLAND
THE SETTLEMENT STRUCTURE BEFORE WORLD WAR II

The roots of modern urban culture in Finland stretch back to the end of the 1200s when Turku developed into an administrative and religious centre. At the end of the Middle Ages there were six cities of which Turku and Vyborg were the largest. Urban population was small in proportion but the cultural significance of the cities was considerable. According to law only Turku had a right to practise foreign trade, but this stipulation was not always followed. Vyborg was an important centre for Russian trade and the peasant population of the south coast regularly sailed to Tallinn, the nearest trading town belonging to the German Hansa.

In the beginning of the 1600s when Sweden was a great power, armed conflicts were common and at least 100,000 Finns died in wars. Only the years of famine were as devastating. Population began to grow when wars and the diseases that followed them abated and the land yielded good crops. Population growth was twice that of Sweden in the beginning of the 1700s (Ahtiainen et al., 1998). The low death rate can be partly explained by the fact that population was not concentrated in built-up areas where the propensity to epidemics was consequently higher (Tarkka et al., 1991: 25).

Russia conquered Finland from Sweden in 1809 and established an autonomous country. The emperor proclaimed Helsinki as capital in 1812. The concentration of the population in the cities increased remarkably. The total number of cities was 29, compared to six in the Middle Ages. Finland attained independence in 1917.

The largest cities grew the fastest after the turn of the 20th century and architects designed impressive Romantic buildings. The population of Helsinki was 65,000 inhabitants at the beginning of the 1890s, but only three decades later the population was already 161,000. In 1920, 84 per cent of the population still lived in the countryside.

REGIONAL POPULATION GROWTH SINCE THE 1950s

The division of labour has changed significantly since the Second World War, due to the waning of the agricultural sector. In four decades (1940-80) the proportion of people working in primary production decreased from 64 per cent to 13 per cent whereas the corresponding change in Sweden took 70 years (Karjalainen, 1986: 11-12). Reconstruction after the Second World War and industrialization during the Korean War were important factors that contributed to structural change in the country. Payment received for war damages was used to benefit the country nationally. This led to a boom in construction and restructuring of industry which, in turn, resulted in the fastest increase in the urban population of all industrialized countries. The location of investment in the metal industry, in particular, determined the main direction of regional development (Valtioneuvoston selonteko eduskunnalle, 1993: 55).

Internal migration grew steadily in the 1950s, while the main direction was still from rural to rural areas (Figure 10.1). Great population waves, caused by 'welfare' migration from rural to urban areas occurred in the late 1960s and early 1970s. Cities in Finland and Sweden absorbed most of these migrants, the largest number of them Baby Boomers entering the labour market. Increasing proportions of women entering the labour force contributed to the change of the structure of business and industry in the country.

Finland reached the level of urbanization of other industrialized countries by the 1970s. In 1995, 81 per cent of the population lived in built-up areas already – few of them were second and third generation city-dwellers.[1] The degree of urbanization in Finland is less than that of Sweden. Sixty three per cent of the Finnish population lived in the cities in 1995 while the corresponding figure for Sweden was 83 per cent (Seppänen, 1996: 55). Around the end of the 1960s and beginning of the 1970s, there was a change in population migration trends away from the large urban agglomerations to smaller size cities (see Peltola 1987). After the massive cumulative migration gain of the previous decades, a turnaround started to occur in 1977 when large cities started losing population in absolute terms.

---

[1] A settlement containing at least 200 inhabitants and with no more than 200 metres between residences is considered as a built-up area (SVT 1998: 94).

Figure 10.1 Net migration in different groups of cities, towns, and rural municipalities in Finland, 1941-98 ('000)

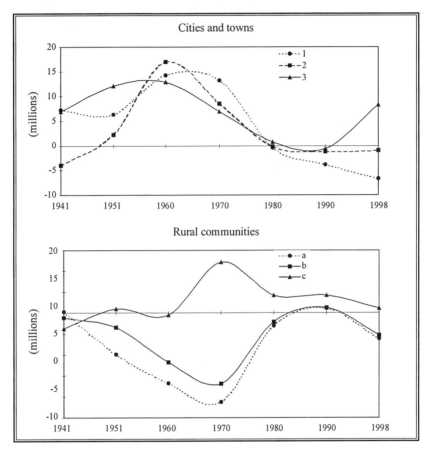

Source : Own calculations

Mass migration to the large cities regained momentum as a result of the improvement of employment opportunities in the cities during the second half of the 1980s. This is referred to as the new migration wave. People systematically found their way from the north to the south and within provinces from rural to regional core areas. As a result of migration losses in the rural areas and small towns, regional convergence increased again. Internal migration within the municipalities increased slightly in the late 1980s. Two thirds of the migration occurred as internal migration, mainly to the built-up areas. This led to the development of new sub-centres within cities which increased the multi-nodality of large urban areas − i.e. deconcentration within core areas (Andersson, 1993: 45). Factors that influenced this scattered construction included locational choices of the people in general, measures of support of social politics and methods of production and design principles in the construction industry (Virtanen, 2000: 54).

In the 1990s the volumes of migration decreased and most migration gains of the urban regions occurred in the satellite municipalities of urban districts (Table 10.1). Commuting areas[2] were defined by Statistics Finland in 1997, each of which consists of a central urban district and a number of districts surrounding it. In 1991, the first of the true depression years, migration decreased. As production decreased and unemployment increased, the Helsinki conurbation started gaining population again. The growth was largely based on immigration. Following the dissolution of the Soviet Union, these numbers increased significantly. The Act on the Municipality of Domicile which came into effect in 1994, also led to an increase in migrants to univer-

Table 10.1 Inter-municipal migration in urban commuting areas and in non-urban municipalities 1990-1999 ('000)

Year	Urban travel-to-work areas					Other semi-rural municipalities
	Total	Urban districts				
		Total	Central municipalities	Satellite municipalities	Urban municipalities without satellite municipalities	
1990	585	1181	-4216	5397	-596	-585
1991	1785	2877	-1441	4318	-1092	-1785
1992	2811	3462	-924	4386	-651	-2811
1993	3963	4857	2266	2591	-894	-3963
1994	10110	11727	10392	1335	-1617	-10110
1995	11589	12826	11451	1375	-1237	-11589
1996	11395	12848	10653	2195	-1453	-11395
1997	10290	12097	7501	4596	-1807	-10290
1998	11333	12693	8422	4271	-1360	-11333
1999	10661	11980	5761	6219	-1319	-10661

Note: The municipal typology for 1999 is applied throughout the table.

Source: SVT, 2000b: 107

[2] These areas are also called 'travel-to-work areas', or 'labour catchment areas'.

sity towns. Earlier, students were not classified as permanent residents, but after the promulgation of the Act the cities in which they studied became their permanent residences.

At the turn of the millennium the country witnessed a dramatic general decrease in its birth rate as well as changes in its regional division of population due to migration. The main migration stream was directed to the large central regions of know-how and of administration in the southern parts of the country, a process that has been accompanied by significant migration losses in several of the small towns. Net migration losses were particularly severe in industrial cities with narrow economic bases and in provincial centres (Laakso, 1998: 13-14, 68). In 1996 only nine out of 85 sub-regional units experienced migration gains. The effects of regional policies and communal development can be seen in the Table 10.2. Cities have become larger while smaller towns have almost disappeared.

Table 10.2 Cities and towns by number of inhabitants in Finland, 1950 - 2010.

Inhabitants		Cities and towns						
		1950	1960	1970	1980	1990	1998	2010
-	4 999	20	13	6	1	1	1	1
5 000 -	9 999	16	16	21	21	27	31	35
10 000 -	19 999	16	16	23	25	28	30	26
20 000 -	49 999	10	16	18	24	25	26	26
50 000 -	99 999	-	3	7	8	7	8	8
100 000 -		3	3	3	5	6	6	6
Total		65	67	78	84	94	102	102

Source: SVT 1991: 44; SVT 1992: 43; SVT 1999: 58 - 78.

In 1966 an official regional policy was introduced which put emphasis on the industrialization of development areas. In the 1970s, it was a legislative requirement for political decision-makers to take regional aspects into consideration. This was a period of great regional policy and welfare-state construction. The regional disparities grew in the 1980s while industrial growth slowed down in core regions. Regional policy emphasized technology and innovation. The concentration of population and economic growth was interpreted as the result of globalization and advantages of concentration. EU regional policy came into effect in 1994 in the form of programme-based policy. It replaced the former national regional policy.

Migration theories and views on regional economic influences of the past have been severely criticized. Concentration, associated with large production and service centres is regarded as an essential ingredient of global market economics in the EU. In contrast to the classical theory, migration has widened the gap in the income between provinces. Migration is more selective than before and has an increasing influence on the population in areas of migration loss; and the economically active population is now more strongly concentrated than ever before (Kangasharju et al., 1999; Korhonen, 1994). Young people tend to select growth centres as their destination which results in ever decreasing birth rates in the outlying rural districts (Okko et al., 2000: 9-11). The down side of concentration is depopulation and the costs of regional restructuring.

THEORIES OF URBANIZATION AND MIGRATION
MAIN THEORIES

Migration and urbanization have been extensively studied in Finland since the beginning of the 1960s. In empirical research in this field emphasis in geographical studies obviously falls on areal aspects. Up to the 1970s deductive hypotheses and statistical analyses dominated the research. Subsequently, the emphasis shifted to social research concentrating on individuals. In the 1970s and 1980s positivistic concepts of behavioral science were based on a philosophical basis. The theories of push and pull emphasize the importance of rational behaviour, but it has been generally found that, depending on the situation, the same factors can both push and pull migrants (e.g. Kytö, 1998: 37; Söderling, 1983: 9; Taylor, 1969: 99).

The evaluations of the research from the 1960s to the 1980s have been criticized for their narrow focus on theories (Paasi, 1981: 2; Vartiainen, 1989a: 6-7, 1989b: 4, 9). In the 1980s and early 1990s there was quite a strong school of thought pursuing the study of functional centres and their spheres of influence. This continued to contribute to production of both empirical and theoretical findings. Much of the research focused on the form of urban structural dynamics, objective and subjective space in the cities and the economics and social restructuring of urban centres (Yli-Jokipii, 1994: 193-4). As the manipulative capacity of computers increased in the 1980s and 1990s computer-generated models became more widespread. However, quantitative methods were shunned in city studies in the 1990s while qualitative methods and an interdisciplinary approach brought new viewpoints to the research (Karisto, 1995: 58; Kytö, 1998: 21).

THEORIES OF URBAN DYNAMICS

Grand theories of population change, demographic transition and historical materialism have been linked with geographical regularities observed or assumed to exist in various spatial systems. The most common of these is the theory of population concentration (Gibbs, 1963). It describes an areal diffusion of towns and a direct relationship between levels of demographic transition and rank-size within an urban system. Palomäki in particular has studied the possibilities of applying the model in Finnish conditions. Palomäki (1972a, 1972b) has revised Pred's (1965) cumulative growth model of the cities reflecting progressive areal influences over time and combined it with the theory of Gibbs to develop a cartographical model of sequence in the urbanization process; a sequence of communicational influences has also been added to the model. The model shows that geographical factors determined the birth of regional differences of the location and degree of development of the central areas as a result of development mechanisms of economic life.

Tervamäki (1987) has studied the quantitative development of migration as a part of a multi-level regional system. Attention was focused on migration between different area types and the directions of migration. The starting point for a multi-level regional point of view was Christaller's system of central places and their hinterlands. In his study, regional differences in the relative migration balance in migration streams between central and peripheral areas proved to be better indicators of migration tendencies than the differences in the absolute migration balance; these indicators described the differences between central and peripheral areas in migration. Vartiainen (1989b: 8) has criticized Tervamäki's trust in the explanatory power of quantitative grouping analysis as well as the results of a compiled municipal classification framework.

In the mobility transition theory of Zelinsky (1971: 219-49) migration is examined as part of the process of social and regional development combined with the stages of demographic transition. According to Zelinsky migration has distinctive characteristics of its own in different stages of social development. Migration from rural areas is mostly centre-oriented, and mostly economically motivated, i.e. in pursuit of either work or education. Migration occurring in the late stage of the transition, however, is more residential oriented, linked to stages of life. It therefore seems as if an individual's priorities are determined by his or her stage in life.

Karjalainen (1989) has developed a model for intra-community migration where the theoretical basis is provided by a dynamic model incorporating elements of the thinking of Zelinsky (1971) and Skeldon (1977). In developing municipalities the internal migration has been stronger than in other groups. Accordingly, in remote rural areas the direction has been either migration to built-up areas or migration within or between the rural areas. The model of Karjalainen is based on the notion that migration flows within a community alter when the community, or some sub-set of it, is growing or modernizing.

Kauppinen (2000) makes use of the concept of a thoroughfare zone. These zones are defined as 'pausing places' which gain migrants as a result of migration between municipalities but lose population to the rest of the municipality. These areas are often the most densely populated ones, but the study does not explain whether the phenomenon is due to the availability of housing stock, the atmosphere of the area, the image of the area, or something else.

The theoretical model of differential urbanization put forward by Geyer and Kontuly (1996) uses net migration flows to identify phases in the urbanization process. It introduces polarization reversal as an intermediate phase of urban development between population concentration and deconcentration in the migration sequence. The model is based on fluctuations between main- and sub-stream migration in different stages of social development. Heikkilä (2003) has tested the model for both urban and rural areas and this combination has explained the regional population dynamics in Finland. The theoretical model is suitable for different regional levels and gives deeper knowledge of the urbanization process. One useful concept that has been introduced in this context is the ideal size of a city. Another topic that has been discussed is the appropriate degree of urbanization.

Söderling (1988) studied internal migration in a country as a whole. He used individual and grouped (areal) social levels to generate multi-level models. The study was based on Allardt's (1976) comparison of welfare-elements of different migrant and municipality types. According to the first model most migration occurs between municipalities with large reserves of welfare resources. Only people that are migrating for non-material reasons are willing to move to municipalities with inferior structural and functional welfare infrastructure. Another multi-level model that was developed reinforces the concentration trends described by the first one. According to the study the most important migration flows occur between dynamic centres.

Andersson (1983, 1988, 1990, 1993) focused his attention on the difference between physical and social space, the interaction between them, and the historical processes that underlie them. In the structural renewal of society the question centres on the re-organization of production and on the local manifestation of global trends. The transition from a Fordist industrial society of mass production to a post-industrial service and information society is seen in the changes in the city's built environment. Andersson has concentrated specifically on the structural dynamics of the city of Turku and developed classification methods using socio-spatial methods of differentiation. Although his theoretical framework originates from the urban ecology tradition, he deals more conspicuously with the process that underlies the differences and changes in the urban structure than in the traditional ecological approach.

According to Peltola (1987) the Finnish population concentration that occurred between 1980 and 1985 can best be explained by a cyclic model resembling Kondratieff's long waves. The basic idea of the Kondratieff-waves is that economic innovation accelerates the accumulation of jobs and population in the largest centres in terms of the efficiency it creates. In Finland where public policy aims to maximize regional balance, spatial imbalance causes the government to counter-act by inducing development in peripheral areas. However, subsequent innovations tend to create new imbalances, which in turn, spawn new cycles.

INDIVIDUAL VERSUS REGIONAL HUMAN CAPITAL

According to Tiebout (1956: 416-24) an individual's choice of place of residence is largely influenced by taxation at the area of destination and to what extent its service structure meets the needs of the prospective migrant. According to this school of thought public services diminish the mobility of private services and migrants are dependent on the areal change of public services and taxation in proportion to the tax-paying abilities of the migrants. Several researchers (see Kytö 1998: 37) have later added new elements to this classical model of consumer behaviour. Additional assumptions have been added before applying it to the study of the regional structure of urban settlement.

Basic economic theories of migration are usually based on the concept of human capital. Sjaastad's (1962) well-known human capital framework considers migration as an investment which produces personal human capital (see also Isserman et al., 1986: 543-80; Jones, 1990). In the family context, migration is a joint welfare maximisation decision (Mincer 1978). The family weighs up the expected benefits and costs of moving, and migration takes place if the benefits exceed the costs. Different psychological costs linked to the change in the economic and social environments are also taken into account in the costs of the migration (Kytö, 1998: 38-9; Laakso and Loikkanen, 2000: 104).

According to Krugman's (1995) idea of endogenic regional growth the intensive use of knowledge and technology results in accumulation of growth. The driving force behind this development is technological change which creates the demand for more advanced human capital. Decreasing transportation costs, increasing commuting, and mobile production factors on the other hand strengthen the centrifugal forces created by land rent. The overall result on the economic geography is much less concentration than what is normally predicted in theory. The increase in the significance of information in industry increases the growth possibilities of large urban concentrations.

Social capital includes the idea of social trust, courses of action of communities, networks of reciprocal action, and social norms that have a significant influence on economic development. The overall applicability of the concept has been questioned and criticized, however, especially the question whether social capital could really be regarded as capital. It is argued that the base of social capital, i.e. the network of reciprocal action, is weakened by migration, lessening trust, decreasing club activities and causing the estrangement of relatives. According to Pehkonen (2001) social capital is a significant factor in migration in the Finnish community. It is particularly important for small villages to attract even a few migrants annually because reciprocal action and versatility created by new migrants improve their sustainability. The significance of social capital has not yet been quantitatively determined.

THE DELIMITATION OF URBAN ZONES

The urbanization of people and the structural change of the business sector have increased the mosaic quality of the countryside. Mechanization, rationalization and international integration of the agricultural sector have transformed life in the countryside (Katajamäki and Kaikkonen 1991). Today, the countryside interacts more readily with cities than in the past and is linked to both national and international development processes. It has indeed been suggested that the functional division between the city and the countryside should be abandoned. Cities and their hinterlands are transformed into network structures of a community system. It is essentially a system in which a network of reciprocal relations occur between organizations located in different nucleated areas (Vartiainen, 1989c: 50-1).

When examining urban settlements it is important to distinguish between administrative, statistical and geographical approaches to the concept. Administrative divisions do not provide an ideal framework for the description of city networks, because in Finland, municipalities have been given autonomy over the usage of the term 'city'. But because municipalities are often large in area, their built-up areas usually only cover a small part of their areas while the rest consists of sparsely populated countryside (Palomäki, 1972b: 20; Rikkinen, 1977: 11).

Geographically it is desirable to classify settlements with similar structures similarly although they might be located in areas that are administratively classified differently. Due to this, a joint Nordic concept of built-up areas covering all urban-like areas regardless of the administrative status of the municipality has been developed. It is based on their population and the visible part of their built-up areas (SVT VI C, 1976: 104: 4). A settlement containing at least 200 inhabitants and with not more than 200 metres between residences is considered as a built-up area. The problem with this is that there are no distinctive boundaries between built-up areas and the countryside. Urban areas should rather be treated as a continuum where urban characteristics become less obvious as one moves further from the city centre. Cities have been outlined also by means of interaction between city and countryside, i.e. systems of central and hinterland areas (Palomäki, 1972a: 29). A criterion for the delimitation of a functional city region is usually the direction and spatial extent of commuting. The labour-market area is formed by municipalities that exceed a limit of, say 15 or 20 per cent of the labour force commuting from the municipality of departure to the city centre (Heikkilä and Korhonen 2000). OECD (see Malinen and Keränen, 1996) defines areas with a population density of less than 150 inhabitants per km² as rural areas. According to this 35 of our cities reach the required population density.

The Research and Development Centre of Kajaani and Suomen aluetutkimus FAR (Keränen et al., 2000) has drawn up a classification of countryside types for the official countryside policy (Figure 10.2). This classification distinguishes areas in terms of their regional structure. It is based on a city network study (Vartiainen and Antikainen, 1989) and on the principal component analysis. In addition, relative and absolute numbers of countryside and city population and as well as the location of centres have been taken into consideration. In a study where different municipal types were compared with one another it was found that the proportion of highly educated people increases as the municipality becomes more urbanized (Data: SVT 2000a). In the centres of city areas the proportion of inter-municipality commuters, as a percentage of employed persons is the lowest, and in the rural areas near to the cities, it is the highest. In the area between the nuclear and the sparsely populated regions the inter-municipality commuting increases. The dependency ratio increases towards the group of municipalities of sparsely populated areas. The mean of unemployment rate in different types of municipalities is highest in sparsely populated areas and in the centres of city areas. The range of variance of tax revenues per inhabitant is quite large inside the different types of municipalities.

The Nordic countries have a fairly long history of analysing regional input-output (Susiluoto, 1999: 37). It has the advantages of independence of long time sequences and connection to the established concepts of accountancy of the national economy as well as offering the possibility for evaluation of the multiplier impacts of migration. It has become one of the main methods in the study of whole regional economies in particular. Regression models with multiple variables, where migration has been one of the factors describing regional development, have been constructed in several studies.

Figure 10.2 Countryside types by municipality, 2001

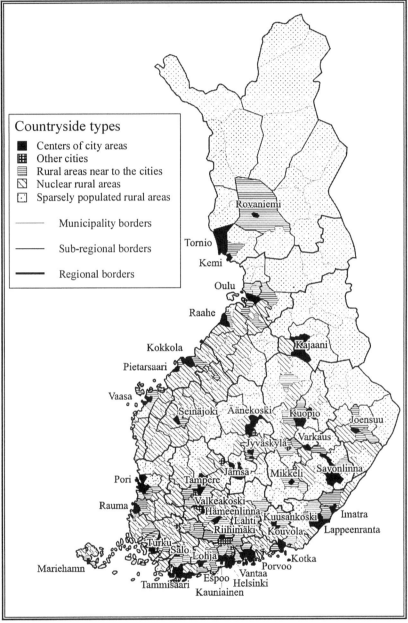

Source: Keränen and Malinen (2001), p. 9

Also panel-data combining cross-section and time-sequence data have been used lately (Moisio, 1998a: 47-8). Pure time sequence analysis is seldom represented in studies. In particular long time sequences are hard to find within several crucial variables (Okko et al., 2000: 32).

The development and connections of variables are illustrated, for example by time-sequence graphs and cross-charting. Different indicators measuring migration and regional economy have been utilized in analysis of the influence of migration. The basis of the development of indicators is that evaluation of regional development becomes a better tool for policy makers. Indicators can consist of both quantitative and qualitative factors. General guidelines for drawing up indicators have been presented in e.g. OECD and EU publications (OECD, 1993; CEC, 1994).

The Nordic research team Edvardsson et al. (2001: 21-2), has constructed a local labour market performance index in order to illustrate the regional adaptability to structural change and to enable comparisons between regions. The index measures the relative labour market performance in different regions. The total performance index is composed of a set of different mobility rates derived from internal gross streams within the local labour markets. In the national context all local labour market mobility measures are compared with a corresponding national average rate. The results show that there are clear differences in the mobilities of the labour market between the Nordic countries. According to the research group this factor is essentially the difference among the forces of the cycles of economic life in the countries (Stambøl et al., 1999: 27-30).

LAYERED EXAMINATION OF URBANIZATION AND MIGRATION
AGE AND FAMILY STATUS
The strong dependence of interregional migration on age and family status can, according to Laakso (1998: 26) be interpreted with the help of a migration theory based on the idea of production of human capital (Isserman et al., 1986; Jones, 1990). People's income over their lifespan depends largely on the educational and occupational choices that were made at the beginning of their careers. Knowledge and skills become increasingly more occupation specific along with increasing age. This leads to a situation where older workers have fewer choices, and the variation of pay options is smaller for older workers than for those at the beginning of their career (Jouhki, 1988: 83-4). In addition the psychological costs of migration are seen to be smaller for the young when compared to the elderly.

The migration propensity declines with advancing stages of life and is at its highest before the children are born and around the time of their birth.

The migration propensity increases again to some extent for the elderly people. In Kainuu county the proportion of elderly people, over 64 years of age, moving from the countryside to the built-up areas was as much as eight times that of those moving in the opposite direction. Many migration events are also brought about by major changes in life such as widowhood and the resulting experience of having to live alone, or simply retirement, and the proportion of elderly people moving from the countryside into the built-up areas has in any case increased simply because of the biased age structure of the rural population (Karjalainen, 1989: 38, 40).

The migration propensity of families with children is considerably lower when compared to others of working age. Single people and working-age children living with their parents migrate at the highest rate (Laakso, 1998: 29). Approximately two thirds of migrants are young people of between 15 and 34 years. Children under 7 years old tend to migrate more because their parents are usually young adults. In contrast the migrations of school children are more rare (Laakso, 1998: 25).

A weakened sense of belonging among young people may be the result of the fact that to a larger degree careers are shaped outside the young people's local regions in the course of their educational and professional lives. Because the options of work and place of residence are increasing it is becoming more important for regions to improve their images in order to attract different educational and occupational groups (Aslesen and Langeland, 2000: 18).

According to Vaattovaara (1998: 82, 138) families with children show significant differences in their choice of residence within a core-peripheral framework. For families with children, single-family housing close to nature is more important than easy access to options of fast commuting by rail. This differentiation is often found in factor ecological urban studies (e.g. Andersson, 1983; Katajamäki, 1990). The age structure of the population and different stages of life have an important impact on the migration of men and women (see Heikkilä, 1997; Naukkarinen, 1974: 121). In areas of great population loss more females than males leave the area which also has a significant impact on birth rates in such areas.

Higher educational levels augment family migration. In two-earner families wives do have some bargaining power in the decision-making process. Personal unemployment and commuting increase the propensity to migrate, and children as well as home-ownership inhibit migration. The wife's unemployment experience and commuting behaviour has a slightly stronger positive effect on family migration than the husband's, and the mobility of the husband decreases with the wife's income. With regard to regional characteristics, migration propensity increases with the area's unemployment rate and share of industry, while agriculture seems to have no effect on family migration (Nivalainen, 2000: 10).

THE ECONOMY

The change of the regional structure has been influenced not only by industry but also by national factors such as the natural environment, narrow resources base and sparse population (Peltonen 1982). In addition, the political actions of each era have been reflected as changes in the location structure of the city system. In the decades of urbanization the small-size cities grew as a result of support by their hinterlands (Peltola, 1986: 127-8).

Migration has been closely linked to regional development, but most of all to the regional labour and housing market. Job opportunities, income level, education possibilities, accommodation options and their costs, public and private services, the living environment and the possibilities for leisure-time activities are essential factors influencing migration decisions and choices of destination (Summa, 1982: 36-8).

Significant attention has been given to the direct impact regional and municipal economies have on migration. Economic trends influence the volume of migration in such a way that during a boom the number of migrants increases while it decreases during depression (Korkiasaari, 1991; Lee, 1966; Stamböl et al., 1997). A study of the impact of the economic depression of the early 1990s on migration type shows that the proportion of migration inside communities increased during the recession, but at the national level it had no visible effect on migration (Kauppinen 2000: 119-20). During the economic recession of 1992 there was more migration from urban to rural areas, while the trend was reversed during the boom period.

Although there is sufficient housing overall, migration sometimes creates a shortage of housing in certain areas. For instance, migration would increase to the Helsinki conurbation during boom periods if the real estate market responded sufficiently to the demand for housing. The cost of housing and infrastructure is approximately 70 000 Euros per migrant in the Helsinki conurbation, of which the share of the municipality is roughly 20 per cent (Lankinen, 1998). According to Moisio (1998b), however, the impact of in-migration on the economic stability of municipalities and on the availability of funds as a whole, remains positive.

The recent increase in inter-regional migration has caused much concern among peripheral regions because of the loss of their educated population, leaving them with an ageing population. Over the short term migration may have a converging effect, but in the long term the effects are likely to be divergent (Pekkala, 2000). Convergence is related to economic upswings, whereas the poorest regions fall behind the rest during recessions. Highly educated migrants tend to create cumulative causation through the effective use of their productive capacity and by generating faster income growth in attractive regions. This tends to reinforce growth in the existing regional growth poles. On a short time span, migration tends to balance out regional income differences, but in the long run they act conversely. The results also indicate that migrants tend to migrate to areas where their income could increase and where their income growth could increase faster.

Small households, people that are less skilled, high unemployment rates, high tenancy levels, and low income levels are characteristics that are associated with social disadvantage. Overall the disadvantaged areas cover approximately 10 per cent of the capital city area. Through the city's own intervention the regional distribution of disadvantaged people has been fragmented on purpose. This is a desirable situation. Fear of segregation as an areal and areally spreading phenomenon is not reasonable, although some centres do give cause for concern (Vaattovaara 1998: 141).

HUMAN CAPITAL AND EMPLOYMENT

Like capital, human capital also tends to withdraw from low productivity areas and gravitate to areas where productivity is high. It has been estimated that Finland loses about 54 million Euros' worth of human capital each year. The total value of human capital invested abroad is around 1.3-1.5 milliard Euros (Kärkkäinen, 1993). Laakkonen (1992) estimates that a 20-year old immigrant brings with him or her 120,000 Euros in the form of know-how. If the immigrant has an academic degree, the contribution may even be up to three to four times higher.

The exchange of population produced by inter-provincial migration weakens the development potential of depressed areas both quantitatively (decrease in population) and qualitatively (decrease in human capital). On average the out-migrants of depressed regions are more highly skilled than the population in the region of origin and those that are moving to depressed areas are often older and more likely to be unemployed than those moving to other regions (Kauhanen and Tervo, 1999: 19).

In the 1960s higher education was deconcentrated to different parts of the country so that young people could study in their own counties. The population, economy and educational facilities are, however, more concentrated in the coastal areas than ever before. Because of selective migration Helsinki, Tampere, Oulu and their neighbouring municipalities are the only true growth centres in the country. Of the university cities even Turku, Jyväskylä and Joensuu are losing highly skilled people. Migrants often form part of the dynamic and rapidly developing group in the enterprises in the area, which leads to the widening of the gap between social differences between the advantaged and the disadvantaged.

In the future the demand for a more highly educated and differentiated labour force is likely to increase the mobility of people even more (Laakso, 1998: 35). To be able to compete effectively, regions must be able to attract and maintain high quality human capital, as well as encourage young people to choose an education that corresponds with the needs of the local labour markets. There are small variations in young people's preferences with regard to education, work or place of residence according to where they live in the country (Aslesen and Langeland, 2000: 15-16).

From a migration point of view it is essential to separate regional unemployment from individual unemployment. The unemployed who moved during the boom period improved their chances of employment by nearly 50 per cent compared to those who stayed where they were. During the depression years the unemployed experienced a weakening of their chances to find employment (Stambøl et al., 1997: 26-7). On average, it takes longer for women to find employment after a move than it does for men, and returns take longer to accrue for women. Higher education is pivotal in securing employment in the migration process. Moreover, men's success in getting jobs depends on the region of destination, while the size of the labour market is more important to women (Nivalainen, 2000: 2-3). In Finland migration of the unemployed will increase only if unemployment in their living area is higher than that of another area (Ritsilä and Tervo, 1999).

Redistribution of wealth through taxation and welfare endowments has led to a comparative equalization of housing and income in the Nordic countries (Stambøl et al., 1997: 23-4). Current high regional unemployment together with an unfavourable prognosis for the future is a strong push factor in the area. In the United States the mobility of the unemployed is higher than in Europe. This is due to the more secure living conditions during periods of unemployment, especially in the Nordic countries (Paasivirta, 2001; Stambøl et al., 1997: 24; Tervo, 1998: 14-15).

The in-migrants of the Helsinki labour market area in 1996 were relatively evenly distributed in the different occupational categories. Half of the migrants had completed secondary education and 37 per cent had a higher education although only 44 per cent of the country's population had completed secondary education and 13 per cent had tertiary education. Of employed in-migrants, 87 per cent maintained their labour market status as employed whereas 5 per cent were unemployed after a year (Figure 10.3). The employment absorbtion rate of in-migrants was 80-96 per cent depending on the occupational group in 1996. In-migrants working in the field of data processing had the best employment rate. Generally, fewer than half of all unemployed in-migrants found employment within a year after migration, a third were still unemployed and one tenth continued with their studies. Of those who migrated as unemployed, 10 per cent became unemployed the year after

Figure 10.3   The changes of labour market status until 1997 of those who migrated in 1996 to the Helsinki labour market area as employed

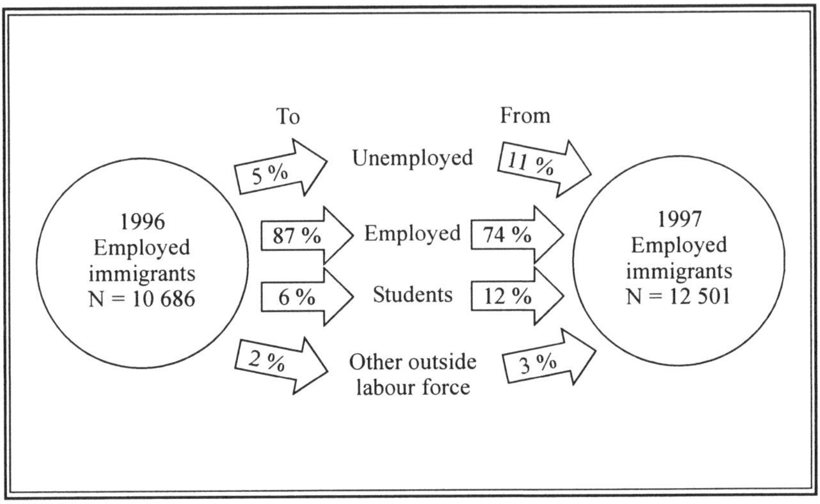

Source: SVT

DEVELOPMENT ESTIMATES AND CONSEQUENCES FOR THE FUTURE

In the following section the need and costs of actions in regional policy will be considered. Although regional balance is an ideal, concentration is seen as an important factor in the country's competitive ability and in the restoring of the economic structure of a country with a small and sparse population (Leppänen, 2001). At the moment Helsinki is the only international primate city of Finland. Forecasts for cities in the EU for the period between 1995 and 2015 show that the fastest growing cities are Lisbon (26.5 per cent) and Helsinki (24.2 per cent) (Seppänen, 1996: 55).

Internal migration, immigration and emigration during the next decades will depend on the development of the country's economy and its international competitiveness, employment opportunities, growth and development of the EU and future migration policy. Migration affects the regional size and age structure of the population both directly and indirectly. Indirect influences are caused, among other things, by the population structure, by variations in the death rate, and in fertility rates. In 1999, 62 per cent of communities had a negative growth rate, i.e. where the death rate exceeded the fertility rate. Statistics Finland has estimated that almost 40 per cent of communities will lose their labour force over the next 30 years, in extreme cases up to 25 per cent (Nieminen 2001: 45). When future regional development is contemplated, it must be borne in mind that the proportion of elderly consumers will increase and that this group's needs will have to be reflected in the planning of entertainment. The increase of their level of wealth and the growth in pension funds also mould the capital and financial markets.

In Eastern Finland and Lapland 'Return Migration Campaigns' have been launched to persuade people who have left the areas, to return to their home regions. Environmentalism, so-called 'lifestyle migration', has been presented as a strong pulling factor. However, the precondition for return migration is generally thought to be that they should be able to find employment in their own occupational field (EVA, 1999: 12-16, 57; Korhonen, 1994: 46-50). If the Return Migration Campaign is successful and becomes more common, it should have a long-term influence on regional development, especially when the campaign has an effect on expatriates and on foreigners. Forecasting emigration and immigration is currently more uncertain than before because new forms of migration are emerging. Factors such as temporary and periodical labour migration, cross-border labour commuting between Euro-regions, asylum seekers, and illegal aliens, are complicating traditional emigration and immigration patterns.

According to Kauppinen (2000) there are three visible trends in theoretical migration thinking. First there is the view that intra- and inter-city migration will become the main forms of migration (Järnegren and Ventura, 1977; Zelinsky, 1971). A shortcoming of these models is that they do not take into consideration the migration to the countryside that began after the middle of the 1970s. In the second school of thought the end point of development is a situation where migration occurs from cities to the surrounding countryside (Gibbs, 1963; Palomäki, 1970). These models in turn have not considered migration between and within centres. The third type is represented by Hautamäki's (1967, 1982) model, where growth in the last stage is strongest in the remote regions, thus resembling the first stage. In the stage new resources were taken into use, settlement grew in the provincial limits of the area. Urbanization didn't occur to a significant degree.

The view is held that the population transition in Finland would have happened in accordance with the vital transition theory if the birth rates had not declined in the years of famine and because of migration (Kultalahti 1990: 114). The birth rate fell rapidly at the end of the 19th century, levelled out in the early years of the 1900s and then declined again in the 1930s, to rise sharply once more in the 1940s with the post-war boom generation. It then decreased rapidly from that time onwards (Karjalainen 1989: 18-19). In Western Europe, fewer babies are born each year than there are deaths, leading to a natural decrease of these populations, except where it is offset by immigration. This situation is due both to the low birth rate and to higher proportions of older people in the population (Figure 10.4 and 10.5). The population prognosis by municipality until the year 2030 was drawn up by SVT (1998) and is based on the population data of 1997. In the prognosis the population of Finland will turn to decline by the 2020s if the deficit cannot be filled with net immigration. According to Nieminen (2001) the annual number of county-internal migration would stay near 250,000 in the future.

Laakso (1998) sees two possible trends in the Finnish population projections for the years 1997-2020. In a projection of a centrally focused regional structure, the regional development is assumed to continue the trend of development in the years 1993-97; thus the central areas would grow at the expense of small towns. According to Laakso urbanization and the stabile regional policies are likely if a high economic growth rate can be maintained. The population of the Helsinki conurbation should grow by approximately 20 per cent in twenty years, of which a little more than 50 per cent would be due to net migration gain and the rest to natural population growth.

The alternative by Laakso is based on relatively balanced regional development where central areas do not receive migration gain and small town areas and the countryside do not suffer from migration loss. This would mean that the population of Helsinki would still grow by 60,000 inhabitants due to natural population growth. In this option regional policies could lead to regionally balanced development provided that investments larger than the current ones are made to prevent further economic regression. According to Laakso the second alternative is a result of slow economic development. If the migration assumptions of centrally led regional development are realised, the proportion of the people over 65 years of age would grow from the current 16 per cent to about one third. At the same time the proportion of children and working-age people would decline by almost the same amount. If balanced development occurred in the country, the age structure of the population would develop in the same direction but the change would be slower.

Moisio (1999: 21) has developed an econometric model for migration on a county level. The results show that migration will continue at a slightly accelerated pace. By using economic variables such as changes of employment and income it is possible to develop dynamic migration and population prognoses. According to Moisio net migration is the most important element in the model describing the role of migration in regional development because it influences the changes of the number and quality of the area's labour force. In addition, attention should be given to the structure of migration because even a net migration gain could have a negative effect on an area's development if its labour force is exchanged for elderly and less skilled people.

The Ministry of the Interior endeavours to increase the balance in migration nation-wide by establishing a national growth centre network of 30-40

Figure 10.4 The change in population structure, 1750-1900

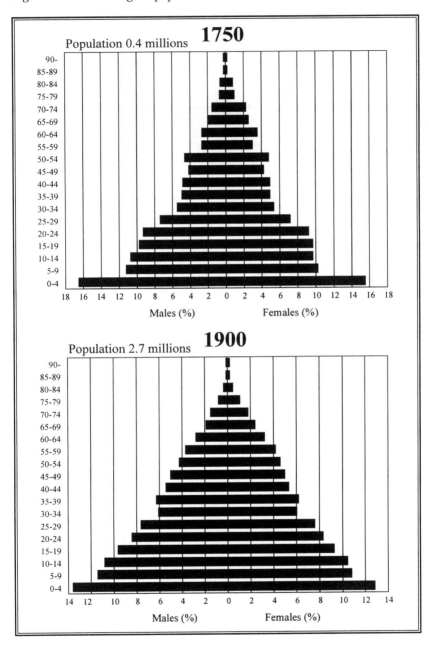

Figure 10.5 The change in population structure, 1999-2050

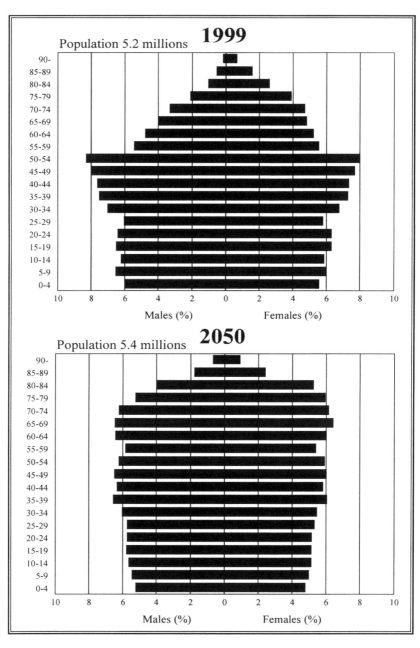

Source: SVT

regional centres to promote the interaction between the countryside and the cities (Salmela, 2001). The goal is to have at least one regional centre in each county; the centre should have a versatile labour market and a stimulating social environment. It is hoped that these regional centres will attract young families (Mainio, 2000). It is also believed that the programme will be more successful if the inhabitants of the regions participate in it. 'Seed money' is provided by the Ministry in cases where promising project proposals are submitted. Although the municipalities may not be able to create many employment opportunities, they can create a pleasant and safe living environment which, it is believed, will attract people and enterprises to the area.

According to Vartiainen (1995: 57) the prognosis for small town regions in urban development is not promising because future development is assumed to favour large cities. The smaller settlements near to the major centres are assumed to develop primarily as satellite centres or as part of the growth zones of the major cities. The government is currently moving away from the welfare state concept, which is causing difficulties for many administrative centres in rural areas that traditionally have relied on welfare services for their expansion (Andersson, 1993: 42).

Finland is unlikely to benefit as much as the rest of Western Europe from the opening up of the labour market through the EU because of the high usage of female labour in the former and the high proportion of part-time workers in the latter. The unemployed form a relatively large proportion of the labour force at present which is not structurally consistent with the needs of the demand of the labour force in the country. According to Konttajärvi (2000) one of the most significant changes in the regional structure is likely to occur in job descriptions. The number of manual jobs has decreased and has been increasingly replaced by so-called information work occupations. The wider use of new telecommunication technology might eventually reduce the concentration of economic activities that have occurred over the last twenty years and should also curb the increase in commuting.

Finland's population is currently ageing rapidly. This will lead to an increase in the demand for services for the aged and for highly skilled workers (Trux, 2001). A process of active immigration recruitment has been initiated to find workers in areas where specific shortfalls are experienced. It is estimated that there will be a shortfall of approximately 20,000 people leaving the labour market annually from 2010 (Mölsä, 2001). However, it is unlikely that the loss of people will be replaced by immigrants. Presently immigrants are concentrated in certain areas, partly because of employment opportunities in Southern Finland (Jaakkola, 2001). As the Western European population ages the need to migrate to countries where demand for labour is greatest will be emphasised everywhere in Europe. Competition for an educated labour force is likely to increase and wage rates, housing and tax benefits are likely to become important factors in this process (Heikkilä, 1997: 173-5).

REFERENCES

Ahtiainen, Marketta, Vuokko Aromaa, Pertti Haapala, Sirkka Kauppinen and Karl-Erik Michelsen (1998), *Suomen historian aikakirja,* Helsinki, Edita.

Alker, H. R. Jr. (1969), 'A typology of ecological fallacies', in Dogan, Mattei and Stein Rokkan (eds), *Quantitative ecological analysis in the social sciences,* Massachusetts, The MIT Press, pp. 69-86.

Allardt, E. (1976), *Hyvinvoinnin ulottuvuuksia,* Porvoo.

Andersson, H. (1983), 'Urban structural dynamics in the city of Turku, Finland', *Fennia,* **161** (2), 145-261.

Andersson, H. (1988), 'Kaupunkitilan luokittelu. Luokittelumenetelmien käyttö kaupungin sosiaalisen tilan ja asumistilan analyysissa', *Turun yliopiston maantieteen laitoksen monisteita,* 7, 42 p.

Andersson, H. (1990), 'Sisäkaupungin rakenteellinen uusiutuminen ja teollisuustilan uuskäyttö', in Andersson, Harri (ed.), *Teollisuustilan uuskäyttö Turun kaupunkikeskustassa,* Turku, Turun kaupunki, pp. 11-82.

Andersson, H. (1993), 'Rakennettu ympäristö – kaupunki rakentamisen modernina projektina', *University of Turku, Täydennyskoulutuskeskus* **A 10**, 116 p.

Antikainen, J. (2001), 'Julkeanko olla käyttämättä paikkatietoa muuttoliikkeen tutkimisessa?', in Heikkilä, E. (ed.), Muuttoliikkeet vuosituhannen vaihtuessa - halutaanko niitä ohjata? *Siirtolaisuustutkimuksia* **A 24**, Institute of Migration, pp. 220-221.

Aslesen, S. and O. Langeled (2000), 'The Regional skill-gap. Educational Preferences and Recruitment Problems in the Regional Manufacturing Industry in Norway', Paper presentated at the 40th European Congress of the European Regional Science Association, Barcelona.

CEC (1994), *Fifth Periodic Report on the Social and Economic Situation and Development of the Regions in the Community,* Luxembourg, European Commission.

Edvardsson, I. R., E. Heikkilä, M. Johansson, L.O. Persson and .L.S. Stamböl (2001), 'Competitive Capitals. Performance of Local Labour Markets - an International Comparison Based on Gross-stream Data', in Heikkilä, E. (ed), Muuttoliikkeet vuosituhannen vaihtuessa - halutaanko niitä ohjata?, *Siirtolaisuustutkimuksia* **A 24**, Institute of Migration, 47-70.

EVA (1999), *Suomen uusjako, raportti aluekehityksestä ja sen vaikutuksista,* EVA Elinkeinoelämän valtuuskunta, 100 p.

Geyer, H. S. and T. M. Kontuly (1996), 'A Theoretical Foundation for the Concept of Differential Urbanization', in H. S. Geyer and T. M. Kontuly (eds), *Differential Urbanization, Integrating spatial models*, London: Arnold, pp. 290-308.

Gibbs, J. (1963), 'The evolution of population concentration', *Economic Geography*, **39** (2), 119-129.

Hautamäki, L. (1967), 'Development of settlement in some rural communes in Western Finland since 1920', *Fennia*, **96** (2), 1-97.

Hautamäki, L. (1982), 'Maaseutukylien kehitysnäkymät', in Koivukangas, Olavi, Kai Lindström and Raimo Narjus (eds), *Muuttoliikesymposium 1980, Siirtolaisuustutkimuksia* **A 8**, Institute of Migration, pp. 148-153.

Heikkilä, E. (1997), 'Educated people and their migration behaviour in an integrated Europe', in L-E. Borgegård, A.M. Findlay and E. Sondell (eds), *Population, planning and policies*, Cerum report, **5**, pp. 169-176.

Heikkilä, E. (2003), 'Differential Urbanization in Finland', *Tijdschrift voor Economiesche en Sociale Geografie*, Forthcoming.

Heikkilä, E. and S. Korhonen (2000), 'The Dynamics of the Finnish Labour Markets in the 1990s', Turku: Institute of Migration. Unpublished.

Isserman A., C. Taylor, S. Gerking and U. Schubert (1986), 'Regional Labor Market Analysis', in Nijkamp, P. (ed.), *Handbook of Regional and Urban Economics I*, Amsterdam: Elsevier Science Publisher B. V., pp. 543-580.

Jaakkola, T. (2001), 'Maahanmuuttajien rekrytoitumispyrkimykset ja sopivan työn saaminen', in E. Heikkilä (ed), *Muuttoliikkeet vuosituhannen vaihtuessa - halutaanko niitä ohjata?* Siirtolaisuustutkimuksia A 24, Turku: Institute of Migration, pp. 191-194.

Järnegren, A. and F. Ventura (1977), *Tre samhällens förändringshistoria: Exploateringen av den fysiska miljön i historisk belysning*, Stockholm: Statens råd för byggnadsforskning.

Jones, H. (1990), *Population Geography*, London: Paul Chapman Publishing Ltd.

Jouhki, H. (1988), 'Työmarkkinat – Markkinoita ja sosiaalisia instituutioita', Jyväskylän yliopisto, *Keski-Suomen taloudellisen tutkimuskeskuksen julkaisuja*, **96**, 160 p.

Kangasharju, A., J-P. Kataja and V. Vihriälä (1999), 'Suomen aluerakenteen viimeaikainen kehitys', Helsinki, *Pellervon taloudellisen tutkimuslaitoksen työpapereita*, **17**, 50 p.

Karisto, A. (1995), 'Elastiset ja epäelastiset kaupungit. Amerikkalainen näkökulma segregaatioon', *Yhteiskuntasuunnittelu*, **3**, 58-60.

Karjalainen, E. (1986), *Muuttoliike ja sen vaikutukset Kuhmon alueelliseen väestökehitykseen 1959-8*', Oulu: University of Oulu, Research Institute of Northern Finland, Research Reports, No. 205, 211 p.

Karjalainen, E. (1989), 'Migration and regional development in the rural communes of Kainuu, Finland in 1980-85', *Societas Geographica Fenniae Nordicae, Nordia Geographical Publications,* **23** (1), 1-89.

Kärkkäinen, E. (1993), *Aivovuoto - yksilön voitto, yhteiskunnan tappio?* Lisensiaatintutkimus, Helsinki: Helsingin yliopisto, Sosiaalipolitiikan laitos.

Katajamäki, E. (1990), *Hyvinvointi Helsingissä - Ensiaskeleita hyvinvoinnin alueellisen jakautumisen kuvaamiseen,* Helsinki: Helsingin kaupungin tietokeskuksen muistioita 1990 (1), 40 p.

Katajamäki, H. and R. Kaikkonen (1991), *Maaseudun kolmastie,* Helsinki: Helsingin yliopisto, Maaseudun tutkimus- ja koulutuskeskuksen julkaisuja A 1.

Kauhanen, M. and H. Tervo (1999), *Who move to depressed regions, an analysis of migration streams in Finland in the 1990s,* Helsinki: Helsinki Labour Institute for Economic Research, Research report, 161.

Kauppinen, J. (2000), *Muuttoliike Suomessa vuosina 1989-1994 koordinaattipohjaisten paikkatietojen perusteella,* Turku: Siirtolaisuusinstituutin tutkimuksia A 22, Institute of Migration.

Keränen, H., P. Malinen and O. Aulaskari (2000), 'Suomen maaseutututyypit', Suomen aluetutkimus FAR, *Selvityksiä,* **20**, 60 p.

Keränen, H. and P. Malinen (2001), *Vuoden 2001 kuntaliitosten vaikutus maaseutututyypit-luokitukseen,* Suomen aluetutkimus FAR, Muistio 13.2.2001.

Konttajärvi, T. (2000), *Pitkän matkan työssäkävijöiden muutto- ja etätyöpotentiaali Suomessa,* Helsinki: Helsingin yliopiston maaseudun tutkimus- ja koulutuskeskus B 20, 124 p.

Korhonen, S. (1994), *Paluumuuttohalukkuus Kainuuseen. Tutkimus Kainuusta 1982-90 muuttaneista henkilöistä,* Oulo: University of Oulu, Research Institute of Northern Finland, Research Reports 120.

Korkiasaari, J. (1991), *Liikkuvuus ja rakennemuutos. Maassamuutto ja työvoiman liikkuvuus osana yhteiskunnan rakennemuutosta,* Työministeriön työpoliittinen tutkimus 11, 185 p.

Krugman, P.(1995), *Development, geography and economic theory,* Cambridge, USA: MIT Press.

Kultalahti, O. (1990), *Yhteiskunta ja alue,* Jyväskylä: Finnpublishers.

Kytö, H. (1998), 'Muuttajan muuttuvat motiivit eräissä suomalaisissa kaupungeissa 1980- ja 1990-luvuilla', *Suomen kuntaliitto, Acta,* **1998** (100), 310 p.

Laakkonen, R. (1992), 'Tarvitseeko Suomi työmarkkinoillaan siirtolaisia', in R. Vuohelainen (ed.), *Eurooppalaisella torilla*, Yrityksen uudistuva toimintaympäristö, WSOY, Porvoo, 41-47.

Laakso, S. (1998), 'Alueiden välinen muutto Suomessa. Muuttajien sopeutuminen työ- ja asuntomarkkinoille vuosina 1993-1996', *Helsingin kaupungin tietokeskus, Tutkimuksia*, **1998** (4), 92 p.

Laakso, S. and H.A. Loikkanen (2000), 'Yritysten sijoittuminen, asukkaiden liikkuvuus ja kaupunkialueiden vuorovaikutus', *Kaupunkipolitiikan yhteistyöryhmän julkaisu*, **2000** (1), 126 p.

Lankinen, M. (1998), 'Muuttoliikkeen vaikutukset kunnan menoihin' in Muuttoliike ja kunnat. *Kunnallisalan kehittämissäätiö, tutkimusjulkaisu*, **15**, pp. 39-82.

Lee, E. (1966), 'A Theory of Migration', *Demography*, **3** (1), 47-57.

Leppänen, J. (2001), 'Yhteiskunnan ohjaus aluerakenteen ja muuttoliikkeen hallinnassa 2000-luvulla', in E. Heikkilä (ed), Muuttoliikkeet vuosituhannen vaihtuessa - halutaanko niitä ohjata? *Siirtolaisuustutkimuksia* **A 24**, Institute of Migration, pp. 200-202.

Mainio, T. (2000), 'Nuorille perheille virikkeellisiä aluekeskuksia', *Helsingin Sanomat* 12.12.2000.

Malinen, P. and H. Keränen (1996), 'Indikaattorisuositus maaseudun elinolojen seurantaan EU-sopeutumiskaudella', *Suomen aluetutkimus FAR selvityksiä*, **13**, 75 p.

Mincer, J. (1978), 'Family Migration Decisions', *Journal of Political Economy*, **86**, 749-773.

Moisio, A. (1998a), *Kuntien menot ja valtionavut, Paneeliaineiston analyysi*, Jyväskylän yliopisto, taloustieteellinen osasto, 111, 108 p.

Moisio, A. (1998b), *Millaiset kunnat kriisissä*. Pellervon taloudellisen tutkimuslaitoksen työpapereita 15, 37 p.

Moisio, A. (1999), *Muuttoliikkeen ennustamisesta*. Pellervon taloudellisen tutkimuslaitoksen työpapereita, 19, 25 p.

Mölsä, J. (2001), *Maahanmuuttajat voivat olla menestystekijä*, Helsinki: Helsingin Sanomat 4.2.2001.

Naukkarinen, A. (1974), Väestönmuutostekijöiden sekä väestörakenteen ikä- ja sukupuolispesifisyys alueellisessa tutkimuksessa', *Terra*, **86** (3), 119-124.

Nieminen, M. (2001), 'Maassamuuton kehityslinjat nyt ja tulevaisuudessa', in E. Heikkilä (ed), Muuttoliikkeet vuosituhannen vaihtuessa - halutaanko niitä ohjata? *Siirtolaisuustutkimuksia* **A 24**, Institute of Migration, 38-46.

Nivalainen, S. (2000), 'Migration and post-move employment in two-earner families', Paper presented at the 40th European Congress of the regional Science Association, Barcelona, Spain.

OECD (1993), *Creating Rural Indicators – Framework, Figures, Findings,* Organisation for economic Co-operation and Development, Rural Development Programme, Draft 22.9.1993.

Okko, P., A. Miettilä and E. Oikarinen (2000), *Muuttoliike pakottaa rakennemuutokseen,* Kunnallisalan kehittämissäätiön tutkimusjulkaisut, 24.

Paasi, A. (1981), 'Spatiaaliset preferenssit ja muuttaminen – maantieteellinen näkökulma', *Siirtolaisuus-Migration,* **1981** (3), 2-12.

Paasivirta, A. (2001), 'Muuttoliike ja työllisyys', in E. Heikkilä (ed), *Muuttoliikkeet vuosituhannen vaihtuessa - halutaanko niitä ohjata?* Siirtolaisuustutkimuksia **A 24**, Institute of Migration, pp. 90-100.

Palomäki, M. (1970), *Kaupungistumisprosessista Suomessa,* Vaasan kauppakorkeakoulu, Maantiede, Tutkimuksia 4, 8 p.

Palomäki, M. (1972a), *Kaupunkimaantiede,* Vaasan kauppakorkeakoulu, Maantiede, Opetusmonisteita 1, 108 p.

Palomäki, M. (1972b), *Kaupungistumisprosessin vaikutus taloudellisten ydinalueiden syntymiseen ja siirtymiseen,* Vaasan kauppakorkeakoulun julkaisuja, 10, 23 p.

Pehkonen, A. (2001), 'Sosiaalisen pääoman merkitys muuttoliiketutkimuksessa', in E. Heikkilä (ed), *Muuttoliikkeet vuosituhannen vaihtuessa - halutaanko niitä ohjata?* Siirtolaisuustutkimuksia A 24, Institute of Migration, pp. 290-293.

Pekkala, S. (2000), 'Regional convergence and migration in Finland 1960-95', *Jyväskylä Studies in Business and Economics,* **4**, 121 p.

Peltola, O. (1986), *Kaupungistumisprosessi Suomessa 1960- ja 1970-luvuilla taajamoitumiskehityksen valossa,* Vaasan korkeakoulu, Maantiede, Tutkimuksia, 114, 164 p.

Peltola, O. (1987), 'Taajamoituminen Suomessa 1980-85', *Proceedings of the University of Vaasa, Discussion Papers,* **87**, 12 p.

Peltonen, A. (1982), *Suomen kaupunkijärjestelmän kasvu 1815-1970, teollistumisen leviämisen vaikutuksista perifeerisen maan kaupungistumiseen,* Societas Scientiarum Fennica, Bidrag till kännedom av Finlands natur och folk, 128, 219 p.

Pred, A. (1965), 'Industrialization, Initial Advantage and American Metropolitan Growth', *Geographical Review,* **IX**, 158-185.

Rikkinen, K. (1977), *Suomen asutusmaantiede,* Otava: Keuruu.

Ritsilä, J. and H. Tervo (1999), *Regional differences in migratory behaviour in Finland,* in A. Alanen, H. Eskelinen, J. Mønnesland, I. Susiluoto and H.

Tervo, *Structures and Prospects in Nordic Regional Economics*, Nordregio, 1999 (5), 121-138.

Salmela, M. (2001), *Ministeriö suunnittelee uusia aluekeskuksia ympäri maata*, Helsinki: Helsingin Sanomat 4.3.2001.

Seppänen, S. (1996), *Helsinki ja Lissabon kasvavat EU-kaupungeista nopeimmin*, in S. Seppänen, K-M Vastamäki and E. Pentinmäki, EU-raporttisarja, Alueelliset menestystekijät, Tilastokeskus, EU-Report Series 1996 (2), 54-56.

Sjaastad, L. (1962), 'The Costs and Returns in Human Migration', *Journal of Political Economy*, 70 (Supplement), 80-93.

Skeldon, R. (1977), 'The evolution of migration patterns during urbanization in Peru', *The Geographical Review*, 67 (4), 394-411.

Söderling, I. (1983), *Maassamuutto ja muuttovirrat. Vuosina 1977-78 kunnasta toiseen muuttaneiden elinolosuhdetutkimus*, Institute of Migration, Siirtolaisuustutkimuksia A 11, 430 p.

Söderling, I. (1988), *Maassamuuton ulottuvuudet. Yksilö-, alue- ja yhteiskuntatason tarkastelu Suomessa vuosina 1977-1978 maassamuuttaneista*, Turku: Annales Universitatis Turkuensis C 65.

Stambøl, L.S., M. Johansson, L.O. Persson and E. Rissanen (1997), *Flytting og sysselsetting i nordiske land*, TemaNord, 1997 (599), 182 p.

Stambøl, L.S., E. Heikkilä, M. Johansson, O. Nygren and L.O. Persson (1999), *Regional arbeidsmarkedsmobilitet i nordiske land*, TemaNord, 1999 (551).

Summa, H. (1982), *Kaupunkien sisäinen muuttoliike muuttotyypeittäin*, Teknillinen korkeakoulu, Yhdyskuntasuunnittelun jatkokoulutuskeskus, B 40.

Susiluoto, I. (1999), Regional input-output analysis, in A. Alanen, H. Eskelinen, J. Mønnesland, I. Susiluoto and H. Tervo, *Structures and Prospects in Nordic Regional Economics*, Nordregio, 1999 (5), 37-40.

SVT VI C, 104, 4 (1976), *Taajamat*, Helsinki: Statistics Finland.

SVT (1993), *Population 1993: 4*, Helsinki: Statistics Finland.

Statistics Finland (1998), *Population projection by municipalities 1998-2030*, Helsinki: Statistics Finland.

SVT (1991, 1992, 1998, 1999, 2000a, 2000b), *Statistical Yearbook*, Helsinki: Statistics Finland.

Tarkka, J., T. Polvinen and H. Soikkanen (1991), *Itsenäisen Suomen historia. 1, Rajamaasta tasavallaksi*, Gummerus: Jyväskylä, Weilin and Göös.

Taylor, R. C. (1969), 'Migration and Motivation, A study of determinants and types', in Jakcson, J. A. (ed.), Migration, *Sociological studies*, 2, pp. 99-133.

Tervamäki, E. (1987), 'Migration in Finland, a multi-level system of regions', *Fennia*, **165** (1), 1-88.

Tervo, H. (1998), *Post-migratory employment prospects, evidence from Finland*, University of Jyväskylä, School of Business and Economics, Working Paper, 187, 18 p.

Tiebout, C. M. (1956), 'A pure theory of local expenditures', *Journal of Political Economy*, **64**, 416-424.

Trux, M-L. (2001), 'Suomen tapaus: monimuotoisuus liiketoiminnassa ja yhteiskunnassa, tulevaisuuden valinnat', in Heikkilä, E. (ed), *Muuttoliikkeet vuosituhannen vaihtuessa - halutaanko niitä ohjata?* Siirtolaisuustutkimuksia A 24, Institute of Migration, 189-190.

Vaattovaara, M. (1998), *Pääkaupunkiseudun sosiaalinen erilaistuminen*, City of Helsinki Urban Facts, Research Series, 1998 (7).

Valtioneuvoston selonteko eduskunnalle (1993), *Suomi 2020 -visioita kansakunnan tulevaisuudesta*, Valtioneuvoston kanslian julkaisusarja, 1993 (4).

Vartiainen, P. (1989a), 'Alueellisen muuttoliiketutkimuksen tienhaarassa', *Siirtolaisuus-Migration*, **1989** (4), 6-13.

Vartiainen, P. (1989b), 'Maassamuuttotutkimuksen itsestäänselvyydet ja vaihtoehdot', *Yhteiskuntasuunnittelu*, **1**, 3-11.

Vartiainen, P. (1989c), 'Yhteiskunnan muutos ja yhdyskuntarakenne', *Joensuun yliopisto, kulttuuri- ja suunnittelumaantiede, Tiedonantoja*, **13**, 111 p.

Vartiainen, P. (1995), 'Kaupunkiverkko. Kuvausjärjestelmän kehittäminen kansallisiin ja kansainvälisiin tarpeisiin', *Ympäristöministeriö, Alueidenkäytön osasto, Tutkimusraportti*, 3, 62 p.

Vartiainen, P. and J. Antikainen (1998), 'Kaupunkiverkkotutkimus 1998', *Sisäasiainministeriö, Kaupunkipolitiikan yhteistyöryhmän julkaisu*, **2**, 64 p.

Virtanen, A. (2000), *Tilasta paikkaan, estetiikasta ekologiaan. Maantieteellisiä tulkintoja eletystä kaupungista*, Turku: Annales Universitatis Turkuensis, C 155.

Yli-Jokipii, P. (1994), 'Trends in Finnish geography in the 1980s and early 1990s in the light of the geographical journals, with a bibliography', *Fennia*, **172** (2), 191-234.

Zelinsky, W. (1971), 'The hypothesis of the mobility transition', *Geographical Review*, **61**, 219-49.

Chapter 11

The Maturing of the Polish Urban System

Z. Rykiel and I. Jażdżewska

THE HISTORICAL BACKGROUND

Three main phases of development of the Polish urban system can be identified (Dziewoński et al., 1984). The first phase started with the crystallisation of the feudal urban network in the thirteenth and fourteenth centuries when most towns were located in Western and Central Europe up to Estonia. The first groups of settlements in Poland date from the tenth century. They represented networks of functional units grouped around local or, occasionally, regional economic, social and political centres. Although originally tribal, they were subsequently transformed into the seats of a strongly integrated military, political and ecclesiastical organisation imposed by the victorious rulers. These centres underlay the original boroughs that, with their subsidiary[1] and supplementary[2] settlements subsequently developed into towns (Dziewoński et al., 1984).

A dense network of towns developed during the period of internal colonization from the twelfth to sixteenth centuries. Most urban areas that developed at the time are still in existence today, which shows how viable they are. Not all of them developed in the same area at the same time. The process of establishment of urban settlements started in the twelfth century in Silesia in the southwest and ended in the sixteenth century in Masovia and Ducal, Eastern Prussia in the Northeast (Dziewoński et al., 1984). The gradual development of human settlements in the country from the southwest to the Northeast occurred over centuries and is the cause of two forces that shaped urban-economic development in Central Europe. One is the traditional declining gradient of economic development, urbanization and living

---

[1] Settlements whose status was linked to a borough.
[2] Settlements that functionally served boroughs, mostly through their services.

standards decreasing in intensity from the Rhine valley as the European economic core[3] in the west, towards the east. The other is the decreasing number of mineral resources and soil fertility from the south to the north. For ages, if not millennia, these factors were responsible for differences in the levels of development of local crafts and industry, including nineteenth-century industrialization, resulting in a decline in the density of urban development[4] from the piedmont regions[5] to the northern plains (Dziewoński et al., 1984).

The capitalist transformation of the original feudal network formed the second phase of urban development. The first capitalist development began when Poland had not existed as an independent state for more than a century, and lasted from 1796 to 1914. During this time the area that later would become Poland again, was politically divided into three empires. Each of the three empires followed different economic policies resulting in a considerable disintegration of the late feudal Polish national urban system and its growing external links. Although the large cities were militarily strategic their growth was limited because they were located in the economic peripheries of the three empires. They served more as fortified military bases than as central places serving regions (Davies, 1985). Because of the differences in economic policy between the three empires, the role and status of the smallest towns were undermined, which in turn reinforced the original inequality in the urban development from west to east. This also affected industrialization in Poland which originally tended to decline in intensity from south to north. In general, therefore, the late nineteenth-century industrialization changed the original west-east gradient in the level of civil sophistication on a sub-continental scale to approximately follow the Prussian-Russian border (Hartshorne, 1933).

The re-integration of the Polish urban system after the restitution of the statehood in 1918 formed the third phase. Within the latter phase, three periods can be distinguished: firstly, the period of the two inter-war decades of capitalist reconstruction and development, secondly, the Communist period of the interregional unification within the national territory that was considerably shifted westwards after the Second World War, and thirdly, the period of the transformation from communism to capitalism after 1989. During this phase the urban central-place functions were largely restored and at the same time

---

[3] I.e. the area, generally known as the 'Blue Banana' originally stretched from Switzerland to the Netherlands but it was subsequently extended from northern Italy to southern England.

[4] The density of the mediaeval urban centres varied from 50 towns per 10000 sq km in the southern mining and early industrial mountains to 15 towns per 10000 sq km in the northern lakelands with their extensive forests and woodlands.

[5] This region covers the area between the Harz Mountains in Germany and the Eastern Carpathians in Romania.

the generally prostrate urban hierarchy of the Communist era, which resulted in a polycentric urban system, became a more pyramidal or centralized hierarchy.

CURRENT CONCEPTUALIZATIONS OF THE URBAN SYSTEM
DEFINITIONS
The definition of the term 'town' in Poland is an entirely legal matter. A town is a settlement which acquired 'urban' status in terms of a Royal Charter or, from the nineteenth century onwards, in terms of a governmental regulation. A population size of 1000 can roughly be regarded as the lower size limit of towns since there are hardly any 'towns' with less than 1000 inhabitants, while non-agricultural 'villages' up to 5000 can be found throughout the country, especially in metropolitan areas and in the south (Table 11.1).

Table 11.1. Polish urban sizes, 1950-98

Year	Number of urban places							
	Total	(Size in thousands)						
		Under 5	5-10	10-20	20-30	50-100	100-200	200 or more
1950	706	393	159	76	50	12	11	5
1960	889*	405	236	138	68	20	13	9
1965	891	369	245	151	78	25	13	10
1970	889	359	220	162	97	27	14	10
1975	810	286	193	157	110	35	15	14
1980	804	264	185	169	111	38	22	15
1985	812	256	184	164	125	43	22	18
1990	830	257	177	177	128	48	23	20
1995	860	269	181	178	139	51	22	20
1998	875	281	181	182	139	50	22	20

Notes: *Political division of Jan.1962

Source: authors

Traditionally,[6] county towns were settlements with well-established administrative functions. After the Second World War until 1973[7] small towns operated independently from civil parishes at the local level. However, since 1973, *de facto*, they were generally considered to be part of larger urban communities. At the same time, while there were 16 provinces, the number of provincial centres first increased from 14 in 1946, to 17 in 1950, and 49 in 1975, and then decreased again to 18 in 1999.

No legal or statistical definition of metropolitan areas or urban agglomerations existed in Poland, except between 1975 and 1998. During this period, four *voivodeships*[8] were recognized as urban. These included the Warsaw metropolitan *voivodeship*, the Łódź and Cracow urban *voivodeships* and *de facto* also the Katowice *voivodeship* with its 90% urban population.[9] During that time the designation and delimitation of urban agglomerations were empirical rather than statistical. Of the many empirical approaches that were reviewed by Korcelli (1967) and Gontarski (1980), the method followed by Iwanicka-Lyra (1969) was the only one that remained unchallenged. It was also found that the Polish urban agglomerations were regional rather than national centres (Rykiel, 1978) since their hinterlands coincided more with the regions in which they were located (Rykiel, 1985a).

THEORIES ON MIGRATION

Traditionally, migration has been regarded as an important indicator of urban growth. This is based on long standing economic theory of migration related to the neo-classical general equilibrium theory in economics. It is generally assumed that individuals migrate to places (regions or towns) with many job opportunities and high wage levels. High in-migration is thus treated as an indicator of the economic attractiveness of the place while high out-migration indicates economically less attractive or stagnating areas. Net migration is therefore a good representation of urban growth.

One of the criticisms that can be raised against this line of reasoning is that it relies only on one group of causes (Cordey-Hayes and Gleave, 1974). It was indicated that, contrary to the assumptions in the classical model, net outflows are dependent on a number of factors that can be related to the entire population of a place rather than only to its economic characteristics (Lowry, 1966). It was also found that in certain instances, outflows tend to correlate

---

[6] I.e. from the 14th century until 1975.

[7] I.e. when civil parishes merged to become larger communities.

[8] I.e. equivalent of administrative provinces.

[9] The metropolitan *voivodeship* applied to the administrative unit which included the national capital; the two urban *voivodeships* were those in which mayors of the regional cities also served as governors of the respective provinces; the *de facto* urban *voivodeship* was classified in terms of the percentage of its urban population.

positively with inflows (Cordey-Hayes and Gleave, 1973). This implies that, at least in more developed countries, migration tends to occur more readily between economically vibrant places while economically weak places tend not to play such an important role in the process (Cordey-Hayes and Gleave, 1974). If net out-migration were a characteristic of weak places, outflows would be negatively correlated with inflows and this would imply that it is the low-paid and unemployed people that are more mobile (Fielding, 1989).

As was indicated by Cordey-Hayes (1975), high in- and out-migration is a characteristic of economically strong places, which produce net migration close to zero. This results from the fact that what is characteristic of strong places is higher mobility of cadres that enter the stochastic learning process in the market and thus gain information not only about the local labour market but also more distant markets. Importantly, mobility is also related to the age structure. Generally younger people are more mobile than older people (Rogers and Willekens, 1978). Because of these factors, trends of population change rather than net migration as a determinant of economic prosperity, are preferred as an indicators of urban evolution in this chapter.

POPULATION REDISTRIBUTION PATTERNS AND TRENDS

THE POST-WAR DEVELOPMENT OF THE POLISH URBAN SYSTEM

The development of the Polish urban system after the Second World War was very much dependent on two macro-structural processes. One was the re-integration of the system after the period when the Polish state did not exist during the nineteenth century and the other was a significant shift of the national boundary towards the west after the Second World War. The integration of the Polish urban system into three empires during the first Industrial Revolution contributed much to an urban system in which there was not one city that absolutely dominated others. The usual primate city structure was, therefore, non-existent at the time.

The post-war expansion of the national territory which triggered a visible east-west shift in the population, significantly increased the spatial mobility of the people. Demographically, the population structure changed. More younger people moved to the territory that had been gained in the west after the war, a phenomenon that resulted in higher degrees of mobility of the affected urban population, especially in the largest cities, than had been the case during the pre-war period (Dziewoński et al., 1977). One of the results was that net migration figures often did not correlate statistically with social and economic indicators of western Polish urban population growth and, therefore, gross migration trends were often a more accurate indicator of population redistribution patterns than net migration data (Rykiel and Żurkowa, 1981).

THE POLITICAL AND IDEOLOGICAL CONTEXT

No explicit economic cycles existed under Communism. However, the cycles of central planning can be taken as a rough equivalent. After the three-year plan of 1947 to 1949 and the six-year plan of 1950 to 1955, a five-year planning system was adopted until the mid-1980s. Importantly however, none of the plans was implemented as initially intended. Political cycles overlapping with planning cycles seem to have been more important in the development of Polish post-war history. They are referred to here as a series of political crises, usually related to or at least convergent with economic tensions. The political cycles in post-war Poland seem to result from a basic contradiction of Communism, i.e. one between the planned developmental expectations of those in power and the aspirations of the people in the improvement of their living standards (Rykiel, 1984a). In spatial terms the contradiction was manifested in a contradiction between urbanization and industrialization (Dziewoński et al., 1977; Jałowiecki, 1982; Pietraszewski, 1982). While, for reasons discussed already, the level of industrialisation kept pace with urbanization in the south, it did not do so in the north (Dziewoński et al., 1977).

Since Communist revolts occurred in less developed countries,[10] industrialization had, apart from its economic function, also an important political-ideological role to play in the legitimization of the regime. The latter refers to the process of the production of the 'workers' class' (i.e. the Leninist equivalent of Marx's 'working classes') that was perceived as the subject of the new system. Paradoxically however, out of the five political crises of 1956, 1968, 1970, 1976 and 1980, only that of 1968 was not underlain by the 'large industrial workers' class' revolt against Communist rule.

The relationship between the political crises and population redistribution patterns in the country was twofold. First, the workers' revolts of 1956, 1970, 1976 and 1980 occurred in the urban centres in which contradictions of the system were the most obvious (Jałowiecki, 1982), i.e. in Poznań in 1956, the sea-side cities in 1970, in Radom in 1976, and in the sea-side cities again in 1980. The main contradiction referred to here was that between industrialization and urban problems caused by the lack of housing. The five revolts, including the one of university students in 1968, occurred in centres where the contrast between the availability of labour production was the greatest (Jałowiecki, 1992). Secondly, following the political crises of 1956, 1970 and 1980, economic policy changed, especially with regard to industrial location and the provision of housing. This in turn changed the scale and direction of migration and also caused the improvement (liberalization) of foreign emigration policy.

---

[10] These occurrences were never anticipated in the classics of Marxism

Various international political events impacted on the Polish urban system, some of them directly, others indirectly. Changes in the political system after the Second World War, changes in the country's boundaries and the associated east-west shift in the population nationally were directly caused by forces from outside the country. Indirectly, the Korean War and the Cold War resulted in high expenditures on defence. This was associated with an extensive programme of heavy industrialization in the early 1950s. These factors influenced urban growth and development in various ways. For political and ideological reasons, large metallurgical complexes were developed near large urban centres of national cultural and religious importance. Because the communities in these cities strongly opposed the new regime,[11] the aim of the development was to 'improve' the local social structure of the cities.

The state ownership of the means of production, especially large industrial enterprises, reinforced the centralization of the political system. The centralization involved an increase in bureaucracy, which was one reason for the highest urban growth in provincial centres. Only three out of seventeen *voivodeship* centres of 1950-75 were not the largest cities in their provinces, yet whether or not they were, they grew faster than their regional counterparts of similar size (Dziewoński et al., 1977). This tendency even gained momentum after the reform of the territorial administration from 1975 to 1998, because during this period the provincial centres increased to forty-nine.

It is interesting however that, as bureaucratic centres, the provincial centres never really attracted ideologically meaningful concentrations of the 'workers' class'. To achieve this goal, industrial development of towns, especially of administrative centres, was always an important ideological objective. Industrial development was the only means the government had to attract meaningful numbers of the workers class to these centres, because in the centrally managed system there was hardly any private ownership, and local governments, which could represent local communities and their interests, were also abolished. The 'socialization', i.e. *de facto* nationalization of commerce in the late 1940s resulted in the complete collapse of the economic base of small towns. Industrialization was the only way in which development could be achieved. This development was reflected in the functional structure of Polish urban areas[12], especially their dominant functions (Jerczyński, 1977).

---

[11] This was done at Warsaw, Cracow and Częstochowa. The former city which was largely destroyed in 1944 is the national capital and it represents a symbol of the Polish nationhood. Cracow is an important cultural centre, an area of conservative opposition and, as a former national capital, the symbol of the continuity of the Polish nationhood. Częstochowa is the location of the nationally important St. Mary's sanctuary.

[12] The industrial sector dominated in most larger centres

Until the late 1980s small non-metropolitan towns continuously experienced economic crises in Poland. Attempts to stimulate their economies were a permanent feature of government policy during the Communist period (Domański, 1997). Due to the scarcity of resources, however, benefits could not be provided to every small town and as a result many of them were in a permanent state of economic depression. Demographically they either stagnated or their population numbers declined (Dziewoński et al., 1957). It was only after the restoration of the system of local self-government in 1990 and the subsequent revival of the local economic initiative that small towns began to prosper again.

The massive migration of people to the largest cities, especially Warsaw, resulted in the emerging of an urban crisis. Disequilibrium in the housing market developed because, strictly speaking, the housing market collapsed after the state took over the responsibility to provide dwellings for the people. To solve the problem in the housing market the Communist government simply applied bureaucratic restrictions on the migration of people to the cities. Such regulations were first applied to Warsaw, then to a few other large cities such as Łódź, Cracow, Poznań, and Gdańsk and finally to Warsaw's suburban zone. Interestingly enough, these regulations never applied to Wrocław and Szczecin in western Poland, with their highly mobile post-war populations.

In the cities where the migration restrictions applied, they were more socially selective than generally limiting. The selection worked in two ways: informally and formally. Informally, people that were not allowed to register as residents of the respective cities did so in the suburban zone while others simply lived in the city illegally. This resulted in constant statistical over-representations of the *de facto* population growth of small suburban towns. Formally, access to the cities was limited to those that were 'indispensable for the functioning of the city'. This bureaucratic regulation resulted in an explicit social selection of potential migrants in terms of their social position. The selection depended on the social stratification in the Communist society and was largely independent of income. As a result potential migrants were divided into the socially stronger and socially weaker (Jagielski, 1978; Rykiel, 1986). The division was based on the primary and secondary segments[13] of a dichotomous labour market (Piore, 1975; Pytel-Tafel, 1991). Paradoxically, as has been indicated elsewhere for Warsaw (Rykiel, 1984b), the administrative restrictions on migration to the city resulted in the reduction of out-migration from the city simply because those who succeeded in getting to the city were

---

[13] Generally, people with well-paid jobs and permanent formal contracts were associated with the primary sector, while those without contracts were mostly associated with the secondary sector.

unlikely to leave. The disequilibrium in the housing 'market' resulted in an expansion of commuting fields (Potrykowska, 1989).

Also the administrative restriction on migration to the largest cities, which was valid until the mid-1980s, resulted in a constant statistical underestimation of the sizes of cities.

Emigration policy was another important factor in urban growth. Generally, the attitude of the Communist regime toward emigration was determined by the level of economic frustration experienced by people during the inter-war period.[14] This resulted in the above-mentioned developmental mission of the government to provide enough jobs locally to reduce the need of local people to migrate to the West. While Poland was generally closed for foreign emigration, except during the occasional periods of revolt, it was the Polish-West German agreement of 1975 that provided the only gap in the Iron Curtain. The agreement made it possible for families that were divided by the post-war border changes to re-unite and it only applied to those Polish citizens who could prove that they had relatives in Germany. This regulation indirectly applied to the inter-war Polish-German borderland which was granted to Poland after the Second World War.

As a result of the re-unification of families the growth of some large cities in Upper Silesia and a few in Lower Silesia was hampered. In certain cases urban populations even declined. Also some small towns in the eastern part of the Opole *voivodeship* lost population. The main difference between the stagnating cities in Upper Silesia and the declining cities of the Opole *voivodeship* was that the former were slightly declining mining towns that permanently lost people to Germany. The majority of the local population in most of these mining towns were people from outside the region. The latter towns were deeply rooted regionally, with their inhabitants migrating, whenever possible, back and forth between Poland and Germany, especially after the political transformation.

THE URBAN PATTERN

As far as interurban migration is concerned the Polish urban system contained two subsystems. The one consisted of a hierarchy of central places based on the Christaller-model which included most of the urban centres in the urban system. Small towns were hierarchically subordinate to sub-regional centres which, in turn, were subordinate to less than four dozen mezzo- and a dozen macro-regional centres. Most of the latter were subordinate to Warsaw, while a few peripheral regional centres served as cores to relatively self-contained

---

[14] Because massive foreign economic migration from Poland was reported in the interwar period, the provision of sufficient number of jobs on the domestic market was an important objective of the Communist regime to legitimize its policies..

regional systems (Rykiel, 1984c). Micro-regional migration sheds[15] based on counties (Rykiel, 1985b) and macro-regional sheds based on pre-1975 *voivodeships* (Żurkowa and Księżak, 1980) were outstanding features of the rural-to-urban migration patterns in the country. The pattern closely resembled the territorial structure of public administration prior to 1975, a phenomenon that is hardly surprising, given the centralist approach of the Communist government. The urban centres in the other subsystem were largely based on non-hierarchical specialized functions and the reach of their activities normally far exceeded the service areas justified by their size.

The largest cities also tend to serve as central places that interact more with their regional systems than with other large cities in the country (Rykiel, 1985a). Although the hierarchical pattern of urban relationships is being distorted by non-hierarchical urban functions in certain instances in the Upper Silesian conurbation they do not invalidate the general hierarchical central-place pattern (Rykiel, 1985b).

Overall, there are three age-specific migration patterns observable in Poland (Rykiel, 1985b). Firstly, the migration of households that contain children is influenced by the children. In the process mental maps are created in the minds of children which ultimately, though unconsciously, will influence their future migration decisions. Secondly, the migration patterns of the youth tend to divert from the hierarchical patterns of migration. Finally, migration of the aged follows the more conservative trends which tend to reinforce hierarchical urban patterns.

Two gender-specific migration patterns have also been identified (Rykiel, 1985b). Women tend to follow a more conservative hierarchical central-place pattern that results from the simple fact that greater numbers of women than men are employed in the tertiary sector.[16] However, women gradually started to migrate beyond the international boundaries of nineteenth-century Poland – which for a long time served as spatial barriers of migration for them – and as a result it reshaped the traditional patterns of migration in the country. Men on the other hand, followed a more specialized, non-hierarchical, industry-oriented migration pattern which mostly affected industrial regions. The latter greatly reshaped the urban system because the massive industrialization that

---

[15] A migration 'shed' is an area, usually contiguous, from which migration of any magnitude is reported to the regional centre in question. It differs from a migration 'region' in that the latter includes only these parts of the migration sheds from which more people migrate to the regional centre in question than to any other centre.

[16] The tertiary sector, which attracts women migrants, is the principal factor determining the hierarchy of central places. On the other hand, industries, in which mostly men are employed, represent specialized urban functions whose hierarchical relationships tend not to be influenced significantly by the central-place pattern.

occurred in the country was not affected by its pre-industrial central-place hierarchy.

Finally, there is only one difference worth mentioning between the migration patterns of people that are less educated and those that are more educated in Poland. Generally the people that fall in the primary educated groups are more restricted by friction of distance than people that are better educated. It is mainly the people with tertiary education that migrate between regional and main cities (Rykiel, 1985a).

During the economic crisis of the 1980s the hierarchical urban system was both simplified and reinforced. During the years of acute shortages in the supply of goods, more migrants and commuters moved to large urban centres while intermediate-sized cities stagnated or even declined.

For a long time very few traces of counter-urbanisation have been detected in Poland. This can be ascribed to two reasons. Firstly, there is not enough variety in the Polish physical environment to cause a significant degree of counter-urbanization. The even distribution of environmental attributes in Poland could be compared to areas such as Florida in the USA or the Black Forest in Germany. Secondly, the large disparities between urban and rural living conditions that persisted for a long period were responsible for mainstream migration up the urban hierarchy rather than down. However, some population growth in tourist areas, mostly along the coast, in the mountains and in lake-districts is an indication of some counter-urbanization[17] occurring in Poland. Since the 1990s, however, rural-to-urban migration has started to decline as a result of industrial re-structuring. This slowdown is accompanied by a slow but permanent increase in urban-to-rural migration. This trend is consistent with the concept of counter-urbanization.

THE IMPACT OF MIGRATION ON URBAN CHANGE
DIFFERENTIAL URBANIZATION

The political, economic and social changes had some effect on the evolution of the Polish urban system over the post-Second World War period. As can be expected, the towns and cities increased in number, density and size, measured both in population and spatial terms (Table 11.1). Poland's urban population increased from 9 605 300 or 38.4 per cent in 1950 to 23 922 800 or 61.9 per cent in 1998. However, although the general decline in the spatial distribution of urban places in Poland from southwest to northeast has not changed significantly since the Middle Ages, minor changes in the general trend can be found in mid-southern Poland, where, as a result of industrialization from the early nineteenth century, a greater concentration of larger middle-sized (over 50 000) and large towns can be found (Figure 11.1).

---

[17] In many cases new urban centres developed in popular areas.

Figure 11.1 Polish urban sizes, 1998

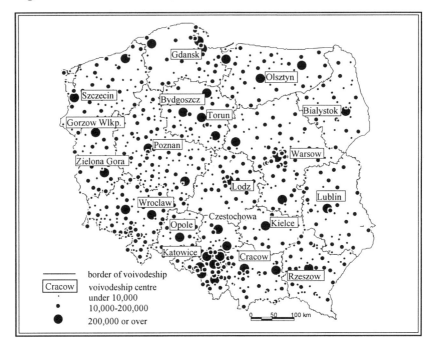

Source: authors

For further analysis, urban places were divided into three size groups, i.e. small towns under 10000, middle-sized towns of 10000 to 100000, and large towns of 100000 or more inhabitants. These are equivalent to the small cities, intermediate cities and primate cities, respectively, defined by Geyer and Kontuly (1993). In Poland the two latter urban categories played an important role in the differential urbanization process. The number of large towns grew from 16 to 42 between 1950 and 1998. The increase in the number of middle-sized towns was even more impressive, from 138 in 1950 to 371 in 1998. The growth in small towns varied since the number of centres between 5000 and 10000 increased by 22 while those under 5000 decreased by as many as 112 over the same period (Figure 11.2).

In the 1950s Poland's urban population grew by 5000000, 42.0 per cent of which was accounted for by natural increase, 33.2 per cent by changes in municipal status and boundaries, and 26.8 per cent by internal net migration (Kosiński 1968).[18] In the 1960s natural increase accounted for 47.0 per cent

---

[18] The total percentage amounts to more than one hundred per cent which is attributed to net international out-migration.

Figure 11.2 Rank-size distribution of Polish towns, 1950 and 1998

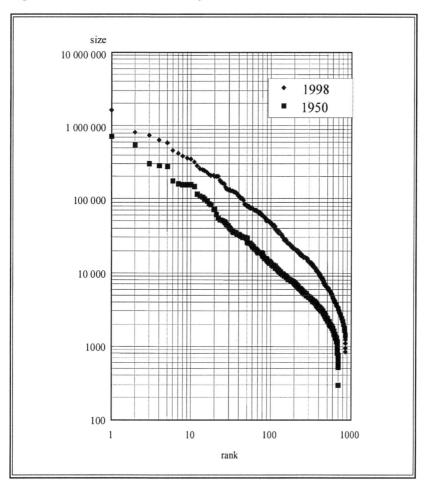

Source: own calculations

of urban growth, 39.9 per cent was accounted for by net migration and 13.1 per cent by administrative changes. In the 1970s migration was the main component of urban growth, and accounted for 49.2 per cent of the change; 41.1 per cent was caused by natural increase and 9.6 per cent by administrative changes. From 1981 to 1984, natural increase was again the leading cause of urban growth (59.8 per cent), followed by net migration (37.4 per cent). Administrative factors played a minor role (2.8 per cent) during this period. Although the numbers of net rural-to-urban migration varied from time to time, it has remained the main migration stream throughout the last fifty years.

Figure 11.3   Gross rural-to-urban and urban-to-rural migration in Poland,
1952-98

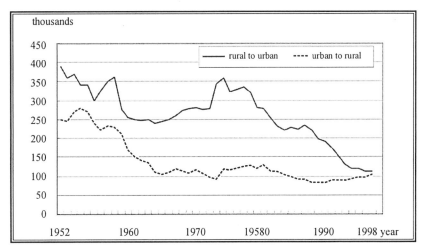

Source: own calculations

It increased in the mid-1970s as a result of industrialization and the
administrative reform that added provincial administrative functions to 32
cities. After 1980 rural-to-urban migration declined while urban-to-rural
migration has stabilized from the mid-1960s onwards (Figure 11.3).

In 1998 net rural-to-urban migration reached its lowest level in Poland's
post-Second World War history. At the same time a minor but stable increase of
urban-to-rural migration has been detected since 1990. This is evidence of
suburbanization[19] and possibly also counter-urbanization. The suburbanization
process applies, as it usually does, to the more affluent and higher educated
people (Jażdżewska, 1999).

Foreign migration is also worth mentioning here. With a few exceptions in
the early 1950s, foreign net migration remained negative in the post-Second
World War period in Poland (Figure 11.4). More people tended to leave Poland
for Germany, Israel, the United States, Canada, France and Britain than
expatriates returned from the USSR and Western Europe (Kosiński 1968). After
the abolition of Communism immigration to Poland doubled, even though the
actual numbers are still relatively insignificant. The largest gains in foreign
migrants are reported in the large cities in the country, especially in Warsaw,
yet upper and Lower Silesian towns are still losing people through international
migration.

---

[19] Note that suburban metropolitan zones are categorized in censuses as 'rural'.

Figure 11.4 Foreign migration in Poland, 1948-98

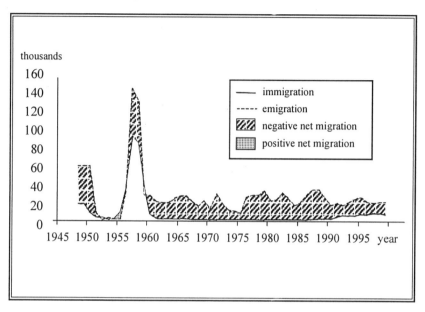

Source: Dziewoński et al.,1977, p.182

Migration between urban areas plays an important part in the maturing of the urban system. Geyer and Kontuly (1993) and Geyer (1996) indicateed how different urban size categories increase and decrease in successive phases of urbanization or urban development over the long term and how economic cycles could play a role in migration patterns, especially during the counter-urbanization phase when the urban system has reached maturity. The analysis of migration trends in Poland is an indication of how sensitive annual net migration is to political, economic and social change (Figure 11.5).

The comparison of the Polish case with the general model provided by Geyer and Kontuly (1993) indicates that Poland was well past the early primate and intermediate primate city stages by the beginning of the 1950s since there was no period in the post-Second World War Polish history in which primate cities dominated the urban system. From the late 1950s until the mid-1970s both large and middle-sized towns developed rapidly and thus this period can be categorized as the advanced primate city stage. Large cities grew, expanded, 'metropolitanized', dominated their hinterlands, and developed into agglomerations. The development of those cities was controlled under Communism by a system of restrictions and commands. Apart from the administrative restrictions that were placed on migration to the largest cities, there were specific regulations that predetermined the division of

Figure 11.5 Annual net migration by city size in Poland, 1952-98

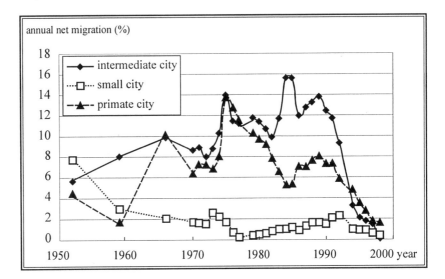

Source: own calculations

labour in certain occupational categories in the 1950s. However, because of inertia, the system was never applied to the letter, which resulted in migrants in the labour market regularly ignoring the restrictions. This resulted in discrepancies between the *de jure* and the *de facto* population statistics.

The early intermediate city stage began in Poland in the mid-1970s and lasted till 1980. It was one of the results of the administrative reform and consequent investment boom at the time. The towns that gained new administrative functions shifted up the urban hierarchy. Towns that served as important transport nodes and those that experienced rapid industrialization grew in importance. During this period eight new large and sixteen middle-sized towns appeared while thirty small towns disappeared. At the same time the populations of small towns declined and migration to them decreased.

Successive changes in the Polish urban system occurred after 1980. The economic crisis, social unrest and finally the Martial Law of 1981 caused a rapid decrease in migration to large and middle-sized towns, while net migration to small towns began to increase. The 1980-82 period can thus be categorized as the advanced, intermediate city stage, i.e. a rapid increase in net migration in middle-sized towns (from 1983 onwards), Somewhat more limited but also clear growth in net migration occurred in large towns (from 1986) and the most limited but stable growth in net migration in small towns (from 1980). A very high natural increase of urban places was also a distinguishing feature of the 1980-85 period. Average annual natural increase accounted for as much as 55.6 per cent of the national figure. The highest urban natural increase of 9.9 per thousand was reported in 1983.

The urban system's transformation also influenced its structure. Since 1993 net migration to the three size categories started to decrease in numbers unprecedented after the Second World War (Figure 11.5 and 11.6). In 1998, 8600 people immigrated while 12500 emigrated resulting in an urban population migration deficit of 3900. The decrease of births and of natural increase are also noteworthy. It was the first time in the post-war period that the urban natural increase turned negative, the lowest being in cities larger than 500000 people.

Figure 11.6 Average net migration by city size in Poland, 1952-98

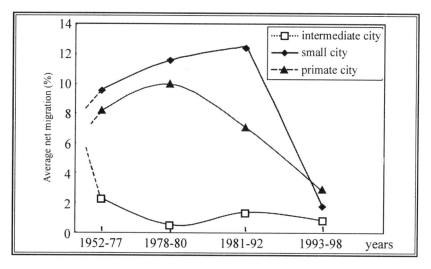

Source: own calculations

SUB-STREAM MIGRATION

Empirical investigations carried out in the 1970s indicated (Rykiel and Żurkowa, 1981) that mainstream migration in Poland was directed upwards in the urban hierarchy. This migration accounted for 50 per cent of interurban migration in 1975 while 31 per cent applied to migration down the hierarchy. The remaining 20 per cent was migration between urban places of equal size. Importantly, however, individual urban settlements of similar size represented different degrees of centrality which might result in even greater degrees of migration upwards in the *de facto* urban hierarchy than the data above suggest.

Rykiel and Żurkowa (1981) indicated that the sub-stream migration down the urban hierarchy is mainly composed of four parts. One represents return migrants who failed in the metropolitan or large urban labour market. This group also includes those that could not adapt successfully to the large urban environment. The second part is represented by migration to small satellite towns within large urban agglomerations. Migration to specialized (non-central-place) centres represents the third part. The final part consists of random moves related to family associations.

A detailed analysis by Rykiel and Żurkowa (1981) indicated the following spatial differences between main and sub-stream migration:

1. Sub-stream migration is much more locally oriented, some even taking place towards satellite towns in the outer urban agglomeration fringe (that could not strictly be regarded as sub-stream migration) ;
2. Sub-stream migration occurs in a wider spectrum of urban hierarchies than mainstream migration;
3. More traditional (historical) patterns of migration are reflected in sub-stream migration which produces a rather different pattern of migratory relationships than in mainstream migration;
4. Some long-distance sub-stream migration in southern Poland between the west and the central east might be one result of kinship links, following the post-war resettlement pattern.

Sub-stream migration from Warsaw, Poznań, Cracow and Łódź was especially limited because of the administrative restrictions that were placed on migration. The situation was different in other large regional centres, especially Wrocław, where the restrictions did not apply. In the case of cities where restrictions did not apply the spatial patterns of sub-stream migration were often very similar to the mainstream migration patterns. Such centres possessed clearly defined migration regions or fields which led to well-defined spatial patterns of migration.

The importance of the traditional pattern of migration deserves additional attention here. It was found that return migrants often followed very similar routes to those that were used by them or their parents while they were still part of the migration mainstream previously (Rykiel and Żurkowa, 1981). However, these migrants that form migration sub-streams do not tend to follow the same complicated process of migration down the urban hierarchy that their predecessors did when they migrated up the urban hierarchy; they often skip certain urban levels in the hierarchy during migration.

Furthermore, changes in the patterns of migration are often determined by changes in the mobility of people overall. The latter begins with commuter patterns that are directly linked to changes in labour markets. In this regard the mainstream migration routes represent a more traditional pattern, although sub-stream migration tends to follow traditional migration patterns more closely than mainstream migration (Rykiel and Żurkowa, 1981). In both cases the process of migration from one hierarchical level of urban areas to the next seems to be simplified, resulting in the establishment of functional urban regions. This tendency is clearly related to improvements in the transportation system and thus to the diminishing of the 'friction of distance'.

THE PERIODS OF DIFFERENTIAL URBAN GROWTH

From the viewpoint of urban growth differentials six distinct phases can be distinguished in the post-Second World War period in Poland, each phase lasting approximately a decade and each clearly related to the planning and political cycles that were referred to earlier in this chapter.

The late 1940s

The immediate post-war period was characterized by massive migration volatility as a result of frantic population re-distribution. Based on these processes, the following changes in the Polish urban system can be identified:
1. general urban decline in eastern and central Poland after the Holocaust because considerable proportions (often the majority) of the population of small towns in those parts of Poland were Jewish;
2. general urban decline in western Poland after the displacement of the German population;
3. rapid growth in some of the largest cities that were extensively destroyed during the Second World War;
4. stagnation of middle-sized towns;
5. stabilization of small towns, based on local initiative after the 'relief' from Jewish competition after the Holocaust;
6. the policy of 're-integration of the re-gained areas'.

The early 1950s

The main processes that underlay urban growth in Poland in the early 1950s include:
1. the post-war baby boom;
2. massive industrialization;
3. the nationalization of commerce;
4. the policy of 'even distribution of productive forces';
5. rural-to-urban migration;
6. massive urbanization.

Based on these processes, the following changes in the Polish urban system can be identified:
1. rapid growth in industrialized large and middle-sized towns;
2. the development of new towns;
3. stagnation or decline of small towns, deprived of local initiative as a result of the nationalization of commerce.

The late 1950s and the 1960s

The main processes that underlay urban growth in Poland in that period included:

1. massive industrialization of some areas, especially the south;
2. administrative restrictions on migration to the largest cities;
3. the policy of 'deglomeration' of the largest urban areas.

Based on these processes, the following changes in the Polish urban system can be identified:

1. the administrative limitation of Warsaw's growth;
2. suburbanization in Warsaw;
3. limited growth in the largest cities;
4. growth in large (but not the largest) cities and conurbations;
5. suburbanization of the largest cities;
6. growth in middle-sized towns under industrialization;
7. continuation of the crisis in small towns.

The 1970s

The main processes that underlay urban growth in Poland in that period included:

1. the policy of 'a moderate polycentric concentration of development';
2. a new investment boom and industrialization followed by a growing economic crisis;
3. a growing urban crisis;
4. the administrative reform of 1975, with the liquidation of county-level government units and the multiplication of *voivodeships* from 17 to 49;
5. opening of some areas to foreign immigration.

Based on these processes, the following changes in the Polish urban system can be identified:

1. metropolitan growth and suburbanization;
2. rapid growth in some middle-sized towns as new administrative centres;
3. stagnation of most middle-sized and small towns as a result of the abolition of county-level public administration and the centralisation of state-owned small business from the provincial to the national level;
4. stagnation of some of the large mining towns as a result of foreign emigration;
5. continuation of the crisis in small towns.

The 1980s

The economic crisis was the main process that underlay urban growth in Poland in that period. This involved the following characteristics of the Polish urban system:

3. stagnation of large cities;
4. decline of city centres as a result of negative natural increase and minor volumes of in-migration;
5. a slight decline of middle-sized towns;
6. stagnation of small towns.

The 1990s

The main processes that underlay urban growth in Poland in that period included:

1. a transformation of the political system;
2. the restoration of the local government system;
3. a rapid privatization of commerce;
4. an inflow of foreign capital.

Based on these processes, the following changes in the Polish urban system can be identified:

1. metropolitan growth;
2. suburbanization of large cities, especially Warsaw;
3. stagnation of heavily industrialized middle-sized and large towns;
4. decline of industrial mill-towns;
5. differential growth in small towns;
6. boom of western border towns.

PERSPECTIVES ON THE URBAN FUTURE
EXPECTED DIFFERENTIAL URBAN GROWTH IN THE EARLY TWENTY FIRST CENTURY

The main processes that underlie the expected urban growth include:

1. the dependent growth strategy adopted;
2. the expected accession to the European Union;
3. the restoration of the county-level government system;
4. a reinforcement of central bureaucracy of the unitary state during the process of the adaptation of EU legal regulations.

Based on these processes, the following changes in the Polish urban system are expected:

1. the growth of Warsaw as the centre of a centralist state;
2. metropolitan suburbanization;

3. decline in the growth of western border towns as a result of the *de facto* liquidation of the Polish-German border as an economic barrier after Poland's accession to the European Union;
4. differences in the growth of large cities as a result of differences in the availability of local social capital and their competitiveness;
5. increasing growth of sub-regional middle-sized towns as county-level centres;
6. differential growth in small towns, based on local initiative and competitiveness.

REFERENCES

Cordey-Hayes, M. (1975), Migration and the dynamics of multiregional population systems. *Environment and Planning, A,* 7, 793-814.

Cordey-Hayes, M. and D. Gleave (1973), Migration movements and the differential growth of city regions in England and Wales. *Regional Science Association, Papers*, **32**, 99-123.

Cordey-Hayes, M. and D. Gleave (1974), *Dynamic models of the interaction between migration and the differential growth of cities.* Laxenburg, Austria: International Institute for Applied Systems Analysis, Research Report RR-74-9.

Davies, N., (1985), *God's playground: a history of Poland.* Oxford: Clarendon Press.

Domański, B. (1997), *Industrial control over the socialist town. Benevolence or exploitation?* Westport, Connecticut – London: Praeger.

Dziewoński, K., M. Kiełczewska-Zaleska, L. Kosiński, J. Kostrowicki and S. Leszczycki (eds), (1957), *Studia geograficzne nad aktywizacją małych miast.* Warszawa: Polska Akademia Nauk, Instytut Geografii, *Prace Geograficzne*, 9.

Dziewoński, K., A. Gawryszewski, E. Iwanicka-Lyrowa, A. Jelonek, M. Jerczyński and G. Węcławowicz (1977), *Rozmieszczenie i migracje ludności a system osadniczy Polski Ludowej.* Wrocław – Warszawa: Polska Akademia Nauk, Instytut Geografii i Przestrzennego Zagospodarowania, *Prace Geograficzne*, 117.

Dziewoński, K., M. Jerczyński and P. Korcelli (1984), The Polish settlement system, in L. S. Bourne, R. Sinclair and K. Dziewoński (eds): *Urbanization and settlement systems. International perspectives.* London: Oxford University Press; 359-376.

Fielding, T. (1989), Migration and urbanization in Western Europe. *Geographical Journal, 155, 60-69.*

Geyer, H. S. (1996), Expanding the theoretical foundation of differential urbanization. *Tijdschrift voor Economische an Sociale Geografie,* **87**, 44-59.

Geyer, H. S. and T. Kontuly (1993), A theoretical foundation for the concept of differential urbanization. *International Regional Science Review,* **15**, 157-177.

Gontarski, Z. (1980), *Obszary metropolitalne w Polsce.* Polska Akademia Nauk, Komitet Przestrzennego Zagospodarowania Kraju, *Biuletyn,* 109.

Hartshorn{,}e R. (1933): Geographic and political boundaries in Upper Silesia. *Annals of the Association of American Geographers,* **23**, 195-228.

Iwanicka-Lyra, E. (1969), *Delimitacja aglomeracji wielkomiejskich w Polsce.* Polska Akademia Nauk, Instytut Geografii, *Prace Geograficzne,* **76**.

Jagielski, A. (1978), Struktura społeczno-ekologiczna miast polskich a koncepcje szkoły chicagowskiej; in Jan Turowski (ed.), *Procesy urbanizacji kraju w okresie XXX-lecia PRL.* Wrocław: Ossolineum.

Jałowiecki, B. (1982), *Strategia uprzemysłowienia a proces urbanizacji. Studium Socjologiczne.* Warszawa: Polska Akademia Nauk, Komitet Przestrzennego Zagospodarowania Kraju, *Biuletyn,* 119, 9-118.

Jażdżewska, I. (1999), *Przemiany funkcjonalne i morfologiczne przestrzeni geograficznej wsi Rzgów w świetle metod numerycznych.* 'Szlakami Nauki', 28. Łódź: Łódzkie Towarzystwo Naukowe.

Jerczyński, M. (1977), Funkcje i typy funkcjonalne polskich miast. (Zagadnienia dominacji funkcjonalnej); in: *Statystyczna charakterystyka miast. Funkcje dominujące.* Warszawa: Główny Urząd Statystyczny, *Statystyka Polski,* **85**, 20-53.

Korcelli, P. (1967), Problematyka regionów metropolitalnych w Stanach Zjednoczonych i w Wielkiej Brytanii. *Przegląd Geograficzny,* **39**, 333-354.

Kosiński, L. (1968), *Migracje ludności w Polsce w latach 1950-1960.* Polska Akademia Nauk, Instytut Geografii, *Prace Geograficzne,* 72.

Lowry, I. S. (1966), *Migration and metropolitan growth: two analytical models.* San Francisco: .

Pietraszewski, W. (1982), *Polska strategia industrializacji?* Warszawa: Polska Akademia Nauk, Komitet Przestrzennego Zagospodarowania Kraju, *Biuletyn,* 119, 119-135.

Piore, M. (1975), Notes for a theory of labour market segmentation; in: R. Edwards. M. Reich and D. Gordon (eds.): *Labour market segmentation.* Lexington: D.C. Heath.

Potrykowska, A. (1989), Funkcjonalne regiony miejskie w krajowym systemie osadniczym; in P. Korcelli and Gawryszewski (eds): *Współczesne przemiany regionalnych systemów osadniczych w Polsce.* Polska Akademia

Nauk, Instytut Geografii i Przestrzennego Zagospodarowania, *Prace Geograficzne*, **152**, 55-75.

Pytel-Tafel, E. (1991), Zróżnicowania społeczne w regionie katowickim; in: Z. Rykiel (ed.): *Studia z geografii społecznej*. Polska Akademia Nauk, Instytut Geografii i Przestrzennego Zagospodarowania, *Dokumentacja Geograficzna*, **3-4**, 67-78.

Rogers, A. and F. Willekens (1978), *Migration and settlement: measurement and analysis*. Laxenburg, Austria: International Institute for Applied Systems Analysis, Research Report RR-78-13.

Rykiel, Z. (1978), *Miejsce aglomeracji wielkomiejskich w przestrzeni społeczno-gospodarczej Polski*. Polska Akademia Nauk, Instytut Geografii i Przestrzennego Zagospodarowania, *Prace Geograficzne*, **128**.

Rykiel, Z. (1984a), *Geografía dialéctica: una perspectiva polaca*. Barcelona: Publicacions i Edicions de la Universitat de Barcelona; Colección Geo-Crítica: Textos de Apoyo.

Rykiel, Z. (1984b), Intra-metropolitan migration in the Warsaw agglomeration. *Economic Geography*, **60**, 55-70.

Rykiel, Z. (1984c), A multi-facetal concept of urban hierarchy: with special reference to the Polish urban system. *Geographia Polonica*, **50**, 15-24.

Rykiel, Z. (1985a), The system of main cities: a critique and an empirical evaluation. *Tijdschrift voor Economische en Sociale Geografie*, **76**, 100-105.

Rykiel, Z. (1985b), *Zagadnienia regionalnych systemów osadniczych*. Polska Akademia Nauk, Komitet Przestrzennego Zagospodarowania Kraju, *Studia*, **88**.

Rykiel, Z. (1986), Ograniczenia meldunkowe jako bariery przestrzenne. *Przegląd Geograficzny*, **58**, 395-409.

Rykiel, Z. (1989), Układ przestrzenny i mechanizmy migracji; in: Z. Rykiel (ed.): *Struktury i procesy społeczno-demograficzne w regionie katowickim*. Wrocław – Warszawa: Polska Akademia Nauk, Instytut Geografii i Przestrzennego Zagospodarowania, *Prace Geograficzne*, **151**, 29-36.

Rykiel, Z. and A. Żurkowa (1981), Migracje między miastami: systemy krajowe i regionalne; in: K. Dziewoński and P. Korcelli (eds): *Studia nad migracjami i przemianami systemu osadniczego w Polsce*. Wrocław – Warszawa: Polska Akademia Nauk, Instytut Geografii i Przestrzennego Zagospodarowania, *Prace Geograficzne*, **140**, 138-188.

Żurkowa, A. and J. Księżak (1980), 'Elementy struktury przestrzennej migracji wewnętrznych w Polsce', Stan w r. 1974. *Przegląd Geograficzny*, **52**, 81-102.

Chapter 12

The Maturing of the Romanian Urban System

I. Ianoş

INTRODUCTION

Historical events in the twentieth century largely determined the current state of the urban system of Romania. There are 266 urban settlements in the country; at the top of the list is Bucharest, a city that is a thousand times larger than Baile Tusnad, which lies at the bottom of the list. Given the arbitrary criteria that are still in use, distinguishing rural settlements from towns remains a challenge. No wonder that, in the absence of size criteria, towns with over 10 000 inhabitants stand side by side with villages that have a population of under 2000. In the past, designating settlements as towns was the exclusive task of the central government. The process continues to be cumbersome because it depends on the competence of decision-makers, and more recently on lobbyists.

Two political events disrupted the evolution of individual towns over the past century, the totalitarian regime that came into effect after the Second World War and the transition towards democracy and the free market system after 1989. The impact of these events on the urban system can clearly be detected in the differentiated manner in which different size towns evolved over time. An interesting phenomenon in recent years is the way in which rural areas have gained population at the cost of urban areas. The question could be asked whether this is the result of counter-urbanization or whether it is a temporary phenomenon linked to the political transition.

GENERATIONS OF TOWNS AND THE URBANIZATION PROCESS

GENERATIONS OF TOWNS

The beginning of visible urban change in contemporary Romania dates back to the Hellenistic period when the port-cities on the Black Sea coast (Hystria, Tomis and Callatis) experienced a period of fast growth. The second generation towns date from the Dacian and Roman-Dacian Periods,[1] most of them reappearing in the early Middle Ages, after the period of diminishing urban growth which was associated with the 'great migration'.

Towards the end of the first millennium urban life became rejuvenated along with the consolidation of the first Romanian System of States. Even before the arrival of the Hungarians in Transylvania cities such as Morisena-Cenad (1030) and Alba Iulia (1097) served as Glad's and Gyla's voievodship-residences respectively. Dobrogea re-entered during the Bizantine rule in the tenth century after it became economically revitalized. Urban demographic stability led to the rejuvenation of urban life.[2]

The most prominent Transylvanian towns date back to the twelfth to thirteenth centuries.[3] During approximately the same period, urban areas in the eastern part of the Carpathians started expanding again.[4] However, most urban settlements in Moldavia and the Romanian area (Tara Romaneasca) that are mentioned in documents date from the period after their consolidation as feudal states, i.e. Siret, Suceava, Harlau, Iasi, Baia, and Targu Neamt in Moldavia, and Campulung, Curtea de Arges, Ramnicu Valcea, Braila, Giurgu, and Pitesti in Muntenia.

A further wave of urban development occurred in the nineteenth century after the Adrianopol Peace Treaty was concluded and Moldavia and Tara Romaneasca were united. The former gave commercial liberty to the Romanian Principalities and the latter led to the independence of the state and an increase in industrial production.

Consequently, the Danube cities and those that lie along the contact line between the plains and the hills experienced an urban explosion from 1831 to 1899. In that time Bucharest, which became the capital, grew by 5.4 times, Turnu Magurele by almost 10 times, Braila by about 8 times, Buzau and Galati by over 7 times, and Ramnicu Sarat by approximately 6 times.

---

[1] These include the 'dava-s' (Arcidava, Buridava, Dierna, Piroboridava, Sucidava, etc.), the 'municipii' ('Roman towns') and the ones known as Roman colony centres (Napoca, Potaissa, Drobeta, Romula, Apulum, Malva, etc.).
[2] Vicina became a well-known city at that time.
[3] They include centres such as Oradea, Arad, Cluj-Napoca, Sibiu, Timisoara, Satu Mare, Orastie, Hunedoara, Brasov, and Fagaras.
[4] Urban centres that are worth mentioning here are Tecuci, Vaslui and Barlad.

Alexandria, Slobozia, and Petrosani emerged as new towns, but other old small towns such as Dragasani, Urziceni, and Rosiori de Vede also became revitalized. Cities in Moldavia such as Dorohoi, Botosani, Husi, and Barlad were also revitalized but they did not develop as fast. Some new small towns also developed, some of them evolving into cities later on.

In the first half of the twentieth century, the urban areas moved into a new era, especially after the Romanian Unitary State had been created. Improved transportation led to the development of industries and services. New cities appeared in the wake of the upsurge of Romanian capitalistic relations. As a result of the establishment of new services and industries, the structure of these urban centres differed largely from those of the former period. From 1912 to 1948, 33 new cities were added to the urban network, many of them having developed between 1923 and 1930.

Cities that have appeared during the totalitarian period were mainly politically inspired, their development closely linked to the industrialization process. Between 1948 and 1966, 31 new cities emerged. Centres such as Onesti, Victoria, and Motru were built from the ground without a pre-existing centre. After 1966, two groups of new cities emerged: those (53 cities) that were declared as new cities after the administrative reform of 1968 and those (23) after the decree of 1989.

Since the post-socialist period, six rural localities have become towns, three of them located in Transylvania (Teius, Baia de Aries and Geoagiu), and one each in the following provinces: Banat (Faget), Muntenia (Otopeni), and Moldova (Murgeni). So, the Romanian urban system today has 266 towns in total (Figure 12.1).

URBANIZATION PROCESS

According to the official data of the Central Statistical Commission, the urban development trends have been, by and large, positive – their rate of development depending on external links and internal political conditions. Romania had been significantly affected by the two world wars. From the late 1940s until 1989 it had one of the most centralized political systems of the entire communist world. The impact of the last ten years of transition on the urbanization process have been equally significant, however, with urban areas striking a new balance, and adjusting their size to their adjoining regional profile.

Due to the effect of the two world wars, the pace of urbanization in the first half of the twentieth century was extremely slow. The total net increase was only approximately 5 per cent. Later on, through direct state intervention in the economy and in urban development policies, urbanization was stepped up progressively. At the end of the totalitarian period, over 50 per cent of the country's population lived in towns, the number of urban settlements growing

Figure 12.1 Urban network and distribution of population, 2000

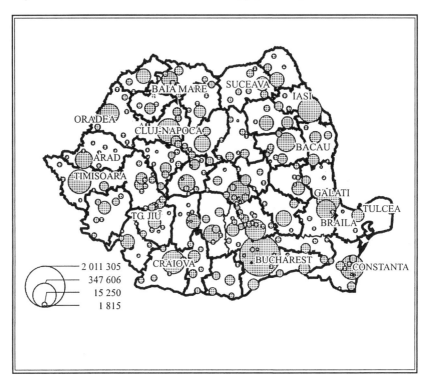

from 110 at the beginning of the century to 263 in 1998 (Table 12.1).
Although the data referring to the process in fact are fairly relative a situation
encountered in the neighbouring countries, too and the extent of ruralism in
Romania is seemingly significant, and on the upsurge due to the difficulties
of the transition period.

Table 12.1 Urban population and the number of urban settlements, 1912-98

	1912	1930	1948	1956	1966	1977	1992	1998
Urban Population (mil.)	2.06	3.05	3.71	4.75	6.74	9.40	12.37	12.35
No. of urban areas	110	142	152	171	236	236	260	263
% Urbanization	16.1	21.4	23.4	31.3	38.2	43.6	54.4	54.9

Source: Recensamantul populatiei si locuintelor din 7 ianuarie 1992, p.3, p.8.

rural population after the collectivization of agriculture, (ii) the forced absorbing of these people through massive industrialization schemes, and (iii) the new macro-regional administrative division. A combination of these factors led to a spectacular promotion of the 1968-established county-seats of Slatina, Vaslui, Zalau, Slobozia, Miecurea-Ciuc, Piatra Neamt, Botosani, and Sfantu Gheorghe on the hierarchical scale (Ianos, 1987). The sizes of these cities grew by three to four times over the 22 years from 1968 to 1990. The very close correlation between town rank and industry proves the determinant role of industrialization in urban development (Ianos, 1993).

THE URBAN SYSTEM AND ITS HIERARCHICAL AND REGIONAL PATTERN
THE HIERARCHICAL PATTERN
Just like other countries, the basic principles that determine the functions of settlements in Romania are hierarchy and centrality. Economic, demographic, service, and political-administrative relations in the urban system of Romania are governed by specific economic, geographical, historical and environmental conditions. Despite the rather long time-intervals between censuses no significant changes occurred in the general hierarchical pattern of the Romanian urban system over the years. Individual changes in settlements were relatively insignificant because particular phases of urban development were eliminated from the equation. The most visible change in this century can be detected between the country's capital and the second city in the national hierarchy: the widening of the gap between the two before the 1948 census has slowed down subsequently.

The 1948-rank/size distribution shows that the growth of intermediate sized cities was less than that of small towns and large cities. That was mainly due to the war and as a result of a period of drought (1945-1947), when intermediate-sized cities in Moldavia, in particular, became depopulated. At the same time, Jews, who mostly lived in Moldavian cities began to emigrate over a short period of time.

Subsequently, concavity was re-established in the upper hierarchy and convexity amongst the middle order cities. The changes that occurred in these distributions become evident if we analyze them comparatively with the adjustment line intersecting the ordinate in the point where Bucharest values are written. Most medium and small towns that were still positioned below this line in 1966 moved to a position above it in 1992 (Figure 12.2). This spectacular shift is due to an enhanced process of urbanization brought about by the industrialization drive. A significant correlation was found between the urban and the industrial hierarchies in 1990, except for Bucharest which holds a special position in both of them (Ianos, 1993).

Figure 12.2 The comparative rank-size distribution, 1966-92

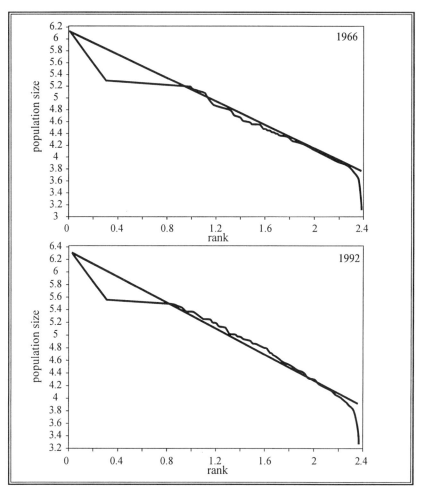

Source: I. Ianoş, 1997

If one compares the capital city to the remainder of the Romanian urbansystem there are two distinct sections in the hierarchy.   One section contains a number of undersized cities that are obviously lagging behind while the intermediate sized cities appear to be relatively oversized. The latter is clearly the result of the demographic explosion that occurred in county-seats and certain specialized industrial centres in 1968.   The remainder of the hierarchy consists of a relatively low number of small towns that appear undersized. If there were more small rural towns, the hierarchy would have appeared more balanced.

A rank/size analysis only offers a general impression of an urban system. It does not supply the information that is needed for an in-depth study of the relations between cities in the system. To do that the urban system's regional configuration needs to be defined to determine the geographical confines of functional subsystems within the hierarchy. In a study of the Romanian urban system two criteria were used: regional functions and polarizing potential. Seven levels of urban development were distinguished (Ianos, 1987).[5] Apart from Bucharest, first-rank cities such as Iasi, Cluj-Napoca, Timisoara, Constanta and Craiova still serve as gravity points in Romania's old historical provinces. This group of cities forms the first hierarchical level (Figure 12.3). In addition, two other big predominantly industrial towns – Brasov and Galati – serve as gravity points outside the historical spheres of influence of the other large centres. The wide-ranging urban functions of these two have singled them out as regional centres. Both cities have a special geographical position: Brasov, Romania's geometrical centre, seems to take over some of Bucharest's administrative functions while Galati, which lies close to Braila, seems to be competing with its neighbour. Two other cities, Ploiesti and Oradea almost reached this hierarchical level, but after 1990 they seem to have lost some of their importance.

Second-rank towns include the county-seats with more than 150,000 inhabitants, as well as Baia Mare and Suceava, which are better equipped for special academic, cultural, economic, legal and administrative services. These cities (more than ten of them in total) complement the regional network of the first-rank settlements. In most cases the former are more than 100 km away from the latter, except for Arad, Ploiesti and Braila.

The remaining county capitals are third-rank cities, except those that are directly competing for this status with the former seats, such as Vaslui and Barlad, Miercurea Ciuc and Odorheiu Secuiesc, and Slatina and Caracal. This rank also contains some intermediate-sized cities such as Roman, Turda, Hunedoara, and Medias. They provide superior industrial and services functions which make them important county nodes.

Fourth-rank towns generally have more than 30,000 inhabitants and provide some advanced urban functions. This category includes all the interwar county-seats, as well as towns that are situated in favourable geographical locations, or which have a strong industrial base which makes them important regional locations. Examples of the former are Medias, Caran sebes, and Rosiori de Vede, while those of the latter are Campina, Turnu -

---

[5] The addition of twenty-three new towns after 1989 and the political and socio-economic changes that followed did not fundamentally alter the structure of the urban hierarchy.

Figure 12.3 The multicriterial hierarchy of towns

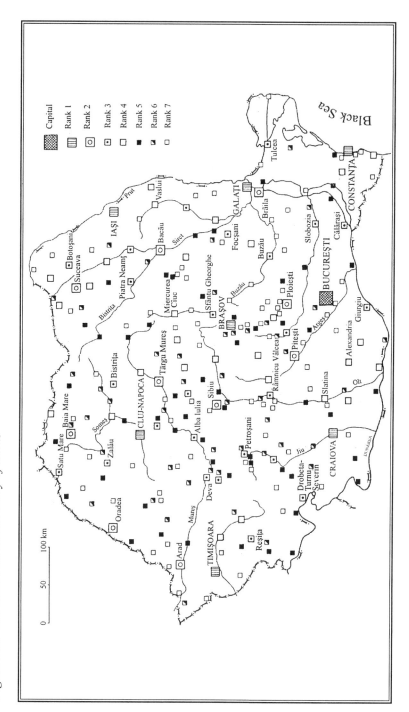

Magurele, and Onesti. Another town that has developed a variety of functions is Mangalia.

Fifth-rank towns are located in a variety of geographical environments and, as a result, have acquired rather specialized economic functions. Centres that are of particular importance in this group include towns with monoindustrial functions (Campia Turzii, Colibasi, Moreni, Tarnaveni, Navodari etc.), multi-industrial structures (Curtea de Arges, Targu Secuisc, Gheorgheni), centres that are of major agricultural interest (Fetesti, Salonta, Dragasani, Tandarei), or localities with a large or strong hinterland, and some with some other industrial activities (Sinaia, Vatra Dornei, Lipova).

Sixth-rank towns generally have less than 20,000 inhabitants. They are only of local importance, but they have some significant economic potential which is largely determined by their geographical position relative to those of the larger urban centres. Many of them are important primary production centres with specialisations such as mining[6] and agriculture.[7] Others provide a variety of functions and are attracting centralized industries from neighbouring cities, or they exploit local soil resources.[8]

Seventh-rank towns have very limited influence in the territory, restricted, as a rule, to their administrative area including one or two surrounding residential communities. Some of them are isolated from the national settlement system (Cavnic, Sulina, Nucet), or are incapable of exerting an important impact on the neighbouring villages (Curtici, Budesti, Mihailesti, Piatra Olt). This category of towns marks the transition from rural-to-urban settlements, and they are insufficiently developed to polarize activities in the areas that they are supposed to serve.

This seven-rank hierarchical structure explains the intricate relations and potential complementarity of regional subsystems within the national urban system.

REGIONAL PATTERNS OF URBAN DOMINATION

The regional pattern explained above (see Figure 12.4) is determined by the relationships between towns and cities based upon administrative areas, the provision of services, and definitive migration patterns of people.

After 1989, the role of county-seats in the co-ordination of regional activities and of large industrial centres causing regional economic polariza-

---

[6] Examples of coal mining centres are Anina, Baraolt, Motru, and Rovinari; ferrous and nonferrous metal centres are Moldova Noua, Borsa, and Balan; salt production occurs at Targu Ocna and Slanic); oil drilling occurs at Videle and Ianca.

[7] Examples here are Segarcea, Nadlac, Insuratei, and Negru Voda.

[8] Topoloveni, Bals, Bailesti, and Odobesti are examples of these towns.

Figure 12.4 The territorial pattern of urban systems

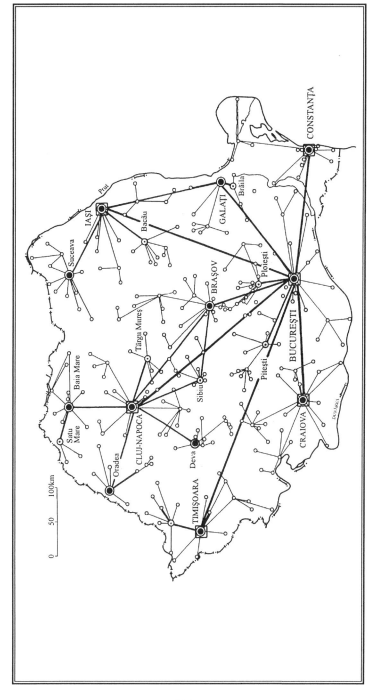

Source: I. Ianoş, Cr. Talangă, 1994

tion decreased. At the same time, centres that historically used to co-ordinate activities in Romania's large provinces became important, especially in the fields of socio-cultural and educational activities.[9]

In the coming years it is expected that the subsystems gravitating around these six large cities will become more defined. It is quite possible that two subsystems might fall apart: the one covering the southeastern part of Transylvania, centering around Brasov city, and the other one extending towards the southern part of Moldavia. The latter may become part of the subsystem controlled by Galati. This could become a reality if this subsystem and the one in the Northeast of Muntenia, centering around Braila, merge functionally. There seems to be a slim chance of it happening because there is powerful competition between these two cities and their economies are not complementary. The urban system of the Hunedoara region is also slowly becoming more defined as Timisoara and Craiova are exerting strong forces of attraction onto the central and southern parts (the Jiu Valley) of the surrounding area respectively.

Four of the regional settlement systems in the country have a mono-central character. The systems that centre around the cities of Iasi and Cluj-Napoca have a bi-central character, while the one in Transylvania is poly-central. The graph presented in Figure 12.5 gives an overview of the structure of the urban system at the regional level. The urban system shows some unique characteristics. In Oltenia and Dobrogea, the second hierarchical level is missing, with the third one being far better developed in Oltenia. To compensate, the fourth level of the structure is also more developed than usual. The upper parts of the urban hierarchy of Banat region reveal an almost linear evolution, with only one town on the first three levels. In Transylvania, levels two, three and four are well represented: the structure of the system is typically arborescent. The regional system of Moldavia is similar to the one in Transylvania, the only difference being the existence of only one second-rank town, hence a different distribution. In Muntenia, the regional system centres around Bucharest, the capital. There are no first-rank towns there, but there are three second-rank towns. Its structure is relatively normal, i.e. descending steadily. Changes in the relation between the two highest-ranking cities in each of the regions from 1966 to 1998 are shown in Table 12.2.

Administrative centres are extremely oversized compared to second-rank cities, particularly in Muntenia. Bucharest is over eight times larger than the second-rank city (Ploiesti). Generally, however, the gap between the first and

---

[9] Iasi in Moldavia, Cluj-Napoca in Transylvania (covering also Crisana and Maramures), Timisoara in Banat, Bucharest in Muntenia, Craiova in Oltenia and Constanta in Dobrogea.

Figure 12.5 A graphical representation of urban hierarchical arrangements

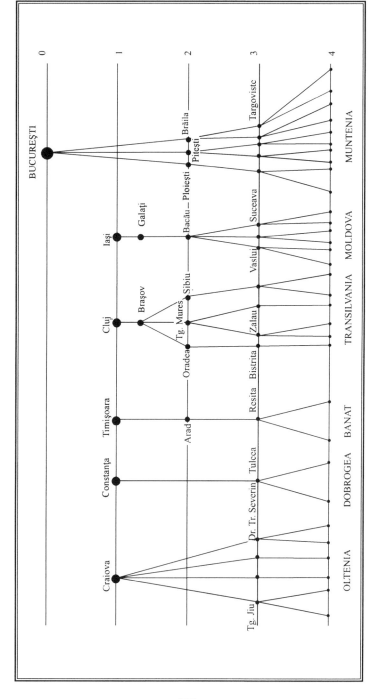

Source: I. Ianoş, Al. Ungureanu, F. Grimm, 1996, with changes.

Table 12.2 Relation between first- and second-rank towns within regional systems, using their population size

Year	Tran-sylvania	Mun-tenia	Mol-davia	Oltenia	Banat	Dobro-gea
1966	1.14	9.30	1.06	3.28	1.38	4.23
1977	1.02	9.05	1.11	2.89	1.57	4.16
1992	1.01	8.19	1.05	2.63	1.76	3.59
1998	1.06	8.02	1.05	2.62	1.76	3.55

Source: Data processed by author

the second-ranking town in all regional systems seems to be narrowing (Oltenia from 3.28 to 2.62; Dobrogea from 4.23 to 3.55). Differences in the ratio between the two upper-ranking towns in the regional systems of Transylvania and Moldavia are slightly decreasing, both towns showing a remarkable proximity (Cluj-Napoca/Brasov and Iasi/Galati, respectively). Values are increasing in the urban system of Banat where the gap between Timisoara and Arad keeps on widening fast (from 1.38 in 1966 to 1.76 in 1998). On the other hand, the situation of second- and third-rank cities is reversed, the ratio being the lowest in the regional systems of Muntenia (Ploiesti is 1.08 times larger than Braila) and Oltenia (Drobeta Tr. Severin is 1.02 times larger than Ramnicu Valcea [10]). The highest values are registered in Dobrogea (Tulcea is 2.05 times as large as Medgidia) and in Banat (Arad, twice as large as Resita). In Transylvania and Moldavia, second-rank towns are some 1.5 times larger than third-rank ones. Trends indicate that values are increasing in Transylvania and decreasing in Moldavia. On the other hierarchical levels the ratios are relatively the same. The differences only lie in the number of centres on each level.

Regionally, urban systems differ in terms of their complexity and in terms of their distinct levels of urbanization and growth rates. The urban hierarchies of Transylvania, Muntenia and Moldavia are not as clearly defined as those in Oltenia, Banat and Dobrogea. What characterizes urbanization in the last three regional systems is the constant faster growth of their administrative centres compared to those in Transylvania and Moldavia. It accounted for over 40 per cent in the total increase of the urban population from 1977 to 1992. In Dobrogea, it was 43.5 per cent and in Banat, 60.6 per

---

[10] It is interesting to note that eight years ago, the ratio between the two cities was the same, but at that time Drobeta Tr. Severin was the smaller of the two.

cent (Table 12.3). In most regional systems the contribution of the main city to the total number of urban population kept on decreasing. The only exception was Banat, where 40 per cent of the urban population live in Timisoara. This is due to three factors, a decrease in the number of small- and medium-town inhabitants, the slow increase of the population in Arad and the spectacular increase in the population of Timisoara. As for Bucharest, which holds 50 per cent of Muntenia's population, it increased by only 14.2 per cent between 1977 and 1992.

Looking at the contribution of main cities to the total number of town inhabitants, we can easily see that co-ordination centres are indeed oversized in relation to their regional urban systems.

Table 12.3 The co-ordination centre and its place within regional urban population systems; contribution to population increases over 1977-92.

Regional system	Main city	Contribution (%)		To urban population increase (1977/1992)
		To urban population		
		1977	1992	
Muntenia	Bucharest	56.1	50.0	14.2
Moldavia	Iasi	17.8	15.7	11.2
Transsylvania	Cluj-Napoca	9.5	9.4	8.8
Oltenia	Craiova	32.8	31.5	28.3
Banat	Timisoara	34.5	38.7	60.6
Dobrogea	Constanta	55.1	51.5	43.5

Source: data processed by the author

INTER-TOWN COMPETITION

As the national and regional urban hierarchies suggest, towns and cities are constantly in competition with one another for a higher position in the hierarchy. There are two forms of competition, direct and indirect, and both are important in the development process. Direct competition usually takes place between two neighbouring towns, each trying to increase its area of influence and its control over the other. When both cities have the same rank in the hierarchy, the same functional composition and similar demographic and economic capabilities, the competition between them is limited to gaining on the other's area of influence. For example, Timisoara and Arad are steadily competing to gain influence over the settlements which lie around Vinga and Periam – both centres that lie inside each other's areas of attraction. The same applies to Braila and Galati, each one trying to dominate the other by encroaching its areas of influence.

Sometimes competition between large cities and adjacent small- and medium-sized towns is mutually beneficial, lower-ranking towns becoming 'pillars of support' to large cities. In such cases they perform complementary functions and contribute to enhance the regional links of the larger cities, such as in the case of the agglomeration of Brasov and Ploiesti. It is not competition *stricto sensu*, but rather a relationship based on specialization or functional complementarily.

Indirect competition occurs when the position of one city on the urban hierarchy improves at the cost of another over a period of time. Urban hierarchies in Romania in 1966 and 1992 looked fairly similar, but in reality, substantial changes had occurred, due to the differences in demographic change in the cities (Figure 12.6). Over all, inter-urban competition, as indicated by rank changes seems to be based on 'prey-predator' rules. The role of the 'predators' is performed by cities that manage to improve their position in the hierarchy, while the role of the 'prey' is played by the losers. Normally, one would have expected the sum of acquired ranks to equal the sum of ranks lost during our two years of study. But whenever new towns appeared during the study period (1966 and 1992) these sums did not tally. In the case of Romania, the sum of lost ranks exceeded that of gained ranks, because one additional town appeared in 1981 and another twenty-three in 1989.[11] A particularly striking aspect of rank changes is the 'violent' upsurge of some intermediate-sized cities to the upper section of the national urban hierarchy between 1966 and 1992. These are the 'predators' – county-seats that were re-established in 1968. Spectacular gains were registered in Slobozia (68 places), Zalau (55 places), Vaslui (44), Miercurea Ciuc (40), and Slatina (34), for instance, with a few others (Navodari 121 places, Motru 88, Mangalia and Tandarei 37) that have suddenly become industrialized, especially after 1975. These centres have experienced population explosions. Their gains in the upper section of the hierarchy were achieved at the expense of former county capitals of the interwar period that were deprived of their status in 1968, and stagnating mining towns (particularly in the Jiu Valley). The lower section of the hierarchy reveals that, between 1966 and 1992, beneficiaries were mostly cities that specialized in machine building (Plopeni, Cugir, Sacele) and in extractive industry (Balan, Moinesti).

Improvements in the rank of cities depend on the increase in their population, which in turn is determined by their economic improvement and in the number of towns and cities in the system. The largest number of

---

[11] Although 52 of the towns were only declared in 1968 it was assumed that they had already existed in 1966.

Figure 12.6 Rank variation of towns between 1966 and 1992

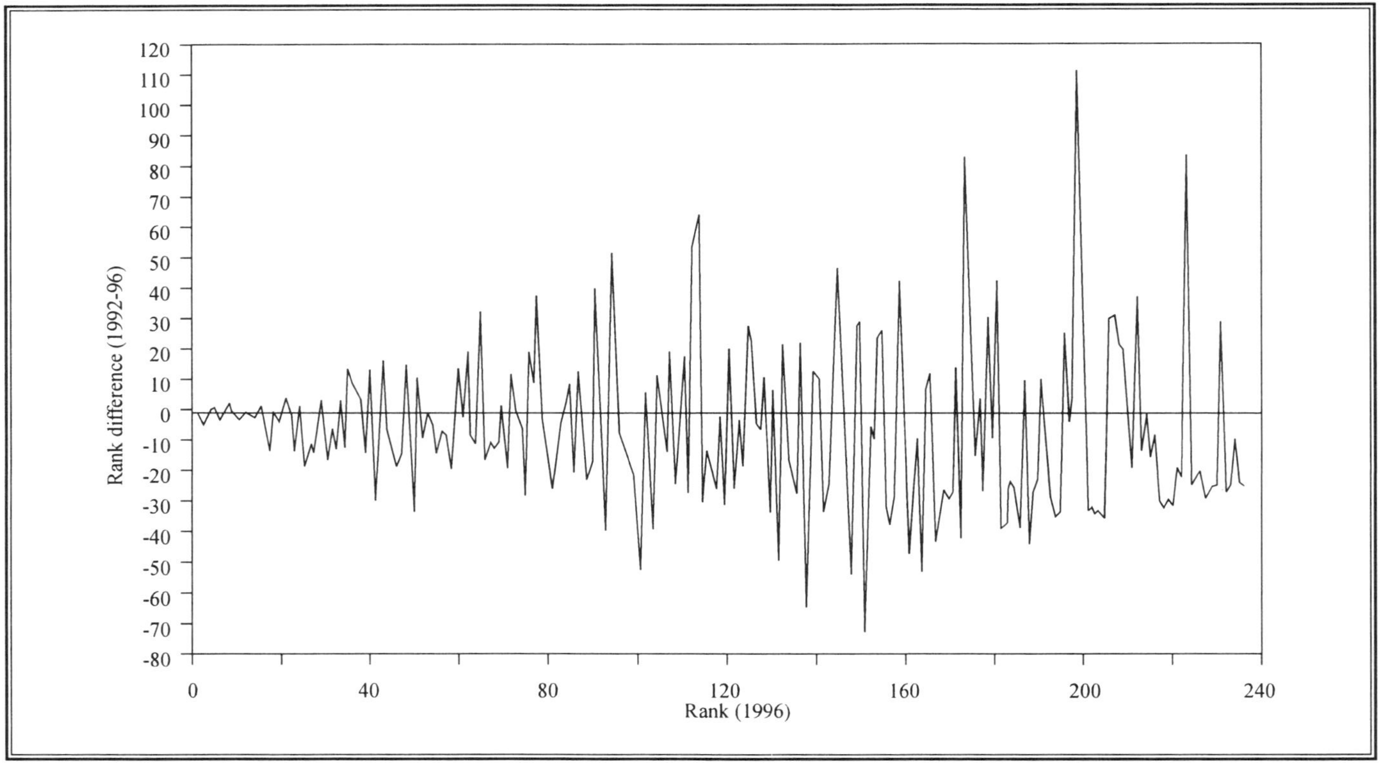

changes in urban rank was recorded in Transylvania followed by Muntenia. In Oltenia, the explosive population growth of some mining (Motru) and machine-building centres (Bals) was equalled by a dramatic decline in certain agricultural towns (Vanju Mare).

In the large urban systems of Transylvania, Muntenia and Moldavia, county-seats emerged as the highest ranking cities, whereas in the smaller systems such as Oltenia, Banat and Dobrogea, county-capitals are the highest ranking cities. Almost throughout the urban network the lower hierarchical segment is dominated by relatively new towns, specialiing in mining and oil drilling,[12] or in industrial manufacturing.[13] Some towns which lie close to large cities, such as Buftea near Bucharest in Muntenia and Targu Frumos near Iasi in Moldavia have profited from their geographical location.

In almost all historical provinces, it was mainly the important agricultural towns that have lost most of their seats.[14] Old mining centres[15] and specialized industrial cities[16] had the same fate.

Due to the current restructuring of industry, cities are expected to undergo further hierarchical changes in the future. Rank fluctuations at national and regional levels will be a response to the present 'order' of the urban systems. A new administrative-regional reorganization would bring about new, more or less artificial, shifts of position. However, it is highly improbable that hierarchical leaps similar to those encountered in the old days will happen again, because urban development is sure to be governed by laws and public consultation rather than political ideology.

TYPES AND DYNAMICS OF THE URBAN FUNCTIONS
A CENTRALIZED DEVELOPMENT POLICY

Differences between the demographic evolution of towns across the country are the result of an excessively centralized sectoral and regional development policy. Right after the Second World War, the urban network reflected a normal relationship between resources, population and infrastructure that had been established in the course of time, although the latter two elements had been influenced by the war.

---

[12] Balan and Uricani in Transylvania, Baicoi in Muntenia, Motru in Oltenia, and Moldova Noua in Banat.

[13] Covasna in Transylvania; Bals in Oltenia; Otelu Rosu in Banat; and Navodari in Dobrogea.

[14] Examples are Cehu Silvaniei in Transylvania, Saveni in Moldova, Costesti and Faurei in Muntenia, Vanju Mare in Oltenia, and Curtici in Banat.

[15] Vulcan and Petrila in Transylvania, Slanic in Muntenia, and Anina in Banat.

[16] Zlatna in Transylvania, Bicaz in Moldova, Boldesti-Scaeni and Comarnic in Muntenia.

But the nationalization of big industrial enteprises in 1948 and the subsequent industrial drive with its focus on the heavy industry altered the ratio between the major economic branches of each and every town. As new socialist relationships were set up in the economy (state units in industry and agriculture, collective farms, state-based centrally controlled services) and in socio-political life, urban functions in the territory were being reduced and restructured. While interwar urban polarization had centred around the tertiary sector, it was the industrial sector that was given priority after the Second World War. In many respects the latter overwhelmed the urban centres.

The socialist slogan: 'harmonious development in all the country's zones' became a *sine-qua-non*, and the first to feel its benefits were the towns. By and large, three major stages marked the development of urban economic activities:

1) The **development of industry, mainly in regional centres**, and the establishment of new industrial cities (1950-1965). The territory of Romania was divided into 16 regions and several hundred counties (after the Soviet administrative organization pattern). The development of county-seats, as the first growth poles, became a priority task. The industrial sector outgrew the commercial, cultural and social sectors in these centres. Several industrial centres started afresh on barren land, and they were immediately turned into cities. Onesti (Gheorghe Gheorghiu-Dej), Victoria, Stei, and Motru together were the symbol of communist economic and social achievement.

2) The industrialization drive; **building large units in county-seats and intermediate-sized towns** (1965-1980). The preferential development of county-seats had led to intra-regional discrepancies. As a result, industrializing intermediate-sized towns was the new policy line after 1965. Many of these towns grew into county centres. As Romania became more and more independent from the former Soviet Union, and the leadership feared a possible Czechoslovakian-type invasion (1968), Ceaussescu's regime decided to opt for a closed, self-sufficient economy, with an industrial sector capable of producing absolutely everything.

3) As foreign encouragement was quick to come in, a vast **industrial investment program** was implemented, which basically changed the structure of urban economic activities.

4) **Industrialization of small-sized towns and rural settlements** scheduled to become agro-industrial centres (1980-1989). The economic policy of the 1980s, with obvious roots in the previous stage, had the establishment of at least one big industrial enterprise in small towns, and low and medium sized ones in future agro-industrial settlements in mind. This second target was reached chiefly by re-locating some industrial

components in rural settlements scheduled for development. To give just two examples: the 'lectromotor' plant in Timisoara and 'rinul' factory in Bucharest set up some of their sections in Lovrin, Jebel, Buzias, and Lehliu-Gara, Nehoiu and Olteni, respectively.

The massive investments that were made in the urban economy, particularly after 1970, brought about radical changes in the structure of activities, and implicitly in the relationships between towns and the surrounding countryside, from where they derived their labour force. Large amounts of funds were also allocated to machine-building (65 per cent), textiles and ready-mades (15 per cent) and food (12 per cent) industries.

Consequently, over 50 per cent of the economically active population in half of Romania's towns and over 40 per cent in more than three-quarters of them (198 towns, i.e. 76.2 per cent) worked in the industrial sector (1992 census data). The farming population was dominant in eleven towns only, numbering more than 50 per cent in only two of them. Insuratei and Mihailesti were raised to the rank of township in April 1989. In four others it reached over 40 per cent. Two years after the fall of the totalitarian regime the workforce still found the building sector attractive. In total it contained almost as many people as education and culture put together. In Cernavoda, for example, 44.5 per cent of the active population worked in the construction of the first nuclear-power plant in Romania and at Cernavoda-Fetesti road section, a first segment of the future Bucharest-Constanta motorway had already been scheduled for commissioning. High degrees of employment in this sector are also found in the Black Sea towns where important industrial and port construction projects are underway (Navodari, Constanta, Basarabi). In the Danubian towns (Calarasi, Harsova, Drobeta Turnu Severin) and the towns located along certain watercourses, big water management works are being carried out (Brezoi, Draganesti-Olt, Nehoi).

The population engaged in commercial activities exceeds the 12 per cent mark only in health resorts and spas, averaging 8.5 per cent throughout the urban network. Education, culture and the arts attract some 5.5 per cent of each town's population, obviously more so in large cities. Taking a closer look at the evolution of town functions over the past fifty years in terms of the highest proportion of economically active people in the main categories, we find it depends on each town's size, position in the network and dominant activities.

THE INDUSTRIAL FUNCTION

Despite the gap between industries and local raw material and labour resources, this function dominates Romania's towns. It is quite impressive to see how many people among the total active population are working in various industrial branches (Ungureanu, 1981). Differences depend upon the size and position of the town in the network. For example, small and intermediate-sized towns (under 50,000 inhabitants) record extreme values. Some are excessively industrialized with one sub-branch profile only, while others have no industry at all. Among the former category (over 70 per cent of their economically active population are employed in industrial activities) are the towns located in the coal-mining basin of the Jiu Valley. Besides the extractive sector, several connex branches (mining equipment, electric and chemistry units) and complementary branches (textiles, ready-mades) have been set up. Next come the towns of the highly industrialized Brasov-Ploiesti area (Zarnesti, Plopeni, Moreni, Azuga, Fieni) and of Sibiu county (Cisnadie, Copsa Mica).

The towns in the second category are either in the lowlands, with a population largely engaged in agriculture (Insuratei, Pogoanele, Negru Voda, Nadlac, Beresti), or in the highlands, where spas and health resorts are numerous (Baile Herculane, Baile Tusnad, Predeal). The main non-industrial town is Cernavoda where, for the time being, the population is mainly engaged in finishing and the construction of the nuclear power station.

Large and intermediate-sized towns have a much more diversified economy. However, in two-thirds of the towns in the north of Romania and in one-third of those in the south, over 50 per cent and 40-50 per cent respectively of the labour force are involved in industry. The populations of large cities (except Galati, Brasov and Oradea) are not working in industry (see Bucharest, Constanta, Cluj-Napoca, Timisoara, Iasi).

In order to get an insight into the regional diffusion of the industrialization process, a comparative look at the town distribution in terms of industrial ratio between 1977 and 1992 shows that until 1977 towns with more than 50 per cent of its people involved in industry were concentrated in Banat region, in southern and eastern Transylvania, and extending into Prahova county. In 1992, one finds them also in Moldavia, and in the northern part of Transylvania (the counties of Salaj, Bistrita-Nasaud and Maramures), but they are much fewer in Oltenia, Muntenia and Dobrogea.

In terms of industrial ratio per town, it is the large cities that usually register decreases of a few percentages, whereas the smallest towns, ignored by past industrial policies, record spectacular increases. Bucharest, Arad, Timisoara and Sibiu fall into the former group, declining by some 2-3 per cent, while the county-seats of Vrancea, Bistrita-Nasaud and Botosani (Focsani, Bistrita and Botosani) benefited from substantial investments during 1970-1978. The funds allocated to the other towns from 1978 to 1992 led to the opening of at least one factory with more than 1,000 employees, resulting in an industrial population growth of 20 to 25 per cent and even more: Beclean, Darabani, Saveni, Panciu.

At the beginning of 1990, it was the large enterprises with over 1,000 employees that prevailed, providing jobs for approximately 70 per cent of the total workforce. Machine-building factories and chemical works (high energy-consumers) were dominant within an otherwise complex industrial profile, until cooperation between industries came to a sudden halt. The dismemberment of the CMEA system and the embargo imposed on Iraq, followed by Yugoslavia led to Romania's industrial decline, partly because the quality standards of the world market could not be fully met.

Subsequent events have further depleted industrial activities, especially in the towns which had previously recorded an economic and demographic boom. In Negresti-Oas, for example, from 6,000 workers, barely 800 are left. In Barlad not more than 16,000 were still working in 1996, compared to 25,000 in 1990.

In this situation it could be said that the industrial function is no longer a major binding force between towns, and that they are likely to decline steadily while the tertiary sector seems to be recuperating. Certain towns have only one industrial enterprise. In cases where they are closing down without the town being able to replace them or stimulate new activities, social conflicts often occur.

The political-administrative function has always had a prominent place in the development and evolution of some towns. After the administrative-regional reorganization of the country in 1968 this function played a major role in stimulating economic life. The new county-seats (but never regional seats) were the first to benefit from investments. They generally experienced an upsurge in economic development, much of it industrial, which generally improved economic interaction between settlements. In the process they became gravity points within the counties and some of them even became regional centres serving more than one county. Administrative coordination at the intra-county level had first been assigned to urban centres, but in cases where there was no large town in an area, this role was performed by rural settlements.

Apart from Bucharest, the following hierarchy of towns could be distinguished in terms of decision-making powers in the country: inter-county functions, county-seats, former county-seats, towns with extended functions, towns with reduced functions and towns performing strictly local functions.

Culture and education also proved to be important factors in the establishment of ties between cities because they tend to elevate living standards far beyond physical boundaries. The number of people engaged in educational and cultural activities has determined the rank of a town in the urban hierarchy over the past fifteen years.

Generally county-seats are prominent cultural and educational centres. Over 6.5 per cent of the economically active population work in these fields in county seats while the percentage increases to 7.5 in large university centres such as Cluj-Napoca, Iasi, and Timisoara. Smaller towns with a strong cultural tradition are mainly located in Transylvania, i.e Beius, Caransebes, Blaj, and Nasaud. Apart from privately run centres of higher learning that were operating in county-seats, several state-sponsored private establishments re-opened after 1990. However, the impact of these institutions is, as a rule, limited to the county in which they are located.

After 1990, some towns, especially health or recreation resorts and spas have developed a special function, namely the organization of national or international congresses, seminars and colloquia.

A strong commercial function, estimated by the level of amenities and population working in this sector is a characteristic of tourist settlements, health resorts and large cities. Over 12 per cent of the commercially active population in the former two urban categories is located in the mountainous and Subcarpathian areas, as well as in the southern coastal area of the Black Sea. In terms of their distribution, commercial towns are more numerous in the western and central-western parts of Romania. Moldavia numbers the fewest. This distribution reflects the income of the people in different areas in the country and their traditions of town life (Dobraca, 2001).

In the past, the commercial function was limited to supplying basic foodstuffs only. Trade was not regarded as a basic economic function and could not be practised under normal market conditions. As is well known, the distribution of products in a socialist economy is strictly centralized. The utopian model of town-building and its organization pattern was based upon the whims of dictators and the services, especially commercial networks, were usually concentrated in the central zone, while outer districts were left with few general or special supply stores.

To compensate for this deficient trading system, a host of small private shops have opened since 1990, very many in the outskirts of towns and cities. Obviously, at the back of people's mind was the desire for fast gains at low costs, presumably a typical mentality of people during the transitional period from a socialist to a market economy, largely facilitated by a legislative void and socio-political instability. Transport, health services, and cultural-religious institutions augmented the nodality of urban areas.

STAGES OF MATURATION OF THE URBAN SYSTEM SINCE 1990

The evolution of the Romanian urban system has been characterized by contradictory converging factors, most of them political-administratively driven. The absence of clear-cut criteria to determine the urban perimeter has often resulted in the arbitrary assessment of the urban phenomenon in Romania.

The post-Second World War period was marked by social-political distortions, due to large-scale nationalization and excessive centralization of industries, the collectivization of agriculture, over-development of the secondary sector to the detriment of the tertiary sector, and control over the planning and development of the tertiary and residential sectors.

Despite its appearance, the urban system went through a difficult period when elements of the cities and their relationships with their hinterlands underwent fundamental changes. A simple way of determining an urban system's evolution is to establish the number of urban areas that have been added to the system over a particular period of time and hierarchical changes that have taken place. In the case of Romania 122 new settlements were added between 1948 and 1990. Although the impact of the number of urban areas that were added to the system was not so apparent at the national level it was noticeable at the regional and departmental level. Interurban interaction did occur but always under strict state guidance and control. No local initiative was allowed in matters such as type of industry, size of enterprise, and extent of services. Everything was coordinated from the centre.

A historical overview of the evolution of the Romanian urban system reveals **two stages of division**. External pressure caused the historical relationship between towns and their own governmental bodies to change suddenly. Utopian models of central-based economic and social leadership were substituted for market-based economic relations while traditional political and social ties remained. This was in total contradiction to the normal evolution process, which caused a rift in development.

Despite the apparent stability, the evolution of the state-controlled urban system was disrupted by contradictions and marked by artificialities. As early as 1968, the system was shattered by internal fluctuations, which continued to grow in intensity until 1990 when the second period of transformation and confusion set in. This second change meant a return to a normal evolution process.

A qualitative and quantitative analysis of this evolutionary process reveals four stages with thresholds in between (Figure 12.7). These thresholds should be viewed as the apexes of critical intervals rather than episodes of sudden transition.

1. **The stage of postwar turbulence** is the interval in which the first transition in the evolution of the Romanian urban system occurred. This was a period when towns were confronted with many contradictions brought about by a change in the system of production and administrative organization. The urban system was further disturbed by the appearance of thirty-three new towns and the disappearance of another fourteen. Of

the latter category, six would regain that status in 1968, but the remaining eight[17] fell out of the urban system for good.

The abolition of the county system and the division of the territory into regions (subdivided into districts according to the Soviet model) and the ensuing changes at that level created a state of turbulence. However, the shock of all those transformations was attenuated because the urban system was not much evolved (only 23.8 per cent of the population lived in towns) and the country was striving to rebuild the war-stricken economy.

Figure 12.7 Main stages in the evolution of urban systems in the socialist period

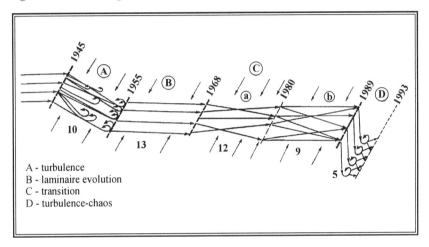

Source: after I. Ianoş, Cr. Talangă, 1994, with changes

2. The brutal intervention of the state in the process of urbanization and territorial development had actually annihilated a normal phase of transition between turbulence and stability. Therefore the 1955-1968 interval can be considered **a laminar stage** in the evolution of towns. They quickly resumed their individual development pace under the new political, economic and social conditions. Occasionally, disruptions would occur when the state violently intervened and favoured the development of large cities, of regional seats, even erecting new towns (Onesti, Motru, Victoria) on altogether barren land.

3. Between 1968 and 1990 **a transition stage** followed when steps were taken by the state to reorganize the territory administratively and

---

[17] I.e. Racari and Filipesti Targ in Muntenia, Plenita in Oltenia, Ostrov in Dobrogea a.s.o.

restructure the urban system. This stage can be subdivided into two periods: from 1968 to 1980, when the new county-seats enjoyed preferential treatment, and from 1980 to 1990, when the hierarchical stability of towns was affected by rank changes.

Early in this stage, the previous laminar, almost rectilinear evolution, became more and more complicated to the effect that a number of towns started developing at different rates. Inter-town relationships, in turn, became more intricate as services activities were left far behind industrial activities. Simultaneously, human pressure on the urban system increased as a consequence of the worsening living conditions in the countryside (after the village had been severed from its supporting territory) and fifty-two settlements were turned into townships. In order to control this artificial urban system, the state took a number of tough steps during 1980-90, three of which had a particular impact: the enforced prioritizing of regional planning programs, priority state-assistance for small towns and especially for the several hundred rural settlements singled out to become future agro-industrial towns, and the founding of twenty-three New Towns in the spring of 1989.

As the processes of regional development became more intricate and the village-town relationships deteriorated, while at the same time the big industries proved to be alarmingly inefficient, policy-makers started to opt for agro-industrial centres. Unfortunately, the same type of industrialization, based on rather bizarre policies of regional distribution, size, and profile, was consistently being implemented.

Urban planning went on almost simultaneously with the administrative reorganization of the territory, and in the process county-seats were given absolute priority. A focal point in this all-embracing program from the second half of the 1980s and throughout the 1990s, was the restructuring of Bucharest city, of small- and medium sized towns, and of rural centres scheduled to become agro-industrial towns.

4. The last interval, defined by the collapse of the totalitarian regime, could be considered as a **turbulence-chaos stage**, due to the impact of radical changes. It is about the shock of transition from the over-centralized system to the market economy and democracy.

THE URBAN SYSTEM UNDER SHOCK OF TRANSITION

During the 1945-90 period, the urban system had developed in a rigid, controlled, manner imposed by a communist mode of production and types of relations. The utopian views on town-building and town-functioning, as well as the interdependence between towns, placed emphasis on the economic component alone, creating an artificial urban system with an unstable hierarchical pattern in its middle and lower sections. Stability has been maintained, with a few exceptions, in the upper level of the hierarchy. As a rule, the changes that occurred were sudden, induced by big production unit-based industrialization.

By the end of 1989, the urban system was in an advanced stage of transition to turbulence (Ianos, 1995). That year had been scheduled as the first in a series meant to witness fundamental shifts in the hierarchical town basis. In April 1989, twenty-three settlements had been declared agro-industrial towns; another five situated in the peri-urban area of Bucharest (Otopeni, 30 Decembrie, Voluntari, Magurele and Branesti), were doomed to follow in the first half of 1990. That was a first step in a vast urban and regional planning scheme to halve the number of villages (down to about 7,000) and increase that of towns (by over 400).

The December 1989 events, and the sudden downfall of the political regime had a decisive influence on the evolution of individual towns and on the urban system as a whole. But the development of new self-control mechanisms to replace the old ones based on a utopian, socialist, town model, ruled by the arbitrary decisions of dictators at each and every hierarchical level, is not an easy matter. It is a very complex process and will probably take a much longer time than expected. In the first place, the property structure needs to be changed and adapted to the new framework, and in the second place townsfolk's mentality and behaviour have to change. If the town resumes its realistic position within the urban network, which implies that it should adjust itself to its realistic size and profile in terms of its internal and external market (hinterland), then normal rural-urban relations can develop.

The abrogation of the restrictive laws that had controlled migration movements was the cause of a first element of turbulence in the urban system. The abrogation of the law restricting people's settlement in large towns (with over 100,000 inhabitants) had an immediate impact. It is a well-known fact that after 1970 large towns had been closed to people seeking permanent residence during the communist period, except for people with specialized knowledge who were officially transferred, party activists, officers and university graduates receiving an appointment based on government consent.

So the large cities are the principal beneficiaries of this abrogation. Between 1989 and 1990 their population increased by 15 per cent: the upsurge was spectacular. The largest influx occurred during the first six months of 1990: Constanta gained 13.7 per cent; Timisoara, 8.2 per cent; Pitesti, 7.4 per cent; Galati, 6.9 per cent, and Craiova, 6.7 per cent. In Bucharest and nine other cities the influx was around 2 per cent. At the same time several industrial centres that had developed explosively during the years of communist regime, such as Colibasi, Calafat, and Mangalia lost the same percentage of people.

The 'assault' on large cities was encouraged also by a post-revolutionary populist policy, which augmented the industrial segment of the population by several hundred thousands. First to feel the impact were not the villages (deserted by skilled people), but rather the small towns of the respective county or/and of bordering counties. For example, the city of Bucharest attracted 80,000 new residents which resulted in negative values in all its surrounding counties (Teleorman, Giurgiu, Calarsi, Ialomita). However, in cases where in-migration was offset by mass emigration of German ethnics (such as Brasov and Sibiu) the population figures of cities remained relatively stable. In the next stage and throughout 1991, population shifts began to slow down, yet not in places like large cities, county-seats and some industrial towns, where the inflow of people continued.

After a lapse of twenty-five years, a law was passed legalizing abortion. This measure affected every town, inclusive of regions known to have demographic excedents and high birth rates indexes. In 1989, over 63 per cent of the total number of towns had recorded a natural increase of over 6 per cent, but two years later (1991) this value was reached in only 21 per cent of them. The number of towns which registered decreases rose from 3.4 per cent to 18 per cent of the total number of urban settlements. Growth of over 10 per cent was observed in six times fewer towns than in 1989, especially in mining centres (Motru, Rovinari, Uricani, etc). Industrial towns expanded mainly during the last three years of communism (Colibasi, Zalau, Navodari etc), as well as certain towns situated in areas with marked demographic excedents such as Harlau, Negresti, Targu Frumos, and Necresti-Oas.

These demographic changes had a significant impact on the entire urban system. Despite a rather short interval, these changes, correlated with the mass migrations of the German population, are quite significant. Up to rank 25, there is remarkable hierarchical stability between the years 1990 and 1992. But this stability was violently shaken (given the normal possibility of change), when Brasov lost five seats in the upper segment and four other towns took their place.

A detailed study of rank changes shows that 53 towns had maintained their hierarchical position, 95 lost positions and 112 gained. Over 10 positions were gained by small industrial towns in which big enterprises of national importance were located – i.e Colibasi, Rovinari, Alesd, Bumbesti-Jiu, Plopeni, and Nehoiu. Other small towns – i.e. old mining centres (Anina, Balan), old industrial centres with high-polluting units (Copsa Mica, Bicaz, and Victoria) and several others with different profiles (Jimbolia, Bocsa, Curtici, Titu, and Sacele) had low negative scores.

Pressure is being exerted on former county-seats to regain the status that they held in the interwar period. The pressure manifests itself in the form of a kind of local patriotism rather than through documented economic or social needs. If these patriotic-driven demands are met the future evolution of the Romanian urban system will become even more complicated. The twenty-one towns that are involved are part of 'a league of counties abusively dissolved by the communist regime', and they are trying to convince Parliament to accept the administrative-regional pattern of the 1930s.

However, decision-makers should carefully consider the consequences before reinstating county-seats. Things have changed since the 1930s: neither the economic and social development of the territory nor the national urban hierarchy is still the same. The country needs a scientific analysis of the possible effects of such a decision.

Urban economic restructuring is not easy for people that have lived for so many years under communism. The industrial sector which is largely based on large production units, is high-energy and raw-material consuming. The chain of relations among industrial enterprises is no longer operative within the same administrative structures and is under centrally controlled management. Therefore, the key to urban revival is industrial restructuring. But this action implies huge financial and social efforts, which Romania cannot afford at present, because it has neither the economic capacity, nor the managerial expertise or capital.

The most serious difficulties cropped up when the CMEA system fell apart. Traditional markets were lost and certain Romanian products proved to be uncompetitive. The surgical, chemical and machine-building sectors which are oversized compared to the actual needs of the country, lowered their output by 40-60 per cent against 1989 levels. The consequences of production reduction are: a lack of capable managers, a lack of a clear-cut transition strategy and spiralling unemployment. The latter was insignificant after 1991 but now it is affecting 11 per cent of the economically active population and prospects are as bleak.

Industrial restructuring does not affect the large cities to the extent it affects the small and intermediate-sized towns. In large cities workers that have been laid off in a struggling industrial sector can perhaps find alternative employment in the tertiary sector which is undersized compared to cities in Western Europe. Smaller towns that are relying on one or two industrial enterprises only face serious social challenges when these industries struggle or collapse. Cugir, Stei, Aiud, and Barlad are examples of such towns with some 35 per cent of their active population out of work. Certain social protection plans have been implemented but the high unemployment rate may eventually lead to serious social conflicts.

Towns that are based on light and food industries which process part of their local products are in a better position. Nevertheless they, too, have been seriously affected by privatization in the agricultural sector and the alarming decline in the production of products such as sugar beet, sunflower, soya, hemp and flax. So far, the small and intermediate-sized towns, in which wood processing and building-materials units operate (such as Beius, Reghin, and Campeni) are advantaged. They have secured internal and external markets for their products, maintained their workforce, and in some cases taken in new employees.

The Land Law, enacted in 1991, had both direct and indirect effects on towns and the urban system as a whole. Among those directly affected are the small towns, located in the lowlands and in the hilly areas, with a poorly developed industrial sector.[18] About 27 per cent of Romania's towns have suffered the direct effects of this law. Large cities, intermediate-sized towns, or centres which have experienced exceptional industrial development during the communist era are indirectly affected. On the one hand, part of their retired population, originating from the countryside, would periodically or permanently return to their native villages to work the plots of land re-appropriated to them. On the other hand, peasants who live in the neighbourhood of towns also received land. This brought down commuting[19] to less than one-third, because commuters were the first to lose their jobs – the management argued that they had a source of income. All these factors considerably reduced the negative impact of industrial restructuring for townsfolk.

Town size and the types of industries located in them play an important role in people's perception of the economic transition. Apart from it, this initial trying period of industrial restructuring is marked by events such as the U.N. embargo on Yugoslavia, or the preferential location of foreign investments. Foreign investments are an important element in revitalizing the economy. However, they impact negatively on the urban system when certain categories of towns or geographical regions are favoured to the detriment of others. Theoretically, at least, preferential localization would bring about positive changes in the national urban hierarchy, and in inter-town relationships.

Investments are largely concentrated in Bucharest (more than 55 per cent), followed by towns in Transylvania. Oltenia province seems to be the least attractive at this time. Towns located along the Danube are very easily accessible because the Danube-Main-Rhine river system provides a direct link between the Black and the North Sea. But foreign investors are reluctant

---

[18] Examples are Vanju Mare, Beresti, Tasnad, Pogoanele, Insuratei, and Budesti.
[19] Commuting was particularly high in the past (approximately 1.8 million people).

to invest in this area. Only Galati, Braila and Macin have attracted significant amounts of foreign capital.

NEW TENDENCIES IN THE RECENT EVOLUTION OF THE ROMANIAN URBAN SYSTEM

To depict the recent changes in the evolution of the urban system a detailed analysis was made of population shifts in the main urban categories, including the rural areas (Geyer and Kontuly, 1993). This analysis shows that people are leaving towns to settle in the countryside. It is by no means an accidental phenomenon: cross-country data indicate a decrease in the urban population since 1996.

Unlike the typical case of the Western countries, however, here we are confronted with an economy that is in transition from a centralized system to a market driven one. This means that a restructuring is taking place in the urban as well as the rural economies. In the rural areas the restructuring is limited to properties (Land Law No. 18/1991) with no regard for economic efficiency. The Land Law has resulted in the creation of new jobs in agriculture through the parceling out of land. Approximately one-third of these owners live in towns.

The very tough industrial restructuring that is under way in the urban areas has led to a labour surplus. Failing industries have reduced the means for these families to survive in town. Those that own land in their native villages tend to return there. The urban-rural migration is therefore a reflection of the changing economic circumstances which result in changes in the relationships between towns and villages in Romania (Ianos, 2000b).

In the aftermath of the 1990 shock-wave, all categories of towns witnessed the steep decline of net migration rates between 1997 and 1998. Negative values have been recorded in all cases. On the other hand, rural settlements as a whole for the first time since the Second World War gained population (Figure 12.8). Although the growth is not very impressive (not more than 2-3 per cent), the record is very significant considering the level they had started from. Back migration affects all towns but more so towns in the southern and eastern parts of the country. In 1999, rural net migration reached 2.7 per cent while that of Bucharest was up 0.1 per cent.

The effects of a return to a market economy and the elimination of centralist restrictions are also reflected in disparities in the ability of towns (by cateory) to attract people. The value of this indicator is visibly similar for all urban categories.

Figure 12.8 Evolution of net migration by groups of settlements

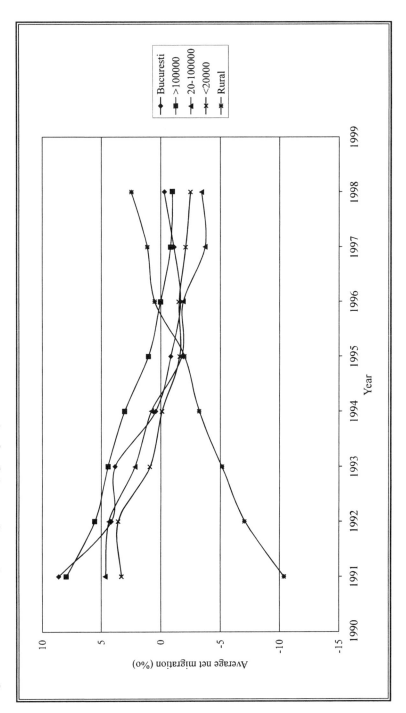

CONCLUSIONS

During the twentieth century the Romanian urban system has been strongly affected by two changes in the socio-economic history of the country: the change from a capitalist to a communist system and back. Additional factors were the two world wars, which deeply affected Romania. Despite these events, the maturing of the Romanian urban system has resulted in new urban forms, showing interesting and surprising changes, but in general the changes have occurred within the limits of the classical models. An entire cycle of urban evolution could be identified. First there was a primate city phase centered around the capital city during the first part of the twentieth century, followed by a shift in importance to the regional centres (1950-70), then to the intermediate-sized and small towns (1970-90) and finally to the revitalizing of the countryside (after 1990). Although the return to the market economy has accelerated the counter-urbanization process the associated urban characteristics are not very clear. Future trends will confirm or disprove the present-day tendencies. Some existing insights may be gained from the location of new foreign investments. New forces of attraction may be uncovered and may eventually lead to new perspectives on the urbanization cycle.

REFERENCES

Bacanaru, I., M. Candea, and G. Erdeli (1976), 'Tendances territoriale et socio-professionelles dans l'evolution de la population urbaine en Roumanie', *Revue Roumaine de Geographie*, **20**, 177-188.

Cucu, V. (1970), *Orasele Romaniei,* Bucarest: Stiintifica.

Cucu, V. and P. Deica (1978), 'Le processus d'urbanisation en Roumanie', *Revue Roumaine de Geographie*, **23**, 239-250.

Dobraca, L. (2001), *Activitatile comerciale in orasele Romaniei. Studiu de geografie umana*, Teza de doctorat (manuscript), Bucarest.

Geyer, H. S. and T. M. Kontuly (1993), 'A theoretical foundation for the concept of differential urbanization', *International Regional Science Review*, **15**, 157- 177.

Ianos, I. (1987), *Orasele si organizarea spatiului geografic. Studiu de geografie economica*, Bucuresti: Editura Academiei.

Ianos, I. (1993), 'A comparative analysis between urban and industrial hierarchy of the Romanian towns', *GeoJournal*, **29**, 1: 49-56.

Ianos. I. (1995), *The Romanian urban system under shock of transition, environment and quality life in Central Europe: Problems of transition*, Conference proceedings, Prague: Albertina Icome, Faculty of Science, Charles University, CD-Rom, 173, Prague.

Ianos, I. (1997), '*Hierarchical distortions within the Romanian urban system*, Urban development and urban life in international perspective', *Geographia Polonica*, **69**, 55-65.

Ianos, I. (2000a), 'Integration and fragmentation processes in the urban systems', in I. Ianos, D. Pumain, J.B. Racine, T*he integrated urban systems and sustainability of urban life* (eds), Bucarest: Editura Tehnica, pp. 67-76.

Ianos, I. (2000b), 'Romanian towns. From the extensive industrialisation to ruralisation?', *The Geographical Journal of Korea*, **34**, pp. 125-136.

Ianos, I. and C. Talanga (1994), *Orasul si sistemul urban romanesc in conditiile economiei de piata,* Bucharest : Institutul de Geografie.

Ianos, I., A. L. Ungureanu, and F. D. Grimm (1996), 'Grundzüge der Stadtgeographie und des Städtessystems Rumäniens, Städte und Städtesysteme in Mittel-und Südosteuropa, xx', *Institut für Länderkunde,* **39**, 172-226.

Pumain, D., L. Sanders, and T. Saint-Julien (1989). *Les villes et auto-organisation*, Paris: Economica.

Sandru, I. and A. Ungureanu, (1967), 'Quelques traits geographiques de l'evolution des villes de Roumanie', *An.st. ale A.I.Cuza, Iasi,* **seria II-b, t.XIII**, 135-144.

Ungureanu, A. (1981), 'Au sujet du rapport entre l'industrialisation et l'urbanisation en Roumanie', *An.st. ale A.I.Cuza, Iasi,* **seria II-b, t.XXVII**, 73-80.

Ungureanu, A. and I. Ianos (1996), 'Characteristic features of the urban system in Romania', *Revue Roumaine de Geographie*, **40**, 3-12.

Chapter 13

The Demographic Transition and Urban Development in Turkey

T. Baycan-Levent

INTRODUCTION

The twentieth century has been a century of major transformations in the world. Since the 1980s the world has seen a transition from industrial to informational societies, from modernism to post-modernism and from nation-states to globalization. All of these have led, on the one hand, to changes in spatial distributions of population and on the other hand, in line with improved means of transportation and advanced communicational and informational systems, have provided for a greater mobility for people. In this sense, the concept of migration has acquired a new meaning. As a result of all this the terms 'rural' and 'urban' need to be redefined as they have undergone a change in meaning due to modern technological developments and modifications in agricultural production. Undoubtedly, in many parts of the world and particularly in developing countries, there are still a multitude of rural areas where industrialization is still absent or where it is still in its infancy. However, in view of continuously altering conditions, it cannot be stated for certain that such areas are likely to ever attract large-scale industrial and urban development at any meaningful scale. Therefore, it seems necessary to evaluate the process of urbanization and the changes in the distribution of population within the framework of existing transitions.

As a developing country, even though the meanings associated with the concepts 'rural' and 'migration' have remained unaltered in Turkey, the tempo of the change in the two environments has accelerated rapidly over the years. The observed tendencies in demographic transformation and the effects of migration in Turkey, as well as the predictions for the future, are similar to experiences in developed countries.

Since the founding of the Republic in 1923, Turkey has experienced substantial changes in its demographic structure. When the Republic was founded in 1923, the population of Turkey was approximately 14 million. Today, Turkey's population is approximately 63 million and according to current projections it is expected to reach 88 million by 2025. Over the past seventy years the spatial distribution, density and size of the population have changed fundamentally, all of which have had profound effects on the social, political, and economic lives of the people, and they are expected to have further consequences in the future. The dynamism of the process of change continues.

The type of population change so far experienced in Turkey, as well as the changes expected to occur in the near and distant future, are described as 'demographic transitions' by demographic and historical literature. The term demographic transition generally refers to the process whereby high fertility and high death rates give way to the deliberate control of the birth rate and to the decline in the death rate. The trends and projections in population indicate that Turkey's demographic transition is almost over. This will have a series of repercussions in a wide array of spheres ranging from trends in social life to economic and political systems. On the other hand, due to this demographic transition, it is expected that Turkey will face the demographic condition known as the 'window of opportunity' (S.I.S., 1995; TUSIAD, 1999). The 'window of opportunity' is a phase in the demographic transition process whereby the steady increase in the supply of the labour force is sustained while there is a precipitous fall in the rate of growth of the population. The projections made by the State Institute of Statistics for the future population structure in terms of three groups of the population, viz. producers, youth and the elderly clearly show the demographic condition that Turkey will face (Figure 13.1). During this period when the labour force and the number of households continue to rise while the structure of the population remains unchanged, it is possible to increase the per capita income rapidly and to provide the same number of citizens with improved services. Therefore, the demographic transformation in Turkey provides for a possible acceleration in its economic development which would enable it to soon take its place among the developed countries. This is the same type of opportunity that Eastern Asian countries took advantage of in the 1970s. However, in order to take advantage of this opportunity, the characteristics of the process should be well understood and correct policies should be devised and implemented.

In the next section of this paper, the stages and the characteristics of the demographic transition process in Turkey will be investigated and the window of opportunity that has been opened by the prevailing conditions will be evaluated. In the third section, which will present an evaluation of the dynamism of urbanization during the last 50 years, the alterations in the ratio of population increase in rural and urban areas, the regional distributions of population, the socio-economic developments, the regional disparities and the dynamics of urbanization during the last ten years will be discussed. In the fourth section, the history of internal migration, variations in migratory movements involving different settlements and the effects of migrations on urbanization will be investigated. The last section will deal with existing demographic transformations, future expectations and predictions within the framework of the outcome of urbanization and migratory movements.

THE DEMOGRAPHIC TRANSITION IN TURKEY

The term 'demographic transition' is generally used to refer to a process that starts with a high fertility and death rate followed by an intermediate phase of faster population growth as a result of a slower death rate than birth rate and ends when both the fertility and death rates are low. The trends in population and projections indicate that Turkey's demographic transition is almost over. According to the report of the State Institute of Statistics (S.I.S.) on demographic structure and development, the Turkish demographic transition (S.I.S., 1995) involves three stages. These can be summarized as follows:

The first stage: In Turkey, the first stage of transition roughly covers the period between 1923 and 1950. Though complete statistics on death rates do not exist for the entire period, there seems to have been a steady decline in death rates, except for a brief reversal during the Second World War period. However, fertility increased significantly from around 5.5 children to 7.0 children during this period. In order to overcome the shortage in the labor force, particularly in agriculture, both families and the State considered high fertility to be necessary. With falling death rates and rising birth rates, the growth rate of the population increased rapidly. Between 1927 and 1955, the population almost doubled, increasing from 13 to 24 million (Table 13.1).

The second stage: The second period of Turkey's demographic transition is dated from about 1955 to 1985. This stage started with the population growth rate at its highest level, 2.8 per cent per year. During the 1950s, fertility began to decline and it has not reversed since then. However, the rate of decline was not fast enough to catch up immediately with the previous decline in death rates, so the population continued to grow. Between 1955 and 1985, the population doubled again, from 24 to 51 million (Table 13.1). Another major development of the second period was rapid urbanization. The urban population increased from 29 per cent in 1955 to 53 per cent in 1985.

The third stage: The second period did not end with any specific event. The downward trends of mortality and fertility continued. However, a definite and irreversible decline in the rate of population growth shows that Turkey

Table 13.1 Overall results of population censuses, 1927–97

Census dates	Population ('000 000)	Annual increase rate %	Number of provinces	City population ('000 000)	Annual increase rate % (city)	Percentage of city population	Village population ('000 000)	Annual increase rate % (village)	Percentage of village population
1927	13.65	-	63	3.31	-	24.22	10.34	-	75.78
1935	16.16	2.11	57	3.80	1.75	23.53	12.36	2.22	76.47
1940	17.82	1.96	63	4.35	2.67	24.39	13.47	1.73	75.61
1945	18.79	1.06	63	4.69	1.51	24.94	14.10	0.91	75.06
1950	20.95	2.17	63	5.24	2.25	25.04	15.70	2.15	74.96
1955	24.06	2.78	66	6.93	5.57	28.79	17.14	1.75	71.21
1960	27.75	2.85	67	8.86	4.92	31.92	18.90	1.95	68.08
1965	31.39	2.46	67	10.81	3.97	34.42	20.59	1.71	65.58
1970	35.61	2.52	67	13.69	4.73	38.45	21.91	1.26	61.55
1975	40.35	2.50	67	16.87	4.17	41.81	23.48	1.37	58.19
1980	44.74	2.07	67	19.65	3.05	43.91	25.09	1.33	56.09
1985	50.66	2.49	67	26.87	6.26	53.03	23.80	-1.06	46.97
1990	56.47	2.17	73	33.33	4.38	59.01	23.15	-0.65	40.99
1997	62.87	1.51	80	40.88	2.87	65.00	21.98	-0.67	35.00

Notes:
City population: Population within the municipal boundaries of provincial and district centres.
Village population: Population of sub-districts and villages that are outside the municipal boundaries of provincial and district centres.
Population in the table is the *de facto* population.

Source: S.I.S. (1999).

entered a third phase of transition during the 1980s. The growth rate decreased to 2.2 per cent during the five-year period, 1985-90. According to the 1997 census, Turkey's population grew at an annual average rate of 1.5 per cent during the 1990-97 period. This represents a significant decrease given the fact that the population had increased at an annual average rate of 2.5 per cent from 1980 to 1985 and from 2.2 per cent from 1985 to 1990. On the other hand, the share of urban population within the total reached 65 per cent while the rate of growth of urban population dropped to 2.9 per cent. Thus, for the first time since the 1950s, the period during which Turkey had its initial experience with rural out-migration, the rate of growth of total population dropped below the 2 per cent mark and the rate of growth of urban population below 3 per cent (Table 13.1).

According to projections (S.I.S., 1995), the population of Turkey is expected to stabilize at around 95 million by the middle of the 21st century. Thus, the population in 2023 will have increased by approximately 7.5 times by the time the transition is completed.

Figure 13.1 Youth, producer and elderly population, 1935-90, with a projection to 2070

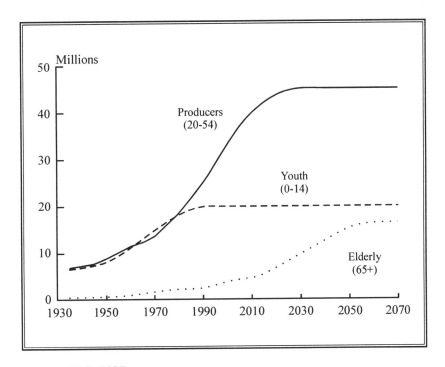

Source: S.I.S. (1995)

URBANIZATION DYNAMICS OF TURKEY, 1950-97

In the 1950s, a process of rapid urbanization began in Turkey, reflecting the influences of mechanization in the agricultural sector, polarization of rural land ownership, rapid population growth, the development of communications linking countryside and city, the industrialization of western port cities as an extension of the western industry and the relatively more advanced social services and employment opportunities in cities as opposed to rural areas. The most notable characteristic of this process is the migration from the countryside to the city. This migration, which began in the 1950s and accelerated in the 1960s, together with the urbanization it produced, was first viewed in Turkey as a positive development, one that constituted a potential and a driving force for development. However, as years went by and internal migration accelerated, the supply of manpower in cities surpassed the demand of the industrial and service sectors for labour, and the growing supply of labour and disorderly nature of urbanization became major problems.

URBAN AND RURAL POPULATION GROWTH RATES FROM 1950 TO 1997

Turkey's population more than triple between 1950 and 1997. What is more important is that the urban population (the population of province and district centres) recorded an almost nine-fold growth. Urban population numerically surpassed the rural population at the end of the 1980s, and since then, the rural population has been decreasing not just proportionally, but also in absolute terms. Since 1980, the rural population has declined from 25 million to 22 million, while the urban population has increased from 20 million to 41 million. Therefore, in terms of the population of the province and district seats, Turkey's urban population increased from 25 per cent of the total in 1945 to 65 per cent in 1997. The high urbanization rate of Turkey has started to slow down since 1990.

In terms of the rate of growth of the population, the rural out-migration exhibited major periodical fluctuations. The annual average rate of growth of the urban population remained at around 4 per cent in general, with a couple of major exceptions, i.e. from 1950 to 1955 and from 1980 to 1985 when the urban population grew at an annual average rate of 5.6 per cent and 6.3 per cent respectively. However, the rate of growth of urban population drastically declined to 2.9 per cent between 1990 and 1997. From 1950 to 1997, the rural population increased merely 1.4 times, at an annual average rate of growth of around 1 per cent.

REGIONAL DISTRIBUTION OF POPULATION FROM 1950 TO 1997

The investigation of the regional distribution of population shows that in the

---

1950-97 period population increased in the Marmara, Mediterranean and Southeast Anatolia regions and decreased continuously in the Black Sea and East Anatolia regions. There was no important change in contributions to population of the Aegean and Central Anatolian regions during the same period (Table 13.2 and Table 13.3). The Marmara Region, with an increase in its contribution to population from 18.2 per cent in 1950 to 25.8 per cent in 1997, is the most populated region of the country. On the other hand, the Black Sea Region with a decrease from 21 per cent in 1950 to 12.5 per cent in 1997 is the most depopulated region (Figure 13.2). It can be said that there is a population shift from the northern and northeastern regions to the western, southern and southeastern regions of Turkey.

Table 13.2 Population of regions by census year in millions, 1950-97

Regions	1950	1955	1960	1965	1970	1975	1980	1985	1990	1997
General Total	20.95	24.06	27.75	31.39	35.61	40.35	44.74	50.66	56.47	62.87
Marmara	3.81	4.47	5.18	5.84	6.84	8.06	9.44	11.10	13.30	16.19
Aegean	3.00	3.43	3.92	4.40	4.87	5.40	5.95	6.75	7.60	8.45
Mediterranean	2.05	2.43	2.87	3.31	3.83	4.56	5.26	6.12	7.03	8.06
Central Anatolia	3.84	4.45	5.15	5.87	6.69	7.63	8.26	9.22	9.94	10.58
Black Sea	4.39	4.81	5.47	6.09	6.59	7.05	7.49	7.96	8.11	7.84
East Anatolia	2.51	2.70	3.09	3.52	3.98	4.43	4.77	5.21	5.35	5.61
Southeast Anatolia	1.35	1.77	2.06	2.37	2.80	3.21	3.57	4.30	5.16	6.13

Source: Various publications of S.I.S. (State Institute of Statistics)

Table 13.3 Regional contributions to population by census year, 1950-97 (%)

Regions	1950	1955	1960	1965	1970	1975	1980	1985	1990	1997
General Total	100	100	100	100	100	100	100	100	100	100
Marmara	18.2	18.6	18.7	18.6	19.2	20	21.1	21.9	23.6	25.8
Aegean	14.3	14.2	14.1	14.1	13.6	13.4	13.3	13.3	13.4	13.4
Mediterranean	9.8	10.1	10.4	10.5	10.8	11.3	11.7	12.1	12.4	12.8
Central Anatolia	18.3	18.5	18.6	18.7	18.8	18.9	18.5	18.2	17.6	16.8
Black Sea	21	20	19.7	19.4	18.5	17.5	16.7	15.7	14.4	12.5
East Anatolia	12	11.2	11.1	11.2	11.2	11	10.7	10.3	9.5	8.9
Southeast Anatolia	6.4	7.4	7.4	7.5	7.9	7.9	8	8.5	9.1	9.8

Source: Various publications of S.I.S. (State Institute of Statistics)

Figure 13.2   Distribution of the population by region in 1950 and 1997 (1950 percentage / 1997 percentage)

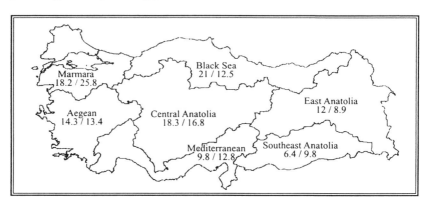

Source: Various publications of S.I.S. (State Institute of Statistics)

SOCIO-ECONOMIC DEVELOPMENT AND REGIONAL DISPARITIES

It is understood that the urbanization process in Turkey is closely related to regional disparities. In general, while the Marmara, the Aegean, the Central Anatolian and the Mediterranean Regions of Turkey have undergone development, some parts of Eastern Anatolia, the Black Sea regions and South East Anatolia, in particular, remain considerably below Turkey's average in terms of income, employment and welfare. While the problems faced in underdeveloped regions are primarily stagnation and lack of investment and services, the developed regions also suffer from unemployment, insufficient infrastructure, informal settlements and environmental problems, which go hand-in-hand with the rapid increase in population.

This kind of polarization has created two sets of problems: problems concerning the 'metropolis' created by excessive growth in developed regions and problems of 'underdeveloped regions'. The developed and underdeveloped region dilemma also causes further deepening of the existing differences. The concentrated migration phenomenon represents the essential dynamic within this dilemma. The people migrating from the rural and underdeveloped regions to the metropolis significantly changed the spatial distributions of the population.

The migration phenomenon, which can be considered as a transfer of labour force and capital, can sometimes hamper development by reducing the market in regions from which people migrate. It can thwart continued investments and can result in a loss of productivity required to promote skilled labour and capital. On the other hand, it puts significant pressure on the population in developed regions, increases the need for public investments and results in additional costs.[1] Consequently, the migration of people, which is primarily responsible for the problems experienced in both developed and underdeveloped regions, creates a problem of settlement throughout Turkey.

In a study conducted by the State Planning Organization (DPT) in 1993, the provinces and regions of Turkey were ranked according to their level of socio-economic development. The study involved 72 provinces. A total of 58 ranking indicators were used in the study and the provinces were classified into 5 separate groups. The numbers of provinces, grouped according to their level of socio-economic development, were as follows: 5 in the first, 11 in the second, 26 in the third, and 17 in the fourth and fifth groups (DPT, 1996). As can be seen in Figure 13.3, the provinces located to the west of the line joining Zonguldak and Gaziantep lie on the first, second and third levels, while the provinces to the east of this line lie on the fourth and fifth levels. It can be said that generally the level of development declines from west to east. In terms of its state of socio-economic development the Marmara Region ranks first among 7 regions of the country. From an industrial and commercial standpoint, Istanbul, which is primarily responsible for the socio-economic development of the region, is the most important city in the country. Commercial and industrial activities diffusing from Istanbul to the region make Marmara the dynamic centre of development and an attraction zone in Turkey. The Aegean Region, which ranks second to Marmara, shows similar tendencies for development. The centre of economic activities in the region is Izmir. Central Anatolia, third in rank, shows a similar socio-economic development to the Aegean Region. Ankara, the capital of the country, is the commercial centre of the region, elevating all economic and social indicators of the region. The Mediterranean Region, ranking fourth, represents Turkey's average. Agriculture, industry and service sectors in the region are in rapid development. The international ports and the free zones in the region contribute significantly to commercial activities. Also, rapidly growing tourism has a great influence on the economic structure of the region. Development is not based on one sole growth pole. Rather, many of the cities in the region have become centres of growth.

The regions that fell below the country's average with respect to socio-economic development are the Black Sea, the Southeastern and the Eastern Anatolian regions. Factors relating to geography and climate and the long distance from developed Western markets are primarily responsible for the stagnation observed in these regions. Therefore, there is an intense migration outward from these three regions, a migration, which has an adverse effect on their development.

---

[1] Additional cost is the cost of the public investment realized because of the ncreasing need.

Figure 13.3 Provinces by socio-economic development level

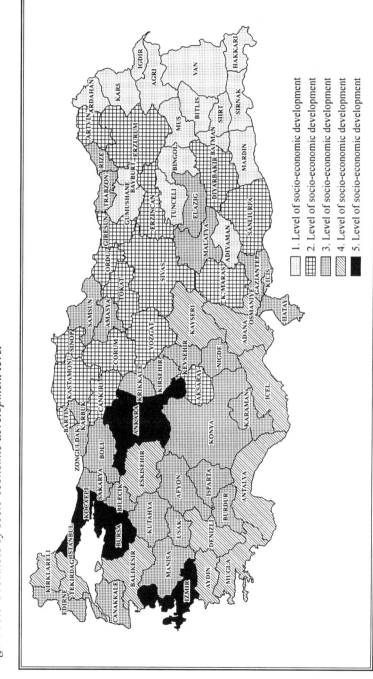

1. Level of socio-economic development
2. Level of socio-economic development
3. Level of socio-economic development
4. Level of socio-economic development
5. Level of socio-economic development

Source: S.P.O. (1996)

One of the important findings of the study conducted by the State Planning Organization is that spatial developmental tendencies in Turkey are governed by dynamics of 'diffusion'. While Istanbul, Ankara and Izmir are the primary centres of development in the country with a place in the first level of development, Kocaeli and Bursa have joined the developmental process and have also become centres of attraction as a result of activities that are diffused from Istanbul. Similar tendencies can be observed in provinces belonging to other levels in a hierarchical order. The activities culminating in development originate in upper level cities and diffuse to lower level ones in time.

POPULATION DISTRIBUTION BY POPULATION GROUPS FROM 1950 TO 1997

When settlements are examined in terms of the sizes of their population, it is clear that the highest increase is in the number of settlements with a population between 100001 and 500000 (Table 13.4). The number of settlements which have a population between 100001 and 500000 increased more than 20 times from 4 in 1950 to 85 in 1997. On the other hand, the number of settlements that have a population of over 500000 increased from 1 in 1950 to 10 in 1997. The number of settlements with populations of between 25000 and 100 000 increased in the period 1950-97, while there was not an important change in other groups with the exception of the settlements with a population between 2001 and 5000.

When the distribution of the population of the country is studied in terms of the share of the population per city size category, it is clear that settlements with than 2000 inhabitants tended to decreased dramatically while the settlements with more than 25000 increased (Table 13.5). The percentage of settlements which had a population under 2000 decreased from 71 per cent in 1950 to 21.9 per cent in 1997. On the other hand, settlements which had a population of between 100001 and 500000 increased from 8.2 per cent to 32.4 per cent over the same period. The percentage of settlements with populations over 500000 had also increased from 1.8 per cent in 1970 to 9.8 per cent in 1997. As a result, it can be stated that according to the 1997 census, 57 per cent of the total population lives in settlements with a population exceeding 25000. The direction of migration, therefore, tends towards intermediate sized cities and metropolitan areas.

In terms of its development characteristics the national urban system was in the 'urbanization phase' from 1950 to 1970 (Figure 13.4). During this period a large proportion of the population lived in settlements with less than 10000 inhabitants, while the term 'urban' was associated with settlements with more than 10000 inhabitants. Another outstanding feature of this period was the growth of large (100001 – 500000) and intermediate-

Table 13.4 Number of cities and villages by population group and census year,
1950-97

Population group	1950	1955	1960	1965	1970	1975	1980	1985	1990	1997
Total	34737	35331	36064	36259	36634	36753	36793	36667	37120	38288
0-2 000	34372	34898	35552	34905	34860	34720	34678	34423	34420	35230
2 001-5 000	165	189	220	948	1368	1424	1448	1512	1817	2016
5 001-10 000	98	123	144	206	161	267	288	333	398	465
10 001-25 000	71	78	91	123	131	194	206	222	257	290
25 001-100 000	26	37	48	63	82	110	128	124	155	192
100 001-500 000	4	5	8	11	29	35	41	45	66	85
500 000+	1	1	1	3	3	3	4	8	7	10

Notes:
Number of cities: Number of provincial centres and district centres. (The district centres within municipal boundaries of metropolises are shown in their respective population groups).
Number of villages: Number of sub-districts and villages (muhtarlik) outside the municipal boundaries of province and district centres.

Source: Various publications of S.I.S. (State Institute of Statistics)

sized cities (10001   100000). On the other hand, large cities before the 1970s (100001   500000) are now becoming intermediate-sized cities, while larger cities (now 500000 +) start to grow. In the next period, between 1975 and 1990, it is observed that both intermediate sized cities and primate cities grew, while previous intermediate-sized cities (10001   100000) are now becoming relatively small and starting to stagnate. It can be said that the country started moving towards the 'polarization reversal phase' (Geyer, 1996) after 1985. Large cities (500 000+) started to decline while intermediate-sized cities (100001   500000) continued to attract people. It is expected that the urban system may enter the counter-urbanization phase in the future.

Table 13.5   Share of population group by total population and census year,
1950-97 (%)

Population group	1950*	1955	1960	1965	1970	1975	1980	1985	1990	1997
Total	100	100	100	100	100	100	100	100	100	100
-2 000	71	66	61.9	57.2	49.8	44.2	41	35.7	29.7	21.9
2 001-5 000	6.4	7.4	7.7	8.5	10	10	9.2	8.7	9.3	9.1
5 001-10 000	3.7	4.1	4.3	4.5	4.5	4.3	4.3	4.5	4.7	4.9
10 001-25 000	5.3	5.4	5.6	6	6.3	7.1	7	6.6	6.8	7
25 001-100 000	5.2	7	8.4	8.8	11	12.4	13.8	11.4	12.8	14.9
100 001-500 000	8.2	10.1	12.1	15	16.6	17.1	18.8	21.5	27.4	32.4
500 001+	-	-	-	-	1.8	4.7	5.9	11.6	9.3	9.8

Notes: The district centres within municipal boundaries of metropolises are shown in
their respective population groups.
* Population outside enumeration districts = 73495

Source: Various publications of S.I.S. (State Institute of Statistics)

Figure 13.4 Differential urbanization in Turkey, 1950-97

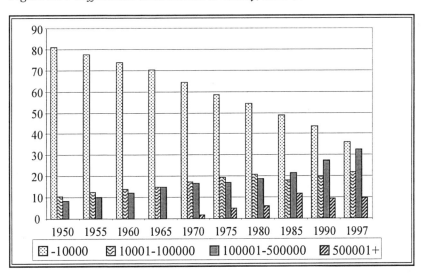

Source :   See Table 13.5

THE LAST DECADE OF URBANIZATION, 1990-1997

The regional distribution of population during the 1990-97 period indicated movement of people characterized by a differentiation on an unprecedented scale. From 1985 to 1990, 12 provinces experienced a decline in their population, as compared to 26 in 1990-97. In 1985-90, 14 provinces had annual average increases of zero to one per cent which rose to 21 during the subsequent period. The Black Sea and the Eastern Anatolian regions continued to lose their population (Figure 13.5).

On the other hand, in 1997, five Turkish cities had a population of over 1 million: Istanbul, Ankara, Izmir, Adana and Bursa, which together accounted for 39.4 per cent of the total urban population. Ankara and Izmir, as compared to the remaining three cities, exhibited a different pattern. During the 1990-97 period, the rate of growth of the urban population of Ankara and Izmir remained below the average rate of growth for the first time. On the other hand, in the same period, the top ten provinces with the most rapid growth rates were Antalya, Adiyaman, Sanliurfa, Kocaeli, Istanbul, Hakkari, Bursa, Yalova, Tekirdag and Sirnak (Figure 13.5). A significant change is observed in this ranking when the population of the centres of these provinces is considered. All of the top ten provinces with the highest population growth rates are in the Southeast (Adiyaman, Sirnak, Hakkari, Bingol, Siirt, Mus, Sanliurfa, Van, Malatya and Batman). Some of these cities recorded annual growth rates of as high as 10 per cent, which is far beyond that which can be considered as natural. Among these, Adiyaman more than doubled its population over a period of seven years. In the absence of any sharp increase in the total province population, the high rates of increase in the populations of provincial centres suggest an intensive intra-province shift of population from rural areas to centres. It is also known that there is significant migration from these provinces to neighbouring ones (Adana, Gaziantep and İçel), and the former cities serve the function of some sort of stopover stations.

The population growth rate by province in the 1990-97 period suggests the existence of three growth poles[2] in Turkey (Figure 13.6) as was indicated by Isik in his study on the recent dynamics of urbanization (Isik and Guvenc, 1999; Isik, 2000). These three growth poles are quite different from one another in terms of dynamics for development:

❑   Istanbul metropolitan area and its hinterland (Istanbul, Kocaeli, Yalova, Bursa, and Tekirdag);
❑   The coastal areas (Izmir, Mugla, Antalya, and Icel);

---

[2] The author uses the concept 'growth pole' as a spatial unit that pulls population and capital from its hinterland and differs from the rest of the country in terms of its potential for rapid growth.

Figure 13.5 Population rates of change, 1990-97 (%)

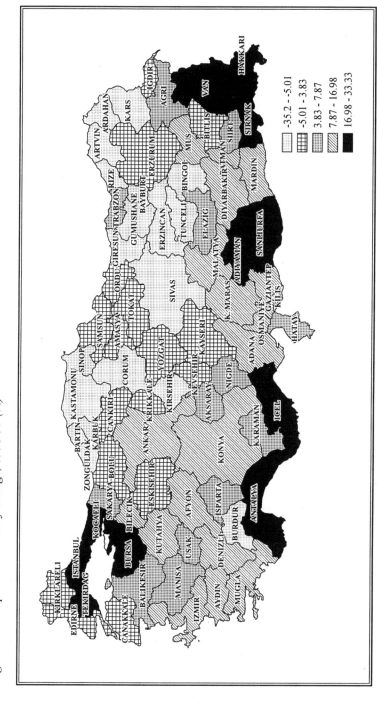

-35.2 - -5.01
-5.01 - 3.83
3.83 - 7.87
7.87 - 16.98
16.98 - 33.33

343

Source: S.I.S. (1999)

Figure 13.6 Annual population growth rates of provinces, 1990-97 (%)

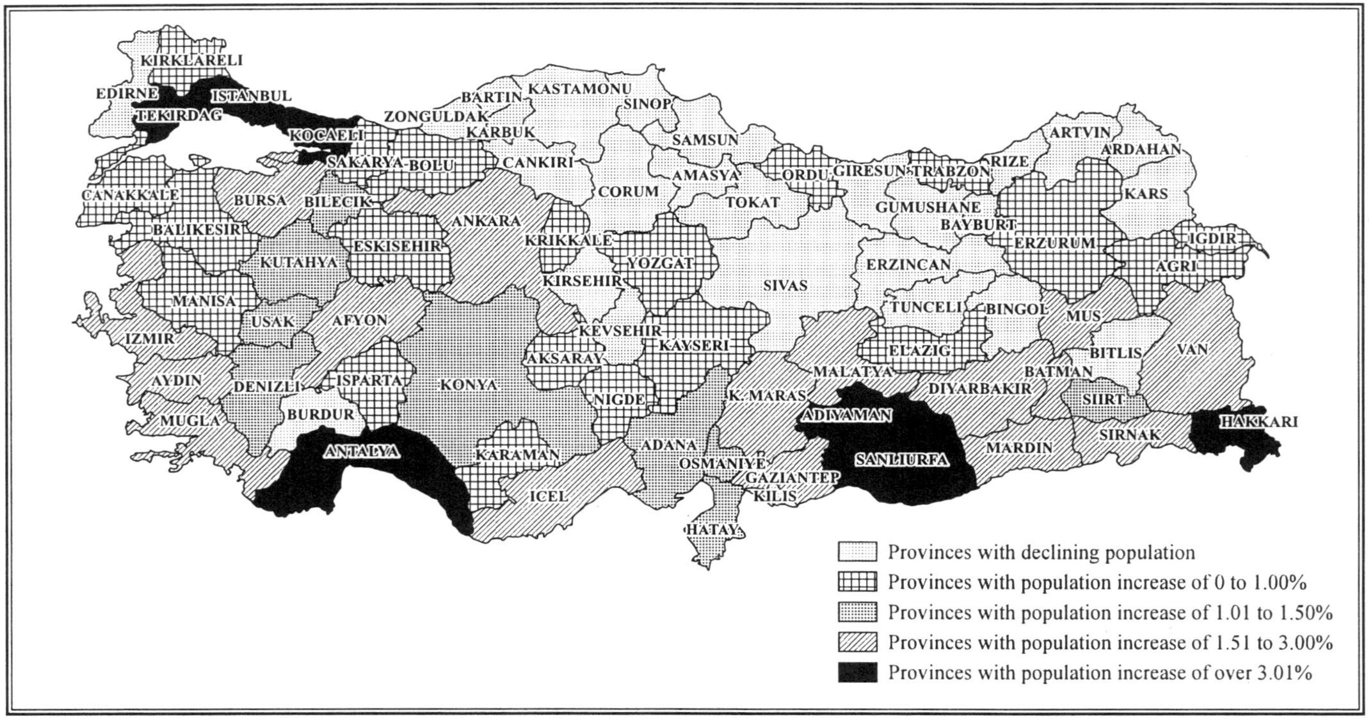

Provinces with declining population
Provinces with population increase of 0 to 1.00%
Provinces with population increase of 1.01 to 1.50%
Provinces with population increase of 1.51 to 3.00%
Provinces with population increase of over 3.01%

Source: S.I.S. (1999)

❑ The southeastern region (Adiyaman, Sanliurfa, Hakkari, Sirnak, Van, Diyarbakir, Malatya, Batman, and Mardin).

An investigation of population movements in provinces and districts during the 1990-97 period has revealed that interregional differences in population growth rates have become more pronounced and the large cities have to some extent ceased to be the sole growth poles which they were in the early years of urbanization. On the other hand, regional centres with high potential for development have come to the fore as important centres for growth.

As a result, the major features of transformation in Turkish settlement structure can be summarized as described in the Turkey National Report and Action Plan, Habitat II; (1) the rising rate of urbanization, (2) concentration in coastal regions, (3) uneven spatial growth, and (4) intensification of the network of relationships between settlements (Habitat II, 1996).

INTERNAL MIGRATION

Migration within the country follows certain fixed patterns. The first is migration from rural to urban areas. This was one of the major trends from the 1950s until the 1980s, but it lost its momentum when the natural population growth in the rural areas started to decline. The decline in rural to urban migration during the 1980s was accompanied by a considerable rise in inter-city migration. This seems to be motivated by a lack of employment opportunities in lagging urban areas and the availability of job opportunities in growing cities and more developed regions of the country. By and large, migrants in this group consist of people that are better qualified and, therefore, a selective process seems to be in operation. As a result this migration leads to a further decline in development locally. In the last decade, a lack of security[3] and the consequent evacuation of villages in Eastern Anatolia has also led to population displacement. In total approximately 300000 people were displaced in this manner over the last decade. Other factors that played a role in the displacement of people include the construction of dams,[4] which forced approximately 75 000 families to move

---

[3] In the last decade, Eastern Anatolia was dangerous to live in because of terrorist activities. As a result of terrorist attacks approximately 30000 people died between 1984 and 2000. This security problem has created two kinds of involuntary migration: (1) people that have fled to safer areas on their own accord, and (2) people that were evacuated from a number of small villages in this region as part of the government's anti-terrorist strategy.

[4] The choice of dam sites sometimes creates problems in Turkey. In certain cases heritage sites are being affected, such as Hasankeyf and Zeugma in the planning of the two new dams.

(Habitat II, 1996) and the Marmara Earthquake on August 17, 1999 which also resulted in the migration of people from the major earthquake zone. However, there are no data currently available on the extent of this evacuation since the results of the 2000 census have not yet been released.

THE HISTORY OF INTERNAL MIGRATION

In various studies on the history of internal migration in Turkey (Icduygu, and Unalan, 1998; Icduygu and Sirkeci, 1999), three fundamental stages seem to have overlapped, each one identifiable in terms of its basic characteristics. The three stages cover the period from 1950 to the early 1960s, the late 1960s until early 1980s, and after 1980. Each of these periods exhibits specific identifiable features that differ significantly from one another.

The internal migration which started and subsequently accelerated in the 1950s could have been caused by momentum gained from the transformation of the rural areas (see Table 13.6 for reasons). Migration that occurred from the late 1960s until the beginning of the 1980s can be ascribed to 'pull factors' caused by changes in urban areas. During the 1980s and the 1990s the process of internal migration entered a new phase caused by the advancements in communication technology and skills which had a profound effect on the migration of people. Figure 13.7 shows the dynamics of migra-

Figure 13.7 Dynamics of migration

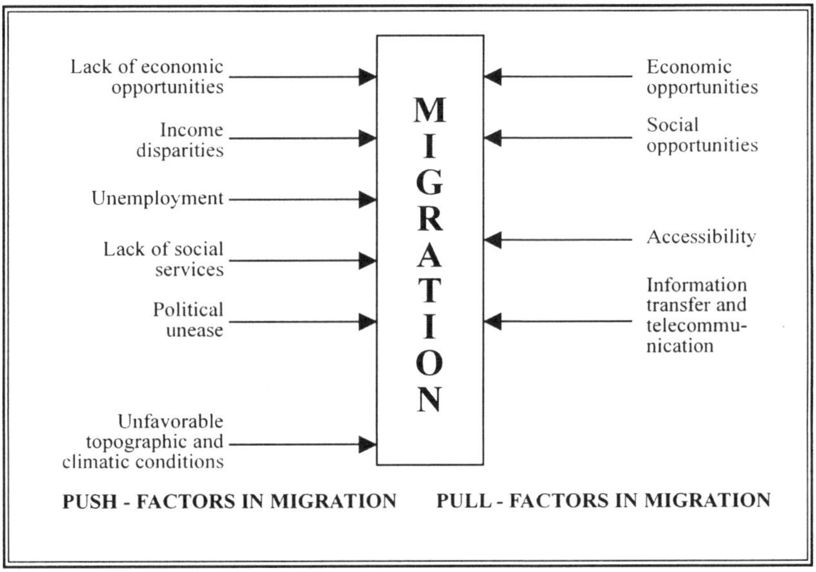

Source: S.P.O. (1991)

tion in Turkey and Table 13.6 summarizes the main characteristics of the three different stages of internal migration.

During the period from 1950 to 1985 Turkey witnessed the increase as well as the loss of momentum of the process of rural to urban migration. From 1945 to 1950, 214000 migrated to the cities. While this number increased many times to 904000 over the next five years, the number remained fairly constant over the subsequent two five-year periods (Table 13.7). There was another sudden increase during 1965-70 when the number of people migrating from rural to urban areas doubled again to 1896000. Over the next two five-year periods the number, once again, did not change considerably and, in fact, diminished a little to 1692000 during 1975 to1980. In the period between 1980 and 1985 the net number of people migrating from rural to urban areas became 1.5 times that of the previous five-year period reaching 2582000 and showed only a slight increase during 1985-90 (S.I.S., 1995). As indicated in Table 13.7, the greatest contribution to the growth of the urban population is through rural-urban migration. An evaluation of the contribution of internal migration to the growth of the urban population shows that during 1945 to1990, rural-urban migration was responsible, on average, for 52 per cent of the urban population growth, whereas 30 per cent of the growth was due to natural increase, 15 per cent to reclassification of places from rural to urban and 3 per cent to net emigration. As these percentages indicate, migration is the most important contributor to urbanization since 1945.

NET MIGRATION BY REGIONS

A 15-year historical review of the net stream of migrations involving five demographic regions of Turkey showed that the migratory trend is negative (net out-migration) for the eastern, northern and central regions of the country, whereas there is a positive trend towards the southern and western regions, particularly towards cities with populations over 500 000 (Table 13.8 and Table 13.9). The western regions are undergoing growth faster than any one of the others and their growth seems to be gaining momentum with the passage of each five-year period. There is a similar tendency in southern regions, but the figures are much smaller. Thus, it appears that the western regions are more attractive to live in than the others. Southern areas are also attractive, but the growth of population there is not as much as in the western parts of the country. There are fewer attractive factors in regions elsewhere.

MIGRATION BETWEEN DIFFERENT TYPES OF SETTLEMENTS

Migration between different types of settlements has been studied by Gedik in relation to three administrative units: provincial centres, district centers and sub-district centres and villages, a total of nine streams of migrations.

Table 13.6 The main characteristics of the stages of internal migration

Push factors developed in rural areas 1950s-1960s	Pull factors developed in urban areas 1960s-1970s-1980s	Increased communication activities influencing the movement of populations 1980s-1990s
Factors culminating in migration: □ Mechanization and modernization of agriculture □ Change in the policy of land-ownership □ Loss of land or ownership of land by specific people □ Development of transportation *Factors causing migration to gather momentum:* □ High population growth □ Low agricultural productivity □ Increased unemployment in rural areas □ Low levels of education	*Factors causing migration to gather momentum:* □ Widening of the gap between rural and urban income □ Increased attraction of urban economy and social life □ Improvement in transport and communication facilities *Consequences of migration in urban areas:* □ Stagnant industries and shortage of employment opportunities □ Insufficient housing for people moving to urban areas □ Inability of urban areas to absorb the rapidly increasing rural population due to factors mentioned above □ The increase in the ratio of employed migrants living as squatters and earning a living illegitimately □ The majority of the labour force migrating to large cities such as Istanbul, Ankara and Izmir □ Intensified urban-urban migration towards the end of the 1970s as compared to rural-urban migration during the 1960s and the 1970s	*Factors affecting migratory movements and the kind of effects produced:* □ Reorganization of the economy as a free market economy; privatization □ Birth of new national and international problems as a consequence of globalization *Migrations with political nature and consequences:* □ Intensification of internal migration caused by political factors which resulted in the distinction between 'involuntary' and 'voluntary' migration □ Insecurity in Eastern and Southeastern Anatolian regions forcing migration of a significant portion of the population, first to neighbouring provinces considered to be more secure, followed by further westward migration towards larger provinces, especially Istanbul, Izmir, Adana and Icel
Basic characteristic of the period: □ Rapid departure from village and village life	*Basic characteristic of the period:* □ The period of structural features and their transformation leaving a mark on problems of internal migration.	*Basic characteristic of the period* □ A period of increased social mobility with continuity in the development of transportation and communication facilities and increased emphasis on individual and social life

Table 13.7 The contribution of migration to urban growth, 1945-90

Period	Net total urban growth	Net internal rural to urban migration		Reclassification of places from rural to urban		Natural increase		Net emigration	
	(1000)	(1000)	%	(1000)	%	(1000)	%	(1000)	%
1945-50	340	214	63	50	15	70	20	6	2
1950-55	1643	904	55	210	13	399	30	130	8
1955-60	1883	964	51	330	18	539	28	50	3
1960-65	1075	1027	49	390	19	608	30	50	2
1965-70	3371	1896	56	650	19	800	24	25	1
1970-75	3953	2072	52	630	16	1176	30	75	2
1975-80	3623	1692	47	440	12	1316	36	175	5
1980-85	5560	2582	46	650	12	2078	37	250	5
1985-90	5960	2654	45	700	12	2061	35	500	8

Notes: * In Turkey, urban is defined according to two different criteria: (1) cities, which is an administrative measure and comprises the areas within the municipal boundaries of the province and district centres, (2) settlements with more than 10 000 inhabitants. The population of places is reclassified from rural to urban whenever the general process of growth raises the population of a place to 10 000 or more.

Source: S.I.S. (1995)

Based on this study, the fundamental trends in internal migration were described and new insights were gained in relation to some of the contradictory findings reported in the literature concerning the developing countries (Gedik, 1996; 1997; 1998). In the exchange of migrants between the three types of settlements they favoured 'higher' order settlements. For example, the provincial centres always experienced net in-migration both from villages and from district centres. District centres always had net out-migration to provincial centres, and received net in-migration from villages, with the exception of the period 1975-80 when there was a net out-migration to villages probably because of the adverse national socio-economic conditions. Villages always lost population to provincial and district centres, except between 1975 and 1980 (Gedik, 1998). Therefore, it can be concluded that the net transfer of migrants from villages and district centers was

Table 13.8 Net migration and rate of net migration 1975-90, by region

	1975-80			1980-85			1985-90		
Regions	Population with permanent residency 1980	Net migration	Rate of net migration %	Population with permanent residency 1985	Net migration	Rate of net migration %	Population with permanent residency 1990	Net migration	Rate of net migration %
Total	38,395,730	0	0	44,078,033	0	0	49,986,117	0	0
West	11,603,753	528,964	47	13,710,562	490,730	36	16,345,907	1,035,038	65
South	4,875,556	68,311	14	5,820,200	93,239	16	6,891,451	180,280	27
Central	9,201,848	-52,602	-6	10,394,339	-69,819	-7	11,470,858	184,844	-16
North	4,841,919	-102,047	-21	5,265,487	-155,387	-29	5,475,966	321,691	-57
East	7,872,654	-442,626	-55	8,887,445	-358,763	-40	9,801,935	708,783	-70

Notes:
West: Aydin, Balikesir, Bursa, Canakkale, Denizli, Edirne, Istanbul, Izmir, Kirklareli, Kocaeli, Manisa, Sakarya, Tekirdag.
South: Adana, Antalya, Burdur, Gaziantep, Hatay, Isparta, Icel, Mugla.
Central: Afyon, Ankara, Bilecik, Bolu, Cankiri, Corum, Eskisehir, Kayseri, Kirsehir, Konya, Kutahya, Nevsehir, Nigde, Tokat, Usak, Yozgat, Aksaray, Karaman, Kirikkale.
North: Amasya, Artvin, Giresun, Kastamonu, Ordu, Rize, Samsun, Sinop, Trabzon, Zonguldak, Bartin.
East: Adiyaman, Agri, Bingol, Bitlis, Diyarbakir, Elazig, Erzincan, Erzurum, Gumushane, Hakkari, Kars, Malatya, Kahramanmaras, Mardin, Mus, Siirt, Sivas, Tunceli, Sanliurfa, Van, Bayburt, Batman, Sirnak, Ardahan.

Source: Demirci and Sunar (1998)

Table 13.9 Net migration to cities with a population over 500 000, 1980-90

City	Five year period	Five year periods of time Net migrants (1000)	Yearly numbers and rates Net migrants (1000)	Migrants per 1000 population
Istanbul	1980-85	601.1	120.2	24.2
	1985-90	666.7	133.3	22.0
Ankara	1980-85	121.6	24.3	11.8
	1985-90	57.0	11.4	4.7
Izmir	1980-85	155.0	31.0	22.8
	1985-90	150.4	30.1	18.6
Adana	1980-85	98.7	19.7	29.5
	1985-90	47.0	9.4	11.2
Bursa	1980-85	77.8	15.6	28.2
	1985-90	125.0	25.0	33.6
Gaziantep	1980-85	39.1	7.8	18.4
	1985-90	47.5	9.5	17.6
Konya	1980-85	42.5	8.5	21.6
	1985-90	21.8	4.4	9.2

Source: S.I.S. (1995)

Table 13.10 The percentages of different streams of migration in terms of the total number of migrants, 1965-85

	1965-70	1975-80	1980-85
From district centre to provincial centre	15.1 (3)	21.3 (1)	20.3 (1)
From provincial centre to provincial centre	11.2 (4)	11.9 (3)	16.9 (2)
From village to provincial centre	17.0 (2)	9.9 (4)	14.2 (3)
From provincial centre to district centre	7.0 (7)	6.5 (9)	9.9 (4)
From district centre to district centre	5.8 (9)	9.2 (7)	9.1 (5)
From village to district centre	10.4 (5)	7.1 (8)	8.3 (7)
From provincial centre to village	9.3 (6)	9.8 (5)	6.7 (8)
From district centre to village	6.2 (8)	9.6 (6)	6.2 (9)
From village to village	17.9 (1)	14.8 (2)	8.5 (6)

Notes: The numbers in parentheses indicate the order of contribution (in descending order). The migrations during the period 1970-1975 were not analyzed by Gedik because of unreliable data.

Source: Gedik (1996)

largely towards provincial centers (Table 13.10). According to this trend, it can be predicted that district centres will also experience reductions in population in future as is the case with villages, but the loss in the former is expected to be less than in the latter (otherwise they would have lost their 'district' status).

One of the important findings in Gedik's study is the significance of the other factors as 'push factors'. It is generally emphasized that 'push factors' include low rural income, inadequate infrastructure, deficient facilities and services which affect the rates of out-migration from rural to urban areas. However, the analysis of the Turkish data by Gedik indicated that factors such as the educational skill and the level of knowledge of the potential rural migrant, facilities of transportation and communication and the presence of previous migrants that are relatives, friends and people from the same village were at least as significant as the push factors mentioned earlier (Gedik, 1996, 1997, 1998). The significance of these factors indicated that the socio-psychological distances seem to be more meaningful than physical distances.

Another important finding in Gedik's study is that there is more urban to urban migration among the total number of migrants in the country. This contradicts the general notion amongst scholars that rural to urban migration is more prominent in less developed countries. In the study of migration between different types of settlements it is observed that city to city migration is most common and has increased from 39.2 per cent to 62.2 per cent between 1965 and 1990, while the percentage of village to city migration among the total number of migrants decreased from 23 per cent to 18 per cent in the last two periods (Table 13.11 and Figure 13.8). According

Table 13.11 Trends in migration between different types of settlement, 1965-90 (%)

Settlement types	1965-70	1975-80	1980-85	1985-90
From city to city*	39.2	48.9	56.2	62.2
From village to city*	27.4	17.0	22.5	17.9
From city to village*	15.5	19.3	12.8	12.6
From village to village	17.9	14.8	8.5	7.3
Total	100.0	100.0	100.0	100.0

Source: Gedik (1996); S.I.S, (1997)

Note: * Includes both the provincial centres and district centres. The migrations during the period 1970-1975 were not analysed by Gedik because of unreliable data.

Figure 13.8 Migration between different types of settlements

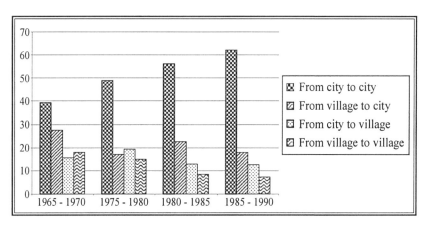

Source: See Table 13.11

to Gedik's study, during the period of rapid urbanization from 1965 to 1970, rural to urban migration was the second most important migration stream with a contribution of 27.4 per cent. On the other hand, about 4 per cent of the village population migrated between villages, a percentage that increased to 17.9 per cent in the period from 1965 to 1970.

Although Geyer and Kontuly (1993) and Geyer (1996) have stressed the importance of counter stream migration in developing countries, it is generally believed urban to rural return-migration does not exist or is of a negligible magnitude in such countries.[5] However, according to calculations done by Gedik, the ratio of the urban to rural counter stream was approximately 50 per cent during the period from 1965 to 1985 (Gedik, 1996, 1997). Moreover, it was observed that return-migration to villages increased significantly between 1975 and 1980 (Table 13.10, Table 13.11 and Figure 13.8). Gedik noted that the return of Turkish workers from Europe and adverse national socio-economic conditions could be responsible for the return of migrants to villages. Another view is that the maximum numbers of out-migration are observed in the least developed regions of Eastern and Southeastern Turkey. However, according to findings of Gedik, the highest rural to urban migration rates between 1965 and 1970 involved the developed regions in the western and central parts of the country, especially the provinces which are close to the three metropolises of Istanbul, Ankara and Izmir. On the other hand, the rural to urban migration rates in the least developed regions in eastern and southeastern parts of Turkey have the lowest value (0-25 per cent).

According to these trends, it can be said that in the future: (1) villages will continue to be depopulated but their role as a source of net migration will diminish, (2) the district centres, similar to villages, will also experience depopulation but the role of district centres in the net overall migration towards provincial centres will continue to increase, (3) an over-all decrease in net migration rates will continue, as the level of urbanization and the proportion of the young mobile population decrease.

On the other hand, another study conducted by Gedik in 1992 indicated that the consequences of migration gradually resemble those in Developed Countries (Gedik, 1992). According to the study, the effects of migration on urban growth are contradictory to those observed for Developed Countries by Lowry in 1966 (Table 13.12). However, the data also indicated that with further developments in Turkey, the migration patterns might approximate those found for Developed Countries.

Gedik emphasized that possible factors behind the observed differences between Turkey and the developed countries are: (1) the differences in demographic characteristics and the resultant age structure, (2) informal

---

[5] Turkey is included in this group.

Table 13.12   A comparison between Turkey and Developed Countries: migration rates to/from urban areas

Developed Countries	Turkey
Relatively constant out-migration rates relative to in-migration rates; relatively constant 'emitting' capacity.	Relatively constant in-migration rates relative to out-migration rates; relatively constant attraction capacity.
In-migration and out-migration rates highly related.	In-migration and out-migration rates not related.
Net-migration more related to in-migration than out-migration rates.	Net-migration is more related to out-migration than in-migration rates.
Large values for net in-migration due to very high in-migration rates, rather than to low out-migration rates.	Large values for net in-migration due to very low out-migration rates, rather than to large in-migration rates.
Large values for net out-migration due to minimum in-migration rates, rather than to large out-migration rates.	Large values for net out-migration due to very high out-migration rates, rather than to low in-migration rates.
Directions of net migration, and out- and in-migration, are positive. Influence of pull-push factors is doubtful.	Clear demonstration of the role of pull-push factors. (Direction of relationship between net migration and in-migration is positive; it is negative between net migration and out-migration).

Source: Gedik (1992)

employment, (3) dependence on friends and relatives, (4) significant influences of intra-regional and stepwise migration on migration patterns.

THE IMPACT OF MIGRATION ON URBANIZATION

Since the beginning of the massive rural out-migration in the 1950s, the development of squatter housing, the Turkish 'gecekondu', has been the most basic phenomenon that helped to alleviate the turbulent effects of mass migration. Gecekondu, which is legally defined as a shelter built on somebody else's land without permission, first emerged in the early stages of Turkey's urbanization process as a basic form of habitation for the newcomers to the city. However, the construction process and the mechanism of establishing gecekondu changed over time and gecekondu became an instrument of urban economic rent. On the other hand, the share of the urban population living in gecekondu dwellings increased from 4.7 per cent in 1955 to 33.9 per cent in 1990 (Table 13.13).

Table 13.13 Gecekondu dwellings and population

Year	Total number of gecekondu dwellings	Gecekondu population	Share of urban population living in gecekondu dwellings (%)
1955	50,000	250,000	4.7
1960	240,000	1,200,000	16.4
1965	430,000	2,150,000	22.9
1970	600,000	3,000,000	23.6
1980	1,150,000	5,750,000	26.1
1990	1,750,000	8,750,000	33.9

Source: Keles (1990)

The construction of the first generation of gecekondu was not market related. This first phase of construction of gecekondu provides very important clues as to the first phase of Turkish urbanization. Rural out-migration occurred as a multilevel process within specific personal networks. The rural immigrant often contacts co-villagers who have already moved to the city and arrives at the city after having being assured of finding a slot in the labour market. On the other hand, the relationship with the rural area is maintained at least temporarily, which has positive effects on the welfare of new arrivals and thus social problems created by internal migration can be easily avoided. However, the characteristics of the first generation gecekondu do not apply to the second generation that emerged in 1970s, the period during which the conditions of construction of gecekondu began to change rapidly.

It has been emphasized in a number of studies that informal housing does not have the same attributes today as it had in the 1950s and 1960s (Keles, 1990; D.P.T., 1991; Tekeli, 1992; Senyapili, 1992; Habitat II, 1996; Ozuekren, 1998; Isik and Guvenc, 1999; Isik, 2000). The gecekondu that the users built to own a place for themselves and their families in the city have, in time, been turned into an instrument of speculation (Table 13.14). Informal and illegal real estate agents (also called the 'land mafia') appeared on the scene, and they were responsible for the second-generation gecekondu. While the demand for housing was driven by the need for shelter at the beginning of the urbanization process, poor squatters improved their dwellings in order to live more comfortably or to obtain extra income by renting rooms in later stages. During this stage, a second or third home was built to secure the future of the children. Likewise, the middle income groups bought second or third dwellings for the same reason. Thus, housing came to be seen as a good investment because the increase in housing prices exceeded the rise in the inflation rate. It can be said that although the first phase of development of gecekondu was in general positive, the second stage seems to carry potential for creation of several socio-economic and urban problems that planners will not be able to solve easily. Competition is strong today for land on the fringes of urban areas among the higher income groups wanting to move away from the congestion, pollution and insufficient infrastructural services in central areas. It can be said that the gecekondu phase of the 1950s is now being repeated in the peripheral areas among middle and high income groups that keep building residences without permits, using their financial power and networks of relations and information.

CONCLUSION

These factors imply that the process of urbanization in Turkey in the 21st century will be very different from that of the past. According to the trends observed in the demographic structure, the dynamics of urbanization and streams of migration in Turkey will face new, different and sometimes unexpected challenges in political, economic and social fields. The concluding remarks on these developmental trends, expectations and projections for the future can be summarised as follows:

DEMOGRAPHIC TRENDS

❑ Population trends and projections indicate that Turkey's demographic transition is almost over. The population growth rate has slowed down and has approached the trends of developed countries. The population of Turkey is expected to stabilize at around 95 million by the middle of the 21st century.

❑ It is expected that the age structure of the population will also change rapidly with the declining rate of growth. The population between ages 20-65, that is the potential labour force, will increase over the first quarter of this new century. As a result, Turkey will face the demographic condition known as the 'window of opportunity' when there will be a rise in the national per capita income while the population growth slows down. This will transform Turkey into a country that can take her place among the developed countries of Europe.

However, demographic change also brings some important problems:

❑ The issue of an aging population is a demographic problem that Turkey has never faced until now.

Table 13.14 Main features of the phases of development of gecekondu

1950s-1960s First phase of construction of gecekondu	1970s-1980s Second phase of construction of gecekondu	1990s
Identity of owner-builder-dweller	Dissapearance of identity of owner-builder-dweller	The changing meaning of gecekondu and its transformation into an instrument of urban economic rent
Tenancy is exceptional	Increase in tenancy, onwership of more than one gecekondu	
Flexibility in the construction and utilization process (changes for user needs)	Disappearance of flexibility in the construction and utilization process with the participation of new social groups and the emerging of a market which has its own special rules	
Construction for their own needs	Construction for others, commercialization of gecekondu	
Construction outside the market mechanism	Construction by a special land-and-construction market for gecekondu	
Construction process on public land by the user's own labour	Construction process on land in urban peripheries by the other groups	
Relatively high environmental quality	A prominent decline in environmental quality with respect to first generation of gecekondu	Deterioration of environmental standards, commercialization of squatter housing at the expense of healthy and safe living conditions and occupation of the most ecologically vulnerable areas, such as forests, flood plains and water basins.
Illegal occupation of public land	The pieces of land in urban peripheries which are parcelled and put on sale by their owners	
Single-storey houses	Transformation from one-storey to multi-storey apartment blocks because of the pardons and construction laws for squatter settlements in the 1980s	
Gecekondu as the result of migration from rural areas to urban areas	Gecekondu as the cause of migration from rural areas to urban areas	
Gecekondu not an instrument of specualtion	Transformation of the gecekondu to an instrument of speculation	

Source : Author

❑ The fact that the young population will cease to grow numerically and then diminish in size will be the source of another change.

❑ According to the trends observed in demographic structure, Turkey will have to change its order of priorities. The social security system, the health system and the health institutions, the educational system and the regional distribution of educational opportunities should be restructured in accordance with expected developments.

URBANIZATION TRENDS

❑ Turkey's urban population increased from 25 per cent to 65 per cent in the last fifty years and today 57 per cent of the total population lives in settlements which have a population of over 25 000. It can be said that in the future the population of the settlements which have a population over 25 000 will continue to increase and spatial distributions of population will continue to change in accordance with these trends.

❑ The urbanization process in Turkey is closely related to regional disparities and these disparities have created two sets of problems: the problems of the 'metropolis' caused by excessive growth in developed regions and the problems of 'underdeveloped regions'. The intensity in migration is central in this dilemma. There is a population shift from the northern and northeastern regions to the western, southern and south-eastern regions of Turkey. According to regional disparities and trends observed in migration, it can be said that the share of population in the Marmara, the Mediterranean and the southeastern regions of Anatolia will increase in the future, while the Black Sea and Eastern Anatolian regions will continue to decrease in population. On the other hand, the problems of the 'metropolis' and the 'underdeveloped regions' will also continue in parallel to regional disparities and streams of migration.

❑ According to the spatial developmental trends which are determined by dynamics of 'diffusion', it can be said that Istanbul metropolitan area and its hinterland, coastal areas and southeastern regions will continue to develop in the future as three growth poles in Turkey. However, the developmental activities, diffusing particularly from these three growth poles, will in time spread to other cities and regions down the hierarchy.

MIGRATION TRENDS

❑ The better means and availability of transportation facilities, together with the developments in communication and informational technologies in the twentieth century, have provided more freedom of mobility for people. In this connection, internal and international migrations are expected to accelerate in Turkey.

❏ Likewise the demographic trends and the effects of migration also increasingly come to resemble those of the Developed Countries.

❏ It is also possible to state that the rural to urban migration that was experienced in Turkey between 1950 and 1980 will continue to decline. However, internal migration is expected to continue between cities.

Based on trends in migration between different types of settlements, it can be stated that in the future:

❏ Villages will continue to be depopulated but their role as a source of net migration will decrease.

❏ The district centres, similar to villages, will experience depopulation but the role of the district centres in net migration rates will continue to increase.

❏ An overall decrease in net migration rates will continue as the level of urbanization and the proportion of young mobile population decreases.

❏ It can be assumed that metropolises such as Istanbul, Ankara, and Izmir will remain important destinations of international migrants. Second metropolis areas such as the Southern Marmara region (Bursa, Kocaeli, Sakarya) and the Cukurova (Adana, İçel, Gaziantep) region will increasingly attract migrants. As a result, Turkey will have to re-organize its order of priorities and pay attention to the restructuring of its institutions according to observed trends and future expectations.

REFERENCES

Demirci, M. and B. Sunar (1998), 'Nufus Sayimlari Ile Derlenen Icgoc Bilgisinin Degerlendirilmesi', *Turkiye'de Icgoc*, Turkiye'de Icgoc: Sorunsal Alanlari ve Arastirma Yontemleri Konferansi, 6-8 Haziran 1997, Bolu-Gerede, Turkiye Ekonomik ve Toplumsal Tarih Vakfi, Istanbul, pp. 125-151.

D.P.T. (1991), *Gecekondu Arastirmasi*, Sosyal Planlama Baskanligi, Arastirma Dairesi (State Planning Organization).

D.P.T. (1996), *Illerin Sosyo-Ekonomik Gelismislik Siralamasi Arastirmasi (1996)*, Bolgesel Gelisme ve Yapisal Uyum Genel Mudurlugu (State Planning Organization).

Gedik, A. (1992), 'The Effects of In- and Out-Migration on Urban Growth in Turkey (1965-85) and a Comparison with the Developed Countries', *Papers in Regional Science*, 71(4), 405-419.

Gedik, A. (1996), *Internal Migration in Turkey, 1965-1985: Test of Some Conflicting Findings in the Literature*, Working Papers in Demography, No: 66, The Australian National University, Research School of Social Sciences, Canberra.

Gedik, A. (1997), 'Internal Migration in Turkey, 1965-1985: Test of Conflicting Findings in the Literature', *Review of Urban and Regional Development Studies*, 9, 170-179.

Gedik, A. (1998), 'Trends in Migration Between Different Settlement Types: Turkey, 1965-90', *38th European Congress of the Regional Science Association, CD-Rom,* August 28-September 1, 1998, Vienna, Austria.

Geyer, H.S. (1996), 'Expanding the theoretical foundation of differential urbanization', *Tijdscrift voor Economiesche en Sociale Geografie,* 87(1), 44-59.

Geyer, H.S. and T.M. Kontuly (1993), 'A theoretical foundation for the concept of differential urbanization', *International Regional Science Review,* 15(2), 157-177.

Habitat II (1996), *Turkey: National Report and Plan of Action,* United Nations Conference on Human Settlements Habitat II, Istanbul.

Icduygu, A. and T. Unalan (1998), 'Turkiye'de Icgoc: Sorunsal Alanlari ve Arastirma Yontemleri', *Turkiye'de Icgoc,* Turkiye'de Icgoc: Sorunsal Alanlari ve Arastirma Yontemleri Konferansi, 6-8 Haziran 1997, Bolu-Gerede, Turkiye Ekonomik ve Toplumsal Tarih Vakfi, Istanbul, pp. 38-55.

Icduygu, A. and I. Sirkeci (1999), 'Cumhuriyet Donemi Turkiye'sinde Goc Hareketleri', *75 Yilda Koylerden Sehirlere,* Turkiye Ekonomik ve Toplumsal Tarih Vakfi, Istanbul, pp. 249-268.

Isik, O. (2000), 'Kentlere, Kentlesmeye ve 21. Yuzyilin Esiginde Turkiye Kentlerine Dair', *Toplum ve Hekim,* 14, 163-175.

Isik, O. and M. Guvenc (1999), 'The changing nature of Turkish urbanization and economic geography on the eve of the 21st century: new challenges and new opportunities', *Turkey's window of opportunity: demographic transition process and its consequences,* Istanbul: Turkish Industrialists' and Businessmen's Association (TUSIAD).

Keles, R. (1990), *Kentlesme Politikasi,* Ankara, Imge Kitabevi.

Ozuekren, S. (1998), 'Informal and formal housing construction in Turkey: blurred boundaries and regulations', in R. Hjerppe (ed), *Urbanization: its global trends, economics and governance,* Government Institute for Economic Research, UNU/WIDER, The Finnish Ministry of the Environment, Helsinki, Vatt Publications, pp.121-134.

Senyapili, T. (1992), 'A new stage of Gecekondu Housing in Istanbul', in Turkish Social Science Association, *Development of Istanbul Metropolitan Area and Low Cost Housing,* Municipality of Greater Istanbul, IULA-EMME-International Union of Local Authorities, Section for the Eastern Mediterranean and Middle East Region, pp. 182-209.

S.I.S. (1995), *The population of Turkey, 1923-1994: demographic structure and development,* Ankara, State Institute of Statistics (S.I.S).

S.I.S. (1999), *1997 Population count administrative division*, Ankara, State Institute of Statistics (S.I.S.).

S.P.O. (1991), *Planning tools of regional development for 1990's in Turkey*, State Planning Organization (S.P.O.) Department of Less Developed Regions.

Tekeli, I. (1992) 'Development of urban administration and planning in the formation of Istanbul Metropolitan Area', in Turkish Social Science Association, *Development of Istanbul Metropolitan Area and Low Cost Housing,* Municipality of Greater Istanbul, IULA-EMME-International Union of Local Authorities, Section for the Eastern Mediterranean and Middle East Region, pp. 3-111.

TUSIAD (1999), *Turkey's window of opportunity: demographic transition process and its consequences*, Istanbul, Turkish Industrialists' and Businessmen's Association (TUSIAD).

C. AMERICAN COUNTRIES

Chapter 14

A History of Recent Urban Development in the United States

W. H. Frey

INTRODUCTION

For a very long time there was a tendency among people in America to concentrate in the large and expanding cities of the United States while inside the cities there was a tendency to decentralize (Clark, 1967). Early on, the higher concentration of industries in certain parts of the country than in others played a major part in the direction of these migration flows. Although there was a gradual shift in focus away from industries to the tertiary and quaternary sectors in the US economy during the second part of the twentieth century, economic development based on factors such as the location of natural and human resources, distances to markets and scale economies kept on attracting people to the large metropolitan areas (Ullmann, 1958; Hoover, 1963; Richardson, 1973). This is perhaps the most important reason why the turnaround in the population concentration trends that was detected for the first time after the 1970 census results came as such a complete surprise (Beale, 1977). In the extensive body of literature that has developed on the migration reversal in the United States subsequently, three prominent characteristics of the phenomenon have been uncovered thus far: (i) de-concentrating streams of people seem to cascade down the urban hierarchy (Frey and Speare, 1988), (ii) the small and medium-sized cities closest to the core regions were the first to absorb de-concentrating migrants (Gordon, 1979), and (iii) the ripple-effect of the reversal was detected throughout the country, even in distant non-metropolitan areas in peripheral regions (Vining and Strauss, 1977; Vining, 1982).

Various factors that are related to the de-concentration trends in America have been highlighted since. They include the location of immigrants in

America (Frey and Liaw, 1998), and the locational dynamics caused by immigrants inside and between cities in the United States (Frey, 1998a; 1998b; 1998c; Frey and Geverdt, 1998). A migration trend that is impacting visibly on the American urban environment currently is the significant 'South to North' immigration, largely from Latin American and Asian origins. The destinations of these immigrants are unevenly distributed within the U.S. and concentrated primarily in selected large 'port of entry metropolitan areas'. Many of these same 'port of entry' areas are losing domestic migrants who are more likely to relocate in faster-growing, but smaller metropolitan areas, as well as non-metropolitan territories. Because the immigrant flows tend to have younger age structures and higher fertility levels than the U.S. native population, their 'port of entry' areas are becoming demographically distinct from the parts of the urban system that are attracting mostly domestic migrants. This chapter contrasts the demographic structures of immigrant 'port of entry' areas with other metropolitan and non-metropolitan areas. In so doing, the U.S. case study illustrates how 'South-to-North' migration is impacting settlement systems in Developed Countries in ways that further isolate immigrant groups from long-standing residents.

The chapter also demonstrates how immigration may serve to reinvigorate previously declining populations in large metropolitan areas that otherwise sustain losses. At the same time, the new immigrant settlement clusters in selected metropolitan areas may be adding a further impulse toward a de-concentration of the native-born population toward metropolitan and non-metropolitan areas that are less populated. This added immigrant-driven impulse toward de-concentration of native-born residents adds a further ingredient to the longstanding population de-concentration in Developed Counties that has been tracked since the 1970s (Champion, 1989; Long and DeAre, 1988; Frey and Speare, 1988, 1992; Fuguitt, Brown and Beale, 1989; Johnson and Beale, 1995).

Within the US, recent immigration is relevant toward accounting for a continued population dispersal. This is not because the immigrants themselves are dispersing. It is because they are prompting a selective dispersal of domestic migrants away from the large immigrant port-of-entry metropolitan areas – a pattern which is also evident in Europe (Champion, 1994). This phenomenon can be attributed, in part, to the increasing dual labour market character of high immigration metropolitan areas such as Los Angeles and New York (Waldinger, 1996). Low-skilled immigrants, many with at most high school education, tend to take poorly-paying service jobs and work in the informal sector. Because these metropolitan areas also tend to serve as advanced service centers, they attract highly educated professional domestic migrants to activities which complement the informal and low-wage sectors that employ the bulk of new immigrants. In the process, low-skilled and lower-income US residents see their wages bid down, and job prospects reduced at the same time that costs of housing and commuting rise. The increased multiethnic nature of these metropolitan areas also leads to the perception that social service costs in these areas are driven up and the potential for inter-ethnic conflict will increase. In response, lower middle class domestic residents of these areas show a propensity to out-migrate (Frey, 1995a).

The destinations of these out-migrants are not always to small metropolitan areas or non-metropolitan territories. Often they relocate to growing metropolitan areas which are less ethnic and do not have a dual economy character. However, the coincidence of heavy immigration in California metropolitan areas, coupled with increased development and diversification of small towns located in non-metropolitan and small metropolitan areas in the states surrounding California and in the Rocky Mountain region, laid the groundwork for selective domestic out-migration into more dispersed settlement areas in the western United States in the early 1990s (Frey, 1995b; 1996).

This chapter presents evidence underlying these trends, based on the most recently available estimates of demographic components of change, as well as race-ethnic and age attributes from the 2000 U.S. decennial census. Following a discussion of data, definitions and methods, separate sections are presented on how these shifts are affecting individual metropolitan areas and how they are impacting on the regional, metropolitan settlement system in the United States. This is followed by a comparison of cohort component projections which contrasts the future demographic scenarios of a large immigrant port-of-entry metropolitan area (Los Angeles) and of a modestly growing metropolitan area which attracted a minimal number of immigrants (Detroit).

DATA, DEFINITIONS AND METHODOLOGY

The data for this chapter draw from (1) estimates of demographic components of change (international migration, net domestic migration, net natural increase) compiled at the county-level by the U.S. Bureau of the Census for the period 1990-99; and (2) decennial census data from the periods 1960, 1970, 1980, 1990 and 2000 for population totals, race-ethnic status, and age. These sources permit us to make an assessment of immigration and domestic migration trends over the 1990s, in comparison to earlier decades.

It should be noted that the 2000 US decennial census results are now in the process of being released and a full evaluation and reconciliation with earlier estimates of components of change has not yet been conducted. Yet there is initial evidence to suggest that the earlier estimates understate the size of net international migration to the U.S. over the 1990s (Cohn, 2001). Because of these discrepancies, this analysis presents parallel tables to those examining immigration and domestic migration components of change over the 1990-2000 decade, with tables showing relative gains of the combined Hispanic and Asian populations, on the one hand, with those of the combined non-Hispanic white and black populations, on the other hand. The Hispanic and Asian populations represent a high percentage of recent immigrants and provide a crude indicator of immigrant patterns, as can be currently assessed with the 2000 decennial census data.

RACE-ETHNIC DEFINITIONS
Statistics in the U.S. make a distinction between race and Hispanic status, so that persons of all major racial groups, such as whites, blacks and Asians can also be classed as Hispanic or non-Hispanic in terms of their ethnicity. In this chapter, we follow the convention of classing groups into mutually consistent categories: Hispanics, non-Hispanic whites, non-Hispanics blacks, and non-Hispanic Asians.

METROPOLITAN DEFINITION
This chapter will employ metropolitan area definitions that were in effect with the 2000 US census. Although we categorize metropolitan areas in selected categories, such as 'High Immigration Metropolitan Areas' (discussed in the next section), the broad categorization of metropolitan and non-metropolitan areas are defined as follows:

The metropolitan population comprises the combined population of all individual metropolitan areas. First used in the 1950 census, the metropolitan area is a functionally based concept designed to approximate to the socially and economically integrated community. As originally defined, individual metropolitan areas included a central city nucleus with a population of at least 50,000 along with adjacent counties (or towns in the New England states) that were economically and socially integrated with that nucleus, as determined by commuting data, population density and measures of economic activity. While most of the nation's present metropolitan areas can still be characterized by this concept, minor modifications to the definition have been implemented to account for special cases and more complex urbanization patterns. Current metropolitan areas are designated as either Metropolitan Statistical Areas (MSA), stand-alone areas; or Consolidated Metropolitan Statistical Areas (CMSAs), combinations of smaller metropolitan units (Primary Metropolitan Statistical Areas) which show commuting relationships with other such units. In 1995, there were 276 metropolitan areas (MSAs and CMSAs) which housed approximately 80 percent of the US population; the residual 20 percent was defined as a 'non-metropolitan' category.

The present analysis will follow the conventional definitions of metropolitan and non-metropolitan with one minor exception. This occurs in the six New England states, where metropolitan definitions, based on towns, preclude the availability of some population data. For this reason, we follow the convention of earlier research, to employ county-based New England County Metropolitan Areas (any NECMAs) to define the metropolitan population in these states.

METHODOLOGY

The methodology for this chapter utilizes: (1) demographic trend and decomposition of changes in population for areas between 1990 and 2000; and (2) multi-state cohort component projections, developed by the author, for individual metropolitan areas. The trend analyses contrast metropolitan areas that are dominated by immigrants, other metropolitan areas and non-metropolitan areas. These categories are further subdivided by major regions of the U.S.: North, South, and West. (The North combines the Northeast and Midwest census regions).

Projections are conducted over the 2000-2025 time span, tracking the components of change for each 5-year period. The methodology draws from a multi-state cohort component framework developed by the author (Frey, 1983) which incorporates domestic migration steams between individual metropolitan areas and other major regions of the country. This application of the framework also incorporates immigration from abroad. The projections are based on a disaggregation of: 5-year age groups, gender, and a race-ethnic classification that includes Hispanics, non-Hispanic whites, blacks, Asians, and other races. The immigration, fertility and mortality components of change are estimated separately for each of these groups, based on U.S. Census estimates and projected future changes built into the Census Bureau's national projections. The domestic migration stream patterns, assumed for these projections, are based on those observed with the 1990 U.S. Census for the 1985-90 migration interval. Results of the projections permit an examination of demographic components of change for each period, and allow conclusions to be reached regarding how individual metropolitan areas differ with respect to dominant demographic components of change, age structure, and race-ethnic composition.

THE DISTINCTIVENESS OF 'HIGH IMMIGRATION METRO AREAS'

While immigration to the United States has always been high, it has changed both in magnitude and character in the last two decades as the result of revisions in immigration legislation in the mid-1960s which were further modified in 1986 and in 1990 (Martin and Midgley, 1994). The increasing number of immigrants, both legal and illegal, from Latin America as well as from Asia have tended to accentuate the concentration of these immigrants into familiar port-of-entry areas where there are like race-ethnic and nationality populations who can provide both social and economic support as well as information about employment in the informal economy. Because the US immigration preference system favors family reunification rather than recruitment based on skills, the most recent immigrant cohorts tend to comprise a disproportionate number of labour force aged persons with at most high school education who are best suited for lower-level service kinds of employment (Briggs, 1992). As a consequence, these immigrants provide competition for less-skilled US residents because they tend to bid down the wages for employment in these large gateway metropolitan areas. This is part of the reason that the high immigration metropolitan areas are showing large domestic out-migration.

A METROPOLIAN AREA TYPOLOGY

What is clear when looking at Table 14.1 is that the nine areas listed as high immigration metro areas (Figure 14.1) are sustaining all or most of their migration-related growth from immigration rather than from domestic, internal migration. These areas are quite distinct from areas which are classed as high domestic migration metro areas (Figure 14.2) or high out-migration metro areas (Figure 14.3). The latter two kinds of areas either gain or lose most of their migration-related population change through domestic migration subject to the pushes and pulls of the economy. High domestic migration metropolitan areas such as Atlanta, Seattle, Raleigh-Durham, and Charlotte are among the fast-rising national or regional 'command and control' corporate or banking centers with significant advanced service components to their economies. Also on this list are places like Las Vegas, Phoenix and Orlando – noted retirement and recreation centers – which are attracting an increasing working aged population lured by new job growth in these areas. And, at the other extreme, Detroit, Cleveland, and other high out-migration metropolitan areas are losing internal migrants due to more sluggish economies.

In contrast to these latter two categories of metropolitan areas, the high immigration metropolitan areas are distinct in a number of respects. First, most of them can be thought of as either global cities or national corporate headquarters and trade centers. Not only do they attract large numbers of immigrants, mostly from Latin America and Asia, but they are also centers of finance and corporate decision-making at a national or worldwide level. Second, it is plain that there is a strong net out-migration of domestic migrants from most if not all of these areas and especially from those areas

Figure 14.1 High immigration metro areas

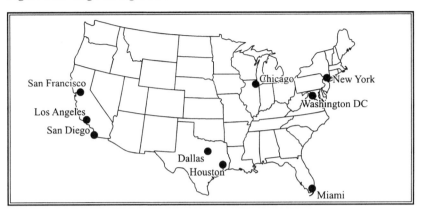

Figure 14.2 High domestic migration metro areas

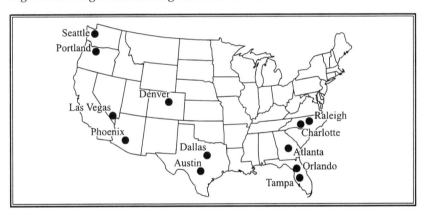

Figure 14.3 High out-migration metro areas

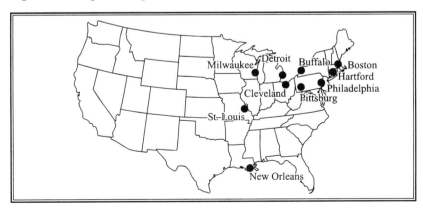

Table 14.1 Metropolitan areas classed by international and domestic migration contributions to population change, 1990-99

Metropolitan Categories Rank		Contribution to 1990-99 Change	
		Net International Migration	Net Domestic Migration
I. HIGH IMMIGRATION METROS [a]			
1	New York	1.408.543	-1,913.850
2	Los Angeles	1.257.925	-1,589.222
3	San Francisco	494.189	-373,187
4	Miami	420.488	-84.884
5	Chicago	363.662	-516.854
6	Washington DC	267.175	-172.425
7	Houston	214.262	85.537
8	Dallas	173,500	235,611
9	San Diego	159.691	-139.649
II. HIGH DOMESTIC MIGRATION METROS [b]			
1	Atlanta	81,037	498.283
2	Phoenix	60,800	396,092
3	Las Vegas	35.506	394.331
4	Dallas	173.500	235,611
5	Denver	50.089	200.658
6	Portland	55,583	198,896
7	Austin	27,114	168,817
8	Orlando	44,244	167.120
9	Tampa	42.088	157.209
10	Charlotte	14.719	154.320
11	Raleigh	16.269	154.049
12	Seattle	90,492	153,946
III. HIGH OUT-MIGRATION METROS [c]			
1	Philadelphia	106,951	-269.874
2	Detroit	76.185	-238.994
3	Boston	137.634	-199.506
4	Cleveland	19.705	-103.945
5	Buffalo	8.927	-82,174
6	Hartford	24.028	-79.177
7	Pittsburgh	8.681	-73.980
8	St. Louis	24.828	-71,014
9	Milwaukee	11.883	-70.223
10	New Orleans	14.128	-70,036

Notes: Metro areas are CMSAs, MSAs, and (in New England) NECMAs, as defined by OMB in June, 2000
a Metro areas with the largest net international migration
b Metro areas with the largest net domestic migration
c Large metro areas with the largest negative domestic migration and not recipients of large domestic international migration

Source: Author's analysis of US Census Bureau County Estimates

which are the largest 'world cities.' This suggests that these areas are taking on a dual city character (Sassen, 1991; Waldinger, 1996) in that their economic and labour force structures will become highly bifurcated between professionals, on the one hand, and lower-level service workers, on the other. In these areas (in contrast to the high domestic migration metropolitan areas) it appears that the recent immigrant population will be taking over more of the latter jobs, while domestic migrants and longer-term residents will be taking the former.

Although the metropolitan areas in each category have somewhat distinct patterns, there is some overlap. One metro, Dallas, appears on both the high immigration metro and high domestic migration metro list. Because of the strong economy of the 1990s in Texas, as well as its continued attraction for immigrants from Mexico and other countries, Dallas draws heavily from both sources. Two high out-migration metros, Philadelphia and Boston, show modestly high levels of immigration which serve to cushion the higher levels of net domestic out-migration.

Further, the metros in each category tend to have distinct regional locations. Those of the high domestic migration metro category are located in the South and the West regions of the U.S., whereas the metros of the high out-migration category are primarily located in the North (New Orleans standing as the exception). This reflects strong economic forces and the greater generation of employment in the 'Sunbelt' (South and West) regions than the more heavily industrialized 'Rustbelt' (North) portions of the U.S., that has characterized the nation's redistribution shifts for several decades. high immigration metros are located in each of the nation's major regions. However, most of them are located in coastal states that have served historic roles as immigrant 'ports of entry'. The role of 'chain migration, along with continued establishment of race and ethnic communities in these areas, allowed them to draw international migrants during periods, such as the 1990s, when most of the domestic migrants moved to more economically robust areas.

RACE-ETHNIC AND AGE DISTINCTIONS

Another way in which the three metropolitan categories differ from each other pertains to their relative attraction for new immigrant minorities--Hispanics and Asians – compared with their attraction for native-born racial groups – whites and blacks (see Table 14.2). It is clear that the high immigration metros dominate in their numeric gains for Hispanics and Asians, compared with metro areas in the other two categories. Moreover, consistent with the domestic migration patterns observed in Table 14.1, high immigration metros show either declines or smaller gains in their white and black populations.

Table 14.2   1990-2000 changes and 2000 sizes of selected race-ethnic groups for categories of large metro areas

Metropolitan Categories Rank		1990-2000 Change		2000 Size (1000s)	
		Hispanics & Asians*	Whites & Blacks*	Hispanics & Asians*	Whites & Blacks*
I. HIGH IMMIGRATION METROS					
1	New York	1,559,497	-398,422	5,283	15,270
2	Los Angeles	2,278,670	-800,482	8,333	7,587
3	San Francisco	852,811	-289,229	2,715	4,059
4	Miami	529,378	77,648	1,632	2,160
5	Chicago	741,078	49,953	1,888	7,123
6	Washington DC	386,288	342,586	888	6,545
7	Houston	676,974	202,184	1,577	3,019
8	Dallas	698,679	411,414	1,319	3,808
9	San Diego	315,467	-79,859	1,011	1,703
II. HIGH DOMESTIC MIGRATION METROS					
1	Atlanta	296,608	795,493	406	3,640
2	Phoenix	473,405	473,062	887	2,253
3	Las Vegas	288,576	379,283	403	1,109
4	Dallas	698,679	411,414	1,319	3,808
5	Denver	256,066	299,260	551	1,970
6	Portland	170,368	239,788	298	1,888
7	Austin	176,977	207,520	372	855
8	Orlando	196,286	189,672	317	1,290
9	Tampa	133,054	158,793	294	2,059
10	Charlotte	84,082	236,742	106	1,373
11	Raleigh	82,429	233,244	107	1,062
12	Seattle	222,631	231,443	486	2,900
III. HIGH OUT-MIGRATION METROS					
1	Philadelphia	210,220	4,546	550	5,542
2	Detroit	108,481	59,817	285	5,047
3	Boston	222,071	26,648	601	5,304
4	Cleveland	38,155	9,582	121	2,780
5	Buffalo	14,087	-46,319	49	1,100
6	Hartford	40,431	-33,188	134	994
7	Pittsburgh	13,714	-71,161	44	2,290
8	St. Louis	28,032	52,494	78	2,489
9	Milwaukee	62,770	-604	142	1,518
10	New Orleans	12,599	24,286	87	1,230

Notes: Metro areas are CMSAs, MSAs, and (in New England) NECMAs, as defined by OMB in June, 2000 (names are abbreviated).
*Asians, Whites and Blacks pertain to Non-Hispanic members of those races.

Source: Author's analysis of 1990 and 2000 US decennial census data.

This pattern is also consistent with the relative 2000 population sizes across metropolitan categories for the two race-ethnic groupings. Again, high immigration metros tend to have greatest numbers of Hispanic and Asian populations according to the results of the 2000 Census. This is especially the case for the New York and Los Angeles metropolitan areas.

Despite these sharp differences across metropolitan categories, new 2000 Census results show higher than expected gains in Hispanic populations in all parts of the U.S. These are reflected in the relatively higher levels of Hispanic and Asian gains shown for metropolitan areas outside the high immigration metro category. For example, the 1990-2000 numeric gains in Phoenix's Hispanic and Asian populations are slightly greater than its gains in the combined white and black population. Although not all Hispanics and Asians are foreign-born or recent immigrants, these 2000 U.S. Census results are consistent with the relative distributions of international migration and domestic migration for Phoenix (shown in Table 14.1).

In like manner, higher than expected gains are shown for Las Vegas, Orlando and Denver, among other metros in the high domestic migration category. It is not yet possible to determine whether these gains are the result of direct immigration from abroad, the secondary migration of the foreign-born, or domestic migration of Hispanic and Asians of second and higher generations. Nonetheless, 2000 Census results show a somewhat greater than expected spreading out of Hispanic and Asian populations away from the high immigration metros.

Table 14.3 shows the ethnic and age characteristics for metro areas in each of the metropolitan categories as reported in the 2000 U.S. Census, along with changes since 1990. With a few exceptions, high immigration metros have a larger percentage of Hispanics and Asians than those in other categories. Aside from Washington, DC and Chicago, Hispanics and Asians account for between one-quarter and over one-half of the populations in each of these areas. In six of the nine areas the combined white and black share of their populations declined by 9 percentage points or more.

Still, there is a surprisingly large Hispanic presence in several high domestic migration metros. This is evident in Phoenix and Las Vegas, which increased their Hispanic and Asian shares by over 8 percent in the 1990s. In like manner, these two areas, as well as Orlando reduced their combined white and black shares by over 10 percent. In high out-migration metros, Hispanic and Asian population percentages tend to be smaller, and 1990-2000 increases are less than in other metropolitan categories. These metro areas are at least 85 percent white and black in their race-ethnic composition.

Age comparisons are somewhat less distinct across these broad areas. High out-migration migration metros have lower shares of their populations

Table 14.3 2000 race-ethnic and age characteristics, and 1990-2000 changes for categories of large metro areas

Metropolitan Categories Rank	% Hispanics and Asians*		% Whites* and Blacks*		% Aged Under 18		% Aged 65 and over	
	Year 2000	Chge since 1990	Year 2000	Chge since 1990	Year 2000	Chge since 1990	Year 2000	Chge since 1990
I. HIGH IMMIGRATION METROS								
1 New York	25.0	5.9	72.4	-8.2	24.7	1.7	12.7	-0.5
2 Los Angeles	50.9	9.2	46.3	-11.4	28.5	1.9	9.9	0.1
3 San Francisco	38.6	8.8	57.7	-11.9	23.6	0.6	11.1	0.1
4 Miami	42.1	7.6	55.7	-9.5	24.3	1.6	14.5	-2.2
5 Chicago	20.6	6.7	77.8	-8.1	26.9	0.8	10.9	-0.5
6 Washington DC	11.7	4.2	86.0	-6.2	25.3	1.4	10.1	0.3
7 Houston	33.8	9.6	64.6	-10.8	29.0	0.2	7.7	0.4
8 Dallas	25.3	9.9	72.9	-11.2	28.0	0.8	8.1	-0.3
9 San Diego	35.9	8.1	60.5	-10.9	25.7	1.3	11.2	0.2
II. HIGH DOMESTIC MIGRATION METROS								
1 Atlanta	9.9	6.2	88.5	-7.6	26.6	0.7	7.6	-0.5
2 Phoenix	27.3	8.8	69.3	-10.2	26.8	0.5	11.9	-0.6
3 Las Vegas	25.8	12.4	70.9	-14.6	25.3	1.0	11.8	0.2
4 Dallas	25.3	9.9	72.9	-11.2	28.0	0.8	8.1	-0.3
5 Denver	21.4	6.4	76.3	-8.1	25.7	-0.1	8.9	-0.3
6 Portland	13.1	6.0	83.4	-8.6	25.7	-0.1	10.7	-1.7
7 Austin	29.8	6.7	68.4	-8.1	25.4	-0.2	7.3	-0.5
8 Orlando	19.3	9.4	78.4	-11.4	24.8	1.0	12.4	-0.5
9 Tampa	12.3	4.5	85.9	-6.0	21.9	1.5	19.2	-2.4
10 Charlotte	7.1	5.2	91.6	-6.2	25.4	0.7	10.2	-0.7
11 Raleigh	9.0	6.1	89.4	-7.5	24.2	1.5	8.6	-0.9
12 Seattle	13.7	4.8	81.6	-8.3	24.8	-0.2	10.3	-0.4
III. HIGH OUT-MIGRATION METROS								
1 Philadelphia	8.9	3.1	89.6	-4.4	25.3	1.0	13.5	0.0
2 Detroit	5.2	1.8	92.5	-3.6	26.4	0.3	11.7	0.2
3 Boston	9.9	3.3	87.6	-5.3	24.0	1.3	12.7	-0.1
4 Cleveland	4.1	1.2	94.4	-2.5	25.3	0.3	14.3	0.3
5 Buffalo	4.2	1.3	94.0	-2.4	24.3	0.8	15.8	0.6
6 Hartford	11.7	3.3	86.5	-4.9	24.2	1.7	14.0	0.6
7 Pittsburgh	1.9	0.6	97.1	-1.5	22.3	0.2	17.7	0.6
8 St. Louis	3.0	1.0	95.6	-2.2	26.3	0.0	12.9	0.1
9 Milwaukee	8.4	3.5	89.8	-4.6	26.5	0.0	12.5	0.1
10 New Orleans	6.5	0.7	92.0	-1.9	26.8	-1.3	11.4	0.4

Notes: Metro areas are CMSAs, MSAs, and (in New England) NECMAs, as defined by OMB in June, 2000 (Names are abbreviated)
*Asians, Whites and Blacks pertain to Non-Hispanic members of those races

Source: Author's analysis of 1990 and 2000 US decennial census data

under 18 and higher shares over age 65 than the other categories. High immigration metro areas tend to have the youngest age structures. Among all of the metropolitan areas on the list, the high immigration metros, Los Angeles, Houston and Dallas lead the rest with more than 28 percent of their populations under 18. High domestic migration metros also exhibit relatively young age structures, although, in some cases, this is moderated by the aging of their large middle-aged baby boom populations (Frey, 2001b).

In sum, distinct demographic dynamic processes are at work for the three categories of metropolitan areas. High immigration metros dominate with respect to attracting immigrants, and in their concentration of Hispanic and Asian immigrant minority groups. Nonetheless, the 2000 U.S. Census results suggests 'spilling out' of the latter into other growing metropolitan areas, perhaps in response to the service, retail, and construction jobs being created by the even larger domestic migration gain exhibited in high domestic migration metros. A systemic view of how these patterns are playing out across the nation's metropolitan and regional settlement grid is taken up in the next section.

IMMIGRATION AND THE SETTLEMENT SYSTEM
This section will evaluate the impacts that immigration and domestic migration components exert on the regional and metropolitan area settlement system of the US. This system includes the three broad regions of the U.S., North, South and West and, within them, a metropolitan status trichotomy that includes the combined high immigration metropolitan areas, all other metropolitan areas, and the residual non-metropolitan territory. This settlement system grid permits us to evaluate the extent to which immigration is being concentrated in the high immigration metro areas, and the extent to which domestic migration disperses across regions and other metropolitan status categories.

SETTLEMENT SYSTEM REDISTRIBUTION TRENDS
Before evaluating these components of change, it is useful to examine the trends over the past three decades in the relative growth and decline of metropolitan and non-metropolitan areas for this settlement system. Table 14.4 indicates that in the 1970s, so-called 'rural renaissance' characterized the settlement system such that, overall, non-metropolitan areas grew faster than either of the two metropolitan categories. This non-metropolitan growth has been attributed to a number of deconcentration and period influences associated with the dispersion of small manufacturing and extractive jobs, and the rise of a large retirement population during the decade (Frey, 1989). A sharp reversal of fortunes for non-metropolitan economies during the 1980s

Table 14.4 Population change by metropolitan status and region

Region* Metropolitan Status**	2000 Size (millions)	Percent 10 year change			Share of US Population				Change in Share 1970-2000
		1970-1980	1980-1990	1990-2000	1970	1980	1990	2000	
NORTH									
High Immig Metros	30.3	-1.6	2.8	9.2	13.5	11.9	11.1	10.8	-2.7
Other Metros	65.3	2.1	3.0	6.2	28.8	26.4	24.7	23.2	-5.6
Non-metropolitan	22.4	7.8	-0.4	5.4	9.7	9.4	8.5	8.0	-1.8
SOUTH									
High Immig Metros	21.4	22.7	21.1	20.8	5.9	6.4	7.1	7.6	1.7
Other Metros	54.2	21.6	16.3	18.7	15.9	17.3	18.4	19.3	3.4
Non-metropolitan	24.6	15.5	2.8	11.5	9.2	9.5	8.9	8.8	-0.4
WEST									
High Immig Metros	26.2	16.4	24.3	12.6	7.9	8.3	9.4	9.3	1.4
Other Metros	28.6	31.2	23.3	26.7	6.9	8.1	9.1	10.2	3.3
Non-metropolitan	8.3	28.1	12.9	20.8	2.3	2.7	2.8	3.0	0.6
					100.0	100.0	100.0	100.0	100.0
UNITED STATES									
High Immig Metros	77.9	8.9	13.9	13.4	27.2	26.6	27.6	27.7	0.4
Other Metros	148.2	12.0	10.6	14.2	51.5	51.8	52.2	52.7	1.1
Non-metropolitan	55.3	13.3	2.6	10.2	21.2	21.6	20.2	19.7	-1.6
					100.0	100.0	100.0	100.0	

Notes:
* Pertains to US Census regions with the exception that 'North' pertains to the combined Northeast and Midwest census regions
** High Immigration Metros are: New York and Chicago in the North: Washington DC, Miami, Dallas and Houston in the South: Los Angeles, San Francisco and San Diego in the West.

Source: Author's analysis of US decennial censuses. 1970 - 2000

substantially reduced their population growth. Still, a new revival of non-metropolitan areas, reflected in new population gains, appears to have occurred during the 1990s. These gains were less attributable to self-contained rural and non-metropolitan economic activities. Rather, non-metropolitan growth in the 1990s occurred in counties that lie just adjacent to metropolitan areas and serve as residences for ex-urban commuters. Likewise, large gains occurred in high amenity non-metropolitan counties which attracted retirees who, in fact, served to create economic growth rather than respond to it (Johnson and Beale, 1995).

From the metropolitan perspective, the slow growth or population declines of the 1970s were attributable to a wholesale downsizing of manufacturing production. As a consequence, some of the largest metropolitan areas in the U.S. sustained unprecedented population losses during the decade. Among those experiencing significant losses were areas we have classed as high immigration metros, although rising immigration did not occur until after this decade had passed.

In the 1980s, there was a selective rebounding of metropolitan area growth. Areas that were most likely to gain were the locations of advanced service activities, including corporate headquarter cities, high-tech incubation centers, and other places that were able to make the manufacturing-to-advanced services transition, or those that were generally diversified enough to weather the 1970s manufacturing 'shakeouts' (Frey, 1993). These included some of the high immigration metros such as New York, Los Angeles, San Francisco, Chicago and Dallas-Fort Worth. Still, the 1980s showed negative patterns for metros areas specializing in particular industries that were not doing well. For example, the reduced mid-decade demand for products of the extractive industries reversed population growth in metro areas such as Houston and Denver.

The 1990s showed some rebounding of the latter two areas which diversified their economies, and there was a more broadly based growth in metropolitan areas of all sizes, especially in the South and West. Still, there were adverse growth impacts associated with the early 1990s recession. It affected metropolitan areas that held significant U.S. government defense installations or areas which did much contract work with U.S. defense agencies (e.g., San Diego, Los Angeles). This is evident from the reduced growth shown for high immigration metro areas in the West during the 1990s decade.

MIGRATION COMPONENTS IN THE 1990s

Yet, perhaps the most important long-term phenomenon of the 1990s which affected both the demographics and economics of selected large metropolitan areas was the impact that concentrated immigration imposed on a few port-of-entry areas. This is clear from the 1990s components of change data shown in Table 14.5. Were it not for immigration in the 1990s, the large high immigration metros in the West would have shown insignificant growth in their populations; those in the North would have sustained declines. In the South, these areas would have gained modestly, but primarily due to natural increase. In short, immigration, combined with natural increase, accounted for most of the population gains in each region's metropolitan areas during the 1990s.

In contrast, small metropolitan areas in the both the South and West regions sustained greater growth from domestic migration than from international migration, and this is even more so the case for non-metropolitan areas in these regions. This pattern is consistent with the scenario where domestic migrants are locating in low-cost, less congested smaller metropolitan areas at the same time that immigration continues to be concentrated. Nationally, 65 percent of all the 1990s immigrants located in the nine high immigration metropolitan areas. These same metro areas house less than 28 percent of the total U.S. population, and less than 23 percent of the combined white and black population of the nation.

RACE-ETHNIC AND AGE DISTINCTIONS

The 1990-2000 decade changes by race-ethnic groups are shown in Table 14.6. As with immigration over the 1990s, Hispanics and Asians are more concentrated in the high immigration metros than whites and blacks. Those in the north and west regions sustained declines in their combined white and black populations; and in the other metros in these same two regions, Hispanic and Asian gains exceeded gains among whites and blacks. This is not the case for other metropolitan areas in the south where the gains of whites and blacks were greater than those for Hispanics and Asians. This is fueled, in part, by a substantial black migration to the south during the 1990s (Frey, 2001a). Moreover, in the non-metropolitan areas of all three regions, the gains for whites and blacks outnumber those for Hispanics and Asians.

Table 14.6 contrasts somewhat with Table 14.5 by showing that the new immigrant minority groups are gaining in all parts of the settlement system, suggesting some 'spilling out' of these race-ethnic groups away from the high immigration metros. Overall, however, these groups continue to remain far more concentrated in these selected metros than the general population.

The impact of this concentrated immigration is reflected in the race-ethnic compositions of high immigration metros, as contrasted with other categories of areas in the settlement system. Table 14.7 indicates one-third of the population of high immigration metros, nationally, is comprised of Hispanics and Asians in contrast to less than 12 percent of other metros and less than

Table 14.5 Demographic components of change by metropolitan status and region, 1990-99

Region* Metropolitan Status*	International Migration	Domestic Migration	Natural Increase		International Migration	Domestic Migration	Natural Increase		2000 Population	1990-1999 Intl. Migration
NORTH										
High Immig Metros	6.4	-8.0	6.7		1,772,205	-2,430,704	1,849,785		10.8	24.3
Other Metros	1.2	-2.2	4.8		709,798	-1,439,108	2,935,179		23.2	9.7
Non-metropolitan	0.3	1.4	2.1		68,040	318,416	436,536		8.0	0.9
SOUTH										
High Immig Metros	6.1	0.3	8.8		1,075,425	63,839	1,556,199		7.6	14.7
Other Metros	1.6	4.5	6.3		741,739	2,448,870	2,906,687		19.3	10.2
Non-metropolitan	0.6	4.1	2.9		133,970	998,283	649,553		8.8	1.8
WEST										
High Immig Metros	8.2	-8.0	10.6		1,911,805	-2,102,058	2,488,664		9.3	26.2
Other Metros	3.4	5.5	9.2		760,073	1,571,516	2,103,253		10.2	10.4
Non-metropolitan	1.9	6.9	6.4		133,710	570,946	439,937		3.0	1.8
									100.0	100.0
UNITED STATES										
High Immig Metros	6.9	-5.7	8.6		4,759,435	-4,468,923	5,894,648		27.7	65.1
Other Metros	1.7	1.7	6.1		2,211,610	2,581,278	7,945,119		52.7	30.3
Non-metropolitan	0.7	3.4	3.0		335,720	1,887,645	1,526,026		19.7	4.6
									100.0	100.0

Notes:
* Pertains to US Census regions with the exception that 'North' pertains to the combined Northeast and Midwest census regions.
** High Immigration Metros are: New York and Chicago in the North; Washington DC, Miami, Dallas and Houston in the South; Los Angeles, San Francisco and San Diego in the West.

Source: Author's analysis of US Census Bureau County Estimates

381

Table 14.6 1990-2000 changes and 2000 sizes of selected race-ethnic groups by metropolitan status and region

Region* Metropolitan Status**	1990-2000 Change		2000 Size (1000s)		Share of US 2000 Population	
	Hispanics & Asians	Whites &Blacks	Hispanics & Asians	Whites &Blacks	Hispanics & Asians	Whites &Blacks
NORTH						
High Immig Metros	2,300,575	-348,469	7,171	22,393	15.7	9.8
Other Metros	1,590,607	1,257,451	3,887	60,223	8.5	26.4
Non-metropolitan	291,572	610,220	643	21,320	1.4	9.3
SOUTH						
High Immig Metros	2,291,319	1,033,832	5,416	15,531	11.8	6.8
Other Metros	2,735,369	5,043,049	6,529	46,666	14.3	20.4
Non-metropolitan	655,161	1,603,859	1,583	22,497	3.5	9.8
WEST						
High Immig Metros	3,446,948	-1,169,570	12,060	13,350	26.3	5.8
Other Metros	2,753,744	2,372,217	7,121	20,278	15.6	8.9
Non-metropolitan	394,783	753,433	1,373	6,244	3.0	2.7
					100.0	100.0
UNITED STATES						
High Immig Metros	8,038,842	-484,207	24,646	51,274	53.8	22.4
Other Metros	7,079,720	8,672,717	17,537	127,167	38.3	55.7
Non-metropolitan	1,341,516	2,967,512	3,599	50,060	7.9	21.9
					100.0	100.0

Notes:
* Pertains to US Census regions with the exception that 'North' pertains to the combined Northeast and Midwest census regions
** High Immigration Metros are: New York and Chicago in the North; Washington DC, Miami. Dallas and Houston in the South; Los Angeles. San Francisco and San Diego in the West.

Source: Author's analysis of 1990 and 2000 US decennial census data

Table 14.7 2000 race-ethnic and age characteristics, and 1990-2000 changes, by metropolitan status and region

Region* Metropolitan Status**	% Hispanics and Asians		% Whites and Blacks		% Aged under 18		% Aged 65 and over	
	Year 2000	Chge since 1990	Year 2000	Chge since 1990	Year 2000	Chge since 1990	Year 2000	Chge since 1990
NORTH								
High Immig Metros	23.7	6.1	74.0	-8.1	25.4	1.5	12.1	-0.5
Other Metros	5.9	2.2	92.2	-3.7	25.2	0.2	13.0	0.1
Non-metropolitan	2.9	1.2	95.2	-2.3	24.9	-1.3	15.4	-0.1
SOUTH								
High Immig Metros	25.3	7.7	72.7	-9.3	26.6	1.1	9.9	-0.3
Other Metros	12.0	3.7	86.1	-5.1	25.3	-0.2	12.4	0.0
Non-metropolitan	6.4	2.2	91.3	-3.3	25.0	-1.5	14.5	-0.2
WEST								
High Immig Metros	46.0	9.0	50.9	-11.5	26.9	1.5	10.4	0.1
Other Metros	24.9	5.5	70.8	-8.4	26.9	-0.2	10.9	-0.1
Non-metropolitan	16.5	2.3	75.0	-4.7	27.2	-2.0	13.0	0.1
UNITED STATES								
High Immig Metros	31.7	7.5	65.8	-9.5	26.2	1.4	10.9	-0.3
Other Metros	11.8	3.8	85.8	-5.5	25.6	0.0	12.4	0.0
Non-metropolitan	6.5	2.0	90.4	-3.3	25.3	-1.5	14.7	-0.2
Total US	16.3	4.5	81.2	-6.2	25.7	0.1	12.4	-0.1

Notes:
* Pertains to US Census regions with the exception that 'North' pertains to the combined Northeast and Midwest census regions
** High Immigration Metros are: New York and Chicago in the North; Washington DC, Miami, Dallas and Houston in the South; Los Angeles, San Francisco and San Diego in the West.

Source: Author's analysis of 1990 and 2000 US decennial census data

seven per cent for non-metropolitan areas. The patterns differ regionally such that all three categories in the West exhibit a greater Hispanic and Asian presence than those in the North and South. This suggests some dispersal of the new immigrant minority groups away from the high immigration metro areas in the West toward smaller-sized places and some non-metropolitan counties. In the North and South, however, there is a sharp difference between the race-ethnic compositions of high immigration metros, on the one hand, and other metros, on the other. Non-metropolitan areas in the north and south, and other metropolitan areas in the south are over 90 percent white and black.   At the other extreme, barely half of the population of high immigration metros in the West is white and black.

The differences in age structures among the categories of the settlement system are sharper than those for race and ethnicity. The youngest areas of the system include high immigration metropolitan areas in the South and West, as well as other metros and non-metros in the latter region. Non-metropolitan areas in each region have the highest shares of their populations aged 65 and above. These areas sustained significant domestic out-migration with relatively little infusion of immigration and the in-movement of new ethnic minority groups that have younger age structures.

In sum, this section has shown that immigration over the 1990s tended to be concentrated within the high immigration metros, although there has been some dispersal of Hispanics and Asians to other metropolitan areas and non-metropolitan areas, especially in the West region. Other metropolitan areas in the South and West have also shown large gains in their white and black populations. Hence, there is a greater representation of immigrant minorities in the high immigration metropolitan areas in all three regions.

PROJECTIONS TO 2025

Although one cannot reliably predict the future demographic patterns associated with immigration and domestic migration across the nation's settlement systems, multi-state cohort component projections provide a way of assessing outcomes if current demographic processes continue. These projections have been performed for individual metropolitan areas: Los Angeles, a high immigration metro area and Detroit, a high out-migration metro. The projections utilize a procedure developed by Frey (1983) that incorporates separate migration components of change. Each metropolitan area projection is part of a multi-state system which includes the metropolitan area, and the four residual census regions of the U.S. Hence, the net domestic migration is shown as a result of this projection, representing the net of exchanges between the given metropolitan area (Los Angeles or Detroit) and all other regions of the U.S.

The contrast between the projected Detroit and Los Angeles migration components over the 2000-2025 period is striking (see Table 14.8). Over the 25 years, metropolitan Los Angeles increases its population by 43 percent wherein international migration accounts for more than half of that gain. Metro Los Angeles is projected to lose domestic migrants over each of the periods of the projection. However, this is more than compensated for by immigration, as well as a significant level of natural increase which reflects its younger age structure and the higher fertility of the larger Hispanic population in the Los Angeles metropolitan area. The Detroit metropolitan area, on the other hand, shows a projected growth of only 8.5 percent over the 25-year period. The bulk of this growth is accounted for by natural increase, although the rate of natural increase in Detroit is only about half of that for Los Angeles. Detroit also has shown negative domestic migration rates slightly higher than those for Los Angeles. In short, Detroit's scenario is one of a steady-state population where natural increase overcomes the net loss that would accrue from the combination of immigration and domestic migration contributions alone.

Figures 14.4 and 14.5 contrast 2025 age structures by race for Los Angeles and Detroit. The difference is quite striking with Los Angeles showing an extremely young age structure where large Hispanic and Asian populations overwhelm the sizes of its combined white and black populations for all ages under 50. Only at the age category of 70 and above, are the Hispanic and Asian populations in Los Angeles smaller than whites and blacks in the year 2025. In Detroit, on the other hand, the projection is dominated by the white and black populations that exhibit a relatively flat age distribution. The youth momentum generated by Hispanics and Asians in Los Angeles is not available to Detroit, which would not attract any new immigrant minorities, according to the projection.

The differences in these two metro area age structures and race compositions hold important implications for the policies related to youth versus the elderly, on the one hand, and the needs of immigrant minorities versus native-born whites and blacks on the other. In Los Angeles, much of the working aged population will be Hispanic and Asian in origin and will be more concerned about issues related to their large child populations. In Detroit, in contrast, the elderly population will hold greater sway in decisions made by the electorate and its leaders. Here racial and multi-cultural matters such as the infusion of bilingual education in the schools or alterations in preferences of the nation's immigration laws, will be far less important than they are for the residents of Los Angeles. In like manner, residents in the nation's clusters of high immigration metros, will hold distinctly different views of national policy priorities, than those parts of the settlement system which have been populated primarily by native-born domestic migrants.

Table 14.8 2000-25 projected demographic components of change for Los Angeles and Detroit Metropolitan Areas*

| | 5-year Periods | | | | | 25-years |
	2000-05	2005-10	2010-15	2015-20	2020-25	2000-25
Los Angeles Metro Area		363,669				
Numeric Change						
International Migration	862,641	737,898	663,674	680,121	743,669	3,688,003
Domestic Migration	-158,139	-213,386	-269,585	-322,330	-369,514	-1,332,954
Natural Increase	811,290	928,442	1,016,496	1,062,274	1,082,548	4,901,050
Total	1,515,792	1,452,954	1,410,585	1,420,065	1,456,703	7,256,099
Percent Change						
International Migration	5.2	4.0	3.4	3.2	3.3	22.0
Domestic Migration	-0.9	-1.2	-1.4	-1.5	-1.6	-8.0
Natural Increase	4.8	5.1	5.2	5.0	4.8	29.3
Total	9.1	8.0	7.2	6.7	6.5	43.4
Detroit Metro Area						
Numeric Change						
International Migration	44,099	37,798	34,013	34,829	38,192	188,931
Domestic Migration	-104,656	-105,491	-106,060	-104,239	-98,670	-519,116
Natural Increase	160,219	155,836	157,282	163,200	161,252	797,789
Total	99,662	88,143	85,235	93,790	100,774	467,604
Percent Change						
International Migration	0.8	0.7	0.6	0.6	0.7	3.4
Domestic Migration	-1.9	-1.9	-1.9	-1.8	-1.7	-9.4
Natural Increase	2.9	2.8	2.8	2.8	2.8	14.5
Total	1.8	1.6	1.5	1.6	1.7	8.5

Notes: *defined as CMSAs

Source: Author's multistate cohort component projection

Figure 14.4 Los Angeles 2025 age structure by race-ethnicity

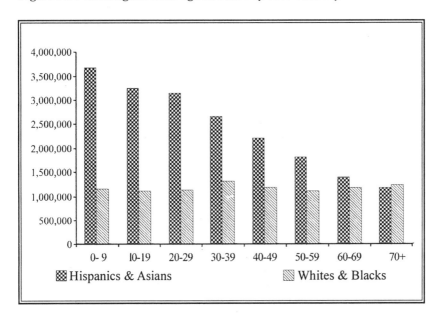

Figure 14.5 Detroit 2025 age structure by race-ethnicity

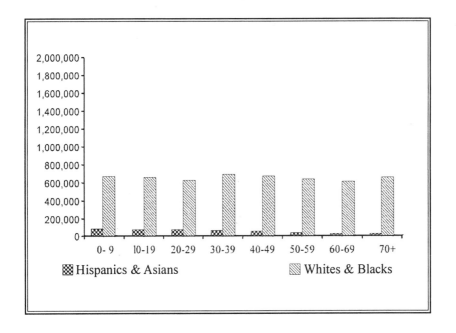

CONCLUSION

In conclusion, we have shown that in the United States, recent immigration continues to concentrate in selected large metropolitan areas in contrast to other parts of the settlement system. We have also shown that this concentrated settlement pattern affects the demographic structure of high immigration metros quite differently from the rest of the country. If current demographic processes are projected ahead, these areas would become increasingly multi-ethnic, have younger age structures, and would likely be involved with different social and economic concerns than other metropolitan areas and non-metropolitan areas that would house a much smaller share of the new immigrant groups. An important aspect of this continued immigration concentration is the potential emergence of dual economies in these high immigration regions, wherein new immigrants continue to cluster, not only residentially but economically in industry and occupational niches that may hold little prospect for advancement (Frey and Liaw, 1998). This chapter documents some of the demographic implications that the new 'South to North' immigration flows are exerting on the US settlement system. The US is not alone among developed nations, in accepting large numbers of developing country-origin immigrants who concentrate in selected 'port of entry' metropolitan areas. Hence, this analysis can serve as a case study of how longstanding urbanization patterns may be altering as a result of emerging international migration trends. Although immigration is often suggested as a remedy for problems endemic to the 'aging' of populations in today's industrialized countries, these arguments fail to take into account the significant demographic differences which can emerge between regions within these nations. These divisions may lead to commensurate social and political divisions, among different parts of the urban and regional system, that will differentially benefit from government programs designed to aid the elderly (e.g. publicly funded pensions), minorities (e.g. affirmative action policies) or the young (e.g. improved education). It suggests that such policy prescriptions need to pay more attention to the internal urban and regional impacts of immigration on these nations' demographic structures.

REFERENCES

Beale, C. L. (1977), 'The Recent Shift of United States Population to Nonmetropolitan Areas, 1970-75', *International Regional Science Review*, **2**, 113-122.

Briggs, V. (1992), *Mass immigration and the national labor market*. Armonk, New York: N. E. Sharpe, Inc.

Champion, A. G. (ed.) (1989), *Counterurbanization: The changing pace and nature of population deconcentration*. London: Edward Arnold.

Champion, A. G. (1994), 'International migration and demographic change in the Developed World', Urban Studies, **31**, 653-677.

Clark, C. (1967), *Population growth and land use,* New York: St.Martin's Press.

Cohn, D. (2001), '2000 illegal residents exceed estimates', *The Washington Post.* March 18, A01.

Frey, W. H. (1989), 'United States: Counterurbanization and metropolis depopulation' in A. G. Champion (ed.), *Counterurbanization: the changing pace and nature of population deconcentration,* London: Edward Arnold, pp. 34-61.

Frey, W. H. (1993), 'The new urban revival in the United States', *Urban Studies,* **30**, 741-774.

Frey, W. H. (1995a), 'Immigration and internal migration "flight" from us metropolitan areas: Toward a new demographic balkanization', *Urban Studies,* **32**, 733-57.

Frey, W. H. (1995b), 'Immigration and internal migration flight "a california case study", *Environment and Planning A,* **16**, 353-75.

Frey, W. H. (1996), 'Immigration, domestic migration and demographic balkanization in America', *Population and Development Review,* **22**, 741 – 763

Frey, W. H. (1983), 'Multiregional population projection framework that incorporates both migration and residential mobility streams', *Environment and Planning A,* **15**, 1613-1632.

Frey, W. H. (2001a), *Census 2000 shows large black return to the south: reinforcing the region's white-black demographic profile,* Research Report 01-473, Ann Arbor, MI: University of Michigan, Population Studies Center

Frey, W. H. and A. Speare, Jr. (1988), *Regional and metropolitan growth and decline in the United States,* New York: Russell Sage.

Frey, W. H. (1998a), 'Black migration to the South reaches record highs in the 1990s', *Population Today,* **26**, 1-3.

Frey, W. H. (1998b), 'New demographic divide in the US: Immigrant and domestic 'migrant magnets', *The Public Perspective,* June/July, 35-39.

Frey, W. H. (1998c), 'The diversity myth', *American Demographics,* June, 39-43.

Frey, W. H. (2001b), 'The Baby Boom Tsunami' *Milken Institute Review* Second Quarter. August, 4-7.

Frey, W. H. and D. Geverdt (1998), *Changing suburban demographics: beyond the "Black-White, city-suburb" typology,* Report No. 98-422, Michigan: Population Studies Centre, University of Michigan.

Frey, W. H. and K-L. Liaw (1998), 'The impact of recent immigration on population redistribution within the United States', in J. P. Smith and B. Edmonston, (eds), *The immigration debate: Studies of economic, demographic and fiscal effects of immigration.* Washington, DC.: National Academy Press, pp.388-448.

Frey, W. H., and A. Speare (1992), 'The revival of metropolitan growth in the United States: An assessment of findings from the 1990 census', *Population and Development Review* **18**, 129-46.

Fuguitt, G. V., D. L. Brown, and C. L. Beale (1989), '*Rural and small town America.* New York: Russell Sage Foundation.

Gordon, P. (1979), 'Deconcentration Without a 'Clean Break', *Environment and Planning A*, **11**, 281-290.

Hoover, E. M. (1963), *The location of economic activity*, New York: McGraw-Hill.

Johnson, K. and C. L. Beale (1995), 'The rural rebound revisited', *American Demographics,* July, 46-54.

Long, L. and D. DeAre (1988), 'U.S. population redistribution: a perspective on the nonmetropolitan turnaround', *Population and Development Review* **14**, 433-50.

Martin, P. and E. Midgley (1994), 'Immigration to the United States: Journey to an uncertain destination', *Population Bulletin*, **49**, 2.

Richardson, H. W. (1973), *Economic Growth Theory.* London: MacMillan.

Sassen, S. (1991), *The Global City.* Princeton, NJ: Princeton University Press.

Ullman, E. L. (1958), 'Regional development and the geography of concentration', *Papers and Proceedings of the Regional Science Association,* **4**, 179-162.

Vining, D. R. (1982), 'Migration between the core and the periphery', *Scientific American*, **247**, 44-53.

Vining, D. R. Jr. and A. Strauss (1977), 'A Demonstration that the current deconcentration of population in the United States is a clean break with the past', *Environment and Planning A,* **9**, 751-758.

Waldinger, R. (1996), _Still the promised city?: African Americans and new immigrants in post-industrial New York.* Cambridge, MA: Harvard University Press.

Chapter 15

The Dynamics of the Canadian Urban System

L. S. Bourne and J. W. Simmons

SETTING THE CONTEXT

Canada presents a challenge to conventional theories of growth and change within a system of cities, and this makes it an informative case study. The country is vast (9.7 million sq. kilometres), spanning an entire continent, physically diverse, and relatively thinly populated (31 million). The modern settlement system is also relatively young and therefore is still evolving. Since European colonization, the settled landscape has unfolded from east to west over some 300 years in a distinctively sequential and linear fashion, and is characterized by strong core-periphery contrasts. Today most of the population lives in a strip of territory roughly 300 kilometres wide along the border with the United States. Indeed, sharing a continent with the world's largest economy and arguably most aggressive culture, presents a series of challenges and opportunities for, and constraints on, territorial development in general and the growth of the Canadian urban system in particular.

This chapter examines the recent evolution of the Canadian urban system with special emphasis on two themes: the intersection of diverse processes in shaping the urban system, and the crucial role of external factors in defining the direction of urban change. The first section of the paper develops a conceptual framework that elaborates on the role of external determinants of change. This is followed by a brief overview of the attributes of the Canadian urban system and the significant processes that have reorganized that system over one hundred years, and especially over the last thirty to forty years. The concluding section illustrates these shifts through a series of case studies of the changing relationships among major subsystems of the Canadian urban system, using economic indices and migration flows.

THE CONCEPTUAL FRAMEWORK

Our generalizations about change in national urban systems are often distorted by a preoccupation with our home urban system and its demographic evolution in the recent past. This emphasis is not surprising. Few databases evaluate more than a handful of countries; few national databases cover more than a handful of time periods; even fewer studies reach beyond population measures to evaluate the impact of economic and political events, let alone events in neighbouring regions and countries.

Canadian studies on urban systems are not exempt from these difficulties, but they do have, in addition to the challenges cited above, some particular advantages. First, since Canada is unusually large, geography really does matter. Location relative to other cities affects a city's economic role, social character and rate of growth, as does the level of access to external urban systems. Second, Canada is a very 'open' system - in demographic, economic and political terms. Flows of immigrants and capital, new export markets, and political events outside the country have produced rapid growth and dramatic shifts within the Canadian urban system. Third, our close familiarity with the literature and reality of change in the U.S. urban system provides a perspective, a template, on change which challenges our generalizations. Many of the processes of urban change that occur in that country do not happen in Canada, and vice versa.

In this context our paper offers some universal generalizations about change in urban systems and provides a number of examples from Canada as illustrations. The urban system is defined here as the set of cities (or more broadly, urban agglomerations or regions) within a country, their social and economic characteristics and their interdependencies. Changes within these systems, in broad outline, can be categorized into two distinct types of processes. The first type, called *urbanization processes*, are observed – in varying degrees in most countries and over most time periods – as the increase in urban population (in both absolute and proportional terms), and a declining rate of urban growth. These processes are largely the spatial outcome of the restructuring of national economies away from primary production (agriculture, resources) to secondary industries (manufacturing) and, more recently, to services.

The declining rate of increase in levels of urbanization observed over the last forty years in Canada, and in most developed nations, reflects several processes, but primarily the decline in fertility rates and the virtual completion of the spatial process of population redistribution (e.g. migration from rural to urban areas). Since the basic causes of urbanization, economic restructuring and the demographic transition, derive largely from forces operating within the urban system, they may also be called *internal processes*.

The second type of change in urban systems, and the most interesting we submit, leads to uneven or differential rates of growth among cities within that system. The latter could include variations in the growth rates of cities of different sizes, although these tend to be minor, or the substantial shifts among the rankings of leading cities and/or among sub-regions of the country. This paper argues that such changes derive principally from the degree of openness of urban systems, that is, the *external processes* of change.

Countries that are relatively closed to the movement of goods, capital and immigrants, have urban systems that are highly stable; changes observed are largely those attributable to urbanization. The variability of urban growth rates within such systems tends to be low relative to the overall average rate of growth. In contrast, urban systems that are relatively open to external influence, such as Canada, have the potential for rapid change, often in directions that are unpredictable. In other words, it is primarily external events that permanently alter the structure and spatial organization of urban systems. One further implication of linking external events to urban growth is that contemporary processes of globalization, including increased trade, capital movements, industrial innovations, information technologies, and flows of immigrants, can only accelerate the impact of external changes on urban systems.

THE ARGUMENT EXPANDED

We can expand the argument here with specific illustrations. Closed, or autonomous, urban systems tend to have limited contact with other countries and thus weak external relationships. As a result they generally change slowly and in more-or-less predictable ways. For example, rates of natural population increase (births less deaths) are relatively stable and have become increasingly uniform over space. The spatial distribution of that increase is heavily dependent on the existing location and age structure of the population. Internal migrants are generated in direct proportion to that distribution, and they tend to move to places that are nearby. The amount of population growth therefore is essentially finite and, to a considerable degree, predictable. Similarly, economic growth takes place largely in sectors and at locations that resemble those in earlier periods. New technological innovations, or new resource finds, may alter the location of economic activity, but at modest rates. As a result, the larger urban nodes within the urban system will be strengthened, their dominance enhanced, and the rank ordering of places will be retained. Patterns of economic specialization within the system will also be maintained as wage and price adjustments resist change. Government policies and major investment decisions will tend to reflect the vested interests and power of existing cities and dominant regions.

Urban systems that are open, in contrast, have relatively high potentials for spatial reorganization. Flows of capital, goods, ideas, information, technologies and people across borders are not subject to the constraints imposed within closed systems. The total population can be augmented by new immigrants, who are in theory free to locate where they like, usually where jobs (or earlier immigrants) are present. Conversely, emigrants are free to leave declining cities and regions for other countries. In parallel, the composition of exports, and the major trading partners of that country, may be in continuous flux. There is no need to restrict production to fit domestic demand; nor does domestic demand need to be met from domestic production. Any change in the sectoral composition of the economy, or in international trading arrangements, will advantage some locations and disadvantage others. This, in turn, will influence the location choices of both domestic migrants and immigrants.

Table 15.1 lists some of the more important kinds of external events and relationships that may influence the spatial structure and growth of national urban systems. The entries are listed in order of the degree to which those relationships can be managed by the governments responsible for that urban system. International migration, for example, while initiated outside the system under study, is highly sensitive to changes in domestic policies and politics. Natural hazards, in contrast, are physically internal but functionally (and politically) external. The degree of control exerted by the nation state may be thought of as a measure of the permeability of the national boundary through tariffs, trading agreements, cultural exchanges, foreign (inward) investment and immigration. The concepts of internal-external determinants of change, and the degree of state control, thus represent a continuum, incorporating a wide range of intermediate situations.

The process of urban system development within most countries fits within this general framework. In Canada, a country with a long history of colonial relations with, and dependence on, first France and Britain and then the United States, the now classic 'staples' model of economic development (Watkins 1963) has emphasized the impacts of successive waves of primary products for export: fish, furs, timber, wheat and minerals. Each product, because it was destined for export markets, often developed by foreign capital, and originated from somewhat different supply locations, imposed a distinct layer of settlement on the urban pattern inherited from earlier periods. Each staple product also drew heavily on the attraction of immigrants as a labour source. The result has been continuous change, intense external dependencies, highly specialized urban and regional economies, and a distinctive core-periphery pattern of development (Davies and Donoghue 1993; Britton 1996; Coffey 1996; McCann and Gunn 1998).

Table 15.1 *External factors in the reorganization of urban systems*

Factor	Impacts
Immigration/emigration:	Accentuates the spatial variation in urban growth and decline. Modifies attributes of border zones. Adds skills and capital.
Trade: (a) Composition	Each production sector has a different spatial pattern.
(b) Prices	Stimulates growth/decline in different economic sectors and regions.
(c) Trading partners	Focus on transportation facilities, and location advantages.
Investment:	
(a) Capital	Permits more rapid urban growth or decline. Imposes global standards on rates of return, risk, and tax structures.
(b) Multinationals	Same cultural, technological and institutional links
(a) Transport systems	Alter relative locations; new linkages
(b) Culture and tourism	Creates new growth sectors and locations
(c) Production innovation	Changes regional comparative advantage
(d) Consumption	Hierarchical diffusion processes
War and the threat of war:	
(a) Destruction	Spatially concentrated
(b) Defence budgets	Spatially concentrated
(c) Boundary changes	Modifies access and linkages
Natural hazards:	
(a) Catastrophes	Immediate, localized destruction
(b) Evolutionary	Drought, erosion, disease slowly alter production within the urban system

With this background, we now turn to a brief description of the Canadian urban system and its recent growth experience in order to explore these arguments further.

THE CANADIAN URBAN SYSTEM

As an urban nation, Canada is relatively young. At the time of confederation (1867) the country had fewer than three million people, and only six cities were of significant size (in order of size: Montreal, Quebec, St. John's, Toronto, Saint John, Halifax). All but one of these cities was east of the Ottawa River; three were in the Atlantic region. As the country expanded westward over the next century, the population increased to 5.4 million in 1901, 11.5 million in 1941 and 21.5 million in 1971; the urban system expanded accordingly, to 28 cities in 1901, 65 in 1941 and 105 in 1971. Most of those new cities arose in Ontario and in the west: the prairies and British Columbia. By 1921 the Canadian population was over 50 percent urban, and by 1941 the urban hierarchy had expanded to produce one city of over one million population (Montreal).

Figure 15.1 and Table 15.2 summarize the current Canadian urban system as of 1996. The national statistical agency, Statistics Canada, identifies 137 urban centres with populations of at least 10,000 (Figure 15.1). These centres are best described as 'functional urban regions' in that they include a central city and those adjacent suburban municipalities that are closely linked to the central city through commuting to work. Of these, 25 have populations over 100,000 and are classified as census metropolitan areas (CMAs). The criteria used to define and delimit CMAs closely parallel those used in the US Census, although some metropolitan regions (e.g. Toronto) are now geographically under-bounded (Bourne and Olvet 1995; Bunting and Filion 2000).

The urban system is of course more extensive than the 137 nodes defined above. It also includes many small towns and rural settlements (note: only three percent of the population is now classified as rural farm). Most of these settlements are incorporated into the hinterlands of larger centres, but are not formally considered here. Nor do we discuss the unique problems of small, isolated, resource-based towns in the vast northern periphery, or those of the country's aboriginal communities (Peters 2001).

The geography of the urban system is unusual in a number of regards other than having a northern periphery. The cities are scattered in a narrow populated band along the U.S. border, while most of the rest of the country ecumene has few urban places and is settled at very low densities. This urbanized band is over 8,000 kilometres long, and in most regions, not more than 300 kilometres wide. Thus, the degree of spatial separation among cities, outside of southern Ontario and Quebec, is extreme. Most Canadian cities, in

Figure 15.1 The size of urban centres, 1999

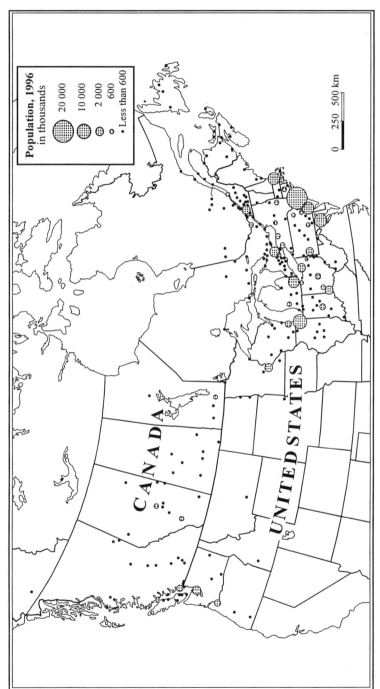

Source: Statistics Canada, Census of Canada, 1995

Table 15.2 Urbanization by region and city size, Canada, 1996

Number of cities						
Population	BC	Prairies*	Ontario	Quebec	Atlantic	Total
>1 million	1	0	2	1	0	4
>300,000	1	3	4	1	1	10
>100,000	2	2	9	3	4	20
>30,000	10	9	13	14	4	50
>10,000	9	11	14	10	9	53
Total	23	25	42	29	18	137
Aggregate population (1000s of persons)						
>1 million	1,832	0	5,274	3,327	0	10,433
>300,000 304	2,351	1,778	672	333	5,438	
>100,000 273	413	1,402	448	531	3,066	
>30,000	573	399	722	650	218	2,563
>10,000	166	182	231	195	177	951
Total	3,148	3,346	9,408	5,291	1,258	22,452
Percentage urban:	84.5	68.3	87.5	74.1	53.9	77.8

Notes: *Includes the Territories

Source: Statistics Canada, Census of Canada 1996

fact, are as close or closer to an American city of the same size or larger population, than they are to an equivalent size Canadian city (Figure 15.1).

Nonetheless, the urban systems of Canada and the U.S. are distinguishable, despite continued economic (and cultural) integration. Numerous studies have shown that various measures of human contact (e.g. telephone calls, airline travel, service delivery, migration) between U.S. and Canadian cities are only one-fifth to one-tenth the magnitude that would be expected (given the size of the cities and their distance apart) without the border. National boundaries still matter. And, most of the flows between the two countries are not symmetrical, in volume or kind. The U.S. has long provided an outlet for Canadian emigrants, especially from slow-growth regions such as the Atlantic region, while immigrants from the U.S. to Canada are few. In recent years, the balance of trade flows in commodities have been heavily in Canada's favour; while flows in services and dividend payments have been overwhelmingly in the U.S.'s favour.

Another unusual feature of the Canadian urban system, which has direct implications for the behaviour of that system, is the immense differences in the size of cities, from 10,000 to almost 5 million, and in the distance between them – as much as 8,000 kilometres. As a consequence, the organization of the urban system is strongly regional and hierarchical, as shown by the linkages in Figure 15.1. These linkages represent the largest outflow from each city, measured as airline trips or migration flows. Within the system, regional centres tend to serve nearby cities and these, in turn, connect to Toronto as the country's dominant economic centre. The most important regional centres are Vancouver, Calgary, Edmonton, Winnipeg, Montreal and Halifax. Linkages define regional hinterlands, while channelling the effects of regional growth upward through the urban hierarchy to the larger centres. Thus, the urban system evolves through competition and differential growth: if, for example, two cities grow at different rates, eventually they exchange size ranks and position as one city captures part of the hinterland of the other. This was the case as Calgary and Edmonton both overtook Winnipeg and captured much of the latter's service area on the prairies.

Table 15.2 summarizes the distribution of urban population in Canada by city size and region. Nearly 78 percent of the population is defined as urban, and of this urban population, 47 percent lives in only four metropolitan regions (Toronto, Montreal, Vancouver, Ottawa-Hull) of over 1 million population. The latter proportion will rise to 55 percent when Edmonton and Calgary pass the one million population threshold. As in most urban systems, the largest cities have the most diversified economies and thus the most stable growth rates (Coffey 1996; Simmons and McCann 2000).

The regional breakdown provided in Table 15.2 is important. Each Canadian region has a different economic base, cultural mix and historical inheritance that affect its response to external forces. The Atlantic region includes some of the earliest settlements in Canada, but its economy is still based on older primary industries: fishing, lumbering, mining. The region's small population and peripheral location discourage the growth of manufacturing or service industries oriented to the national market. The relative lack of economic growth in the region has meant that cities remain small. Halifax is the largest at 350,000, and the region attracts few immigrants. History, geography and politics have conspired to restrict economic (and political) integration within the region.

Quebec provides a different trajectory. As the second largest province (population 7.4 million in 2001) in Canada, Quebec and Montreal dominated the Canadian core region for more than a century. However, as Canada's colonial and trade relationships shifted from Europe to the U.S., the province of Ontario (with 11.7 million) and specifically the Toronto region (with 4.8 million) have moved ahead. With French as the official language of the workplace in Quebec, recent immigrants (especially Asian and Caribbean), and American capital, have increasingly gone to Ontario. As a result, Ontario has grown rapidly and its economy has become closely integrated with the U.S. economy and the northeast manufacturing belt, especially through the location of American branch-plants and, specifically, the location of the automobile industry. As well, rapid economic growth has attracted more than half of Canada's recent immigrants.

To the west, growth of the urban system is largely driven by the boom-and-bust cycles typical of the primary sectors. The prairie region has been based on agriculture (typically slow growing), but Saskatchewan and especially Alberta have become significant producers of oil and gas. Edmonton and Calgary have boomed as a result. British Columbia (B.C.) is also dependent on primary products, but its economy is more diversified with expanding fishing, lumbering, mining and energy sectors that are oriented to markets in Asia. Most cities in B.C., but especially Vancouver, have also absorbed large numbers of Asian immigrants. As a broad generalization of external influences, Montreal could be seen as oriented to markets and investment sources in Europe and the U.S. northeast, Toronto to the mid-Atlantic and mid-west regions in the U.S., and Vancouver to Asian markets and the Pacific Rim generally.

PERIODS AND PATTERNS OF URBAN GROWTH

Each census reveals a somewhat different pattern of urban growth. Table 15.3 summarizes trends in the most recent census period, 1991-96. Overall, Canadian cities (CMAs and CAs) grew by 6.2 percent over this period, compared to 3.9 percent for the non-urban population. The process of urbanization, as defined above, continues, but at a slow rate. Among city-size groups, differences in growth rates are modest, although in this period the largest metropolitan areas (those with over one million population) grew more rapidly than the rest, and small cities and towns (population <30,000) showed the lowest rates of growth. This is the first time since the early 1980s that growth rates have been significantly and positively correlated with city size, an indication perhaps of a reversal of earlier decentralization trends and a return to a period of further metropolitan concentration. Also note that the variations in growth rates among regional urban subsystems are much greater than among city-size groups, with B.C. growing at twice the rate of the national system, Ontario slightly above average, and the other three regions growing much more slowly. The Canadian urban system is clearly still undergoing substantial reorganization by city size and region.

The table also records the variability of growth rates within each region and city-size category, as measured by the coefficient of variation (ratio of the standard deviation to the average for cities in each row or column). As expected, cities in the core region of Canada (Ontario and Quebec) display less variation in growth rates than do cities in the periphery the Atlantic region, the prairies and B.C. In the case of B.C., however, the average growth rate is so large overall that it obscures the high standard deviation.

Table 15.3 Urban growth by region and city size, Canada, 1991-96

Aggregate Growth Rate (per cent)							
Population	BC	Prairies*	Ontario	Quebec	Atlantic	Total	C.of V.
>1 million	14.3	---	9.0	3.7	---	8.1	0.47
>300,000	5.7	4.2	4.5	4.1	3.7	4.3	0.53
>100,000	21.1	2.5	6.9	2.3	1.1	5.7	1.27
>30,000	15.2	2.8	1.3	2.0	3.6	4.7	1.36
>10,000	5.1	2.6	4.2	1.3	-0.3	2.6	1.85
Non-urban	12.9	3.8	7.0	3.3	2.0	6.2	0.95
C.of V.	0.51	1.21	0.70	0.82	1.85	0.95	---

Notes:

*Includes the Territories

C.of V.= Coefficient of Variation (defined as the standard deviation/mean)

Source :   Statistics Canada, Census of Canada, 1996 and 1996

Over a longer period, however, the short-term fluctuations may cancel each other out or they may cumulate into substantial rates of change sufficient to produce shifts in the way the urban system is organized and the way that cities are linked together. Table 15.4 outlines changes over the twenty-five years from 1971 to 1996. In aggregate, the population of cities in

Table 15.4 Urban growth by region and city size, Canada, 1971-96

Aggregate Growth Rate (per cent)							
Population	BC	Prairies*	Ontario	Quebec	Atlantic	Total	C.of V.
>1 million	69.2	---	60.6	19.7	---	44.6	0.53
>300,000	---	62.3	37.3	34.0	---	47.4	0.70
>100,000	55.4	54.5	36.2	9.9	20.0	34.0	0.85
>30,000	120.3	28.1	44.7	36.2	55.6	51.1	1.02
>10,000	99.2	58.4	35.9	31.9	53.2	50.3	1.11
Total	77.0	59.1	47.7	23.9	31.6	44.7	1.04
C.of V.	0.78	0.85	1.02	0.86	0.86	1.04	---

Notes:

*Includes the Territories

C.of V. = Coefficient of Variation (defined as the standard deviation/mean)

Source: Statistics Canada, Census of Canada, 1971 and 1996

the initial urban system grew by roughly 45 percent, but with relatively small variations among the city-size groups. The correlation between city-size (log 1971) and growth is only –0.073. Larger cities do, however, grow in a more regular fashion.

The other expected pattern is the inverse relationship between city-size and variability in growth rate. The coefficients of variation for cities in the three smallest size categories are more than twice the levels for larger places. Thus, increasing city size is important not primarily for what it tells us about average growth rates but about the predictability of those rates, and thus about the vulnerability of smaller places to extreme fluctuations of growth and decline (Bourne 2000). This vulnerability is particularly evident in the boom-bust cycles typical of the country's more remote resource-based communities (Randall and Ironside 1996).

If we disaggregate this time period into shorter periods there is evidence to support the argument of 'period-effects' in terms of the balance of urban and non-urban growth rates, and in the direction of net migration flows, but the evidence is not particularly strong. For example, the early post-war period, basically the 1950s through to the early 1970s, could be described as a period of rapid growth almost everywhere in the country, but with extensive urban growth and metropolitan concentration. Migration flows during the 1960s were, on balance, directed to the larger urban centres. The 1970s, in contrast, ushered in an era of modest deconcentration, with rapid growth of many medium and smaller urban centres, and much of the nation's resource-based periphery. This short period was as close as Canada came to displaying the properties of polarization reversal or 'counter-urbanization'.

The 1980s and 1990s, following severe recessions in the first years of both decades, witnessed an equally modest return to a period of metropolitan economic renewal and population concentration. The latter trend, however, appears to have been driven largely by foreign immigration flows into the major metropolitan centres, rather than by domestic migrants. Even during the 1990s, the Toronto and Montreal metropolitan areas lost domestic migrants to small cities and towns in their immediate hinterlands, and to most cities in the west. They also lost in the migration exchange in all age categories other than the under-29 years age cohorts.

At the same time, substantial and consistent differences can be observed in growth rates among different regions of the country. Indeed, these have been sufficient to modify the urban system over the short span of twenty-five years. Cities in B.C. have grown at twice the rate of those in the Atlantic provinces and three times as fast as those in Quebec. The overall shift of population from east to central and western regions in Canada continues the historical sequence of settlement, but it also mirrors differences in the resource base of the regions and the growing significance of markets in the U.S. and Asia.

Differences in the growth rates of cities in the upper echelons of the urban hierarchy are of considerable significance since they both reflect and generate a reorganization of the hierarchical linkages among places. During this period, Toronto solidified its position of national dominance over Montreal, continuing a process that began in the 1920s or earlier. Montreal's hinterland, with a few exceptions, is now largely restricted to the province of Quebec. In the prairies, Winnipeg (700,000) was once the dominant regional centre but has lost that position to Edmonton (925,000) and especially to Calgary (950,000). At the upper level of the hierarchy in the west, Vancouver (2 million) has extended its reach into the prairies. In the Atlantic region, Halifax has moved into a clearly dominant position, ahead of St. John's (Newfoundland) and Saint John (New Brunswick).

Over an even longer term, the last 100 years, these changes have accumulated into the present day urban system. Table 15.5 summarizes these complex patterns in terms of average growth rate (the urbanization process) and various measures of variations in these rates (defined above as urban change). First, note the decline in the average growth rate of Canadian urban areas since 1901. The decade from 1901 to 1911 was the most intense period of settlement expansion and urbanization in the country as waves of European immigrants surged into the cities and as the western frontier was opened. Second, the high value for the coefficient of variation suggests that this was also a period of extraordinary changes in the nation's urban system.

Table 15.5 Spatial reorganization of the urban system and levels of external influence, Canada, 1901-96

Decade	Number of Cities	Growth Rate			Immigrants/ Population	Net Immig.	Export Growth
		Mean	S.D.	CofV			
1901-11	28	52.3	69.0	1.32	28.9	15.1	29.9
1911-21	42	39.6	29.9	0.75	19.4	4.3	75.4
1921-31	50	26.5	20.9	0.79	13.7	2.6	4.5
1931-41	59	19.7	17.7	0.90	1.4	0.9	140.4
1941-51	65	31.3	17.3	0.55	4.8	1.5	20.4
1951-61	78	39.1	22.2	0.57	5.7	4.4	27.0
1961-71	105	23.8	30.9	1.30	9.6	6.7	104.5
1971-81	127	13.2	23.0	1.74	7.8	4.0	90.8
1981-91	141	8.1	11.4	1.41	8.5	5.5	4.6
1991-96*	137	8.2	11.8	1.44	8.1	6.5	153.0

Notes: *Values extrapolated to 10-year rates; all cities over 10,000 population.
S.D.=Standard Deviation; C.of V.=Coefficient of Variation

Source: Statistics Canada, Census of Canada, 1901 and 1996

An entirely new urban subsystem emerged in western Canada, and very quickly Winnipeg and later Vancouver moved into the upper ranks of Canadian cities.

Following this decade, and especially during the great depression of the 1930s, the rate of reorganization levelled out until the 1950s and 1960s. The 1951-61 period produced another surge of urbanization as the post-war Baby-Boom peaked, and as Canadians left the farms for the cities. They were joined by new waves of immigrants from Europe. Following the baby-boom, when fertility rates were among the highest in the western world, rates of natural increase dropped sharply (producing lower urban growth rates), while continued high levels of immigration added to the variation in those growth rates. In other words, urbanization processes gave way to urban change.

THE DEMOGRAPHY, MIGRATION AND IMMIGRATION

Figure 15.2 documents the shift in the components of population growth, and the demographic transition that lie behind the most recent shifts in the patterns of urban growth. The decline in rates of natural increase has reduced the volume of population growth generated locally, and as the population ages the level of domestic migration, especially long-distance migration, has been reduced. Note that the volume of 'net' domestic migration – measured here as the sum of positive net inter-provincial migration flows - is now only about 50,000 persons per year. With net immigration levels now at 175,000 persons per year, this means that immigration adds three to four times as many net migrants to the urban system as does domestic migration.

Note also the shift in importance of natural increase and immigration as contributors to national population growth. In the 1960s, for example, approximately 80 percent of growth was attributable to natural increase, and only 20 percent to immigration. At the end of the 1990s, immigration accounted for over 50 percent of national growth. Equally important, that flow of immigrants has three distinctive properties that have direct impacts on the urban system. First, the immigrants are now drawn overwhelmingly from non-traditional source countries (e.g. in Asia, Africa, Caribbean); second, more are arriving as the result of chain migration (e.g. through kinship networks, family reunification), and as refugees; and third, they are heavily concentrated in a few large metropolitan areas or 'gateway' centres (Toronto, Vancouver, Montreal). Most cities in the rest of the country (including those in Quebec outside of Montreal), receive few immigrants.

These new immigrant groups have not only changed the components of growth but they have added to the skills (or human capital) pool and introduced a much greater differentiation in social, ethnic and cultural

Figure 15.2 *Migration and shifts in the Canadian population growth, 1961-99*

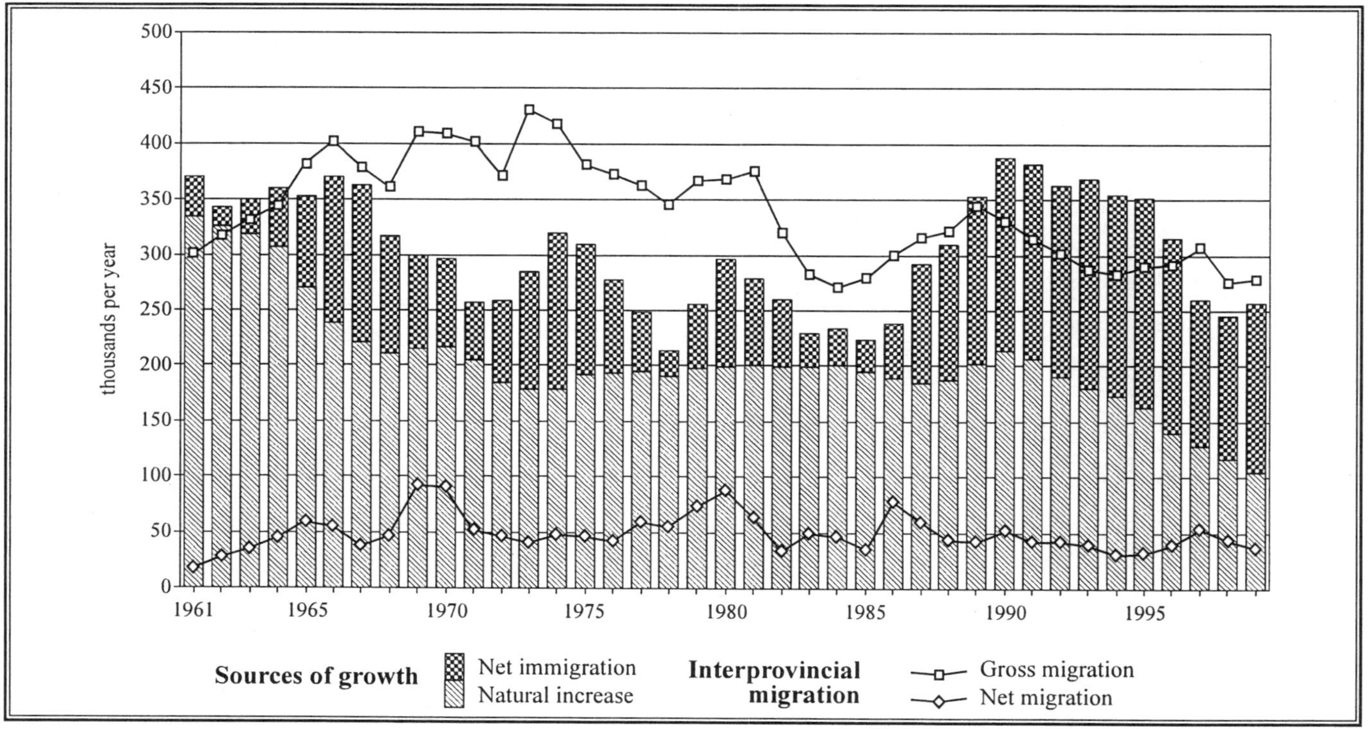

Source: Statistics Canada, Census of Canada, 1961 and 1999

characteristics among places within the urban system. The implications of these cultural transitions are the subject of increasing research and policy interest (Ley 1999; Bourne 2001).

Domestic migration flows within the urban system continue to reflect past directions and linkages (origins and destinations), but with modest swings due primarily to regional business cycle effects. It is difficult to generalize beyond the patterns that we have come to expect in migration research: the bias in the kinds of movers toward younger age cohorts, and the bias in locations selected people tend to move to areas with jobs, and to smaller places in amenity-rich locations for reasons of life style and/or retirement. Most of the latter locations are in or near the major metropolitan areas.

Moreover, each major metropolitan region has a more-or-less unique migration regime (Table 15.6). Each tends to draw different combinations of in-migrants from (and out-migrants to) metropolitan and non-metropolitan areas, and different balances of domestic and foreign migrants (Bourne and Flowers, 1999). Toronto, for example, in the last decade garnered 85 per cent of its growth (over 90,000 people annually) from immigration, while it lost heavily in the domestic migration exchange. The impact of the severe recession in the late 1980s and early 1990s in the industrial heartland is clearly evident. Montreal also lost through domestic out-migration, but surprisingly at a

Table 15.6 The changing components of metropolitan population growth in Canada, 1986-96

Metro area		Pop. Growth %	Contribution to Growth (%)			Total Growth (000s)
			N.Inc.	N.Mig.	N.Immig.	
Toronto	1986-91	13.4	47.2	-24.9	77.7	461
	1991-96	9.4	31.4	-24.0	92.5	365
Montreal	1986-91	7.0	54.6	-14.8	60.2	206
	1991-96	3.7	39.8	-40.7	100.9	118
Vancouver	1986-91	16.1	27.9	17.9	54.0	221
	1991-96	14.3	15.7	5.3	79.1	229
Ottawa	1986-91	12.4	37.2	24.6	38.1	106
	1991-96	7.3	43.4	2.4	54.2	69
Calgary	1986-91	12.3	55.8	3.7	40.4	83
	1991-96	9.0	36.0	13.8	50.3	68

Notes: N.Inc.=Natural increase; N.Mig.=Net domestic migration; N.Immig.=Net immigration.

Source: Census of Canada 1996; Bourne and Olvet, 1995

lower rate than Toronto; the difference is that it receives even fewer in-migrants and immigrants. It also retains fewer of its immigrants in the first five years after their landing than either Vancouver or Toronto. Vancouver, in contrast, has gained from both domestic and international migration, while Ottawa's growth is fuelled largely by natural increase and domestic migration. In some cities, notably Toronto and other cities in southern Ontario, there is evidence that domestic out-migration increases as the level of immigration increases (Bourne 2001).

THE ECONOMY

Figure 15.3 shows the parallel transition in terms of the economy. Over time the average growth rate of that part of the national economy (GDP) destined for the domestic market has declined, while imports and the more volatile component of economic growth, exports, have increased their share. Since the introduction of the Free Trade Agreement (FTA) with the U.S., and the subsequent North American Free Trade Agreement (NAFTA) with the U.S. and Mexico, exports have risen from 22 percent of Canada's output to over 45 percent. Export sales can, and often do, shift from one sector to another over time, and therefore from one location of origin to another. For example, note the wide fluctuations in the export volumes of two critically important Canadian commodities: energy (oil and gas) and automobiles.

Over the last decade or more, exports have also grown at a much higher rate than inter-regional flows within the country (Figure 15.4). This suggests a relative weakening of the linkages that tie Canadian cities and regions together, and closer integration of regional economies in Canada with those of other regions, especially in the U.S.

To some observers these trends raise serious questions about the viability of the nation state. Specifically, they focus attention on the future of equalization relationships between the country's 'have' and 'have-not' regions (called the Canadian social contract), and thus the persistence of regional inequalities, and the creation of new forms of powerful regional urban subsystems that increasingly behave as separate states (Courchene and Telmer 1998; Polese 2000). At the very least, these trends confirm the increasing importance of external factors in urban and regional development outlined above.

Figure 15.5 indicates that while exports may increase national growth rates, as well as levels of personal and corporate income, they also import a considerable amount of volatility into the economy, and thus into the nation's geography. The effects on the urban system of changes in export regimes can also be dramatic. Different parts of the urban system will grow at different rates, depending on the composition (sectors), prices and locations of export growth.

Figure 15.3 GDP growth of different sectors in Canada, 1971-2000

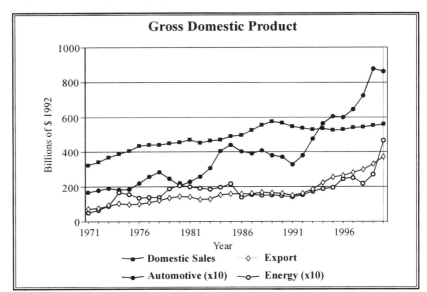

Source: Statistics Canada, Census of Canada, 1971-2000

Figure 15.4 Interprovincial and international trade flows, 1984-99

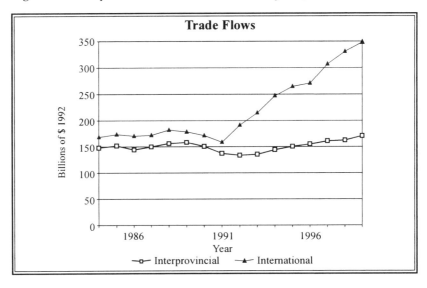

Source: Statistics Canada, Census of Canada, 1984-1999

Figure 15.5 Local and international trade of Canada, 1972-2000

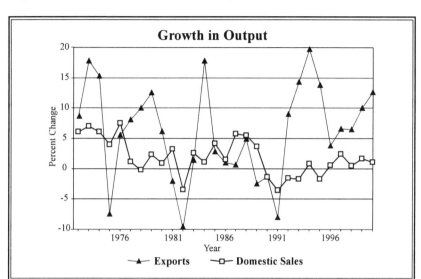

Source: Statistics Canada, Census of Canada, 1972-2000

THE PROCESSES REVISITED: FOUR CASE STUDIES

In the earlier sections we have demonstrated how short-run variations in urban growth rates can accumulate into substantial reorganizations of the urban system. As well, we have demonstrated how these changes are associated with shifts in the external relationships of urban systems. Yet, for a clearer sense of the processes involved in urban system change, their volatility over time, and the complex interactions between external and internal forces of change, we develop a series of case studies of the major relationships acting to redefine subsystems of the Canadian urban system. Each case begins by tracking changes in the demographic indicators for the urban subsystem, as these are reflected in variations in population growth and migration flows from year to year, and these changes are then linked to events occurring inside or outside the region and the country. The case studies are of four provinces (regions), each of which represents an urban subsystem focused on a major city or cities: southern Ontario (Toronto), Quebec (Montreal), Alberta (Calgary and Edmonton), and British Columbia (Vancouver).

The case studies illustrate the intersection of three distinct types or patterns of urban systems linkages: the cultural/demographic, the economic and the political (i.e. the state). These three dimensions, broadly defined, jointly shape the spatial patterns of growth within the Canadian urban system. The first, the cultural/demographic, describes flows of people, ideas, human capital, and information, and include migration, telephone and other communication exchanges. The volumes of these flows, in turn, are largely shaped by a combination of factors, such as differences in city-size, economic base and social structure, and of course, by distance.

But in Canada these flows are further modified by the language barrier that separates Francophone (primarily Quebec) and Anglophone regions, and they are even more constrained by the international boundary to the south. Flows of information across the language barrier are reduced by a factor of two to four times, compared to regional boundaries without a language divide, while flows across the U.S. border are reduced by a factor of six to eight.

The economic flows include all elements of production and consumption, such as the movement of raw materials from the periphery to the country's core region, or their shipment directly to international markets, and the flow of manufacturing parts and producer services within the southern Ontario-southern Quebec core region. These flows are only modestly affected by language barriers or international boundaries, but they are intensified by the regional pattern of economic specialization, and by regions exhibiting differential levels of urbanization. Cities in the core region, for example, are closely interconnected, while non-core cities are much less so, the latter for reasons of distance and the relative lack of complementarity in their economic bases. In the periphery, primary products destined for export often move out of the country by the most direct route, while goods destined for consumers tend to filter down the urban hierarchy from their usual place of origin in the major regional centres, and especially in the cities of Central Canada. In 1984 the level of exports (in goods) was equivalent to roughly 90 percent of the value of interprovincial trade flows, but by 1999 they were twice as large.

The political system refers to the movement of money, and political influence, within and among political jurisdictions. Revenues flow to governments from individuals and firms, while transfer payments and public services flow in the opposite direction (Simmons 1984; Simmons and McCann 2000). Public expenditures in Canada are roughly 40% of GDP. Clearly, the geography of the national political system, and the different roles of the various levels of government in Canada (federal, provincial, regional and local), are both significant here. Provincial boundaries are evident in different levels of taxation and public expenditure. Net transfers within the political system shift money from the larger and wealthier cities and regions to smaller centres and rural areas, and especially to poorer regions (e.g. equalization payments).

Of course, as the level of public expenditures declines as a proportion of GDP, the impact of the political system on the pattern of growth in the urban system is reduced. And, as the relative importance of different levels of government shifts, most recently towards the provinces, the potential for the spatial redistribution of growth is altered, and at the national level, is significantly reduced. As a result, regional differences in income and standard of living may increase once again.

The case studies illustrate how changes within the urban system can originate within each of these three dimensions. We begin with Ontario, the largest region and the home of the largest urban region, Toronto, and the region most closely linked to the United States market (Figure 15.6). As Ontario, and especially southern Ontario, has come to dominate the Canadian urban system over the last thirty years, it has also become the demographic reservoir and the migration 'swing' region for the rest of the urban system. Ontario provides domestic migrants to areas of the country that are growing (typically in the west), and absorbs migrants from regions in decline (typically in the east and Quebec). Ontario is also typically the leader in both return and onward migration flows (Newbold and Liaw 1990) across the country. But Quebec was losing domestic migrants from the 1950s onward while Toronto was attracting them. Ontario, especially the Toronto region, was also increasingly attractive to immigrants (Figures 15.6 and 15.7).

By the 1970s these trends were accelerated by a series of political events that, among other effects, frightened Anglophones in Montreal. A surge of relocations, of individuals and firms, out of the province, was the result, as shown by the domestic migrant profiles for both provinces (Figure 15.7).

Figure 15.6 Migration trends, Ontario, 1966-99

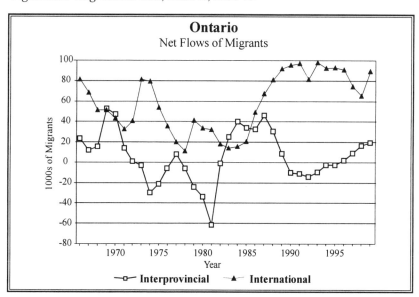

Source: Statistics Canada, Census of Canada, 1966-1999

Figure 15.7 Migration trends, Quebec, 1966-99

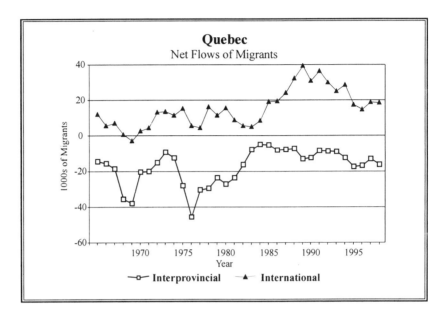

Source: Statistics Canada, Census of Canada, 1966-1999

After a few years of recovery, the election of a separatist party to power in the provincial government in 1976 led to a second surge of out-migration to Ontario, notably Toronto, and the west. These trends were reinforced by a decline in domestic in-migration rates, and by only a modest rebound in immigration levels. Montreal intensified its links to Francophone communities within Quebec, but weakened its links to the rest of the country. Meanwhile, Francophone elites replaced the Anglophone elites within the Montreal economy and power structure. By 2001, the Toronto metropolitan area had a population of 4.8 million (with over 5.8 million in the greater Toronto region) compared to 3.6 million in the Montreal region.

The recent and dramatic growth of exports to the U.S. from the early 1990s, especially in automobiles and auto parts, has stimulated economic and population growth. Trans-border competition and integration have intensified. Ontario, as a result, has become more dependent on the U.S. market for economic growth, as well as on international migration for labour and population growth. As a result, it is less and less concerned with maintaining its dominant role in the Canadian economy and within the national urban system.

While Quebec's economic role within Canada resembles that of Ontario, the key events in the relative decline of Montreal were often more political than economic. In 1961 the Montreal metropolitan region had a population of roughly 1.7 million, while Toronto had only 1.5 million. The two metropolises shared the national hinterland, providing goods and services

The relationship between the Ontario urban subsystem, focused on Toronto, and that in Alberta, focused on Calgary and Edmonton, is a classic example of the core-periphery dynamic. Alberta contains most of Canada's oil and gas deposits. When energy prices are high, producers invest heavily in new production facilities, as well as new office buildings, and new jobs are created. In addition, the provincial government collects more revenues and uses these to build roads, schools and hospitals. Yet much of the capital for energy investments, as well as the labour force, comes from Ontario, Canada's largest pool of consumers, capital and potential migrants.

The result has been an inverse relationship between growth in Alberta and the west and growth in Ontario (Figure 15.6). The boom times for Alberta lasted from 1974 (the first oil crisis) until 1981 (see Figure 15.8). At that time the federal government introduced the National Energy Program (NEP) that froze oil and gas prices in an attempt to redistribute revenues from the Alberta government. The result was a reversal of migrant flows back to Ontario and other eastern regions. Later the policy was withdrawn, and with the subsequent escalation in energy prices during the late 1990s Alberta has again undergone an economic boom, and is again attracting substantial flows of in-migrants from the rest of the country. Surprisingly, the province has attracted fewer international migrants than might have been expected during

Figure 15.8 Migration trends, Alberta, 1966-99

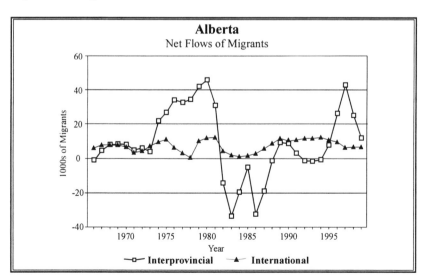

Source: Statistics Canada, Census of Canada, 1966-1999

Figure 15.9 Migration trends, British Columbia, 1966-99

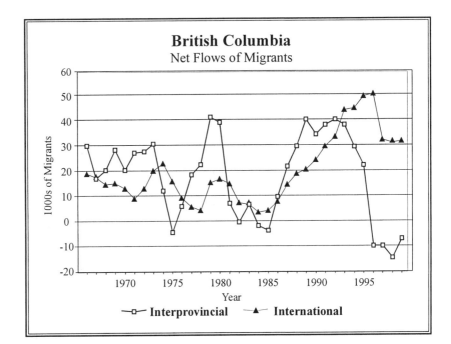

Source: Statistics Canada, Census of Canada, 1966-1999

a boom, in part because it did not already have a large base of recent immigrants.

British Columbia, in contrast, has always been home to substantial concentrations of immigrants, especially Asians, and when the political circumstances in Hong Kong generated uncertainty during the early 1990s the province attracted a huge influx of new immigrants (Figure 15.9). By 1995 over 50,000 immigrants a year were coming into Vancouver, bringing with them a substantial infusion of skills and capital. The concomitant prosperity attracted large numbers of domestic migrants as well. After the smooth transition of Hong Kong to China, however, the level of immigration declined, as did other sectors of the B.C. economy linked to Asian exports, and the province went into decline. Domestic net migration flows also declined, with fewer arrivals from Ontario and Quebec and more leaving for Alberta.

Nonetheless, this recent surge of growth cemented Vancouver's position as Canada's third-ranked city, despite the challenges posed by the growth of Edmonton and Calgary. It also re-affirmed its dominant position within the urban hierarchy of western Canada, and as the country's gateway to the Pacific region.

CONCLUSIONS AND A LOOK AHEAD

National urban systems are in continuous evolution, driven by factors deriving from both inside and outside the system. Internal, or domestic, factors have been largely responsible for the continuing growth in urban population, measured either in absolute or relative terms. However, to understand, let alone explain, how urban systems alter their spatial organization, their hierarchical relationships, and the rank-ordering of cities, we argue that researchers must look to events outside the system, as demonstrated by this study of Canada. Other researchers have made similar arguments in different contexts (e.g. Rozenblat and Pumain 1999).

To summarize the arguments with which the paper began, and the empirical evidence presented above:

1. urban growth has the potential to be highly volatile; and thus urban systems can evolve rapidly.
2. differentials in growth rates are higher for regions (i.e. urban subsystems) than among city-size groups. Based on the Canadian experience, the former are the more interesting kinds of urban system change.
3. Variations in growth rates are greater within urban systems that are more open to external influence.
4. Globalization increases the likelihood of change within urban systems. Indeed, the most recent wave of globalization beginning in the 1970s may have stimulated much of the 'counter-urbanization' effect, at least in the initial stages, by favouring peripheral locations over traditional core regions. This effect has been reversed in recent years, however, as core regions and the larger metropolitan areas have shown renewed economic fortunes (and increased immigration).
5. National governments can only control, or even influence, changes in their urban systems if they can manage the flows of stimuli across their borders.
6. Future studies of urban systems must incorporate research on linkages to neighbouring urban systems – e.g. continental approaches, as well as examine the imprint of global economic competition, new trade and financial agreements, and political events.

In the Canadian case we are likely to see the continuation of past trends in urban growth over the next few decades. The urban system in Canada is certain to witness further changes in its spatial organization and linkages. It is likely to become, by most indices, more regionally fragmented, with increasingly strong economic linkages to neighbouring regions in the U.S., and to the U.S. urban system in general. Immigration will generate an increasing share of population growth and redistribution, especially for the larger metropolitan areas.

We are also likely to see the emergence of a more formal and tightly integrated North American urban system, focused on New York, Los Angeles, Dallas-Houston and Chicago (and perhaps Mexico City) as the high-order control centres. Canadian metropolitan areas will occupy second tier positions. Yet the national boundary will continue to matter, at least for the immediate future. Geography will also continue to be a dominant influence; distance too still matters, even in an era of new technologies, effortless telecommunications and frictionless e-space.

The challenge of maintaining, and managing, a national urban system will grow. Cities in the system will become more socially distinct, largely due to differential rates of growth and decline, highly concentrated immigration flows and widespread population aging. Income inequalities and social polarization are likely to increase within the larger metropolitan regions, even as they decline between those regions. At the same time these cities will become more similar in economic terms as overall levels of economic specialization decrease.

With national population growth rates declining, most areas of the country, and many small towns and cities, will witness little or no growth in the future (Bourne and Rose 2001). Net migration rates will also decline, and become even more selective in terms of the age and occupational characteristics of out-migrants, and their destinations. This will leave some places, especially small towns and cities in peripheral regions, with even more skewed age profiles and truncated labour force structures. The country will have to find ways to assist these places in adapting to population shrinkage and aging.

Finally, metropolitan concentration will continue, especially for higher-order services (e.g. producer services), high-tech functions, and skilled workers. This is a response in part to the pressures from global competition for scale economies and in part to the social and cultural attractions of larger cities. But concentration will be combined with widespread decentralization of population and production capacity at the local and regional scale. Indeed, we might anticipate a future Canadian urban system dominated by five 'extended' metropolitan regions: Toronto-Hamilton-Oshawa, Montreal, Vancouver-Victoria, Ottawa-Hull, and Calgary-Edmonton – even as these places become increasingly subservient to the U.S. urban system.

REFERENCES

Bourne, L. S. (2000), 'Living on the edge: Multiple peripheries in the Canadian urban system', in Y. Gradus and H. Lithwick (eds.) *Developing frontier cities – global perspectives*, Amsterdam: Kluwer Publishers, pp. 77-97.

Bourne, L. S. (2001), 'On migration, immigration and social sustainability: the recent Canadian experience', in R. B. Singh (ed.) *Urban sustainability in the context of global change,* Plymouth, U.K., Science Publishers, pp. 261-282.

Bourne, L. S. and A. Olvet (1995*), The Canadian urban system revisited: a statistical analysis*, Research Paper 192, Centre for Urban and Community Studies, University of Toronto.

Bourne, L. S. and M. Flowers (1999), *Changing urban places: Mobility, migration and immigration in Canada*, Research Paper 196, Centre for Urban and Community Studies, University of Toronto.

Bourne, L. S. and D. Rose (2001), 'The changing face of Canada: The uneven geographies of population and social change', *The Canadian Geographer*, **45**, 105-119.

Britton, J. N. H. (ed) (1996) *Canada and the global economy*, Montreal: McGill-Queens University Press.

Bunting, T. and P. Filion, (eds) (2000), *Canadian cities in transition*, Second Edition, Toronto: Oxford University Press.

Canada, Energy, Mines and Resources, Surveys and Mapping Branch (nd), *National atlas of Canada,* Fifth Edition, Ottawa, Geographical Services Division.

Coffey, W. (1996), *Employment growth and change in the Canadian urban system, 1971-1994*, Ottawa: Canadian Policy Research Network.

Courchene, T. and C. Telmer (1998*), From heartland to North American region state*: *The evolution of Ontario*, Toronto: University of Toronto Press.

Davies, W. K. D. and D. Donoghue (1993), 'Economic Diversification and Group Stability in the Urban System: The Case of Canada', *Urban Studies* **30**, 1165-86.

Foot, D. and D. Stoffman (1996), *Boom, Bust and Echo*, Toronto: McFarland Walter and Ross.

Gertler, M. (2001), *'Urban economy and society in Canada: Flows of people, capital and ideas'*, Ottawa: Policy Research Secretariat, and Canadian Policy Research Network (mimeo).

Ley, D. (1999), 'Myths and Meanings of Immigration and the Metropolis', *The Canadian Geographer*, **43**, 2-19.

McCann, L. and A. Gunn (1998), *Heartland and hinterland. A geography of Canada*, Third Edition, Toronto: Prentice-Hall.

McCann, L. and J. Simmons (2000), 'The core-periphery structure of Canada's urban system', in T. Bunting and P. Filion (eds), *Canadian cities in transition*, Second Edition, Toronto: Oxford University Press, pp. 76-96.

Newbold, B. and K. L. Liaw (1990), 'Characterization of primary, return and onward provincial migration in Canada: Overall and age-specific patterns', *Canadian Journal of Regional Science*, **13**, 17-34.

Norcliffe, G. (2001), 'Canada in a global economy', *The Canadian Geographer*, **45**, 14-30.

Peters, E. (2001), 'Geographies of aboriginal people', *The Canadian Geographer*, **45**, 138-144.

Polese, M. (2000) 'Is Quebec special in the emerging North American economy? Analysing the impact of continental economic integration on Canadian regions' *Canadian Journal of Regional Science,* **23**, 188-212.

Randall, J. and G. Ironside (1996), 'Communities on the edge: An economic geography of resource-dependent communities in Canada', The *Canadian Geographer*, **40**, 17-35.

Rozenblat, C. and D. Pumain (1999), 'Expansion of multinational firms in the European urban hierarchy, 1990-1996', in A. G. Aguilar and I. Escamilla (eds), *Problems of megacities: Social inequalities, environmental risk and urban governance*, Mexico City: Institute of Geography, Universidad Nacional Autonoma de Mexico, and the International Geographical Union, Commission on Urban Development, pp. 5-20.

Simmons, J. (1984), 'Government and the Canadian urban system: Income tax, transfer payments and employment', *The Canadian Geographer*, **28**, 18-45.

Simmons, J. (1992), *'The reorganization of urban systems: The role and impacts of external events'*, Research Paper 186, Toronto: Centre for Urban and Community Studies, University of Toronto.

Simmons, J. and L. McCann (2000), 'Growth and transition in the Canadian urban system', in T. Bunting and P. Filion (eds), *Canadian cities in transition*, Second Edition, Toronto: Oxford University Press, pp. 97-120.

Watkins, M. (1963), 'A staple theory of economic growth,' *Canadian Journal of Economics and Political Science,* **26**, 132-148.

Chapter 16

Evolution and Maturing of the Mexican Urban System

A. G. Aguilar and B. Graizbord[1]

INTRODUCTION

Urbanization associated with developing countries over the last five decades has been one of rapid urban growth and rural to urban migration flows. In the larger developing countries urban concentration accelerated after the Second World War, due to advances in the industrialization process. Industrialization, considered to be an indispensable factor for the 'take off' in economic development, tends to concentrate in a limited number of cities, if not in one only, and urban primacy became a common feature, particularly in Latin America.

However, after the 1970s signals of a new stage in the evolution of the urban system from a very concentrated pattern to decentralization and polarization reversal started to appear in certain countries in Latin America. As Leven (1990:182), suggested 'the advantages of larger size are not limitless; eventually certain disadvantages of size would emerge and, depending on circumstances, the net advantages of scale would be reached at some finite population.'

The theoretical insight offered by Leven in such a parsimonious statement justifies an investigation into (i) changes in the Mexican urban system, (ii) the way cities have changed in size and function, and (iii) how the urban

---

[1] The authors gratefully acknowledge the contribution of Irma Escamilla, Clemencia Santos, and Milton Montejano in the analysis of the data and in the compilation of the figures.

population has evolved in terms of its socio-economic and demographic attributes. As technological and organizational changes occur in the production process, geographic responses can be seen not only through time but through space as well. Thus, our analysis of the Mexican urban system is organized not only in terms of city sizes, but also by geo-economic regions and from a centre-periphery point of view.

Our interest will be: (i) to discuss the stages of evolution and signs of maturation of the Mexican urban system; (ii) to find out if cities by size are becoming similar in terms of their population attributes (Leven 1990:189); (iii) to describe how the urban system and some particular cities have experienced the transition from a more industrial to a more service-oriented economy; (iv) to examine the relative importance of and differences between core and periphery and among the main urban subsystems in Mexico. The framework for analysis is the proposal of 'differential urbanization' (Geyer and Kontuly 1993) that recognizes a cyclical process in which the timing whereby different city size ranks are to change and become recipients of main and subsidiary migration flows (streams) follows a sequence starting from the centre and highest rank size and spreading to the periphery and lower rank sizes.

This process of city and population growth is explained by migration or population decentralization, but also by economic activities and market developments, as was pointed out recently by Fujita, Krugman, and Venables (1999:128-129). The idea is based on the central-place hierarchy concept, and not only on some special natural locational advantages such as ports as transportation hubs (*op. cit.*:129). According to them increasing population density in a territory plays a significant role in an urban system's evolution.

The chapter is divided into five sections. This short introduction sets the framework for the analysis. The second section, based on historical events, describes how the Mexican urban system was structured, emphasising the 'outset of rapid urbanization' and concentration, a process that prevailed throughout most of the first half of the twentieth century. The third refers to the development of the 'modern' urban system in more detail, mainly through a review of the literature. The fourth section analyses the specific changes in the urban system occurring during the second half of the twentieth century through socio-economic and demographic variables by city-size categories. Finally, some perspectives on the urban future are offered in the last section.

THE EARLY DEVELOPMENT OF THE MEXICAN URBAN SYSTEM

The aim of this section is to highlight historical events that shaped the early formation of the Mexican urban system, particularly from pre-colonial times up to the first half of the twentieth century. Three main stages can be identified: (i) the *Pre-Colonial and Colonial Period*, referring to the time before the Spaniards conquered Mexico in 1521 to the year of Mexican Independence in 1810; (ii) the *Independent Era*, from the early nineteenth century up to the beginning of the Mexican Revolution in 1910; and (iii) the *Outset of Rapid Urbanization*, comprising most of the first half of the twentieth century, from 1910 up to 1940.

(1) The Pre-Colonial and Colonial Period.

Just before the Spanish conquest in the sixteenth century, Tenochtitlan, in the valley of Mexico, with about 300,000 inhabitants, was the most important urban settlement of an empire[2] that extended over a large portion of the Meso-american region.[3] Simultaneously, there were also important settlements associated with the *Maya* people in the Yucatán Peninsula; the *Tarascos* in the present states of Michoacán, Jalisco, Colima, and Guanajuato; and the *Zapotecs* and *Mixtecs* in the state of Oaxaca. Two aspects have to be emphasised. Firstly, these large-scale communities adopted the political form of 'city-states' where a large commercial and religious settlement tended to dominate several agricultural localities and small political-religious entities; apparently, there was very little economic interaction between the different cultures and entities (Scott 1982: 25). Secondly, large-scale urban cultures were particularly important in the central region of Mexico,[4] which played an historical role in the formation of future urban agglomerations as Spaniards consolidated most of the pre-colonial spatial order. The best example is Tenochtitlan, later re-founded as Mexico City, the capital of New Spain.

During the 300 years of the colonial period, the urban development axis moved to the North and towards the Gulf of Mexico. Cities were mainly developed to perform political and administrative functions and to provide trading partners with Spain, as well as to exploit mineral resources.[5]

Two main trends can be identified: (i) consolidation of former inhabited spaces and (ii) the foundation of dispersed new settlements (see López Austin and López Luján 1996; García Castro 1993: 133-134). In the first place, the

---

[2] An empire called Culhua-Mexica, also known as Aztec.
[3] The region covers the area from the northeast of Central America to the present Mexican states of Sinaloa, San Luis Potosí, and Tamaulipas
[4] It is estimated that by 1521, the population in central Mexico was 2.5 million in a highly-dispersed pattern (Unikel et al. 1976: 17).
[5] The same sort of economic functions were distinguished for other colonial towns in Latin American countries (see Castells 1973: 19).

early distribution of cities largely coincided with that of Indian settlements. The best example is Mexico City, which, as the seat of government and ecclesiastical authorities, consolidated a pre-eminent role in this period as a political, administrative, and financial centre for Spain's large colonial territory in the Americas. In other words, Colonial Mexico inherited and maintained the central region (or *altiplano*) as an historical and geographical nucleus. In several regions, old Indian pueblos co-existed with the new Spanish settlements, mainly in the central portion of the country and in the lowlands of the Yucatán Peninsula, where the Maya groups developed.

Secondly, mining towns (*reales de minas*) were established close to important silver mining sites; among those were Taxco, Pachuca, Zacatecas, and Guanajuato. They acted as 'company towns' and are good examples of an enclave economy. The mining centres served as a first phase of the colonization of the northern part of the country. One region structured during the colonial period with an important agricultural and cattle-raising sector was the *Bajío*; the discovery of rich mineral resources in this region, its fertile soils on a large plain, and the support of the colonial government were fundamental incentives for colonizing this territory and setting the conditions for further urban growth.

In the eighteenth century, the colonial urban network presented all the characteristics of an 'immature' urban system.[6] The lack of a good road infrastructure inhibited the development of interurban links, resulting in a weak commercial exchange among urban areas, and one city, the capital, dominated the area. The high cost of transport was an important barrier for commercial activities between regions,[7] reflecting a predominant agricultural economic base and a rural society. Secondly, 90 per cent of the population lived in settlements with less than 10,000 inhabitants. Therefore, the 'urban' concentration of commercial activities and mining was dominated by five or six main cities (see Figure 16.1) in a milieu of unarticulated and weak regional markets.[8] Migration to cities occurred, but Mexico City absorbed most of it, particularly from the central region of the country. In the second half of the eighteenth century, at least 40 per cent of its inhabitants had been born outside the city limits (Pescador 1993: 115-117). By the same date its population reached more than 100,000 inhabitants.

---

[6] This statement is put forward by Pescador (1993: 112).
[7] For example, a caravan of horses could take six weeks to go from Mexico City to Guadalajara or to Zacatecas; and no less than nine weeks to go from Tula to Monterrey or Parral (Pescador 1993: 109-110).
[8] The presence of merchants and commercial activities was particularly important in Guadalajara and Veracruz; Puebla was a textile centre with half of its population employed in this industry by 1793; and the *Bajío* manufactured mainly cotton, wool, and leather (Morse 1973: 22; Moreno Toscano 1973: 178-179).

Figure 16.1 Main cities and roads in the eighteenth century

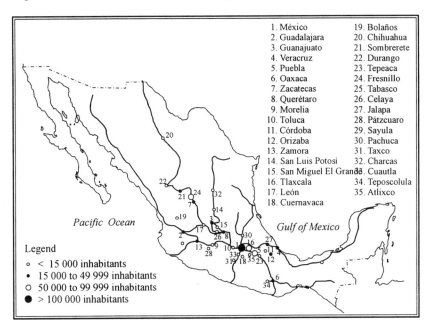

1. México	19. Bolaños
2. Guadalajara	20. Chihuahua
3. Guanajuato	21. Sombrerete
4. Veracruz	22. Durango
5. Puebla	23. Tepeaca
6. Oaxaca	24. Fresnillo
7. Zacatecas	25. Tabasco
8. Querétaro	26. Celaya
9. Morelia	27. Jalapa
10. Toluca	28. Pátzcuaro
11. Córdoba	29. Sayula
12. Orizaba	30. Pachuca
13. Zamora	31. Taxco
14. San Luis Potosi	32. Charcas
15. San Miguel El Grande	33. Cuautla
16. Tlaxcala	34. Teposcolula
17. León	35. Atlixco
18. Cuernavaca	

Pacific Ocean

Gulf of Mexico

Legend
o   < 15 000 inhabitants
•   15 000 to 49 999 inhabitants
O   50 000 to 99 999 inhabitants
●   > 100 000 inhabitants

Source: Pescador, 1993, p. 111

(ii) The Independent Era

It was not until the second half of the nineteenth century, during the *Porfiriato,* that important changes occurred and new regional centres emerged. In the second half of the nineteenth century moderate economic growth was facilitated by foreign investment and the development of the transport network, particularly railroads.[9] The development of ports linked to the railroad network and the proliferation of mining towns in the North led to the expansion of regional markets and urban growth.

Railroad expansion played an important role in stimulating the growth of cities at a higher pace than Mexico City in the central and northern part of the country (Guadalajara, Veracruz, Monterrey, San Luis Potosí, and even Mérida in the South). [10] Old mining towns in the North gave way to new

[9] Before the Revolution, 33 per cent of foreign investment was in railroads, and 24 per cent was in extractive industries (Scott 1982: 31).

[10]San Luis Potosí prospered due to its commercial links with the port of Tampico, which had a significant number of U.S. merchants; Mérida experienced rapid growth because of the commercial plantations of sisal (Moreno Toscano 1973: 186).

centres in Coahuila, Durango, and Sonora, Torreón-Gómez Palacio in *La Laguna,* and Monterrey, which became a traditional heavy-industry location. Veracruz, one of the main railroad network nodes, concentrated almost all export and import maritime freight (see Figure 16.2).

Figure 16.2 The railway network before and after 1900

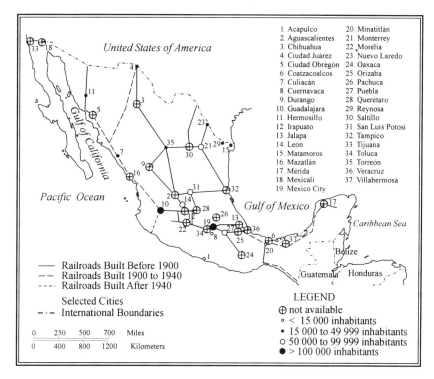

Source: Scott, 1982, 0.29

At this stage, Mexico City became the predominant city in the urban system, increasing its population from 200,000 in 1877 to 400,000 in 1910. In other words, whereas the primacy index between the two main cities in the early nineteenth century was slightly over 2, by the end of that century the same index was well above 3, more closely approaching a pre-eminent condition (see Unikel et al. 1976: 24). Macro-economic and spatial changes during the *Porfiriato* had a lasting effect on the structure of the Mexican urban system. A communications network was established, facilitating interactions between the centre and the northern regions. The heavy dependence on exports to the United States inhibited to a great extent the formation of a balanced urban system, and cities which were the largest at the beginning of the twentieth century, were to retain their prominence thereafter.

(iii) The Outset of Rapid Urbanization

The first decades of this period were characterized by relatively slow urban growth, due to domestic and external events. The 1910-21 Revolution and the 1929 world economic depression had negative impacts on exports and affected the pace of urban growth. After the 1920s, in a period of reconstruction, consolidation, and institution building, the largest cities, particularly Mexico City, diversified and strengthened their social, economic, and cultural functions and accelerated their urbanization trends.

Urban population grew at a more rapid rate than the total population between 1900 and 1940, from 1.4 to 3.9 million inhabitants. But the number of cities increased from 33 in 1900 to 55 in 1940. Most of the urban growth was concentrated in the larger cities. While in 1900 there were only two cities with over 100,000 inhabitants concentrating 33 per cent of the total urban population (representing 10.5 per cent of the total), by 1940 there were 6 cities of the same size concentrating 12 per cent of the total urban population (20.0% of the total) (Unikel et al. 1976: 30-31). By 1940, Mexico City had reached a population of 1.5 million and the primacy index increased to 6.65 (for two cities).

Improved accessibility reinforced the main cities. During the first half of the twentieth century the railroad network remained roughly the same, but road transport grew significantly. Both the national road system and the railroad network emphasized North-South linkages, hindering East-West movements. This structure reflected both physical-geographic conditions and inertial forces from the *Porfiriato* period (Scott 1982: 42). Cities located along the transport network were favoured in terms of their functions, experiencing urban growth and reinforcing their linkages with Mexico City. Two main regions where this process occurred can be identified: (i) the central portion of the country connecting cities like Guadalajara, Aguascalientes, San Luis Potosí, the *Bajío*, and those along the roads to Veracruz (East) and Acapulco (West); (ii) those comprising the North-Central and north-eastern corridors in a comprehensive network including Tampico, Monterrey, Torreón, Chihuahua, and border towns to the Northeast, fairly distant but potential market towns. On the other hand, two main regions remained isolated. One comprised the North-western states, since the Sonora-Baja California road system was not connected to the main network until 1942. The other to the Southeast, including the Yucatán Peninsula, remained isolated until 1938 when the railroad system was linked to the central network.[11] Maritime transport was significant and remained so for cities along the Gulf of Mexico.

---

[11] Referring to this aspect, Scott (1982: 41) points out that the national road network linked only thirty-three of the fifty largest cities in 1940. The Northwestern and Southeastern regions having fewer roads than other areas.

Table 16.1 Urban population by urban size groups, 1910 and 1940

Size of settlement	Number of urban places		Population of urban places			
	1910	1940	1910	1940	1910	1940
2,001-2,500	396	n.a.	1,313,794	n.a.	8.67	n.a.
2,501-5,000	n.a.	438	n.a.	1,486,648	n.a.	7.56
5,001-10,000	123	165	848,124	1,101,778	5.59	5.61
10,001-20,000	40	55	518,124	757,170	3.42	3.85
20,001-50,000	22	29	714,786	876,281	4.71	4.46
50,001-100,000	5	9	362,845	672,552	2.39	3.42
100,000+	2	4	590,534	2,002,240	3.9	10.19
Total	588	700	4,348,341	6,896,669	28.68	35.09

Notes: n.a. = not available

Source: Scott (1982, p. 48)

THE DEVELOPMENT OF THE MODERN URBAN SYSTEM, 1950-2000

URBANIZING TRENDS 1950-1970: CONCENTRATION AND METROPOLITAN GROWTH

In the late 60s, Unikel (1971) initiated systematic studies of urbanization and city growth in Mexico. His work was permeated by ideas which were paramount at that and earlier times in developed countries: primate city growth as a fact and 'concentrated decentralization' (Rodwin 1972) as a wish.

By the 1950s, Mexico City already had 3 million inhabitants, while only Guadalajara and Monterrey surpassed the 250,000-population mark. Industrialization policies were publicly supported and industrial growth was accompanied by population concentration in Mexico City, with heavy periphery-to-centre migration flows.

It was in the 1970s that a metropolitan growth trend as a form of urbanization began, affecting Mexico City and a few secondary cities. Unikel (1971) and other authors (e.g., Carrillo Arronte 1971) were able to identify main trends: rural-urban migration flows, mostly to the country's capital as of the 1940s and to very few other cities later on, and concentrated efforts, both public and private, but mainly by the State, to trigger an industrialization process in the country by taking advantage of scale and external economies in Mexico City. Unikel referred to a massive rural-urban flow (3 million migrants during the 1960s) to Mexico City which experienced an average annual growth rate of 5.7 per cent (5.5 per cent during 1950-60), an historical peak. He was also able to trace signs of contiguous peripheral growth in twelve urban centres (Unikel et al., 1976:135): Mexico City, Monterrey, Guadalajara, Puebla, Orizaba-Córdoba, Veracruz, Chihuahua, Tampico, León, Torreón, Mérida, and San Luis Potosí. The first three had over 500,000 inhabitants. Three additional cities (Tijuana and Mexicali in Baja California and Ciudad Juárez in Chihuahua) were experiencing growth followed by intensive linkages with their twin cities across the border, rather than expanding physically to other contiguous municipalities on the Mexican side.

In the early eighties, an extensive review of the literature[12] constituted a good starting point to speculate on the possibilities of decentralized urban growth in the Mexican urban system (Graizbord 1984). It was expected that intermediate-sized cities would show a relative growth rate surpassing that of the large metropolitan centres in the country. Stage models by Hall (1980), Drewett (1980), Berry (1980), and Berry and Dahman (1977) provided a framework to explain general sequences in urban development. They visualized a 'U'-shaped trend, – first rural-to-urban, then urban-to-urban, and finally urban-to-rural migration. Later on, the stage model was conceptually expanded to include the possibility of more than one cycle of stages,[13] not only nationally and internationally but also at the regional and local level (Geyer and Kontuly, 1993; Geyer, 1996, 1998). Population redistribution patterns at the latter levels could be described as 'similar migratory modes involving different regions in the country or different migration modalities in

---

[12] Including several papers referring to urbanization and counter-urbanization (Berry 1976), a 'clean break with the past' (Vining and Strauss, 1977), 'deconcentration without a clean break' (Gordon, 1979), the halt in the metropolitan phenomenon (Alonso, 1978), polarization reversal (Richardson, 1980), etc..

[13] In addition to mainstream migration patterns implied in earlier stage models, the concept of 'differential urbanization' included sub-stream migration flows that either serve as an early indication of a new phase of urban development that is about to begin, or as an indication of the last traces of a past phase. Six stages of urban evolution are suggested in the model.

one region' (*op. cit.* 1984: Figure 1 on page 44 and page 46). Contrary to what was initially considered as a concentrating tendency *ad infinitum*,[14] deconcentrating trends in urban growth patterns were seen as more than a possibility.

With the onset of deconcentration, defined as 'polarization reversal' in the Third World environment (Richardson, 1980) and as 'counter-urbanization' in the First World[15] (Vining and Strauss, 1977), the urbanization process acquired a new dimension. Some (Gordon, 1979) thought at the time that no such break was evident, but rather that an undulatory process in metropolitan growth affecting other cities within the regional influence of dynamic urban centres was more likely under way. In fact, inspired by Berry (1972), both processes were recognized as parallel and it was speculated that, in the case of the Mexican urban system, hierarchical diffusion within the urban system, as well as a contiguous process taking advantage of opportunities offered by location relative to the main metropolitan centres, was a possible scenario for the near future (Graizbord, 1984). The idea of a 'U' shape (Alonso, 1980) describing the evolutionary process in mobility over time, as was pointed out by Zelinsky (1971) and considerations by Rutledge Vining twenty or more years earlier, were sufficient references as a basis for such an hypothesis. In fact, Ledent (1982) had identified a point of inflection in rural-urban migrations for Mexico for the 1975-80 period which was also a good reason to consider the possibilities of a rather new approach to the Mexican urbanization process by looking at small- and intermediate-sized cities in the national urban system (see Aguilar, Graizbord and Sánchez-Crispín, 1996 and 1997).

What was treated as a remote possibility for an underdeveloped country was later stated as a generalization by Gilbert (1993). This author identified five basic trends characterizing more recent urbanization processes in developing countries: (i) urbanization rates were increasing in most of the African and Asian countries, but decreasing in Latin America; (ii) migration trends had been modified as the possibilities for long-distance daily commuting to work have increased;[16] (iii) suburbanization and spatial deconcentration have resulted in a polycentric urban structure in most of the metropolitan areas; (iv) primate cities and old metropolitan areas reduced their population growth rates; (v) last but not least, Gilbert was convinced that those changes have not necessarily been deliberate, since explicit urban

---

[14] By Garza (1980) in the case of Mexico.

[15] At the time Vining and Strauss referred to migration deconcentration in the USA as 'a clean break' with past trends.

[16] That is the case for Mexico City (Acuña and Graizbord, 1999; Graizbord and Molinatti, 1998), but also for Guadalajara, Monterrey, Puebla, and other cities along the León-Querétaro industrial corridor in the Central-Western region of Mexico.

policies had not been effective or have disappeared from the developing countries' political agendas.

In the case of Mexico rapid population growth at average annual rates of 2.8 per cent during 1950-95 reached a peak of 3.2 per cent in 1950-70. During these two decades, the urban population grew at almost 5 per cent annually, while the rural population (in settlements with 2,500 or fewer inhabitants) was growing at an average rate of 1.5 per cent. At that pace, 8 out of every 10 new inhabitants ended up as urban dwellers. Thus, in terms of demographic growth, the second half of the twentieth century can be divided into two periods: 1950-70 and 1970-95 (Cabrera 2000). From 1950 to 1970 most of the demographic factors experienced positive changes: life expectancy rose from 51.9 years to 63.1; infant mortality was cut back from 116 one-year-old deaths per thousand to 73 (albeit with big differences persisting between urban and rural figures) and so on. But the main factor was rural-to-urban migration, with numerous origins and very few destination points. Nearly 50 per cent of total rural migration ended in Mexico City and 20 per cent in Monterrey and Guadalajara. Due to these migration flows, by the year 1970, Mexico's rural population increased much faster amongst younger people (15 years and less) and slightly faster amongst the older people (65+) than the urban population. The country also became predominantly urban, still exhibiting great differences between the rural and urban populations and increasing inequalities by region.

DECENTRALIZATION 1970-95. EARLY STAGES OF INTERMEDIATE-SIZED CITY GROWTH

The country's population reached 91.2 million in 1995. According to the latest census data, Mexico today has a population of 100 million people. Demographic planning (i.e., 'family planning', as birth control was euphemistically termed), with the main objective of reducing the country's very high fertility and birth rates, was institutionalised by law and by the creation in 1974 of CONAPO (*Consejo Nacional de Población*, or National Population Council). From then on, growth rates were reduced to reach 2.6 per cent in 1995 for the country's total, 0.8 per cent for the rural and 3.5 per cent for the urban population. Population growth slowed down, inhabitants became relatively older, and the younger cohorts shrank. Fertility for both the rural and the urban populations dropped substantially from 6.3 children per woman to 3.1 for the country as a whole and from 7.7 to 4.4 and from 5.7 to 2.8 for the rural and urban populations, respectively. The country is now almost 70 per cent urban, but still bears witness to wide social differences not only between central and peripheral regions but also by sectors and between ethnic groups. A greater number of people living in more and bigger cities seems to be a continuing trend (see Figures 16.4 and 16.5). At the same time, growth rates are being reduced in every rank-size group, especially in those with over one million inhabitants, which, since the seventies, have been exhibiting rates similar to the country's total (see Figures 16.3 and 16.4).

The faster growth of middle-size cities in the 1980s and early 1990s demanded attention not only from the government sector in the form of urban-regional policies, but also new interpretations and emphasis from academic works on this particular urban level of the hierarchy. Several analyses highlighted the process of urban dispersion in the country (see Aguilar, 1992; Aguilar and Rodríguez, 1995), and the promotion and growth of intermediate-sized cities   (see Aguilar, Graizbord and Sánchez-Crispín, 1996 and 1997).

Later in the 1990s, while in Mexico a counter-urbanization tendency was seen as temporary with strong agglomeration forces acting in favour of the primate city (Garza 1999), some signs of differential urbanization were highlighted. This phase apparently corresponds to the following one defined by Geyer (quoted in Geyer and Kontuly, 1993): 'early signs of deconcentration being apparent while concentration forces are still dominant and signs of continuing concentration after dispersion has set in as the predominant migration pattern'. At the same time 'the sequence of tendencies observed in the development of urban systems, first toward concentration and then toward dispersion or deconcentration is not limited to systems at the national level, but can also manifest itself at each of the lower levels of territorially organized subsystems because the same spatial forces operate at both national and subnational levels' (Geyer and Kontuly *op. cit.* p. 160). In fact, a deconcentration of urbanization in the functional region of Guadalajara (Mexico's second largest metropolitan area) was reported with intermediate- and small-sized cities growing at faster rates (Arroyo and Velásquez 1992).

DECONCENTRATION OR COUNTER-URBANIZATION 1985-2000
Recently, Tuirán (2000) was able to identify differential growth in Mexico's larger metropolitan areas. After referring to the controversy and analysing migratory trends in two periods based on general information, he was able to report that Mexico City 'observed an unfavourable migratory balance' in both the 1987-92 and 1992-97 periods. The net migration balance of Guadalajara, Puebla, and Torreón 'was positive during 1987-1992 but changed to negative during the second period'. Toluca, 'with a positive balance in the 1987-92 period registered a balance close to 0 in 1992-1997'. Monterrey 'was the only one of the six selected cities with a positive balance in both periods' (Tuirán 2000:56). His conclusions are relevant to the present discussion. He reported the following tendencies:

i   Migration towards the metropolitan peripheral rings of the selected cities originating in the 'rest of the country,[17] slowed down in both five-year periods analysed. The size of those flows decreased both in absolute numbers and in rates in all cases. Puebla was the only city in which a small positive increment was observed.

ii   Migration from the metropolitan peripheral rings towards 'the rest of the country' increased between the first and second periods. This flow increased in all six cases. With the exception of Mexico City, larger numbers of migrants resulted in higher migratory rates.[18]

iii Migration to central cores originating in the 'rest of the country' diminished from 1987-92 to 1992-97. Except for Monterrey, all cities experienced a drop in the number of migrants and in migratory rates.

iv   Migration from the central cores to the 'rest of the country' slowed down in both periods. Except for Puebla, the other cities experienced a decreasing migratory flow reflecting a phase out of this decentralizing process.

v   Metropolitan mobility between central core and peripheral rings also slowed down between the 1987-92 and 1992-97 periods.

In short, except for Monterrey, where migratory flows from the 'rest of the country' to both the central core and the peripheral rings were still prevalent in both periods, in the other cities considered movements from the central core to the peripheral rings decreased and those to the 'rest of the country', either from the central core or from the peripheral rings, got stronger and in some cases quite significant.

Mexico City, the primate city, experienced the three stages of the first urbanization phase as proposed by Geyer and Kontuly (1993). During the third stage, when the city's mono-centric urban structure could no longer sustain and diseconomies (congestion) appeared, Mexico City developed into a typical multi-centered structure. This complex structure reached a 'megalopolitan' status once its peripheral rings merged to the metropolitan area of Toluca, a city 60 km away. As pointed out by Graizbord and Mina (1994) and Aguilar (1999 and 2000), as well as by Garza (1999) and Negrete (1999), during the eighties the central region showed signs of rapid growth; some intermediate-sized cities within the region grew rapidly, reaching the

---

[17] Based on Berry and Dahman's center-periphery migration model (1977), Tuiran divided the country into metropolitan (central core and peripheral rings), and non-metropolitan (urban and rural) areas. For simplicity we refer to 'central core', 'peripheral rings', and 'rest of the country'.
[18] Average annual rate per thousand inhabitants. These rates result from dividing the number of migrants by the total population at the beginning of the respective period.

500,000 inhabitants mark due to migratory flows originating in both the primate city and their contiguous regions.

One can, of course, view Mexico's differential urbanization process as being at the 'concentrated dispersion' or intermediate-sized city phase because some typical signs of this phase are emerging. 'Urban growth [is taking] place [not only] in intermediate-sized cities fairly close to the primate cities' (Geyer and Kontuly 1993), but also in independent cities in distant regions far away from the primate city, which by now is growing at a much slower rate than most (if not all) intermediate-sized cities of the Mexican urban system. The fact that Mexico City's manufacturing employment is decreasing is a clear indicator of this phenomenon. In this sense, the country's urbanization process cannot be categorized as continuing urban sprawl, not even on a regional (central-region)[19] scale.

EVOLUTION OF THE MEXICAN URBAN SYSTEM IN THE SECOND HALF OF THE 20th CENTURY

DEMOGRAPHIC GROWTH BY CITY-SIZE AND CORE-PERIPHERY CATEGORIES

In the second half of the twentieth century population growth by city-size categories shows three main periods: concentration in the primate cities; first trends of polarization reversal to a reduced number of urban centres; and a dominance of intermediate-sized cities and regional metropolitan areas.

In the period 1950-70, the largest metropolitan areas established overall dominance, registering the highest growth in the system with rates of approximately 5 per cent, and concentrating 25 per cent of the total population at the end of the period. Those metropolitan areas were attracting a large percentage of migrants, with Mexico City metropolitan area at the forefront (see Figures 16.3 and 16.4). A weak urban hierarchy developed with intermediate-sized and large cities concentrating a small proportion of the population (about 10 per cent in each category), while small-sized cities concentrated more than 20 per cent.

The above mentioned trends are good enough to accept that this period corresponds to the primate city stage with a clear dominance of the core, represented by the three main metropolitan areas, over the periphery (see Table 16.2).

Between 1970 and 1990 the most important changes occurred in the main metropolitan areas. Growth slowed down in large cities and intermediate-sized cities started growing faster. Migratory flows led to both economic

---

[19] The central region comprises the *Distrito Federal* and the states of Mexico, Morelos, Hidalgo, Tlaxcala, Puebla, and Querétaro, an area of nearly 100,000 square kilometers.

diversification and changes in their urban spatial structure. Those urban centres closer to the main metropolitan areas responded first to polarization reversal. In fact, the outer cores of Mexico City, Guadalajara and Monterrey grew much more rapidly than their inner cores, reaching a more 'mature' phase in the following decade (see Table 16.2). Thus, intermediate-sized cities adjacent to the primate cities, and also those with exceptional locational attributes or the presence of natural resources (oil or tourism) in some distant regions, had better chances to develop, showing features of the 'advanced primate city stage'.

After 1990, the pace of growth in all the urban categories and main metropolitan areas continued to slow down. Large cities consolidated their position as regional centres and their growth tended to accelerate during the last period with intermediate-sized cities following very close by. On the other hand, small-sized cities are maintaining their non protagonist role. In general, the basic trend in the urban system is a larger concentration of population in outer cores (metropolitan peripheral rings) and an expansion of metropolitan areas.

These recent trends in the Mexican urban system tend to coincide still with the 'intermediate-sized city stage' of the Geyer-Kontuly model. But the primate city is losing population vis-à-vis the large and intermediate-sized cities, while urban centres within the main metropolitan regions are now growing faster than the central city. One main difference from the model is that small-sized cities have been growing steadily at low rates and do not show signs of accelerating their growth in the short term.

SOCIO-ECONOMIC CHANGES BY CITY-SIZE CATEGORIES

Our aim in this section is to show to what extent the redistribution of urban growth (concentration to deconcentration) in the period 1950-90 has produced changes in some socio-economic variables by city size. Five variables were selected for analysis: employed population by income, economic sector, and qualification levels, educational levels and age groups (see Figure 16.5). To the extent that there has been a deconcentration process, the socio-economic characteristics of the main metropolitan areas tended to spread out to the urban periphery, and trickle down the Mexican urban system hierarchy.

During the 1940s Mexico adopted an economic model that stimulated import-substitution industrialization (ISI) which mainly affected large cities. By 1950 this process was under way and its effect was already present. The main metropolitan areas attracted most of the main urban productive activities, concentrating 61 per cent of government functions, more than 35 per cent of all commercial and service activities, and 38 per cent of manufacturing activities. The next level of cities in the hierarchy (large cities)

Figure 16.3 Population change by rank-size, 1950-95

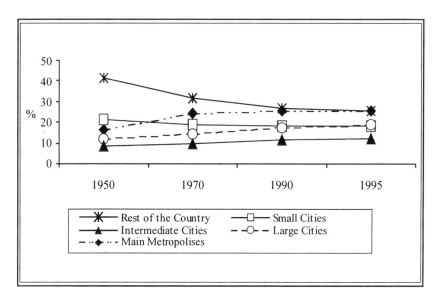

Source: Bureau for Geographical and Statistical Data: Mexico

Figure 16.4 Evolution of population by rank-size, 1950-95

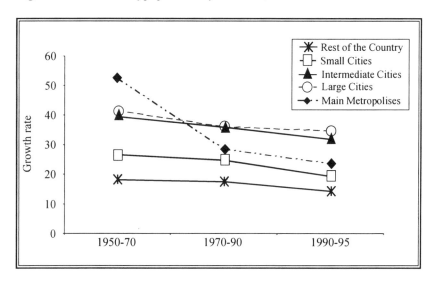

Source: Bureau for Geographical and Statistical Data: Mexico

Table 16.2 Population 1950-70-90 and growth rates 1950-70 and 1970-90 by rank size*

	1950 Total	1950 %	1970 Total	1970 %	1990 Total	1990 %	Growth rate 50-70	Growth rate 70-90
Main metropolises	4,264,906	16.54 (100.00)	11,879,365	24.63 (100.00)	20,787,521	25.58 (100.00)	5.26	2.84
ZMCM	3,391,602	(79.52) 13.16	9,091,189	(76.53) 18.85	15,226,800	(73.25) 18.74	5.05	2.61
Inner core (DF)	3,050,442	89.94	6,874,165	75.61	8,235,744	54.09	4.15	0.91
Outer core (MMEM)	341,160	10.06	2,217,024	24.39	6,991,056	45.91	9.81	5.91
ZMG	483,675	(11.34) 1.88	1,533,485	(12.91) 3.18	2,987,194	(14.37) 3.68	5.94	3.39
Inner core (MG)	380,226	78.61	1,199,391	78.21	1,650,205	55.24	5.91	1.61
Outer core (MMG)	103,449	21.39	333,094	21.79	1,336,989	44.76	6.04	7.18
ZMM	389,629	(9.14) 1.51	1,254,691	(10.56) 2.60	2,573,527	(12.38) 3.17	6.02	3.66
Inner core (MMO)	339,282	87.08	858,107	68.39	1,069,238	41.55	4.75	1.11
Outer core (MMMO)	50,347	12.92	396,584	31.61	1,504,289	58.45	10.87	6.89
Large cities	3,137,660	12.17	7,060,983	14.64	14,320,997	17.63	4.14	3.60
Intermediate cities	2,172,962	8.43	4,708,021	9.76	9,520,806	11.72	3.94	3.58
Small cities	5,386,666	20.90	9,314,399	19.31	14,967,708	18.42	2.78	2.40
Rest of the country	10,817,060	41.96	15,262,470	31.65	21,652,613	26.65	1.74	1.76
Mexico	25,779,254	100.00	48,225,238	100.00	81,249,645	100.00	3.18	2.64

Notes:
* Main Metropolises: ZMCM (Metropolitan Area of Mexico City), ZMG (Metropolitan Area of Guadalajara), ZMM (Metropolitan Area of Monterrey). Large Cities: more than 500,000 excluding the three main metropoli. Intermediate Cities: 100,000 to 499,999. Small Cities: 15,000 to 99,000. Rest of the Country: all municipal units not included in the above categories.

Source: National Bureau for Statistics and Geographical Information, Mexico.

also attracted a significant proportion of these activities, almost a quarter of the total. On the other hand, many small-sized cities were closely linked to agriculture and mining and provided commercial goods to the local communities.

Larger urban centres present obvious comparative advantages. They contained the highest proportion of the most educated and qualified section of the population, i.e. those with secondary, high school and university education, and contained the highest percentage of specialized professional and technical personnel. In fact, there was a direct relationship between the level of education of the population and urban size. In contrast, the higher proportion of illiterate and lowly qualified people was concentrated in rural areas and small-sized cities (65 per cent of the population with a low levels of qualification).

By 1970 the level of economic concentration in the largest city of the Mexican urban system reached its peak. In the context of rapid urbanization some economic sectors became more concentrated in the main metropolitan areas. Examples of the latter were manufacturing and commercial activities: more than 40 per cent. Although large and intermediate-sized cities lost some industrial vigour, they increased their share of other important urban functions like wholesale and retail, services, and government. Signs of an urban-based economy were already under way in larger cities that were performing central place functions and their bureaucratic sector expanded significantly.

Of the three main urban subsystems, of which Mexico City, Guadalajara and Monterrey formed the gravity points, Mexico City was the unchallenged 'core' with about 37 per cent of the manufacturing activity, and a similar proportion of retail and service activities. Their inner cores concentrated more than 75 per cent of these economic activities.

Urbanization increased the provision of formal schooling through vast investments in education. Secondary high school and university graduates contributed to the country's social development as their total numbers increased substantially in the urban hierarchy as a whole. Even so, main and large cities still held the larger proportion. In general, provision of education to the middle classes benefited and enhanced their social mobility. But rural migration to these centres increased their percentage of illiterate population while rural areas experienced a small reduction in its non-educated population.

At the stage of high concentration, the main metropolitan areas were showing unequivocal signs of economic development with a substantial consumer market, and a larger proportion of medium and high-income groups as well as the largest percentage of highly skilled and highly paid work force in them. Their national share of medium and highly qualified

Figure 16.5 Socioeconomic changes by city-size categories

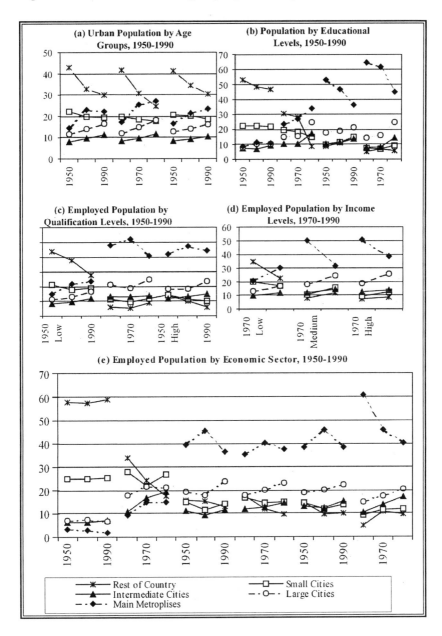

Source: Based on official figures of Census Population Data. National Bureau of Geographical and Statistical Data. Mexico.

An expanding medium stratum in those cities (more than 50 per cent of the country's total) was indicating rising income levels and a possible reduction of inequality as the more skilled workers responded positively to employment opportunities. The main metropolitan areas were also the places of residence of the richest people as 51 per cent of the population with the highest income were concentrated there. However, at the time when larger cities attracted the best-qualified population, they were also receiving a high proportion of the least qualified migrants. These groups were less and less incorporated into the formal productive sector and remained involved in marginal activities, increasing the income inequality effect. On the other hand, small-sized cities and rural areas exhibited high levels of inequality during rapid urbanization. Not having produced on a significant scale the agglomeration economies offered by larger cities, they were not able to offer substantial employment opportunities. A large proportion of the labour force in small-sized cities and rural areas in 1970 were people that fell in the low income and low qualified groups. As a consequence, a clear polarization in the urban hierarchy was observed during the period, i.e. concentration of more affluent people in the main metropolitan areas and poorer people in the smaller urban centres and rural areas. Large and intermediate-sized cities showed some economic expansion but their proportion was far from that of the rest of the urban hierarchy.

The main metropolises showed an increasing share of all age groups, particularly the youngest group (0-11 years), due to high urban growth rates. Also the increase in the economically active group (12-64 years) reveals strong employment generation during the phase of economic expansion.

The data for 1990 show how the process of urban deconcentration has had a positive socio-economic effects on the Mexican urban system. Main metropolitan areas lost their preponderance in the urban system, benefiting the rest of the urban hierarchy in terms of productive activities, population with higher incomes, and more educated and qualified urban residents. All economic sectors became less concentrated in the main metropolitan areas and lost relative weight. The cases of manufacturing and government are particularly notable because these sectors decreased by approximately 9 and 6 per cent respectively from 1970 to 1990. Two important factors contributed to this process: an economic crisis in the early 1980s, and the adoption of an export-oriented model that culminated in the North American Free Trade Agreement (NAFTA) with the United States and Canada, resulting in a more open economy.

The loss of relative economic importance of the three main urban subsystems speaks for itself. The economic concentration of manufacturing, retail and services in the main metropolitan areas lost between 4 and 9 percentage points in the period 1970-90, in favour of the rest of the urban hierarchy. In terms of metropolitan expansion, the outer core in each metropolis increased its concentration of productive activities significantly, reaching more than half the city total, as in Monterrey in 1990 (see Table 16.2).

Direct foreign investment, diseconomies of scale in the largest cities, and the provision of infrastructure, made other urban centres good alternatives for industrial relocation. Large and intermediate-sized cities expanded their concentration of manufacturing as well as of commercial and service activities. Large cities increased their share of manufacturing by 5.5 per cent. Small-sized cities and rural areas were apparently poorly affected by economic redistribution as they presented a very insignificant change in their share of these economic growth sectors. Some even showed a decrease.

The urban periphery increased its share of highly educated people due to the demands of the new specialized economic activities. This was not only a result of new higher education facilities but also due to receiving urban migrants with good education that responded to the employment opportunities in these urban centres. In contrast to the previous years, these large, intermediate-sized and small-sized cities also attracted non-educated migrants, increasing their share of illiterate people. These processes provide evidence of how the 'pull' factor of the main metropolitan areas diminished, and how middle classes left the largest cities for alternative destinations.

The economic deceleration in the main metropolitan areas caused a reduction in the proportion of medium and high-income population, and an increase of low-income groups. Data tend to indicate a social polarization in these urban agglomerations: at the time they became the residence of many highly paid employees like corporate executives and financial leaders, but informal activities and poorly paid occupations proliferated.[20]

Economic expansion spread out to the lower levels of the hierarchy and caused an important incremental increase in the medium and high-income groups particularly in small-sized cities. This was highly related to rapid urban growth and the arrival of new productive enterprises. But interestingly enough small-sized cities and rural areas lost a certain proportion of their more qualified people, who surely migrated to larger urban centres. This converted the former locations into reserves of cheap labour force for particular labour-intensive industrial activities, as in the case of assembly plants *(maquiladoras)* that have recently started to establish in them.

In this period, the distribution of all age groups apparently entered a phase of decelerating concentration. Rural areas continued their diminishing trend in all the age groups while intermediate-sized and large cities showed an

---

[20] On the expansion of the informal sector, social polarization, and increased instability of the labour force in Mexico City, Guadalajara, Monterrey and Puebla, see Aguilar (1997).

incremental increase in the proportion of all the age groups, and the working population in the large cities went up by 4 per cent. With a slower growth rate in the main metropolitan areas, the share of the youngest population dropped, but their proportion of working and older age groups reached the highest values in the period: 27 per cent of the working population concentrated in these cities, the highest share in all categories.

CORE-PERIPHERY MIGRATORY STREAMS

Additional signs of the Mexican Urban System (MUS) entering a 'mature' phase of dispersion or deconcentration are given by recent migratory flows. Contrary to a bottom-up flow pattern (from smaller to bigger urban centres) as in the 1950s and 1960s, new patterns of migration that differ from traditional rural-urban or peripheral-core trends have emerged during the 1980s and 1990s.

From a counter-urbanization and differential urbanization perspective, main migratory streams that are either horizontal, i.e. from one centre to another of the same size, or from the largest cities down the urban hierarchy, have been observed in recent years. Subsequent to the rural to urban migration phase, flows followed intra-regional decentralization trends. This has been experienced in Mexico in the '70s and '80s. During that time Mexico City's urbanized area expanded significantly. Also, some small-sized settlements in the vicinity grew enormously as population moved from the central city inner core to the metropolitan fringe and beyond. More municipalities were added and an extensive metropolitan area developed during this period. This trend is still continuing today and more and more municipalities 30-40 and even more kilometers away from the central city are incorporated into the larger metropolitan area, in a contiguous or a functional manner (Graizbord and Mina 1994). By the late '80s the inner core of the metropolitan area lost population, and became the most important origin of migratory flows to the metropolitan fringe or to destinations within the Central Region, but also to the rest of the country as well.

Based on a census that was held in 1990, an account of regional and urban migration flows during 1985-90 is given in Figures 16.6 and 16.7.[21] Almost 3.5 million people moved across state boundaries to change their place of residence.[22] Most important of those movements are those related to the primate city's inner core (Distrito Federal or Federal District). In fact, a little

---

[21] We have divided the country in a Core Region Subsystem (which includes the non-contiguous Central, Western, and Northeast regions) and a Peripheral Region Subsystem (including the Central-Northern, Northern, Southeast, and the Yucatan Peninsula).

[22] Information of such moves within state boundaries (inter-municipal) was not captured in the census.

more than a million people (1,035,758) left the Federal District. This is a totally unexpected phenomenon. The central city districts (or *delegaciones*) started to show signs of negative growth since the 1970s but as a whole Mexico City did not lose population in absolute terms during this time; most residential movements stayed within its boundaries. Having received no more than 300,000 new residents during the period (half of those originating from within the Central Region), Mexico City's inner core lost population in absolute terms for the first time in history. It became an important origin rather than the most important destination for people that are changing their place of residence.

On the other hand, of a total of 1,035,758 people leaving Mexico City's inner core (Federal District), 66 per cent stayed within the Central Region, half of whom ended up in municipalities of the Mexico City metropolitan area's (MCMA) peripheral rings. The remaining 34 per cent settled in other regions and urban subsystems: 7 per cent in other regions within the Core Region Subsystem, and 27 per cent in the Peripheral Central-Northern region's[23] large, medium sized and small-sized cities, and in the Northern region's[24] larger cities.

Although small, the Central Region (i.e. the main agglomerated region) also showed a slight negative balance. More than 1.6 million people left while slightly less than 1.5 million moved into this region. Of those, 298,235 settled in Mexico City's inner core (Federal District), and 731,705 in its peripheral rings. Of the remaining immigrants, 209,805 settled in the four large urban centres within the region (i.e. the metropolitan areas of Puebla, Toluca, Cuernavaca, and Querétaro), 42,533 in intermediate-sized cities (Tehuacán and the metropolitan area of Cuautla, Pachuca and Tlaxcala), more than 77,601 in small-sized cities of 15 to 100 thousand inhabitants, and 112,315 in rural communities in the rest of the region.

Two other regions, the Central Northern and the Southern showed a negative migration balance. In contrast, the Northern gained around 230,000 migrants, attracted by *maquiladoras* activity. The Yucatan Peninsula also ended up with a positive migration balance, due mainly to the urban expansion and development of Cancun, the most important tourist destination pole in the region and the country.

It is interesting to look at the state and regional migration O-D matrix.[25] It reflects the strong and weak attraction forces operating within each region.

---

[23] Includes the states of Aguascalientes, Guanajuato, San Luis Potosí, Zacatecas, Michoacán and Veracruz.
[24] Includes the states of Baja California, Sonora, Chihuahua, Sinaloa, and Durango.
[25] The matrix shows the probability of a migrant to change his/her residence in the 5-year period, crossing regional boundaries or not, and end up in a particular city size or in another central (core) or peripheral region.

These forces affect interstate migration and cause people to remain in, or leave their 1985 residences. Despite the changing trends, it is still the Central Region that shows strong attraction for cross-state migration (42 per cent of all migrants). Next are the Northern and the Central-Northern regions with 16 and 15 per cent, in that order. All the rest received less than ten per cent each.

Many migrants to the Yucatan Peninsula, the South East, the North, Central North, Northeast, and the West originated in the inner core (Federal District), displaying not only polarization reversal tendencies but also signs of counter-urbanization and differential urbanization processes.

The balance by core and peripheral regions subsystems then is as follows (see Figure 16.6a, b, c):

❑ Fifty eight per cent of the total number of migrants from 1985 to 1990 settled in the Core Region and 42 per cent in the Peripheral Region Subsystem. A one percent difference, or 28,703, constituted the balance in favour of the periphery, in terms of immigrants versus out-migrants.

❑ Of those migrants that left the core (2,044,210 in all), 65.6 per cent stayed within the core and 34.4 per cent ended up in the periphery (a ratio of 1.9), while of those leaving the periphery 52.7 per cent remained in the periphery and 47.3 were attracted by the core (a ratio of 1.1).

Recently, the Mexican Urban System (MUS) shows signs of maturity. The main metropolis (MCMA) in the Central Region and the other two in the Western (GMA) and the Northeast (Monterrey metropolitan area), as well as large urban centres show negative population growth rates as well as negative migration balances in favour of intermediate-sized and small-sized cities and rural settlements in both urbanized and rural areas in the Core and in the Peripheral Region subsystems. Compared to the 1970s and previous decades, this is clearly a reversal of past trends.

In terms of city size distribution (see Figure 16.6d,e, f), the three main metropolitan areas (Mexico City, Guadalajara, and Monterrey) received 36 per cent of the total number of migrants. Suburban and metropolitan peripheral ring locations were preferred by the majority. On the other hand, one out of four of the total settled in large cities of more than 500,000 inhabitants (excluding the three largest metropolitan areas), 15 per cent in medium-sized urban centres (100,000 to 499,999) and 13 per cent in small-sized cities (15,000 to 99,999). These three categories amounted to more than half of all migratory flows over the period. The remaining 11 per cent, or 382,480 migrants, choose rural areas as a destination: 4.3 per cent or 165,311 in the Core and 5.7 per cent or 217,169 in the Peripheral Region Subsystem.

Most migrants to the Core Region concentrated mainly in the main metropolis (63 per cent), while large and medium-sized cities in the core region were the final destination of 21 per cent and only 16 per cent settled in small-sized cities and in rural areas. Thirty nine percent of migrants to the

Figure 16.6 Regional and city size distribution of migration flows originating in core and peripheral regions, 1985-90

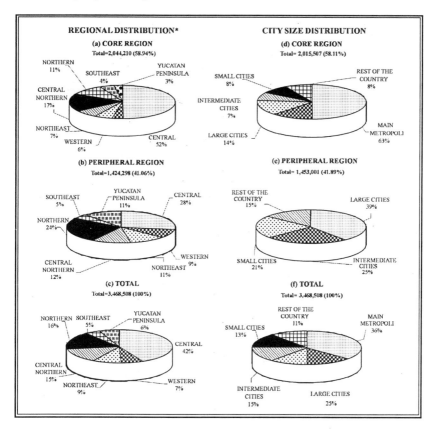

Source: National Bureau for Statistics and Geographical Information (INEGI), Mexico, 1991: XI Censo General de Población y Vivienda, 1990, Tomo I.

Notes: *Regions of Mexico display as follows:
CORE REGION: Central Region, Western Region, and Northeast Region.
PERIPHERAL REGION: Central Northern Region, Northern Region, Southeast Region and Yucatan Peninsula Region.
CENTRAL REGION: Distrito Federal, México, Puebla, Morelos, Tlaxcala, Hidalgo, Querétaro.
WESTERN REGION: Jalisco, Colima y Nayarit.
NORTHEAST REGION: Coahuila, Tamaulipas, Nuevo León.
CENTRAL NORTHERN REGION: Guanajuato, Aguascalientes, San Luis Potosí, Zacatecas, Veracruz, Michoacán.
NORTHERN REGION: Baja California Norte, Baja California Sur, Sonora, Chihuahua, Sinaloa, Durango.
SOUTHEAST REGION: Guerrero, Oaxaca, Chiapas

peripheral region chose large cities as their destination, 25 per cent decided on medium-sized cities, 21 per cent preferred small-sized cities, and 15 percent rural settlements as destinations.

The balance by city-size categories is, therefore, the following (see Figures 16.6d, e, f and 16.7).[26]

1) The distribution of the 3,468,508 cross-state migrants for the period 1985-90 still favoured the three metropolitan areas and the large cities in the country (36.1 and 24.7 per cent, in that order). Despite this fact, almost 4 out of 10 migrants settled in decentralized locations (medium, small and rural settlements).

2) From a total of 1,341,317 migrants with an origin inside the Core Region, 287,209 (21.4 per cent) resettled in decentralized locations, and 162,569 (12.1 per cent) in large cities, while the remaining 891,539 (66.5 per cent) preferred a metropolitan area within the core. Of 674,190 migrants from outside the core, 185,688 (27.5 per cent) chose a decentralized location as a destination, 127,876 (19 per cent) a large city, and 360,626 (53.5 per cent) a metropolitan area.

3) From a total of 702,893 migrants with an origin in the Core Region 58.9 per cent settled in a decentralized location, and 41.1 in a large city in the Peripheral Region. Of 750,108 originating within the periphery 62.8 per cent decided for a decentralized location and only 37.2 per cent for a large city.

4) Another feature of these recent migration trends is that related to out-migration from Mexico City's inner core (Federal District). A total of 1,035,758 people moved out during the five-year period from 1985 to 1990. Seven out of ten preferred to stay within the Core Region. A total of 519,477 changed from an inner core residence, probably without changing work, to a peripheral ring location within the MCMA. Three out of ten moved into the Peripheral Region. Of those, four out of ten preferred to move to large cities, one out of four to medium-sized cities,

---

[26] We have divided both the core region subsystems and the peripheral region subsystems into the following city-size categories according to their 1995 municipal population (see Figure 16.6): main metropoli (Mexico City Metropolitan Area, Guadalajara Metropolitan Area, and Monterrey Metropolitan Area); large cities (all 500,000 plus, excluding the above category); intermediate-sized cities (all 100 to 499,999); small cities (all settlements with 15 to 99,999 inhabitants); and the rest (all municipalities not included in the above categories). The reader should be aware of the difference when we refer to the country's totals by category or the core region and peripheral region subsystem's totals. The main metropoli is a category pertaining only to the Core Region Subsystem: Central region (Mexico city metropolitan area), Western region (Guadalajara metropolitan area), and Northeastern region (Monterrey metropolitan area).

Figure 16.7 Total migration flows between core and peripheral regions, 1985-90

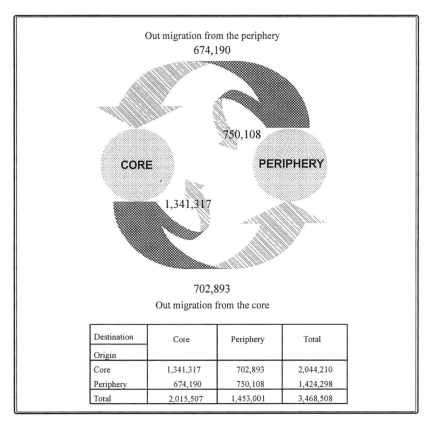

Destination Origin	Core	Periphery	Total
Core	1,341,317	702,893	2,044,210
Periphery	674,190	750,108	1,424,298
Total	2,015,507	1,453,001	3,468,508

Source: National Institute of Statistics, Geography and Informatics (INEGI). XI Censo General de Población y Vivienda, 1990, Tomo I, Mexico, 1991.

two out of ten to small-sized cities, and the remaining 15 per cent settled in rural areas.

Of all the human settlements in the MUS (almost 200,000), small-sized rural settlements are becoming an important destination to urban and metropolitan migrants. A systematic study is necessary to determine the particular characteristics of these trends, but it is expected that these rural areas and small settlements are close to urban and metropolitan origins. The medium-sized and large cities as well as the metropolitan areas are attracting population, the latter at a very slow rate between 1970 and 1990. On the other hand, the share of migrants to small-sized cities and rural areas is relatively small and their growth rates are below the national urban growth rate. This is also the case for the inner cores of the main metropolitan areas for the last two decades (0.91, 1.61 and 1.11 per cent for Mexico City, Guadalajara and Monterrey, respectively).

While Mexico City maintained an annual average growth rate of 5.05 per cent during the 1950s and 1960s, compared with the country's 3.18 per cent, Guadalajara and Monterrey were growing above the national average at 5.94 and 6.02 per cent, respectively (see Table 16.2). From 1970 to 1990 all inner cores were losing population in relative terms. Their growth rate was below the national average of 2.64 per cent per year. Still, the average annual growth rate of Guadalajara and Monterrey metropolitan areas, as well as that of their and Mexico City's suburban and metropolitan peripheral rings were above the national annual growth rate. This implied a decentralization trend within metropolitan areas with rates of up to 7.18 per cent for Guadalajara, 6.89 per cent for Monterrey, and 5.91 per cent for Mexico City metropolitan municipalities in their respective peripheral rings.

A deconcentration trend is becoming apparent also if we look at the large and intermediate-sized cities. Both groups of cities experienced a lower annual growth rate than Mexico City during the first period (1950-1970). Even compared to the main metropolitan areas (2.84 per cent) the annual growth rate of larger and intermediate-sized cities was high, 3.60 and 3.58 per cent respectively. Not so for small-sized cities. Compared to the national average, they have lagged behind with relatively low rates of growth during the 1950-70 and 1970-95 periods. The growth of this urban category, indicative of a more advanced phase of urban maturity, has not yet 'taken off', and it looks far away as local governments are still politically and economically weak without being able to play their role as providers of public goods and services, and effectively create agglomeration economies and competitive advantages.

PERSPECTIVES ON THE URBAN FUTURE

In this chapter we have tried to demonstrate how the Mexican urban system has expanded and matured, especially since the 1970s. New urban centres have been added to the lower ranks while many of those that already existed, developed and moved up through higher ranks. During the process of expansion various layers of territorially organized core-peripheral subsystems developed in the urban system from the macro-level through the regional to the sub-regional and local levels. Examples of different constellations of polarized regions, each one at a different level of spatial aggregation, are to be seen in Mexico City together with Guadalajara and Monterrey at the national level, and the latter two, in turn, as central nodes in lower order sub-systems. The development of the urban system since the middle of the 20th century occurred in different phases. First concentration, then a limited degree of urban dispersion or polarization reversal and, finally, more widespread urban deconcentration that apparently corresponds to an intermediate-sized city stage of urban development.

There are several reasons why it is believed that the Mexican urban system will remain in the current intermediate-sized city stage, and will not move on to the counter-urbanization phase in the short and medium terms.[27] The first group of factors to consider is the prevailing government internal economic policy and the external factors that potentially impact upon it. During the 1990s, urban deconcentration was accelerated as a result of the adoption of an export-oriented economic model that favoured foreign investment, the beginning of new manufacturing and new large scale migration towards secondary cities and some regional metropolitan areas.

The proximity to, and commercial relationship with the United States have induced rapid urban growth in the north of the country and are likely to continue to do so in the future. Good examples of this are the two north-south oriented development axes that both start in Mexico City, the one connecting San Luis Potosí, Monterrey and Laredo and the other San Luis Potosí, Torreón, Chihuahua, and Ciudad Juárez. Large investments in manufacturing such as large automobile assemblies have started along these economic corridors in recent years.

In addition, all the cities along the northern border, each one representing a potential source of cheap labour, have started to develop as favourable locations for assembly plants in an east-west direction. The neo-liberal orientation of the new government that took office at the end of 2000 makes domestic businesses and regional trade markets accessible to foreign business people. This makes urban locations and subsystems with exceptional locational attributes and good infrastructure in the central and northern regions more favourable than locations deeper into the country. It will also consolidate the process of concentrated deconcentration in the largest city subsystems as they become spatially and economically more integrated.

Another element is the lack of proper attention to the rural sector in large parts of the country, notably in the regions with high rainfall. Since the Import Substitution Industrial model has been phased out, many workers have left this sector, some moving into the cities, others migrating to the United States. As a result the rural areas have run out of their former strong work force. In addition, the rural areas do not offer good quality services, which contributes to their problems. Unfortunately there are no signs that this process will be reversed in the near future or even the medium term. In view of this, wide sweeping counter-urbanization from the main metropolitan areas to the impoverished rural areas and small-sized towns looks highly unlikely.

---

[27] An important factor in this statement lies in the large core-periphery sub-systems that have developed in Mexico in a remarkable way.

Counter-urbanization might happen in the near future but mainly in locations relatively close to the primary city or other large metropolitan areas.

The Mexican population has been growing since the 1950s. The fastest growth since the Second World War was recorded from 1950 to 1970 when the Mexican population doubled. Due to a declining growth rate it took another 30 years to double again. Over the last two decades (1970-90) the Mexican population growth rate kept reducing while the urban population continued to grow. In 1970 the total population grew at a rate above 3 percent; in 2000 it was 1.7 per cent. Although the rate at which the population of the country grows is likely to keep declining, the population will continue to concentrate in urban areas. According to projections there will be 125 million people in the country by 2025 and by 2050 more than 130 million (CONAPO, 1998: 18). It is difficult to project 50 years ahead but it is likely that at least 75 per cent of the population will be living in cities (not necessarily in large or metropolitan urban areas) and that migration, already showing counter-urbanization trends, will still be playing an important role in the distribution of the urban population.

So far, the preliminary results of the 2000 Census provide an indication of what urban development trends could be expected in the future. Most people (26 per cent) held residence in cities with more than 500 thousand inhabitants, followed by urban centres between 100 and 500 thousand (21 per cent). This is an indication that intermediate-sized cities and regional metropolitan areas will continue to attract large numbers of people in years to come. The metropolitan character of many of them is expected to be reinforced and the urban system will reach an advanced intermediate-sized city stage.

Another remarkable feature of urban development is the increasing demographic and economic concentration that occurs in the large central area of the country, covering 13 states.[28] In 2000, 58 per cent of the total population and 60 per cent of the GDP occurred in this region (Puig Escudero, 2001: 5). One of the important implications of this is that urban agglomeration in the core region sub-systems of Mexico City and Guadalajara will intensify. This should augment their polycentric metropolitan character resulting in further suburbanization and urban growth along the metropolitan fringe. Also, the states of Nuevo León (Monterrey metropolitan area) and Baja California (with some important border cities) in the North will stand out as important activity centers in the future.

Referring to the impact of technology on urban development it is Berry's (1996: 684) contention that '[t]he underlying process that has driven the

---

[28] These states are: Aguascalientes, Colima, Distrito Federal, Estado de Mexico, Guanajuato, Hidalgo, Jalisco, Michoacan, Morelos, Puebla, Queretaro, Tlaxcala and Veracruz.

accompanying transformation of urban structure is endogenous (i.e., internally driven)'. In developing countries this mostly does not apply. In such countries technological innovations are in most cases adopted first and sometimes only in the primate cities. Usually they are externally initiated, either through branches of multinational corporations that are established in the country or by means of pressure by the State to innovate and to adopt (imported) technologies in its efforts to industrialize the country and to keep up with the 'rest of the world'.

In a globalized economy[29] all sources of technological innovation are internal. However, the initiating sources are often located in the developed world. It appears to us as an imperative to focus our research efforts on assessing the capacity or 'ability of cities' to adjust to changes in demand derived from technological innovations and, in the framework of differential urbanization, to identify changes in intercity migratory flows within the 'maturing' urban system related to economic, social, and/or environmental variables.

Whether Mexico's urban system will enter the more mature counter-urbanization phase, in which small-sized cities, not only those closer to the primate city or the large secondary urban centres, experience relatively faster growth rates and attract migrants from local regions and higher-ranked cities remains to be seen. So far, only large and medium-sized cities have experienced a higher population growth relative to the rest of the urban system. The fact is that rural-to-urban migration in Mexico has ceased to be a major contributing factor to urbanization. Urban-to-urban migratory flows are already apparent and the still weak urban-to-rural or metropolitan-to-small-sized cities migration is becoming more evident through the increasing population growth rates in small-sized cities, as well as by the increasing proportion of manufacturing jobs and the changing sectoral structure of employment in small-sized cities. Another sign, as depicted in Geyer and Kontuly (1993: Figure 2, p. 165), is apparent in the slowing-down of general urban growth rates for all cities in the Mexican Urban System.

---

[29] The consolidation of global or world cities (Friedmann 1995) does not preclude differential urbanization processes. Such processes refer to the functional role of some cities in economic globalization that the world has been experiencing at the end of the twentieth and beginning of the twenty-first centuries.

REFERENCES

Acuña, B. and B. Graizbord (1999), 'Movilidad cotidiana de trabajadores en el ámbito megalopolitano de la ciudad de México', in J. Delgado and B. Ramírez (coords.), *Territorio y cultura en la ciudad de México*, vol. I, Mexico City: UAM and Plaza y Valdés, pp. 195-205.

Aguilar A. G. (1992), 'La dispersión del proceso urbano', *Ciudades*,. **12**, Red Nacional de Investigación Urbana, 24-30.

Aguilar A. G. (1997), 'Metropolitan growth and labour markets in Mexico', *GeoJournal*, **43**, 371-383.

Aguilar A. G. (1999), 'Mexico City growth and regional dispersal: The expansion of largest cities and new spatial forms', *Habitat International*, **23**, 391-412.

Aguilar, A.G. (2000), 'Megaurbanización en la región Centro de México', *El Mercado de Valores*, **60**, 77-86.

Aguilar, A.G., B. Graizbord, and A. Sánchez-Crispín (1996), *Las ciudades intermedias y el desarrollo regional en México*, Mexico City: Instituto de Geografía-UNAM, El Colegio de México, CONACULTA.

Aguilar, A.G., B. Graizbord, and A. Sánchez-Crispín (1997), *Política pública y base económica en seis ciudades medias de México*, Mexico City: El Colegio de México.

Aguilar A.G. and Rodríguez F. (1995), 'The dispersal of urban growth in Mexico, 1979-1990', *Regional Development Studies*, **1**, 1-26.

Alonso, W. (1978), 'The current halt in the metropolitan phenomenon', in C. Leven, (ed), *The mature metropolis*, Massachusetts: Heath and Co., pp.23-41.

Alonso, W. (1980), 'Five bell shapes in development', *Papers, Regional Science Association,* **45**, 5-16.

Arroyo, J., W. Winnie and L. A. Velázquez (1986), *Migración a centros urbanos en una región de fuerte emigración: El caso del Occidente de México*, Guadalajara, México: Universidad de Guadalajara.

Arroyo, J. and L. A. Velázquez (1992), 'La migración hacia Guadalajara y la transición de los patrones migratorios en el occidente de México' in Arroyo, J. and L. A. Velásquez (comps.), *Guadalajara en el umbral del Siglo XXI*. Guadalajara, México: Universidad de Guadalajara, pp. 189-222.

Berry, B. J. L. (1965), 'City size distribution and economic development', in J. Friedmann and W. Alonso, (eds), *Regional development and planning*, Cambridge, Mass.: MIT Press, pp.138-252

Berry, B. J. L. (1972), 'Hierarchical diffusion: The basis of developmental filtering and spread in a system of growth centers' in P. English and R.

Mayfield, eds., *Man, space, and environment*, New York: Oxford University Press, pp.340-359.

Berry, B. J. L. (1976), *Urbanization and counter urbanization*, Beverly Hills, CA: Sage.

Berry, B. J. L. (1980), 'Urbanization and counterurbanization in the United States', *Annals of the American Association of Political and Social Sciences*, **451**, September 1980, 13-20.

Berry, B. J. L. (1996), 'Technology-sensitive urban typology', *Urban Geography* **17**, 674-689.

Berry B. J. L. and H. Dahman (1977), 'Population redistribution in the United States in the 1970's, *Population and Development Review*, **3**, 443-471.

Borchert, J. (1967), 'American metropolitan evolution', *Geographical Review,* **57**, 301-332.

Breeze, G. (ed.) (1972), *The city in newly developing countries: Reading on urbanism and urbanization.* Englewood Cliffs, N.J.: Prentice-Hall.

Cabrera, A. G. (2000), 'Del México rural al México urbano. Historia y destino demográfico', *El Mercado de Valores,* **60**, 22-33.

Carrillo Arronte, R. (1971), 'La estrategia del desarrollo regional de México: Evolución, magnitudes y perspectivas' in M. Wionczek, (ed), *La sociedad mexicana: Presente y futuro*, Mexico City: Fondo de Cultura Económica, pp.414-441.

Castells, M. (ed) (1973), *Imperialismo y urbanización en América Latina*, Barcelona: Editorial Gustavo Gilli.

Commons A. (1981), 'Límite de los Cuarteles en 1930-1970 y de las Delegaciones que se formaron en 1970', *Boletín de la Sociedad Mexicana de Geografía y Estadística*, **CXXVII**, 19-36.

Commons A. (1995), 'La Población de Nueva España en 1790', *Tempus*, Revista de Historia de la Facultad de Filosofía y Letras, **3**, 7-112, Mexico City: UNAM.

CONAPO (1998), *Proyecciones de la Población de México, 1996-2050*, Mexico City: Consejo Nacional de Población.

Drewett, R. (1980), 'Changing urban structures in Europe', *Annals of the American Association of Political and Social Sciences,* **451**, September 1980, 45-51.

Friedmann, J. (1995), 'Where we stand: A decade of world city research' in P. Knox and P. Taylor, (eds), *World Cities in a World System*, Cambridge, Mass.: Cambridge University Press, pp. 21-47.

Fujita, M., P. Krugman, and A. Venables (1999), *The spatial economy. Cities, regions, and international_trade*, Cambridge, Mass: MIT Press.

García Castro, R. (1993), 'Patrones de poblamiento en la Nueva España', in CONAPO (eds), *El poblamiento de México. Una visión histórico-demográfica*, vol. II, Mexico City: Secretaría de Gobernación, pp. 132-151

Garza G.. (1980), *Industrialización de las principales ciudades de México*, Mexico City: El Colegio de México.

Garza, G. (1999), 'Globalización económica, concentración metropolitana y políticas urbanas en México', *Estudios Demográficos y Urbanos*, CEDDU, El Colegio de México, **14**, 269-311.

Garza G. and S. Rivera (1994), *Dinámica Macroeconómica de las Ciudades en México*, Aguascalientes, México and Mexico City: INEGI, El Colegio de México, Instituto de Investigaciones Sociales-UNAM.

Geyer, H.S. (1996), 'Expanding the theoretical foundation of differential urbanization', *Tijdschrift voor Economische en Sociale Geografie*, **87**, 44-59.

Geyer, H.S. (1998), 'Differential urbanization and international migration: an urban systems approach', in C. Gorter, P. Nijkamp, and J. Poot, (eds), *Crossing borders: regional and urban perspectives on international migration*. Aldershot, Hants: Ashgate, pp.161-184.

Geyer, H. S. and T. M. Kontuly (1993), 'A theoretical foundation for the concept of differential urbanization', *International Regional Science Review* **15**, 157-177.

Gilbert, A. (1993), 'Third World Cities: The changing national settlements system', *Urban Studies*, **30**, (3/5), 721-740.

Gordon, P. (1979), 'Deconcentration without a "clean break"', *Environment and Planning A*, **11**, 281-290.

Graizbord, B. (1984), 'Perspectivas de una descentralización del crecimiento urbano en el sistema de ciudades de México', *Revista Interamericana de Planificación* **XVIII**, (71), 36-58.

Graizbord, B. and A. Mina (1994), 'Los ámbitos geográficos del componente migratorio de la ciudad de México', *Estudios Demográficos y Urbanos*, CEDDU, El Colegio de México, **9**, 609-628.

Graizbord, B. and C. Molinatti (1998), 'Movilidad megalopolitana de fuerza de trabajo', in R.M. Zenteno (coord.), *Población, desarrollo y globalización*, Mexico City: Sociedad Mexicana de Demografía, El Colegio de la Frontera Norte, pp. 211-220.

Hall, P. (1980), 'New trends in European urbanization', *Annals of the American Association of Political and Social Sciences,* **451**, September 1980, 45-51.

INEGI (1994*), Estadísticas históricas de México*, Tomo I, Aguascalientes, México: Instituto Nacional de Estadística Geografía e Informática.

INEGI (1990), *XI Censo general de población y vivienda, 1990*, Aguascalientes, México: Instituto Nacional de Estadística Geografía e Informática.

INEGI (1996), *Conteo de población y vivienda 1995*, Tabulados Básicos, Aguascalientes, México: Instituto Nacional de Estadística Geografía e Informática.

Ledent, J. (1982), 'Rural-urban migration, urbanization, and economic development', in A. Rogers and J. G. Williamson (eds), *Urbanization and development in the Third World*, Laxenburg, Austria: IIASA, pp.507-538.

Leven, C. L. (1990), 'Changing urban purposes in historical perspective' in D. Shefer and H. Voogd (eds), *Evaluation methods for urban and regional plans*, London: Pion, pp.175-190.

López Austin, A. and L. López Luján (1996), *El pasado indígena*, Mexico City: Fondo de Cultura Económica, El Colegio de México.

Mastache, G. and R. Cobean (1993), 'Sociedades urbanas y población', in CONAPO, *El poblamiento de México. Una visión histórico-demográfica*, Tomo I, Mexico City: Secretaría de Gobernación, pp. 164-189.

McGreevey, W. P. (1973), 'Un análisis estadístico de hegemonía y log-normalidad en la distribución de tamaño de las ciudades de América Latina', in R. Morse (ed), *Las ciudades latinoamericanas. II. Desarrollo histórico*, Mexico City: SepSetentas No. 97, pp. 225-242.

Moreno Toscano, A. (1973), 'Desarrollo del sistema urbano, 1750-1920. México', in R.M. Morse (ed), *Las ciudades latinoamericanas. II. Desarrollo histórico*, Mexico City: SepSetentas No. 97, pp. 172-196.

Morse, R. M. (1973), 'Patrones de la urbanización latinoamericana. Aproximaciones y generalizaciones tentativas', in R. M. Morse (ed), *Las ciudades latinoamericanas. II. Desarrollo histórico*, Mexico City: SepSetentas No. 97, pp. 11-55.

Negrete, M. E. (1999), 'Desconcentración poblacional en la región Centro de México', *Estudios Demográficos y Urbanos*, CEDDU, El Colegio de México, **14**, 313-352.

Pescador, J. J. (1993), 'Patrones demográficos urbanos en la Nueva España', in CONAPO, *El poblamiento de México. Una visión histórico-demográfica*, Tomo II, Mexico City: Secretaría de Gobernación, pp. 108-131.

Puig Escudero A. (2001), 'La población en el Año 2000', *Demos, Carta Demográfica sobre México*, **13**, Mexico City: IISUNAM.

Richardson, H. W. (1980), 'Polarization reversal in Developing Countries', *Papers of the Regional Science Association*, **45**, 67-85.

Rodwin, L. (1972), 'Urban growth strategies reconsidered', in N. M. Hansen (ed.), *Growth centers in regional economic development*, New York: The Free Press, pp.1-19.

Scott, I. (1982), *Urban and spatial development in Mexico*, Baltimore, Maryland, U.S.A.: The Johns Hopkins University Press.

Secretaría de Industria y Comercio (1971*), IX Censo general de población, 1970*, Mexico City: Dirección General de Estadística.

Secretaría de Economía (1952), *VII Censo General de Población, 1950*, Mexico City: Dirección General de Estadística.

Tuirán, R. (2000), 'Tendencias recientes de la movilidad territorial en algunas zonas metropolitanas de México', *El Mercado de Valores*, **60**, 47-61.

Unikel, L. (1971), 'Urbanización y urbanismo: Situación y perspectivas' in M. Wionczek (ed), *La sociedad mexicana: Presente y futuro*, Mexico City: Fondo de Cultura Económica, pp.254-288.

Unikel, L., C. Ruíz and G. Garza (1976), *El desarrollo urbano de México. Diagnóstico e implicaciones futuras*, Mexico City: El Colegio de México.

Vining, D. and A. Strauss (1977), 'A demonstration that the current deconcentration of population in the United States is a clean break with the past', *Environment and Planning A*, **9**, 751-758.

Zelinsky, W. (1971), 'The hypothesis of the mobility transition', *Geographical Review*, **61**, 219-249.

Chapter 17

Urbanization and the Redistribution of Population in Brazil: Recent Changes and Trends[1]

R. Baeninger

INTRODUCTION

Over the last thirty years Brazil has experienced a relatively high urban population growth rate which contributed, on the one hand, to the development of large metropolitan areas and, on the other hand, to the expansion of a diversified national urban network. The latter has led to the acceleration of growth in regional and sub-regional centres and, at the same time, a slowdown in population growth in the large urban centres in recent years.

Until the 1970s the urbanization process and the process of spatial redistribution of the Brazilian population were characterized by accelerated growth in mainly the large cities and metropolitan areas. However, since the 1980s the growth of these cities has slowed down significantly while other areas have started to attract migrants. In recent years, the urban system has been reshaped by a new wave of population redistribution, a complex pattern of interaction between cities which has led to the emergence of new metropolitan areas and the formation of non-

[1] This paper is a product of the sub-project 'Migration, Urbanisation and Environment in the New Axis of the State of São Paulo: the Tietê-Paraná Waterway', with the support of National Council of Scientific and Technological Development (CNPq) - process number 520045/00-9 - and of the project 'Population Redistribution and Environment in São Paulo and the Centre West' (PRONEX), currently underway in the Population Studies Center (NEPO-UNICAMP).

metropolitan urban agglomerations in the 'interior' of the country. In the process these growing urban areas have not only been able to absorb but also to retain a large proportion of the migrants that previously tended to migrate to the major metropolitan areas.

BRAZILIAN URBAN GROWTH FROM 1940 TO 2000

The historic outline of the evolution of the Brazilian urban system in this section will reveal different phases and characteristics of the urban development process over the past half century. The intensity and sequences in the process of urbanization and spatial redistribution of the Brazilian population over the last fifty years will show how concentration occurred in specific areas. Following the transformations that have occurred in the Brazilian society as a whole, the dynamics of the urban development process have also changed over time. Until the 1930s, when the primary export phase of Brazil came to an end, the location of cities and the spatial economic structure of the country was largely determined by commercial activities linked to sugar, cotton and coffee production (Cano, 1977).

As a result of economic integration, interaction between regions, and the evolving of the national market, the incipient industrial economy subsequently demanded new patterns of urbanization. New industrial development strategies required the fusion of the market. To unite regional markets and to improve communication the road network had to be expanded. This led to a significant expansion of the urban network throughout the country (Faria, 1983).

Industries tended to concentrate in large population and administrative centres that were ideally located for export. During the consolidation of the national market, the industries were mainly located in the Southeast, especially in São Paulo, Rio de Janeiro and Belo Horizonte. Most of these changes in the national productive structure occurred after 1960, a process that was associated with the expansion of the secondary sector and the subsequent subordination of agriculture. The industrial base started to diversify while traditional branches started to lose their relative importance (Cano, 1988). Urbanization intensified in the country.

The urban population of Brazil increased significantly until the 1970s. In 1940, 12.8 million people were living in the urban areas, but 69 per cent of the population still lived in the rural areas. The urban population had increased to more than 110 million by 1991 and has approached the 138 million mark in 2000 (Table 17.1). Only 18.8 per cent of the total population (around 32 million people) are currently living in rural areas. Until the 1970s, a growing percentage of the Brazilian population flocked to the primate cities. This influx of people to the urban areas, particularly during the 1970s, is locally known as the period of 'urban explosion' (Martine, 1987).

Table 17.1 Total urban and rural population of Brazil, 1940-2000

Year	Population (million)			Growth Rates (% per year)		
	Total	Urban	Rural	Total	Urban	Rural
1940	41,236	12,880	28,356	2.33	3.84	1.58
1950	51,994	18,783	33,162	3.05	5.32	1.54
1960	70,191	31,534	38,657	2.87	5.15	0.60
1970	93,139	52,084	41,054	2.48	4.44	-0.62
1980	119,002	80,436	38,566	1.93	2.96	-0.66
1991	146,917	110,876	36,042	1.35	2.11	-1.16
1996	157,080	123,082	33,997	1.93	2.85	-1.62
2000	169,544	137,697	31,847	-	-	-
1991/2000	-	-	-	1.61	2.42	-1.30

Source: FIBGE, Demographic Censuses 1940 to 2000 and Count Population, 1996.

POPULATION DISTRIBUTION OF BRAZIL, 1940-2000.

In an attempt to curb population concentration in the country a policy of expansion of agricultural frontiers was adopted in Paraná, around the 1930s. A similar policy was followed in the central belt a decade later in Mato Grosso do Sul, Goiás, and Maranhão, and in Amazon after 1970. The ending of agricultural activities in the Paraná frontiers and in the Centre-West was already evident in the 1960s, while in the case of Amazon, it occurred during the first half of the 1980s. As a result a large part of the rural population that previously had lived in these areas moved to the large Brazilian urban centres in the Southeast (Martine, 1987). It is estimated that around 50 million people left the rural areas between 1950 and 2000 (Rigotti and Carvalho, 2001, p. 7).

On the other hand, the urbanization process in Brazil created an impressive urban network that differs from that of other countries in Latin America that experienced urban primacy (Faria, 1983; Villa and Rodríguez, 1994). The dynamism and complexity of the process, characterized by the fast growth of the cities, resulted in the multiplication of urban areas. The number of settlements in the country increased from

1889 in 1950 to 3991 by 1980. A majority of them are small centres with less than 20 thousand inhabitants. Only 22 per cent of the urban population lived in 87.6 per cent of all the Brazilian cities compared to 31 per cent in the 13 largest cities with more than 500 thousand inhabitants each. Approximately 54 per cent of the population lived in the 95 intermediate-sized and large cities in 1980.

The enormous exodus of the people from the rural areas since the 1950s led to the acceleration of urbanization. The urban population growth rate increased from 3.8 per cent per year in the 1940s to 5.32 per cent per year from 1950 to 1960. During this period urbanization peaked in the country. Since then the urbanization rates have started to decrease steadily from 5.15 per cent per year in the 1960s to 4.44, 2.96, and 2.42 per cent respectively in the following decades. Similarly, the country's average annual fertility rate declined from 3.05 per cent per year in the 1950s, to 2.48 in the 1970s and 1.93 and 1.6 per cent in following decades. Despite the decline in the fertility and urban growth rates the level of urbanization of the Brazilian population continued to increase from 45 per cent in 1960, to 56, 67, 75, and 82 per cent in each of the following decades, while the rural population declined from 1.54 per cent per year in the 1950s to -1.3 per cent per year by 2000.

The fast urban growth of the period up to the 1970s not only led to the depopulation of the rural areas but they also became increasingly desolated. The displacement of people from rural areas pointed to a changing but disfunctional and unviable agricultural economy. A policy of agricultural modernization, which had been vigorously applied since the early 1960s, combined with the ending of agriculture in the agricultural frontiers, resulted in a strong concentration of people and the metropolitanization of the larger of the large cities (Martine, 1987, p. 29).

As was pointed out earlier the urbanization of the Brazilian population before 1970s was mainly determined by three factors: the progressive downsizing of rural occupation coupled with urban growth, notably of regional centres, population movements to agricultural frontiers, and the continuous process of metropolitanization.

Some of the trends that had been observed prior to 1970, particularly the movements of people to agricultural frontiers and the large stream of migrants from the rural areas to the cities, independent of their size, started to change during the 1970s. New urban-to-urban population movements such as commuting, return migration and intra-metropolitan relocations started to emerge. Although the huge influx of people to the large metropolitan centres started to slow down, most analysts still believed that rural-urban migration and metropolitan growth would continue. Catastrophic economic and social scenarios were formulated.

The decline in living conditions of the majority of the Brazilian population, the scale of metropolitan problems, the accelerated growth of the large cities all pointed to economic and social chaos which was predicted for the future. However according to Deddeca and Brandão (1992) these predictions were not realised. Instead, the 1991 census showed that the growth rate of metropolitan regions, especially the larger ones, was on the decline in comparison with other cities in the country. The decline in migration to large metropolitan areas reduced the pressure that had been expected in the South-Eastern Region and its metropolitan areas and it also reduced the disastrous effects of an economic crisis that had been expected in the Central-Southern Region (p.16). These trends contributed to changes in the perceptions of people about the continued growth of large urban areas in the Third World. The growth of small- and intermediate-sized cities, as shown by the 1991 and 2000 census results, as well as the reality of a new regional dynamism in the State of São Paulo changed the views of people who had previously anticipated a disaster in the metropolitan areas of the region in the future. However, the emergence of new urban agglomerations and metropolitan sub-centres, and particularly the growth of small municipalities, will probably lead to new urban challenges in the future.

REGIONAL DISPARITIES IN URBANIZATION

Due to an uneven socio-economic geography urban development did not occur in all the regions of Brazil in the same way. In 1960, for instance, when 45 per cent of the total population was urbanized, the South-Eastern Region was already more than 50 per cent urbanized, while only 34 per cent of the people in the North-East lived in urban areas (Table 17.2). Urban development occurred mostly in the large regions of the country after the 1980s where more than half of the population were living in urban areas (see the politico-administrative map, Figure 17.1). Over the years the North and the North-East kept on lagging behind, because by 2000, when the South-East was almost 90 per cent urbanized, the former regions were still trailing behind by approximately 20 per cent. This demonstrates distinct differences in the phases of urban development in the different regions of Brazil.

As regards the rural population, the Northern Region was the only one that recorded a significant growth rate. Its rural population grew by 3.35 per cent per year due to the opening up of the Amazonian Frontier. The rural North-East grew slowly at a rate of 0.52 per cent per year. All the other regions lost some of their rural populations. The rural population in the South decreased at a rate of -2.5 per cent per year as a result of the ending of agricultural activities in the agricultural frontier of Paraná. The

Table 17.2 Degree of urbanization and growth rates of the rural population, regions of Brazil, 1950-2000

Indicators	BRAZIL	Regions				
		North	North-East	South-East	South	Centre-West
Degree of urbanization (%)						
1950	36.2	31.5	26.4	47.5	29.5	24.4
1960	44.9	37.4	33.9	57.0	37.1	34.2
1970	55.9	42.6	41.8	72.7	44.3	50.7
1980	67.6	50.3	50.5	82.8	62.4	70.8
1991	75.5	59.0	60.6	88.0	74.1	81.3
1996	78.4	62.0	65.0	89.0	77.0	84.0
2000	81.2	69.7	69.0	90.5	80.9	86.7
Annual growth rates of the rural population (%)						
1940-50	1.58	1.80	1.84	0.64	2.97	2.98
1950-60	1.54	2.37	1.02	1.06	2.90	3.89
1960-70	0.60	2.11	1.10	-1.88	2.20	3.14
1970-80	-0.62	3.35	0.52	-1.99	-2.48	-1.24
1980-91	-0.66	2.04	-0.28	-1.52	-2.01	-1.05
1991-96	-1.16	-0.35	-1.40	-0.91	-1.31	-1.49
1991-2000	-1.30	-0.54	-1.38	-1.02	-1.98	-1.50

Source: FIBGE, Demographic censuses of 1940 to 1991 and population count of 1996.

South-East, particularly São Paulo, already had seen a decline in the rural population as early as 1970. Between 1980 and 1991 all the regions registered negative rural growth rates, except the Northern Region. This trend continued into the 1990s (see Table 17.2).

Figure 17.1 Map of Brazil

The overall growth rate of the national population decreased from 2.48 per cent per year in the period from 1970 to 1980, to 1.93 per cent per year between 1980 and 1991. During the same time periods the rural exodus increased from -0.62 to -0.66 per cent per year. In contrast, the growth rate of the urban population of Brazil, despite its decline, remained at a high level: 4.44, 2.97, and 2.42 per cent per year in the 1970s, 1980s, and 1990s respectively.

From 1980 to 1991 the Northern Region stood out as one that kept on attracting rural population (3.85 per cent per year). This demonstrates the potential importance of the agricultural frontiers as rural areas of attraction during the 1980s, particularly Rondônia and Pará. The North was the only region with a positive growth rate during the 1980s (2.04 per cent per year). Also the urban population growth rate of this region surpassed those of the other regions. Growing at an average rate of 5.37 per cent per year, 59 per cent of the population of this region lived in urban areas by 1991. From 1991 to 2000 the urban population growth rate of this region was 4.8 per cent per year. In a national context this region also made a growing contribution. It accommodated 4.43 per cent of the national population in 1970, 5.57 per cent in 1980, 6.53 per cent in 1991, and 7.62 per cent in 2000 (Table 17.3).

This significant increase in the population of the Northern Region was largely caused by immigration to the region towards the end of the 1970s until 1986. According to Martine (1994) migration to this agricultural frontier had practically come to an end by 1986 because of the government's policy to slow down growth in the frontier regions. According to him various problems were being experienced in other regions as well. These included: (i) the ending of subsidies (incentives) in agriculture in Amazon, (ii) inherent difficulties in the economic development of the region and the lack of technological know-how among farmers in the rural areas, (iii) the abolition of fixed minimum prices by the government for agricultural products and of transport costs to stabilize 'economic market mechanisms', (iv) the cost of industrial subsidies in the Zona Franca de Manaus, and (v) national and international protests against policies that allowed deforestation in Amazon.

Settlement in the Amazon frontier region differed from that in other frontier regions because there was a faster than expected increase in the urban population in this area. Migration also did not predominantly consist of people coming from, or heading for rural areas. The fast expansion of the garimpo (diamond mining) and of forestry, commerce, and the service sector, and even the narcotráfico (drug trafficing) added to the attractiveness of certain locations in the region (Martine, 1994: 13-14).

From 1980 to 1991 the North-East and Central-Western regions registered population growth rates of 1.83 and 3.01 per cent per year respectively. These growth rates were higher than of the South-East and the South which recorded 1.77 and 1.38 per cent per year respectively. In the case of the North-East the recent movement of people to the region is linked to the Pólo Petroquímico de Camaçari (a petroleum pole), tourism and the production of fruit for the export market (Araújo, 1995). The expansion and diversification of the economy of the North-East enabled the region not only to absorb more migrants, but also to attract return

Table 17.3 Total population, urban and rural, growth rates (% per year) and relative distribution (%)

	BRAZIL	Regions				
		North	Northeast	Southeast	South	Centre-West
1. Population						
1970						
Total	93,139,037	4,121,966	28,111,927	39,853,498	16,496,493	4,555,153
Urban	52,087,092	1,754,553	11,752,916	28,965,601	7,304,586	2,309,436
Rural	41,051,945	2,367,413	16,359,011	10,887,897	9,191,907	2,245,717
1980						
Total	119,002,706	6,623,397	34,812,356	51,734,125	19,031,162	6,801,666
Urban	80,436,409	3,332,429	17,566,842	42,840,081	11,877,739	4,819,318
Rural	38,566,297	3,290,968	17,245,514	8,894,044	7,153,423	1,982,348
1991						
Total	146,825,475	10,030,556	42,497,540	62,740,401	22,129,377	9,427,601
Urban	110,990,990	5,922,574	25,776,279	55,225,983	16,403,032	7,663,122
Rural	35,834,485	4,107,982	16,721,261	7,514,418	5,726,345	1,764,479
2000						
Total	169,544,443	12,919,949	47,679,381	72,262,411	25,071,211	11,611,491
Urban	137,697,439	9,005,797	32,919,667	65,418,765	20,290,287	10,070,923
Rural	31,847,004	3,914,152	14,759,714	6,851,646	4,780,924	1,540,568

Table 17.3 continued

Growth Rates (% per year)

1970/1980						
Total	2.48	4.86	2.16	2.64	1.44	4.09
Urban	4.44	6.62	4.10	3.99	4.98	7.64
Rural	-0.61	3.35	0.52	-1.99	-2.48	-1.24
1980/1991						
Total	1.93	3.85	1.83	1.77	1.38	3.01
Urban	2.97	5.37	3.54	2.34	2.98	4.31
Rural	-0.66	2.04	-0.28	-1.52	-2.01	-1.05
1991/2000						
Total	1.61	2.88	1.28	1.58	1.40	2.34
Urban	2.42	4.81	2.75	1.90	2.39	3.08
Rural	-1.30	-0.54	-1.38	-1.02	-1.98	-1.50

2. Total Population

	Relative Distribution in Brazil (%)					
1970	100.00	4.43	30.18	42.79	17.71	4.89
1980	100.00	5.57	29.25	43.47	15.99	5.72
1991	100.00	6.83	28.94	42.73	15.08	6.42
1996	100.00	7.17	28.49	42.66	14.99	6.69
2000						

Notes: The current politic-administrative division of the country in 1970, 1980, 1991 and 1996.

Source: FIBGE, demographic censuses of 1970 to 2000 and population count of 1996.

migrants from the South-East, especially São Paulo and Rio de Janeiro.

It is important to point out that the 1980s were marked by a decrease in absolute numbers of the rural population in the North-East from 17.2 million to 16.7 million. In this region the growth rate of the rural population declined from 0.52 per cent per year in the 1970s to -0.28 per cent per year in the 1980s, and it reached a low of -1.38 per cent per year from 1991 to 2000. Despite the decrease in this population, almost half of the rural population of Brazil live in this region. On the one hand, the North-Eastern region experienced a significant economic, social and demographic transformation during the 1980s. The urban growth rate of 3.55 per cent per year in the region was well above the national average of 2.97 per cent per year for that period. The level of urbanization of the population in the North-East, which was 42 per cent in 1970, increased to 50.5 per cent in 1980 and 60.6 per cent in 1991, and by 2000 it had reached 70 per cent.

The higher population growth that was recorded in the Central-West region from 1980 to 1991 can be ascribed to its status as an agricultural frontier and the new dynamism of grain and meat production that was associated with it. As the commercial and industrial sectors are strongly linked to the expanding agricultural sector in the region, the growth of the former sectors had an important impact on its urban system. In 2000, 87 per cent of its population was urbanized. In fact, the growth rate of the urban population of the Central-West was significantly higher than the national average over the last three decades. The population of Central-West as a share of the total of the population of Brazil also increased over the last decades, growing from 4.9 per cent in 1970, to 6.8 per cent in 2000. According to Martine (1994) two distinct economic-demographic growth factors contributed to this increase in urbanization: (i) the boom in the production of soya beans in the state of Mato Grosso – which caused urbanization to increase faster than in states that did not experience the same agricultural dynamism such as Goiás and Mato Grosso do Sul – and (ii) the new capital status of Brasilia since the 1960s.

Despite a decline, the urban population of the South-East still increased by 2.34 per cent per year. At the same time its rural population continued to decline in absolute terms from 8.8 million in 1980 to 6.8 million in 2000, which shows that the region's urban population continued to increase in relative terms. By 2000, 90 per cent of the population of the South-East lived in urban areas and the South-East was still the home to 42.7 per cent of the Brazilian people.

On average, the population growth rate of the Southern region, during the 1980s, was 1.38 per cent per year; its rural growth rate was negative (-2.0 per cent per year). This was partially due to the large rural exodus from Paraná which had already started during the 1970s. By 2000 the growth rate of the population had increased to 2.4 per cent per year, while 80 per cent of the people in the region lived in urban areas. The high level of urbanization is largely due to industrial development which increased urbanization in the South in the last decade, especially in Santa Catarina and Paraná (Bandeira, 1994).

During the 1990s all Brazilian regions started experiencing a decrease in population growth, especially in the urban Northern Region: from 6.6 per cent per year in the 1970s to 4.8 per cent per year from 1991 to 2000. Actually, the South-Eastern and Southern Regions registered urban population growth rates below the national average (2.0 per cent per year), while the urban growth rate of all the others was higher than the national average.

The total population growth rates of the Northern and Central-Western Regions were higher between 1991and 2000 than in the other regions in the country, i.e. around 2 per cent per year. In the North-East and Southern Regions the total rates were lower than the average of the country, while that of the South-East equalled the national average during this period. The higher than national average growth rates of the former two regions could be ascribed to the growth in their rural populations. At the same time the rural population growth rates of the South-East and Southern Regions remained negative. The inverse of the tendency was experienced in the case of the Northern Region where its rural population only started registering negative growth rates in the 1990s.

In this manner, Brazil displayed different rhythms of growth and decline in its regional populations during the 1980s and early 1990s, where the growth in urban areas played a fundamental role in the spatial redistribution of the population at the national level. Significant in all this is the lower than national average growth rates recorded in the South-Eastern Region over the last fifteen years, as is evident in states that contain three of the largest metropolitan areas in the country, namely São Paulo, Rio de Janeiro and Belo Horizonte. In fact, the 1991 census results of the metropolitan areas indicated an increasing inflexion of the urban pattern, i.e. tendencies of a progressive concentration of the population in the large cities. In this context, the decrease in the migratory movements has been an important factor.

MIGRATION PATTERNS IN BRAZIL

From 1986 to 1991 around 3.2 million Brazilians moved from one state to another. Over the next five years this volume decreased to 2.7 million (Table17. 4).

Table 17.4 In-migration and out-migration by region, 1986-91 and 1991-96

| Regions | Inter-Regional Migration | | | | Migration | |
| | In-migration | | Out-migration | | Intra-Regional | |
	1986-91	1991-96	1986-91	1991-96	1986-91	1991-96
North	408,696	310,370	277,478	249,526	144,447	133,865
Northeast	477,915	384,291	1,354,449	1,237,023	459,777	319,643
Southeast	1,426,934	1,219,899	786,796	622,009	726,557	552,341
South	285,264	254,718	470,655	285,228	268,410	223,610
Central-West	627,286	505,884	336,717	281,376	186,955	187,408
Brazil	3,226,095	2,675,162	3,226,095	2,675,162	1,786.,26	1,416,867

Source: FIBGE, Demographic Census 1991 and Population Count of 1996.

Overall, the volume of interstate and out-migration between the states of Brazil is on the decrease, especially in the case of the Southern Region where the number of out-migrants has decreased from more than 470,000 people in the first five year period (1986-91) to 285,000 between 1991 and 1996. Even in the case of the North-East a slight decrease in out-migration has been observed (from 1.3 million to 1.2 million migrants).

Interstate migration is also on the decrease (from 1.7 million people to 1.4 million). This points to an increase in the importance of intra-state migration because the economic opportunities within the states have increased as a result of governmental policies, especially in the Southern and Central-Western Regions. Within the Southern Region significant population shifts in the states of Paraná and Rio Grande do Sul to Santa Catarina have been recorded. Similar shifts in Goiânia and Distrito Federal in the Central-Western Region have also been recorded.

Significant changes had therefore taken place in the migration patterns in Brazil over the last half of the 1980s and the first half of the 1990s. Although no significant changes in the direction of the main migratory flows occurred, prominent features of this period were the return of out-migrants that left São Paulo for the states in the North-Eastern Region earlier. Another prominent feature of this period was the correlation between migratory patterns and the economic dynamism of regions. As a result, Santa Catarina, Espirito Santo, Roraima and Goiás were new states that were added to the number of receptor states in the country.

Of the total number of Brazilians (26,854,055) that indicated at least one change in municipal residence during the 1980s, 60.7 per cent moved from one urban area to another (Table 17.5). This is indicative of the strong tendency towards urbanization. In the South-East, urban-to-urban migration as a share of the total has been even higher, i.e. 79 per cent in Rio de Janeiro and 70 per cent in São Paulo.

Despite the predominance of urban-to-urban migration in the North and North-Eastern Regions, inter-municipal rural-to-urban and rural-to-rural movements have reached significant proportions during the 1980s. Rural-to-rural movements represented more than 20 per cent of the total migratory movements in the case of Rondônia, Pará, Maranhão and Alagoas, while more than 15 per cent of migrants in Paraná and Mato Grosso fell into this category from 1980 to 1991. This is an indication of the relative importance of the rural character of the economies of those states.

In the period from 1980 to 1991, almost five million people left the Brazilian rural areas, i.e. approximately 18 per cent of the total number of migrants in Brazil. Approximately 28 per cent of all migration from rural-

Table 17.5 Migratory movements according to rural or urban area, states of Brazil, 1981–91

States	Migratory Flows						Total
	Urban-urban	Rural-urban	Urban-rural	Rural-rural	Ignored with destination		
					Urban	Rural	
Rondônia	219,563	64,411	73,449	163,504	3,517	3,600	528,044
(%)	41.58	12.20	13.91	30.96	0.67	0.68	100.00
Acre	31,195	15,351	4,888	9,797	839	166	62,236
(%)	50.12	24.67	7.85	15.74	1.35	0.27	100.00
Amazonas	146,038	46,645	10,104	6,709	6,600	710	216,806
(%)	67.36	25.51	4.66	3.09	3.04	0.33	100.00
Roraima	41,577	7,009	10,469	8,140	1,495	839	69,529
(%)	59.80	10.08	15.06	11.71	2.15	1.21	100.00
Pará	414,422	153,695	226,757	237,800	8,205	4,463	1,045,342
(%)	39.64	14.70	21.69	22.75	0.78	0.43	100.00
Amapá	31,631	15,047	4,150	4,470	984	224	56,506
(%)	55.98	26.63	7.34	7.91	1.74	0.40	100.00
Tocantins	122,431	45,888	33,200	48,960	2,265	1,149	253,893
(%)	48.22	18.07	13.08	19.28	0.89	0.45	100.00
Maranhão	232,881	158,747	178,574	259,512	5,162	6,241	841,117
(%)	27.69	18.87	21.23	30.85	0.61	0.74	100.00
Piauí	170,988	101,575	31,428	55,791	3,199	1,184	364,165
(%)	46.95	27.89	8.63	15.32	0.88	0.33	100.00
Ceará	554,403	238,907	82,423	124,133	8,561	1,493	1,009,920

Table 17.5 continued

(%)	54.90	23.66	8.16	12.29	0.85	0.15	100.00
Rio Grande do Norte	244,087	98,629	56,018	59,695	2,312	907	461,648
(%)	52.87	21.36	12.13	12.93	0.50	0.20	100.00
Paraíba	279,722	106,679	45,832	60,670	3,914	714	497,531
(%)	56.22	21.44	9.21	12.19	0.79	0.14	100.00
Pernambuco	729,478	203,679	97,824	130,202	8,730	1,861	1,171,774
(%)	62.25	17.38	8.35	11.11	0.75	0.16	100.00
Alagoas	173,817	98,035	44,199	83,403	2,842	1,541	403,837
(%)	43.04	24.28	10.94	20.65	0.70	0.38	100.00
Sergipe	175,376	52,508	18,739	32,309	991	167	280,090
(%)	62.61	18.75	6.69	11.54	0.35	0.06	100.00
Bahia	819,542	313,832	162,468	218,415	14,234	3,630	1,532,121
(%)	53.49	20.48	10.60	14.26	0.93	0.24	100.00
Minas Gerais	1,667,102	430,957	226,044	220,211	25,814	6,798	2,576,926
(%)	64.69	16.72	8.77	8.55	1.00	0.26	100
Espírito Santo	391,268	110,711	34,554	66,341	4,259	847	607,980
(%)	64.36	5.68	5.68	10.91	0.70	0.14	100
Rio de Janeiro	1,130,499	176,876	44,726	32,106	46,120	1,969	1,432,296
(%)	78.93	3.12	3.12	2.24	3.22	0.14	100
São Paulo	4,386,265	1,094,369	267,471	336,318	151,954	9,291	6,245,668
(%)	70.23	4.28	4.28	5.38	2.43	0.15	100

	Urban	Urban	Rural	Rural	Urban	Rural	
Paraná	1,092,667	395,146	134,057	302,639	10,836	1,999	1,937,344
(%)	56.40	20.40	6.92	15.62	0.56	0.10	100
Santa Catarina	525,859	192,415	61,381	128,982	6,921	1,972	917,530
(%)	57.31	20.97	6.69	14.06	0.75	0.21	100
Rio Grande do Sul	1,019,319	317,797	92,199	152,194	11,023	1,625	1,594,157
(%)	63.94	19.94	5.78	9.55	0.69	0.10	100
Mato Grosso do Sul	296,427	76,462	48,484	75,040	4,550	1,173	502,136
(%)	59.03	15.23	9.66	14.94	0.91	0.23	100
Mato Grosso	414,578	124,723	84,021	140,360	6,372	2,264	772,318
(%)	53.68	16.15	10.88	18.17	0.83	0.29	100
Goiás	729,872	185,310	98,349	89,862	12,807	2,016	1,118,216
(%)	65.27	16.57	8.80	8.04	1.15	0.18	100
Federal District	252,282	64,846	19,025	14,632	3,395	741	354,921
(%)	71.08	18.27	5.36	4.12	0.96	0.21	100
TOTAL	12,294,764	4,890,745	191,083	3,062,555	357,930	59,592	26,856,651
(%)	60.67	18.21	8.16	11.40	1.33	0.22	100

Source: FIBGE, Demographic Census of 1991: Special Tabulations, NEPO/UNICAMP..

to-urban areas in the country occurred in the North-Eastern Region. Put together, rural-to-urban migration in all the other states counted for more than 10 per cent of the total amount of migration in the country. The rural exodus in São Paulo was higher than one million. This represented 17 per cent of all migration.

Although less significant in relative terms, urban-to-rural migration in the country as a whole represented 8 per cent of all migration, involving around two million people from 1981 to 1991. In the Northern states urban-to-rural flows formed 16 per cent of their total migration, which amounted to 363 thousand migrants. One can see in this region the State of Pará, where the urban-rural migration represented 21.7 per cent of its migratory flows (more than 200 thousand people), the reflection of the agricultural frontier in Amazon, as well as the areas of *garimpo* (diamond mine) as contributors to new ways of migration towards rural areas.

Among the states of the North-East, urban-to-rural migration in Maranhão was on a relatively high level from 1981 to 1991. A total of 178,000 people were involved in this type of migration, i.e. 21 per cent of the total in the state. At that time Maranhão was still regarded as an expanding agricultural frontier and explicit policies of population attraction increased the migration to this rural area.

In urban-to-rural migration, 267,000 and 226,000 migrated to São Paulo and Minas Gerais, respectively. The State of São Paulo stood out in this regard. As it is the most urbanized state in the country the definition of 'rural' in São Paulo is somewhat problematic because there are areas with a distinct urban character that were classified as rural. Two population groups were particularly important in the urban-to-rural migration flow. Firstly, residents forming part of the middle and upper-middle class tend to migrate to secured condominiums in rural areas to avoid the violence, pollution and chaos in the urban centre. Secondly, as a mechanism for surviving, poor people tend to migrate to rural areas because rural land is more readily available and affordable than land in the city and because of the scarcity of employment opportunities in the commercial and industrial sectors. In this way, the urban-to-rural migration patterns in the State of São Paulo serve as an indication of new modalities that can be added to the traditional migration flows in the country.

THE METROPOLITAN SLOWDOWN

Despite the fact that the Brazilian metropolitan areas have attracted and held large populations for several decades, their population growth began to decrease between 1970 and 1980. In fact, the average metropolitan growth rate declined from 4.7 per cent per year during the 1960s to 3.8

per cent the following decade, a growth level that was well below the average Brazilian urban population growth rate of 4.44 per cent per year for the 1970s. In spite of this, 5,705,021 people still migrated to the metropolitan areas between 1970 and 1980, a figure that represented 22.5 per cent of all inter-municipal migration in the country.

The 1970s the regions of Belém, Fortaleza, Salvador, Belo Horizonte, São Paulo and Curitiba registered growth rates higher than or close to the average growth rates of the urban population at the time. The absolute population increase in those regions between 1970 and 1980 was 8.3 million people, which corresponded to a 30 per cent increase in the national urban population overall.

During the 1980s and 1990s the growth rates of the Brazilian metropolitan population continued slowing down. It reached an average growth rate of 1.99 per cent per year between 1980 and 1991 and 1.79 per cent per year from then on up to 2000. The deceleration undoubtedly had an influence on urban development. The first indications that the Brazilian urban population growth was gaining momentum during the 1970s continued into the 1980s and 1990s. Urban growth was 2.97 per cent per year from 1980 to 1991 and 2.42 per cent from 1991 until 2000 while the population growth of metropolitan areas declined (Table 17.6).

The deceleration trend can be seen in the 1980-91 data. During this period the metropolitan growth rates were far below the metropolitan average growth, i.e. 1.88 per cent per year, and 1.26 per cent, respectively, against 1.99 per cent per year for the average Brazilian metropolitan population growth rate.

The results of the Census of 2000 suggest that the deceleration of the metropolitan population during the previous decade continued into the 1990s, especially in São Paulo, Rio de Janeiro, and Porto Alegre. The growth rates of these cities were (1.61, 1.14, and 1.61 per cent per year respectively between 1991 and 2000) were well below the national urban and the metropolitan average of 2.42 and 1.79 per cent for the period. However, the growth rates of Recife, Belo Horizonte, and Fortaleza metropolitan regions remained relatively stable throughout the period, while Curitiba's growth rate increased from 3.03 per cent per year in the 1980s to 3.46 per cent in the 1990s. The metropolitan growth rate in all the other regions decreased.

Despite the fact that the resident population of the nine old metropolitan areas increased from 23,717,028 to 50,164,717 between 1970 and 2000, the deceleration of the metropolitan process is revealed by significant losses of metropolitan populations in relative terms. The national metropolitan population which accounted for 45.56 per cent of

Table 17.6 Total population and growth rates (% per year), metropolitan regions, 1970-2000

METROPOLITAN REGIONS	TOTAL POPULATION				PERCENTAGE OF GROWTH		
	1970	1980	1991	2000	1970-1980	1980-1991	1991-2000
TOTAL	23,730,895	32,126,519	39,759,370	46,657,093	3.79	1.99	1.79
São Paulo	8,139,730	12,588,725	15,444,941	17,833,511	4.46	1.88	1.61
Rio de Janeiro	6,891,521	8,772,265	9,814,574	10,871,960	2.45	1.26	1.14
Recife	1,791,322	2,347,146	2,858,147	3,249,754	2.74	1.22	1.44
Belo Horizonte	1,658,482	2,609,583	3,436,060	4,251,350	4.70	2.42	2.39
Porto Alegre	1,574,239	2,285,140	3,038,792	3,507,624	3.84	2.16	1.61
Salvador	1,147,821	1,766,614	2,496,521	3,018,326	4.43	3.04	2.13
Fortaleza	1,036,779	1,580,074	2,307,017	2,920,923	4.29	2.67	2.66
Curitiba	821,233	1,440,626	2,000,805	2,716,288	5.80	3.03	3.46
Belém	669,768	1,021,486	1,401,305	1,794,981	4.30	3.43	2.79
TOTAL URBAN	52,084,984	80,436,409	110,990,990	137,697,439	4.44	2.97	2.42

Source: FIBGE. Demographic Censuses 1980. 1991 e 2000

the Brazilian urban population in 1970 decreased to 33.88 per cent in 2000. The largest losses were registered in the metropolitan areas of the State of São Paulo and Rio de Janeiro. Despite some regional oscillations, metropolitan reconcentration was never observed during the 1990s (Matos and Baeninger, 2001, p. 17).

THE BRAZILIAN URBAN NETWORK

Based upon the overall distribution of the population in the larger regions of Brazil it is possible to determine the relative importance of non-metropolitan agglomerations and smaller cities in the spatial reorganization of the population (Table 17.7).

When the entire urban system, ranging from metropolitan areas to non-metropolitan urban agglomerations, intermediate-sized cities, and other small towns, is considered, 36.3 per cent of the total population is concentrated in the metropolitan areas. Another 22.6 per cent live in non-metropolitan urban agglomerations and intermediate-sized cities. The remainder of the total population (41.1 per cent) reside in the other municipalities.

Although Brazil is a highly urbanized country with 80 per cent of its population living in urban areas, the data in Table 17.7 show how dispersed the population actually is when the entire urban network is considered. The increasing importance of non-metropolitan areas indicates their substantial potential to absorb and retain people. Through the densification of the urban network they contribute to the reduction in the growth of metropolitan areas, and in turn, begin to play an important role in the intra-regional redistribution of the Brazilian population. This new urban configuration includes the filling in of local or regional 'expansion areas' and thereby brings a new spatial dimension to the urbanization process, i.e. the formation of new spaces that incorporate more than one municipality.

By the year 2000, there were 18 metropolitan areas and 31 non-metropolitan urban agglomerations in the country, 14 of which were located in the South-East (Map 1). There were 61 intermediate-sized city districts (urban centres) located outside metropolitan concentrations and agglomerations which indicates their importance even in economically depressed areas such as the North-East where there are 12 such centres.

Urban areas of all sizes in Brazil, from metropolitan areas to small towns (less than 20 thousand habitants) and cities (more that 20,000 inhabitants) have been growing from 1991 to 2000. The particular population growth rate of each size-category of cities serves as an indication of the ability of the various groups of cities to accommodate

Table 17.7 Population according to the Brazilian urban network morphology, 1980-2000

Morphology	Number of Municipalities in 2000	Total Population			Relative Distribution (%)				Growth Rates (% per year)
		1980	1991	2000	1980	1991	2000		1980-91
BRAZIL	5,507	119,002,706	146,816,455	169,544,443	100.00	100.00	100.00		1.93
Metropolitan Regions(*)	203	40,561,170	51,566,033	61,549,587	34.08	35.12	36.30		2.21
Urban Non-Metropolitan Agglomerations	178	11,519,524	16,670,309	20,353,120	9.68	11.35	12.00		3.42
Urban Centres	62	10,892,419	14,821,581	18,043,223	9.15	10.10	10.64		2.84
Other Municipalities	5,064	56,029,593	63,758,532	69,598,513	47.08	43.43	41.05		1.18

Notes: (*) Includes the old and new metropolitan areas (18 areas).

Source: FIBGE. Demographic Censuses 1980 to 2000. The morphology is based in IPEA/IBGE/NESUR-UNICAMP (2000).

people. While metropolitan areas of Brazil grew at a rate of 2.0 per cent per year during this period, the other categories, i.e. the non-metropolitan urban agglomerations, urban centres (cities with more 500,000 inhabitants), and the non-primate cities (cities that are not urban agglomerations) grew at 2.24, 2.16, and almost 1.00 per cent per year respectively.

Looking at the population growth of cities in the Brazilian regions, non-primate municipalities in the North grew the fastest of them all, i.e. at 2.55 per cent per year. This rate is higher than those of the metropolitan areas of South-Eastern Brazil. Such places provide basic services to prospective migrants and are now becoming service centres at the local and even sub-regional levels. However, the spatial arrangement of cities in the region is clearly influenced by Belém and Manaus (NESUR-IE/UNICAMP, 1998; Moura and Moreira, 1998), although the other state capitals are also important in this regard. All of them have grown by more than 3 per cent per year from 1991 to 2000. Moura and Moreira (1998) call the emerging new non-metropolitan small cities in this region evidence of a new 'rural revival'.

In the North-East, the metropolitan areas have experienced growth rates similar to those of non-metropolitan urban agglomerations and intermediate-sized cities (around 2 per cent per year in the 1990s). Although the non-primate municipalities accounted for 61.0 per cent of the regional population in 2000, concentration of people in this urban category declined, in favour of municipalities located within urban concentrations.

This metropolitan concentration in the North-East reflects the idiosyncrasies of regional urbanization. The 1980s witnessed an acceleration in rural-to-urban migration which led to a significant decrease in the local rural population (from 17,245,514 inhabitants in 1980, to 16,721,621 in 1991, and dropping further to 15,575,505 in 1996). Part of the population that left the rural areas of the region between 1980 and 1996 was absorbed by the local urban areas, mostly by the regional metropolitan areas. The urban population growth rate of the North-East was 2.5 per cent per year between 1991 and 1996, far above the national average of 2.1 per cent per year for the period.

The recent economic growth of certain areas in the North-East, especially those related to (i) the petrochemical complex of Camaçari, (ii) the textile centre of Fortaleza, (iii) the mineral-metallurgical complex of Carajás, (iv) the agro-industrial centre of Petrolina/Juazeiro, and (v) the areas marked by modern cereal agriculture, tourism, and export oriented fruit production, have all contributed to the growth and diversification of the region's economic structure (Araújo, 1995; Pacheco, 1998). They all contributed to the expansion of tertiary activities and increased the population absorptive capacity of this region.

The metropolitan growth of the South-East is the lowest among all of the large regions of Brazil. The growth rates are fairly even across different urban categories (see Table 17.5), ranging from 1.51 per cent per year to 1.73 per cent in spite of the predominance of non-metropolitan urban growth. A more homogeneous diffusion of urbanization constitutes a strong characteristic of the region, a trait related to the emergence of new urban agglomerations, and the increased density of urban areas, strategically located in the urban network.

The long history of concentration of economic activities in the South-East, especially in São Paulo, Rio de Janeiro and part of Minas Gerais, made the South-East the most urbanized region of Brazil. In 1996, 89.3 per cent of its population or 9,825,958 people lived in urban areas which include the three most important national metropolitan areas. Currently, the large metropolitan areas are shrinking and new roles are being assigned to them.

In the South of Brazil the growth of metropolitan areas (3.13 per cent per year in the 1991-2000 period) was higher than all the other urban categories, especially when compared to the non-primate cities (0.09 per cent per year in the same period). Its recent economic dynamism is impacting positively on urban development in the region. New development centres are being formed in all the States. In this context, the shoe manufacturing pole in Vale dos Sinos, the mechanical industry in the metropolitan region of Porto Alegre and in the north-east of Santa Catarina, the petrochemical complex of Triunfo, in Rio Grande do Sul, the oil refinery of Araucaria, and the industrial district of Curitiba in Paraná are good examples of such development poles (Pacheco, 1998).

The new economic restructuring followed by a demographic recovery of the area, especially in the state of Paraná, had a significant impact on the southern urban system. According to the results of a study by IPEA/IBGEINESUR-IE/UNICAMP (1998: 107) 'the main characteristic of the southern urban network is the combination of an increasing number of densely populated municipalities in urban agglomerations – spaces qualified as both population and economic concentration areas' which diverted historical population shifts away from the regional metropolitan areas.

The manifestation of new socio-spatial dynamics in the Brazilian urban system can clearly be seen in the evolving of Brasilia's hinterland and in the process of regional metropolitanization in the Central-Western Region. In the 1990s, 53.5 per cent of the regional population lived in this group of cities compared to 40.1 per cent in the 1981-91 period. In fact, the annual growth rate of the Central-Western metropolitan areas (Brasilia and Goiânia) was 4.57 per cent from 1991 to 2000, the highest in the Brazilian urban network for the period. Marked by the expansion, modernization, and urbanization of the agricultural frontier the Central-West experienced a rural outflow of people since the 1970s. During that time the region's urban population grew at a rate of 7.6 per cent per year, higher than the rate of Northern Brazil for the same period (6.6 per cent per year). Between 1980 and 1991, the urban population growth rate started to decrease to 4.3 per cent per year but it still remained above the national average of 3.0 per cent. This trend continued during the early 1990s when the urban growth rate of the Central-West declined to 3.0 per cent compared to the Brazilian average of 2.1 per cent per year. This general movement towards the cities is a result of the prevailing economic dynamics in the region, a highly capitalized and automated agricultural sector that concentrates on the production of commodities. It does not rely heavily on manual labour and it transforms land uses and property values, resulting in the emptying of the rural areas and the stimulation of migration towards the large urban centres (NESUR-IE/UNICAMP, 1998, p. 59).

The growing focus on grain and meat production in the region and the polarizing of the tertiary and industrial sectors had a significant impact on the urban system, as 86 per cent of the people of the Central-West lived in urban areas in the year 2000, second only to South-Eastern Brazil (90.5 per cent).

SPATIAL DECONCENTRATION: REVERSION, INVERSION OR NEW POLARIZATION?

The changes that have been observed in the patterns of population redistribution and economic activities have resulted in complicated processes of spatial deconcentration, or, in Richardson's terms (1980), polarization reversal, facilitating the deconcentration of industrial activities and people outside metropolitan areas. In fact, in the case of São Paulo, the effect of the reduction in economic opportunities in the city and, at the same time, governmental policies stimulating deconcentration to the interior of the country, could be seen in the low rate of population growth in the largest metropolis in the country.

The discussion about polarization reversal, however, although emphasizing deconcentration of population and economic activities, in reality seems to be directed to economic factors and tied to the idea of the migration-employment relationship. Redwood (1984: 35) says: 'the reversion of polarization implies in the redistribution of the population to the interior, a national urban hierarchy. It is, then, strictly associated with the spatial distribution of economic activities through time, particularly in the context of a Developing Country where the people tend to follow their employment' (see also Matos, 1994, p. 17).

In fact, this seems to have been the predominant tendency at the beginning of the economic deconcentration process (Diniz, 1993). One can say that the 1970s were marked by industrial polarization reversal accompanied by an incipient process of population deconcentration. The example of São Paulo is very clear in this regard. When industry moved to the interior of the country in the 1970s it led to significant metropolitan migration flows to the interior. The impacts of this process and the socio-spatial development that followed involved different phases of agglomeration and dispersion (Matos, 1995). This led to significant changes in the composition of São Paulo which included a possible polarization inversion or industrial reconcentration in the modern services and high technology sectors (Diniz, 1993; Cano 1995). As a result the focus in São Paulo is shifting away from employment opportunities for the less qualified.

Currently, the dispersion of population and of economic activities gives rise to a completely new pattern of polarized development. In comparison, the impact of industrial development forces on the emergence and expansion of regional agglomerations in the 1980s and the 1990s are not as clear as they were during the 1970s. The creation of new communication mechanisms and the homogenization of life styles make the direct relationships between industrial development patterns and migration trends less obvious, and it makes other factors more important in the decision to migrate. As a reflection of interurban relations and of social processes, regionalization has come to play an important role in decision-making processes, and it often affects the currents and volume of internal migration (Ebanks, 1993). Commuting also impacts on the urbanization process because it increases the range of living and working options in the interior.

CONCLUSIONS

Productive restructuring at the international level has impacted significantly on the evolution of urban space at the local, regional and national levels in recent years. This evolution has been brought about by major changes in economic, political and social interaction patterns as they adjust to blend in with global changes. Urban dynamics have also changed. The tempo at which technological transformations have occurred has intensified. Small and intermediate-sized cities are playing a more important role in regional dynamics and this has changed the direction and composition of migration flows.

These new scenarios are changing the contours of the cities. In many instances an understanding of local changes requires a broader understanding of regional, metropolitan and even global dynamics. Changes in the urban functions of cities, in terms of economic activities and changes in the spatial redistribution of people are often fundamental in the strengthening of regional economies.

This new urban dispensation represents important transformations in the dynamics of population redistribution processes. There is consequently a need at present for a revision of traditional concepts such as rural versus urban areas, push and pull areas, and origin and destination areas, all of which were previously strongly anchored in urban-rural relations. In fact, so many fundamental changes have occurred over the last twenty years in urban-rural relationships that the methods of analysis that are currently used to unravel social reality need to be reviewed. At the centre of this change is the predominance of urban-to-urban migration flows. New kinds of population movements are emerging which are currently not fully comprehensible in terms of traditional concepts of urban areas, hinterlands, and migration patterns.

One of the first changes one can identify is the disappearance of the traditional rural area. Today rural is an extension of urban. On the one hand, crops and production patterns are determined by the dynamics of international markets. Service and leisure activities, on the other hand, involve the so-called rural area. In this context, the geographic unit of analysis is no longer the city or the 'urban' area, but the municipality which involves both the urban and rural areas of a place. This redefinition allows one to identify the contributions of internal population movements in the formation of the new spatial dimensions of the city and, in a wider context, the configuration of local, regional and national urban networks.

In order to understand this new spatial configuration, the concepts of push- and pull-factors and origin/destination areas need to be revisited. Urban-regional dynamics create and recreate spaces where the circulation of goods and services and of population produces a new territoriality. In this case, the links between cities and their periphery redefine the meaning and explanations of the departing and arrival points of migrants.

In the context of these transformations, the predominance of the urban population, independent of city size, has generated an 'homogenization' of demographic indicators such as degree of urbanization, mortality rates, and fertility rates in different places. This shows how important it is to find new ways of understanding the spatial redistribution of the population in the urbanization process.

REFERENCES

Araújo, T.M.B. (1995), 'Nordeste, Nordeste: que Nordeste?', in R. Affonso and P.L. Barros Silva (eds), *Desigualdades Regionais e Desenvolvimento (Federalismo no Brasil)*, São Paulo: FUNDAP/ ED. UNESP, pp. 125-156.

Azzoni, C. (1986), 'Indústria e Reversão da Polarização no Brasil'. *Ensaios Econômicos* **58**, São Paulo: IPE/USP.

Baeninger, R. (1999), Região, Metrópole e Interior: Espaços Ganhadores e Espaços Perdedores nas Migrações Recentes no Brasil 1980/1996. Doctoral Thesis. IFCH/UNICAMP, Campinas.

Bandeira, P. S. (1994), 'A economia da Região Sul', in R. Affonso and P. L. Silva (eds), *Desigualdades regionais e desenvolvimento (Federalismo no Brasil)*. São Paulo: FUNDAP, UNESP. p. 225-51.

Benko, G. and Lipietz, A. (1994), 'O novo debate regional: Posições em confronto', in G. Benko and A Lipietz (eds), As Regiões Ganhadoras Distritos e Redes: os novos paradigmas da geografia econômica. Celta Editora, Oeiras, pp. 3-15.

Benko, G. (1996), *Economia, Espaço e Globalização: na aurora do século* **XXI**. Editora Hucitec, São Paulo.

Bilsborrow, R. E. (ed.) (1996), *Migration, urbanization and development: new directions and issues*. New York : UNFPA/Kluwer, 1996.

Brito, F. (1997), *População, espaço e economia numa perspectiva histórica: o caso brasileiro*. Doctoral Thesis: CEDEPLAR/UFMG-Faculdade de Ciências Econômicas, Belo Horizonte

Camarano, A. A. (1998), 'Movimentos Migratórios Recentes na Região Nordeste', in Encontro Nacional sobre Migração, Curitiba, Anais, ABEP/IPARDES, pp. 189-208.

Cano, W. (1977), *Raízes da Concentração Industrial em São Paulo*, São Paulo: TA Queiroz.

Cano, W. (1988), *A Interiorização do Desenvolvimento Econômico de São Paulo, 1920-1980*. Fundação SEADE

Cano, W. (1995), 'Auge e inflexão da desconcentração econômica regional', in R. Affonso and P. L. B. Silva (eds) *A federação em perspectiva: ensaios selecionados*. São Paulo: Fundap, pp. 399-416.

Cano, W. (1996), 'Migrações, desenvolvimento e crise no Brasil'. Campinas : Instituto de Economia/UNICAMP (mimeo)

Carvalho, J. A. M. and J. I. Rigotti (1998), 'Análise das metodologias de mensuração das migrações', in Encontro Nacional sobre Migração, Curitiba. Anais. Curitiba: IPARDES/ABEP.

Castells, M. (1989), *The informational city, information technology, economic restructuring and the urban-regional process*. Oxford: Basil Blackwell.

CELADE (Centro Latinoamericano de Demografia) (1994), *Dinâmica de la población en las grandes ciudades en América Latina y Caribe*. Santiago de Chile: Documentos Docentes.

Cunha, J. M. P. (ed) (1999), Projeto *Mobilidade e redistribuição espacial da população no Estado de São Paulo: características recentes, padrões e impactos no processo de urbanização*. Campinas : NEPO /UNICAMP. 273p. (Final Report)

Deddeca, C. S. and S. M. C. Brandão (1992), 'Crise, transformações estruturais e mercado de trabalho'. Campinas : CEDE/UNICAMP, 1992 (mimeo).

Diniz, C. C. (1993), 'Desenvolvimento poligonal no Brasil; nem desconcentração, nem contínua polarização'. *Nova Economia - Revista do Departamento de Ciências Econômicas da UFMG*, **31**, 11, Belo Horizonte.

Diniz, C. C. (1993), 'Dinâmica regional recente e suas perspectivas', in Affonso, R. and P. L. B. Silva, A federação em perspectiva: ensaios selecionados. São Paulo: Fundap, pp.417-429.

Ebanks, E. G. (1993), *Determinantes Socioeconómicos de la Migración Interna*. Santiago de Chile: CELADE.

Faria,V. (1983), 'Desenvolvimento, Urbanização e Mudanças na Estrutura do Emprego: a experiência brasileira dos últimos 30 anos', in Sorj , B. and M.H. Almeida, *Sociedade e Política no Brasil Pós-64*. São Paulo: Editora Brasiliense.

Faria, V. (1991), 'Cinqüenta anos de urbanização no Brasil: tendências e perspectivas'. *Novos Estudos CEBRAP* **29**, 98-119.

Fundação IBGE . *Demographic Censuses 1940 to 2000*, Rio de Janeiro.

Fundação IBGE (1995), *Pesquisa Nacional por Amostra de Domicílio*. Rio de Janeiro: PNAD.

Fundação IBGE (1997), *Contagem Populacional de 1996*. Rio de Janeiro.

Fundação IBGE/DPE/DPIS/DICAD/DEMOG (1997), *Movimentos migratórios segundo o Censo Demográfico de 1991 e Contagem da População de 1996*. Rio de Janeiro : IBGE (mimeo).

Gottdiener, M. (1990), 'A teoria da crise e a reestruturação sócio-espacial: o caso dos Estados Unidos', in Valladares, L. and E. Preteceille (eds), *Reestruturação Urbana: tendências e desafios*. Nobel/IUPERJ, São Paulo, pp.59-78.

Gottdiener, M (1993), *A produção social do espaço*. São Paulo: EDUSP.

Greenwood, M. (1980), 'Migrações internas nos Estados Unidos; uma revisão da literatura', in A. M. Moura (ed), *Migração interna; textos selecionados*. Fortaleza: Banco do Nordeste do Brasil, pp.733-77.

Harvey, D. (1992), *Condição Pós-Moderna*. São Paulo: Editora Loyola.

IPEA/IBGEINESUR-IE/UNICAMP (1998), *Caracteristicas e Tendências da Rede Urbana no Brasil*. Instituto de Economia-UNICAMP.

Martine, G. (1987), *'Migração e Metropolização'*. Revista São Paulo em Perspectiva, São Paulo: Fundação SEADE.

Martine, G. (1992), *Processos recentes de concentração e desconcentração urbana no Brasil: determinantes e implicações*. Documento de Trabalho 11, Brasília, Instituto SPN, 1- 29.

Martine, G. (1994), *A redistribuição espacial da população brasileira durante a década de 80*. Textos para Discussão 329, Brasília, IPEA,. 43p.

Martine, G. (1995), 'A evolução espacial da população brasileira', in R. B. A. Affonso and P. L. B. Silva (eds), *Desigualdades regionais e desenvolvimento (Federalismo no Brasil)*. São Paulo: FUNDAP/Ed. UNESP, pp.61-91.

Matos, C. de (1994), *Capital, población y territorio. Seminário distribución y movilidad territorial de la población y desarrollo humano*. Bariloche, Argentina: Fundación Bariloche / CENEP / PROLAP.

Matos, R. E. S. (1995), *Dinâmica migratória e desconcentração da população na macrorregião de Belo Horizonte*. xx: Belo Horizonte. CEDEPLAR (tese de doutorado).

Matos R. E. S. and R. Baeginger (2001). *Migração e Urbanização no Brasil: Processos de Concentração e Desconcentração Espacial e o Debate Recente*. Session Brazilian Demography. XXIII General Conference IUSSP. (CD-ROM). Salvador, Bahia.

Negri, B. (1996), *Concentração e desconcentração industrial em São Paulo (1880-1990)*. Campinas: Ed. UNICAMP.

Negri, B. and C. A. Pacheco, (1993), 'Mudança Tecnológica e Desenvolvimento regional nos Anos 90: da interiorização do desenvolvimento à nova dimensão espacial da indústria paulista' (Relatório Final). Projeto Desenvolvimento Tecnológico e Competitividade da Indústria Brasileira. Mexico City: SCTDE/ FECAMP/ UNICAMP/ IE, Campinas.

NESUR-IE/UNICAMP (1998), *Caracterização e Tendências da Rede Urbana no Brasil Estudo Regional: Norte*. Relatório 6. Campinas, outubro (mimeo). (Núcleo de Economia Social, Urbana e Regional)

Pacheco, C. (1993), 'Evolução Recente da Urbanização e da Questão regional no Brasil: implicações econômicas para a dinâmica demográfica'. Anais da IV Conferencia Latinoamericana de Población. Ciudad de México.

Pacheco, C. A. (1998), *Fragmentação da Nação*. Mexico City: Campinas: Instituto de Economia/UNICAMP.

Pacheco, C. and N.L. Patarra, (1998), 'Movimentos migratórios anos 80: novos padrões?' in Encontro Nacional sobre Migração (eds), Anais. Curitiba : ABEP/IPARDES.

Pacheco, C.A. and N.L. Patarra (2000), *Tendências da Urbanização e do Crescimento Populacional Brasileiro: População em Idade Escolar*. Mexico City: Instituto de Economia/UNICAMP.

Patarra, N.L., R. Baeninger, L. Bógus, and P. Jannuzzi, (1997), *Migrações, Dinâmica Urbana e Condições de Vida*. Mexico City: Instituto de Economia-UNICAMP.

Piore, M. and C. Sabel (1984), *The second industrial divide*. New York: Basic Books.

Preteceille, E. and L. Valladares (1990), 'Introdução', in Valladares, L. and E. Preteceille, eds., *Reestruturação Urbana: tendências e desafios*. Nobel/IUPERJ, São Paulo, pp.7-13.

Redwood III, J. (1984), *Reversion de polarizacion, ciudades secundarias y eficiencia en el desarrollo nacional: una vison teorica aplicada al Brasil contemporaneo*. Revista Latinoamericana de Estudios Urbanos Regionales, **11**, Santiago.

Richardson, H. W. (1975), *Economia Regional, teoria da localização, estrutura urbana e crescimento regional*. Rio de Janeiro: Zahar Editores.

Rigotti, J. I. R and J. A. M. Carvalho, (1998), 'As migrações na grande Região Centro-Leste', in Encontro Nacional sobre Migração. Anais. Curitiba : ABEP/IPARDES, pp.67-90.

Rigotti, J. I. R. and D. Sawyer (2001), *Migrações Rurais-Urbanas no Brasil.(CD-ROM) Session Brazilian Demography*. XXIII General Conference IUSSP, Salvador, Bahia.

Santos, M. (1990), 'A metrópole: modernização, involução e segmentação', in Valladares, L. and E. Preteceille (eds), *Reestruturação urbana: tendências e desafios*. São Paulo: Nobel/IUPERJ, pp. 183-191.

Santos, M. (1997), *Técnica, espaço, tempo: globalização e meio técnico-científico informacional*. São Paulo: Editora Hucitec.

Sassen, S. (1988), *The mobility of labor and capital*. Cambridge: Cambridge University Press.

Singer, P. (1973), *Economia política da urbanização*. São Paulo: HUCITEC.

Townroe, P. M. and D. Keen (1984), 'Polarization reversal in the state of São Paulo, Brazil', *Regional Studies*, **18**, 1, pp.45-54.

Villa, M. and J. Rodriguez (1994), 'Dinámica sociodemografica de las metrópolis latinoamericanas', in *Grandes ciudades de América Latina: dos capítulos*. Documentos Docentes, Santiago de Chile, Centro Latinoamericano de Demografia-CELADE, Naciones Unidas-FNUAP.

D. ASIAN COUNTRIES

Chapter 18

Migration and the Development of the Japanese Urban System, 1950-2000

A. J. Fielding

INTRODUCTION

The years 1994 and 1995 have a special significance in the history of modern Japanese migration. For the first time since the Second World War, the Tokyo metropolitan region, which had been gaining more than 350,000 people a year through internal migration in the early 1960s, became an area of net population loss by internal migration as more people left the capital region than entered it. This paper traces the post-war history of migration within Japan, focussing especially on the importance of flows to and from the capital city-region. It attempts to explain the four main phases of this migration: (i) the very rapid Japan-wide urbanization associated with the rural depopulation of the 1950s and 1960s; (ii) the so-called 'turnaround' phenomenon of the 1970s, when net gains to the largest urban regions either disappeared or were, as in the case of Tokyo, drastically reduced; (iii) the renewal of net migration gains to the Tokyo metropolitan region in the 1980s; and (iv) the recent and sudden change to net loss for this same region in the mid-1990s.

THE JAPANESE URBAN SYSTEM

Japan has a long and distinguished urban history. At a time when Europe was in its dark ages, a magnificent capital city was being built in central western Japan at Nara,[1] only to be followed by the building of the even greater city of Kyoto, the imperial capital of Japan for the whole of its Medieval and Early Modern Periods, attaining its finest hour during the Heian period from 794 to

---

[1] The Nara period lasted from 710 to 794.

1185. Moreover, despite the rapid urbanization associated with Mercantilist trade and capitalist industrialization in western Europe, for a time during Japan's semi-feudal Edo period (1600-1868) the largest city in the world was not London or Paris, but the Tokugawa Shogun's city of Edo (present day Tokyo) (Masai 1990). How tragic, therefore, that most of the landscape and built-form legacy of this earlier urban history was lost (obliterated is a better word) either in the course of Japan's violent modernization, or through natural disasters (such as the great Kanto earthquake and fire that struck Tokyo in 1923), or through the massive American fire- and nuclear bombing of Japanese cities at the end of the Second World War.

After 1945, city-people flocked back into the cities from the countryside where they had sought safety from the bombing. They were followed over the next 25 years by millions of others, mostly young people from rural backgrounds attracted to the cities by the many job opportunities that accompanied Japan's miracle state-sponsored postwar economic growth. We see, today, the product of that rapid postwar urbanization: a sophisticated system of cities, dominated spatially and functionally by Tokyo, and connected by massive flows of goods, people and information. Many of these flows are channeled along major axes of development, notably the Tokaido axis linking the Tokyo-dominated Kanto region of eastern central Japan to the Osaka-dominated Kansai region of western central Japan, but also the western extension of this axis down the north shore of the Inland Sea to the city of Fukuoka in northern Kyushu. Figure 18.1 shows the main spatial features of this urban system. Using just the largest and second largest out-migration streams from each prefecture, it reveals first the importance of Tokyo,[2] especially to people living in the north and east of Japan (Touhoku), but more generally to those living in the peripheral regions of the country. Secondly, it shows the significance of Osaka[3] as the destination for inter-prefectural migration streams in central western Japan. Finally, it demonstrates the role of provincial cities such as Sendai, Nagoya, Hiroshima and Fukuoka as the foci in smaller, regional migration systems.

The degree to which the urban system is dominated by Tokyo is shown effectively in Figure 18.2. Here the vertical position of a city is a measure of its importance with respect to employment in private sector head and branch offices. Tokyo clearly towers over the rest, and Osaka and Nagoya seem almost insignificant by comparison. The lines have a thickness that reflects the proportion of head offices located, for example in Tokyo, that have branch offices in that other city. This reveals the importance of the main provincial cities (in addition to Osaka and Nagoya), notably Sapporo (regio-

---

[2] The population of the four prefectures which make up the metropolitan region totals 32.7 million.
[3] The population of the four prefectures of the Osaka region totals 18.2 million.

Figure 18.1 The spatial structure of the Japanese urban system

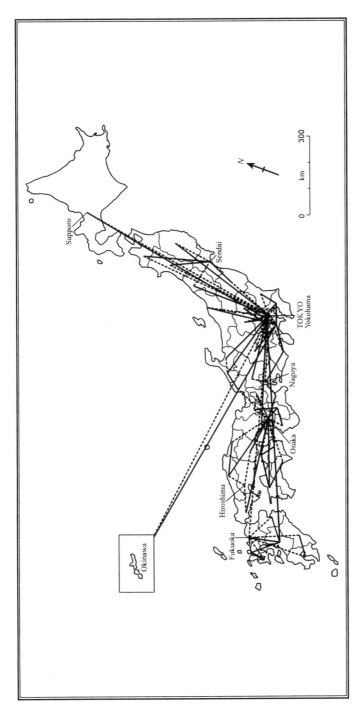

Notes: First and second order prefectural out migration flows, 1996.

Source: Statistics Bureau, Annual Report on the Internal Migration in Japan derived from the Basic Household Registers.

Figure 18.2 The hierarchical structure of the Japanese urban system

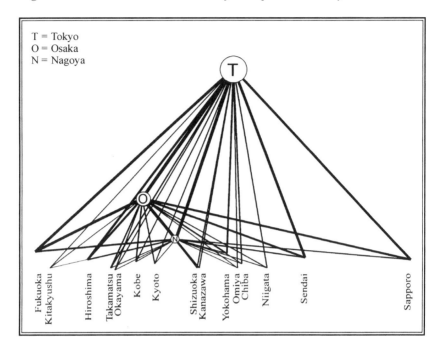

Notes: The vertical position of each city reflects the numbers of employees in the head and branch offices of major private sector companies, and the thickness of the lines reflects the percentage of the head offices of firms located in Tokyo, Osaka and Nagoya respectively that have branch offices located in each of the other Japanese cities.

Source: Abe, 2000.

nal capital of Hokkaido), Sendai (regional capital of Touhoku), Hiroshima (regional capital of Western Honshu) and Fukuoka (regional capital of Kyushu).

MIGRATION AND THE JAPANESE URBAN SYSTEM

Figure 18.3 shows the way that internal migration was implicated in the development of the post-war urban system in Japan. In the case of the three largest cities, Tokyo, Osaka and Nagoya,[4] the period witnessed the increasing under-bounding of the emerging urban region by the cities' administrative areas, the prefectures. Not surprisingly, it is Tokyo that shows this feature earliest and to the highest degree. For this reason it is sensible to follow the

---

[4] The population of Nagoya's Aichi prefecture is 6.9 million

Figure 18.3 Migration efficiency for selected prefectures, 1955-90

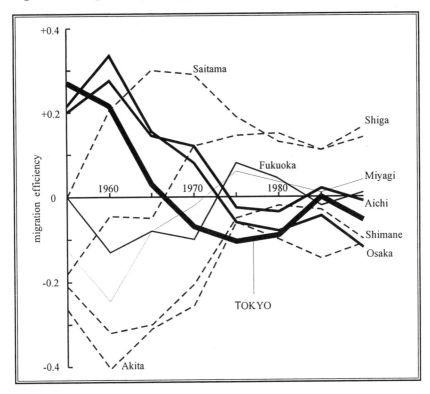

Notes: 'Migration efficiency' is net migration expressed as a proportion of total migration (i.e. in-flow minus out-flow, divided by in-flow plus out-flow).

Source: Based on data presented in Outomo, 1996, Nihon no Jinkou Idou, page 71.

Tokyo curve alongside that for Saitama prefecture.[5] In 1955 Tokyo showed strong net migration gains while Saitama was in net migration balance. During the high period of urbanization, Tokyo moved from high gains to net losses, while local decentralization resulted in very high gains for Saitama. By 1975, however, the gains in Saitama were being matched by the losses in Tokyo, and it was only when Tokyo ceased to lose in the mid and late 1980s that the region as a whole began once more to gain. A similar, but later and more muted relationship can be seen for the Osaka-Shiga pair of prefectures. Shiga[6] was a net loser by migration until the mid-1970s but subsequently

---

[5] Population 6.8 million, located contiguous with, and to the north and northwest of Tokyo.

[6] Population 1.3 million.

benefited from the decentralization of population and employment from the core area of the Kansai region centred on Osaka.

How remarkably different are the curves for the provincial cities of Fukuoka[7] and Sendai![8] When Tokyo, Osaka and Aichi were gaining at their fastest rates around 1960, the prefectures of these medium-sized provincial cities were losing by migration. By 1975 both prefectures were gaining, and they have largely continued to gain since, despite some local decentralization to nearby prefectures.

That leaves the smallest places in the Japanese urban system. Figure 18.3 shows the curves for two prefectures, Shimane[9] and Akita,[10] that are typical of peripheral regions, dominated by forested, mountainous terrain and small-scale agriculture. Both of these prefectures are located on the Japan Sea coast (i.e. the coast that faces Asia) and are therefore a considerable distance away from the heavily populated and urbanized Pacific coastal belt. Until 1970, these were areas of rapid and massive out-migration. But since 1975 these areas have seen only small losses due to migration, though their top-heavy age-structures often imply excess deaths over births. Many less peripheral and less rural prefectures show curves that have net losses in the pre-1970 period followed by small net gains after 1975.

EXPLAINING THE RECENT MIGRATION HISTORY OF THE TOKYO METROPOLITAN REGION

The remainder of this chapter[11] focuses on Figure 18.4, which shows the pattern of net internal migration gain and loss for the Tokyo, Osaka and Nagoya metropolitan regions (note: not prefectures) for the period 1954-97. Four periods can be identified: (i) 1950s and '60s – high net gains in all metropolitan regions; (ii) 1970-80 – sudden decline in net gains in the early 1970s, followed by low gains for Tokyo, and net losses for the other two metropolitan areas; (iii) 1980s – only Tokyo shows a return to strong net gains; and (iv) the early-mid 1990s – Tokyo's net gains decline sharply and turn into net loss, before turning again into slight net gain.

CONCEPTUAL FRAMEWORK

To make sense of these migration trends we need a conceptual framework

---

[7] Prefecture population 5.0 million.

[8] Myagi prefecture, population 2.3 million.

[9] Population 0.8 million.

[10] Population 1.2 million.

[11] This part of the chapter is a development of a paper given to the Asian Urbanization Conference, SOAS 1997 (see Fielding and Ishikawa 1997).

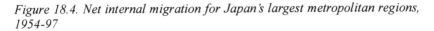

Figure 18.4. Net internal migration for Japan's largest metropolitan regions, 1954-97

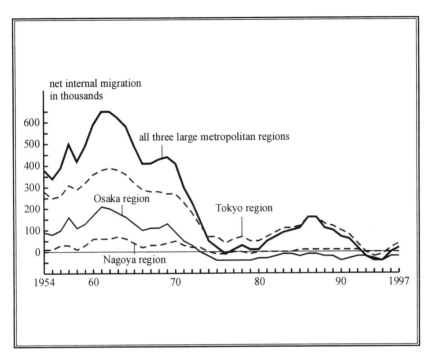

Notes: The Tokyo region consists of the four prefectures of Tokyo, Kanagawa, Saitama and Chiba; the Nagoya region of the three prefectures of Aichi, Gifu and Mie; and the Osaka region of the four prefectures of Osaka, Hyogo, Kyoto and Nara

Source: Management and Coordination Agency, Statistics Bureau 1998, Annual Report on Internal Migration in Japan

that captures the root causes of metropolitan migration in the contemporary period. Figure 18.5, based upon an earlier study by the author on migration to and from South East England, represents an attempt to provide such a framework. The main features of this approach are (i) the importance it places on economic forces in explaining migration flows. Note that this does not imply that other forces are unimportant (for example, state or regional policies or local cultural factors), only that the root causes of migration are predominantly economic; and (ii) that these economic forces can be usefully divided into t term – business cycle-related changes in housing and labour markets; (b) medium-term – economic restructuring and the changing spatial divisions of labour; and (c) long-term – globalization and the underlying structure of economic space.

Figure 18.5 *Processes of economic change and migration to and from Tokyo, 1960-2000*

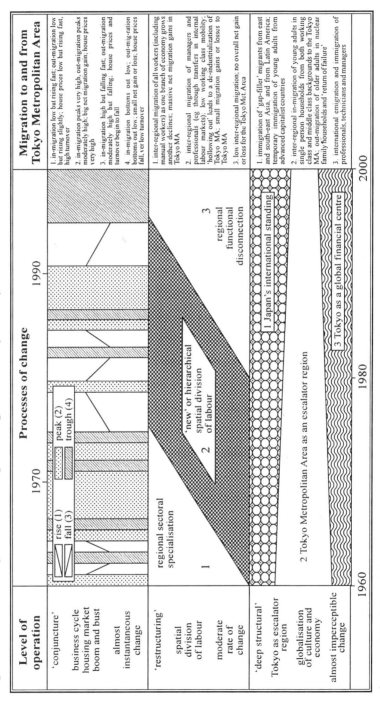

Source: Own interpretation

INTER-REGIONAL MIGRATION AND THE TOKYO METROPOLITAN CITY-REGION

The question can then be asked whether the processes discussed within the framework developed in Figure 18.5 can help us to explain the patterns revealed in Figure 18.4.

Period 1: the 1950s and 1960s

(i) Short-term: *the effects of business-cycle related changes in housing and labour markets on migration flows to and from the Tokyo metropolitan region*

There is an intimate relationship between internal migration and economic growth in postwar Japan. It was to a significant degree due to the almost unlimited supply of rural labour on to the urban industrial labour markets that high rates of profit, rapid capital accumulation, and high levels of investment in new plant and machinery were achieved in the high growth period between 1950 and 1973. These rural migrants constituted the cheap, plentiful and manageable workforce that underpinned the success of Japanese manufacturing industry, which in turn produced national GNP growth rates of around 10% per annum for much of this period. At the regional level and over short time-spans, however, it was growth in GDP which seems to have stimulated migration. For the Tokyo Metropolitan Area (TMA[12]) there is a strong positive correlation between in-migration and the business cycle (r = + 0.81) for the period 1956 to 1993 (Fielding and Ishikawa, 1998), and the relationship is strongest for the earlier period when the peaks and troughs in the GNP curve preceded those in the migration curve, indicating that the direction of causality was more in the direction of GNP influencing migration than *vice versa*. Since the 1950s and 60s were years of high GNP growth it is only to be expected then that there would be large net migration gains to the capital city-region.

(ii) Medium-term: *the effects of economic restructuring and changing spatial divisions of labour on migration to and from the Tokyo metropolitan region*

During the early post-war period, Japan experienced rapid rural depopulation and a massive concentration of population and employment growth in the largest metropolitan city-regions (for example Tokyo, Osaka and Nagoya), as these areas became the locations of Fordist mass-production consumer goods industries. Patterns of regional development and migration during this period can be interpreted with the assistance of the concept of regional sectoral specialization. Under regional sectoral specialization (which dominated in the 1950s and 1960s) there was inter-regional migration of all kinds of workers (but especially manual workers) as one branch of the economy grew and another declined (for example, as the vehicle and consumer electrical

---

[12] It consists of the four prefectures of Tokyo, Kanagawa, Saitama and Chiba.

goods industries expanded and agriculture declined). The Tokyo region, with its highly favourable employment structure, experienced net migration gains at this time (see Fielding, 1998).

(iii) Long-term: *the effects of the underlying structure of economic space on migration to and from the Tokyo metropolitan region*

Tokyo dominated the early post-war space-economy of Japan. Large regional income differentials favoured the capital city-region as did job opportunities and the prospects for upward social mobility. The fact that Japanese economic growth was, to a significant degree, assisted by state policy only served to further enhance the status of Tokyo since it was here that the top bureaucrats in the key ministries exercised their considerable authority.

Period 2: the 1970s

(i) Short-term: *the effects of business-cycle related changes in housing and labour markets on migration flows to and from the Tokyo metropolitan region*

The sharp downturn in in-migration to Tokyo preceded the oil crisis of 1973-74 (see Figure 18.4), but the slowdown in the economy probably also contributed subsequently to maintain that downturn.

(ii) Medium-term: *the effects of economic restructuring and changing spatial divisions of labour on migration to and from the Tokyo metropolitan region*

In the late-Fordist period (late 1960s and 1970s), Japan, like other advanced capitalist countries, experienced a geographical decentralization of industrial and service employment. This was partly in response to a spatial standardization of the conditions of production (for example, state-sponsored infrastructure investment in peripheral and rural regions, and an upgrading of health and education services in non-metropolitan areas), and partly due to labour shortages in the largest metropolitan cities. Coinciding with the emergence of counter-urbanization in other advanced capitalist countries, this produced the famous U-turn migration in Japan (that is, the sudden appearance of return migration and counter-stream migration flows: this is neatly demonstrated by the sudden decrease in migration efficiency rates around 1970 in Figure 18.3). Net migration gains to the Tokyo region declined sharply, particularly so in the early 1970s, but this decline stopped short of producing a net loss to the region, resulting instead in very low net migration gains by the mid-1970s. Patterns of regional development and migration during this period can be interpreted with the assistance of the concept of the new (or hierarchical) spatial division of labour.

> This explanation puts class relations and class conflict centre-stage. What determines the differential ('uneven') development of cities and regions, and therefore the geography of employment and the migration of people, is the search

for profitability ('the logic of capital accumulation'). This search for profit forces firms to restructure their activities in such a way as, among other things, to minimise their labour costs and maximise their control of labour. After the twenty-five years of rapid post-war growth, located mostly in the large metropolitan cities, employees in these cities were in short supply, they were far too expensive to employ to remain competitive in international markets, and being well-versed in the struggle between labour and capital, they were extremely difficult to manage. The obvious solution to the problem was to decentralize routine production of goods and services to branch plants and back offices in regions where reserves of 'green' labour (previously non-employed women and young people) were to be found. These reserves were located in old industrial regions, in the urbanized countryside around the large metropolitan cities, in former resort towns, and, more generally, in rural and peripheral regions. .... Under the new spatial division of labour, which came to dominate in the 1970s, the inter-regional migration of professionals and managers became more important (particularly as a result of intra-organizational transfers) and the migration of manual workers became less important; a major de-industrialization of Tokyo, combined with counter-urban shifts in both manufacturing and service sector employment led to a sharp decline in the net migration gains of the Tokyo metropolitan region (adapted from Fielding, 1998, pages 42 and 45).

(iii) Long-term: *the effects of the underlying structure of economic space on migration to and from the Tokyo metropolitan region*
The concentration in Tokyo of the most prestigious universities added to the attractiveness of the capital city-region, further enhancing the upward social mobility prospects for those who migrated there. But the income differentials favouring Tokyo had diminished somewhat since the early post-war period, thus reducing its attractiveness.

Period 3: the 1980s
(i) Short-term: *the effects of business-cycle related changes in housing and labour markets on migration flows to and from the Tokyo metropolitan region*
The rapid, land and asset-based, speculative 'bubble economy' growth of the Tokyo economy in the late 1980s attracted migrants from all over Japan but especially from the Touhoku region. When the boom came to a sudden end the attractiveness of Tokyo as a destination region became much reduced. Migration to Tokyo seems to be negatively related to land prices: as prices rise, net migration falls (Fielding and Ishikawa, 1998).
(ii) Medium-term: *the effects of economic restructuring and changing spatial divisions of labour on migration to and from the Tokyo metropolitan region*
Inter-regional migration patterns in Japan in the 1980s reveal the effects of its capital city becoming one of the three main 'global' cities within an increasingly globalized world economy. Tokyo, unlike the Osaka and Nagoya

city-regions, showed marked net migration gains in the mid-late 1980s, associated with the growth in producer services employment. The capital city-region, due to the concentration there of company headquarters, the key institutions of financial capital, central government offices, and the main sites of cultural production (both high and popular culture), now became very different from the other major cities within Japan. And this difference, reflected, for example, in very high living (especially housing) costs, resulted in new barriers to inter-regional migration. Patterns of regional development and migration during this period can be interpreted using the concept of regional functional disconnection.

> When regional sectoral specialization dominated, there were strong inter-regional economic linkages arising from sectorally specialised production for the national market – most goods and services were produced in one region of the country and consumed by those living in another region. Under the new spatial division of labour there were also strong inter-regional linkages, but this time they were linkages within production organizations, as decisions taken at one location were carried out at another. However, with regional functional disconnection (emerging since the mid-1970s) the emphasis is on the weakening of inter-regional linkages as production at one location within a country like Japan becomes more and more connected with suppliers and customers located in other countries, and production becomes more likely to be determined from outside the country. Under regional functional disconnection, inter-regional labour migration is reduced by divergence in regional housing and labour markets, resulting in a pattern of low net inter-regional gains or losses. Whether a region gains or loses from migration now depends on neither the market relations between regions (as under regional sectoral specialization) nor the planned relations between regions (as under the new spatial division of labour) within the country, but on the success or failure of the region to attract capital and labour which is globally mobile' (adapted from Fielding 1998, page 45).

(iii) Long-term: *the effects of the underlying structure of economic space on migration to and from the Tokyo metropolitan region.*

As an 'escalator region' Tokyo played an important role in the formation of Japan's professional and managerial middle classes. An 'escalator region' is a region which has a labour market that favours the rapid upward social mobility of the men and women who work there. Individuals step on the escalator by migrating there at the start, or in the early stages, of their careers. See Fielding, 1999.

Period 4: the early- and mid-1990s

(i) Short-term: *the effects of business-cycle related changes in housing and labour markets on migration flows to and from the Tokyo metropolitan region*

The poor performance of the economy in the early 1990s, combined with growing uncertainties in the banking and construction sectors, reduced the attractiveness of the Tokyo region to migrants. In addition, many large Tokyo-based companies applied a stop on recruitment until the economy returned to a growth path. This especially hit the job prospects of university graduates, those most likely to be looking towards Tokyo for their first employment (Fielding 2000).

(ii) Medium-term: *the effects of economic restructuring and changing spatial divisions of labour on migration to and from the Tokyo metropolitan region*

In the period since the mid-1970s, the processes of economic restructuring have increasingly reflected the 'hollowing out' of the Japanese economy due to foreign investment by Japanese companies in East and South East Asia, and in Western Europe and North America. The negative effects of this hollowing out are especially strong in the Tokyo region since it is there that the costs of labour and overhead costs are highest. Nevertheless, the loss of Fordist manufacturing jobs and the degree of import penetration has been far less in Japan than other advanced capitalist countries. Hence Tokyo remains a significant industrial region with many new jobs in high-tech industries partially compensating for the massive job losses from traditional sectors. There seems to be a positive correlation between manufacturing job loss and out-migration from the Tokyo region (Fielding and Ishikawa, 1998).

(iii) Long-term: *the effects of the underlying structure of economic space on migration to and from the Tokyo metropolitan region*

Tokyo in the 1990s remained the principal site for career advancement and for relatively well-paid low-level jobs. But by now there were others who were keen to take up these job opportunities. Tokyo was the main destination for the very rapidly expanding 'newcomer' populations of immigrants from countries in East and South East Asia and Latin America (Fielding and Mizuno 1995). It was also, and remains, the main destination for skilled international migrants. As it became increasingly international in its business connections, Tokyo was seeing an increasing proportion of its jobs, both those at the top and those at the bottom of the income distribution, being taken not by inter-regional migrants within Japan, but by international migrants.

CONCLUSIONS

The conceptual framework in Figure 18.5 has served us well. Undoubtedly,

some of the patterns and processes of inter-regional migration in Japan are different from those found in other advanced capitalist countries. But the main features of the migration profile of Tokyo shown in Figure 18.4 are fairly well explained by a combination of economic processes depicted in

Figure 18.5, some of them very short-term in nature, some of them played out over the medium-term, others so deep-rooted that they change hardly at all between one generation and the next.

REFERENCES

Abe, K. (2000), 'The Japanese urban system from the standpoint of large private firms' head offices and branch offices, 1995', *Geographical Review of Japan*, **73B**, 62-84.

Fielding, A. J. (1998), 'Counterurbanization and social class', in P. Boyle and K. Halfacree, (eds), *Migration into Rural Areas: Theories and Issues.* Chichester: John Wiley, pp. 41-60.

Fielding, A. J. (1999), *Migration and social mobility in contemporary Japan*, British Association for Japanese Studies, Winchester: Annual Conference, mimeo.

Fielding, A. J. (2000), *Migration and the life course in contemporary Japan*, British Association for Japanese Studies, Birmingham: Annual Conference, mimeo.

Fielding, A. J. and Ishikawa, Y. (1997), *Migration and urban development in Japan: the case of the Tokyo metropolitan region*, Asian Urbanization Conference, SOAS, August 1997, mimeo.

Fielding, A. J. and Mizuno, M. (1995), *Japanese migration and the economic development of the East Asian region.* University of Sussex, Geography Research Paper 23, 40pp.

Ishikawa, Y. and Fielding, A. J.(1998), 'Explaining the recent migration trends of the Tokyo metropolitan area', *Environment and Planning A*, **30**, 1797-1814.

Masai, Y. (1990), 'Tokyo: from a feudal million city to a global supercity', *Geographical Review of Japan*, **63B**, 1-16.

Outomo, A. (1996), *Nihon no Jinkou Idou.* Tokyo: Oukurashou Instsukyoku.

Statistics Bureau (various years) Japan, Annual report on internal migration. Household registers.

Chapter 19

Migration and the Urban System of South Korea

H. W. Richardson, C. C. Bae and M. Jun

INTRODUCTION

South Korea has undergone a major transformation since the end of the Korean War. Propelled by a long era of export-oriented industrialization, its per capita income rose from subsistence levels (in the 1950s comparable with the living standards of Sri Lanka) to advanced economy levels by the 1990s. The economy finally sputtered in the wake of the Asian financial crisis of 1997, and has not yet recovered. Over the period of four decades, the capital of Seoul and the surrounding metropolitan region dominated the spatial landscape. Although agglomeration economies and other market forces were very important, the role of the national government was also influential. The changes in Seoul's metropolitan spatial structure were molded by government investments in transportation (e.g. bridges across the Han River, subways and suburban rail lines), a strategy for decentralizing both industrial establishments and educational facilities, a very restrictive Green belt policy, and a very impressive New Towns construction program. On the whole, these policies enabled the Capital Region to adapt its spatial structure to continuing growth forces without having to incur the core city congestion that would have compelled much earlier interurban and interregional decentralization trends. As a result, the Seoul metropolitan area still accounts for 45 percent of the national population and more than one-half of the urban population in this highly urbanized country.

CHANGES IN THE NATIONAL URBAN HIERARCHY

Although Seoul became the national capital centuries ago, its population remained small (96,000 in 1648, 174,000 in 1753, 204,000 in 1852, and

444,000 in 1935). Korea remained overwhelmingly rural (the urbanization level slowly rose from 3.3 percent in 1789 to 10.1 percent in 1935) until after the Second World War. However, after 1945 urbanization soared, from 19.6 percent in 1944 to 88.8 percent in 1995 (for a review of urbanization trends in Korea up to the mid-1980s, see Richardson and Hwang, 1987).

Table 19.1 shows how the urban hierarchy in South Korea has changed since 1960.[1] Although the cities above 1 million increased in number from 2 in 1960 to 7 in 1999, their share of the urban population peaked in 1980 (at 66.3 percent). No size class experienced a continuous increase or decline in its urban population share over the 40-year period; the obvious explanation was the distortions resulting from 'urban size class jumping' (i.e. moving up from one size class to a higher size class) given a modest pool of cities (e.g. only 40 cities in 1980). The most striking changes were the increase in the number of cities in the 1980s (from 40 to 73), the associated temporary spike in the share of the smallest size class group (50,000 –99,999), and the sharp rise of the urban population share of cities between 100,000 and 1,000,000 in the 1990s.

Figure 19.1 and Table 19.2 presents the population data for cities larger than 250,000 (in 1995) between 1960 and 1995 and provisional 2000 Census estimates for the seven cities larger than 1 million. It should be noted that Incheon (in addition to Seoul) forms part of the Capital Region; it is separated out because this port city has a long, independent history long before the Capital Region spread out.[2] Also, Table 19.2 ignores ten other cities larger than 250,000, all of them within the Capital Region and that are a large part of the Seoul decentralization story. These cities are Sungnam (889000 in 1995), Bucheon (779,000), Suweon (756,000), Anyang (591,000), Koyang (518,000), Koyang (518,000), Ansan (510,000), Kwangmyun (351,000), Pyongtaek (313,000), and Euijeongbu (276,000); most of these are located south of the Han River, a tribute to the success of the decentralization strategies.

The data in Table 19.2 illustrate the powerful trends of urbanization over the past forty years. The population of Seoul has more than quadrupled; those of Pusan, Incheon and Gwangju have more than tripled; Daegu has almost quadrupled, while the population of Taejon has increased almost six-fold. The remaining million-plus city, Ulsan, located in the South East, did not even exist before 1970. Some of the cities around 500,000 grew even faster, for example, the Southeastern steel city of Pohang, but the growth of some of

---

[1] A qualification is that the data refer to municipalities not to metropolitan areas.
[2] Incidentally, Incheon is likely to become more important in the future as a result of the opening of the new international airport near Incheon to replace Kimpo Airport as Korea's international hub.

Table 19.1 Changes in the national urban hierarchy, 1960-99

Year	1960			1970			1980			1990			1999		
City Size POP('000)	No. of cities	POP ('000)	%	No. of cities	POP ('000)	%	No. of cities	POP ('000)	%	No. of cities	POP ('000)	%	No. of cities	POP ('000)	%
>1,000	2	3,609	51.6	3	8,482	65.6	4	14,213	66.3	6	20,691	64.4	7	22,873	55
500-1,000	1	677	9.7	2	1,145	8.9	2	1,380	6.4	6	3,477	10.7	10	6,634	16
250-500	2	715	10.2	2	676	5.2	7	2,366	11.0	7	2,345	7.3	19	6,031	14.5
100-250	4	705	10.1	11	1,371	10.6	21	3,033	14.2	22	3,455	10.7	35	5,388	13.0
50-100	18	1,291	18.5	4	1,255	9.7	6	442	2.1	32	2,216	6.9	8	632	1.5
Sum	27	3,997	100	32	12,929	100	40	21,434	100	73	32,154	100	79	41,558	100

Source: Adapted from Choi, Jae-Heon (2000)

Figure 19.1 Cities with population > 250,000 in South Korea

Table 19.2. City populations, 1960-2000 ('000)

Year	1960	1965	1970	1975	1980	1985	1990	1995	2000
National Population	24,989	29,192	30,882	34,707	37,436	40,448	43,411	44,609	46,125
Capital Region	5,195	7,011	8,894	10,029	13,302	15,825	18,587	20,189	21,346
Seoul	2,445	3,803	5,433	6,890	8,364	9,639	10,613	10,231	9,891
Pusan	1,164	1,430	1,842	2,453	3,160	3,515	3,798	3,814	3,664
Daegu	677	848	1,064	1,311	1,605	2,030	2,229	2,449	2,480
Incheon	401	529	634	800	1,084	1,387	1,818	2,308	2,476
Gwangju	314	404	494	607	728	906	1,139	1,258	1,352
Ulsan	-	-	157	253	418	551	682	967*	1,014
Jeonju	188	221	258	311	367	426	517	563	-
Cheongju	92	124	141	193	253	350	478	531	-
Pohang	60	66	78	134	201	261	318	509*	-
Changwon	-	-	-	-	112	174	323	481*	-
Masan	158	155	187	372	387	449	494	441*	-
Cheonan	-	71	77	97	121	170	211	330*	-
Jinju	87	107	119	155	203	227	256	330	-
Iksan	-	-	-	-	-	-	-	323*	-
Kumi	-	-	-	-	105	142	206	311	-
Gyeongju	76	86	90	108	122	128	142	274	-
Gunsan	90	103	110	155	165	186	218	267	-
Jeju	68	88	104	135	168	203	233	259	-
Kimhae	-	-	-	-	-	78	106	256*	-

Source: Republic of Korea, National Statistical Office

Notes: * The populations of these cities have been affected by annexations in 1995, usually of part or all of the surrounding county.

these cities is distorted by annexations of surrounding rural counties in 1995.

It is difficult to identify comparative urbanization trends merely by eyeballing the data in Table 19.2. This is easier to do by reorganizing the data into quinquennial growth rates (Table 19.3) and converting these to an index where the growth rate of the Seoul metropolitan area (Capital Region) is the reference region (=1.00). Prior to 1975, Seoul grew faster than the Capital Region as a whole. After then, its share declined quickly, growing at only 58 percent of the Capital Region's rate by the late 1980s, then declining absolutely in the 1990s. As for the Capital Region itself, it experienced deceleration from one five year period to the next, although the rate of deceleration was relatively stable until the 1990s (mirroring the trend in national population growth). However, in the early 1990s, national population growth plunged, and growth in the Capital Region followed, with its population expanding by less than 9 percent during the period 1990-95 and less than 6 percent in the period 1995-2000.

How did the secondary cities perform over recent decades? The fifth largest city, Taejon, is the only one that has grown faster than the Capital Region in each quinquennium, if only barely faster prior to 1975. Its growth has been fueled, in part, by its selection as the site for the nation's largest Science park; the park was founded in 1974, and the first establishments began to move in from around 1979. Pusan, the second largest city, grew much faster than the Capital Region, from 1965 to 1980, but then its growth plummeted as its expansion possibilities hit the tight constraint of its large Greenbelt. Incheon started to accelerate in the 1970s, but its location within the Capital Region ensured that it would benefit from the metropolitan decentralization of Seoul. Daegu's growth rate fluctuated relative to the reference norm from one period to another, while Gwanju began to grow relatively faster in the 1980s. The new city of Ulsan has consistently grown much faster in each quinquennium since it emerged in the 1970s. Descending the urban scale, the picture is mixed. All the large secondary cities grew more slowly than the Capital Region in the 1960s, but several have grown faster since. By the 1990s, all were growing faster than the Capital Region; this was partly because of the dramatic deceleration in the Capital Region's growth rate (because many of the growth rates experienced by some of the cities were relatively modest). In other cases (e.g. Kimhae, Gyeongju), the growth rates were distorted by annexations.

THE GROWTH OF SEOUL AND THE CAPITAL REGION AND ITS CHANGING SPATIAL DISTRIBUTION.

Seoul more than doubled its population in the second half of the 1930s (from

Table 19.3 City growth rates and index, 1960-95

Period	1960-65		1965-70		1970-75	
Population	Rate	Index	Rate	Index	Rate	Index
Nation	0.168		0.058		0.124	
Seoul MA	0.350	1.00	0.269	1.00	0.229	1.00
Seoul	0.555	1.59	0.429	1.60	0.268	1.17
Pusan	0.229	0.65	0.288	1.07	0.332	1.45
Daegu	0.252	0.72	0.255	0.95	0.232	1.02
Incheon	0.318	0.91	0.198	0.74	0.262	1.14
Taejon	0.379	1.08	0.289	1.08	0.245	1.07
Gwangju	0.286	0.82	0.221	0.82	0.23	1.00
Ulsan	-	-	-	-	0.608	2.66
Jeonju	0.173	0.49	0.167	0.62	0.209	0.91
Cheongju	0.347	0.99	0.135	0.50	0.369	1.61
Pohang	0.11	0.31	0.176	0.65	0.73	3.19
Changwon	-	-	-	-	-	-
Masan	-0.02	-0.06	0.207	0.77	0.99	4.33
Cheonan	-	-	0.074	0.27	0.264	1.15
Jinju	0.23	0.66	0.114	0.42	0.296	1.29
Kumi	-	-	-	-	-	-
Gyeongju	0.13	0.37	0.054	0.20	0.199	0.87
Gunsan	0.137	0.39	0.071	0.26	0.405	1.77
Jeju	0.288	0.82	0.194	0.72	0.293	1.28
Kimhae	-	-	-	-	-	-

Table 19.3 Continued

1975-80		1980-85		1985-90		1990-95	
Rate	Index	Rate	Index	Rate	Index	Rate	Index
0.079		0.08		0.073		0.028	
0.217	1.00	0.19	1.00	0.175	1.00	0.086	1.00
0.214	0.99	0.152	0.80	0.101	0.58	-0.036	-0.42
0.288	1.33	0.112	0.59	0.081	0.46	0.004	0.05
0.224	1.03	0.265	1.40	0.098	0.56	0.099	1.15
0.355	1.63	0.28	1.47	0.311	1.78	0.27	3.13
0.286	1.32	0.329	1.73	0.212	1.21	0.212	2.46
0.199	0.91	0.245	1.29	0.257	1.47	0.104	1.21
0.656	3.02	0.317	1.67	0.238	1.37	0.418	4.85
0.179	0.82	0.162	0.85	0.212	1.22	0.089	1.03
0.314	1.45	0.383	2.02	0.364	2.09	0.112	1.30
0.497	2.29	0.296	1.56	0.219	1.25	0.601	6.98
-	-	0.554	2.92	0.863	4.94	0.49	5.69
0.04	0.18	0.16	0.85	0.1	0.57	-0.106	-1.23
0.246	1.13	0.412	2.17	0.242	1.39	0.563	6.53
0.311	1.43	0.121	0.64	0.125	0.72	0.29	3.37
-	-	0.349	1.84	0.451	2.58	0.511	5.93
0.125	0.58	0.045	0.24	0.113	0.64	0.931	10.8
0.068	0.31	0.123	0.65	0.175	1.00	0.222	2.57
0.242	1.11	0.21	1.11	0.147	0.84	0.111	1.29
-	-	-	-	0.363	2.08	1.414	16.4

444,000 to 935,000), lost population during the Second World War, then increased its size by 60 percent in the four years after liberalization from the Japanese. During the Korean War, the population changed little, impacted by war-related mortality, flight from Seoul to safer areas in the South, and refugees from the North. Then the border was sealed, so subsequent growth was a combination of natural increase and in-migration (initially from rural areas).

Table 19.4 shows the population of Seoul City, the Capital Region (Seoul plus Kyunggi province), and South Korea as a whole between 1955 and 1995. Up to 1990, Seoul's population increased by an average of nearly 2.6 million each decade, peaking at 10.613 million in 1990, and accounting for 24.5 percent of the national population. In the first half of the 1990s, on the other hand, Seoul's population declined for the first time since the Second World War. The Capital Region (or Seoul metropolitan area) has continued to expand its share of the national population from 18.3 percent in 1955 to 45.3 percent in 1995, with absolute growth during the same period from 3.93 million to 20.19 million. However, the Seoul metropolitan area's share of the nation's urban population has been declining (from 62.2 percent in 1955 to 50.9 percent in 1995, although much of the decline occurred before 1975), evidence of a modest degree of interurban decentralization. Yet, as pointed out below, the Capital Region continues to experience net in-migration, although the numbers have fallen off dramatically in the 1990s.

On a different point, with respect to many variables, the Capital Region's share of national economic activity (jobs, housing stock, gross regional product, automobiles, hospitals, roads, etc.) is not much different from its population share (Table 19.5); with respect to other variables (e.g. densities, the concentration of public agencies, savings, government investment institutes, headquarters of large firms, number of manufacturing firms, information technology output) the Capital Region's share is significantly higher.

One of the major reasons why Seoul has continued (until very recently) to grow has been its capacity to reduce core city congestion via decentralization. Table 19.6 compares suburbanization of population and decentralization of employment in 1981 and 1996 for three zones within Seoul City (the CBD, a First Ring and a Second Ring) (Choi, Geun-Hee, 2000). The 1981 data clearly reveal the well-known phenomenon that people suburbanize faster than jobs decentralize, while within the employment sector construction and producer services were much more centralized than the other employment subsectors. By 1996, however, although decentralization had increased markedly both for people and jobs, employment decentralization had almost caught up with suburbanization. The most striking change was in producer services. In 1981, producer services were heavily located in the CBD; by

Table 19.4 Population in the Capital Region, 1955-95 ('000)

YEAR	A Nation	B Seoul	B/A Share	C Kyunggi	C/A Share	D Capital Region	D/A Share	E Urban pop in ROK*	D/E Share
1955	21.502	1.569	7.30%	2360	10.98%	3929	18.27%	6.321	62.16%
1960	24.994	2.445	9.78%	2750	11.00%	5195	20.78%	8.840	58.77%
1965	29,193	3,803	13.03%	3108	10.65%	7011	24.02%	12.303	56.99%
1970	31,469	5,536	17.59%	3358	10.67%	8894	28.26%	15.385	57.81%
1975	34,709	6,889	19.85%	4040	11.64%	10929	31.49%	20.876	52.35%
1980	37,449	8,367	22.34%	4935	13.18%	13302	35.52%	24.876	53.47%
1985	40,467	9,646	23.84%	6179	15.27%	15825	39.11%	29.983	52.78%
1990	43,411	10,613	24.45%	7974	18.37%	18587	42.82%	34.622	53.69%
1995	44,609	10,231	22.93%	9958	22.32%	20189	45.26%	39,635	50.94%
2000	46,125	9,891	21.44%	11,455**	24.83%	21346	46.28%	n.a.	

Source: Kwon. Y.W.. p.68

Notes: * from Table 3-2, p.70: ** Includes Incheon City

Table 19.5 Capital region's share of nation c. 1995

Population	45.3%
Households	44.7%
AdministrativeArea	11.8%
Population Density	380.0%
Residential Buildings	44.7%
Automobiles	47.7%
Road	24.2%
GRP	46.2%
Employment	48.6%
Public Agencies	55.1%
Savings	65.5%
Financial Self-sufficiency	133.0%
Hospitals	45.7%
Area	11.8%
Manufacturing Firms	55.1%
Top 100 Firm Headquarters	95.0%
Small Firms	55.2%
Value Added for IT Industries	62.9%
Government Investment Institutes	80.0%

Source: Varied

Table 19.6 The distribution of population and employment in Seoul, 1981-96

Year		1981 (%)			1996 (%)	
Area	CBD	1st Ring	2nd Ring	CBD	1st Ring	2nd Ring
Population	6.1	43.4	50.5	3.2	26.1	70.7
Employment	36.3	26.4	37.2	18.1	20.0	61.8
of which:						
Manufacturing	20.1	30.6	49.3	18.9	24.1	57.8
Utilities	17.4	21.7	60.9	6.3	25.0	68.7
Construction	61.3	9.8	28.9	20.0	12.7	67.3
Producer Services	54.7	18.8	26.5	21.8	14.2	64.1

Source: Choi (2000)

1996, almost two-thirds were in the Second Ring. This reflects the growth of the business subcenter, Kangnam, south of the Han River; this development was facilitated by policy interventions such as the construction of more bridges over the Han River and expansion of the subway system.

Using a different criterion, the Gini coefficient for the dispersion of population among zones changed little in the Seoul metropolitan area (from 0.805 in 1980 to 0.801 in 1995), while it fell substantially with respect to employment (0.877 in 1980 to 0.823 in 1995). Interestingly, during the same period population in Kyunggi province became more concentrated (with the Gini rising from 0.653 to 0.760) as a result of the development of five dense New Towns: Bundang, Ilsan, Jungdong, Pyongchon and Sanbon (Jun and Bae, 2001). Moreover, population and employment exhibit different patterns of decentralization; employment density data suggests rapid job growth between 15 and 30 kilometers from the CBD, while population soars between 30 and 50 kilometers from the CBD (Jun and Bae, 2001). This suggests a sprawling pattern of development coexisting with significant jobs-housing imbalances.

MIGRATION PATTERNS

The story of interregional migration in Korea is the way in which the Capital Region (Seoul metropolitan area) has continuously sucked in migrants from the rest of the country. The macroregional data for 1970-95 are summarized in Table 19.7. They show that the Capital Region has gained net migrants in every year during that period, usually within the range of 300,000 to 400,000 a year until 1990, when net in-migration began to drop off sharply. All the other macroregions had negative net migration with the exception of the Central West (including the Taejon metropolitan area) after 1993 and the Southwest (the Cholla provinces) in 1994.

However, the pattern of migration has changed dramatically in recent decades. In the late 1960s, 50 percent of migrants were rural-to-urban and 18 percent were rural-to-rural; only 22 percent were urban-to-urban. By the 1990s, the proportions were 12, 2 and 79 percent, obviously a change that reflected the intense urbanization that occurred in Korea during these decades (Table 19.8). Stepwise migration has not played much of a role in Korea because of the small geographical size of the country.

The annual report on internal migration statistics for 1999 (Republic of Korea Bureau of Statistics, 2000) reveals that three of the six largest cities (Seoul, Pusan and Taegu) all experienced negative net migration in 1999, while net migration into Incheon, Kwangju and (especially) Taejon was positive. However, negative net migration from the core cities meant intraregional decentralization much more than dispersion throughout the

Table 19.7 Interregional net migration, 1970-95

Year	Capital Region	North East (Kangwon)	Central West (Chung Cheong)	South West (Cholla)	South East (Kyung Sang)	Jeju Island (Jeju)
1970	389 412	-36 222	-95 137	-177 642	-77 257	-3 154
1971	373 916	-34 994	-95 033	-160 144	-79 833	-3 912
1972	173 874	-30 734	-47 328	-78 019	-18 444	651
1973	240 385	-35 802	-72 079	-112 527	-17 060	-2 917
1974	347 011	-49 300	-92 078	-155 619	-44 437	-5 577
1975	587 653	-60 210	-158 772	-270 638	-88 132	-9 901
1976	365 916	-41 882	-100 984	-157 851	-58 157	-7 042
1977	336 615	-45 713	-99 762	-158 238	-24 507	-8 395
1978	362 857	-50 777	-122 100	-185 220	4 876	-9 636
1979	331 825	-50 280	-101 426	-169 826	-5 440	-4 853
1980	288 203	-24 510	-77 307	-153 997	-31 041	-1 348
1981	270 432	-22 376	-88 779	-112 461	-45 372	-1 444
1982	311 714	-29 808	-89 453	-126 389	-62 933	-3 131
1983	398 095	-44 683	-102 747	-159 137	-89 618	-1 910
1984	371 792	-42 202	-100 566	-154 469	-70 353	-4 202
1985	297 590	-28 504	-69 543	-121 463	-74 646	-3 434
1986	272 659	-33 499	-61 768	-120 374	-53 453	-3 565
1987	321 035	-45 132	-77 314	-162 505	-33 226	-2 858
1988	314 362	-52 482	-75 099	-145 586	-39 465	-1 730
1989	317 233	-57 933	-63 465	-138 261	-57 343	-231
1990	276 204	-47 637	-37 862	-124 933	-68 900	3 128
1991	220 581	-38 030	-19 960	-106 831	-58 536	2 776
1992	169 368	-24 845	-4 132	-85 757	-56 339	1 705
1993	151 529	-24 586	15 455	-76 864	-63 805	-1 729
1994	54 027	-18 471	6 288	9 207	-48 906	-2 145
1995	69 172	-9 350	23 436	-33 300	-46 663	-3 295

Source: Bureau of Statistics, Migration Statistical Yearbook, 1970-95.

Table 19.8 Migration flows and patterns among urban and rural areas ('000)

Period	1965-70	1970-75	1975-80	1985-90	1990-95	1995-99
Rural to Urban (%)	1,827 (50.1)	1,754 (44.3)	2,524 (44.9)	2,424 (39.7)	2,329 (33.4)	1,232 (12.2)
Urban to Urban (%)	787 (21.6)	1,087 (27.4)	1,856 (33.0)	2,318 (38.0)	3,527 (50.6)	8,009 (79.4)
Urban to Rural (%)	387 (10.6)	558 (14.1)	681 (12.1)	889 (14.6)	743 (10.7)	694 (6.9)
Rural to Rural (%)	649 (17.8)	563 (14.2)	558 (9.9)	469 (7.7)	368 (5.3)	153 (1.5)
Total (%)	3,650 (100)	3,962 (100)	5,619 (100)	6,100 (100)	6,967 (100)	10,086 (100)

Source: Kang (2000)

country. The data for the Capital Region in Table 19.9 illustrate this point very well. In the late 1960s, migrants poured into the Capital Region from the rest of the country, and intraregional suburbanization was very modest. By the early 1990s, although the Capital Region continued to gain from the rest of the country, the migration flow from Seoul to the rest of the Capital Region was 3.5 times larger than the flow in the opposite direction.

Figure 19.2 shows that the contribution of in-migration to Seoul metropolitan area's population growth has declined significantly since the 1970s, now accounting for little more than one-half of the metropolitan region's growth. Yet equally important is the deceleration in the region's population in the early 1990s, to only 58 percent of the rate experienced in the late 1980s. However, this was matched by an equivalent decline in net in-migration. The metropolitan region continues to grow, but at a much slower rate. Within the metropolitan region, decentralization continues at an impressive rate. The dominance of the Seoul metropolitan region in Korea has been so sustained that the standard description of the evolution of national urban systems (Geyer and Kontuly, 1993) applies only in a truncated fashion.

Analysis of migrant characteristics is handicapped by the lack of income data. As a generalization, migrants to Seoul (and other large cities) tended to

Table 19.9 Migration in the Seoul metropolitan area ('000)

	1965-70	1970-75	1975-80	1980-85	1985-90	1990-95
[A] Kyunggi/ Incheon Seoul	251	242	311	393	504	425
[B] Seoul Seoul	122	299	436	722	984	1,473
[C] Out of M.A. Seoul	940	852	944	952	829	624
[D] Seoul Out of M.A	126	225	317	358	392	455
[E] Out of M. A. Kyunggi/Incheon	224	296	469	578	719	662
[F] Kyunggi/ Incheon Out of M. A	70	90	126	166	229	336
[From C+E] Out of M.A. M.A.	1,164	1148	1,413	1,530	1,548	1,286
[From D+F] M.A. Out of M.A.	196	315	443	524	621	791

Source: Kang (2000)

Figure 19.2 Migration's contribution to the Capital Region's growth

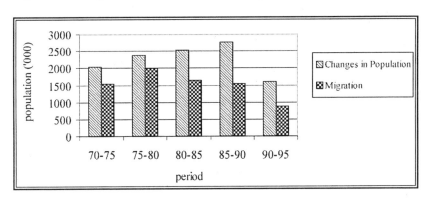

Source: Tables 19.4 and 19.7

be more motivated by upward mobility (they were younger, less likely to be married, held lower occupational positions, were interested in more education, and were less likely to be homeowners); migrants out of Seoul to the surrounding region tended to exhibit the opposite characteristics (older, professionals, more likely to be married, and homeowners). However, the differentials were not extreme (Jun and Bae, 2001). The reasons for migration have also changed over time: prior to 1980 educational opportunities dominated; recent surveys show that economic opportunities are now the primary motivation, and educational reasons (after a successful strategy for decentralizing educational institutions) have faded into relative insignificance.

SOUTH KOREA AS AN OUTLIER

Analysis of urbanization trends in South Korea suggests that the country is somewhat of an outlier. The application of universal spatial concepts such as differential urbanization, counter-urbanization, polarization reversal and migration turnarounds (Ishikawa, 2001) is subject to severe qualifications in this special case. Korea is different from the norm for several important reasons.

First, the country is very small (Wheaton and Shishido, 1981, and other urban analysts have demonstrated that territorial size has a significant influence on the urban size distribution). Its longest axis, from Seoul in the far northwest to the port of Pusan on its southeastern tip, is less than 400 kilometres; at its widest point, the country is 240 kilometres wide. Moreover, about 80 percent of the country's land area is mountainous and cannot be developed. Furthermore, for historical, nationalistic (i.e. food security), rural nostalgia and even irrational reasons, the government is very protective of the remaining rice paddy. Accordingly, there is very little land available for urban development. This fact in itself promotes neither concentration nor dispersal; it all depends on the size of the patches of flat, non-prime-agricultural land.

Second, however, the land constraint problem in Korea is even more serious because of the effects of the long-established green belt policy. In 1971, an initiative promoted by President Park Chung Hee established Green belt around 14 cities, amounting to 5.4 percent of the national territory (Bae, 1998). Since then, development inside those Green belt has been prohibited, although a Greenbelt Reform Committee in 1998 has set in motion some modest relaxations. In many cities, the green belts have not inhibited growth because of the availability of land within the green belt's inner boundary. However, in Seoul and Pusan the impacts have been severe. Seoul's green belt is a band approximately 10 kilometres wide that begins 15 kilometres from Seoul's CBD. Although some land within the Greenbelt is hilly and more suitable for recreational use, much of the land is suitable for development. However, the green belt policy forced development to leapfrog, resulting in higher commuting costs, additional pollution, and an unnecessarily large sprawling metropolitan region (Jun and Bae, 2000). Nevertheless, these impacts in Seoul merely resulted in spatial land use inefficiencies. In Pusan, the consequences were much more serious. Almost one-half of the land within the city of Pusan was within the green belt. This meant that development was severely constrained, pushing residential development up the mountain slopes and spoiling ridgelines. More important, it became much more difficult for Pusan to grow. Its size (easily the second city in Korea) and its location (the most distant city from Seoul) made it an ideal countermagnet, but land constraints have prevented it from fully playing this role.

Third, South Korea is a distorted national urban system because of the historical accident of the separation of the North and the South. Since the Second World War, the Pyongyang-Seoul axis has withered (Pyongyang is the current capital of North Korea). An important component of the green belt policy for Seoul was to prohibit development in the area to the north of Seoul, because of national security concerns about proximity to North Korea. After the Korean War, Seoul experienced rapid growth because of refugees arriving from North Korea.

Fourth, migration streams in South Korea have been impacted by external shocks more than by endogenous forces. The end of the Korean War was the most important of these shocks. Another important influence was the centralization of higher educational institutions and the better quality high schools in Seoul in the 1960s and 1970s. Migration surveys revealed that during this period concern for children's education was the primary motivation for moving to Seoul. However, in more recent years, the Korean government has implemented a strategy of building up universities and other educational institutions in the provinces. Even though the best institutions are still found in Seoul, the decentralization program has had an impact. Now, educational reasons are an almost trivial reason for migration to Seoul compared to the search for economic opportunities (Kwon, 1998). In addition, industrial location policies since the 1970s have been very proactive in promoting export-oriented industries in the south east and labour-intensive industries in the south west as a means to slow down migration to Seoul.

Fifth, South Korea is an extreme case of urban primacy. The Seoul metropolitan area accounts for 51 percent of the national urban population. Even though this share peaked early, it has declined little since 1975. There are several reasons for this. Migration patterns were a facilitator. Seoul acted like a funnel pulling in migrants from the rest of the country and then spilling them out into suburban neighborhoods, satellite cities and other nodes within the Seoul metropolitan area (Kwon, 2000).

Although the green belt policy inhibited close-in suburbanization and made Seoul a less attractive destination because of its impact in terms of higher land prices, congestion and housing prices, the government's other actions helped the Seoul metropolitan area to accommodate a rising population. Transportation investments ranged from building more bridges across the Han River, thereby stimulating development to the south, to the construction of more subway lines and a suburban rail system. A New Towns policy constructed five new towns (Sanbon, Bundang, Pyongchon, Jungdong and Ilsan) within the short period 1989-92 to accommodate 1.18 million people, building 294,000 houses on development sites totalling 4,846 hectares (at a gross density of 26 units per acre).

The government also helped to promote industrial decentralization by developing satellite industrial towns at Banweol and Kuro. Not that the government managed this decentralization process perfectly. The Ministry of Construction and Transport (its research arm, the Korean Research Institute of Human Settlements, and its implementation agency, the Korean Land Corporation) in charge of land use acted more or less independently from the Economic Planning Board responsible for industrial development. The result was severe job-housing imbalances at the district (ku) level, with the consequence of significant excess commuting. Employment/population ratios (1996 data) even within Seoul City varied widely between 8.79 in Choong Ku and 3.56 in Chongro (the CBD districts), 2.43 in Kangnam down to 0.34 in Nowon, 0.36 in Eunpyung and Tobong and 0.37 in Kangbook (Choi, G.-H., 2000); the differentials were even wider in the rest of the metropolitan region. Overall commuting distances increased by 38.8 percent in the Seoul Metropolitan Area between 1980 and 1995 (from an average of 13 to 18 kilometres), largely because of intra-metropolitan migration out to the suburbs, although even non-mover commutes increased by 10.2 percent because of workplace changes (Jun and Bae, 2001). The extensions to the Seoul subway system (e.g. the new Line 5 which is 55 kilometres long) also resulted in longer commutes (Bae, Jun and Park, 2001).

KOREA'S URBAN FUTURE

Many factors will affect future urbanization trends in Korea, but we will mention five. The first is the influence of globalization. Since the 1960s, rapid economic development and urbanization in South Korea have gone hand in hand. However, some degree of liberalization of the Korean economy in the 1990s opened it up to globalization trends. In the long run this may have beneficial effects, but the financial crisis of 1997 was a short-run consequence. By 2000 the economy had undergone a substantial recovery, but in 2001 it faltered again. Several of the chaebols (Korea's giant conglomerates) had to undergo financial restructuring and dispose of some assets. The impact on urban development was noticeable. As revealed in a case study of the city of Daegu, there was a significant decline in employment (especially in manufacturing and construction) and a flattening of employment density gradients (because of differential employment losses in the central city and the suburbs; Kim, 2000). This finding is not surprising (it applies in the United States too): central cities perform badly in recessions but do better in economic booms. Globalization influences in Korea mean more cyclical fluctuations than in the past, and the safest locations to weather the economic storms (both for firms and households) are found in the suburbs. In addition, the Korea Research Institute of Human Settlements' recent research orientation to rezoning land use (including within the green belts) is primarily motivated by a strategy to improve global competitiveness.

This decentralization force is reinforced by the second factor, the information technology (IT) revolution. There is an unresolved debate about whether telecommunications and transportation are complements or substitutes. In the United States, there is an emerging consensus that they are complements. But the Korean situation is less clear because of the severe traffic congestion in Seoul, Pusan and other large cities. Yet the opportunities for the growth of telecommuting are problematic because of the quasi-authoritarian tradition of the close supervision of employees and higher priority of face-to-face communications in Korea than in the West. However, decentralized workplaces offer the opportunity for shorter commutes while taking advantage of the IT revolution to sustain close inter-firm business contacts. Employment decentralization is expected to be much more rapid than in the past.

A third factor is migration attitudes. Historically, Seoul was the employment and education Mecca for all migrants. But economic development, information technology, the decentralization of educational institutions, and many other changes have transformed the provincial landscapes of Korea. At the same time, housing and other living costs, traffic congestion, air pollution and other large city externalities have revised opinions about life in Seoul. In the late 1960s (with respect to interregional migration) 50 percent of migrants were rural-to-urban; this had declined to less than 13 percent by the early 1990s. On the other hand, urban-to-urban migration had increased from 22 percent to 79 percent (Kwon, 2000). Much of the latter was not from other cities to Seoul, but the reverse. Job opportunities and quality of life considerations are making cities other than Seoul increasingly attractive as migrant destinations, although Seoul retains its appeal, especially to elite groups. For example, Taejon's Science Park has had difficulty retaining scientists and technologists, although Taejon is a pleasant, amenity-rich metropolitan region only one-and-a-half hours south of Seoul.

The fourth consideration is the future of the green belt policy. Already, the green belts have been abolished in the seven smallest cities, something of a symbolic gesture because in these cities the green belt was not a binding constraint. The test is what happens in Seoul and Pusan. Analysis is underway, but the attention to agricultural land preservation and environmental concerns are not promising for the prospect of significant relaxations in these two metropolitan areas (Jin and Park, 2000). President Kim Dae Jung made a campaign promise to relax the green belts, but it was not specific. He is much less popular than at the time of his election, and dramatic changes seem unlikely. Yet the growth of Pusan is strangled by the huge green belt within the city boundaries, and abolishing the green belt in Seoul would reduce commuting times and land (and housing) prices. As an example of the irrationality of the current green belt boundaries (drawn arbitrarily and quickly in 1971), in Hanam City (only 15 kilometers from downtown Seoul) 98.5 percent of the land is within the green belt, preventing the city from growing.

Finally, and most important of all, the great unknown with respect to Korea's future urbanization trends is the reunification issue. As pointed out above, South Korea's urban system is truncated because of the lack of all contact, both physical and telecommunicational, between the South and the North. No one knows when, or even if, reunification will occur. Unless preventive action is taken, reunification with open borders will undoubtedly result in a flood of migrants to the Seoul region (estimates range between three and five million) with massive consequences for both the housing and labour markets. Potential preventive measures include infrastructure and industrial investments in the North, building low-income housing settlements just north of the DMZ (Demilitarized Zone), and partial closure of the border after reunification for a transitional period. Once the transition period is over, the national urban system may change dramatically, in part to promote increased connectivity with Russia and China. This would require a restucturing of the transportation system on a North-South axis that would have significant urban growth repercussions. In addition to new cities near the DMZ, the Seoul-Pyongyang axis would be reinforced (Choi, J.-H., 2000). Also, there is talk of a new capital for a unified Korea, perhaps at or near Kaeshong, located in the north close to the border, and the earlier capital of Korea during the Koryo Dynasty centuries ago.

CONCLUSIONS

The standard principles of spatial analysis discussed in this book have limited application to the special case of Korea. The evolution of the model of differential urbanization remains incomplete; polarization reversal took a long time to show itself, at least over a broad range of secondary cities; and counter-urbanization may never take place, except in the restricted sense of the urban development of areas freed up by green belt relaxations, and even in such cases great efforts will be taken to preserve agricultural land.

South Korea has undergone a radical transformation of its economy since the end of the Korean War, bringing its population up to living standards comparable with those found in long-established developed economies. Its population has more than doubled during this period, and its urban population has increased more than six-fold over the same period. What is surprising is that the dominance of the Seoul metropolitan area increased continuously over recent decades (at least up to the 1990s), while the share of Seoul City has remained more or less stable since 1980. There has been a high rate of decentralization within the Capital Region, so all its growth is now taking place outside Seoul City. It remains to be seen whether the very recent significant slowing down of the Capital Region will continue. If reunification occurs sooner rather than later, the dominance of Seoul could be reinforced even more, partly because of heavy immigration from the North, partly because of the re-establishment and subsequent reinforcement of the Seoul-Pyongyang axis. On the other hand, Taejon, Incheon and Kwangju are now attracting net migrants, and there is potential for this to happen in other secondary cities in Korea. Much will depend upon the rate of recovery in economic growth and on the geographical distribution of that growth. The liberalization of the economy, the reduction in central control, the declining influence of the chaebols and more emphasis upon small-firm growth may result in more decentralization of economic activity than in the past; this would have important repercussions on the future distribution of population.

REFERENCES

Bae, C. C. (1998), 'Korea's Greenbelts: Impacts and options for change', *Pacific Rim Law and Policy Review,* 7, 479-502.

Bae, C. C., M. J. Jun, and H. Park (2001), *The Impact of Seoul's Subway Line 5. Seoul:* Seoul Development Institute.

Choi, G. H. (2000), 'Urban spatial changes and post-industrialism: the case of Seoul,' in Korean-American Urban Forum, *Contemporary urban issues in Korea: Issues, strategies and policies.* Seoul: Korean-American Urban Forum, pp. 3-29.

Choi, J. H. (2000), 'The development and prospect of the Korean urban system', *Journal of the Korean Urban Geographical Society,* 3 (1), 33-42.

Geyer, H. S. and T. M. Kontuly (1993), 'A theoretical foundation for the concept of differential urbanization', in N.M. Hansen, K.J. Button, and P. Nijkamp (eds), *Modern Classics in Regional Science: Regional Policy and Regional Integration, Vol.6,* Cheltenham: Edward Elgar, pp. 157-177.

Ishikawa, Y. (2001), 'Migration turnarounds and schedule changes in Japan, Sweden and Canada', *Review of Urban and Regional Development Studies,* **13**, 20-33.

Jin, Y. and J. Park (2000), 'The reform of green belt policy: Korean experiences', in Korea Regional Science Association - Korea Research Institute for Human Settlements, *Urban growth management policies of Korea, Japan and the U.S.A.* Paper and Proceedings of the International Workshop, Seoul: Seoul National University, pp. 125-139.

Jun, M. and Bae, C. C. (2000), 'Estimating the commuting costs of Seoul's greenbelt', *International Regional Science Review,* **23** (3), 300-315.

Jun, M. and Bae C. C. (2001), 'Suburbanization, intraurban migration and commuting: the case of Seoul'. Paper presented at the Association of the Collegiate Schools in Planning Conference, Cleveland, Ohio.

Kang, B. (2000), 'Is city growth manageable?' in Korea Regional Science Association - Korea Research Institute for Human Settlements, *Urban growth management policies of Korea, Japan and the U.S.A.*, Paper and Proceedings of the International Workshop, Seoul: Seoul National University, pp. 355-373.

Kim, J. (2000), 'The effects of external shocks on non-megalopolis spatial structure: The case of Taegu Metropolitan Area', in Korean-American Urban Forum, *Contemporary urban issues in Korea: Issues, strategies and policies.* Seoul: Korean-American Urban Forum, pp. 31-37.

Kwon, S. (2000), 'Migration and the role of large cities in Korea with reference to geographic flow and social mobility', *Journal of the Korean Urban Geographical Society,* **3**, 57-68.

Kwon, Y. W. (1998), *Study of the Capital Region,* Korean: Sudo Kwon Yonku. Seoul: Han Wool.

Nam, Y. (2000), 'Internal structure of the Korean metropolis', *Journal of the Korean Urban Geographical Society,* **3**, 21-32.

Republic of Korea, Bureau of Statistics (annual), *Migration statistical yearbook.*

Republic of Korea, National Statistical Office (quinquennial), *Population Census.*

Richardson, H. W. and Hwang, M. (eds) *(1987), Urban and regional policy in Korea and international experiences.* Seoul: Kon-Kuk Univerrsity Press.

Wheaton, W.C. and H. Shishido (1981), 'Urban concentration, agglomeration economies, and the level of economic development', *Economic Development and Cultural Change,* **30**, 17-30.

Chapter 20

Urbanization and Migration in India: A Different Scene

S. Mukherji

DISTRESSED MIGRATION AND THE URBAN CRISIS IN INDIA

Unlike the developed countries in the West, where rural-to-urban migration and urbanization are associated with a vertical shift in the labour force from the agricultural sector to the urbanized-industrial sector, migration in the developing countries, such as India, often occurs from the rural peasant sector to urban informal sectors. This is a typical manifestation of underdevelopment, poverty, and spatial disorganization of the economy of the underdeveloped sectors of the society, which arose partially as a result of past colonization and its adverse consequences on space economy (Mukherji, 1981: 1-43). Such displacements from the rural to urban areas are occurring, not in response to any structural change within the labour force, as is happening in the West, but as a dislocation of uprooted workers and peasants from the marginalised countryside to involuted urban centres. This displacement in India is a typical characteristic of urban growth that has out-paced industrialization. It is a symptom of underdevelopment, not development, and it tends to compound further underdevelopment. Certain traditional theories and perspectives of urbanization (rural-to-urban) migration, as developed in the West do not fully explain the true picture and processes of migration and urbanization in a Developing Country like India. Hence, this chapter presents a different story.

The crucial problems of distressed migration from villages to metropolitan areas and the associated problems of unbalanced urbanization and extreme urban decay in India need the urgent attention of scholars and planners before such maladies reach catastrophic proportions. Several factors complicate the scenario. First, massive numbers of poor, landless, illiterate and unskilled agricultural labourers and petty farmers from the backward states such as Uttar Pradesh, Bihar, Orissa, Gujarat, and Andhra Pradesh make their way to large metropolitan areas such as Calcutta, Bombay, Delhi, and Madras, bypassing small towns, small cities, and district centres. The latter currently fail to provide even minimum employment to a large majority of these migrants. Such massive rural to metropolitan migration of people is typical of migration in India. It leads to acute urban involution and causes urban congestion, urban decay, the proliferation of filthy urban slums and pavement dwelling, extreme urban squalor and very poor levels of living conditions for the masses in Indian cities. Because the Indian metropolitan areas and cities have failed to provide the migrants with minimum shelter space and minimum subsistence, the overflow of urban poverty, unemployment, extreme housing shortages, and frequent breakdowns of essential urban services such as water, electricity, sewerage, and transport are visible everywhere in these large centres.

Secondly, such phenomena occur because the Indian metropolitan areas and large cities generally are unable to generate enough employment in the capital-intensive industrial sector. Consequently, the vast majority of the incoming illiterate and unskilled migrants are absorbed in the urban informal sectors. Such informal sectors are characterized by very low wages, low productivity, cut-throat competition, insecurity and exploitation. Although such migration helps to avoid starvation in the rural areas, it does not significantly improve the migrants' economic circumstances. Nor does it permit their upward social mobility. The migrants are indeed moving from rural poverty to urban poverty.

Thirdly, as a result, Indian metropolitan areas have became involuted rather than evolved, i.e., they have grown merely in population, not in prosperity. Cities are becoming over-blown villages, without an urban culture or urban functional characteristics.

Fourthly, Indian metropolitan areas and large cities are fast degenerating into extreme filth and indescribable squalor. Competition in over-populated areas leads to shortages of even the most basic shelter space, water, sanitation and electricity among the illiterate and unskilled peasant migrants in the slums.

Fifthly, Indian metropolitan areas are very fast becoming the scene of extreme social and economic inequalities, where a small minority live in abundant affluence and the masses in abject poverty.

These situations may create a dangerously eruptive situation, conducive to the unleashing of extreme social disorder, severe class conflict, crime, widespread violence and even urban civil war, and therefore warrant in-depth studies and strategic planning. In short, if the problems of massive poverty-driven migration, acute urban congestion, urban failure, and urban inequalities in India are not faced and effective action taken, the entire process will fast reach the maximum level of entropy at which the entire system might break down.

The purpose of this chapter is:

❑ to provide an overall scenario of ongoing trends of rural-urban migration and urbanization in India in order to highlight the main problems;

❑ to unfold the underlying socio-economic-spatial processes of such poverty-induced migration and of lopsided urbanization in India, especially in terms of agricultural backwardness, regional disparities, spatial disorganization, polarized industrialization, and related factors of the space economy, in order to evolve clear thinking about the ongoing causal processes and their consequences; and

❑ based upon such understanding, to identify and to recommend alternative development policies and planning strategies for relieving such problems of distress migration and lopsided urbanization in India.

RECENT TRENDS OF URBANIZATION IN INDIA
URBAN INEQUALITY
Two recent noteworthy studies on the problems of rapid urbanization in India are those of the National Commission on Urbanization and the National Institute of Urban Affairs (1988). They have done commendable work by identifying the ongoing problems of lopsided urbanization and also made some useful recommendations as to how the problems could be addressed. Two of the statements that the Commission made are: (a) a map of distribution of growing urban centres should be made, that would represent a fairly well-balanced distribution of urban settlements, where growth is equitably shared (Interim report, 1988, p.10) and (b) that urbanization must be viewed as a positive phenomenon, not a negative one (National Commission on Urbanization, 1988, Vol II, p.31-32).

Both of these statements are debatable, however. The Commission has taken the view that urbanization helps to promote national economic development, and as such, large and small cities must be supported by finance, infrastructure and avenues for employment. It therefore recommended a strategy of promoting new growth centres and strengthening existing metropolitan areas, in the hope that by adopting such a strategy, along with supportive measures, the Indian cities will: (a) create employment, (b) open up hinterlands, (c) generate wealth with equity, (d) be engines of growth, and (e) be catalysts of social transformation and modernization of the economy and society (National Commission on Urbanization, 1988, Vol II, pp.38-39). However, these views do not address the reality that Indian cities cannot yet fulfil such desirable functions.

The Commission failed to determine the true nature and mechanisms of urbanization and rural-urban migration, and believed that migration of distressed people to metropolitan slums could be contained by development in district centres. Urbanization and migration are complex processes, which arise from the complex webs of spatial, social, economic and political forces. Although detailed data on these dimensions and processes are not available, the following data give some perspective on the problem.

Table 20.1 shows that India had 3609 towns and cities in 1991. It also indicates a very rapid increase in the number of class I cities (having populations of 100 000 or more people) during the last century, while the number of smaller cities and towns remained relatively stable or declined.

Table 20.1   Number of urban agglomerations by size class, India , 1901-91

Census year	All classes	I	II	III	IV	V	VI
Year	Total	(Above 100,000)	(50,000-99,999)	(20,000-49,999)	(10,000-19,999)	(5,000-9,999)	(<5,000 Pop)
1901	1811	24	43	130	391	744	479
1911	1754	23	40	135	364	707	485
1921	1894	29	45	145	370	734	571
1931	2017	35	56	183	434	800	509
1941	2190	49	74	242	498	920	407
1951	2795	76	91	327	608	1124	569
1961	2270	102	129	437	719	711	172
1971	2476	148	173	558	827	623	147
1981	3245	216	270	738	1053	739	229
1991	3609	296	341	927	1135	725	185

Notes: Excludes Assam and Jammu & Kashmir

Source: Census of India, 1991, Series - 1, Paper - 2 of 1991, Provisional population totals: rural urban distribution, pp. 30

India's urban population rose from a small figure of 25.6 million in 1901 to 212.8 million in 1991, i.e. 26 per cent of the total population. General consequences of such rapid urbanization are socio-economic and environmental problems (Bose, 1976: 70-143). UN projections show that if Indian urbanization continues at this rate, 46 per cent of the total population (634 million people) will be urbanized by 2030 (UN, 1998). Keeping the problems of the proliferation of slum areas and the degradation of the environment in mind, this is not a very happy prospect.

A total of 65 per cent of the total urban population of the country lives in Class I cities. These cities are also growing relatively faster than smaller cities and towns, and they enjoy a lion's share of the country's capital, investments, resources, and growth efforts. Such a situation has led to acute urban iniqualities and lopsided urbanization over the national space (Figures 20.1 and 20.2). The underlying social, economic, and political processes will be discussed in a later section of this chapter.

Urban inequality refers to the iniquitous distribution of the country's total urban population among different sized categories of towns. Table 20.2 presents information on the accelerating process between 1901 and 1991. The figure shows increasing urban inequality, i.e. greater and greater numbers of urban population are polarized into the largest metropolitan areas, and small towns/cities show a decreasing share. The government's planning perspective has a very strong pro-metropolitan bias, at the expense of smaller towns/ cities (Figure 20.1). This map shows 23 million-cities of India (1991), which dominate the entire national space. The Gini concentration ratio of urban inequality had a very unequal start (0.559 in 1901), which became further engrossed (0.658 in 1951). After Independence, even after ad-hoc attempts at decentralization, urban polarization continued unabated (0.720 in 1991). Table 20.2 indicates that in 1901, approximately 21 per cent of the country's total urban population lived in the smaller 60 per cent of towns and the largest one per cent towns had almost 21 percent. In 1991, the smaller 60 per cent of all towns had only 11.50 per cent, while the largest one per cent towns had 35 percent. This is evidence of increasing polarization in the urban system, inequality that has impeded India's urban development. When an extreme pro-metropolitan development bias persists and the flow of capital rushes mainly towards a few selected cities, villages and the national economy are bound to be affected negatively.

Overall, the decadal variation in the urban population has declined from 47 per cent in 1971-81, to 36 per cent in 1981-91 (Table 20.3). But smaller towns of less than 20,000 people (Classes V and VI) indicate a negative growth rate during 1981-91. Class I cities showed the highest continuing decadal positive variation in urban population compared to all other town size categories from 1961 to 1991. The 1991 census examined the decadal growth rate of common towns during 1971-81 and 1981-91 and found that Class I cities/agglomerations are growing (34.49 per cent) faster than towns in Classes II to VI (28.4 per cent to 31.6 per cent) (Census of India, Paper 2, p.60 and p. 419). These trends reflect neglect of small towns and intermediate cities, in terms of economic development, which in turn jeopardised their economic viability and spatial harmony.

SUBURBANIZATION
According to the 1991 census, the patterns show that:

Figure 20.1 Administrative divisions and million cities of India, 1991

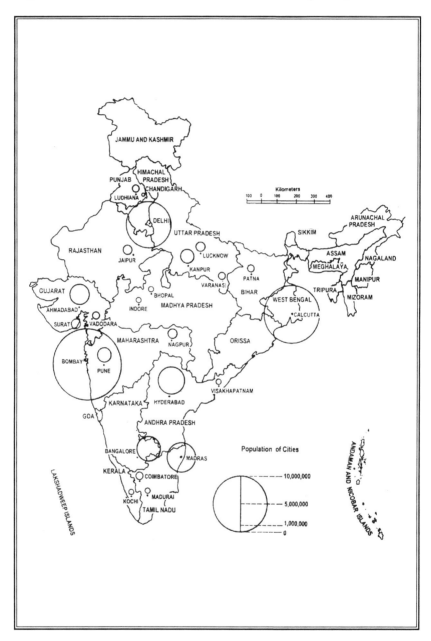

Source: Census of India, 1991.

Figure 20.2 Level of urbanization in India, 1991

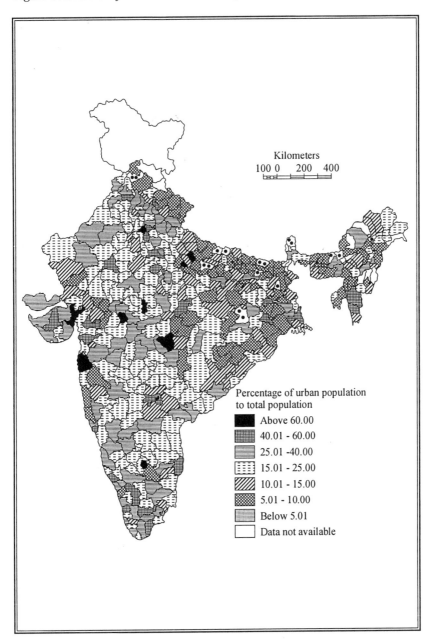

Source: Census of India, 1991.

Table 20.2   Acceleration of urban inequality in India, 1901-91

Year	Gini concentration ratio of urban inequality	Total urban population in 60% smallest towns (per cent)	Total urban population in 5% urban category (per cent)	Total urban population in 1% largest urban category (per cent)
1901	0.559	20.50	41.00	20.8
1951	0.658	15.50	51.00	27.3
1991	0.720	11.50	57.00	34.7

Source: Computed from Census of India 1991, paper 2 of 1991: Rural-urban distribution. Estimated especially on the basis of three Lorenz curves of three years, 1901, 1951, and 1991.

Table 20.3 Percentage decadal variations of urban population in different classes of city, India, 1961-91

Year	Class I	II	II	IV	V	VI	All Classes
1961 - 71	53.51	34.06	30.34	18.22	-	-	37.91
1971 - 81	54.35	55.73	30.85	27.54	10.75	20.71	46.23
1981 - 91	46.87	28.14	25.30	10.72	17.82	65.73	36.09
					- 1.27	-	
						27.70	

Source: Census of India, 1991, Paper 2 of 1991, p. 34.

❑   million-cities in general grew faster than both class I cities and small towns;

❑   moderate million-cities (3-5 million) grew much faster than other metropolitan areas;

❑   the apparent slower growth rate of the largest four metropolitan areas was deceptive as some of their immediate suburbs grew at 200 per cent and sometimes even exceeding 600 per cent.

These findings substantiate an earlier observation that a strong pro-metropolitan bias in urban and national economic planning in India has accelerated growth primarily of already over-crowded metropolitan areas, at the expense of smaller towns (less than 20,000), smaller cities and intermediate cities (50,000-99,999), or even Class I cities (above 100,000).

It is usually believed that Greater Bombay grew from 8.2 million in 1981 to 9.9 million in 1991, showing a decadal growth rate of only 20.21 per cent. But the Greater Bombay urban agglomeration recorded a population of 12.6 million in 1991, registering a much higher growth rate of 33.43 per cent. The census data therefore gave a flawed impression that recently both natural increase and migration had slowed down for Bombay. In reality, the new migrants are settling in the suburbs, e.g. Kalyan, Thane, Mira Bhayandar and New Bombay, some of which registered over 500 percent growth during 1981-91; and Greater Bombay still remains their main centre of attraction and employment. Similarly, new towns and suburbs of Calcutta have registered unprecedented high growth (e.g. Bidhannagar, Salt-lake City, Joka, Gopalpur, Khalishani, etc.). Calcutta proper is already saturated and failed to attract new migrants. It is therefore an illusion that migration to Calcutta and the other large metropolitan areas such as Delhi and Madras is slowing down. Based on these trends the following conclusions can be drawn:

❑ these metropolitan areas are still growing at an alarming rate,
❑ they still remain important centres of survival for large masses of migrants from far-flung rural areas,
❑ they still remain an important source of employment for the distressed rural migrants, and
❑ Satellite towns/new towns/suburbs of large metropolitan areas are still growing swiftly mainly because these are primarily used as nighttime dormitory places for the millions of daily commuters and new migrants, who are compelled to move to the metropolis. This overpopulation of the large urban metropolitan areas of India is indicative of a process of anti-development, an over-exploitation of urban infrastructure and the urban environment.

In spite of long-term attempts made by government to induce decentralization from 1951 to 1991 people kept on migrating to large cities (Figure 20.2). Contrary to what National Commission on Urbanization (1988) believes, the level of urbanization in India is neither spatially well distributed, nor is its growth pattern well balanced over time (1971-91). The evidence presented in this chapter points to a rather polarized and concentrated pattern of population redistribution around a few chosen and favoured metropolitan areas, ports and administrative centres. A comparison of two maps also indicates that 'spread of urbanization' from such designated 'growth poles' or 'growth centres' did not percolate down the urban hierarchy, nor did it spread over the entire national space. Evidently, the 'trickle-down effect' did not occur in India since these nodes are more intimately linked with each other and with international centres than with villages and small towns within their respective hinterlands.

To summarize, it is the continuation of the same process of population concentration at only a few chosen nodes, at the expense of 600,000 small villages and 3600 small towns of India that warrants changes in the thinking of planners in these domains. Some of the issues that are relevant in this regard will be discussed in the next section.

DISTRESSED MIGRATION, WEAK URBAN ECONOMIC STRUCTURE AND POLARIZED INVESTMENT

POVERTY-INDUCED MIGRATION

With reference to rural-urban migration, especially to large cities, a complex scenario emerges. In the rural sector, factors such as demographic explosion, increasing land inequality, continuous fragmentation of land holdings, and the lack of rural industries and rural non-agricultural employment have virtually compelled the small farmers and landless agricultural labourers to leave the tottering villages and crowd into the cities. They increasingly gravitate towards larger metropolitan areas, skipping smaller towns and cities because they know that more employment is available in larger cities. But their dreams remain unfulfilled and they end up in city slums. Bastees (slums), squatter settlements and shanty towns in India's largest metropolitan areas demonstrate the truth of this. In short, this process can be termed the process of 'poverty-induced migration' (Mukherji, 1985a, 1993), an example of an excessive form of the universal concept of 'productionism' (Hart, 1983; Geyer and Kontuly, 1993; Geyer, 1996).

In the urban sector, on the other hand, economic weakening has occurred due to a weak urban economic base, a rapid urban population growth rate, and heavy emphasis only upon foreign export activities (of mainly raw materials), while the development of internal domestic markets is neglected. The result is the growth of only light branches of industries, and low levels of technology. In India, urban growth has occurred without internal economic strength (Mukherji, 1977: 5-61) and without sufficient development of the right kind to provide sufficient employment opportunities to the poor. Indian Class I cities and metropolitan areas serve as focal points of collection of raw materials for export, rather than as poles of development to diffuse growth impulses to their respective hinterlands (Berry, 1966). Since these cities have rather limited employment generating capacities due to capital-intensive industrialization and a limited absorptive capacity in the organized sector, immigrating labour often finds work only in bazaar-type or informal sector activities, as porters, domestic servants, tea-stall boys, hawkers, vendors, construction workers, and the like. So, 'urban involution'

(Mukherji, 1985b, 1993), rather than evolution, is taking place. That is why it has earlier been said that the cities and metropolitan areas of India are becoming merely over-blown villages without internal consolidation and prosperity (Mukherji, 1977: 5-61). Urban decay, urban atrophy, and declining levels of human consumption are acutely associated with present-day urbanization in the country. In sum, polarized economic development occurs in limited regions of India, dominated by the four so-called colonial cities (Calcutta, Bombay, Delhi and Madras). As is the case with most large cities of the world, especially coastal cities, these cities are imperfectly related to their respective hinterlands and they fail to generate significant development waves to the deeper periphery.

During successive Five Year Plans (1951-2001) there has been an increasingly uneven distribution of production enterprises and an excessive 'polarized accumulation of capital' (Mukherji, 1993) in these few large urban metropolitan areas, ports, and administrative centres, at the expense of smaller cities, smaller towns, and the countryside. But this capital has not been used to create employment for the unskilled and semi-skilled incoming migrants. Where capital was available, most of it was not channelled towards industrialization in the cities, but to collect agricultural goods and commodities from the surrounding hinterland for petty trade and low-grade commerce. Capital-intensive industrialization in Indian cities is capable of generating only very few employment opportunities. Consequently, the majority of the unskilled/semi-skilled and illiterate/semi-literate migrants who move from far-flung rural areas of UP, Bihar, Madhya Pradesh, and interior states to those urban nodes are not able to find employment. They normally end up in the poverty-stricken urban informal sectors or in low-grade tertiary activities. It is truly a migration from rural poverty to urban poverty.

Hence, the three basic elements of the urban system in India, i.e., rural-urban distressed migration, weak economic structures of Indian metropolitan areas, and polarized economic growth are causally linked. In the next sections the causal connections between the three sub-systems of India's urban system will be unravelled to identify more promising policy prescriptions for the alleviation of the current unacceptable human conditions of the Indian migrants.

PROBLEMS COMPOUNDED

As was mentioned earlier, Class I cities generally have weak economic bases associated with loosely structured economic activities. A large proportion of the workers in the cities are engaged in informal commerce and service activities and a very minor proportion pursue manufacturing. These facts are substantiated by Tables 20.4 and 20.5 showing the 1981 situation. The manufacturing sector comprises 20 to 43 per cent of workers, while the poverty-induced tertiary sectors comprise as much as 54 to 73 per cent, or more. Twenty per cent or more of the adult population even in million-cities are estimated to be non-workers. This is the situation of the metropolitan areas such as Calcutta (9.1 million in 1981), Bombay (8.2 million), New Delhi (5.6 million), and Madras (4.3 million). The condition deteriorates even further with decreasing city size. As regards migration, several observations can be made from the data.

❑ In most metropolitan areas the bulk of the migrants come from rural areas.

❑ For larger metropolitan areas the volume of inter-state migration exceeds that of intra-state migration. Rural migrants therefore mostly come from far-flung rural areas.

❑ Intra-state migration still forms the rule for smaller metropolitan areas.

❑ Employment was the most important reason for migration and a large segment of the migration that occurred for 'family reasons' is suspected to be employment-linked migration.

❑ Between 40 and 80 per cent of migrants in the listed cities are illiterate or semi-literate, both males and females (Table 20.4).

❑ They have little skill or training and, as such, most of them are absorbed in low-grade processing activities, indigenous transport, petty trade, or low-grade services (Table 20.4). Very few are engaged in administrative, professional or technical services.

These conditions which have been gaining momentum since 1981 and into the 1990s (Tables 20.6 and 20.7) are typical of the cancerous development of metropolitan areas and of urban involution in India (Mukherji, 1981, 1985a, 2001). The distress forms of migration referred to above merely help as a short term survival strategy, but there is very little scope for their vertical social mobility or improvement, even after long periods of stay in the city (Mukherji, 1985c). No cold statistics can adequately describe the sorrow and agony associated with the processes of massive city-ward migration of illiterate/semi-literate peasants and labourers to bastees and squatter settlements, places that are saturated with urban unemployment, inability to afford daily necessities, and declining basic human values.[1]

The path into the future seems very steep, not only in South Asia, but also in South-East and East Asia, because similar trends of very rapid urbanization, massive influx of migrants from rural areas, and very rapid growth of industrialization and urbanization is also taking place in places

---

[1] McNeil (1995) and the United Nations (UN, 1986a; 1986b; 1986c; and 1987) came to similar conclusions recently.

Table 20. 4 Absorption of illiterate and semi-literate migrants in low-grade urban informal sectors, 1981 (lifetime migrants who moved for employment)

Metropolis	Male migrants					Female migrants				
	No. of male migrants	Illiterate (%)	Semi-literate (%)	Tot (3+4)	Absorbed in low grade work	No. of female migrants	Illiterate (%)	Semi-literate (%)	Tot (8+9)	Absorbed in low grade work
(1)	(2)	(3)	(4)	(5)	(6)	(7)	(8)	(9)	(10)	(11)
1. Calcutta	670,059	38.4	41.3	79.7	84.7	24,638	72.5	16.0	88.5	89.0
2. Bombay	1,414,655	24.2	44.4	68.6	79.6	43,283	42.5	21.5	64.0	66.5
3. Delhi	676,016	30.9	32.5	63.4	72.3	22,493	54.2	11.1	65.3	65.8
4. Madras	340,249	11.4	37.5	48.9	62.6	13,256	28.1	15.6	43.7	48.2
5. Bangadore	104,626	15.7	21.3	37.0	50.2	5,902	36.3	8.8	45.1	50.1
6. Ahmadabad	222,820	21.9	42.2	64.1	76.4	4,126	39.7	12.6	52.3	53.2
7. Hyderabad	266,137	17.8	32.5	50.3	63.5	16,039	30.6	11.4	42.0	50.7
8. Pune	158,693	18.9	34.3	53.2	72.2	5,344	43.0	12.8	55.8	59.3
9. Kanpur	66,348	13.1	37.3	50.4	59.5	2,304	24.8	18.9	43.7	44.9
10. Nagpur	79,644	21.6	32.5	54.1	61.5	2,723	43.4	9.2	52.6	54.5
11. Jaipur	116,638	33.5	30.6	63.9	73.7	1,218	52.3	8.4	60.7	62.1
12. Lucknow	59,443	23.8	24.2	48.0	54.5	1,607	28.4	17.2	45.7	46.4

Source: Computed from census of India (1981). All-India, Migration Tables, D-10 and D-12 Series.

Table 20.5 *Economic structure of cities and nature of city-ward migration, 1981 census (males and females)*

City	% of literate	% of workers	% of adult nonworkers. age 15.95	Percentage of total workers as:				Migration, 1981			
				Primary workers	HH indust. workers	Manufac-constr. workers	Trade/service workers	Out of employment migration		Out of employment migration	
								Employment as reason for migration (%)	% of illite-rate	% <H.S. education	% engaged in low-grade work
1	2	3	4	5	6	7	8	9	10	11	12
1. Calcutta	65.5	30.5	21.2	1.3	2.6	34.0	62.1	27.0	39.6	40.4	82.2
2. Bombay	68.2	34.7	16.8	0.2	2.5	43.1	54.2	38.8	24.7	43.6	77.2
3. Delhi	68.0	32.1	19.9	1.5	1.7	33.9	62.9	50.4	31.7	31.8	72.1
4. Madras	67.4	28.2	23.2	2.5	2.1	29.1	66.1	28.1	12.0	36.7	69.2
5. Bangadore	62.9	29.8	22.2	2.7	2.8	40.7	46.2	29.8	18.5	31.3	62.8
6. Ahmadabad	61.2	28.7	23.3	1.8	2.1	46.9	49.2	28.5	22.2	41.7	76.0
7. Hyderabad	55.7	28.2	23.8	2.4	1.6	28.4	67.6	25.0	16.8	20.6	50.5
8. Pune	67.1	30.3	21.7	3.1	2.3	40.4	54.2	23.5	19.7	33.6	71.8
9. Kanpur	55.3	27.5	24.5	3.3	3.6	32.1	61.1	27.9	33.5	30.3	78.6
10. Nagpur	65.9	26.8	25.2	4.7	8.6	25.9	60.7	17.9	13.5	36.7	59.0
11. Jaipur	53.9	27.4	24.6	2.4	4.0	21.1	72.5	29.1	39.0	42.0	79.1
12. Lucknow	57.3	27.7	24.3	3.3	5.3	16.9	74.4	26.5	23.9	24.0	54.3

Source : Census of India, 1981

Table 20.6 Percentage and volume of migration according to literacy level (0-5 years durations), 21 million cities, 1991

| Sr. No. | City/UA | Population, 1991 | Duration of residence 0-5 years (1986-91) | | | | | |
| | | | Total Migrants | Literates % | | Illiterates % | | |
				Males	Females	Males	Females
1	Hyderabad	4,280,261	321,965	71.01	57.20	28.99	42.80
2	Vishakhapatnam	1,051,918	134,320	72.58	59.40	27.42	40.60
3	Patna	1,098,572	83,763	80.75	68.76	19.25	31.24
4	Delhi	8,375,188	770,369	69.41	57.35	30.59	42.65
5	Ahmadabad	3,297,655	193,423	71.00	63.69	29.00	36.31
6	Surat	1,517,076	214,223	66.41	51.87	33.59	48.13
7	Vadodra	1,115,265	104,240	73.06	66.70	26.94	33.30
8	Bangalore	4,086,548	321,830	77.34	64.50	22.66	35.50
9	Kochi	1,139,543	87,390	79.69	83.27	20.31	16.73
10	Greater Bombay	12,571,720	845,538	69.61	56.44	30.39	43.56
11	Pune	2,485,014	191,885	70.26	61.19	29.74	38.81
12	Nagpur	1,661,409	70,738	78.87	69.66	21.13	30.34
13	Ludhiana	1,012,062	105,632	57.40	60.18	42.60	39.82
14	Jaipur	1,514,425	112,913	77.00	60.15	23.00	39.85
15	Madras	5,361,468	326,781	79.41	69.15	20.59	30.85
16	Coimbatore	1,135,549	82,410	81.57	70.53	18.43	29.47
17	Madurai	1,093,702	56,390	78.87	69.58	21.13	30.42
18	Kanpur	2,111,284	75,890	75.92	61.24	24.08	38.76
19	Lucknow	1,642,134	122,573	77.15	66.52	22.85	33.48
20	Varanasi	1,026,467	17,950	85.59	65.30	14.41	34.70
21	Calcutta	10,916,272	378,315	71.85	64.76	28.15	35.24

Source: Census of India, 1991. Migration tables. D- series, R.G. Office, New Delhi, 1999.

Table 20.7 Major metropolitan growth in India, 1951-91

Rank in 1991	UA/City (1,000,000 + Population)	1951	1961	1971	1981	1991
1	Greater Bombay	2.966	4.152	5.970	8.243	12.571
2	Calcutta	4.669	5.983	7.420	9.194	10.916
3	Delhi	1.437	2.359	3.647	5.729	8.375
4	Madras	1.542	1.944	3.169	4.289	5.361
5	Hyderabad	1.130	1.249	1.796	2.545	4.280
6	Bangalore	786	1.206	1.664	2.921	4.086
7	Ahmadabad	877	1.206	1.752	2.548	3.297
8	Pune	608	790	1.135	1.686	2.485
9	Kanpur	705	971	1.275	1.639	2.111
10	Nagpur	485	690	930	1.302	1.661
11	Lucknow	496	655	813	1.007	1.642
12	Surat	237	317	493	913	1.517
13	Jaipur	304	410	636	1.015	1.514
14	Kochi	177	292	505	685	1.139
15	Coimbatore	287	448	736	920	1.135
16	Vadodara	211	309	467	744	1.115
17	Indore	310	394	560	829	1.104
18	Patna	326	414	551	918	1.098
19	Madurai	370	490	711	907	1.093
20	Bhopal	102	222	384	671	1.063
21	Vishakhapatnam	108	211	363	603	1.051
22	Varanasi	369	505	635	797	1.026
23	Ludhiana	153	244	401	607	1.012

Source: Census of India, 1991, Series - 1, Paper - 2 of 1991, Provisional Population Totals: Rural Urban Distribution pp. 39

540

such as Bangkok, Jakarta, and Manila (Mukherji, 2000; UN, 1995a; 1995b; 1995c).

INDIA'S URBAN FUTURE
According to Table 20.7 Bombay had already crossed the 12.5 million mark by 1991, with Calcutta, Delhi and Madras following suit. The growth of the main cities of India seems to have increased unabated, because in 2001 Bombay's population has reached about 18 million, closely followed by Calcutta (13 million), Delhi (12 million), Madras (8 million) and another 27 new million cities being added. According to UN estimates, Bombay will be the second largest city in the world by 2005, with a population of 21 million, and 26.2 million in 2015 (UN, 1998) (see Table 20.8).

Detailed data of the 2001 census on migration, the economic structure of cities and metropolitan areas and growth in them are not yet available, and as such, their current situation cannot be examined at present. However, in India nothing changes overnight, and the above-mentioned interrelationships currently hold true. Based on the information available, the metropolitan areas still appear to have very low work participation rates (for both men and women), a sizeable segment is engaged in primary and household activities, and it is feared that these are coupled with a proliferation of the poverty-ridden tertiary sector.

The rural situation has not improved much either, since rural development and regional planning steps in India are marked by ad-hocracy that has not borne fruit thus far.

SOCIO-ECONOMIC SPATIAL PROCESSES OF UNDERDEVELOPMENT AND POVERTY-INDUCTION
PROCESSES OF UNDER-DEVELOPMENT AND SPATIAL DISORGANIZATION
Figure 20.3 provides the basis of the entire discussion of this section. It is a schematic diagram showing the macro processes of under-development, and labour migration of females and males in low-income countries, such as India and similarly placed Third World nations. The discussion is brief.

In order to understand the current urban situation in India it is crucial to realize that under-development is not a lower stage of development, nor a lagging behind, but rather a product of a 'specific development', induced by the penetration of the capitalist-colonial world economy. In India, this penetration came in the form of mercantile capitalism, and through successsive annexations, exploitation and consolidation, which gave rise to monopoly capitalism. The latter first took hold in coastal ports and foreign enclaves but soon all the country's economic activities were given a total

Table 20.8 Indian Urban Future, 2000-30

Year	2000	Rank	2005	Rank	2010	Rank	2015	Rank	2030
Total Urban Population (millions)	286	-	330	-	380	-	435	-	634
Percent Urban	28.4	-	30.5	-	33.0	-	35.9	-	45.8
Population (Metros) Bombay Calcutta Delhi	18.0 12.9 11.7	2 9 14	20.9 14.1 13.4	2 8 12	23.7 15.6 15.2	2 10 11	26.2 17.3 16.9	2 10 11	NA NA NA

Source: U.N. (1998) , World Urbanization Prospects, UN, New York, pp. 83-143.

orientation to export promotion, mainly to the benefit of the colonial powers. Calcutta, Bombay and Madras ports were set up and were utilized for this purpose.

Capitals, ports, and intermediary urban centres were used as collecting points for resources and raw materials from agricultural regions, plantations, and mines. Arteries of railways and roadways were constructed, but only to aid this draining out from outlying rural areas in the hinterland. Penetration thus reached all parts of the country, where its effects were noticeable in the following three ways: (a) the introduction of commercialized farming and the concomitant exploitation and coercion of labour, (b) the introduction of permanent land settlement and private ownership of land in a society where systems were blissfully absent earlier, which induced land inequality. These mechanisms initiated the process of marginalization of a vast majority of traditional uncompetitive cultivators, who were eventually relegated to share-

Figure 20.3 A schematic diagram of macro-processes of under-development

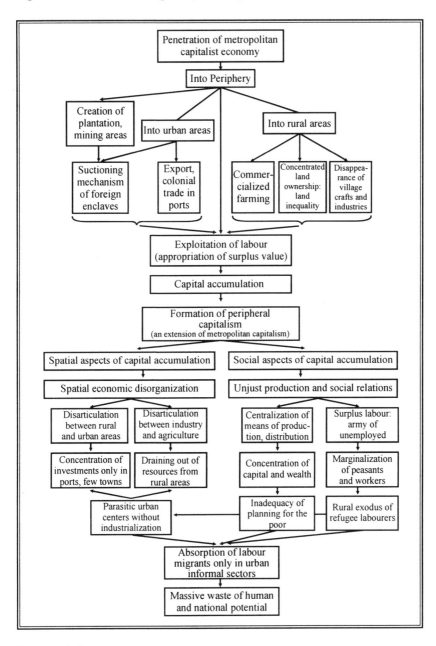

Source: Author

croppers, tenant-farmers, or landless agricultural labourers, and (c) neglect of the traditional indigenous village crafts and industries to facilitate advances for an evolving mercantile and competition oriented market economy.

The introduction of market oriented agriculture resulted in the massive exodus of marginalized peasants, labourers, and village artisans from the countryside, most of whom ended up in slum areas of the coastal ports and capitals. After India had gained its independence subsequent governments of India persisted with market economy principles resulting in the perpetuation of the same patterns of labour migration to this day. Market forces pushed down labour prices in both agriculture and industries in rural and urban areas. Profit margins of commercial enterprises remained high while the per capita income of the masses always remained low.

PERIPHERAL CAPITALISM

Over time, private accumulation of capital led to the formation of peripheral capitalism in a vigorous form within the country. This is an extension of metropolitan capitalism to the periphery. But the periphery became complementary and dominated, as it operated within the framework of competition from the central metropolitan capitalism. This domination and complementarity brought out two kinds of crucial distortions in peripheral capitalism which had not yet been found in metropolitan capitalism. These are (i) social and (ii) spatial dimensions of the process of capital accumulation. The social dimension has brought out unequal production and social relations between the owning class and non-owning class and has aggravated socio-economic inequalities between them. Concentration of the means of production (land, labour, capital) among a privileged few has led to the prosperity of a small segment of the owning class on the one hand, and released an army of surplus labour and unemployed on the other hand. As the concentration of capital and wealth continued unchecked, more and more peasants/workers became marginalized. Finally, a massive exodus of such refugee labourers took place from pauperized villages to urban slums and to other relatively developed zones.

Spatial dimensions of capitalistic accumulation during colonial times have resulted in the disorganization and disintegration of the spatial structure of the economy. Spatial organization usually refers to order in the spatial arrangement of rural and urban settlements in the settlement system of a country. This includes economic activities of people and places, trade linkages and the transport network serving them, land uses, the functional attributes of places and people, and the complex inter-relationships between all those variegated elements. Spatial disorganization, on the other hand, implies distortions, disequilibriums, disharmony, antagonism, decay, dependency and a lack of internal cohesion and consolidation in the spatial organization of the country. Before colonization, India had her own natural, indigenous, internally cohesive and integrated spatial organization of the economy. Internal regions within the country were inter-dependent, complementary and evolving, contributing to the growth and development of the country as a whole. It was not externally linked and dependent. It can be strongly argued that this internally cohesive space economy, in spite of a number of negative economic and regional constraints, might have developed into a more spatially integrated structure, had India not been introduced to market economy principles.

Just as a human being who is externally dependent, is not free to internally develop self determination, similarly a nation like India which was externally linked and dependent, could not develop its own spontaneous, self-sustaining, internally organized economy and society. Internal development pre-supposes freedom from external dependency, for an individual or a nation.

An attempt has been made to show that the former national spatial structure of India was pulled out of shape and substituted by a market economy induced from outside (Mukherji, 1981, pp. 1-65). This was mainly achieved through suctioning mechanisms by which raw materials were collected and exported to the world market at throw-away prices. Consequently, certain new ports/cities emerged and grew up at the expense of the former towns/cities. Certain specific regions became favoured and prosperous while the interior regions of the country were neglected. Marked regional disparities and imbalances have sprung up and the gulf between growing regions and lagging regions widened. In such a situation, labour migration of males and females occurred, and is still occurring, from lagging regions to relatively favoured regions. These are the end results of induced spatial disorganization created by colonialism, capitalism, export-orientation, external dependency and induced poverty and underdevelopment.

DISTORTIONS IN THE SPACE ECONOMY
Three crucial distortions occurred in the spatial organization over time: (i) a distinct bias towards continued export activities which usurped a major part of capital investments that otherwise could have been channeled to other sectors; (ii) a mushrooming of low-grade tertiary activities which arose from special contradictions newly introduced by peripheral capital; and (iii) a distortion towards growth of only light branches of industries and low level technology. The linkages between rural and urban areas were severely disarticulated, as were those between industry and agriculture. Consequently, internal contradictions flourished. Growth of the national economy was retarded. Urban growth occurred without development. Parasitic urban centres have grown and multiplied without industrial strength and without a strong economic base.

In the final analysis, at present migration of rural refugee labourers has occurred to a few coastal ports and 'parasitic' urban centres. Since there are only limited employment opportunities under capital-intensive industrialization, most of the labour migrants find work in the urban informal sector. Through competition from male migrants, females are further pushed out and relegated to the bottom of the informal sector. Urban unemployment overflows, creating concurrently a dangerous involutionary situation. Thus, migration of labourers, both males and females, in an underdeveloped economy is taking place from rural poverty to urban poverty, from one stress region to another, further compounding poverty and underdevelopment. This is a poignant story. The waste of human and national potential is massive (Figure20.3).

UNDER-DEVELOPMENT IN THE POST-INDEPENDENT ERA

The forces that were set in motion by historical adversaries, still largely determine labour migration and urbanization trends in India. This is so because the development measures that were taken during successive Five Year Plans were not adequate to ameliorate the condition of acute poverty, spatial disorganization, widespread unemployment, increasing land inequality, and the neglect of the poor farmers/labourers in stagnating states (U.P., Bihar, Rajasthan, etc.). So there still is a considerable rural exodus of uprooted labourers (both males and females) from backward states to relatively favoured/prosperous states and to a few large inland urban centres, coastal ports, and administrative capitals, such as Calcutta, Bombay, Delhi, Madras, Hyderabad, Bangalore, Lucknow, Kanpur, and Ahmadabad.

After 53 years of post-colonial planning, the country's economy continues to be oriented towards export of mainly raw materials. Railways and roadways still feed mainly export centres or primary cities, instead of the interior areas. Consequently, internal trade circuits remain stagnant. Breaks in the settlement hierarchy persist. As in the colonial era, investments and industries continue to be polarized in only a few selected and favoured nodes. Rarely have there been vigorous attempts at rural development, or attempts for development of hitherto neglected states and regions. Numerous villages are therefore reeling under poverty, unemployment, and under-employment. No wonder that masses of illiterate, unskilled, and poor labourers keep crowding in to the largest metropolitan areas to find a job, no matter how unskilled or low the pay, or how unbearable the filthy urban slums.

As in the past, small towns and cities of India today still primarily act as agricultural collecting centres for further movement of raw materials to coastal exporting centres, rather than as poles of development to diffuse development impulses to surrounding hinterlands. Evidently, these nodes lack the spatial linkages that are necessary for rural development. Rural migrants have to make a quantum jump from rural villages to coastal metropolitan areas, bypassing intermediate-sized towns and cities, because, just like the flow of capital and commodities to such coastal metropolitan areas, labourers are also compelled to move under the forces of the same suctioning mechanism.

Further, as Dos Santos puts it: 'the concept of dependence itself cannot be understood without reference to the articulation of dominant interests in the hegemonic centres and in the dependent societies…Domination is practicable only when it finds support among those local groups who profit by it. Dependence defines internal situation and is structurally linked to it. The only solution therefore would be to change its internal structure' (Dos Santos, 1973: 76-77). Clearly, it is peripheral capitalism within an underdeveloped country which maintains dependence and hinders all efforts for developmental change in the internal structure: the structure of the non-egalitarian society, the structure of concentrated ownership of means of production; and the structure of spatial disarticulation and imbalances.

Planning is not yet for the poor. As Desai stated: '[T]he state instead of becoming a funnel to pump out resources from the rich for distributing them to the poor, in fact works in the opposite direction through an elaborate system of deficit financing, loans (foreign or internal) and indirect taxation - a system which hurts the poor most' (Desai, 1974: 89-99). Desai further remarked that, 'under the mixed economy such items as agriculture, industry and trade were left to the private sector, while creation of elaborate infrastructure and heavy and strategic industries were taken up by the state sector. But, such creation mainly helps them to make their super-profits (Desai, 1974: 94-9). Whatever developmental planning has been attempted during the last 54 years (1947-2001) has actually increased the gulf between the rich and the poor; and whatever regional developmental programmes have been undertaken, are characterised by adhocracy and maintenance of the status quo. In fact, they have increased regional inequalities, instead of narrowing them down (Prakasa Rao, Mishra and Sundaram, 1974: 79-120).

A proper understanding of the complexity of the processes is necessary. Only with that may we be able to find ways and means of correcting the mechanism of underdevelopment and spatial disorganization. The majority of past and present urban and migration studies do not uncover the spatial, social, economic, and political processes that underlie the poverty-induced migration in the formerly colonized Third World countries. We need to evolve a different theoretical perspective in order to come up with planning strategies that will alleviate the current human and economic problems in India.

GLOBALIZATION AND MIGRATION OF THE POOR

THE FUTURE SCENARIO

Under the present trends of liberalization, privatization, and globalization, it is clear that resources, capital, investments, and growth will increasingly concentrate in the mega cities and elitist consumption-oriented industries of India. In the process all-round development of the interior countryside and hinterland of India will be neglected, and as a consequence, much more pronounced forms of the above mentioned kinds of distressed migration and urban involution will be manifest in the future (Mukherji, 1995: 1-45). The true nature of these three processes are seldom carefully inspected, investigated and properly understood.

The process of liberalization has indeed placed the common people at the mercy of international market forces, is oblivious of the issue of equity and social justice, and has been widening the gaps between the rich and the poor. Secondly, the process of privatization that involves disinvestment of public sector utilities at throw-away prices, has actually usurped huge amounts of public money and benefited a handful of private industrialists and corporate bodies, at the cost of the masses of the poor. Thirdly, the present-day processes of globalization are hurting the poor most, as the prices of daily necessities are soaring beyond the reach of the common masses. New investments if any are primarily concentrated in elitist-consumption oriented industries in a few large metropolitan areas. This capital and these investments are not available for agricultural regeneration or rural development. Rural areas, thus devoid of any developmental efforts and capital investments, are reeling under abject poverty, acute unemployment and underemployment and widespread illiteracy. The masses of poor and dispossessed farmers and labourers are thus further compelled to crowd in the city slums and construction sites around large cities for their barest subsistence. A recent study of migrant workers in Gujarat revealed the agonizing results of migration under globalization and privatization.

CORE AND SUBURBAN GROWTH (1961-91)

The largest cities in the world appear to grow through a cycle of four stages: (1) urbanization with the core of the city growing faster than the ring of the city; (2) sub-urbanization with the ring of the city growing faster than the core of the city; (3) counter-urbanization with declining growth in the core as well as in the ring of the city; and (4) re-urbanization with the core of the city growing faster than the ring of the city. Studies show that European and North American cities have reached the third and fourth stage of the urban transition (UN, 1998: 29). Compared to these situations, however, as Table 20.9 and Figures 20.4 to 20.7 reveal, the four largest Indian metropolitan areas seem to still follow the second stage of urban transition; that is suburbanization. In these cities the intermediate zones and suburbs were growing much faster than the cores from 1961 to 1991.

However, there is a marked difference in the underlying causes of these trends in the Indian metropolitan areas compared with the trend of suburbanization in cities in the West. First, the suburbs of the Indian metropolitan areas have been growing very rapidly, not because of rapid growth of automobile ownership, as has happened in the Western cities, but because of the very steep rise in the prices of urban land and very acute housing shortages in the core of Indian metropolitan areas. Prices of residential plots and house rents in Bombay are the highest in the world, surpassing even those of Tokyo and New York. So the process and the context differ.

Secondly, Table 20.9 and Figures 20.4-20.7 also reveal that in most of the Indian metropolitan areas: (i) the core of the city is relatively small in size, while the intermediate zones and suburbs are spread over a much larger area; (ii) the core has often reached a saturation level, sometimes leading to negative growth compared to very rapid population explosion in the ring or suburbs; (iii) in each of the metro cities a large number of illiterate people live in both the core and in the suburbs but comparatively more illiterate people have settled in the suburbs because it is cheaper to live there; (iv) the bulk of the poor people are compelled to live in 'kaccha' houses or in non-brick, non-cemented make-shift houses built of rags (canvas, tin-sheets, or the like), compared to 'pucca' houses (or cemented houses); (v) the type of housing materials used by the residents in different zones (core versus ring) is a clear indicator of their relative socio-economic status. Unlike cities in the West, it is primarily the poorer segments of the Indian urban society that live in the outer rings. The existence of a substantial proportion of illiterate people, both in the core of the city and in the ring, also indicates the basic difference between Western and Indian metropolitan cities. However, there are historical similarities between cities in the West and what is happening in India now. As happened in the industrial cities in the West during the early stages of the Industrial Revolution, it is the illiterate and unskilled migrants that are crowding into the Indian 'El-dorados'. These basic similarities and differences must be noted.

POLICY SIGNIFICANCE OF THE SITUATION

The problem of stagnating rural areas and polarization of capital, investment, and growth efforts in only a few chosen metropolitan areas have resulted in a massive rural-to-metropolitan migration in India over the years. It is doubtful whether such crucial problems can be relieved simply by adopting a few palliative measures. Policies of efficient urban management alone, or infrastructure development at some centres, or continuing the policy of

Table 20.9 Core and suburbs in four largest metros of India, 1961-91

	1991 TOTPOP	Growth rate	Literate	Illiterate		Pucca (brick) houses	Kuccha (non-brick) houses
Gr. Mumbai UA	12,598,750	52.83	70.78	29.22	Gr. Mumbai UA	70.30	29.70
Gr. Mumbai (MC)	9,925,891	20.41	71.28	28.72			
UA-MC	2,672,859		68.93	31.07			
Core of core	1,260,196	-10.94	75.48	24.52	Gr. Mumbai	69.32	30.68
Core	1,066,546	-7.93	75.18	24.82	Thane Part	73.51	26.49
Intermediate zone	7,599,149	34.02	70.03	29.97			
Fringe/Suburbs	2,672,859		68.93	31.07			
Calcutta UA	11,021,918	19.88	68.79	31.21	Calcutta UA	51.84	48.16
Calcutta MC	4,399,819	33.13	70.18	29.82			
UA - MC	6,622,099	12.45	67.86	32.14			
Core	352,303	-1.03		27.97	Calcutta UA	58.61	41.39
Intermediate zone	4,047,516	37.25	70.02	29.98	North 24 par.	50.41	49.59
Fringe/Suburbs	6,622,099	12.45	67.86	32.14	South 24 par.	36.71	63.29

					Nadia	43.54	56.46
Delhi UA	8419084	46.95	63.57	36.43	Part in Haora	41.29	58.71
NDMC	301297	10.35	71.70	28.30	Part in Hugli	51.48	48.52
Delhi Cantt.	94393	10.83	70.90	29.10	Delhi	84.27	15.73
DMC	7206704	32.28	64.20	35.80			
Urban outgrowths	816690	33.57	54.17	45.83			
Core of core	301297	10.35	71.70	28.30	Delhi UA	84.27	15.73
Core	94393	10.83	70.90	29.10			
Intermediate zone	7206704	47.55	64.20	35.80			
Fringe/suburbs	816690	67.75	54.17	45.83			
Madras (UA)	5421985	26.41	71.33	28.67	Madras UA	60.54	39.46
Madras MC	3841396	17.24	71.65	28.35			
Madras UA-MC	1580589	56.07	70.56	29.44			
Core	259798	-9.74	69.75	30.25	Madras MC	65.58	34.42
Intermediate zone	2619074	26.30	70.66	29.34	Chengleput Part	48.30	51.70
Fringe/suburbs	2543113	31.92	72.18	27.82			

Source: Primary Census Abstract of India, Census of India, 1951-91

Figure 20.4 Population growth in Greater Bombay, according to 1991 census

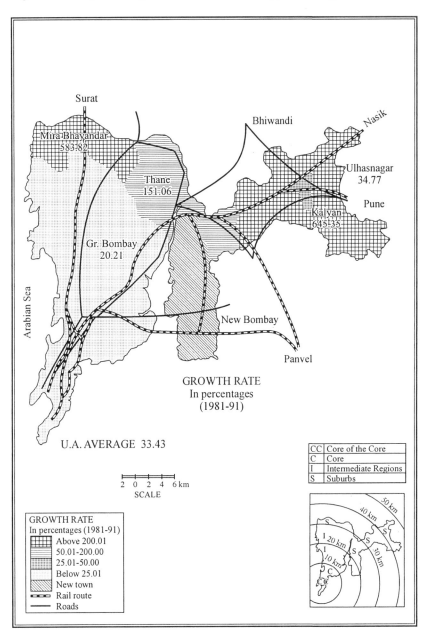

Source: Census of India, 1991.

Figure 20.5 Population growth in Calcutta, according to 1991 census

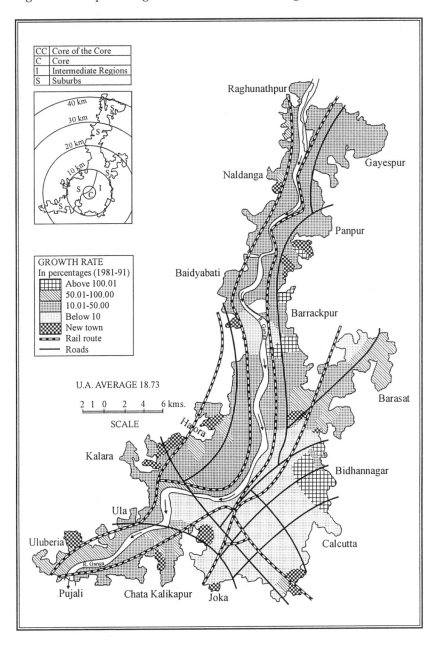

Figure 20.6 Population growth in Delhi, according to 1991 census

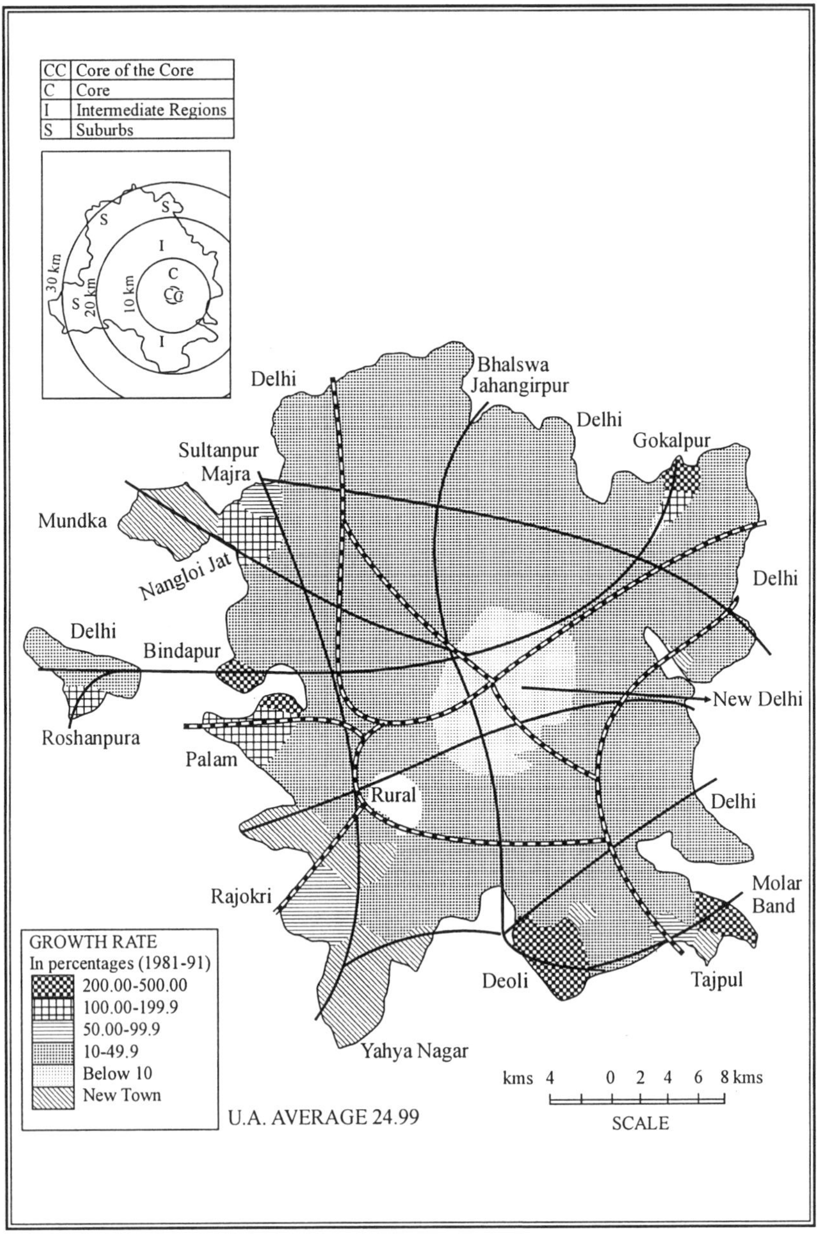
CC Core of the Core
C Core
I Intermediate Regions
S Suburbs
30 km
20 km
10 km
Delhi
Bhalswa Jahangirpur
Delhi
Gokalpur
Sultanpur Majra
Mundka
Nangloi Jat
Delhi
Delhi
Bindapur
New Delhi
Roshanpura
Palam
Rural
Delhi
Rajokri
Molar Band
Deoli
Tajpul
Yahya Nagar
GROWTH RATE
In percentages (1981-91)
200.00-500.00
100.00-199.9
50.00-99.9
10-49.9
Below 10
New Town
U.A. AVERAGE 24.99
kms 4 0 2 4 6 8 kms
SCALE

Source: Census of India, 1991.

Figure 20.7 Population growth in Madras, according to 1991 census

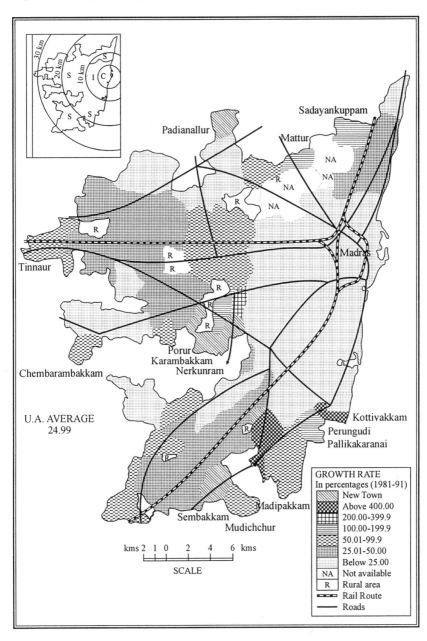

Source: Census of India, 1991.

industrial concentration in the mega cities is unlikely to have the desired effect over the shorter term. The severity of the problem requires a paradigm shift: i.e. a gradual but complete reversal of the current pro-urban development bias in our planning and more effective decentralization of capital, investments, growth efforts, and industrial locations in favour of intermediate- and small-sized cities, small towns and rural villages (Mukherji, 2000: 10-22). A more even and equitable distribution of production units over the entire national space is necessary instead of the continuation of the current and past trends in which a few metropolitan areas like "Black Holes" gulp down all the available capital investments, materials, resources, and growth efforts of the entire nation. In short, it calls for the maximum possible reversal of all the flows of capital, control, innovations, and growth efforts from the metropolis towards the smaller urban centres and the poor countryside. Nothing less than these stringent measures will bring relief of the current problems (Mukherji, 2001: 150-227).

CONCLUSION

This study has discussed acute problems of rural-to-metropolitan distressed migration and involutionary urbanization in India. It has also discussed the patterns of phenomena, the underlying mechanisms, and also the human dimensions of the problems involved. The study has also suggested strategies to alleviate some of the problems. In conclusion, it may be stated that such migration-urbanization problems cannot be fully addressed unless we also realize that these are the consequences of imbalances in the spatial economy of the country which, in turn, is the consequence of excessively polarized economic activities and resources at a few nodes, and improper policies. Many efforts are required to bring about essential changes and restructure the spatial organization of economic activities over the national space of the country. This means more emphasis on the development of internal domestic markets and internal growth, rather than excessive reliance only upon the external market and export activities. It will also require a re-orientation of trade and transport links, resource-use, investment and growth, credit services and subsidies, and functions of urban centres away from the present-day excessive concentration on larger metropolitan areas, rather than emphasizing growth and development in rural and small urban settlements that were hitherto neglected. There is an urgent need for efforts to provide greater welfare to the poor and to raise their purchasing power. In short, it requires a more equitable distribution of income, wealth, means of production and consumption. As Swami Vivekananda said more than one hundred years ago (1893), 'this implies the total elimination of poverty from India (and similar countries) and making all people, especially the poor, the humiliated, and the downtrodden, free from all kinds of bondages and fully liberate them to achieve a fully realized and upwardly transformed human and spiritual life' (Swami Vivekananda, 1893).

REFERENCES

Berry, B. J. L. (1966), *Essays on Commodity Flows and the Spatial Structure of the Indian Economy*. University of Chicago Research Paper No. 111, Chicago: University of Chicago Press.

Bose, A. (1976), *India's Urbanization, 1901-2001*. New Delhi: Tata Mcgraw-Hill.

Census of India (1967), *Census of India (1961), District Primary Census Abstract, (Calcutta, Bombay, Delhi, and Madras)*, New Delhi: Registrar General's Office.

Census of India (1982), *Census of India (1981), India, Series I, General Economic Tables, B series*, New Delhi: Registrar General's Office.

Census of India (1988), *Census of India (1981), India, Series I, Part V (A and B) (i) to (viii), Migration Tables, D-1 Series*, New Delhi: Registrar General's Office.

Census of India (1988) *Census of India 1981*, India, Series I, Part V (A & B) (i) to (viii), Migration Tables, D-I series, D-III Series. New Delhi: Registrar General's Office.

Census of India (1989), *Census of India (1981), India, Series I, Part V (A and B) (vi) to (viii), Migration Tables, D Series*, New Delhi: Registrar General's Office.

Census of India (1991), *Census of India 1991*, India, Series I, Part V (A & B) (i) to (viii), Migration Tables, D-I series, D-III Series. New Delhi: Registrar General's Office.

Census of India (1992), *Census of India (1991), India, Series I, Provisional Population Totals: Rural and Urban Distribution, Paper 2 of 1991*, New Delhi: Registrar General's Office, pp. 1-94.

Census of India (1998), *Census of India (1991), India, D-Series, Migration Tables*, New Delhi: Registrar General's Office (Unpublished). Also see some published volumes on Census 1991 Migration Tables (published in 2000).

Desai, A.R. (1974), 'An alternative approach to development', in A. Bose, P.B. Desai, and J.N. Sinha (eds.), *Population in India's Development, 1947-2000*, New Delhi: Vikash Publishing Co., pp. 89-99.

Dos Santos, T. (1973), 'The Crisis of development theory and the problem of dependence in Latin America', in H. Bernstein (ed), *Underdevelopment and Development in Third World*, Harmondsworth, Middlesex, England: Penguin Books Ltd., pp. 72-77.

Geyer, H.S. (1996), 'Expanding the theoretical foundation of differential urbanization', *Tijdschrift voor Economische en Sociale Geografie*, **87** (1), 44-59.

Geyer, H.S. and T.M. Kontuly (1993), 'A theoretical foundation for the concept of differential urbanization', in N. Hansen, K.J. Button and P. Nijkamp, *Modern Classics in Regional Science: Regional Policy and Regional Integration, Vol. 6*. Cheltenham: Edward Elgar, pp.157-177.

Hart, T. (1983), 'Transport and economic development, the historical dimension', in K.J. Button and D. Gillingwater (eds), *Transport, location and spatial policy*, Aldershot, Hants: Gower, pp.12-22.

McNeil, M. (1995), 'Bombay: one City - Two Worlds', The Urban Age: *The Human Environment of Cities*, **3**, 1-4.

Ministry of Urban Development, India (1988), *Report of National Commission on Urbanization, Vol.I-II and Interim report*, New Delhi.

Mukherji, S. (1977), 'Spatial Disorganisation and Internal Migration in India: Alternative Strategies for Restructuring the Space Economy and Development', Paper presented at ESCAP Expert Group Meeting on Population and Economic Development in Sub-National Areas, Bangkok: UN-ESCAP, pp. 1-56.

Mukherji, S. (1977), 'Summary of Migration and Spatial Disorganisation in India', in *Asian Population Study, Report of Expert Group Meeting, 40*, pp. 17-18.

Mukherji, S. (1981), *Mechanisms of Underdevelopment, Labour Migration and Planning Strategies in India*, Calcutta: Prajna.

Mukherji, S. (1985a), 'The process of wage labour circulation in Northern India', in G. Standing (ed), *Labour circulation and labour process (International Labour Office)*, London: Croom Helm, pp. 252-289.

Mukherji, S. (1985b), 'The syndrome of poverty and wage labour circulation: The Indian scene', in R. M. Prothero and M. Chapman (eds), *Circulation in Third World Countries*, London: Routledge and Kegan Paul, pp. 279-299.

Mukherji, S. (1993), 'A Canonical Model of Migration and Regional Disparities in India: Linking Spatial Structure to Spatial flows', in K B. Pathak, U.P. Sinha, and A. Pandey (eds.), *Dynamics of population and family welfare*, Bombay: Himalayan Publishing House, pp. 203-234.

Mukherji, S. (1995), 'Poverty-Induced Migration and Urban Involution in ESCAP Region', Paper presented to *UN-ESCAP Expert Group Meeting on Linkages between Poverty and Population in ESCAP Region*, Bangkok: UN-ESCAP, Sept 1995, pp. 1-45.

Mukherji, S. (2000), 'Underdevelopment and Migration in India: Urban and Regional Planning Strategies Required', *Geographical Review of India*, Calcutta University, vol 34 (Sept 2000), pp. 10-22.

Mukherji, S. (2001), *Causal Linkages Between Migration, Urbanisation, and Regional Disparities in India: Required Planning Strategies*. Bombay: International Institute for Population Sciences Research Monograph No 29, May 2001, pp. 1-227.

National Institute of Urban Affairs (1988), *The State of India's Urbanisation*, New Delhi: NIUA, pp. 68-70.

Prakasa Rao, V.L.S., Mishra, R.P., and Sundaram, K.V. (1974), *Regional Developmental Planning in India: A New Strategy*, New Delhi: Vikash Publishing House, pp. 79-120.

United Nations (1998), *World Urbanization Prospects: The 1996 Revision*. New York: United Nations, Tables A1 to A15, p. 29, and pp. 83-143.

Vivekananda, Swami (1883), *The Complete Works of Swami Vivekananda*, Calcutta: Udbodhan Karyalaya, Centenary Edition, 1963, Vol 1-8.

E. AFRICAN COUNTRIES

Chapter 21

Current Perspectives on Urban Change in South Africa[1]

H. S. Geyer and I. J. van der Merwe

THE EARLY HISTORY OF URBAN SETTLEMENT

Several waves of urban development mark the history of human settlement in South Africa. For centuries different Black tribes moved out of the south-central territories of Africa to the southern part of Africa. Records of the presence of Black people in the south-eastern parts of what is presently known as South Africa, date back to the sixteenth century (van Warmelo, 1946).

Although some traces of the remains of single black villages have been found in different parts of the South African area, large concentrations of Blacks lived in the mountain region of the Transkei, the sub-tropical areas below the eastern escarpment along the east coast, as well as the north-central highlands of the territory (Malan and Hattingh, 1975). Traditional black rural settlements were occupied on a communal basis by people who entirely depended on subsistence farming for their existence.

In the middle of the seventeenth century, the Dutch, who traded with India, started settling in the south-western tip of South Africa where the first White colony in southern Africa was formed. Soon afterwards white farmers started spreading along the southern coastal areas until they ran into large permanent Black rural settlements in the East London area, around 1770. As

[1] Recognition is hereby given to the National Research Foundation of South Africa for its financial assistance in this study. The usual disclaimer applies to this chapter. The authors also want to thank Laetitia Oosthuizen and Laurette Coetzee who generated some of the graphics displayed in this chapter and Wilhelm Rost and Tiaan Schutte who assisted in analyzing the data.

the White farming community spread, rural agricultural towns were established to provide goods and services to the farming communities.

Tension between the Dutch farming community, the Blacks on the eastern border area, and the British who took control of the colonized area up to the Orange River in 1806, eventually resulted in the 'Great Trek', a process of organised out-migration that lasted from approximately 1836 to 1838. In this endeavour, a large group of Dutch farmers were persuaded by their leaders to leave the area and move to unoccupied territory to the north of the Orange River. Farms were delimited as far as they went and rural settlements that provided goods and services to the farmers soon followed. During the period newly settled areas were politically divided into different administrative areas that were eventually consolidated into the four 'Boer Republics', each area with its own administrative headquarters.

Within a matter of a few years, after large diamond deposits had been discovered in 1871 and gold in 1884, new mining settlements that grew rapidly sprang up in various locations in the country. This completed the main urban structure. By that time four groups of settlements had developed – traditional and commercial farming communities that laid the economic foundation for a wide distribution of agricultural service centres of the Christaller-Lösch-type, administrative centres and large mining settlements. These settlements formed the backbone of the urban system as we know it today.[2]

Although manufacturing, associated with agriculture, occurred in agricultural centres from the beginning, it was the expanding mining sector that first really stimulated large scale manufacturing, causing mining towns to grow into cities. A crippling drought in the late 1920s, followed by the Great Depression, led to large numbers of people leaving their farms to find employment in the booming mining sector. The Second World War further stimulated industrial development, and attracted more redundant labour from the rural areas. As the urban system evolved and urban communities grew and matured, recreational needs developed which in turn led to the development of leisure centres in areas with a pleasant climate and pleasing natural environments, thus completing the South African human activity framework.

---

[2] It is clear that the exploded image of layers of human activities, shown in the Human Activities Model in Chapter 1 (Figure 1.1), serves as a framework for one to distinguish between different elements of the human settlement system, but not as a framework to explain the sequence in the settlement pattern, because in the South African example, the layers of human activities shown in the model did not follow chronologically.

THE IMPACT OF APARTHEID ON THE REDISTRIBUTION OF POPULATION

Different phases of political-economic development can be distinguished in the South African history (van der Merwe, 1983).[3]

☐ In the agrarian period before 1870 an overwhelming majority of the population was involved in agriculture, many of them literally living off the land. Advanced agricultural techniques of the time were implemented by some of the European farmers, especially those that arrived from Europe later during this period, but most other communities employed primitive techniques.

☐ The second period, from 1871 until 1910, was one of political-industrial transition. Mining activities started after diamonds and gold had been discovered and the British government expanded and consolidated its power over the entire South African territory.

☐ The industrial centralization phase lasted from 1911 to 1960. Large-scale industrialization, boosted by mining activities and two world wars, attracted migrants to mining centres and major ports, turning them into metropolitan areas. Meanwhile the policy of racial segregation progressed through various phases and culminated in what later became known as the 'Homeland' Policy (Figures 21.1A and B).

☐ The period from 1961 to 1976 could be regarded as the industrial decentralization phase. Homeland consolidation plans were finalized and a vigorous industrial decentralization policy was implemented to reduce the rate of Black urbanization (see the National Physical Development Plan, Figure 21.2).

☐ During the political-economic transformation phase, from 1977 to 1993, the country progressed from a fragmented regional system of segregated government, through various stages of governmental consolidation to a unified state with a democratic government.

☐ The socio-economic restructuring phase started in 1994.

☐ 'Spatial development initiatives' were taken in 1996 (see Figure 21.3) to provide some national spatial development guidance. Although the implementation of the initiatives received some attention they were not vigorously pursued. Since the beginning of the phase of economic reconstruction and development the redistribution of income and land to lagging communities has been a central objective of the government.

---

[3] See Geyer (1994) for a more detailed discussion of the political phases of South Africa over the past five decades and the spatial economic consequences of recent political changes.

Figure 21.1 The South African Bantustans, 1913 and 1967

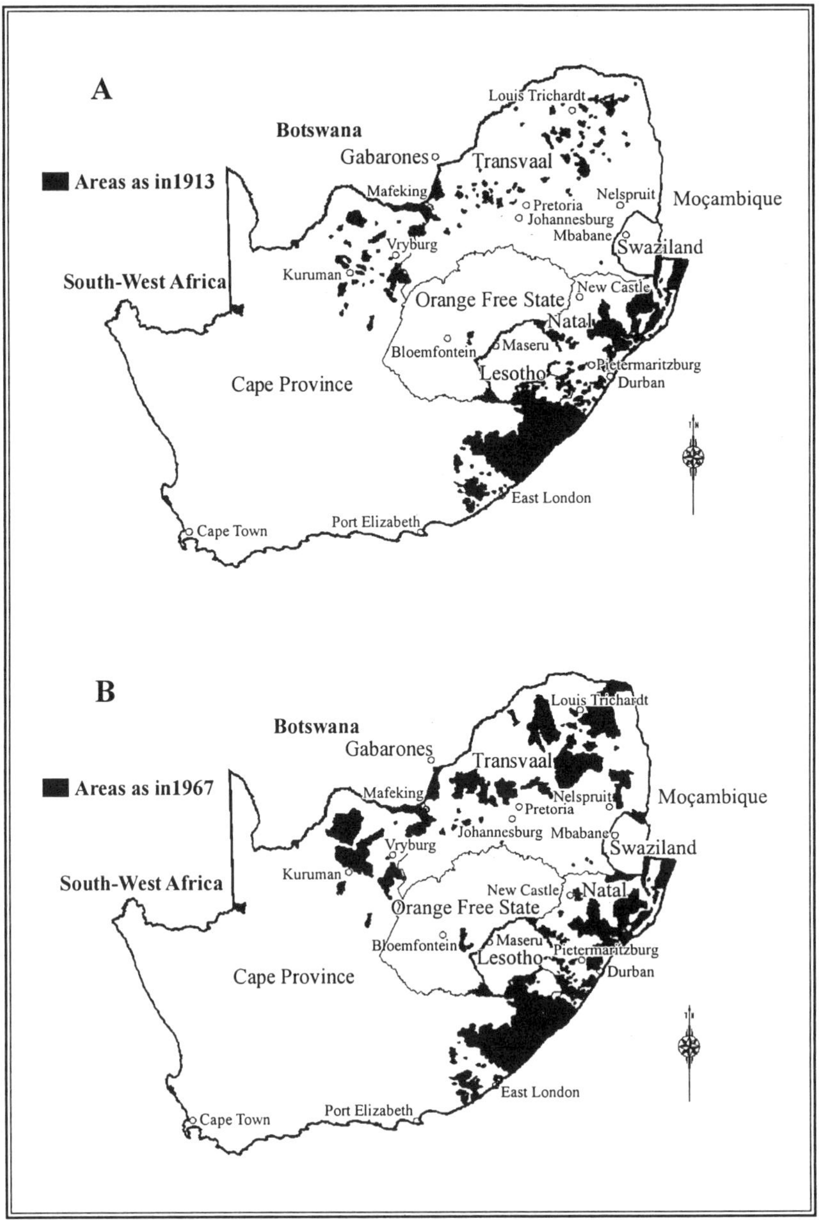

Source: Smit and Booysen, 1981.

Figure 21.2 The National Physical Development Plan, 1975

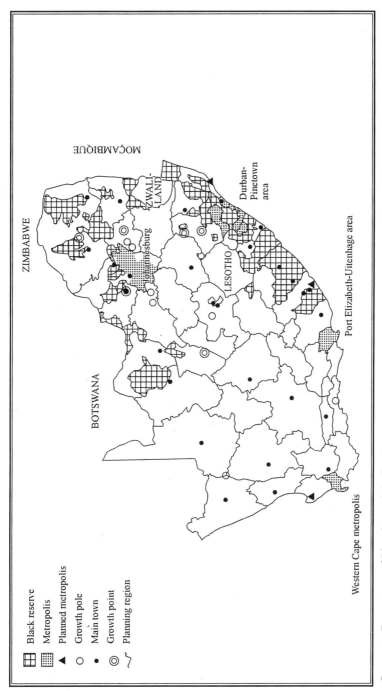

ZIMBABWE

MOÇAMBIQUE

BOTSWANA

SWALI-
LAND

LESOTHO

Johannesburg

Durban-
Pinetown
area

Port Elizabeth-Uitenhage area

Western Cape metropolis

Black reserve
Metropolis
Planned metropolis
Growth pole
Main town
Growth point
Planning region

Source: Department of Planning and the Environment

567

Figure 21.3 Spatial development initiatives and tax holidays, 1996

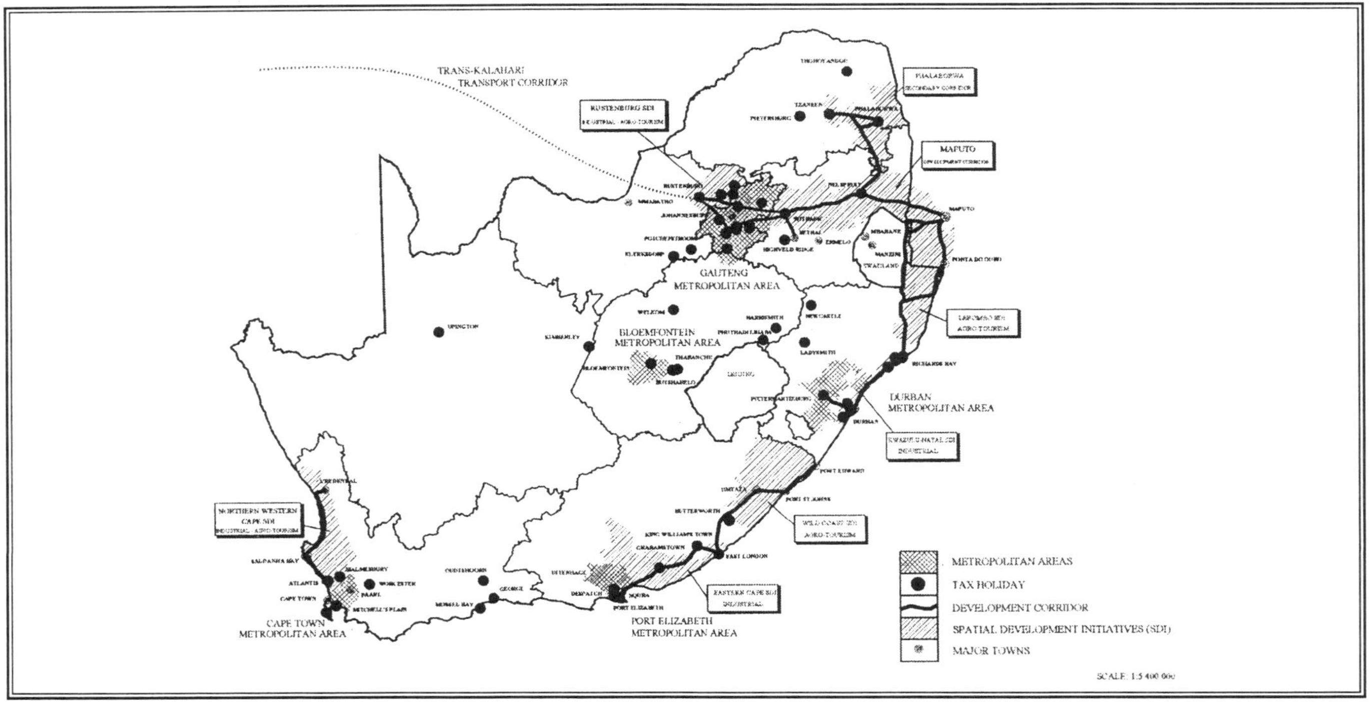

Source: Department of Trade and Industry

Spatial segregation proved to be a significant factor in population redistribution patterns in the history of South Africa. Racial segregation did not start when the National Party, branded the 'apartheid government', came into power in 1948. The first legislation to control the movement of people came in 1760, when the Slave Pass Law was passed, and from then until the apartheid era came to an end in 1993, legislation was continually passed and revised[4] to limit the movement or the settlement of Black people in different parts of the country (Smit and Booysen, 1981; Geyer, 1989a, 1994; Lemon, 1991).

The period after 1960 deserves special attention because policy changes that were made altered the urban scene more significantly than at any time before in South African history. First the government announced its independence from Britain in 1961. At the same time it announced its departure from the Commonwealth of Nations and declared its intention to put the country on the road to 'separate development', an approach whereby the Black tribes were to be given an opportunity to forge their own future on their own land. The aims of the policy of apartheid were firstly to identify land for the different tribes, based on the consolidation of the areas where large concentrations of them had previously resided (Figures 21.1A and B), then to allow them to be emancipated politically within their own 'Homelands', and finally to allow them to co-exist as independent states with the rest of South Africa within a commonwealth of South African nations.

From 1960 to 1970 economically non-active Blacks located in White controlled areas were repatriated to Black 'Homelands'. Four of the ten Bantustans gained independence, but most refused to exercise the option. An entire network of restrictive and incentive measures, so-called 'sticks and carrots', was designed in an effort to reduce the influx of Black migrants from the Bantustans. First, freehold was prohibited for Blacks outside the Bantustans – only leasehold was permitted, and only in the north-east of the country.[5] This political policy was adopted to prevent Black people from getting a foothold on what was regarded as 'white' controlled land. At the same time the government invested heavily in housing for Blacks in the Bantustans and in civil infrastructure in the so-called 'industrial growth points' that were identified along the boundaries of Bantustans (Geyer, 1989b). To give them the best chance of succeeding, many of the growth points were located on development axes between major metropolitan areas and secondary cities (Geyer, 1987).

---

[4] Numerous laws and regulations were passed during the nineteenth century to restrict African movement and / or urban settlement in Natal, the Cape province (as British colonies) and in Transvaal and the Orange Free State (as Boer Republics).
[5] The Eiselen line was drawn to show the area that was to be reserved for Coloured settlement in the Cape province (Smit and Booysen, 1981: 32).

Before 1975, industrial growth points were only identified on the 'White' side of the Bantustan borders to prevent White entrepreneurs from investing within the Bantustans, and in doing so, jeopardizing the concept of separate development (see South Africa, 1975). As a result, large numbers of Blacks who previously had lived deep inside the Bantustans, were attracted to locations close to the industrial development points. Most of these Black concentrations were still located on the Bantustan side of the borders, however (Geyer, 1989a; 1989c). Because of the industrial and commercial development on the 'White' side of the borders, little economic development occurred in the Black agglomerations inside the Bantustans. In the late 1970s, pressure from Bantustan leaders led to the expansion of the growth point concept. Additional growth points were identified, mostly within the Bantustans this time, and almost all of them at twin locations adjacent to existing growth points outside the Bantustans (South Africa, 1981).

Not much industrial development ever occurred within the Bantustans on any meaningful scale. This can mainly be ascribed to security risks. Entrepreneurs from abroad and White entrepreneurs from South Africa were reluctant to invest large amounts in the Bantustans and the local people lacked capital and expertise to do so themselves. This resulted in an uneven distribution of population spatially and economically.

URBAN DEVELOPMENT TRENDS

In 1996 approximately 38 million people were counted in South Africa, of whom 58 per cent lived in urban areas (Figure 21.4). The annual growth rate of the urban population overall is 3.1 percent (Statistics South Africa, 1997), but this is not a true reflection of real situation. Not unlike many former colonial countries soon after their independence, South Africa currently still exhibits a dualistic population character.

The level of urbanization and the annual growth rate of especially the White population are similar to those found in the most advanced parts of the First World, while the same parameters of the Black population resemble those of Third World countries generally (Table 21.1). While it is unlikely that much more urbanzation will occur among the Whites, due to their current high level of urbanization, there is still some scope for an increase in urbanization amongst the Coloureds and Asians.

The large rural Black population, however, still offers significant potential for urbanization. The country currently faces the pressure of over-urbanization, a phenomenon that is often experienced in developing countries (Todaro, 1982; Gugler, 1990). This poses one of the greatest current challenges of South Africa. With an urban population increasing by approximately one million per annum, employment opportunities, housing

Figure 21.4 Distribution of urban population in South Africa, 1991

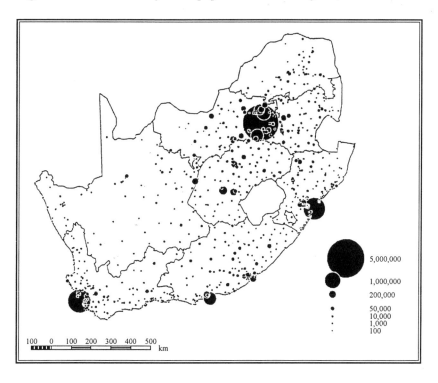

Source: Statistics South Africa

Table 21.1 Comparative urbanization tendencies in South Africa, 1996

	Urban population (million)	Urbanization level (%)	Urban growth rate (p.a.)
World	2 286	43%	2.5%
First World	525	77%	0.9%
Third World	1 483	36%	3.4%
South Africa	22.0	58%	3.1%
Black	14.0	50%	4.0%
White	4.7	92%	1.1%
Coloured/Asian	3.7	87%	2.1%

Source: Department of Constitutional Planning

and services will have to be provided at an exceptional rate.[6]

When the rank-size distribution of the approximately 800 urban settlements in South Africa (Figure 21.5) is compared to Berry's (1961) classical study on the classification of rank-size distributions of different countries, it is clear that the South African system is still in a primary stage of development, i.e. an urban system in which a relatively small number of high order centres dominate the rest of the urban areas, hierarchically and economically.[7]

The functional hierarchy of urban areas in South Africa (Geyer, 1996) also confirms the view expressed in the introduction to this chapter that (non-central) urban areas that originate from 'locational constants' (Richardson, 1973) more often than not become the dominant centres in an urban system. Ports that serve as international economic gateways to the South African interior, mining and political-administrative centres have generally become the economically dominant centres in the system.

The three metropolises in particular are attractive to urban migrants. The Pretoria-Witwatersrand-Vereeniging complex, with 5.7 million inhabitants in 1991, is the most prominent primate city. It represents approximately one third of the country's urban population. This is followed by the two other large agglomerations, i.e. Cape Town (2.0 million) and Durban (1.8 million). Together these three metropolises accommodate approximately two thirds of the country's urban population.

Globally, these three urban complexes form only a small fraction of the more than 250 cities in the world with a population exceeding one million inhabitants. The Gauteng metropolitan area (Pretoria-Witwatersrand-Vereeniging) is rated approximately twentieth in the world in terms of its population, while Cape Town fills the 85th position (United Nations, 1989). South African cities are, therefore, relatively small in international terms, but at the current rate of urbanization, some of these cities may soon count under the larger agglomerations of the world. Johannesburg, especially, is currently regarded as a third order city in global terms (Beaverstock et al., 1999). In

---

[6] This is one of the critical issues this study wants to address, because the question may be raised whether the provision of services should be provided at the scale where urban newcomers reside at present or whether the government should be cautioned about a more-than-likely large scale step-wise migration of mainly African people from small towns to larger towns and cities in due course, once people come under the impression (Todaro, 1982) that the chances of obtaining employment in larger towns and cities may be greater than in small rural towns.

[7] According to the Beaverstock-analysis (1999), for instance, the Pretoria-Johannesburg megalopolitan complex serves as a minor global world centre, while none of the other South African metropolitan areas appear under any of the individual categories listed in the study.

Figure 21.5 Urban rank-size distribution of South Africa, 1991

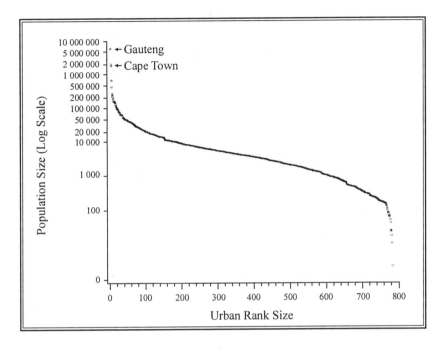

Source: Statistics South Africa

contrast, numerous small rural towns lead an increasingly precarious existence
as many of their economically enterprising inhabitants are migrating to the
larger cities (Dewar, 1996).

An analysis of commercial, industrial and service development within
former White and Black urban areas in South Africa in 1996 confirmed that most
former White controlled towns and cities were generally well provided with
central industrial and commercial goods and services while most former Black
towns and cities are lagging far behind (Figure 21.6).

DIFFERENTIAL URBANIZATION PATTERNS

Recently, the differential urbanization model was introduced (Geyer, 1989b,
1990, 1996a, 1998; Geyer and Kontuly, 1993). Contrary to previous views that
main- and sub-stream migration are often system-based and are mostly of the
migration/return-migration variety (Lee, 1966; Nogle, 1994), the model
suggests that main- and sub-streams can be the result of different population
groups migrating for entirely different reasons. Sometimes main- and sub-
stream migration occur in diagonal directions, sometimes in opposite directions,
but sometimes they can occur in the same direction for different reasons.

Figure 21.6 Provision of services in a selection of SA urban centres, 1996

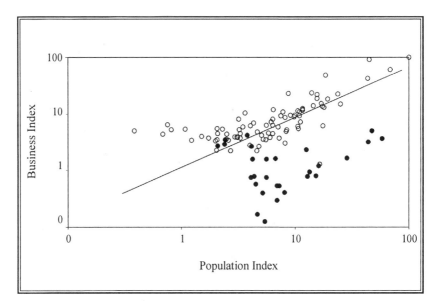

Source: Own calculations, 1996

Productionism[8] or environmentalism[9] (Hart, 1983) is often the underlying cause for differential urbanization patterns.   In the process of differential urbanization, counter-urbanization can be, for instance, the dominant migration stream, while at the same time, urbanization can occur as a sub-stream. An example of this was found in the USA in the early 1970s when African Americans and Hispanics continued to urbanize (i.e. migrate from the rural South to the large metropolitan areas in the North) while counter-urbanization was already taking place as a dominant trend (Berry, 1976). An example of main and sub-stream migration taking place in the same direction has also been found in the USA more recently. While many older, high income people are still leaving the large urban agglomerations in the North to settle in the warmer, less congested South (i.e. a counter-urbanization trend), African Americans – the lower income group – have also started migrating to the same areas (Beale, 1982). The increase in the availability of employment opportunities as a result of the former trend is more than likely an important

---

[8] Productionism oriented migration refers to people's need to move to areas for socio-economic mobility reasons (Fielding, 1991). More of the younger, less affluent people usually fall into this category.

[9] Environmentalism oriented migration refers to people's need to move to environmentally more desirable locations. More of the older and/or more affluent people usually fall into this category.

reason for the occurrence of the latter migration sub-stream, while that factor is of less importance to the counter-urbanizing group.

In South Africa, differential urbanization trends have also been observed at the national (Geyer, 1989b; 2003) and the regional levels (Geyer, 1990). The long term differential urbanization trends at the national level are shown in Figures 21.7-21.9. In the study results three urban categories were distinguished: small sized towns (SSTs), intermediate sized cities closer to the major metropolitan areas (Sat ISCs), intermediate sized cities further away from the major metropolitan areas (Per ISCs), and core areas, the latter being divided into the inner (INC), the intermediate (IMC), the outer core (OTC), and the core fringe (CFR) zones. The study results show a continuing concentration of Blacks[10] in the core areas of the country, much of it occurring in the inner zones of the metropolitan areas, while there was a steady decline in the growth of Whites in these cities since the 1970s (Figure 20.7 and 8). Figure 21.8 shows that the bulk of White population growth in the metropolitan areas occurred towards the metropolitan fringe while the growth column of this group in the inner core zone lies in negative territory. Until the 1970s the population share of the rural areas continued to decline (Figure 21.9), while the small, intermediate and core areas continued to gain population proportionally. This is a strong indication that the country found itself firmly in the urbanization phase (Geyer and Kontuly, 1993; Geyer, 1996). Since the 1970s, though, the proportional decline of the rural areas and the proportional increase in the metropolitan areas stopped, while the smaller cities in the country gained population proportionally. This is an early indication that South Africa was approaching the polarization reversal phase during the late 1980s, early 1990s (Geyer, 2003). However, the political changes that were to follow worked against the trend, because due to the increased influx of Blacks to urban areas of all sizes after 1985, the shares of Blacks had increased relative to all other groups in all urban categories by 1991.

Other interesting patterns of demographic change occurred in the same urban zones between 1970 and 1991. All three main urban categories, i.e. core areas, intermediate- and small-sized cities, gained almost equally in young, middle-aged and older people throughout the period in real terms, although small-sized cities gained slightly more young and middle-aged people between 1980 and 91 (Figure 21.10A). Between 1970 and 1980 small sized-towns and cities lost a large number of unemployed and unskilled people as a result of the repatriation of such people to the Bantustans during this period (Figure 21.10B). By 1991 many of these people had returned, however. The income distribution of the population remained relatively equal in all three urban categories, although in real terms, only the lower

---

[10] As a group Blacks represent the lower income group in the country.

Figure 21.7 Proportional growth of urban groups, 1951-91

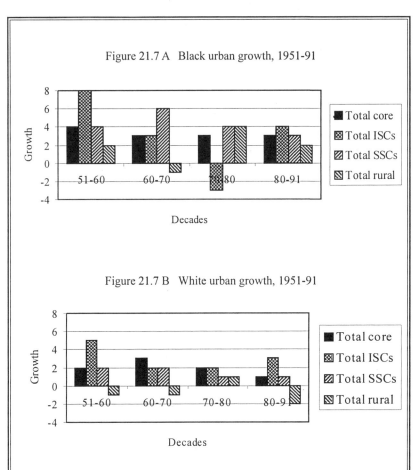

Figure 21.7 A   Black urban growth, 1951-91

Figure 21.7 B   White urban growth, 1951-91

Source: Statistics South Africa

income categories increased significantly from 1980 to 1991 (Figure 20.10C). The metropolitan areas gained mostly in the lower and medium level occupation groups between 1980 and 1991, mostly in the inner and suburban areas (Figure 20.10D). Although metropolitan areas gained some highly skilled workers from 1980 to 1991, the dramatic decline in the numbers of workers in this category over all during the period is an indication of the brain drain that started to occur since the mid-1980s. This factor is directly related to international migration trends.

Figure 21.8 Space-time distribution of urban growth in South Africa, 1951-91

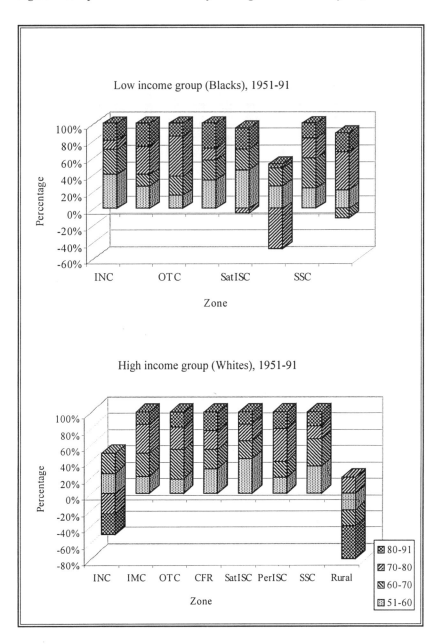

Figure 21.9 Proportional growth of urban groups, 1904-91

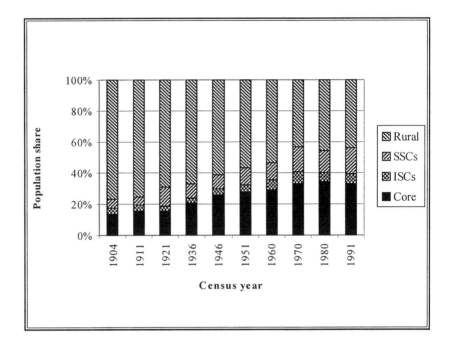

Source: Statistics South Africa

INTERNATIONAL MIGRATION

In international labour migration the emphasis in functional theory has always been on the factors that are taken into consideration by individuals when migration is contemplated. In dependency theory, the focus is largely on the dominating economic impact capitalism has on lagging communities (Goss and Lindquist, 1995; Portes and Walton, 1981). Economic imbalance, whatever the reason for its existence, results in the attraction of labour from lagging areas to prosperous areas. Despite the system of apartheid, South Africa has always been a popular destination for prospective migrants from neighbouring states, especially males (Murray, 1981; Crush, 1987).

Since the abolishing of apartheid, though, the popularity of South Africa as an international destination in the Southern African sub-continent has increased manifold. This is generally regarded by the government as a threat to economic stability and appropriate steps have been taken to reduce the immigration of unskilled labour. The need for gender-sensitivity in the formulation of international migration policy has been voiced, however (Dodson, 2000).

Normally international migration is a significant factor in urban development in the developed world since international migrants usually

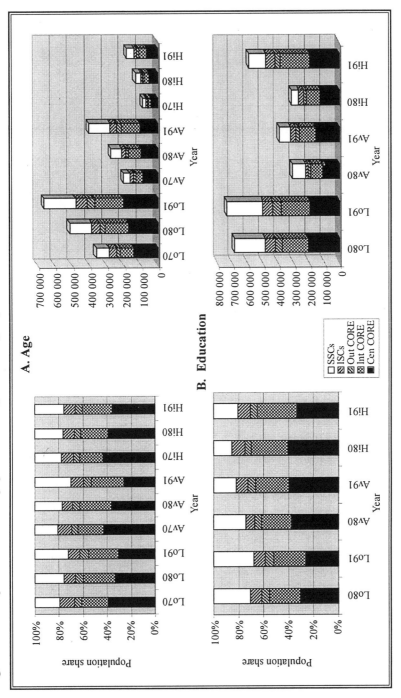

Figure 21.10 Proportional and real population change in urban groups, 1951-91

579

Figure 21.10 Continued

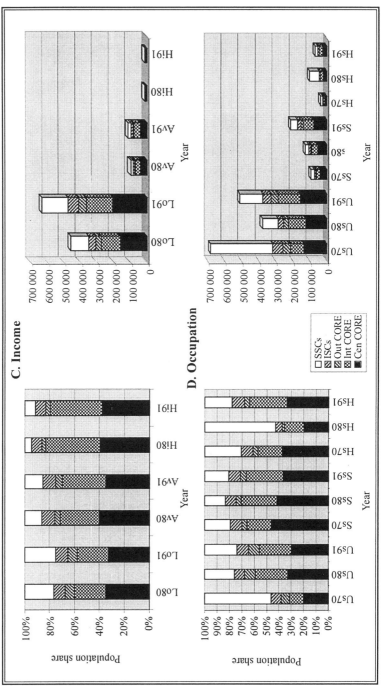

C. Income

D. Occupation

Legend:
☐ SSCs
▨ ISCs
▨ Out CORE
▨ Int CORE
■ Cen CORE

Source: Statistics South Africa

580

tend to settle first in large urban agglomerations of host countries (Champion, 1994). This does not seem to be the case in South Africa at present. Although reliable statistics in this regard are unobtainable, indications are that large numbers of rural migrants are currently infiltrating areas in South Africa that are contiguous to economically struggling neighbouring countries. At the same time large numbers of especially White people are leaving the country, a factor that is still an unknown quantity, although unofficial numbers are substantial.

CIRCULATION

Temporary migration patterns have always played an important part in population redistribution patterns in South Africa. Two forms of circulation need to be highlighted: compulsory and induced circulation. Apartheid was directly responsible for the first and indirectly responsible for the latter. From the outset the mining industry has shaped compulsory temporary population settlement policy. In 1871, when labour was needed by the mining industry after diamonds had been discovered in Kimberley, the British authorities introduced the hostel system for the first time to accommodate Blacks on a temporary basis. The reason was that the Black population was not considered to be ready for formal urban settlement at the time (South Africa, 1948).

This set the pattern for contracting labour by the mining industry for the next hundred years. Because of adverse conditions in the mines, not enough labourers could always be recruited locally. Extensive recruitment drives were launched deep into the rural areas of the country to find the required labour.[11] Contracted migrant labourers were accommodated in hostels for single persons and they were obliged to return home after their term had expired (Leys, 1974), a system that caused concern up to the end of the apartheid era (Penderis and van der Merwe, 1994). Escaping the traditional communal system at home (Schapera, 1947) and earning cash were two of the main advantages of the system. Breaking up social patterns in general and households in particular, were some of the serious disadvantages.

During the apartheid era, a combination of factors was responsible for voluntary circulation. Push factors included population pressure, which combined with traditional agricultural methods devastated the natural environment. This ultimately led to huge differences in living standards between metropolitan areas and Bantustans (Geyer and du Plessis, 1994).

---

[11] This approach tied in with the popular neo-classical model of labour transfer between the rural and industrial sectors to reduce unemployment in the former sector and to provide the necessary labour for the expansion of the latter (Lewis, 1954; Ranis and Fei, 1961).

The possibility of finding employment in the urban areas,[12] on the other hand, served as pull factors. In many respects, voluntary circulation caused greater social disruption within the peripheral society than induced circulation. Whereas the mining sector concentrated on the recruitment of young unmarried men, it was the more established married men that often left the Homelands to find temporary employment in the 'White' areas. Women, children and the aged largely remained in the rural areas. The custom of polygamy often resulted in men having families in both the urban and rural areas, something that is generally accepted and is widely practised to this day in many Black societies.

POST-APARTHEID URBANIZATION

During the latter part of the 1970s the policy of apartheid started disintegrating from within. Strife among former political partners and political exhaustion as a result of continued political pressure from inside and outside the country led first to the dilution of the concept and finally to its abandonment towards the beginning of the 1990s (Tomlinson, 1990; Christopher, 1992; Geyer, 1994). Indications of a disintegrating government leadership, unwilling to further enforce influx control measures, resulted in a flood of migrants to the cities. In the beginning the large urban agglomerations absorbed most of the migrants, but subsequently, urban areas of all sizes gained migrants. By 1991, 30.7 per cent of all Blacks in the three largest metropolitan areas were living in squatter camps (Geyer, 1993a). In the beginning, uncontrolled squatting which led to tension among affected communities, triggered the social rearrangement of residential areas in many parts of South African cities (Geyer, 1993a).

The 1994 elections brought further sweeping changes to the social and economic urban environment. Further influx of rural migrants occurred, most of them settled on the outskirts of cities (Crankshaw, 1993). This resulted in an 'inverted' urban structure, the urban poor living on the fringes of the cities while the more affluent live inside the cities close to employment opportunities (Geyer, 1993b), a situation that currently places huge challenges on social and spatial decision makers (Cape Town Metropolitan Council, 2000; Pillay, 1995). Declining home-based economies of the former Bantustans tend to augment the process (Cross and Bekker, 2000).

On a national scale particular migration patterns are emerging. Urban areas of all sizes are gaining migrants, an overwhelming majority of them Blacks originating from rural areas. A significant proportion of the migrants that locate in small rural towns originate from nearby commercial or traditional farming areas which points to step-wise migration (Geyer, 2000).

---

[12] See Todaro (1969; 1982) for the impact of the 'bright lights' syndrome on migration tendencies in the developing world.

Redundant labourers in the agricultural sector are settling in the nearest towns[13] to enable them to retain strong social and financial ties with their kin on the farms for the sake of survival, a tendency that has even been observed in small satellite urban settlements on the fringes of the large metropolitan areas (Geyer, 2000a).

The huge volumes of new Black migrants in rural towns cannot be sustained by their shrinking economies. A population profile of 1500 Whites to 37000 Black residents in 1997 (Krige, 1997), when the ratio was only 1500 to 4400, in 1980, is not unusual. Because the local governments of most of these rural towns were on the brink of total economic collapse, steps were taken by the central government (South Africa, 1999) to incorporate small economically non-viable rural settlements into the jurisdiction areas of larger towns and cities based on more realistic magisterial district boundaries (Geyer et al., 2000). While this move may delay the further economic-administrative disintegration of the former settlements (Geyer, 2000), it is increasing the burden of some of the larger towns and cities that are already struggling financially (Geyer, 2002). Adding the negative economic effects[14] of a spiraling death rate caused by AIDS (Figure 21.11), the South African cities are facing a tough time ahead.

Figure 21.11 Impact of AIDS on mortality rates in South Africa, 1990-99

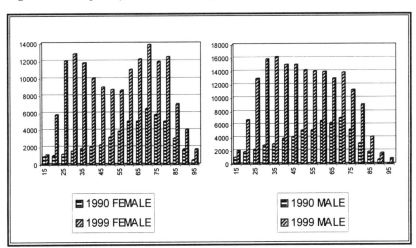

Source: The Sunday Times, July 2, 2000

---

[13] This resembles the first phase of migration anticipated by Lewis (1954) and Ranis and Fei (1961) in their labour migration model.

[14] Exceptionally high proportions of young people in the sexually active age groups are dying. They would have formed the future economically active component of the country's labour force.

Significant population shifts can be observed at the national level. Since the early 1990s, a visible relocation of the White investment in real estate has been taking place to unaffected areas in the coastal regions of the Western and Eastern Cape province. Many of the former migrants are highly skilled professionals or affluent people that are near or past the retirement age (Cross and Bekker, 2000). This is due to the large-scale influx of Blacks to cities in the northern parts of the country and the subsequent increase in violence in those areas. However, since this population shift has taken place significant volumes of Black migrants have also started settling in coastal towns and cities in the Western Cape in recent years. As if in a delayed reaction, new squatter settlements are currently mushrooming near the high income holiday resorts and retirement villages along the coast of the Western and Eastern Cape province.

Similar patterns are observed at the micro urban level nationally. Certain areas closer to traditional Black residential areas as well as isolated affluent areas elsewhere are increasingly becoming racially integrated. Invasion[15] of formal housing areas through illegal squatting by lower income groups during the first half of the 1990s led to the degeneration of many parts of urban areas all over the country (Morris, 1994; Cranksaw, 1993). More often than not this has sparked the relocation of the people who previously lived in those areas. Security high-density housing is becoming particularly popular in new high-income residential development.

There seems to be a divide between academic and policy analysts on the one hand and residents on the other on the issue of spatial integration. The former see the transformation of the urban structure as a priority and a central issue in the establishment of a non-racial South African society, while the latter tend to focus on common identities and the re-establishment of stable communities (Lochnert, et al., 1998; Geyer, 2001). The overall picture is one of increasing social polarization and a rearrangement of the urban environment into new racially homogenous settlements, both at the micro and macro level (Lochnert, et al., 1998).

Interesting changes are also taking place in the micro economic urban environment. Wherever large-scale informal commercial development occurs, formal commerce and industry find it difficult to survive. This more often than not results in the spatial re-location of formal commercial and industrial businesses from central city areas to security oriented development in suburban centres. Visible shifts have occurred in the Johannesburg, Pretoria and Cape Town metropolitan areas in recent years. The main factors playing a role here are unfair competition and the tendency of the criminal element to take refuge in an uncontrolled informal commercial environment.

---

[15] Invasion takes on various forms. Often formal housing is invaded as in Hillbrow, Johannesburg and Sunnyside, Pretoria, forcing property owners out of business by non-payment tactics, or squatting occurs illegally on open land.

RECONSTRUCTION AND DEVELOPMENT

The urban and regional restructuring that has occurred in South Africa since the first democratic election was held in 1994, has been fundamental but not painless. Many people that were denied space or could not afford housing in the urban areas previously are now given the opportunity to obtain land. Providing basic infrastructure to lagging communities has been a priority of the government since its inception. Although the provision of infrastructure in peripheral areas may reduce the current high levels of rural-urban migration, further expansion of civil services in small rural towns and villages may hold substantial risks.

Indications are that the present over-urbanization that is caused by the stepwise migration of unskilled people to rural towns is triggering the abandoning of these settlements by the economically enterprising components of the population (Krige, 1997). The decrease in employment opportunities as a result of this displacement is likely to cause the new Black migrants to leave these settlements over the medium-term as well, turning rural towns into mere medium-term 'transit-locations' for migrants en route to larger urban centres. Whatever the time scale, a gradual reduction in the huge numbers of Black migrants that are currently living in rural towns seems inevitable. The government's current emphasis on Local Economic Development should delay this process, however.[16]

In terms of the government's current policy of restitution and redistribution (Horn, 1998), former long-term farm labourers can obtain tenure rights on commercial farms. This could jeopardize the commercial farm labour market, because former labourers do not need to work on the farms any longer. Without this labour commercial farming is not sustainable, and this could result in the further collapsing of the commercial agricultural sector, eventually forcing more and more people, both former farm owners and their former workers, to migrate to the cities. The allocation of sizeable portions of agricultural land to people in the restitution process could also create pockets of destitution if the process is not accompanied by continued technical assistance. If it is not, these people could eventually also be forced to migrate to the cities. With proper planning and the right kind of technical assistance though, peasant farming could mean a new start for many of the formerly disenfranchised (de Beer, 2001).

Also, the establishment of new settlements in between existing towns and villages, without taking into consideration the impact these new settlements may have on the balance between surrounding rural towns and their hinterlands in the region, may have significant economic consequences for

---

[16] Self-help schemes are an important instrument in creating employment and at the same time providing shelter in a post-developmental urban economic development framework (Seethal, 1996).

the survival of both. The creation of rural pockets of poverty will have obvious consequences for both the government and surrounding agricultural communities. Whenever rural restitution is considered, appropriate planning steps will have to be taken to ensure the social and economic viability of new settlements after the process has been completed (de Beer, 2001). Throughout the process of reconstruction and development trade-offs between dynamic and static redistribution[17] (Killick, 1981) will always have to be borne in mind (Geyer, 1988).

Self-help informal housing seems to be the only viable option to provide shelter to the masses that are seeking accommodation in developing countries around the world (Gilbert and Gugler, 1989) as in South Africa. Many examples can be found where urban residential areas that started out as informal settlements, were upgraded by residents in time to eventually be transformed into stable formal settlements (Eckstein, 1990).

CONCLUSION

Despite the political changes that have taken place in recent years, the South African city still bears the imprint of a frontier colonial Third World city, an urban form that has gone through different phases of development (Davies, 1981; Western, 1986; Krige, 1988; Bernstein and McCarthy, 1990; Lemon, 1991; Swilling et al., 1991; Simon, 1992; van der Merwe, 1993):

In the *Colonial era* settlers regarded cities as their cultural domain and structural ethnic separation was a reality (Christopher, 1983). This urban form served as the foundation for the evolution of the segregated and later the apartheid-city in South Africa.

The *Segregated City* evolved spontaneously from the Colonial City structure. It is a fragmented city with mixed zones and scattered ethnic enclaves within certain neighbourhoods. These cities were highly segregated and segregation indices of Whites fluctuated between 70 and 80 per cent (Christopher, 1990).

The *Apartheid era* cities were highly structured and divided, with White segregation indices increasing to 93 per cent (Christopher, 1990). Equivalent figures in Africa at the time were between 70 and 75 per cent, while in most First World cities the segregation levels ranged between 50 and 60 per cent.

In the *Post-Apartheid City* forced segregation on ethnic grounds is being replaced by the spontaneous separation of people according to socio-economic status and individual cultural preference. Based on experience elsewhere this does not imply total residential integration (Lemon, 1991).

---

[17] Static redistribution refers to direct redistribution of wealth without any form of *quid pro quo* performance while in dynamic redistribution an increase in productivity is required (Geyer, 1988).

Current demographic changes are increasingly transforming South African cities into Third World city structures. The economic structure and social environment are swiftly becoming Africanized.

As long as the White population remains strongly represented in the urban areas in South Africa the dualistic colonial structure of the cities is likely to remain intact.[18] However, the hybridizing of First, Second and Third World urban features is likely to increase in the urban environment of South Africa in the future (Bernstein and McCarthy, 1990; Swilling, Humphries and Shubane, 1991; Simon, 1992; Dewar and Uytenbogaardt, 1991; McCarthy, 1992; Smith, 1992; Tomlinson, 1990).

REFERENCES

Beale, C.L. (1982), 'U.S. population: Where we are; Where we're going', *Population Bulletin*, **37**, 1-59.

Beaverstock, J.V., R.G. Smith and P.J. Taylor (1999), 'A roster of world cities', *Cities*, **16**, 445-458.

Bernstein, A. and J. McCarthy (1990), *Opening the cities: Comparative perspectives on desegregation*, Indicator project South Africa. Johannesburg: Urban Foundation.

Berry, B. J. L. (1961), 'City size distributions and economic development', *Economic Development and Cultural Change*, **9**, 573-588.

Berry, B. J. L. (1976), 'The Counterurbanization Process: Urban America since 1970', *Urban Affairs Annual Review*, 11, 17-30.

Cape Town Metropolitan Council, (2000), *Building an equitable city: urban development principles for the city of Cape Town*, Cape Town: City of Cape Town.

Central Statistical Service (1997), see Statistics South Africa.

Champion, A. G. (1994), 'International migration and demographic change in the Developed World', *Urban Studies*, **31**, 653-677.

Christopher, A. J. (1990), 'Apartheid and urban segregation levels in South Africa', *Urban Studies*, **27**, 421-40.

Christopher, A. J. (1983), 'From Flint to Soweto: Reflections on the colonial origins of the apartheid city', *Area*, **15**, 145-149.

Christopher, A. J. (1992), 'The final phase of urban apartheid zoning in South Africa, 1990/1', *South African Geographical Journal*, **74**, 29-34.

Crankshaw, O. (1993), 'Apartheid, urbanisation and squatting on the southern Witwatersrand', *African Affairs*, **92**, 31-51.

---

[18] This is an urban structure with a developed component reminiscent of the First World Western city, economically dominating a dependent Third World component.

Crankshaw, O. and C. White (1995), 'Racial segregation and inner city decay in Johannesburg, *International Journal of Urban and Regional Research*, **19**, 622-638.

Cross, C. and S. Bekker (2000), *En waarheen nou?:Migration and settlement in the Cape Metropolitan area (CMA).* Occasional Paper, No. 6., Stellenbosch University.

Crush, J. (987), The struggle for Swazi labour 1890-1920', Kinston and Montreal, McGill-Queen's University Press.

Davies, R. J. (1981), 'The spatial formation of the South African city', *Geo-Journal supplementary issue*, **2**, 59-72.

De Beer, S. M. (2001), *Rural settlement models for South Africa.* Masters Thesis, Urban and Regional Planning, Potchefstroom University.

Dewar, D. (1996), *Small towns in development: A South African perspective.* Development Paper 122. Johannesburg: Development Bank of Southern Africa.

Dewar, D. and R. S. Uytenbogaardt (1991), *South African cities: A manifesto for change*, University of Cape Town: Urban Problems Research Unit.

Dodson, B. (2000), 'Porous borders: gender and migration in Southern Africa', *South African Geographical Journal*, **82**, 9-22.

Eckstein, S. (1990), 'Urbanisation revisited, inner-city slum of hope and squatter settlement of despair', *World Development*, **18**, 165-181.

Geyer, H. S. (1987), 'The development axis as a development instrument in the Southern African development area', *Development Southern Africa*, **4**, 271-301.

Geyer, H. S. (1988), 'On urbanization in South Africa', *The South African Journal of Economics*, **56**, 154-172.

Geyer, H. S. (1989), 'Apartheid in South Africa and industrial deconcentartion in the PWV area', *Planning Perspectives*, **4**, 251-269.

Geyer, H. S. (1989a), 'Differential urbanization in South Africa and its consequences for spatial development policy', *African Urban Quarterly*, **4**, 276-292.

Geyer, H. S. (1989b), 'Industrial development policy in South Africa, the past , present, and future', *World Development*, **17**, 379-96.

Geyer, H. S. (1990), 'Implications of differential urbanization on deconcentration in the Pretoria-Witwatersrand-Vaal Triangle metropolitan area, South Africa', *Geoforum,* **21**, 385-396.

Geyer, H. S. (1993a), 'African urbanization in metropolitan South Africa – differential urbanization pespectives', *GeoJournal*, **30**, 301-308.

Geyer, H.S., (1993b), 'Urban infusion as a policy option for future uban development in South Africa: the Witwatersrand metropolitan area as an example', *Geographica Slovenica*, **24**, 243-257.

Geyer, H. S. (1994), 'Development ideology and the political transition in South Africa – changing perspectives', *Planning Perspectives*, **9**, 377-404.

Geyer, H. S. (1996), *A central place study of South Africa*, Pretoria: Statistics South Africa. Unpublished.

Geyer, H. S. (1996a), 'Expanding the theoretical foundation of differential urbanization', *Tijdschrift voor Economische en Sociale Geografie*, **87**, 44-59.

Geyer, H. S. (1998), 'Differential urbanization and international migration: an urban systems approach', in C. Gorter, P. Nijkamp, and J. Poot (eds) *Crossing borders: regional and urban perspectives on international migration*. Ashgate: Aldershot, pp. 161-184.

Geyer, H. S. (2000), *A settlement strategy for the North West province*, Mmabatho, Department of Local Government and Housing, North West province, South Africa. Unpublished.

Geyer, H. S. (2000a), *A socio-economic survey of the Western Gauteng province*. Westonaria: *Western Gauteng Services Council, South Africa*. Unpublished.

Geyer, H. S. (2001), 'Development planning transition in South Africa', in H. C. Marais, Y. Methien, N.S. Jansen van Rensburg, M.P. Maaga, G. F. de Wet, C. J. Coetzee (eds), *Sustainable social development: Critical dimensions*. Pretoria, Network Publishers, pp. 143-152.

Geyer, H. S. (2002), 'The changing South African urban sceneen – from Verwoerd to Mandela', *Petermanns Geographische Miteilungen*, Forthcoming.

Geyer, H. S. (2003), 'Differential urbanization in South Africa – a further exploration. *Tijdschrift voor Economische en Sociale Geografie*, Forthcoming.

Geyer, H. S. and T. M. Kontuly (1993) A theoretical foundation for the concept of differential urbanization. *International Regional Science Review*, **15**, 157-177.

Geyer, H. S., and D. J. du Plessis (1994), 'Existence level differentials and the spatial industrial restructuring of South Africa. *Development Southern Africa*, **11**, 599-616.

Geyer, H. S., M. Orkin, P. Lehohla and J. Kahimbaara (2000), 'Revisiting the magisterial district boundaries of South Africa', *Development Southern Africa.* **17**, 263-276.

Goss, J. and B. Lindquist, (1995), 'Conceptualizing international labor migration: a structuration perspective', *International Migration Review*, **29**, 317-351.

Gugler, J. (1990), 'Overurbanization reconsidered', in J. Gugler (ed), *The urbanisation of the Third World*, Oxford: Oxford University Press, pp.74-92.

Hart, T. (1983), 'Transport and economic development, the historical dimension', in K. J. Button, and D. Gillingwater, (eds), *Transport, location and spatial policy*, Aldershot, Hants: Gower, pp.12-22.

Horn, A. C. (1998), 'The identity of land in the Pretoria district, 19 June 1913: implications for land restitution', *South African Geographical Journal*, **80**, 9-22.

Killick, T. (1981), *Policy economics, a textbook of applied economics on developing countries,* London: Heinemann.

Krige, D. S. (1988), *Die transformasie van die Suid-Afrikaanse stad,* Bloemfontein: University of the Free State.

Krige, D. S. (1997), 'Post-apartheid development challenges in small towns of the Free State', *South African Geographical Journal*, **79**, 175-178.

Lee, E. S. (1966), 'A theory of migration', *Demography*, **3**, 47-57.

Lemon, A. (ed.) (1991) *Homes apart: South Africa's segregated cities,* Cape Town: David Philip.

Lewis, A. (1954), 'Development with unlimited supplies of labour', *The Manchester School*, **22**, 139-192.

Leys, R. (1974), 'South African gold mining in 1974: the gold of migrant labour', *African Affairs*, **74**, 196-208.

Lochnert, B., S. Oldfield and S. Parnell (1998), 'Post-apartheid social polarisation: the creation of sub-urban identities in Cape Town', *South African Geographical Journal*, **80**, 86-92.

Malan, T. and P.S. Hattingh, (1975), *Swart tuislande in Suid-Africa,* Pretoria: Africa Institute.

McCarthy, J. (1992), 'Urban geography and socio-political change: Retrospect and prospect', in C. Rogerson and J. McCarthy (eds) *Geography in a changing South Africa: Progress and prospects.* Cape Town: Oxford University Press.

Morris, A. (1994), 'The desegregation of Hillbrow, Johannesburg 1978-82', *Urban Studies*, **31**, 821-834.

Murray, C. (1981), *Families devided: the impact of migrant labour in Lesotho.* Cambridge: Cambridge University Press.

Nogle, J. M. (1994), 'The systems approach to international migration: and application of network analysis methods', *International migration*, **32**, 329-342.

Penderis, S. P and I. J. van der Merwe (1994), 'Kaya Mandi Hostel, Stellenbosch: place, people and policies' *South African Geographical Journal*, **76**, 33-38.

Pillay, U. (1995), 'The spaontaneous settlement question in South Africa: insights from the international experience', *South African Geographical Journal*, **77**, 45-50.

Portes, A. and J. Walton (1981), *Labor, class, and the international system*, New York: Academic Press.

Ranis, G. and J. C. H. Fei, (1961), 'A theory of economic development', *The American Economic Review*, **51**, 533-565.

Richardson, H. W. (1973), *Economic growth theory*, London: MacMillan.

Richardson, H. W. (1977), *City size and national strategies in developing countries*. Washington DC.: World Bank Staff Working Report.

Richardson, H. W. (1980), 'Polarization Reversal in Developing Countries', *Papers of the Regional Science Association*, **45**, 67-85.

Schapera, I. (1947), *Migrant labour and tribal life: a study of conditions in the Bechuanaland Protectorate*. London: Oxford University Press.

Seethal, C. (1996), 'Reconstruction and postdevelopmentalism in South Africa: the case of informal settlement in Pietermaritzburg-Msunduzi' (1990-1995)', *South African Geographical Journal*, **78**, 64-74.

Simon, D. (1992), '*Reform in South Africa and modernization of the apartheid city*', in D. Drakakis-Smith (ed), *Urban and regional change in Southern Africa*. London: Routledge.

Smit, P. and J. J. Booysen (1981), 'Swart verstedeliking: proses, patroon en strategie', Cape Town: Tafelberg Printers.

Smith, D.M. (ed) (1992) *The apartheid city and beyond: Urbanization and social change in South Africa*. London: Routledge.

South Africa (1975), *The National Physical Development Plan*, Pretoria: Department of Environmental Planning.

South Africa (1981), *The Good Hope Plan*, Pretoria: Department of Foreign Affairs.

South Africa (1998), *Spatial Development initiatives*: Department of Trade and Industy. www.polity.org.za

South Africa (1999), www.demarcation.org.za

Statistics South Africa (1904 – 1991) Official census reports.

Statistics South Africa (1997) *Census '96: Preliminary estimates of the size of the population of South Africa*. Pretoria.

Swilling, M., R. Humphries, and K. Shubane, (eds.) (1991) *Apartheid city in transition*, Cape Town: Oxford University Press.

The Sunday Times (2000), 'Young, gifted and dead'. 2 July-Issue.

Todaro, M. P. (1969), 'A model of labor migration and urban unemployment in less developed countries', *American Economic Review*, **59**, 138-148.

Todaro, M. P. (1982), *Economics for a Developing World: an introduction to principles, problems, and policies*. Harlow, Essex, U.K.: Longman.

Tomlinson, R. (1990), *Urbanization in post-apartheid South Africa*. London: Unwin Hyman.

United Nations (1989), *Prospects of world urbanization*. Population Studies 112. New York.

van der Merwe, I. J. (1983), *Die stad en sy omgewing*. Stellenbosch: University Publishers.

van der Merwe, I. J. (1993), 'The South African city' in relation to international city form', *Development Southern Africa*, **10**, 481-496.

van Huyck, A. (1987), 'New directions for national shelter policies', in I. Rodwin (ed), *Shelter, settlement and development*. Boston: Allen and Unwin, pp.340-358.

van Warmelo, N. J. (1946), 'Grouping and history', in I. Schapera (ed), *The bantu-speaking tribes of South Africa*. Routledge, Broadway House, London.

Western, J. (1986), 'South African cities: A social geography', *Journal of Geography*, **85**, 249-255.

Index